The series Lecture Notes in Computer Science (LNCS), including its subseries Lecture Notes in Artificial Intelligence (LNAI) and Lecture Notes in Bioinformatics (LNBI), has established itself as a medium for the publication of new developments in computer science and information technology research, teaching, and education.

LNCS enjoys close cooperation with the computer science R & D community, the series counts many renowned academics among its volume editors and paper authors, and collaborates with prestigious societies. Its mission is to serve this international community by providing an invaluable service, mainly focused on the publication of conference and workshop proceedings and postproceedings. LNCS commenced publication in 1973.

Jeremy Gibbons
Editor

Trends in Functional Programming

26th International Symposium, TFP 2025
Oxford, UK, January 14–16, 2025
Revised Selected Papers

Springer

Editor
Jeremy Gibbons
University of Oxford
Oxford, UK

ISSN 0302-9743 ISSN 1611-3349 (electronic)
Lecture Notes in Computer Science
ISBN 978-3-031-99750-1 ISBN 978-3-031-99751-8 (eBook)
https://doi.org/10.1007/978-3-031-99751-8

This Springer imprint is published by the registered company Springer Nature Switzerland AG
The registered company address is: Gewerbestrasse 11, 6330 Cham, Switzerland

Preface

This volume contains revised versions of selected papers that were presented at the 26th International Symposium on Trends in Functional Programming (TFP 2025), held at the University of Oxford from 14th to 16th January, 2025. TFP was co-located with the 14th International Workshop on Trends in Functional Programming in Education (TFPIE 2025), which took place on 13th January.

TFP is an international forum for researchers with interests in all aspects of functional programming, taking a broad view of current and future trends in this area. It aspires to be a lively environment for presenting the latest research results and other contributions. TFP reviewing is a two-phase, single-blind process where authors may either submit a full paper for review before the symposium, or submit an extended abstract before the symposium, followed by a full paper afterwards incorporating feedback from both the pre-symposium reviews and the presentations. Each paper receives at least three reviews per round. One paper over which I had a conflict of interest was handled separately by the Symposium Chair, Jason Hemann.

This year we received 35 submissions in total. Of these, 28 were presented at the symposium, along with three keynote talks: *Things We Never Told Anyone about Functional Programming*, by Mike Sperber from Active Group; *Literate Programming and Cultural Practice*, by Graham Nelson from St Anne's College, Oxford; and *A Verified Foreign Function Interface Between Coq and C*, by Kathrin Stark from Heriot-Watt University.

After the post-symposium review phase, revised versions of 20 papers were selected for inclusion in these proceedings. The final selections spanned a wide variety of topics including semantics, design, implementation, teaching, and programming. In addition to the 20 submitted papers, I am delighted to be able to include papers from Mike Sperber's and Graham Nelson's keynote talks.

By tradition, TFP offers two prizes. The *John McCarthy Prize* for the best paper overall was awarded to Matthew Pickering, Rodrigo Mesquita, and Adam Gundry for the paper *Explicit Level Imports*. And the *David Turner Prize* for the best student paper was awarded to Ellis Kesterton and Edwin Brady for the paper *Heapless Functional Programming*.

All of this was only possible thanks to the hard work of the authors, the insightful contributions of the Programme Committee members, the thoughtful advice from the TFP Steering Committee, and the generous support of our sponsors. Funding and organizational support for the event were provided by The Research Institute on Verified Trustworthy Software Systems (VeTSS) and Epic Games. Sincere thanks to everyone for making this year's symposium a success.

May 2025 Jeremy Gibbons

Organization

Programme and General Chair

Jeremy Gibbons	University of Oxford, UK

Symposium Chair

Jason Hemann	Seton Hall University, USA

Publicity Chair

Peter Achten	Radboud University, The Netherlands

Steering Committee Chair

Marco T. Morazán	Seton Hall University, USA

Steering Committee

Peter Achten	Radboud University, The Netherlands
Stephen Chang	University of Massachusetts Boston, USA
Jurriaan Gibbons	University of Oxford, UK
Jurriaan Hage	Heriot-Watt University, UK
Kevin Hammond	IOG, UK
Jason Hemann	Seton Hall University, USA
John Hughes	Chalmers University of Technology, Sweden
Pieter Koopman	Radboud University, The Netherlands
Hans-Wolfgang Loidl	Heriot-Watt University, UK
Greg Michaelson	Heriot-Watt University, UK
Marco T. Morazán	Seton Hall University, USA
Wouter Swierstra	Utrecht University, The Netherlands
Phil Trinder	University of Glasgow, UK
Nicolas Wu	Imperial College London, UK
Viktória Zsók	Eötvös Loránd University of Sciences, Hungary

Programme Committee

Peter Achten	Radboud University Nijmegen, The Netherlands
Edwin Brady	University of St Andrews, UK
Laura Castro	University of A Coruña, Spain
Youyou Cong	Institute of Science Tokyo, Japan
Paul Downen	University of Massachusetts Lowell, USA
João Paulo Fernandes	New York University Abu Dhabi, UAE
Ben Greenman	University of Utah, USA
Jurriaan Hage	Heriot-Watt University, UK
Jason Hemann	Seton Hall University, USA
Zhenjiang Hu	Peking University, China
Hans-Wolfgang Loidl	Heriot-Watt University, UK
Kazutaka Matsuda	Tohoku University, Japan
Alejandro Serrano	47 Degrees, Spain
Nick Smallbone	Chalmers University, Sweden
Alley Stoughton	Boston University, USA
Wouter Swierstra	Utrecht University, The Netherlands
Niki Vazou	IMDEA Software Institute, Spain
Marcos Viera	Universidad de la República, Uruguay
Viktória Zsók	Eötvös Loránd University of Sciences, Hungary

Sponsors

TFP 2025 was sponsored by The Research Institute on Verified Trustworthy Software Systems (VeTSS) and Epic Games.

A Verified Foreign Function Interface Between Coq and C (Abstract of Invited Talk)

Kathrin Stark
Heriot-Watt University

Abstract. One can write dependently typed functional programs in Coq, and prove them correct in Coq; one can write low-level programs in C, and prove them correct with a C verification tool. In this talk, I will present the Verified Foreign Function Interface (VeriFFI) and demonstrate how to write programs partly in Coq and partly in C, and interface the proofs together. VeriFFI then guarantees type safety and correctness of the combined program. It works by translating Coq function types (and constructor types) along with Coq functional models into VST function-specifications; if the user can prove in VST that the C functions satisfy those specs, then the C functions behave according to the user-specified functional models (even though the C implementation might be very different) and the proofs of Coq functions that call the C code can rely on that behavior. VeriFFI is joint work with Andrew Appel and Joomy Korkut.

Contents

Teaching

Invited Papers

Things We Never Told Anyone About Functional Programming

Michael Sperber(✉)

Active Group GmbH, Tübingen, Germany
sperber@deinprogramm.de
https://www.deinprogramm.de/sperber/

Abstract. Functional Programming—what is it good for? Programming is the writing of programs. Judging from the papers and most books on functional programming, functional programming excels as a tool for writing short programs—up to a hundred lines maybe. We also know that there are large functional code bases at large companies, and folklore has it that this also works quite well. Yet there is precious little literature on how to go from a hundred lines to a million lines of functional code. This hinders the adoption of functional program by newcomers, who ask questions like:

- How do I find module boundaries?
- How do I organize teams for functional projects?
- How do I onboard newcomers?
- How does functional software development apply to qualities and requirements beyond functionality?

Successful practitioners rely on folklore and experience for the answers to these questions, but precious little is written down in findable places and accessible formats.

This paper is a call to action: The functional programming community needs to do a better job at outreach—find the gaps in our published knowledge, write down what is undocumented and talk to other communities who deal with large-scale software development.

Keywords: Functional Programming · Software Architecture · Domain-Driven Design

1 Introduction

This paper is about using functional programming to implement software systems, specifically software systems that fulfill externally specified requirements, i.e. requirements that are not inherently about the use of functional programming.

Real-world software systems in active use tend to live long, at least several years. As their maintainers adapt them to new and changed requirements, these systems grow correspondingly. The issues facing such systems are different from

J. Gibbons (Ed.): TFP 2025, LNCS 15652, pp. 3–15, 2026.
https://doi.org/10.1007/978-3-031-99751-8_1

the ones facing the small programs typically printed in research papers. These issues have been extensively studied in the field of *software architecture* [34], if mostly from practical angles due to the difficulties of conducting meaningful comparative studies on large software projects.

As software systems grow, changing them tends get more and more expensive per unit of requirements fulfilled, due to a phenomenon called *coupling* [44]: Inter-dependencies between the parts of a system become more numerous, requiring changes in one part to be accompanied by corresponding changes in other parts, thus "coupling" these parts together.

Consequently, any technique or technology claiming to support the development of such systems must not just support their initial construction, but also their evolution over time. As such, they must grapple with coupling, and support developers in keeping it low or reducing it once it has grown to detrimental levels.

This is particularly important as the requirements imposed on a software systems do not merely concern functionality (i.e. the relationship between input and output), but also other qualities of the system, such as reliability, safety, usability, efficiency etc. [38].

2 Creating Software Systems

Software systems are (presently) created by people, and large software systems are created by large groups of people. This makes the organization of the humans involved in a software project a crucial factor in its success. As the group designing a software system grows, it will typically split into several sub-groups or *teams* to manage the inherent complexity. This raises several questions:

- How should the labor be divided up between the teams?
- What is a good team size?

As to the first question, there are two obvious extreme answers:

- Assign *technical competencies* to each team, i.e. front-end, backend, operations.
- Assign *features* to each team.

("Feature" is a shorthand for a user-visible addition to the system that fulfills requirements running in production.)

The first option typically means that multiple teams have to collaborate to implement a feature. The second option means that each team needs to contain all technical competencies required for the assigned features.

The organizational principle addressing the above questions that is most cited in the software architecture community is *Conway's Law* [8], specifically the following sentence:

> Any organization that designs a system (defined more broadly here than just information systems) will inevitably produce a design whose structure is a copy of the organization's communication structure.

Concretely, this law (not really a "law" in the colloquial sense) is based on the observation that communication within teams of the organization is more efficient than between teams, and thus will produce designs that have boundaries that correspond to the boundaries between teams. Most organizations seem to have settled on teams not larger than 10 people for the law to hold, with 5–7 being more typical [15].

Consequently, Conway's Law favors organizations that assign features to each team (*feature teams*), as feature teams—in principle at least—can produce features avoiding the overhead of inter-team communication.

Another body of evidence in support of feature teams is the *Accelerate* study [13] that concluded that the following four factors are the most important determinants for the performance of software delivery in an organization:

1. delivery lead time
2. deployment frequency
3. time to restore service
4. change fail rate

The two first factors are slightly surprising: Roughly, they mean that an organization is more effective if it ships features more quickly rather than "more thoroughly" with elaborate processes and sign-off requirements. This also favors feature teams, as they can—again, ideally—deliver features without waiting on other teams. Focusing thus on *velocity* often leads to better results than focusing on the leverage of competency teams, even though it means that any given competency needs to be replicated among many teams.

Note that feature teams are not an all-or-nothing proposition: Most organizations will have certain competencies bundled in teams, with the most recent trend being *platform teams* to manage the complexity of modern cloud platforms [36]. They are a good default, however.

It is easy to imagine a code base that will destroy the advantage of the feature-teams approach through coupling: Conway's Law says that each team will typically manage an identifiable part of the code base. If the parts managed by two teams are strongly coupled, each change one team makes to implement a feature requires a change in the other team's code base, causing overhead and waiting.

So in summary, an effective software organization needs the following:

- connecting requirements and software;
- programming in the small to implement features;
- a software architecture with low coupling when programming in the large and in the long; and
- an organizational structure aligned with the design of system.

3 Programming in the Large and in the Long

The upshot of the previous section was that one of the primary goals of software architecture should be to reduce coupling. This section reviews techniques, successes and failures of the software architecture community to do this.

Software architecture considers coupling mostly between the building blocks of a software, where the term "building block" is loosely defined.[1] Coupling should be low, but of course some coupling is necessary for building blocks to make use of each others' functionality. Within a single software deployment artifact (called *monolith* henceforth), many programming languages provide constructs that make these building blocks explicit, usually called *modules* [3].

The notion of coupling is somewhat problematic in that it refers to the future of the program: Some future features or changes might only require changes in a single building block, indicating low coupling. Others might require changes in multiple building blocks, indicating high coupling. So unless all future changes are known (and they usually are not) any strategy that purports to reduce coupling is necessarily a heuristic.

The study of such heuristics has been around for a long time, often under the heading of *modularity*—low coupling between modules. The best-known example is David Parnas's classic paper [32], which contrasts two different heuristics: One is to establish module boundaries between the steps of a processing pipeline, the other to hide information about design decisions that are difficult or likely to change—with the objective of allowing that decision to be changed later.

Paradoxically, the modern software architecture community sees getting decisions "right" as central [5], which seems to indicate that the field of software architecture has given up on Parnas's original goal. Anecdotally, this is because industrial software projects find it difficult to develop modular software, at least within a monolith. Witness in particular the recent rise of the term "modulith" to refer to modular monoliths, implying that the default monolith is unmodular.

Further testament to the difficulty of modularizing monoliths is the rise of *microservice* architectures since about the end of the 1990s [42]. Such architectures consist of many monoliths that interoperate over the network. One possible benefit of using microservices is horizontal scalability for performance reasons. More often however they are used because they leverage Conway's law to make the development of the system more efficient: Each microservice is under the management of a single team. (One team may manage several microservices, but not the converse.)

As a microservice is (ideally) a self-contained monolith, its development requires little interaction with different teams. In particular, a team does not typically need to coordinate deployment with other teams, making for short delivery lead time and high deployment frequency, the first two tenets of the Accelerate study discussed in the previous section.

One particular style of microservice architecture is *Self-Contained Systems*, where each microservice is a self-contained autonomous web application, sometimes called a *vertical* [35]. The overall system assembles the vertical user interfaces into a (seemingly) coherent whole. The code bases of the different verticals share very little, and communication is mostly through asynchronous feeds, rather than synchronous remote-procedure calls or REST interfaces. The result-

[1] Coupling inside a building block is *cohesion*, where high cohesion is usually desired.

ing system can function even if not all of its verticals are operational, again facilitating the teams developing and releasing independently.

Note that moving from a monolithic architecture to one with microservices entails serious trade-offs: Network communication is significantly slower than intra-monolith calls. Developers need to deal with the vagaries of a distributed system. Whereas communication between the modules of a monolith enjoy the direct support of the programming language, inter-microservice communication needs to address issues such as serialization and choreography. Moreover, comprehensive testing is much more difficult in such a setting.

Microservice architectures make coupling more difficult compared to a monolith, as making use of functionality of a different system is so much work. However, coupling is not impossible and again it is easy to imagine a system organization with high coupling between microservices.[2] Consequently, the question of a good heuristic for placing building-block boundaries remains relevant even in a microservice architecture.

Many large software-development organizations turn to *Domain-Driven Design* (DDD) [11] for such heuristics. The DDD community has developed a rich arsenal of techniques for splitting the domain of a software system into *subdomains*. Subdomain boundaries are usually in places where the vocabulary used by the domain experts shift, and where notions of shared entities change.

For an example, consider the domain of an e-commerce website. (E-commerce tends to be a DDD hotbed.) As users travel through the site, they cross invisible boundaries from one subdomain to the next: On the landing page, they can browse among suggested products, they enter specific searches, look at product details, put products in a shopping cart, and then proceed to checkout. Each of these is typically a different subdomain, and each one has its own notion of "product".

A traditional "enterprise" IT system would have a central database with all information about a product, which would have to be jointly administered throughout the domain, causing high coordination overhead. Splitting into subdomains allows implementing separate building blocks (called *bounded contexts*) for each. Each bounded context can have a separate data model and database for products, enabling efficient specialization and—more importantly—decoupling. Bounded contexts are a good match for a microservice or Self-Contained Systems architecture.

Note that the DDD techniques for identifying subdomains are "only" heuristics with the expectation of low coupling between them. DDD has been quite effective in practice at achieving this goal, but anecdotal evidence suggests that not all DDD-designated boundaries are in exactly the right place. In a microservice architecture, these boundaries are quite difficult to move.
To summarize:

- The building blocks of a software system should be loosely coupled to enable effective division of labor and team cooperation.

[2] This is sometimes called a "distributed monolith", again implying that the monolith is always unmodular.

- Achieving loosely-coupled building blocks in a monolith is difficult in practice.
- Many large software architectures use microservices to establish strong separation of building blocks.
- Moving from a monolith to microservices has negative side effects, but the trade-offs are still often in favor of microservices.
- Domain-Driven Design is a set of techniques for splitting a large domain and system so that development aligns with Conway's law.

4 FP—What Is It Good For?

The previous section made no mention of functional programming: The field of (practically applied) software development and software architecture is dominated by object-oriented programming, and has largely gone untouched by functional techniques. Yet, there are obvious areas where functional programming can make significant contributions to software architecture.

4.1 Coupling and Immutability

Assignment and mutation are among the biggest contributors to coupling, as they create hidden temporal dependencies, which are especially pernicious in the face of concurrency.

While object-oriented programming has acknowledged the advantages of immutability [4], the predominant basic programming model in most projects is still pervasively mutable. Domain-Driven Design makes heavy use of the distinction between (immutable) value objects and (mutable) entities with explicit identity. However, where to actually draw the line between the two is often unclear, and practitioners favor different taxonomies to decide on one or the other.[3]

Moreover, functional data structures [31] are not generally used in object-oriented projects, even though they would fall squarely within the "favor immutability" dictum.

Consequently, many software projects would benefit from a functional style that minimizes mutability and uses functional data structures instead of the traditional mutable collection libraries.

4.2 Data Instead of Objects

One way to understand the difference between object-oriented programming and functional programming is that, while object-oriented programming is about

[3] This exposes a deeper issue with object-oriented programming, which is predominantly based on the metaphor of physical objects. Objects inside a computer program are always *representations* of those objects or their state, and this distinction is insufficiently reflected in the object-oriented model.

the physical-objects metaphor, functional programming is about *data*—explicit, immutable representations or descriptions of aspects of our domain.

This distinction is about more than immutability: Many aspects of object-oriented software are not objects. In particular, processes are not, whereas functional programming has a whole taxonomy for representing processes with monads, applicatives, and arrows. Consequently, a possible rallying cry for functional programming is "everything is data".[4]

4.3 Data Modeling

Functional programming has developed a rich discipline of structuring data, as exemplified in the *How to Design Programs* approach to teaching programming [12]. *How to Design Programs* features a taxonomy of data based on the distinction between *sums* and *products* [37]. (Called "itemizations" and "compound data" in the book.) This approach is extraordinarily effective in crafting data models that align with requirements, create good user experiences, and remain flexible in the face of changes.

Surprisingly, object-oriented software development has not developed a similar discipline.[5] Worse, it has largely abandoned object-oriented analysis [14] in favor of ad-hoc designs. In particular, many object models lack a notion of sums, so pervasive in functional programming, especially in languages with algebraic data types.[6]

Of course, functional programming has long gone significantly beyond simple products and sums, in particular with combinator models, in use since at least 1982 [22], and folklore for at least 25 years [33]. Combinator models have applications in many domains [28].

Combinator models solve a frequently occurring problem in software projects, namely that the object/data models (which have degenerated to mere collections of attributes) require modification whenever new requirements arrive or the existing ones change. A combinator model provides a "construction kit" for domain entities rather than a fixed set of monolithic representations, reducing the need to change the software. Since sums are rarely used in object-oriented programming, combinator models are beyond the reach of most real-world projects.

Functional data models also provide a different perspective on bounded contexts: In object-oriented programming, objects and behavior belong inextricably together. Behaviors are often associated with specific bounded contexts. Consequently, this creates pressure on the developers to completely separate data models between different bounded contexts, even if they share meaning and need

[4] It used to be "functions are first-class values", which has become no longer distinctive through the introduction of lambda expressions in most object-oriented languages.

[5] When the DDD community mentions "modeling" (particularly "collaborative modeling"), this typically refers to the modeling of *processes*, not the entities that take part in them.

[6] Of course, sums are expressible as a class hierarchy. However, sums are not a natural outcome from object-oriented analysis. Moreover, creating class hierarchies is largely discouraged in contemporary object-oriented design [17].

to be kept consistent. In functional programming, behavior is typically separate. Moreover, denotational design [9] can establish a common understanding of what pieces of data actually mean.

To summarize, many projects could benefit from the richer, more flexible data models afforded by functional programming.

4.4 Abstraction

Another conspicuous difference between the practice of object-oriented programming and functional programming is the attitude towards abstraction: Current object-oriented practice is generally to avoid abstraction. Anecdotal evidence suggests that abstraction often "goes wrong" in software projects, creating complex object hierarchies. In particular, DDD practitioners commonly advise to stick to the immediate requirements from "the business", and to avoid adding new terms or functionality beyond them [26].

In contrast functional programming routinely applies abstraction to make software more flexible and gain insights into the structure of the domain.

4.5 Mathematics

Functional programming routinely employs mathematics as a source of inspiration for finding useful abstractions that are applicable in many domains. (Again, explicit use of mathematics is rare in real-world projects.) Furthermore, mathematics can also raise assurance for the consistency and correctness of the software through the use of formal methods.

4.6 Teaching and Systematic Programming

There are many introductory textbooks on functional languages [1,25,40]. Moreover, the *How to Design Programs* approach to teaching programming [12] has revolutionized programming pedagogy by focusing on systematic design using *design recipes*, a set of named techniques that take learners from problem statements to solution programs in easy-to-follow and mostly mechanical steps.

Design recipes have wider implications than just the "teachability" of functional programming: Systematic programming is a useful concept in itself. Systematically constructed programs are less prone to error, and easier to read and manage by others. In object-oriented projects, the equivalent—but much weaker—concept would be the use of a "pattern language", a project-specific set of rules prescribing similar solutions to recurring problems [27].

Arguably, the more of a software system is constructed systematically, the higher its code quality will be, with positive implications for maintainability and thus its architecture. While there is still room for pushing the envelope on systematic techniques [19], the existing body includes mostly techniques for constructing functional programs.[7]

[7] The second edition of the design recipes book [12] omitted the section on imperative programming, ostensibly because it was not as effective in the classroom as the rest of its material.

5 A Note on Modularity

The previous section contains an obvious omission: Can functional programming contribute to good modularity? It depends, and to examine the issue of modularity, we need to first discuss how to assess "good modularity" realistically. Remember that "good modularity" means low coupling, and low coupling means that typical future changes are local to few modules. Few projects (if any) are sufficiently disciplined to follow Parnas's heuristic for module boundaries.

An effective proxy for a project's modularity is its static dependency graph [27]. The more connected it is, the higher the coupling, and the worse the modularity. Moreover, certain architectural patterns, such as *layers* or *hexagonal architecture* [7] forbid direct dependencies between certain modules.

While there is some indication that functional programs have less dependencies than object-oriented ones [16], excessive dependencies are certainly a problem in real-world functional software systems. Aside from sheer discipline, teams can try to keep dependencies under control by automatically testing the dependency graph for architectural conformance with tools, or enforcing conformance via constraints expressed in a sufficiently expressive module system.

As an example, excessive dependencies are certainly a problem in Java-based projects, which traditionally have a mostly flat namespace. One contributor is, ironically, modern IDEs. These exhaustively index all parts of a project, making any part of a project instantly accessible. This makes it trivial for programmers to create a dependency spanning many modules and potentially violating architectural constraints.

To address this problem, the Java ecosystem features tools such as ArchUnit [2] for unit-testing the dependency graph. Moreover, the module system introduced in Java 9 allows expressing constraints on dependencies, including those from architectural patterns. (That said, many projects make no use of the module system.)

The availability of tools and language features to similarly help reduce dependencies is at best spotty among functional languages. The best candidate may be the OCaml module system [30], which has unfortunately not seen widespread adoption in other functional languages.

6 A Blueprint for Functional Software Design

This section contains a list of tenets of functional software design summarized from the previous sections. These techniques are specific to functional programming yet independent of a particular functional language, and can serve to explain and differentiate software construction using functional programming.

Note that this is just one particular, opinionated list, and others are possible. Specifically, it does not cover the popular techniques using functional programming to implement DDD [18,41], which are different from the techniques originating from the functional programming community.

To summarize, functional design ...

- is bottom-up,
- starts with functional qualities,
- represents everything as data,
- employs data modeling using sums and products,
- embraces abstraction,
- creates combinator models,
- uses algebraic structures, and
- formulates properties mathematically.

Some elaboration of these tenets follows.

Functional Design is Bottom-Up. This statement concerns the construction of software systems, not that of individual functions: Published accounts of practical applications of functional programming usually focus on conceptual modeling of the domain [10,23,33] rather than starting with a macro-architectural template and the filling in the gaps, as is customary in DDD projects.

Functional Design Starts with Functional Qualities. Most accounts of functional design describe the implementation of *functionality* rather than a comprehensive plan on how to fulfill requirements on other qualities. The inherent low coupling of functional code allows tackling these requirements later, in line with the order in which they come into focus [21].

Functional Design Represents Everything as Data. "Data" (i.e. descriptive, immutable values) here is first of all in opposition to mutable "objects" with state. Moreover, many things are data in functional programs that are not data or objects in object-oriented programs: Functions are data, as well as common abstractions that describe processes or effects. See Sect. 4.2.

Functional Design Employs Data Modeling Using Sums and Products. This needs saying as using sums in data modeling is not very common in non-FP projects. See Sect. 4.3.

Functional Design Embraces Abstraction. Abstraction is a key element in functional programming, and present in almost all published accounts of functional programs. See Sect. 4.4.

Functional Design Creates Combinator Models. Combinator models are a particular form of abstraction, applied to data modeling, virtually unknown outside of functional programming 4.3.

Functional Design Uses Algebraic Structures. Functional design routinely makes use of algebraic structures such as monoids [43], applicative functors [29], arrows [24], or monads [39].

Functional Design Formulates Properties Mathematically. This is in opposition to the common practice of specifying behavior through examples. Note that the focus is (currently) on the formulation of properties, not so much their formal verification [6].

7 A Call to Action

Hopefully, this paper has shown that functional programming can make significant contribution to the construction of practical software and their architecture. Unfortunately, this potential has so far largely gone unrealized through the insularity of the functional programming community.

Clearly, we have done too little to communicate techniques for large-scale functional software construction—with the exception of a few books [18,20,30, 41], which are mostly specific to particular functional languages.

Consequently, we should engage with other communities—the DDD and software architecture communities in particular. We should not just communicate what FP has to offer, but also listen to the techniques and technologies common in the object-oriented DDD world, and analyze how they could cross-pollinate.

Moreover, the body of knowledge needed to construct large-scale functional projects is far from complete. One particularly pressing question is whether the low coupling afforded by immutability and strong module systems can make splitting out modules as microservices superfluous.

We should more generally investigate how the DDD notion of bounded contexts can translate into functional code, and how functional techniques and language design can help implement them in practical projects. This concerns in particular keeping data models separate between bounded contexts but still consistent. Moreover, it is presently unclear what the best way is to combine the top-down approach of DDD with the bottom-up approach of functional design.

There is much to do. Let's go to work.

References

1. Abraham, I.: F# in Action. Manning (2024)
2. ArchUnit: Unit test your Java architecture. https://www.archunit.org/
3. Barnett, T.O., Constantine, L.L.: Modular Programming: Proceedings of a National Symposium. Information & systems Institute (1968)
4. Bloch, J.: Effective Java. Pearson, 3rd edn. (2017)
5. Brown, S.: Software Architecture for Developers. Leanpub (2022)
6. Claessen, K., Hughes, J.: QuickCheck: a lightweight tool for random testing of Haskell programs. In: Proceedings of the Fifth ACM SIGPLAN International Conference on Functional Programming, pp. 268–279. ICFP '00, Association for Computing Machinery, New York, NY, USA (2000)
7. Cockburn, A., de Paz, J.M.G.: Hexagonal Architecture Explained. Humans and Technology Press (2024)
8. Conway, M.E.: How do committees invent? Datamation (1968). https://www.melconway.com/research/committees.html

9. Elliott, C.: Denotational design with type class morphisms (extended version). Tech. Rep. 2009-01, LambdaPix (2009). http://conal.net/papers/type-class-morphisms
10. Elliott, C., Hudak, P.: Functional reactive animation. In: Proceedings of the Third ACM SIGPLAN International Conference on Functional Programming. Association for Computing Machinery, New York, NY, USA (1997)
11. Evans, E.: Domain-Driven Design: Tackling Complexity in the Heart of Software. Addison-Wesley (2003)
12. Felleisen, M., Findler, R.B., Flatt, M., Krishnamurthi, S.: How to Design Programs. MIT Press, second edn. (2018)
13. Forsgren, N., Humble, J., Kim, G.: Accelerate: The Science of Lean Software and DevOps: Building and Scaling High Performing Technology Organizations. IT Revolution Press (2018)
14. Fowler, M.: Analysis Patterns: Reusable Object Models. Addison-Wesley Professional (1996)
15. Fowler, M.: Two pizza team. https://martinfowler.com/bliki/TwoPizzaTeam.html (2023)
16. Gabasova, E.: Comparing F# and C# with dependency networks. https://evelinag.com/blog/2014/06-09-comparing-dependency-networks/ (2014)
17. Gamma, E., Helm, R., Johnson, R., Vlissides, J.: Design Patterns. Prentice-Hall, Elements of Reusable Object-Oriented Software (1994)
18. Ghosh, D.: Functional and Reactive Domain Modeling. Manning (2016)
19. Gibbons, J.: How to design co-programs. J. Funct. Program. **31** (2021)
20. Granin, A.: Functional Design and Architecture: Examples in Haskell. Manning (2024)
21. Harrer, M.: Quality Tactics. Leanpub (2024)
22. Henderson, P.: Functional geometry. In: Proceedings of the 1982 ACM Symposium on LISP and Functional Programming, pp. 179–187. LFP '82, Association for Computing Machinery, New York, NY, USA (1982)
23. Hudak, P.: The Haskell School of Expression: Learning Functional Programming through Multimedia. Cambridge University Press, 4th edn. (2000)
24. Hughes, J.: Generalising monads to arrows. Sci. Comput. Program. **37**(1–3), 67–111 (2000)
25. Hutton, G.: Programming in Haskell. Cambridge University Press, 2nd edn. (2016)
26. Khononov, V.: Learning Domain-Driven Design: Aligning Software Architecture and Business Strategy. O'Reilly (2021)
27. Lilienthal, C.: Langlebige Softwarearchitekturen. Dpunkt Verlag, 4th edn. (2024)
28. Maguire, S.: Algebra-Driven Design. Leanpub (2020)
29. McBride, C., Paterson, R.: Applicative programming with effects. J. Funct. Program. **18**(1), 1–13 (2008)
30. Minsky, Y., Madhavapeddy, A.: Real World OCaml: Functional Programming for the Masses. Cambridge University Press, 2nd edn. (2022)
31. Okasaki, C.: Functional Data Structures. Cambridge University Press (2008)
32. Parnas, D.L.: On the criteria to be used in decomposing systems into modules. Commun. ACM **15**(12), 1053–1058 (1972)
33. Peyton Jones, S., Eber, J.M., Seward, J.: Composing contracts: an adventure in financial engineering (functional pearl). In: Proceedings of the Fifth ACM SIGPLAN International Conference on Functional Programming, pp. 280–292. ICFP '00, Association for Computing Machinery, New York, NY, USA (2000)
34. Richards, M., Ford, N.: Fundamentals of Software Architecture: An Engineering Approach. O'Reilly (2020)

35. Self-contained systems (SCS). https://scs-architecture.org/
36. Skelton, M., Pais, M.: Team Topologies. IT Revolution Press (2019)
37. Sperber, M., Wehr, S.: Data modeling with sums and products. https://funktionale-programmierung.de/2024/11/25/sums-products-english.html (2024)
38. Starke, G., et al.: arc42 quality model. https://quality.arc42.org/
39. Wadler, P.: The essence of functional programming. In: Proceedings of the 19th ACM SIGPLAN-SIGACT Symposium on Principles of Programming Languages, pp. 1–14. POPL '92, Association for Computing Machinery, New York, NY, USA (1992)
40. Whitington, J.: OCaml from the Very Beginning. Coherent Press (2013)
41. Wlaschin, S.: Domain Modeling Made Functional. O'Reilly Media (2018)
42. Wolff, E.: Microservices: Flexible Software Architecture. Addison-Wesley Professional (2016)
43. Yorgey, B.A.: Monoids: theme and variations (functional pearl). In: Proceedings of the 2012 Haskell Symposium, pp. 105–116. Haskell '12, Association for Computing Machinery, New York, NY, USA (2012)
44. Yourdon, E., Constantine, L.L.: Structured Design. Prentice-Hall (1979)

Literate Programming and Cultural Practice

Graham Nelson(✉)

St Anne's College, University of Oxford, Oxford, UK
graham.nelson@st-annes.ox.ac.uk

Abstract. The desire to comment is a human impulse, seen also in art forms from music and visual art to film and literature. Syntaxes for commentary appear almost at once in the history of programming. Comments lie in the zone of the inexpressible, saying what cannot be said in a programming language, and the need for them can never entirely be designed away by new languages. The most audacious case for commentary remains Donald Knuth's radical proposal for "literate programming", which recasts the programmer as essayist. Emerging from Knuth's thinking about ideas of perfectibility, publication, and the sacred, this manifesto was in part a rebuttal of structured programming. Though it failed to achieve dominance, its ideas remain stimulating, and show an eerie convergence with today's norms – GitHub being in some respects its triumph after all. Practical experience with large-scale LP is mixed, but it still has much to teach us.

Keywords: comments · history of programming languages · literate programming · Donald Knuth

{-

It's really a very great privilege for me to speak at Trends in Functional Programming, but please consider this as an intermission, because my subject today is not functional, in either sense of that word, not trendy, and may not even be programming. I speak in praise of the humble comment, which, I hope to persuade you, we too easily overlook.

1 The Artist and the Comment

Let us begin with a story: It's 1910, and in a log cabin in Toblach, in the Italian Tyrol, Gustav Mahler is composing his tenth symphony. Mahler turns fifty this month, but his heart is failing and he knows it. Within a year he will be dead, buried next to his daughter Maria, who had died of diphtheria. His wife Alma is having an affair with the architect Walter Gropius. The symphony is in F♯ major, a difficult key for any orchestra, with six sharps on the clef. The final

J. Gibbons (Ed.): TFP 2025, LNCS 15652, pp. 16–46, 2026.
https://doi.org/10.1007/978-3-031-99751-8_2

movement is extreme and skeletal, with a desperately lonely melody for flute.[1] On the last page of the score, the source code for Symphony No. 10, Mahler writes (see Fig. 1):

> für dich leben! für dich sterben! [To live for you! To die for you!]

Who are these words addressed to? They did not add a single note to the music. Mahler probably hoped he would live long enough to orchestrate this score (though he did not), but this is not a simple aide-memoire like "TO DO: Add more bassoons". Ostensibly, he was speaking to Alma. She, after all, would inherit this pile of paper when he was gone, when she was free to marry Walter. But Alma had become symbolic to him, a symbol of devotion betrayed.[2] Perhaps the words are more universally directed: a Beethovenian testament, a cry to the world, for the conductors and flautists to come. If so, it worked. Audiences are moved by these words even today. The comment, though it has no function in the music, nevertheless reaches us in a sort of side-channel attack.

Another story. Words woven into visual art, like newspaper headlines in a Cubist painting, or the inscription *Et In Arcadia Ego* on the tomb in Poussin's masterpiece, or perhaps even van Gogh's flamboyant signature *Vincent*, are surely part of the work itself. But what about words on the back of a canvas? In 1927 the Scottish artist Francis Cadell wrote the following on the reverse of his latest landscape:

> THE AVENUE, AUCHNACRAIG
> by
> F.C.B.Cadell
> Absorbent ground. NEVER varnish.

Cadell was a working painter – he sold this one to a local ship-owner, and it last changed hands for £84,000 in 2016 – but here he is, long after he was paid, still wanting us to feel a duty of care to his work.[3]

Literature next. Footnotes in non-fiction books are not, I think, comments, but the penultimate chapter of Thomas Hardy's novel *The Return of the Native* ends with a singular footnote which is. Casually breaking the fourth wall, Hardy openly tells us not to believe the happy ending we have just read. He had only married off the hero and heroine because *Belgravia* magazine, which was serialising the book in 1878, made him do it:

> The writer may state here that the original conception of the story did not design a marriage between Thomasin and Venn [...] Readers can therefore

[1] One should not over-interpret, and all compositional sketches are thin, but few doubt that Mahler's mental state in that wooden room reached a condition we can only dimly glimpse: see for example Fischer (2011).

[2] Alma lived on until 1964, and was slut-shamed in a satirical song by Tom Lehrer: her reputation has never escaped 1910 or the untruths she (sensibly) told about it. But she too has biographers and a point of view; and she did not burn the drafts.

[3] This example of artistic commentary was identified by the Christie's specialist Olivia Ghosh (2022).

Fig. 1. Mahler's final bars, with its comments clearly visible. Just below the final melodic leap upward, he has written: "Almschi!". These comments appear on two surviving sketches, so the composer must have copied them at least once.

> choose between the endings, and those with an austere artistic code can assume the more consistent conclusion to be the true one.

Here we have a comment which markedly changes the meaning of Hardy's work, despite changing nothing in its substance.

I promise this is my last example: the release of the movie *Barry Lyndon* in 1975. Stanley Kubrick, who directed, personally signed a letter which begins "Dear Projectionist" to accompany the reels of film as they were driven from cinema to cinema. He writes:

> An infinite amount of care was given to the look of "Barry Lyndon"; the photography, the sets, the costumes; and in the careful color grading and overall lab quality of the prints, and the soundtrack – all of this work is now in your hands, and your attention to sharp focus, good sound, and the careful handling of the film will make this effort worthwhile.

This is more of a `README.md` file than a comment but that's a distinction without a difference. Kubrick is respectful, but demanding. He wants his collaborators on the movie, even those he will never meet, to share his vision. The letter goes on to give instructions recognisably like installation notes for a program.[4]

Programs are inarguably cultural production, but to call them works of art – akin to symphonies, paintings, novels, or movies – is to say more than that. Clearly they do not exist just to be admired, so some might argue that they are functional things, not artworks. And yet they are not anonymous objects, like pots or spanners. They do not somehow exist independently of us: they are created by us, and for human reasons. For money, for passion, for exhilaration, to show our prowess, to claim territory, to satisfy our need to organise things, to make visions come into being. Often enough, it's the creative act itself that matters to us, and the resulting program is just a by-product, which we might then throw away, or at most keep a sentimental copy of.

Of all the traditional forms of art, programming is surely closest to writing, as the words we use to describe it testify. The verb "to write", rather than, say, "to design" or "to compose", has been used of programs at least since 1950. Kernighan and Plauger's formative *The Elements of Programming Style* (1974) was modelled directly on Strunk and White (1959), the writing guide assigned by almost all American universities. Interactive programs allowing source code to be modified seem always to have been called "text editors",[5] a term implying both "text" – i.e., the substance of writing – and "editing" – i.e., the way to correct that substance.

Moreover, our lived experience of coding does seem to match up to this. To find the cleanest, most concise line through some problem is not unlike writing a poem. To plan out software architecture is not unlike plotting a novel, and stocking it with subsystems like characters who each have their own profession. And, just as a novel can be About something – about Fate, or Remorse, or Ambition – even though it never openly says so, programs often have central dogmas, or golden rules, even though no single line of code expresses that. *Everything is a file*, say, or *trust nothing from this input.*

Lastly, just as the visual artist can choose from charcoal, oils, acrylics, and such, so the programmer also has a choice of medium. We tend to call those possible media "languages", another revealing choice of word. A good deal of this talk will be about programming languages, and about what scope they offer for commentary. The best languages, I tend to think, are those which lean in to the artistic impulse within what we are doing. My dream programming language – and there's a human word, dream: lambda-calculus doesn't dream, only we dream – my dream language is certainly one that it's possible to reason about,

---

[4] Projection had long been an obsession of Kubrick's: see Mikics (2020). The letter here was turned up by Jay Cocks (2011), after technical choices in the Blu-Ray release proved contentious. Kubrick wasn't the only director to write such letters: see Mills (2021) for David Lynch on *Mulholland Drive*, 2001. "Projection Department: I understand this is an unusual request yet I do need your help.".

[5] For example, the PDP-1's Text Editor and Corrector, by Daniel L. Murphy in 1962–63, arguably the first full-featured line editor; or the CD-6600's "text-editing and manipulation program", the first screen editor, by Edgar Irons and Frans Djorup in 1967.

and thread-safe, and all of that good stuff. But it is also a language which somehow meets the humanity of creation.

2 The Syntax of the Comment

Jean Sammet, who was born in 1928, wrote her magisterial, 800-page history of programming languages in 1969. The film *2001: A Space Odyssey* was presenting the computer both as demigod and design icon, while the real-life Apollo Guidance Computer had three times navigated people to the moon. The IBM corporation had become so essential to the US economy that anti-trust laws were being used to rein in its monopoly. For Sammet, the story of computing was one of a ferment of small-scale invention back in the past – really just proofs of concept – leading to a formidably capable present. This is also how we feel, and how almost everyone in this story has always felt. Sammet, Perlis, Liskov, Backus, and many others now called "pioneers" did not imagine themselves in an unclaimed wilderness. They were town planners reorganising an existing community, whose problems were those of maturity, not youth.[6]

Computing power has grown by perhaps seven orders of magnitude in a single professional lifetime. Hardware developments constantly outstrip our ability to keep up, and languages have had to react: to make programming cheaper (1950s), more algorithmically correct (1960s), more portable (1970s), larger-scale (1980s), longer-lasting (1990s), safer (2000s), better tuned for constrained devices (2010s), more reliably concurrent (2020s). Language use nevertheless shows great conservatism, not because languages are durable but because people are, and so are their social structures.[7] Fundamental features of programming languages tend to be of even longer standing, copied from each language to the next.

The history of the comment is a case in point. Jean Sammet remarked that a facility for comments exists in almost all of the first two hundred languages, but if anything they first appeared five years earlier still, back in what we might call prehistory. The examples in the seminal 1951 textbook *The Preparation of Programs for an Electronic Digital Computer* (Wilkes, Wheeler, and Gill, 1951) are printed in a standardised format with one column of "orders" and another of commentary:

[6] See Sammet (1969). Sammet is less remembered now than Grace Hopper, but probably had greater influence over COBOL. She was instrumental in setting up the ACM's conferences on the History of Programming Languages, whose proceedings are an invaluable source of first-hand testimony. In the pages to come, I draw often on *HOPL I*, Wexelblat (1981), and *HOPL II*, Bergin and Gibson (1996).

[7] Mid-career programmers resist paradigm shifts, and learn new languages only as variants on those they already know. Systems like Medicaid or the London Underground hang on to the same code for decades.

	Orders		*Notes*
	G	*K*	
start → 0	A	N	Set $x = 200$
1	T	1 N	
20 → 2	A	4 N	Set initial value of $h = 2^{-4}$
3	T	2 H	
4	B	4 θ	Call in subroutine B to evaluate integral
5	F	350 F	

...and so on. The word "orders" now has a disconcertingly military ring, but in England the computer had been born in an Army hut, and Turing, Wilkes, and others of their generation all saw war service, even if as back-room boys. The writing of clear orders was a basic skill taught in staff colleges, and engineers who could call on factory assistance were similarly taught to write "work orders". The basic typographical design of this book – orders on the left, explanation on the right – was much imitated. Assembly-language syntax as it later developed, with line comments in parallel text to the right of what we now call "instructions", has a similar shape even today.

The earliest programming languages hoped instead to be self-explanatory. As such, comments seem not to appear in technical reports on the Laning and Zierler system, 1952, or FLOW-MATIC, 1955.[8] In their tentative way, these proto-languages can each be seen as attempting to shift explanatory matter about a program so that it becomes the program itself. Thus, physics formulae written in the marginal comments of assembly language become syntax for Laning and Zierler: flow charts do not describe FLOW-MATIC but turn into it.

Though FORTRAN, 1957, had similar aspirations, it was built for laboratory problems where not even formulae were self-explanatory. Comments were an early and prominent feature of the language. In FORTRAN, any line with a `C` in the first column is a comment:

```
C      THIS IS A COMMENT.
```

Programmers would write longhand on special pads of IBM-printed paper, which they then gave to key-punch operators to turn into card decks. These pads, and sometimes the blank cards as well, had a pre-printed "C for Comment" arrow pointing to column 1. Perhaps that speaks to a syntax easily bungled, but it also implies a firm expectation of usage.[9]

The other great survivor language from that era, COBOL, was drafted by a "task group" drawn from the Department of Defense, IBM and other large vendors – what President Eisenhower was shortly to call "the military-industrial

[8] Laning and Zierler (1954) and Sperry (1958).

[9] IBM documentation, such as the FORTRAN reference manual (Backus et al., 1957), lends great corporate solidity and assurance to its project, and so inducts the novice into company ways of going about things.

complex" (1961). The group's memo of "Problems to be Considered", 1959, includes this arresting design question:

```
Is extraneous wording - for example, commentary or
misspellings or different connectives - allowed?
```
[10]

Much could be unpacked from this compound question, such as the implication that compilers should not halt lightly over trivial errors, or the origin of COBOL's optional "noise words" – an ability to use prepositions or not as the writer pleases. There seems no great certainty here that comments were necessary for the sort of data-processing that the task group envisaged. But if they were, one possibility would be for COBOL to follow assembly language, and treat any spare text to the right of a "statement" as a comment. We might be tempted to call that a self-evidently bad idea,[11] but much remained open to doubt in 1959. Early COBOL provided a `NOTE` statement, for a much tidier form of comment, but one which could only be used in procedural code. Data structures and file formats could therefore not be commented, being in the `DATA DIVISION` and not the `PROCEDURAL DIVISION`.[12] Jean Sammet later regarded this as one of COBOL's greatest mistakes, which, in a language which also lacked function arguments, is saying something.

In the end, COBOL landed where FORTRAN had. The `NOTE` statement was dropped and instead COBOL once again adopted a special character in column 1:[13] but the marker was an asterisk `*` and not a `C`. This was probably an improvement, making a punched card look more distinctive, and it rather caught on. The IBM/360 assembler used it, for example, as did the simulation language GPSS, 1961. Louis Pouzin, who invented the term "shell", also chose an asterisk for RUNCOM, 1965, which became the MULTICS shell, and has not one but two comment forms:

```
*       THIS IS A COMMENT.
$       THIS IS PRINTED ON THE CONSOLE.
```

The second is in fact a print statement, what Unix shells call `echo`, printing the commentary on the user's console rather than ignoring it. Pouzin, interestingly, regards both as comments: to him, printing was not computation.[14]

Later shells, and other line-oriented Unix tools like awk and Perl and RATFOR, changed the asterisk `*` to a hash character `#` instead, which seems to have

[10] This memo, with some characters broken by a weak typewriter ribbon so that the first hyphen resembles an ellipsis, is photo-reproduced as pp. 226-27 of *HOPL I*.

[11] Witness the confusion that this added to System/360 Job Control Language, 1964, "the worst computer programming language ever devised by anybody, anywhere" (Fred Brooks).

[12] *HOPL I*, pp. 268 and 272.

[13] Or strictly speaking, column 7, but this was the first available since columns 1 to 6 were reserved for sequence numbers used only by key-punch operators.

[14] See Pouzin (1965). He was visiting MIT at the time, and wrote in English, but he was very much a Frenchman, as can be seen from his manual, where the example program names include `TOMATO`, `ONION` and `GARLIC`.

been a decision made at Bell Labs in 1971, probably by Ken Thompson. Computers could store source code in memory now, and with punched cards falling out of use, line boundaries lost much of their specialness, especially since Unix (unlike IBM mainframes) regarded files as very long lines rather than fixed-width rectangular grids. When no longer constrained to be used in column 1, `*` looked like a multiplication sign, or like the Kleene star, while the letter `C` looked like a variable name. Clearly we needed new syntax.

One option was to spell it out. ALGOL had done something similar since 1958:[15]

```
comment This is a comment ;
```

In particular, ALGOL may win the palm as the first widespread language with a multiline comment syntax: but that syntax wasn't a very good one. Both the opening token, `comment`, and the closing token, `;`, look too much like part of the comment. BASIC, which began around 1963 with just 15 statements, was not much better.[16] One of those statements was `REM`, short for "remark":

```
10 REM THIS IS A COMMENT
```

Even as a nonsense-word, `REM` suffers from the same issue that `NOTE` and `comment` do: it looks like prose, and therefore like part of the comment. Better would be to delimit comments with some symbol, some weird glyph which wouldn't clash with either code or English prose. The trouble was to find one.

This trouble was exemplified by ALGOL 68, a language designed by a committee of professors who met up every few months in one romantic locale after another, from St Pierre de Chartreuse to Novosibirsk, somewhat in the way that music labels used to form would-be supergroups of legendary musicians, packing them off to exotic locations together to record.[17] ALGOL 68 was a sprawling and incoherent design, of no practical use, but to a historian it looks better in the rear-view mirror. Its indecision can be revalued as "fertility", and its lack of adoption as "influence". Its approach to commentary certainly runs true to form. The `comment` keyword was deprecated (though not removed) in favour of a pair of matching markers either side of the remark being made. Thus:

```
# This is a comment #
```

However, `# ... #` was only one of four different possibilities. ALGOL 68's preferred delimiter was actually the American cent symbol `¢`:

```
¢ And this is a comment ¢
```

[15] See Perlis and Samelson (1958).

[16] Dartmouth (1964).

[17] See *HOPL II*. To continue this metaphor, Niklaus Wirth was the one who quit the band and recorded a solo album instead: briefly called ALGOL-W, this became Pascal.

¢ could hardly be faulted for distinctiveness, and the embedded "c for comment" made for a visual mnemonic; unfortunately, the non-alphanumeric keys on even a deluxe Teletype Model 37 (1968) did not run to such exotica.[18] As the ASCII character set became dominant, so the ability of language designers to draw on such glyphs went away. Even # was not universally available, since English typewriters had the £ sign instead. And so ALGOL 68 allowed that as well. Had the language ever been seriously used, the result would have been programs with mongrel collections of comment syntaxes scattered throughout.

```
£ Seriously? This is a comment? £
```

Given all this past experience, it is easy to see how a language designer in around 1970 might rule out both words and single characters as comment syntax. In need of something easily typed yet distinctive from both code and text, such a designer would then arrive quite naturally at using pairs or triples of punctuation signs to open and close our comments.

COBOL, when it finally moved away from punched cards and fixed column positions, switched from the singleton `*` to the pair `*>`, so the ghost of its asterisk lives on. That same ghost perhaps also lives in the now-widespread `/* ... */` notation. Often associated with C, 1973, this actually goes back at least to the IBM-sponsored language PL/I, which rolled slowly out in the mid-1960s. Since `/*` can occur in a C expression – if `x` is an integer and `y` is a pointer to another integer, then `x/*y` ought to perform a division – C's borrowing of `/* ... */` was arguably a mis-step, though it now seems a heresy to say so. The notation might have been discarded as an oddity, much as Pascal's use of the pair `(*` and `*)` was gradually supplanted by `{` curly braces `}`. But once Kernighan and Ritchie's much-loved book *The C Programming Language* (1978) had been published, with its very liberal use of comments in its many code examples, a style had been set for the 80s and 90s. `/* ... */` was to be copied by many further languages, from Java to CSS to Go.

More important than PL/I's choice of punctuation marks was that it allowed what we might call "lexical comments", that is, it allowed comments to occur anywhere outside of identifiers or literals: perhaps even in the middle of a statement or expression. The IBM manual (1966) includes this example:

```
LABEL:  /* THE BLOCK OF CODING BETWEEN
BEGIN-END IS USED FOR PAYROLL CALCULA-
TIONS */
    BEGIN;
    ...
    END;
```

It's easy to miss how radical this is. In FORTRAN or COBOL, a single punched card either was a comment or it was not. In PL/I, comments and code

[18] The author of this article is in a position to report that it is hard to force LaTeX to produce a cent sign in a typewriter font even today.

can mingle freely. But this comes at a cost, because it makes commentary a purely lexical feature of the language, which has to be stripped out very early in compilation. Thus an annotated syntax tree for a PL/I program can no longer faithfully represent it, since it cannot contain the comments. That makes automated refactoring, and code visualisation, harder: which may not have mattered in PL/I days, but is more relevant for (say) the C++ or Rust ecosystem today. To take another example, if BASIC had allowed lexical comments then interpreters on 1980s microcomputers would have been unable to store BASIC programs in tokenised form. On a computer with perhaps 4K to 16K free for program storage, this would have been a considerable loss.

Just as C did not invent `/* ... */`, so C++ did not invent `//` for line comments, that is, comments terminated by a line ending. `//` exists in some forms of Job Control Language, and in everyday programming it goes back at least to Martin Richards's admirably lucid specification for BCPL (1967):

```
// This is a line comment, ending when the line does.
```

Numerous other globs have been tried over the years. Among functional languages, Miranda used a double-vertical-stroke `||`, and Haskell rotated that into a double-hyphen `--`:[19]

```
|| A line comment in Miranda.
-- A line comment in Haskell.
```

The success of some comment syntaxes rather than others is not only down to tradition: some simply work better. Lua is a much-loved language, for example, but its multi-line comment syntax `--[[ ... --]]` is unlikely to be repeated, and nor will HTML win any imitators. One reason for survival is simple practicality: `//` is quick to type, a double-tap next to the shift key. Another way to win the hearts of coders is with ASCII art, as if we are drawing speech bubbles around our comments:

```
/* Admire the visual enclosure of my two slashes, */
/* and the mirror-symmetry of these begin and end tokens. */
{- Isn't this multi-line comment from a Haskell program
   a little like a notice pinned to a wall by drawing pins?
-}
```

Alternatively, one might hope to be memorable by imitating typographic conventions familiar already from books:

```
-- A long dash, from Haskell, Ada, or SQL,
-- imitates a French speech mark.
[Square brackets, in Inform, imitate the way books print text
which is a clarification and not really part of a quotation.]
```

[19] Honestly, I don't know how Haskell writers manage: I mean to say, how are you going to decrement your global variables while reading them if you haven't got the minus-minus operator?.

To sum up this historical survey, there have been three main developments: the "line comment", 1957, where opening syntax marks a line as a comment; the "multi-line comment", 1958, where a comment has both opening and closing syntax; and "lexical comments", 1966, in which either line or multi-line comments can appear in arbitrary syntactic positions. Over that same period comments were realised first to be necessary, 1951, then to need their own syntax, 1957, which all parts of a program might need, 1960, and with delimiters visually unlike both source code and prose, 1966, while being possible to type on an ASCII keyboard, 1968.

By 1970 at the latest, then, the evolution of comment syntax was complete: but only from a compiler's point of view. In the decades since, it has become common for other programs dealing with source to look for additional syntax inside of comments – documentation generators, text editors, testing harnesses, and so on. Comments have been hijacked for use as language extensions by third parties. From that point of view, we should let go of the naive idea that the interior of a comment is only a syntactic desert of waste characters.[20]

In particular, users have always wanted to pretty-print their programs, and special comment syntaxes may be used there, too. ANSI COBOL, 1974, and some earlier implementations, used a secondary comment character (`/` instead of `*`) to mean "if printing this program out, start this comment on a fresh page". A more contemporary example is provided by Swift, where `/** ... */`, note the extra `*`, and `///`, note the extra `/`, signal that the commentary should be read as if marked up with Markdown:[21]

```
/// Which is *emphatically* a [good idea](principles.md).
```

These rudimentary ideas of chapter division, of headings, or of using boldface and italic, lie only on the very fringe of programming language syntax. But they point the way to literate programming, to which we will return.

3 The Need to Comment

How and why comments have been used is harder to trace than their syntax, and harder to pin down to specific dates or people. Who now knows what hacker first twigged that the comment could be abused as a rapid way to deactivate lines of code when debugging, by "commenting them out"? It was probably after about 1963, because one can hardly *temporarily* punch a `C` or `*` onto column 1 of a punched card. But who that trailblazer was, we cannot now say.

Leaving that supposedly temporary use for the comment aside, what in practice do we need comments for? We begin with what we might call technical needs.

[20] An early example of this would be that line 1 in a Unix line-based language can be a "shebang" comment, an opening line beginning `#!`, which discloses what language the program is written in.

[21] Markdown, a cynic might observe, has the benefit that no mark-up syntax is ever erroneous, only bizarre: and this avoids the awkward question of whether a compiler could ever throw a syntax error over the contents of a comment.

3.1 The Zone of the Inexpressible

Comments are used to express what is inexpressible in the formal syntax of a language. They convey meanings for which there is no notation: but new languages bring new notations, and capture new meanings. The zone of the inexpressible has therefore shifted, contracted, and expanded over seven decades of language design.

(1) *As programming languages become more expressive, so the zone of the inexpressible contracts.*

(i) The invention of the programming language was a huge contraction all by itself, capturing many aspects of assembly language previously tracked only by comments. The variable name made it unnecessary to comment register usage. Explicit control constructs made it unnecessary to comment every branch. Expressions with operators made simple formulae legible without side-notes.

(ii) Another early use of comment lines was to make a heading, a fence, or a conceptual divider. FORTRAN code in the wild, for example, often contains lines such as:
COBOL shifted many such dividers into formal language syntax, requiring programmers to write compiler-checked lines such as `IDENTIFICATION DIVISION`, `DATA DIVISION`, and so on. Less obtrusively, ALGOL and Pascal gained **`begin`** and **`end`**, while C and C++ adopted braces, to demarcate regions of code: first on the small scale (with loop bodies and functions), then the large (with classes and modules).

```
C       **** GAUSSIAN ELIMINATION SUBROUTINE ****
```

(iii) A further systematic use of early comments was to specify calling conventions for subroutines or functions. These too could be moved into syntax, where they became type declarations and function prototypes, and then, as theoretical interest grew in pre- and post-conditions, design by contract: cf. Eiffel, 1985; Scala, 2004; or Kotlin, 2011.

(iv) There seems to be some interest today in moving "beware!" comments, of the kind which conscientious coders add to high-performance functions without guard-rails, into the formal syntax of languages. We see this in the rise of keywords like **`unsafe`** to mark code contaminated by uninitialised memory, for example.

(2) *On the other hand, as the size and reach of programs grows, so the zone of the inexpressible expands, and this is managed with new forms of commentary.*

(i) Programs have grown vast, with all the problems of coherence and comprehensibility that this brings.[22] Source code struggles to express the place of a unit within the whole. In many large projects, the source code's directory structure, an implicit form of commentary in itself, has to do this.

[22] The Linux kernel in 2025 is larger than Unix system 1 by a factor of about ten thousand, the scale difference between a chair and Mount Everest.

(ii) Programs run against a huge backdrop of supporting libraries and remote services. Interfaces therefore proliferate. We have expectations about their behaviour, but often can't express those well. API writers now put real effort into choosing identifier names which act, in a half-functional, half-commentary way, as documentation. Identifier names have ballooned in size:

```
UnitAcceleration.metersPerSecondSquared
Locale.commonISOCurrencyCodes
```

Language ecosystems attempt to enforce these practices with style guides, but they are essentially voluntary, and in that sense are comment.

(iii) Pervasive source control, and the popularity of GitHub in particular, has given programs a new and wider perimeter. A "program" which might once have been a tarball of source files is now accompanied by metadata – issues, commit names, commit history, pull request discussions, installation notes, internal documentation, and so on. The periphery is now defined by what does, and does not, go into the repository, not just by what is compiled.

3.2 Emotion and Opinion

Technological change, then, changes the technical reasons to write comments, but there are also social reasons, and society changes too:

(i) There have been successive waves of immigration into the population of coders: by corporate salary-men (and women), by the first CS college graduates, by counter-cultural free-thinkers, by teenagers, by entrepreneurs.
(ii) New generations have new performative styles. Those raised on the snark of social media understand the emotional meaning of comments differently from those trained on view-slides and typewritten memos.
(iii) Peer pressure, respect, and participation work differently at different social distances. Collaborators in one room may write comments laced with a private jargon, whereas collaborators on different continents have to address themselves to strangers.
(iv) Discourse about programming remains overwhelmingly in English, but all the same, native speakers may already be a minority among coders, and this must eventually change the stylistics of commentary.[23]

[23] Coding outside of the English-speaking world began early. Contributions to the International Algebraic Language, a working title for ALGOL, were made from Darmstadt as early as 1955: popular in western Europe, ALGOL also went on to became the dominant programming language in the Soviet Union after the Khrushchev Thaw. Pascal, 1970, was created in German-speaking Switzerland, and Prolog, 1972, in France. But one shouldn't overstate this internationalism. Lua, Brazil 1993, is the only language to break through from south of the equator, and Ruby, Japan 1995, is a rare specimen from Asia. In any case, most languages today, regardless of origin, use English keywords such as `for` or `method`, use English API or library names, and are documented in English.

(v) Fashion changes: pair programming, daily standups, code review, and other such practices come and go, and the corporate desire for all its workers to work uniformly waxes and wanes.

With all that duly acknowledged, human nature does not change, and perhaps the following selection of comments, arranged by personality type, will have a certain timeless quality. We have all been all of these people: I accuse nobody.

The Boilerplate-Maker. That is, the compliance lawyer, who stamps the top of every last file with two dozen lines of legalese:

```
Copyright (C) 2016-2024 Free Software Foundation, Inc.
This file is part of the GNU C Library.
The GNU C Library is free software; you can redistribute...
etc.
```

The Simultaneous Translator. Often an assembly-language coder, who clarifies each line of source, in effect re-narrating it in English:

```
.readCharacterFromCurrentInputBufferLoop
    BIT .escapeFlag         ; check ESCAPE flag
    BMI .setEscapeAndExit   ; if (ESCAPE flag set) then branch
                            ; (set escape condition and exit)
    LDX .currentInputBuffer; get current input buffer number
    JSR .readFromEconet     ; get byte from current input
    BCC .pullAndReturn      ; if (valid char found) then exit
```

The Scholiast. This is the person writing in the margin of somebody else's program, trying to make sense of it, adding notes like / ∗ presumablyfailsifx < 0 ∗ / or `/* why? */`.
The Professor. Because authority matters:

```
-- See R. Rivest, ‘‘The MD5 message-digest algorithm,’’
-- IETF Network Working Group, RFC 1321, April 1992.
```

The Guilty. The urge to own up to a quick-and-dirty solution is unaccountably strong. Even relative temples of hygiene such as the Glasgow Haskell Compiler have plenty of comments like these:

```
-- Slight inefficiency here haha
{- Technically, we should state that we depend
on all the indefinite libraries we used to
typecheck this. However, this field isn't
really used for anything, so we leave it
blank for now. -}
```

The Procrastinator. Unlike The Guilty, The Procrastinator fully intends to mend ways:

```
// To do: Check for error codes
// Placeholder class
// Not implemented yet
```

The Victim. Whereas The Victim wants you to know that society is to blame:

```
/* because glibc is totally BORKED */
/* THE CLIENT MADE ME DO THIS */
/* this code is cursed */
```

The Puritan. This is the coder who takes a principled stand against comments in any code-base, and is determined to contribute no new ones. Comments are not checked by the compiler for truth, or sincerity, or redundancy, and that disturbs the Puritan. Even if what we say is true now, maybe it won't be true later, and then the program will contain falsehoods. Code which only makes sense in the light of a comment is bad code. Comments increase the clutter on the screen. You're muddying your code, not clarifying it. Comments are a code smell, a sign that refactoring is needed.[24]

These are caricatures, but we can see the human needs within them: even the Puritan, whose human need is to deny that we have needs. But whether people love or hate to comment, they generally share a mindset that comments are an exceptional act, something you're pushed into by circumstance. That is the mindset which literate programming aims to make a decisive break from.

4 The Other Way Around

Suppose, then, that we turn things inside out, and stop thinking of comments as an exception. In the doctrine of "literate programming", a source file opens in a comment, and the material in it is primarily commentary. In this looking-glass world, instead of using an escape syntax to enter a comment, now we use an escape syntax to enter code.

In "bird-style" syntax for literate Haskell, a greater-than sign > is used: the Haskell 98 report credits this idea to Richard Bird, who had contributed it to Orwell in around 1984–85.[25]

```
map f applies a function f to each entry in a list,
returning the result as another list. If the function f
takes the type a to the type b, then map f will have to
take a list of a to a list of b:
```

[24] Puritans are in many ways admirable people, right up to the point where they start burning non-Puritans. Every large project has a contributor who secretly wants to delete other people's comments.

[25] See Peyton Jones (2003). Orwell is almost unique in *requiring* programs to be literate: to quote §16 of Wadler and Miller (1990), "In most programming languages, comments are indicated by some special symbol. In Orwell, it is the other way around.".

```
> map :: (a -> b) -> [a] -> [b]

Either a list is empty or it contains a first element, x,
and then a tail xs which may or may not be empty. We need
to define map in both cases:

> map f [ ] = [ ]
> map f (x : xs) = f x : map f xs
```

A more modern style would be to indent the code by one tab stop, which, you would not be the first to notice, makes the file look even more like Markdown.

Now, in principle, this pulling inside-out gives us no extra expressive power. There is an obvious duality between writing:

```
Either a list is empty or it contains a first element, x,
and then a tail xs which may or may not be empty. We need
to define map in both cases:

> map f [ ] = [ ]
> map f (x : xs) = f x : map f xs
```

and writing the same thing in non-literate Haskell:

```
-- Either a list is empty or it contains a first element, x,
-- and then a tail xs which may or may not be empty. We need
-- to define map in both cases:

map f [ ] = [ ]
map f (x : xs) = f x : map f xs
```

We have simply given up a life of code diversified by comments for a life of comments diversified by code. So it shouldn't make a difference: but it does. Comment-world is now our home, it's where we live, it's not somewhere we visit. We are no longer writing a program with some marginal notes: we are writing an essay which incorporates a program. If you've never tried this, give it a go: like snorkelling, or country dancing, you'll feel self-conscious at first, but you'll get the hang of it.

All the same, full-on literate programming is more than that. What we have so far is limited, in the same way that a scripting language without branches or loops isn't Turing-complete. There are things it can never do. So if you'll forgive me, I propose the following criterion:

A system for literate programming is Knuth-complete only if it allows code to be reordered and restructured for clearer presentation.

In that sense Orwell and Literate Haskell are not Knuth-complete. I invoke the magic name of Knuth because, as we'll see, Donald Knuth was and probably still is the main proponent of LP.

What then do I mean by "reordered and restructured"? That sounds radical, and it is. The following fragment is what we will call a *paragraph* from a literate program:

```
@<Resolve an ambiguous reading@> =
    int passed_readings = 0;
    @<Set up the list of readings to test@>;
    @<Recurse to try each reading in turn@>;
    if (Dash::problems_have_been_issued()) return
NEVER_MATCH;
    if (passed_readings > 0) @<Preserve successful readings@>
    else @<Give up with no readings possible@>;
```

Paragraphs can have names, and this one is called "resolve an ambiguous reading". It contains other paragraphs – those are not functions calling each other; they are contiguous code, including each other. The point is to make the structure clearer by progressively hiding and then revealing the details. Knuth called a mass of paragraphs like this, all including each other, a "web" – he was writing ten years before Tim Berners-Lee reclaimed the word – but the dependency graph of paragraphs is actually a tree.

To compile this so-called web, we don't need a new compiler: we need a preprocessor called a *tangler*. The tangler turns the web into a file of orthodox source code, which is then run through a compiler. Tangling is the step which literate Haskell doesn't have, and is why I say it's not Knuth-complete. Tangling may have seemed unnecessary to a language where sequence is less explicit and code is already served up in teaspoon-sized portions. Or maybe tangling just looked too shallow, too much like macro expansion. Like flared trousers, macros have made a big comeback lately, but people of a certain age still think they look very 1970s.

Donald Knuth's original tangler was part of a system called WEB, for use with programs in Pascal, but he now uses an adaptation called CWEB, for programs in C. Why, you might wonder, was any adapting necessary? What does the tangler care whether it's rearranging C or Pascal? If you do wonder that, you're mostly right, and I refer you to Norman Ramsey's NOWEB tool, a more language-agnostic tool written in 1989. But the main reason CWEB differed from WEB is that tangling was only one thing it did: the other was *weaving*, which turns a web into an attractively readable version for human eyes. In LP, then, the programmer edits a web, which can then either be tangled and then compiled in order to be run, or woven and then typeset in order to be studied.

WEB was first distributed as a tool for building Knuth's two typographic programs, TeX and Metafont. Woven, then printed in hard covers, these now form volumes B and D of Knuth's five-volume *Computers and Typesetting* (1986). They are a fascinating read, though perhaps not as Knuth intended. They offer a vivid snapshot of the trials of writing system software in circa-1980 Pa, but are also redolent of older coding styles which Knuth had learned in the age of memory soup. Stacks abound, and so do hard limits, with memory micro-managed almost down to the bit level: it's evident that Knuth does not wholly share Wirth's ideas of abstraction, and he adds features to WEB to circumvent any constraints of Pascal which chafe him. The books are also filled with bravura coding tricks, especially in numerical approximations. TEX paragraph 108, for example, relies on the fact that 100×2^{18} is roughly 297^3. Metafont, particularly, is written with the superbness of a maestro performing on a stage (see Fig. 2). Whether these books leave the reader *understanding* their programs is another matter, but they certainly communicate the texture, personality, and motivation within. Above all, as Van Wyk noted (1990), they have "verisimilitude": they are not paraphrases or descriptions of TEX and Metafont, they *are* TEX and Metafont.

44 PART 7: ARITHMETIC WITH SCALED NUMBERS METAFONT §116

116. Here is a typical example of how the routines above can be used. It computes the function

$$\frac{1}{3\tau}f(\theta,\phi) = \frac{\tau^{-1}\bigl(2+\sqrt{2}\,(\sin\theta - \frac{1}{16}\sin\phi)(\sin\phi - \frac{1}{16}\sin\theta)(\cos\theta - \cos\phi)\bigr)}{3\,\bigl(1+\frac{1}{2}(\sqrt{5}-1)\cos\theta + \frac{1}{2}(3-\sqrt{5}\,)\cos\phi\bigr)},$$

where τ is a *scaled* "tension" parameter. This is METAFONT's magic fudge factor for placing the first control point of a curve that starts at an angle θ and ends at an angle ϕ from the straight path. (Actually, if the stated quantity exceeds 4, METAFONT reduces it to 4.)

The trigonometric quantity to be multiplied by $\sqrt{2}$ is less than $\sqrt{2}$. (It's a sum of eight terms whose absolute values can be bounded using relations such as $\sin\theta\cos\theta \le \frac{1}{2}$.) Thus the numerator is positive; and since the tension τ is constrained to be at least $\frac{3}{4}$, the numerator is less than $\frac{16}{3}$. The denominator is nonnegative and at most 6. Hence the fixed-point calculations below are guaranteed to stay within the bounds of a 32-bit computer word.

The angles θ and ϕ are given implicitly in terms of *fraction* arguments *st*, *ct*, *sf*, and *cf*, representing $\sin\theta$, $\cos\theta$, $\sin\phi$, and $\cos\phi$, respectively.

```
function velocity(st, ct, sf, cf : fraction; t : scaled): fraction;
  var acc, num, denom: integer;  { registers for intermediate calculations }
  begin acc ← take_fraction(st − (sf div 16), sf − (st div 16));  acc ← take_fraction(acc, ct − cf);
  num ← fraction_two + take_fraction(acc, 379625062);  { 2^28 √2 ≈ 379625062.497 }
  denom ← fraction_three + take_fraction(ct, 497706707) + take_fraction(cf, 307599661);
      { 3 · 2^27 · (√5 − 1) ≈ 497706706.78 and 3 · 2^27 · (3 − √5) ≈ 307599661.22 }
  if t ≠ unity then num ← make_scaled(num, t);  { make_scaled(fraction, scaled) = fraction }
  if num div 4 ≥ denom then velocity ← fraction_four
  else velocity ← make_fraction(num, denom);
  end;
```

Fig. 2. Paragraph 116 of *Metafont: The Program*, (Knuth, 1986c).

Weaving today more often involves rendering programs as websites than publishing them as books, but there continue to be delightful exceptions, often with code worked into elegant page designs. The designer of the beautiful *Physically Based Rendering: From Theory to Implementation* (Pharr, Jakob, and Humphreys, 2004), a model library of ray-tracing algorithms, shows a particularly keen visual eye (see Fig. 3). There are also near misses at LP, such as the *Algorithm Design* textbook by Richard Bird and Jeremy Gibbons, which, though not a program as such, was woven from literate Haskell by lhs2TEX, and also tangled into a form which was type-checked if not actually executed. Jeremy is our host today and I hesitate to call his book "semi-literate", but it's clearly somewhere on a spectrum. As a program, the Glasgow Haskell Compiler also comes tantalisingly close to LP, with somewhat structured commentary, and woven versions of a sort which do appear online.

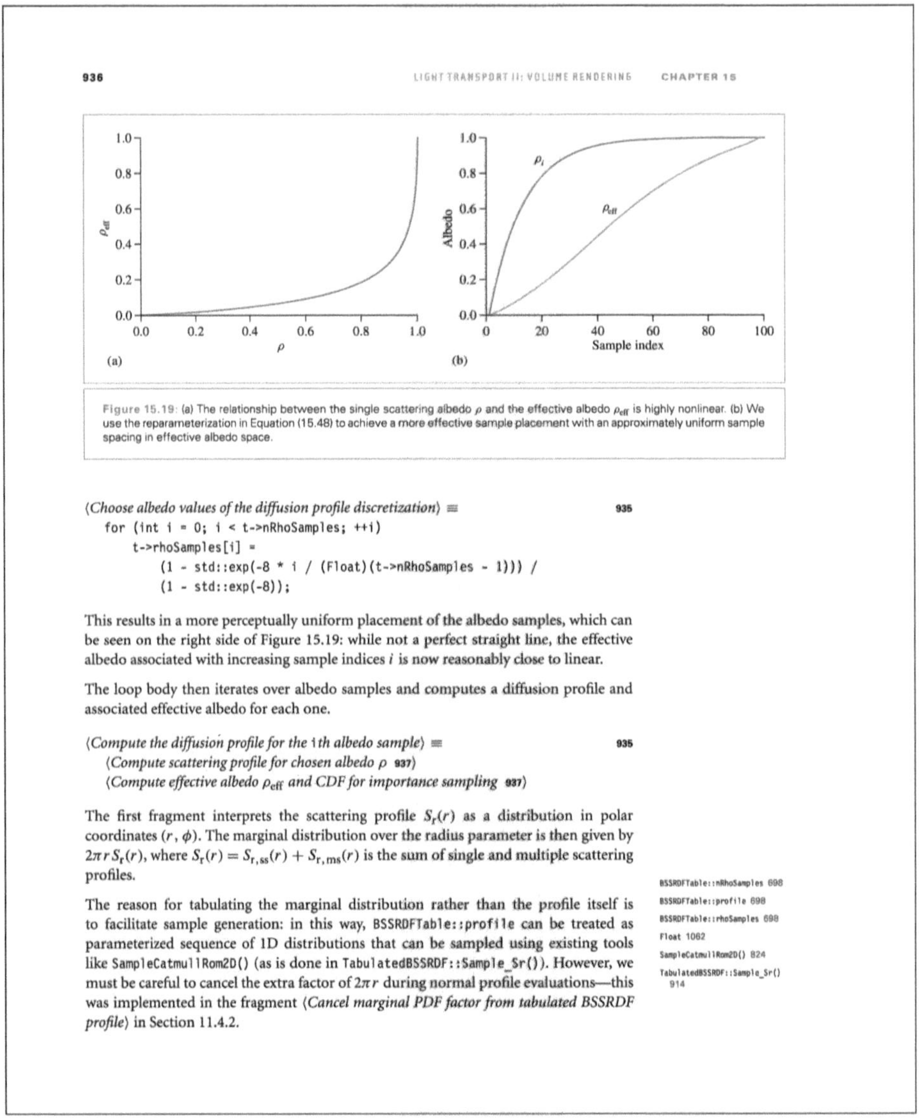

Figure 15.19: (a) The relationship between the single scattering albedo ρ and the effective albedo ρ_{eff} is highly nonlinear. (b) We use the reparameterization in Equation (15.48) to achieve a more effective sample placement with an approximately uniform sample spacing in effective albedo space.

⟨*Choose albedo values of the diffusion profile discretization*⟩ ≡ 935

```
for (int i = 0; i < t->nRhoSamples; ++i)
    t->rhoSamples[i] =
        (1 - std::exp(-8 * i / (Float)(t->nRhoSamples - 1))) /
        (1 - std::exp(-8));
```

This results in a more perceptually uniform placement of the albedo samples, which can be seen on the right side of Figure 15.19: while not a perfect straight line, the effective albedo associated with increasing sample indices i is now reasonably close to linear.

The loop body then iterates over albedo samples and computes a diffusion profile and associated effective albedo for each one.

⟨*Compute the diffusion profile for the* `i`*th albedo sample*⟩ ≡ 935
⟨*Compute scattering profile for chosen albedo* ρ 937⟩
⟨*Compute effective albedo* ρ_{eff} *and CDF for importance sampling* 937⟩

The first fragment interprets the scattering profile $S_r(r)$ as a distribution in polar coordinates (r, ϕ). The marginal distribution over the radius parameter is then given by $2\pi r S_r(r)$, where $S_r(r) = S_{r,\text{ss}}(r) + S_{r,\text{ms}}(r)$ is the sum of single and multiple scattering profiles.

The reason for tabulating the marginal distribution rather than the profile itself is to facilitate sample generation: in this way, `BSSRDFTable::profile` can be treated as parameterized sequence of 1D distributions that can be sampled using existing tools like `SampleCatmullRom2D()` (as is done in `TabulatedBSSRDF::Sample_Sr()`). However, we must be careful to cancel the extra factor of $2\pi r$ during normal profile evaluations—this was implemented in the fragment ⟨*Cancel marginal PDF factor from tabulated BSSRDF profile*⟩ in Section 11.4.2.

`BSSRDFTable::nRhoSamples` 698
`BSSRDFTable::profile` 698
`BSSRDFTable::rhoSamples` 698
`Float` 1062
`SampleCatmullRom2D()` 824
`TabulatedBSSRDF::Sample_Sr()` 914

Fig. 3. A little *Physically Based Rendering*.

5 Donald Ervin Knuth

To see how these ideas were born, and why, we have to step back and talk about Donald Knuth. His early accomplishments in the analysis of algorithms, and in the semantics of programming languages, much influenced by Noam Chomsky, won him the Turing Award in the early 70s, but his greatness lies really in his long cultural presence since that time.

Donald Ervin Knuth was born in 1938, between Donald Duck (1934) and Donald Trump (1946): Don was a fairly common boy's name in his generation. His middle name, though, is a more unusual German one, and we'll come back to that. He is a compulsive writer. He writes in a refreshing, welcoming style, with the voice, perhaps borrowed from Mark Twain, that you hear in the boy inventor characters of American children's books, like Tom Swift; or the amateur-engineer heroes of the science fiction of Edward E. Smith or John W. Campbell. In this milieu, innovation is a healthy pastime, with every American boy a potential Ford, or another Edison. Knuth is happy to talk about himself when asked, so that there is a wealth of autobiographical detail in the *Selected Papers*. He has been interviewed on tape and now on, for example, Lex Fridman's podcast, for nearly four decades and has become very skilled at it. He presents such an open persona that his interviewers are too charmed to push back. Talking with him, which I certainly felt was a privilege, reminded me of a similar evening I once spent with Seamus Heaney. It felt like personal contact even though it wasn't really. Knuth projects a gentle shyness in person – his wife Jill is the more outgoing of the two – but he has lively eyes in his frog-like face, and a quiet charisma which I have to say that I immediately warmed to.

So much for his outward manner. The first thing to say about Knuth's inner self is that he is possessed of a Renaissance-level belief that he embodies universality. If Knuth had a motto, it would be: "Everybody should do this." He learned on a computer with drum memory, and he thinks we should. He is a literate programmer, so we should be. He likes the Computer Modern Roman font, so every book of computer science proceedings should be typeset with it. Because he logs and categorises every bug in his code, we should do that too. This conviction of being a prototype is something you can also see in other American geniuses of the twentieth century – Linus Pauling, or Richard Feynman, for example – but Knuth covers it better with modesty. Just the same, his self-belief is mountainous, and we need to remember that when assessing his claims.

The second thing to say about Knuth is that he is at a profound level a Lutheran, born in the German part of Wisconsin. Lutheranism is a religion of the book, mediated through communal prayer and communal music. Knuth's father was a devout man, and (simplifying the story slightly) became a printer by trade: he and his son printed Church leaflets together, and they were both organists. The most prized possession of history's greatest organist, J. S. Bach (1685–1750), was a bound set of the printed works of Martin Luther: conversely, Knuth's most valued possession is a church organ. In due course Knuth wrote a theological tract of his own, *3:16* (1991), a Bible study looking only at Chap. 3 verse 16 of each book: Genesis 3:16, Exodus 3:16, and so on through. He justifies this as a stratigraphic way to make a statistical sampling of the Bible, but it reminds me more of his advice to students to pick a random memory location in a computer and understand exactly what happens to the bits stored there as programs are loaded and run. To Bach, the Bible and the Church calendar were God's perfect mechanism, they were the gears of the universe, and I think Knuth shares that sense. He once said that to write a program is to create a whole world.

That hope of completeness, of sufficiency, certainly lies behind his supposedly seven-volume *The Art of Computer Programming*, even though it's now 63 years since the publisher commissioned it. Like the team of French mathematicians writing up all of maths under the name "Nicholas Bourbaki" (1934–), Knuth set out to write up all of computer science, but to do so alone: he has been halfway through an ever-expanding Volume 4 for nearly half a century now.[26] The *Art* has gradually turned into a Bible itself, something we venerate as an object on our shelves, and indeed, Knuth created his entire digital typesetting system in order to bring Volumes 2 and 3 closer to perfection as physical artefacts. Knuth once said that he thought God wanted him to finish this book. That's the kind of thing that people who see angels say.

So Knuth grew up not only with ink in the blood, as the saying has it – he was born to print books – but also with a sense that the making of books is a sacral act. From that point of view, turning computer programs into books has a kind of rightness. Knuth wants their mechanisms to be visible, in the way that the Bible makes the mechanisms of the world visible.

And of course on a practical level, he also needed a way to publish the source code of his new program *TEX in book form. It wasn't vanity that led him to publish TEX: The Program* (1986b). Tony Hoare had asked him to do so in 1978, pointing out the shortage of real-world programs for students to study. Individual numerical procedures were sometimes included in journal articles, and a handful of academically interesting programs or subroutine libraries did become technical reports, offprints, or low-circulation tracts.[27] But Hoare was right to see these as being basically toys rather than production software. Even in the 1980s, computer users rarely saw source code written by strangers. At best, they saw short snippets in *BYTE* magazine, or *Dr Dobbs's Journal*, or one

[26] So far we have Volumes 1, 2, 3, 4A and 4B: Knuth (1968), Knuth (1969), Knuth (1973), Knuth (2011), Knuth (2022). Fascicle 7 of Volume 4, on constraint satisfaction, came out a few weeks after this talk was delivered (2025). Addison-Wesley describes it as "the first third of what will eventually become hardcover Volume 4C", with 4D to 4F projected to follow. Since 1973, then, Knuth has set himself to distill the applied theory of all known combinatorial problems, which has turned out to be a combinatorial explosion all by itself. The twenty-first century Fascicles have been delightful reads, as they have appeared one by one, and this is work of lasting value regardless of its impossibility of completion. Still, I can't escape the feeling that Volume 7 of the *Art*, on compilers, was the one most needed by the programmers of 1973, and also the one Knuth was best-placed to write.

[27] For example, an ALGOL 60 implementation of a model ALGOL 60 compiler had appeared in Holland, though with little explication: Kruseman Aretz et al. (1973).

of the Bell Labs books. Knuth's insight here, and in this he saw further than Hoare, was that the ability to publish your own code would democratise being a computer scientist, in the same way that YouTube would later democratise broadcasting. Just as $\TeX$ let you print your own maths, WEB let you publish your own programs. After all, if tiny Lutheran churches in Wisconsin could make their own leaflets, so could you.

6 Shall We Be Structured, or Literate?

"I must confess," Knuth wrote when he announced the rather passive-aggressive term "literate programming", "that there may also be a bit of malice in my choice of title." He explains that he felt coerced into structured programming because he couldn't bear to think of his own programs as "unstructured". Well, said Knuth, surely nobody wants to be "illiterate" either?

The story of "structured programming" could be told in a number of ways: as a clash of mass movements, government vs industry vs academia, in which individuals barely matter, or as a tussle for dominance between a handful of charismatic professors. It might even be possible to argue that nothing really happened except for a quite natural evolution of tooling as software rose in scale. Culturally, though, it's undeniable that by 1980 structured programming had risen to become the dominant way people spoke about virtue in the writing of software. Whatever it was, it was good practice in an almost moral sense of the word "good". This was an ideological movement comparable to, for example, the valorisation of "open source" at the turn of the twenty-first century.

Briefly, then, it had long been folklore that some clean model of computation could implement any program, and in 1966 a rigorous proof was published that every computable function can be made out of `if` and `while` constructs alone. This news buttressed a feeling that maybe `goto` statements – unconditional, unmotivated branches from one part of a program to another – could be phased out from future programming languages. The Dutch computer scientist Edsger Dijkstra, who verged on being a mystical guru and who had devoted followers, then declared in 1968 that `goto` statements were not just unnecessary but damaging.[28] As with many great figures of history, he himself never used the words he is most famous for saying – "Go To Statement Considered Harmful" was a sub-editor's headline – but they sum him up better than the more nuanced things he did say. In this famous polemic Dijkstra writes, and he gives no evidence whatever except to insinuate that big people agree with him, that the ability to use `goto` is "an invitation to make a mess". His opening salvo gives the flavour:

> For a number of years I have been familiar with the observation that the quality of programmers is a decreasing function of the density of **go to** statements in the programs they produce. More recently I discovered why the use of the **go to** statement has such disastrous effects, and I became convinced [...]

[28] Dijkstra (1968).

...and so on. Knuth strongly disagreed. The structure theorem, he pointed out, had an unconstructive proof – in fact Dijkstra agreed about that. Knuth counter-proved that for some computable functions, unstructured implementations use less storage and run faster. Besides, didn't some programs read better with branches?[29] Knuth was genuinely pained to see processor cycles thrown away, but he was also in a massive personal bind here. His unfinished textbook used assembly language to showcase algorithms. If Dijkstra's "pseudocode" became standard as an expositional technique – which of course it did – then *The Art of Computer Programming* would be obsolete before he was even finished. All the same, Dijkstra was the older man, and Knuth was respectful of him, and was the more willing to learn. In a comical exchange of letters they persuaded themselves that deep down they agreed. Knuth said it was like having all his sins forgiven.

The professors of the 1970s were people who had been born into a world where milk was delivered by horse and cart. And now they saw banking and air traffic control running on great big COBOL programs, in a world slipping away from human oversight. Those programs, they suspected, were not well written. That sense of having uncorked a bottle which, maybe, we shouldn't have uncorked, coincided with a wider moral panic. Tony Hoare and his followers, by the 1980s, were talking about bugs in code as being an existential threat to human life. Today, a misdesigned radiation therapy machine for cancer patients: tomorrow, a nuclear accident. In movies, tellingly, computers were not just instruments of an Orwellian state, they were liable at any point to break free of their shackles and become sociopaths. They threatened the whole world, usually with, once again, nuclear missiles. To Hoare, only logical theory could save us from accidental doom. There's an English professor in the 1983 movie *WarGames*, rather nicely played by John Wood, who's a little like Hoare, in fact: having done prodigious things to create his computer, he is now the only one to realise its danger. This is essentially the story of Robert Oppenheimer, and once again shows how the nuclear panic, and the computer panic, were conflated.

How, then, should we make things safe? A consensus emerged that it was theory to the rescue, as in the famous cartoon on the cover of the "Dragon book", Aho and Ullman's *Principles of Compiler Design* (1977), where the knight is labelled with logical precepts and the dragon represents complexity. Spoiler alert: the knight wins. In reality, though, well-understood and theory-heavy tasks such as compilation were the exception, not the rule, and dreams of verifiable software were of greater moral than practical value: what Niklaus Wirth later called "symbols of hope for the drowning".

The fundamental issue here was trust. What could be relied upon? Hoare wanted programmers to write increasingly rigid logical specifications, not trusting even themselves: the paranoid style in computer science. Knuth had a more positive vision. He wanted programmers to explain themselves to each other, in a sort of fellowship of trust, with everyone sharing a common Bible of algorithms

[29] Parsers based on finite state machines are the usual example offered, but it has to be said that not very many programs are like that.

that he, of course, would provide. Structure, to Knuth, did not mean compliance with the Böhm-Jacopini Theorem of 1966. It meant making a human choice of how to divide up big programs into understandable pieces.

Ironically, this idea came to Knuth from an apostle of Dijkstra. In 1973, the Belgian computer scientist Pierre-Arnoul de Marneffe had sent Knuth a technical report of his proposed scheme for "holon programming". The report is a long and diffuse document, whose implications are not easy to grasp, but Knuth replied in 1974 making clear that he had read it carefully. "Holon" is a word de Marneffe had got from Arthur Koestler's philosophy book *The Ghost in the Machine* (1967). Koestler is writing about the mind-body problem, not about computing, and says that complex systems are made up of "holons", which are pieces of the whole. de Marneffe thought, well, programs are complex systems, we should compose those out of holons as well. In the following excerpt, de Marneffe explains his understanding of "holon", and the passage gives, I think, a sense of his convoluted, faintly metaphysical cast of mind:

> A complex system must be a hierarchic ordering of functions (holons) with the following features:
> A) "Hierarchy": Each holon is composed by other holons which are "refinements" of the former holon. These holons are submitted to some rigid rules; they perform the "detail" operations which, put together, compose the function of the former holon.
> B) "Tendency to Autonomy": Each holon has the ability to check its "environment" before performing its function; it may modify its behaviour according to test results. There exists a clear distinction between a "state description" and a "process description." The holon function corresponds to the process description; but it checks if the environment upon which it acts, belongs to its expected state description.
> C) "Tendency to Integration": The holon integrates with other holons in the hierarchy according to a flexible strategy. This integration must be understood as a will to close cooperation with the other holons for the emergence of a "tougher" and more efficient component.

It is not immediately clear how to apply these ideas, but in practice "hierarchy" was the one Knuth latched onto, and holons are what became the named paragraphs of literate programming.[30] The one extant copy of this report was unavailable until 2024, so de Marneffe is only now being reappraised.[31] Reading it now, I find myself bound to wonder: if Dijkstra, rather than Knuth, had picked up this idea and run with it, languages like Pascal and Oberon and Mesa and Modula-3 might have adopted holons, and history might have been different.

Or, maybe not. The golden age when professors genuinely led programming culture, which began in perhaps 1960, was ending anyway. Computerised office

[30] I should say, paragraph is my word; Knuth sometimes called them modules, sometimes sections; the word holon died with de Marneffe.

[31] de Marneffe (1973). Mitch Gerrard has done historians a considerable service by pursuing Knuth's copy of this report, transcribing it and publishing it: see `holon-scribe/holon-programming` at GitHub.

work and home video games brought us vast numbers of small programs in Z80 and 6502 machine code, written by self-trained hackers. Try telling those guys not to use branches. Professors, in the end, don't get to decide cultural norms.

7 The Failure and Success of Literate Programming

We are stuck with the term "literate programming" now, for good or bad,[32] and also with the words "web", "weave" and "tangle". Knuth enjoys picking up random quotations like shiny shells he's found on the beach, and he got all three of these terms of art from this one:

> Oh, what a tangled web we weave,
> When first we practise to deceive!

This couplet is from *Marmion*, an epic Scottish-history poem by Sir Walter Scott, whose first edition in 1808 was an almost emerald green. The dye soaked into its cover used so much arsenic that librarians now have to keep this book in special bags, and readers must wear gloves.[33] A similar fate has befallen Knuth's own book on *Literate Programming* (1992) – it's an awkward selection of his papers which takes a long time to come to the point, and is rather makeshift as a manifesto. The book remains in print, but is a little bit toxic to read. My good friend Peter Jeavons got out the copy from the departmental library here and lent it to me in about 2008. I was never the same again: perhaps I should have worn gloves.

But plainly LP did not have the same effect on very many other people, and certainly did not become dominant. Nelson Beebe's bibliography of LP (2002) shows 250 papers up to 2002, so the idea wasn't ignored after 1984, and a few large projects did try it, notably the Axiom theorem-prover and a C compiler called lcc. But this is a drop in the ocean. Why, then, did LP lose out?

1. LP is radical and unfamiliar.
2. LP has no fancy ideas, like functor or monad. If Knuth had used the word "holon" more and the word "macro" less, LP might have looked shinier to other professors.
3. LP breaks tooling, like text editors and IDEs. Not badly, but enough to chafe.
4. As Christopher Van Wyk pointedly observed,[34] nobody is ever satisfied with anyone else's LP tool, they always end up writing their own. (Noweb is perhaps an exception.)

---

[32] Despite Knuth's substitution of the term "structured documentation" in the title of the CWEB manual, Knuth and Levy (1993).

[33] Scott (1808): a bestseller in six cantos somewhat anticipating Byron, it flung its antihero Lord Marmion, a courtier of Henry VIII, into the Battle of Flodden Field.

[34] "Unfortunately, no one has yet volunteered to write a program using another's system for literate programming": Van Wyk (1990).

5. Early LP tools had dismayingly old-school syntax, showing off Knuth's love of creating more and more escape characters.
6. Most people are not writing programs with a deadline measured in academic years. Most people have to clear 20 tickets from Jira by Monday.
7. LP is individualistic. Modern code is written by large, loose teams.
8. LP assumes all code is equally interesting. It really is not.
9. LP assumes that code should read like a mathematical journal. That's what Knuth loves best, but it's not everybody's cup of tea.
10. Reasons 1 to 9 could be mitigated: this one can't. Most coders are not writers, and most writers are not coders.

In making his visionary and wholly impractical proposal, then, Knuth was a little like those 18th-century French intellectuals who wanted to create a new utopia in America, where everyone would live in peace and harmony because they would all be philosophers. He daydreamed about a *Reader's Digest*-like journal of the future which would carry the best new programs for people to read. That didn't happen.[35] And yet the front page of Hacker News today is, at least in part, a contents page of fun stuff to look at over on GitHub. And while we could argue about the extent to which GitHub weaves code, it certainly does syntax-highlight it, and it uses social pressure to get programmers to write Markdown-formatted `README.md` files. So, rather like those Enlightenment dreamers, perhaps Knuth did see his ideas seep into the future after all.

I will close this talk by giving my own experience, for what that is worth. My one program of note is a programming language called Inform. It's used only by writers of interactive fiction, not for general-purpose programming. Inform once made it to number 47 in the TIOBE index, a popularity chart for languages, but is usually not even in the top 100. Still, it has real-world users and a Jira bug-tracker and forums and feature requests and all of that, so I think it's a fair case study of what literate programs might look like today, and I offer the following lessons learned.

Lesson 1: *Tooling is needed which can scale.* I started out using CWEB, Knuth's approved port of WEB. But those first-wave tools were built for essay-sized programs: say, 300 source lines of code. They were only just able to handle TeX and Metafont, which were dissertation-sized, at around 30,000 SLOC each. Inform has about 300,000 SLOC, and even that's on the small side for a modern compiler. CWEB just can't handle it. Doug McIlroy once called one of Knuth's programs "a sort of industrial-strength Fabergé egg": Knuth loves miniaturist bit-twiddling to cut down on memory use, even if it incurs hard limits. Well, I hit those limits.

[35] A few items in the TeX user-group newsletter *TUGboat* hardly count. More mainstream was the occasional LP column in *Communications of the ACM*, edited by Christopher Van Wyk (the former student of Knuth, who is not the South African poet of the same name): but while the column began in good spirits with Van Wyk (1987), it ended ruefully at its sixth appearance, Van Wyk (1990).

Another sort of scaling is that an undifferentiated mass of text is unreadable when it's long enough: imagine *War and Peace* without chapter divisions. As a rule of thumb, each order of magnitude of SLOC needs another level of hierarchical division. So Inform is (1) a project which (2) has multiple webs, each having a contents page of (3) multiple chapters divided into (4) multiple sections, each of which has (5) subheadings containing (6) paragraphs. That's six levels of hierarchy; early LP tools like CWEB only provide three.

In particular, there's no such thing as a single program any more. Real-world projects are agglomerations – consider git, or Docker, for example – and often have sidekick or initialisation files which are just as important as the executed code. So you won't have one web, you'll have many.[36]

And so, after two years of trying to rewrite CWEB, I gave up and made my own tool. It's called "inweb", and it's okay, but no better than that. I hope to improve it later in 2025, but it does tangle at scale and weave to HTML. You can, for example, use a GitHub action to re-weave a GitHub Pages website of your program each time you push a commit to your web.

Lesson 2: *LP is easily abused.* If you're writing your own preprocessor anyway, it's impossible to resist the urge to use it for fixing what annoys you about C, or Haskell, or whatever. Knuth used WEB to add macros to Pascal, a feature Wirth had not wanted Pascal to have. This ability to customise maybe makes Knuth, and indeed me, biased as witnesses. When you use your own tool, you can scratch your own itches. Other users don't get the same consideration.

Lesson 3: *LP works best when you lean into the enjoyment of it.* This can be awfully self-indulgent, but there's a real satisfaction in finding ways to present your code, and to give informal proofs that it works. Writing code in a prose context also changes it stylistically. You find yourself using extended metaphors, in particular. A dull bit of memory-management code in Inform, for example, has the idea of a warehouse divided into rooms to give a solidity to the explanations. Knuth, similarly, uses an extended metaphor comparing TeX's parser to the human digestive system, with teeth, a throat, and a stomach.[37] Sometimes you end up rewriting your code to make your analogy more apt, and it's almost always better code as a result.

There's nothing new about coding by metaphor, of course. Most of the 23 *Design Patterns* in the famous catalogue (Gamma, Helm, Johnson, and Vlissides, 1994) have names like Factory, Builder, Bridge, Decorator. Those are metaphors from the world of human life. Functional programmers do this too, because categories are to mathematics what metaphors are to language. Categories recognise similar-looking structures which occur all over maths, just as metaphors recognise similar-looking structures all over life. A big selling point of the 1995 book, and it claims to have sold half a million copies, is that readers get to use an agreed set of evocative words like Façade as identifiers in their own code. As I

[36] My contribution to the lexicon of LP is the word "colony" for a collection of related webs – I believe naturalists call really large-scale spider infestations "colonies".

[37] He stops there, I'm happy to say.

argued earlier, use of identifier names can be commentary in disguise. Well: literate programmers have the space and the scope to describe their own picturesque patterns, not just recite the 23 magic words.

Lesson 4: *Literate programs have no secrets, no dark corners.* Perhaps it's a vanity, but I want my code to be maintainable after I die. Inform has been used since 1993, and I'm already older than Gustav Mahler ever was. I think LP has helped to get my often-amateurish code into a state where it's reasonable to expect that any maintainers coming after me will be able to cope.[38]

With that said, something you either love or hate about LP is that it makes you feel that even the boring parts of your code have to be neat as a pin. It's as if you're expecting a royal visit to your university, and you're worried that the Queen might open some door at random. So you paint all of the walls, and you wash all of the floors, just in case. I'm okay with that myself, but my users sometimes think my time is misapplied. As my friend Richard Evans once said, man, you gotta stop coding as if God is looking over your shoulder.

Lesson 5: *However you might want them to be, literate programs are not like novels.* It is a mistake to be overly seduced by the idea of "publication" – an idea that first you write in private, then you publish, then you're done. It frustrated my users that I kept the Inform repository private until I had the complete thing in order. I got actual hate mail.

But the real trouble happens afterwards. The idea of a program being finished can act as a drag anchor, stopping it from moving forwards. Consider TEX itself, which has only had bug fixes since 1986. *TEX: The Program* has been treated as a publication much like the John Updike novel of that year, *Roger's Version*, which is also still reprinted. Nobody thinks to bring the novel up to date – to give the characters mobile phones, perhaps, or mention Taylor Swift. The only maintenance which *Roger's Version* needs from one printing to the next is to correct any typos. In this respect software is not like a novel after all, and it must not be treated as such. Plain TEX has atrophied now into a ruinous state which cannot cope either with Unicode or modern fonts. If Knuth had taken the idea of "publication" of a "finished program" less literally, that need not have happened.[39]

---

[38] Cf. Knuth (2021) on maintaining code from 1980: "I was overjoyed to see how well the philosophy of literate programming has facilitated everything. This multifaceted program was written 40 years ago, yet I could still get back into TEX's darkest corners without trouble [...] I can't help but ascribe most of TEX's success to the fact that it has enabled literate programming.".

[39] This paper, for example, was typed in xelatex, one of several modernising forks of TEX. Knuth neither approves nor forbids these tools, and lends his authority only to the original Pascal code, which he presents as converging onto a final state. Knuth (2021) reports on version 3.141592653, with no further changes scheduled until 2029: "there's always a reason to change anything that isn't trivial. But one of TEX's principal advantages is the fact that it does not change".

8 Conclusion

Literate programming, then, is a minority sport. But it has some excellent use cases. Reference code for cryptography, for example, or the formalisation in the Lean theorem-prover of mathematical proofs. It can also do a nice job on culturally important code of the past, to give a guided tour of, say, Unix system 6, or *Super Mario Brothers*. In education, I think it would help tutors to demonstrate algorithms, and students to explain their submissions.

If I can add a little polemic of my own: try it some day. If you're making little DSLs with Racket, maybe think about making them literate. If you're writing an IDE or a code editor, make it play nicely with preprocessors. If you're writing a code visualiser, like kramdown, give it a syntax-highlighting mode like "Markdown but with Haskell in the code quotes", not just a choice between "Haskell" or "Markdown with plain code quotes". There are many little affordances which could easily be added to existing infrastructure which would make LP more comfortable.

If I have come to understand one thing through working with literate programming, it is this: The comment syntax is the most expressive in any programming language, not the least functional. Whether comments are asides, or long notes like the ones in the source code for GHC, or whether they flow into whole essays or books, comments are a point of contact between the human act of creation and the substance of what is created. When we design programming languages, we barely think about commentary at all. I say we should.

And with that, I reach the end of my own comment, and I hand back to the functional part of this conference.

`-}`

Acknowledgments. This article is slightly expanded from a keynote talk given otherwise largely as written, except that slides have been paraphrased and citations added. I'm grateful above all to Jeremy Gibbons for his generosity in inviting me to speak at Trends in Functional Programming 2025, and to many other speakers for their comments and discussions between sessions. Jeremy also kindly read and commented on a draft of this article. I owe a particular gratitude to my old friend Peter Jeavons, who at key points helped me along this road, and who is, in his modest way, as public-spirited a professor as any named above. Opinions, of course, are my own.

References

Aho, A.V., Ullman, J.D.: Principles of Compiler Design. Addison-Wesley (1977)

Backus, J.W., et al.: The FORTRAN Automatic Coding System for the IBM 704 EDPM: Programmer's Reference Manual. International Business Machines Corporation (1957)

Beebe, N.: A bibliography of literate programming (2002). http://www.math.utah.edu/~beebe/

Bergin, T.J., Gibson, R.G.: HOPL II: The Second ACM SIGPLAN Conference on History of Programming Languages. Addison-Wesley (1996)

Dartmouth. BASIC. Technical report, Dartmouth College Computation Center (1964)

de Marneffe, P.-A.: Holon programming: a survey. Technical report, University of Liège (1973)

Dijkstra, E.W.: Go to statement considered harmful. Commun. ACM **11**(3), 147–148 (1968)

Fischer, J.M.: Gustav Mahler. Yale University Press (2011)

Gamma, E., Helm, R., Johnson, R., Vlissides, J.: Design Patterns: Elements of Reusable Object-Oriented Software. Addison-Wesley (1994)

Ghosh, O.: What to look for on the back of a painting: an expert guide (2022). https://www.christies.com/en/stories/what-to-look-for-on-the-back-of-a-painting-821e1638846944fb9a2b05aad53854fe

IBM. IBM System/360 operating system PL/I language specifications. Technical report, International Business Machines Corporation (1966)

Kenny, G.: Stanley Kubrick's letter to projectionists on "Barry Lyndon" (with update) (2011). https://somecamerunning.typepad.com/some_came_running/2011/06/test.html

Kernighan, B.W., Plauger, P.J.: The Elements of Programming Style. McGraw-Hill (1974)

Kernighan, B.W., Ritchie, D.: The C Programming Language. McGraw-Hill (1978)

Knuth, D.E.: The Art of Computer Programming, Volume 1: Fundamental Algorithms. Addison-Wesley (1968)

Knuth, D.E.: The Art of Computer Programming, Volume 2: Seminumerical Algorithms. Addison-Wesley (1969)

Knuth, D.E.: The Art of Computer Programming, Volume 3: Sorting and Searching. Addison-Wesley (1973)

Knuth, D.E.: Computers and Typesetting. Addison-Wesley (1986a)

Knuth, D.E.: TEX: The Program. Addison-Wesley (1986b)

Knuth, D.E.: Metafont: The Program. Addison-Wesley (1986c)

Knuth, D.E.: 3:16: Bible Texts Illuminated. A-R Editions (1991)

Knuth, D.E.: Addison-Wesley, Literate Programming (1992)

Knuth, D.E.: The Art of Computer Programming, Volume 4a: Combinatorial Algorithms Part 1. Addison-Wesley (2011)

Knuth, D.E.: The TEX tuneup of 2021. TUGboat **42**(1), 7–10 (2021)

Knuth, D.E.: The Art of Computer Programming, Volume 4b: Combinatorial Algorithms Part 2. Addison-Wesley (2022)

Knuth, D.E.: The Art of Computer Programming, Volume 4, Fascicle 7: Constraint Satisfaction. Addison-Wesley (2025)

Knuth, D.E., Levy, S.: The CWEB System of Structured Documentation. Addison-Wesley (1993)

Kruseman Aretz, F.E.J., Ten Hagen, P.J.W., Oudshoorn, H.L.: An ALGOL 60 Compiler in ALGOL 60: Text of the MC-Compiler for the EL-X8. Mathematisch Centrum Amsterdam (1973)

Laning, J.H., Jr., Zierler, N.: A program for translation of mathematical equations for WHIRLWIND I. Technical report, Massachusetts Institute of Technology (1954)

Mikics, D.: Stanley Kubrick: American Filmmaker. Yale University Press (2020)

Mills, T.: David Lynch's projection instructions for Mulholland Drive (2001) (2021). https://www.openculture.com/2021/01/david-lynchs-projection-instructions-for-mulholland-drive-2001.html

Perlis, A.J., Samelson, K.: Preliminary report - International Algebraic Language. Commun. ACM **1**(12), 8–22 (1958)

Jones, S.P.: Haskell 98 Language and Libraries: The Revised Report. Cambridge University Press (2003)

Pharr, M., Jakob, W., Humphreys, G.: Physically Based Rendering: From Theory to Implementation, 3 edn. Morgan Kaufmann (2004)

Pouzin, L.: RUNCOM - a macro-procedure processor for the 636 System. Technical report, Massachusetts Institute of Technology (1965)

Richards, M.: The BCPL reference manual. Technical report, Massachusetts Institute of Technology (1967)

Sammet, J.E.: Programming Languages: History and Fundamentals. Prentice-Hall (1969)

Marmion, S.W.: Archibald Constable. William Miller and John Murray (1808)

Sperry. FLOW-MATIC programming system. Technical report, Sperry Rand Corporation (1958)

Strunk, Jr., W., White, E.B.: The Elements of Style. Macmillan (1959)

Van Wyk, C.J.: Literate programming. Commun. ACM **30**(12), 1000–1010 (1987)

Van Wyk, C.J.: Literate programming: an assessment. Commun. ACM **33**(3), 361, 365 (1990)

Wadler, P., Miller, Q.: An introduction to Orwell 6.0. Technical report, Oxford University Computing Laboratory (1990)

Wexelblat, R.L.: History of Programming Languages. Academic Press (1981)

Wilkes, M., Wheeler, D., Gill, S.: The Preparation of Programs for an Electronic Digital Computer. Addison-Wesley (1951)

Language Design

Explicit Level Imports

Matthew Pickering(✉), Rodrigo Mesquita, and Adam Gundry

Well-Typed LLP, London, UK
{matthew,rodrigo,adam}@well-typed.com

Abstract. Cross-stage persistence rules are commonly admitted in multi-stage programming languages. These rules codify the assumption that all module and package dependencies are available at all stages. However, in practice, only a small number of dependencies may be needed at each particular stage.

This paper introduces Explicit Level Imports, a mechanism which gives programmers precise control about which dependencies are required at each stage. Imports are annotated with a modifier which brings identifiers into scope at a specific level. This precision means it is straightforward for the compiler to work out what is exactly needed at each stage, and only provide that. The result is faster compilation times and the potential for improved cross-compilation support.

We have implemented these ideas in GHC Haskell, consider a wide variety of practical considerations in the design, and finally demonstrate that the feature solves a real-world issue in a pragmatic way.

Keywords: Staging · Modules · Compile-time code generation · Haskell

1 Introduction

Haskell is a pure, lazy, functional programming language that supports compile-time code generation using *staged metaprogramming*, a feature called Template Haskell [11]. Staged compilation enables writing code-generating programs (meta-programs) in a safe and expressive way, by writing programs in the host language that themselves generate host language programs.

In practice, the primary use of Template Haskell is to avoid writing boilerplate. Programmers, in their libraries, write metaprograms that accept program fragments as inputs (typically a representation of a type), and generate code that is needed to use that library. Template Haskell is used to generate type class instance definitions, generate lenses for use as record accessors, and many other mundane tasks. This common pattern looks like the following:

```
import Control.Lens.TH (makeLenses)
import App (S)
data T = MkT { _foo :: S }
$(makeLenses ''T)   -- generates foo :: Lens T S
```


J. Gibbons (Ed.): TFP 2025, LNCS 15652, pp. 49–69, 2026.
https://doi.org/10.1007/978-3-031-99751-8_3

Here the *makeLenses* function is imported from a library, and used in a declaration splice to generate some definitions (here a lens binding, but a similar pattern is often used for TH-based deriving of type class instances). The function call *makeLenses ''T* will be evaluated at compile-time, during the compilation of the containing module, and its result will be a representation of declarations to be inserted into the program at the location of the splice.

At the moment, the compiler must generate executable code for the dependent module *App* before it starts type-checking this module, because in principle, running the splice might end up executing code from *App*. This has a variety of negative consequences:

- Using Template Haskell causes compile-time performance to suffer due to unnecessary (re)compilation. This is particularly relevant for interactive use of the compiler within an IDE such as Haskell Language Server.
- Cross-compilation is significantly complicated by the need to compile and execute code on the target platform during the build process, as there is no way to execute splices on the host.
- Modules needed exclusively at compile-time must still be linked into the final executable, since any imported module could be used at runtime.

The primary idea of this paper is that the language should make it evident to the compiler which dependencies are needed at runtime and which are needed at compile-time. Once the programmer can be explicit about when each dependency is needed, then the compiler can provide just what is required.

Our proposed language extension will allow the programmer to be explicit about the fact that `makeLenses` is used only in a splice, whereas *App* is imported normally and is definitely not executed in splices:

import splice *Control.Lens.TH* (*makeLenses*)
import *App* (*S*)

Not only does this make the code easier to understand, but moreover the compiler can now tell from the imports that the module depends only on the interface of *App*, not on its implementation. Correspondingly, it is possible to start type-checking the module as soon as *App* has been type-checked (before code generation has been completed), and changes to the implementation of *App* that do not affect its interface do not cause recompilation of the importing module.

In practice, many Haskell programs enable `TemplateHaskell` solely to be able to call functions from external packages in top-level splices. Thus versions of this example occur frequently, and using the new feature will merely require the programmer to add the **splice** keyword to a few imports.

1.1 Contributions

In a staged programming language, the type checker uses a level discipline to ensure that evaluation is well-staged [16]. All variables are introduced at a level, and program contexts require variables to be used at a specific level. The result is a system guaranteeing that compile-time fragments (top-level splices) can be fully evaluated before any runtime fragments (the normal program).

Cross-stage persistence (CSP) rules allow the transport of variables between levels. The admitted CSP rules place constraints on the implementation of the language. For GHC Haskell, baked into the current CSP rules is the assumption that if module M depends on N, then N must be compiled before M, and therefore M is free to use anything from N at compile-time. As demonstrated by the previous example, this is a powerful assumption and a strong constraint on the implementation, as admitting this rule *requires* all dependencies to be compiled, available and ready for compile-time evaluation.

Our first contribution is to name and identify `ImplicitStagePersistence` as a potentially undesirable language feature, and one from which programmers should be able to opt out. Under our new feature `NoImplicitStagePersistence`, imported identifiers are restricted to being used *only* at the level they are explicitly bound at (thus forbidding imported identifiers from occurring within top-level splices or quotes by default). See Sect. 3.

Once `ImplicitStagePersistence` is controlled, programmers will not get very far writing metaprograms, as CSP is used ubiquitously to transport imported variables between levels. Therefore we also introduce a language extension `ExplicitLevelImports`, which provides explicit annotations on imports to make variables available at a specific level:

- **import splice** A will make bindings from A available in top-level splices.
- **import quote** B will make bindings from B available in quotations.

These extensions will both be specified precisely in terms of levels in Sect. 4.

Together, `NoImplicitStagePersistence` and `ExplicitLevelImports` solve the shortcomings of Template Haskell presented above, by introducing a finer-grained mechanism for the programmer to control the level at which imported identifiers are introduced, and by restricting identifiers used in expressions to those explicitly bound at the correct level. We have implemented these extensions in the Glasgow Haskell Compiler (GHC) and proposed them to the GHC Steering Committee to be officially accepted as GHC extensions.[1]

2 Background

In this paper we are mostly concerned with *untyped* Template Haskell [11], an extension to Haskell [5] that adds support for metaprogramming.

Template Haskell has support for generating and inspecting expressions, declarations, patterns, types and names. Quotations in these contexts allow users to inspect and manipulate the syntax of these forms, and splices allow users to combine syntax together in order to form larger programs. By judicious combination of quotes and splices, the user writes a program generator (metaprogram) that will be executed during compilation in order to generate part of the final program.

[1] See GHC Proposal #682: Explicit Level Imports.

2.1 Syntax

An expression $e :: a$ can be quoted to generate the expression $[\![\ e\ ]\!] :: Q\ Exp$. Conversely, an expression $c :: Q\ Exp$ can be spliced to extract the expression $\$(c)$ that c represents. Template Haskell also has support for quoting declarations $[\![\ d\ ]\!]_D :: Q\ Dec$, patterns $[\![\ p\ ]\!]_P :: Q\ Pat$, types $[\![\ t\ ]\!]_T :: Q\ Type$, term-level names $'n :: Name$ and type-level names $''N :: Name$.

Intensional code analysis and construction is also supported: after quotation, the user can inspect and manipulate the syntax tree directly, for instance, the *Exp* type is a normal algebraic datatype that represents Haskell expressions.

A *top-level splice* is a splice ($\$(\cdot)$) not surrounded by any quotations. This marks a location in a program where a metaprogram will be evaluated and the resulting program inserted. For example, the declaration $x = \$(c)$ contains a top-level (expression) splice, since it has no enclosing quotes, whereas $[\![\ \$(c)\ ]\!]$ does not contain a top-level splice.[2]

2.2 Levels

In order for a program generator to be executed at compile time, it must depend only on other information available at compile time. A *well-staged program* is one where the compile-time portions of the program can be fully evaluated before the runtime portions.

Every declaration and every (sub-)expression in a program is assigned an integer *level*. These levels are checked by the type-checker in order to ensure that the program is well-staged. The top-level declarations in a module are at level 0. Similarly, any normally-imported bindings are at level 0. The level is increased by 1 when inside a quote and decreased by 1 inside a splice. In short:

- $\$(e)$ is at level n iff e is at level $n-1$
- $[\![\ e\ ]\!]$ is at level n iff e is at level $n+1$

Therefore the level of an expression can be calculated as the number of quotes surrounding the expression minus the number of splices.

For example, in the call to $\$(makeLenses\ ''T)$ from our introductory example, the expression at a whole is at level 0, so $makeLenses\ ''T$ is at level -1, so T is at level 0 again. (While a name quote $''T$ uses a different syntax to quotation brackets $[\![\ \cdot\ ]\!]$, it is still a quote form, so it increases the level.)

2.3 Stages

A *stage* is a moment in time for which a module is compiled. We will write $M@S$ to indicate that module M is compiled for stage S.

In this paper we will typically talk about two-stage evaluation where there are distinct compile-time and runtime stages (C and R, respectively). Compile-time and runtime are distinct stages as programs being executed at compile time

[2] This use of "top-level splice" is standard terminology [11,18], even though it does *not* mean the splice is necessarily a "top-level declaration" within the module.

may need to be compiled in a different way from those being executed at runtime (e.g. using dynamically-linked object files for compile time, but statically-linked object files for runtime).

For example, when compiling the program in the introduction, the main module *Main@R* should create two dependencies: *Control.Lens.TH@C* and *App@R*. When type-checking without producing runtime code (e.g. under `-fno-code`, or in a language server), *Control.Lens.TH* must be compiled for execution at compile time, but it is enough to typecheck *App* without generating code for it.

In a cross-compilation setting, the need for the stage distinction is even clearer, because the runtime stage needs programs that run on the target architecture, whereas the compile-time stage expects programs to run on the host. Cross-compilers may benefit from three or more stages (see Sect. 5.7).

Levels and stages are often confused in literature but for clarity it is important to distinguish between them [16]. Both may be represented as numbers, but levels are offsets (differences relative to common reference point), whereas stages are absolute values. Levels are a type-system concept as part of the specification of valid programs, whereas stages are an implementation detail of the compiler.

The particular stage structure is not the primary focus of this work, but the implementation is constrained by the assumptions made in the design of the level system about which modules will be available at each stage. More permissive rules lead to more programs being accepted but more requirements placed on making modules available at more stages. Less permissive rules make it harder to write level-correct programs but place fewer requirements on which modules are required.

2.4 Cross-Stage Persistence

If an identifier is used at a level different from the level at which it is bound, the program is level-incorrect, but Template Haskell provides two implicit mechanisms that are used to attempt to fix its level via *cross-stage persistence* (CSP) [15]:

Path-based persistence: allows global definitions at level m to be made available at a different level n in two cases:

- If $n > m$, intuitively because all global definitions will still exist in the defining module even if references to them are spliced at a future stage. For example, this allows a module to define a top-level identifier and refer to it in a quote in the same module.
- If $n < m$ and the definition was *imported* rather than being defined in the current module, intuitively because the dependency order on modules ensures the definition must have been compiled already. For example, this allows an imported identifier to be used in a splice.

It is not possible for a global definition to be used in its defining module at a level earlier than its definition, because that would require parts of the module to be compiled to executable code before other parts were type-checked.

Serialisation-based persistence (Lift): locally-bound variables can't be persisted using path-based persistence, but when the variable's type is serialisable, its value can be serialised to persist it to *future* stages. This serialisation is defined as the *lift* method of the *Lift* type class. For instance, the following program is level-incorrect as x is bound at level 0 but used at level 1. However, it is fixed by serialisation-based persistence, which transforms the program into one where x is used at level 0 by the compiler automatically inserting a call to *lift*:

$$\mathit{tardy}\ x = [\![\ x\ ]\!] \quad \Longrightarrow \quad \mathit{tardy}\ x = [\![\ \$(\mathit{lift}\ x)\ ]\!]$$

All base types such as *Int*, *Bool*, *Float*, etc., instantiate *Lift*, and user types can instantiate it automatically with the `DeriveLift` extension (which will generate code that relies on path-based persistence).

It is not possible for a locally-bound variable to be used earlier than the stage at which it is bound, e.g. $[\![\ \lambda x \rightarrow \$(x)\ ]\!]$ is irredeemably stage-incorrect.

Example: The following program requires both implicit mechanisms in order to be accepted. *Path-based persistence* explains why the occurrence of *suc* in examples *one* and *anotherOne* is accepted (since it is defined at level 0 but used at level 1), and why *anotherOne* can be used in a top-level splice (since it is imported at level 0 but used at level −1):

```
module M2 where
  suc :: Int → Int
  suc = (+1)

  one :: Q Exp
  one = [[ λx → suc x ]]

  anotherOne :: Int → Q Exp
  anotherOne y = [[ suc y ]]
```

```
module M3 where
  import M2 (anotherOne)
  two = $(anotherOne 1)
```

Serialisation-based persistence explains why the y in *anotherOne* can be moved from a value that exists at level 0 to one that exists at level 1. The compiler will implicitly introduce a call to *lift*:

$$\mathit{anotherOne}\ y = [\![\ \mathit{suc}\ y\ ]\!] \quad \Longrightarrow \quad \mathit{anotherOne}\ y = [\![\ \mathit{suc}\ \$(\mathit{lift}\ y)\ ]\!]$$

And *lift* will take care of converting the compile-time y into a runtime value.

2.5 Implications of Cross-Stage Persistence for Stages

When compiling, the build system receives demands for the compilation of modules at particular stages. Then by reading the module header, further demands are placed upon the imported modules. It is a key design constraint that the entire build plan for a multi-module program can be determined solely by reading the module headers (e.g. import statements), without needing to perform a full name resolution or type-checking pass.

Serialisation-based persistence elaborates a level-incorrect program into a level-correct one that the user themselves could have written. Therefore it does not impose any requirements or use any assumptions about the stages for which modules are compiled.

However, modules using path-based cross-stage persistence place strong requirements on the set of dependencies that must be demanded. Consider two modules B and C that use cross-stage persistence:

module A **where** $\{a = 1 :: Int\}$

module B **where**
  import A
  $foo = a$
  $bar = [\![\ foo \ ]\!]$

module C **where**
  import B
  $c :: Int$
  $c = \$(bar)$

Cross-stage persistence means that any identifier in scope may be used in a top-level splice or a quotation. When compiling $C@R$, bar from B is used only in a top-level splice, but this can't be determined from the module header. Instead, since C imports B, the build system must presume that both $B@R$ and $B@C$ are needed. Similarly, if compilation of $B@C$ is required, then it is also necessary to compile $B@R$ because the foo identifier appears in a quote and is persisted from level 0 to level 1 (so the resulting program may splice foo and hence it may appear at runtime).

Ultimately, cross-stage persistence forces the build system to compile all modules and require all dependencies for all stages, even if the final program uses only a small fragment of its dependency tree at any particular stage.

3 Implicit Stage-Persistence Considered Harmful

Implicit stage persistence seems convenient at first, but is the root of many performance and cross-compilation issues in practice. If imported identifiers can be arbitrarily used at any stage, the compiler must pessimistically assume they will be used at all stages, and therefore it needs to compile all modules in a project for both runtime and compile-time.

Our design allows implicit path-based cross-stage persistence to be disabled. Identifiers must be used at precisely the level they are bound, and no other levels. Instead, we should be able to explicitly control the level at which identifiers from a module are imported. By being very precise about which levels modules are needed at, there are many real-world advantages:

1. Currently, if a module enables `TemplateHaskell`, then all imported modules are compiled to object code before name resolution takes place. This ensures that any top level splices that may be encountered are able to be fully evaluated. This is a pessimisation because most of the imported identifiers, which we have taken such pains to ensure we can run, will not actually be used in a top-level splice. Proposals to increase build parallelism (such as #14095) are

far less effective in projects that use `TemplateHaskell`, because name resolution depends on code generation for all dependencies. By distinguishing the small fraction of imported modules whose code is executed only at compile time, we are able to improve this pessimisation.

2. GHC offers an `-fno-code` flag that instructs the compiler to parse and type-check Haskell modules, but not to generate code, so as to offer quicker feedback to the user. However, any modules imported by a module using `TemplateHaskell` must be compiled to object code, despite the fact that we will not generate object code for the module itself. By distinguishing imported modules whose code is executed only at compile time, we can eliminate or significantly reduce this unnecessary work.
3. IDEs such as Haskell Language Server face similar problems: they are interested only in the result of type-checking, but when `TemplateHaskell` is enabled, many modules have to be unnecessarily compiled to bytecode.
4. Currently, when cross-compiling modules that use TemplateHaskell, all splices are executed on the target even though compilation takes place on a separate host. This is a source of significant complexity. This work is a step towards properly distinguishing dependencies that need to be compiled for and executed on the host from those compiled for the target.

4 Specification

The purpose of this work is to design a different level system which allows finer grained control of which imported identifiers are available at which level, and hence, which modules will be required at specific stages. In order to do this, we introduce two new language extensions: `NoImplicitStagePersistence` disables path-based cross-stage persistence and forces the programmer to ensure their programs are level-correct explicitly (getting performance benefits as a result); `ExplicitLevelImports` allows for explicit level control via imports.

4.1 ImplicitStagePersistence

When the language extension `ImplicitStagePersistence` is disabled for a module (e.g. using `-XNoImplicitStagePersistence`), path-based cross-stage persistence will be disallowed by the compiler. That is, use of a binding at a level other than the level at which it was defined or imported will result in a type error. In particular, bindings imported using traditional **import** statements or defined at the top-level may not be used inside of top-level splices, nor within quotes.

For example, the following is accepted with `ImplicitStagePersistence`, but rejected under `NoImplicitStagePersistence`:

```
import B (foo)       -- foo :: Q Exp
data C = MkC

quoteC = [[ MkC ]]   -- Error: MkC defined at level 0 but used at level 1
spliceC = $(foo)     -- Error: foo imported at level 0 but used at level −1
```

`ImplicitStagePersistence` is enabled by default in all existing language editions in order to preserve backwards compatibility. In modules which enable `NoImplicitStagePersistence` it is an error to use `DeriveLift` on a type unless all its definition is imported at both level 0 and level 1. This is discussed in more detail in Sect. 6.2.

When a module uses `TemplateHaskell` with `NoImplicitStagePersistence`, the module dependencies no longer need to be pessimistically compiled and loaded at compile time. Instead, the modules that are needed at compile-time versus runtime are determined by the explicit **splice** and **quote** imports relative to the module being compiled, which are enabled by `ExplicitLevelImports`.

4.2 ExplicitLevelImports

The `ExplicitLevelImports` extension introduces two new import modifiers to the import syntax, **splice** and **quote**, which control the level at which identifiers from the module are brought into scope:

- A **splice** import of *A* imports all bindings of *A* to be used *only* at level −1.
- A **quote** import of *B* imports all bindings of *B* to be used *only* at level 1.

For example, the following is accepted with `ExplicitLevelImports`:

```
import quote Foo (bar)   -- bar is introduced at level 1
import Foo (baz)         -- baz is introduced at level 0
import splice Foo (qux)  -- qux is introduced at level −1
foo = baz ⟦ bar ⟧ $(qux)
```

`ExplicitLevelImports` implies `NoImplicitStagePersistence`, to ensure users importing modules just at the correct levels benefit from the compiler performance benefits by default. Nonetheless, it is permitted to enable together `ExplicitLevelImports` and `ImplicitStagePersistence`. This allows **splice** and **quote** imports to be used, but `ImplicitStagePersistence` still allows cross-stage persistence (and thus the compiler must still assume all modules are needed at all stages). This combination is supported to allow gradual migration of code bases following the change, and for corner cases such as programmatic code generation, where the programmer may wish to use the syntax of **splice** and **quote** imports without obliging the whole module to be level-correct.

4.3 Names and Exports

Name resolution ("renaming") does not take account of the level at which an identifier was imported when disambiguating ambiguous names, even though this is sometimes more conservative than necessary. For example, the following program is rejected:

```
import A (x)
import splice B (x)
foo = $(x) x
```

In this case, there is, in principle, no ambiguity because *A.x* isn't allowed to be used in the top-level splice, and *B.x* isn't allowed to be used outside the splice. However, we choose to reject this disambiguation to keep the design simple and prevent any confusion about what is in scope. This position is conservative, and can be relaxed in the future if more flexibility appears worthwhile. This choice follows GHC's Lexical Scoping Principle, which requires that it is possible to determine the binding site of an identifier without type-checking. A positive consequence of this design choice is that if a program is accepted with `ExplicitLevelImports`, it will be accepted after erasing all **splice**/**quote** keywords and using `ImplicitStagePersistence` instead of `ExplicitLevelImports`.

Exports: Under `NoImplicitStagePersistence`, modules can only export bindings available at level 0. For example, the following program is rejected because *bad* is imported at level −1 but used at level 0:

```
module M (bad) where
  import splice N (bad)
```

4.4 Type-Class Instance Resolution

Type-class instances are available at the levels they were imported, much like identifiers, can only be used at those levels under `NoImplicitStage Persistence`. In detail:

- Instance resolution views the set of instances from all imports together and thus instances from normal and leveled imports must agree with each other.
- After instance resolution has selected an instance, it is checked which levels the instance is available at and an error is raised if the instance is not available at the correct level.
- Instances defined in the current modules are at level 0, just like top-level variable definitions in a module.

This design for instances mirrors the situation for name resolution. As with ambiguous names, it would in principle be possible for the type-checker to make use of level information to accept more programs, but this seems like an undesirable level of complexity. Consider the following example modules:

```
                    module Normal where          module Splice where
module X where      import X                     import X
  data X = MkX      instance Show X where        instance Show X where
                      show _ = "normal"            show _ = "splice"
```

The following program, in principle, could be accepted since the overlapping instances for *Show X* in the *show* call are available at different levels, however, we choose to reject the program (just like we do for ambiguous names):

```
import X (X (..))
import splice X (X (..))
import Normal ()           -- imports instance at level 0
import splice Splice ()    -- different instance at level −1
s1 = show MkX
```

On the other hand, the following program imports the same *Show X* instance at both level 0 and level -1, allowing it to be used at both levels. It is accepted:

```
module X where
  data X = MkX deriving Show
module Bottom where
  import X (X (..))            -- imports instance at level 0
  import splice X (X (..))     -- imports the same instance at level −1
  import splice Language.Haskell.TH.Lib (stringE)
  s1 = show MkX                -- Uses instance at level 0
  s2 = $(stringE (show MkX))   -- Uses instance at level −1
```

Exports of class instances: Only instances available at level 0 are re-exported from a module, just like for identifiers. For example, the following is rejected in the call to *show* since no instance for *Show X* is in scope:

```
                    module Normal where           module Splice where
module X where      import X                      import X
  data X = MkX      instance Show X where         instance Show X where
                      show _ = "normal"             show _ = "splice"
```

Even though *Y* has access to the instance at level −1, it does not re-export it. Thus *Bottom* does not import the instance. This is necessary for a clean separation between stages, because instances may exist only at compile-time or only at runtime, just like identifiers.

5 Examples

5.1 Splice Imports

A "splice" import is prefixed with **splice**. In this example, identifiers from *A* can be used only in top-level splices and identifiers from *B* cannot be used in quotes or splices:

$$\begin{array}{ll} \textbf{import splice}\ A\ (foo) & \text{-- } foo :: Int \rightarrow Q\ Exp \\ \textbf{import}\ B\ (bar) & \text{-- } bar :: Int \rightarrow Q\ Exp \end{array}$$

$$\begin{array}{ll} x = \$(foo\ 25) & \text{-- Accepted} \\ y = \$(bar\ 33) & \text{-- Error: } bar \text{ imported at level 0 but used at level } -1 \end{array}$$

Thus:

1. When compiling module *Main* only identifiers from module *A* will be used in top-level splices. Therefore, only *A* (and its dependencies) need to be compiled to object code before starting to compile *Main*.
2. When cross-compiling, in principle *A* needs to be built only for the host and *B* only for the target.

If the same module is needed to be used at different levels then two import declarations can be used:

import *C*
import splice *C*

5.2 Quote Imports

A quote import is prefixed with **quote**. In this example, identifiers from *A* can be used only in quotes, while identifiers from *A* cannot be used at the top-level or in splices:

$$\begin{array}{ll} \textbf{import quote}\ A\ (foo) & \text{-- } foo :: Int \rightarrow Int \\ \textbf{import}\ B\ (bar) & \text{-- } bar :: Int \rightarrow Int \end{array}$$

$$\begin{array}{ll} x = [\![\ foo\ 25\ ]\!] & \text{-- Accepted} \\ y = [\![\ bar\ 33\ ]\!] & \text{-- Error: } bar \text{ imported at level 0 but used at level 1} \end{array}$$

When a quote such as $x = [\![\ foo\ 25\ ]\!]$ is spliced, i.e. $z = \$(x)$, its contents will be needed to execute the program at runtime ($z = foo\ 25$, so evaluating z at runtime requires *foo* to be available).

5.3 Top-Level Definitions

A binding introduced at the top-level has level 0. Therefore, as a consequence of `NoImplicitStagePersistence`, it can not be used either in a quotation (at level 1) nor in a top-level splice (at level -1).

$$plusFive\ x = 5 + x$$

$$tenQ = [\![\ plusFive\ 5\ ]\!] \quad \text{-- Error: } plusFive \text{ is defined at 0 but used at 1}$$

A constant which is defined at the top-level can be persisted to future stages by use of serialisation-based persistence. For example, the constant *five* can be used in a quote since it is implicitly persisted using *lift*.

$$\mathit{five} = 5$$
$$\mathit{doubleFive} = [\![\ \mathit{five} * 2\ ]\!] \quad \Longrightarrow \quad [\![\ \$(\mathit{lift}\ \mathit{five}) * 2\ ]\!]$$

In Sect. 7.1, we reflect briefly on how the design could be extended in order to lift this restriction.

5.4 Module Stages

In Sect. 2.3 we said that modules were compiled for either the *C* or *R* stages. Levelled imports make it possible to be precise about what stages we need dependencies.

- The main module is compiled for *R*. This is where the *main* function lives and the entry-point to running the resulting executable.
- A normal import does not shift the stage at which the dependent module is required.
- If a module *M* splice imports module *A*, then compiling *M@R* requires compiling module *A@C*.
- If a module *M* splice imports module *A*, then compiling *M@C* requires compiling module *A@C*.
- If a module *N* quote imports module *B*, then compiling *N@C* requires compiling module *B* at *N@R*.
- If a module *N* quote imports module *B*, then compiling *N@R* requires compiling module *B* at *N@R*

Stage arithmetic is saturating. Thus, when there are two stages, a quote import corresponds to requiring the module at *R*, and a splice import to requiring a module at *C*. When there are more than two stages then the imports can have different meanings depending on the stage a module is compiled for. The compiler can then choose appropriately how modules needed at *C* are compiled and how modules needed at *R* are compiled. For example:

- In `-fno-code` mode, *C* modules may be compiled in dynamic way, but *R* modules are not compiled at all.
- When using a profiled GHC. *C* modules must be compiled in profiled way but *R* modules will be compiled in static way.

Cross-compilation settings may benefit from introducing more stages, as discussed in Sect. 5.7.

5.5 Module Stage Offsetting

The interaction between stages and level offsetting can be understood more clearly through an example. Module *A* splices *foo* from module *B* which both quotes *bar* from module *C* and uses *baz* from *D*:

```
module A where
  import splice B (foo)
  x = $(foo 10)
module C where
  bar = 42
module D where
  baz 0 = True
  baz _ = False

module B where
  import D (baz)
  import quote C (bar)
  foo x
    | baz x = [[ bar * 2 ]]
    | otherwise = [[ bar ]]
```

In *A*, *foo* can be used within a splice (level −1) because of the splice import (−1). In *B*, *bar* can be used within a quote (level +1) because of the quote import (+1) Now, consider compiling *A*@*R*.

- *B* is required at stage *C*, as it is splice imported from *A*@*R*.
- *C* is required at stage *R*, as it is quote imported from *B*@*C*.
- *D* is required at stage *C*, as it is normally imported from *B*@*C*.

Therefore in order to compile *A*@*R*, we have performed dependency resolution and require *B*@*C*, *C*@*R* and *D*@*C*.

The perhaps curious case is *D*: is it needed at compile-time or runtime? It does not use a splice import, so one could think it is needed at runtime – but here is where the distinction between the import level offset and base stage is relevant. *D* is only being imported as a dependency of *B*, which is at *C* stage. This makes *D* *also* at the *C* stage! Note how *baz* is needed at compile time just to define *foo*, which is properly **splice** imported.

The levels of all modules in the transitive closure of a **splice**-imported module are offset by −1. Conversely, **quote** imports offset the levels by +1, thereby making all the levels align correctly.

5.6 , stages and

The `TemplateHaskellQuotes` extension is a refinement of the `TemplateHaskell` extension in which you may only write non-negative contexts (i.e. quotations). A more refined specification is possible if you observe that `TemplateHaskellQuotes` only persists identifiers forwards. If a module enables `TemplateHaskellQuotes` and `ImplicitStagePersistence` then the module and immediate dependencies are required at current and future stages but not previous stages.

Consider this example, where *M*1 has enabled both `TemplateHaskellQuotes` and `ImplicitStagePersistence`:

```
module M1 where
data T = MkT Int
instance Lift T where
  lift (MkT n) = [[ MkT $(lift n) ]]
```

```
module M2 where
import M1
foo = MkT
```

Under the revised rule, if we require $M2@R$:

- We require $M1@R$ due to the **import** $M1$ declaration.
- $M1@R$ enables `ImplicitStagePersistence` and `TemplateHaskellQuotes` so therefore places a requirement on compiling $M2@R$.

If `TemplateHaskell` was enabled, we would also require $M2@C$ because `TemplateHaskell` allows you to write a -1 context, and hence persist identifiers to negative as well as positive levels.

5.7 Cross-Compilation

Cross-compilation conceptually involves at least three stages:

- a compile-compile-time stage for programs that run on the host at compile-time and generate programs for the host,
- the normal compile-time stage that executes on the host and generates programs for the target,
- the normal runtime stage that executes on the target.

(One can imagine more exotic cross-compilation systems where more than three stages are used, although this is likely to be rare in practice.)

GHC's current implementation strategy for cross-compilation is to compile all splices for the target and execute them there. This requires having a target environment (or equivalent virtual machine) around at compile time, which is complex and limits contexts in which Template Haskell can be cross-compiled. Instead, ideally the compiler would execute splices on the host, but this requires significant implementation work.

A key reason for distinguishing stages and levels is that stages are an implementation detail, about which the level system is agnostic. Thus it should be possible for (cross-)compiler implementors to change the number of stages without modifying the level system, but benefiting from the fact that the level system ensures the program is well-staged. While our work does not directly make changes to GHC's support for cross-compilation, it lays the foundations for future work to change the implementation strategy.

6 Discussion

6.1 Case Study:

The pandoc library is a medium-sized package that contains approximately 200 modules. It uses `TemplateHaskell` in a light manner in order to embed some data files and derive some JSON instances.

Modifying the package to use `ExplicitLevelImports` required little effort and involved modifying the imports of the 5 modules in the project which use `TemplateHaskell`.

Previously, type-checking the library component (by loading it into GHCi using the `-fno-code` option) would needlessly compile the majority of modules to bytecode, as one module near the root of the module graph used `TemplateHaskell`. Following our changes, bytecode generation is no longer necessary and the time is reduced from 17.4 s to 9.5 s.

From looking at the imports of modules, it can be observed that no modules from the `pandoc` library are used in compile-time evaluation and only a few external packages are needed at compile-time. This is a very common situation in practice, and one where the extensions are at their most effective.

6.2 Implicit Lifting and Deriving *Lift* instances

Lift instances are used to provide serialisation-based cross-stage persistence. For example, a typical *Lift* instance looks like:

```
data MInt = Some Int | None
instance Lift MInt where
  lift :: MInt → Q Exp
  lift None = ⟦ None ⟧
  lift (Some x) = ⟦ Some $(lift x) ⟧
```

The presence of this instance means the following declaration will be accepted:

```
foo :: MInt → Q Exp
foo x = ⟦ x ⟧    ⟹    foo x = ⟦ $(lift x) ⟧
```

Defining a *Lift* instance requires the datatype constructors to be available both at compile-time and runtime, so defining *Lift* within the same module as the datatype itself requires path-based cross-stage persistence. Operationally, *None* and *Some* are needed both at compile-time and runtime since they are both matched on at compile time, and also persisted to be spliced in the future into a program that can make use of them at runtime. As a result, it isn't possible to define or derive a (non-orphan) *Lift* instance under `NoImplicitStagePersistence`.

An orphan *Lift* instance can be defined thus:

```
module N where
  import M
  import quote M
  instance Lift MInt where
    lift :: MInt → Q Exp
    lift None = [[ None ]]
    lift (Some x) = [[ Some $(lift x) ]]
```

```
module M where
  data MInt
    = Some Int
    | None
```

This isn't technically problematic, rather it is just a result of what *Lift* means. However, it means some users may need to modify their use of *Lift* instances if they wish to benefit more from `NoImplicitStagePersistence`. Users are free to use `ImplicitStagePersistence` in selected modules to allow defining *Lift* instances, but doing so means all the dependencies of the module will need to be available both at compile-time and runtime.

As a general rule, *Lift* instances should be defined only for simple datatypes near the root of the module hierarchy of an application.

Just as `NoImplicitStagePersistence` allows users to disable implicit path-based cross-stage persistence, it would make sense to have an extension flag to disable implicit lifting (serialisation-based persistence). This would allow the programmer to ensure they are explicit about where calls to *lift* occur in their programs, which is sometimes desirable when using staging for runtime performance.

A possible alternative design choice, taken by MacoCaml [1,19,20], would be to have datatype definitions available at every stage. This would allow *Lift* instances to continue to be accepted, and more generally allow data constructors to be implicitly persisted between levels. However, it would require the compiler and build system to support dependencies on the datatypes of a module independently from the rest of the module, which adds significant complexity, especially since some modules may be otherwise completely unneeded at a particular stage.

6.3 Future Work: Level-Correct Package Dependencies

The **splice** and **quote** imports in this work make it possible to express which module dependencies are required at which stages, within the Haskell language.

However, large Haskell programs are typically organised into multiple packages, using the Cabal package system to describe their dependencies. While our proposed feature delivers significant benefits to the compilation process for a single package, it would ultimately make sense to expose level distinctions in Cabal package dependencies, so that Cabal could build package dependencies only for the stages at which they are required. This would primarily be of value in cross-compilation scenarios.

In the interests of keeping the work manageable, changes to Cabal are out of scope of the current paper, but we believe it lays a foundation for future work to improve Cabal's cross-compilation support.

6.4 Future Work: Typed Template Haskell

Typed Template Haskell (TTH) [18] is an extension of Template Haskell that allows using type-safe staged programming for program optimisation. Its typical use cases are rather different from untyped TH, since in particular it does not support declaration splices.

The same level checks can be used for typed quotes and splices as for the untyped case. However, when using TTH and explicit level imports, the programmer can introduce level errors that cannot currently be worked around. For example, the following program contains a stage error as the evidence for *Show a* is bound earlier than it is used, but it is currently mistakenly accepted by GHC:

$$\mathit{foo} :: \mathit{Show}\ a \Rightarrow \mathit{Code}\ Q\ (a \rightarrow \mathit{String})$$
$$\mathit{foo} = [\![\ \mathit{show}\ ]\!]$$

The language of constraints is not yet expressive enough to communicate that the *Show a* evidence needs to be available at a later stage. Fixing this problem will require significant additional effort to resolve other known issues with TTH [9].

6.5 Level Inference

Our design requires programmers to be explicit about the levels at which identifiers are imported. One might instead ask whether the **splice** and **quote** markers on imports could be inferred, thereby relieving the programmer of this obligation, without the costs of fully implicit stage persistence.

In principle, the compiler could begin compiling a module before any of its dependencies were available, then when a dependency was required, it could suspend compilation of the module, request the dependency at the appropriate stage, then later resume compilation when the dependency was available. However, this would be complex to implement and a radical departure from GHC's compilation model, which as discussed in Sect. 2.5 requires that the build plan can be constructed merely by reading module headers.

6.6 Imports with Explicit Level Numbers

Using the system described here, it is possible to import identifiers only at levels -1, 0 or 1. This means it is not possible to directly import an identifier for use in a splice contained within another splice, e.g. $\$(\mathit{foo}\ \$(\mathit{bar}))$, which requires *bar* to be available at level -2.[3] It is possible to work around this, e.g. by **splice**-importing *baz* from a separate module that defines $\mathit{baz} = \mathit{foo}\ \$(\mathit{bar})$, and which can itself **splice**-import *bar*.

[3] Nested quotes are in any case not supported in GHC due to a separate restriction.

An alternative design would be to allow even finer grained control of splice imports so that usage at level -2 or lower could be distinguished, for example by writing **import splice** 2 *SomeModule* (*bar*). The only real obstacle to adding this to our design is deciding upon a suitable syntax. However, adding this feature would increase the complexity of the extension, and in practice multiple levels of splices are very rare, so we consider the workaround adequate.

7 Related Work

The idea to use import modifiers to accept the level of identifiers originates from Racket [2]. The option of using explicit phasing was then introduced into the R6RS report [13], although many implementations ignore explicit phasing annotations. The community attitute shifted towards implicit phasing [4] and the R7RS report did not require implementations support explicit phases [12]. Our system allows a user to opt into either the implicit or explicit phasing approach on a per-module basis.

We are also inspired by MacoCaml [1,19,20] which suggests an import modifier similar to **splice**. Our work brings those ideas to Haskell, and tackles the challenges faced when integrated leveled imports into Haskell, building on language design discussions in the GHC proposals process.[4]

7.1 Multiple Levels Within a Single module

The design in this paper requires each module to exist at a single level, which may sometimes necessitate users introducing more modules than would be ideal.

One possible design that mitigates the need for module-level granularity of imports, inspired by the Racket [2], MacoCaml [1,19,20] and MetaFM [14] languages, is the introduction of an additional **macro** keyword that introduces bindings at a different level. A **macro** annotated binding would introduce a binding at the -1 level, without requiring it to be **splice** imported from a different module.

Our design lays out the foundation for well-leveled programs, and is forward-compatible with such a **macro** keyword, or other possible features that relax Haskell's identification of compilation units with source files, such as the proposed Local Modules feature.[5]

Another angle is to allow users to define their own level contexts, an idea proposed for Racket [3]. In the future it would also be interesting to explore extending this system to different stages. This could be useful in order to support embedding other modal languages into Haskell.

[4] See GHC proposals #243: Stage Hygiene for Template Haskell and #412: Explicit Splice Imports.

[5] See GHC proposal #283: Local Modules.

7.2 Module Generation

Functors in ML family languages allow users to parameterise modules. It's therefore a natural consideration to remove the abstraction overhead by using ideas from staging [6,10,17]. Modules are neither first-class nor parameterised in Haskell but Explicit Level Imports could be considered a simple form of module generation: by making a demand on a module at a particular stage, the compiler will generate it for that stage. The choice is either to wholly include a module or not include it at all.

In ML family languages, modules and module functors are a primary means of abstraction. In Haskell, a similar role is instead played by type classes. Therefore the ideas in these papers are more suitably considered to apply to modifications to type class mechanisms than modules themselves. For example, you can see parallels in techniques used in CFTT [7] or Staged SOP [8].

Package-level abstraction is implemented for GHC in the Backpack [21] extension, which currently sees little practical use. Similar ideas might also be useful in reviving interest in this area.

8 Conclusion

We have presented the design of Explicit Level Imports, a simple system that allows programmers to be precise about module dependencies when using Template Haskell. By using explicit dependencies, the modules required for each stage are evident to the compiler. This leads to important practical benefits gained by separating runtime from compile-time dependencies. The system described has been implemented and verified to achieve significant practical improvements to projects using Template Haskell. In the next stage of the project we aim to finish the implementation and contribute the feature upstream to GHC.

Acknowledgments. We thank the participants in the GHC proposal process, in particular John Ericson, Sebastian Graf, Simon Peyton Jones and Arnaud Spiwack, for their helpful comments on the GHC proposal that preceded this paper. The participants of TFP, including Daphne Preston-Kendal, provided some useful additional references and conversations. Thanks also to Mercury for funding this work.

References

1. Chiang, T.J., Yallop, J., White, L., Xie, N.: Staged compilation with module functions. Proc. ACM Program. Lang. **8**(ICFP), 3674649 (2024). https://doi.org/10.1145/3674649
2. Flatt, M.: Composable and compilable macros: you want it when? ACM SIGPLAN Notices **37**(9), 72–83 (2002)
3. Flatt, M.: Submodules in Racket: you want it when, again? In: Proceedings of the 12th International Conference on Generative Programming: Concepts and Experiences, pp. 13–22. GPCE 2013, Association for Computing Machinery, New York, NY, USA (2013). https://doi.org/10.1145/2517208.2517211

4. Ghuloum, A., Dybvig, R.K.: Implicit phasing for R6RS libraries. In: Hinze, R., Ramsey, N. (eds.) Proceedings of the 12th ACM SIGPLAN International Conference on Functional Programming, ICFP 2007, Freiburg, Germany, October 1-3, 2007, pp. 303–314. ACM (2007). https://doi.org/10.1145/1291151.1291197
5. Hudak, P., et al.: Report on the programming language Haskell: a non-strict, purely functional language version 1.2. ACM SigPlan Notices **27**(5), 1–164 (1992)
6. Inoue, J., Kiselyov, O., Kameyama, Y.: Staging beyond terms: prospects and challenges. In: Proceedings of the 2016 ACM SIGPLAN Workshop on Partial Evaluation and Program Manipulation, pp. 103–108 (2016)
7. Kovács, A.: Closure-free functional programming in a two-level type theory. Proc. ACM Program. Lang. **8**(ICFP), 659–692 (2024)
8. Pickering, M., Löh, A., Wu, N.: Staged sums of products. In: Proceedings of the 13th ACM SIGPLAN International Symposium on Haskell, pp. 122–135 (2020)
9. Pickering, M.T.: Understanding the Interaction Between Elaboration and Quotation. Ph.D. thesis, University of Bristol (2021)
10. Sato, Y., Kameyama, Y., Watanabe, T.: Module generation without regret. In: Proceedings of the 2020 ACM SIGPLAN Workshop on Partial Evaluation and Program Manipulation, pp. 1–13. PEPM 2020, Association for Computing Machinery, New York, NY, USA (2020). https://doi.org/10.1145/3372884.3373160
11. Sheard, T., Peyton Jones, S.: Template meta-programming for Haskell. In: Proceedings of the 2002 ACM SIGPLAN Workshop on Haskell, pp. 1–16. Haskell 2002, ACM, New York, NY, USA (2002). https://doi.org/10.1145/581690.581691
12. Shinn, A., Cowan, J., Gleckler, A.: Revised [7] report on the algorithmic language scheme (2013)
13. Sperber, M., Dybvig, R.K., Flatt, M., van Straaten, A., Findler, R., Matthews, J.: Revised [6] Report on the Algorithmic Language Scheme, 1st edn. Cambridge University Press, USA (2010)
14. Suwa, T., Igarashi, A.: An ML-style module system for cross-stage type abstraction in multi-stage programming. In: Gibbons, J., Miller, D. (eds.) Functional and Logic Programming. FLOPS 2024. LNCS, vol. 14659, pp. 237–272. Springer, Singapore (2024). https://doi.org/10.1007/978-981-97-2300-3_13
15. Taha, W., Sheard, T.: Multi-stage programming with explicit annotations. In: Proceedings of the 1997 ACM SIGPLAN Symposium on Partial Evaluation and Semantics-based Program Manipulation. pp. 203–217. PEPM 1997, ACM, New York, NY, USA (1997).https://doi.org/10.1145/258993.259019
16. Taha, W., Sheard, T.: MetaML and multi-stage programming with explicit annotations. Theor. Comput. Sci. **248**(1–2), 211–242 (2000). https://doi.org/10.1016/S0304-3975(00)00053-0
17. Watanabe, T., Kameyama, Y.: Program generation for ML modules (short paper). In: Proceedings of the ACM SIGPLAN Workshop on Partial Evaluation and Program Manipulation, pp. 60–66 (2017)
18. Xie, N., Pickering, M., Löh, A., Wu, N., Yallop, J., Wang, M.: Staging with class: a specification for Typed Template Haskell. Proc. ACM Programm. Lang. **6**(POPL), 1–30 (2022)
19. Xie, N., White, L., Nicole, O., Yallop, J.: MacoCaml: staging composable and compilable macros. Proc. ACM Program. Lang. **7**(ICFP), 604–648 (2023)
20. Yallop, J., White, L.: Modular macros. In: OCaml Users and Developers Workshop, vol. 6 (2015)
21. Yang, E.Z.: Backpack: towards practical mix-in linking in Haskell. Ph.D. thesis, Stanford University (2017)

Heapless Functional Programming

Ellis Kesterton(✉) and Edwin Brady

University of St Andrews, St Andrews, UK
{erk4,ecb10}@st-andrews.ac.uk

Abstract. Typed functional programming languages like Haskell and OCaml make heavy use of the heap at run-time. This makes them largely unsuitable for *systems programming*, where resources are limited and programs are often expected to run on bare-metal. This paper demonstrates how a (slightly restricted) high-level, pure, functional language can be compiled to machine code which does not use the heap at all. Despite usually requiring a heap at run-time, features such as higher-order functions, polymorphism and typeclasses are all supported by the surface language. This is made possible through *partial evaluation* [12]: by carefully reducing the program at compile-time, we can eliminate these high-level features entirely, resulting in a residual program which is trivial to compile to stack-based machine code. This paper describes the operation of this partial evaluator, justifies its design, and introduces a novel type system which guarantees that the partial evaluator will always succeed in removing all heap-using features.

1 Introduction

At the core of most functional languages is a set of high-level features including higher-order functions, polymorphism and algebraic data types. Most of the time these features are a boon: they allow the programmer to write concise, maintainable, readable code. However, all of these features typically require a heap at run-time. This is problematic if we want to use functional languages for *systems programming*, where it is common to target environments with limited resources and real time constraints. Consider the following Haskell program:

```
main :: IO ()
main = do
    n :: Int <- readInt
    m :: Int <- readInt
    printInt (n + m)
```

While this program may appear simple, it implicitly makes use of a wide variety of high-level (heap-using) features. Alone, using do-notation requires typeclasses (to resolve the Monad instance), higher-order functions (for the implicit calls to >>=) and polymorphism (also for >>=)! It is clear that every non-trivial

J. Gibbons (Ed.): TFP 2025, LNCS 15652, pp. 70–92, 2026.
https://doi.org/10.1007/978-3-031-99751-8_4

Haskell program will use the heap in some capacity – features such as higher-order functions are too ubiquitous to avoid. Does this mean that high-level functional programming is entirely reliant on the heap? This paper demonstrates that this is not the case.

Reconsider our example from a computational perspective: it is unclear why a program which adds two integers should need a heap at all! In this case, features such as typeclasses and higher-order functions are only abstractions for the programmer; they are not adding any real computational value. We show that most of the time we can actually use these abstractions for free. Through careful partial evaluation at compile-time, it is possible to transform a large class of high-level functional programs into equivalent low-level programs which do not require the heap at all. We make use of the type system to ensure that input programs always fall into this transformable class, guaranteeing that partial evaluation will always succeed at removing high-level features. Compiling a desugared version of the earlier example with our prototype implementation produces identical machine code to the following Rust program[1].

```
fn main() {
    let n = readInt();
    let m = readInt();
    printInt(n + m);
}
```

2 Contributions

The goal of this paper is to describe a method for designing and implementing high-level functional languages which do not use the heap at run-time. We believe this goal is worthwhile as not every low-level environment can feasibly support the high amount of heap allocations typically required by a functional language – by only using the stack, it becomes possible to use functional programming in these restricted environments. We hope that this work will help facilitate the design of functional languages which are suitable for systems programming on low-resource devices such as microcontrollers.

We focus on the design and implementation of a core language $\mathcal{C}$, which aims to be an elaboration target for high-level strict functional languages. Specifically, we make the following contributions:

- We define a strict, polymorphic, higher-order core language $\mathcal{C}$ which serves as an elaboration target for surface languages. $\mathcal{C}$ has a novel type system which guarantees that it can be compiled to stack-based code.
- We describe a pipeline which compiles $\mathcal{C}$ programs down to machine code. We primarily focus on how partial evaluation can be used to eliminate all of $\mathcal{C}$'s high-level features (higher-order functions, polymorphism) at compile-time.

[1] We are assuming that `readInt` and `printInt` are externally defined primitives in both code snippets.

- We informally describe how one could build a practical surface language on top of $\mathcal{C}$. We cover how common features such as typeclasses (incl. monads), implicit polymorphism and data types can be implemented.

We have implemented a prototype for the approach described in this paper, whose source code is publicly available[2].

3 Core Language

3.1 Outline

This section will define the core language $\mathcal{C}$ and describe how it can be compiled to stack-based machine code. The compilation process from $\mathcal{C}$ to machine code is broken down into several distinct steps (occurring in the following order):

1. Partial Evaluation
2. Uncurrying
3. Lambda Lifting
4. Code Generation

At the core of our approach lies a *partial evaluator*. By carefully performing reductions on the input program at compile-time, we can completely eliminate high-level features such as higher-order functions and polymorphism. By eliminating these features at compile-time, we no longer need to deal with the problem of representing them at run-time. The result of partial evaluation is therefore a program written in a very restricted subset of $\mathcal{C}$, greatly simplifying the rest of the compilation process. So that we can guarantee that partial evaluation will eliminate all occurences of these high-level features, we slightly restrict $\mathcal{C}$ programs through the type system. These non-standard typing rules will be justified in detail throughout the remainder of this section.

After partial evaluation, we follow up with two auxiliary source-to-source transformations: uncurrying and lambda lifting. These steps remove curried and nested functions respectively, and are implemented using well-studied algorithms. Unlike standard approaches to uncurrying [9], the type system and partial evaluator guarantee that the input is in a restricted form where function definitions are maximally η-expanded and there are no partial applications, which greatly simplifies the process. Our approach to lambda lifting is entirely standard, and ultimately the choice of algorithm is irrelevant. Quadratic-time algorithms have been specified in detail in existing literature [22].

Finally, the result of lambda lifting is compiled to machine code. At this point in the pipeline the language is extremely restricted, with only first-order top-level function definitions remaining. Compilation is therefore trivial using standard techniques for first-order languages – our sample implementation uses a straightforward conversion to Rust [14] to complete the compilation process.

---

[2] Download link: https://github.com/eayus/heapless.

3.2 Syntax

The core language $\mathcal{C}$ is an extension of System F_ω with let-bindings (both regular and recursive), products, base types, and primitive operations. We assume the obvious strict semantics. The full syntax is given in Fig. 1. In general, we use a single colon for annotating expressions with their type (e.g. $e : \tau$), and we use a double colon for annotating types with their kind (e.g. $\tau::\kappa$).

Order	o	$\in$	$\{1, 2, 3\}$	
Kind	κ	$::=$	$\star_o$	type
		$\mid$	$\kappa \to \kappa$	type constructor
Base Type	ι	$::=$	`Unit`	unit
		$\mid$	`Int`	integer
		$\mid$	`Bool`	boolean
		$\mid$	`World`	world token
Type	τ	$::=$	ι	base type
		$\mid$	$\tau \to \tau$	function type
		$\mid$	$\forall\alpha :: \kappa.\tau$	quantification
		$\mid$	α	type variable
		$\mid$	$\lambda\alpha :: \kappa.\tau$	type abstraction
		$\mid$	$\tau\ \tau$	type application
		$\mid$	$\tau \times \tau$	product
Expr	e	$::=$	x	variable
		$\mid$	$\lambda x : \tau.e$	application
		$\mid$	$e\ e$	application
		$\mid$	$\Lambda\alpha :: \kappa.e$	type abstraction
		$\mid$	$e\ \tau$	type application
		$\mid$	$\langle e, e\rangle$	pair
		$\mid$	**let** $\langle x, y\rangle$ = e **in** e	pair destructuring
		$\mid$	**let** x = e **in** e	let binding
		$\mid$	**let rec** x = e **in** e	recursive let binding
		$\mid$	**if** e **then** e **else** e	branching
		$\mid$	$\langle\rangle$	unit
		$\mid$	n	numeral
		$\mid$	**true** $\mid$ **false**	truth
		$\mid$	op $\vec{e}$	primitive
Context	Γ	$::=$	$\emptyset$	empty context
		$\mid$	$\Gamma, \alpha :: \kappa$	bind type
		$\mid$	$\Gamma, x : \tau$	bind term

Fig. 1. Syntax of the core language $\mathcal{C}$.

The reason for choosing System F_ω as the base for our core language is that it is expressive enough to support all of the high-level features we are interested in via trivial elaboration. Notably, the type-level evaluation facilities of System F_ω can be used to implement typeclasses, discussed in detail in Sect. 6.3.

As a further syntactic convention, throughout the paper we will often give examples in Haskell-like syntax rather than $\mathcal{C}$. This is to aid readability, as programming directly in a core language is very terse. We assume the natural elaboration from the Haskell-like syntax to $\mathcal{C}$, which mostly amounts to inferring things like explicit type applications and type binders; inferring whether a definition is bound with `let` or `let rec`; and ASCII rather than unicode syntax (i.e. `Type1` rather than $\star_1$).

3.3 Type System

The kinding and typing rules for $\mathcal{C}$ are given in Figs. 2 and 3 respectively. The typing rules for primitive operations (including constants and arithmetic/logic operations) are omitted for brevity, assuming the usual types.

The most unusual part of the type system is the kind $\star_o$, indexed by an *order* o. The full justification for this system is given in Sect. 4.5, but we give an intuitive overview here. The basic premise is that we want to differentiate first-order and higher-order terms. Types are categorised by their kind by their kind as follows.

- $\star_1$ Basic types, such as `Int`, `Bool`, etc.
- $\star_2$ First-order function types, modulo currying. `Int -> Int -> Bool` is included in this kind, but `(Int -> Int) -> Int` is not.
- $\star_3$ Everything else, including higher-order function types and types using universal quantification.

Intuitively, the kinds form a hierarchy where kinds with a higher number are more permissive in the types they allow. This hierachy is realised through the sub-typing rule for kinds KIND-SUB, meaning each kind is included in the one above.

Most of the rules are straightforward, however some of the rules require some special attention. In general, types with kind $\star_3$ should be *contagious*, meaning that if they are used as a component of a composite type, then the composite type should also have kind $\star_3$. For example, a product type where one of the elements is a higher order function (of kind $\star_3$) must also be considered higher order, and hence be given the kind $\star_3$. This is to ensure that higher-order functions and polymorphism are still removed, even when they are used as part of another type (such as a product). Formally, we represent this in the typing rules as taking the maximum of two orders (see max in KIND-PROD and KIND-ARROW). The typing rule TYPE-LET-REC makes use of the kinding information attached to types to enforce that recursive functions are not higher-order and do not use universal quantification in their type – the justification behind this rule is described in detail in Sect. 4.4.

3.4 Handling IO

IO functions are an important part of any practical language. In general, impurity does not mix well with program manipulation and partial evaluation – even

$$\text{KIND-BASE}\quad \frac{}{\Gamma \vdash \iota :: \star_1} \qquad \text{KIND-FORALL}\quad \frac{\Gamma, \alpha :: \kappa \vdash \tau :: \star_i}{\Gamma \vdash (\forall \alpha :: \kappa.\tau) :: \star_3} \qquad \text{KIND-VAR}\quad \frac{(\alpha :: \kappa) \in \Gamma}{\Gamma \vdash \alpha :: \kappa}$$

$$\text{KIND-ARROW}\quad \frac{\Gamma \vdash \tau_1 :: \star_i \qquad \Gamma \vdash \tau_2 :: \star_j \qquad k = max(min(i+1, 3), j)}{\Gamma \vdash \tau_1 \rightarrow \tau_2 :: \star_k}$$

$$\text{KIND-ABS}\quad \frac{\Gamma, \alpha :: \kappa_1 \vdash \tau :: \kappa_2}{\Gamma \vdash (\lambda \alpha :: \kappa_1.\tau) :: \kappa_1 \rightarrow \kappa_2} \qquad \text{KIND-APP}\quad \frac{\Gamma \vdash \tau_1 :: \kappa_1 \rightarrow \kappa_2 \qquad \Gamma \vdash \tau_2 :: \kappa_1}{\Gamma \vdash \tau_1 \tau_2 :: \kappa_2}$$

$$\text{KIND-PROD}\quad \frac{\Gamma \vdash \tau_1 :: \star_i \qquad \Gamma \vdash \tau_2 :: \star_j \qquad k = max(i, j)}{\Gamma \vdash \tau_1 \times \tau_2 :: \star_k} \qquad \text{KIND-SUB}\quad \frac{\Gamma \vdash \tau :: \star_i \qquad i < j}{\Gamma \vdash \tau :: \star_j}$$

Fig. 2. Kinding rules for $\mathcal{C}$.

something as simple as inlining a let-binding can become problematic if the bound expression has a side-effect. The most popular solution in modern functional programming is the IO monad, but it isn't trivial to represent at run-time without a heap. Instead, we thread a linear[3] `World` token throughout the program, similar to the approach used by Clean [15]. At run-time the `World` token can be treated as the unit type. In Sect. 6.4 we show how to reintroduce the IO monad in the surface language userspace.

Note that the typing rules presented in this paper do not enforce the linearity of the world token – this is done intentionally to keep the presentation of the type system concise. However, real implementations should enforce this property properly, as we do in our sample implementation. We use an approach which supports linearity "on the arrow" using multiplicities, almost identical to the approach used in Linear Haskell [4].

4 Partial Evaluator

4.1 Rules

We characterise the partial evaluator by a set of source-to-source reduction rules on $\mathcal{C}$. The notation $t \rightsquigarrow u$ means that subterms matching the pattern t should be replaced with u during partial evaluation. Unless specified otherwise, there are no restrictions on where these reductions can take place, meaning that we reduce under binders by default. Occasionally, rules may have an attached side-condition which restricts when the rule should be applied – this means the rules

[3] In this context, the distinction between linear and unique types is irrelevant, as only one `World` will ever be present.

$$\frac{(x : \tau) \in \Gamma}{\Gamma \vdash x : \tau}\ \text{TYPE-VAR} \qquad \frac{\Gamma, x : \tau_1 \vdash e : \tau_2}{\Gamma \vdash \lambda x.e : \tau_1 \rightarrow \tau_2}\ \text{TYPE-ABS} \qquad \frac{\Gamma \vdash e_1 : \tau_1 \rightarrow \tau_2 \qquad \Gamma \vdash e_2 : \tau_1}{\Gamma \vdash e_1\ e_2 : \tau_2}\ \text{TYPE-APP}$$

$$\frac{\Gamma, \alpha :: \kappa \vdash e : \tau}{\Gamma \vdash (\Lambda\alpha :: \kappa.e) : (\forall\alpha :: \kappa.\tau)}\ \text{TYPE-FORALL} \qquad \frac{\Gamma \vdash e : \forall\alpha :: \kappa.\tau_1 \qquad \Gamma \vdash \tau_2 :: \kappa}{\Gamma \vdash e\ \tau_2 : \tau_1[\alpha \mapsto \tau_2]}\ \text{TYPE-INST}$$

$$\frac{\Gamma \vdash e_1 : \tau_1 \qquad \Gamma \vdash e_2 : \tau_2}{\Gamma \vdash \langle e_1, e_2 \rangle : \tau_1 \times \tau_2}\ \text{TYPE-PROD} \qquad \frac{\Gamma \vdash e_1 : \tau_1 \times \tau_2 \qquad \Gamma, x : \tau_1, y : \tau_2 \vdash e_2 : \tau_3}{\Gamma \vdash (\texttt{let}\ \langle x, y \rangle = e_1\ \texttt{in}\ e_2) : \tau_3}\ \text{TYPE-LET-PROD}$$

$$\frac{\Gamma \vdash e_1 : \tau_1 \qquad \Gamma, x : \tau_1 \vdash e_2 : \tau_2}{\Gamma \vdash (\texttt{let}\ x = e_1\ \texttt{in}\ e_2) : \tau_2}\ \text{TYPE-LET}$$

$$\frac{\Gamma, x : \tau_1 \vdash e_1 : \tau_1 \qquad \Gamma, x : \tau_1 \vdash e_2 : \tau_2 \qquad \Gamma \vdash \tau_1 :: \star_2}{\Gamma \vdash (\texttt{let rec}\ x = e_1\ \texttt{in}\ e_2) : \tau_2}\ \text{TYPE-LET-REC}$$

$$\frac{\Gamma \vdash e_b : \texttt{Bool} \qquad \Gamma \vdash e_t : \tau \qquad \Gamma \vdash e_f : \tau}{\Gamma \vdash \texttt{if}\ e_b\ \texttt{then}\ e_t\ \texttt{else}\ e_f : \tau}\ \text{TYPE-IF}$$

Fig. 3. Typing rules for $\mathcal{C}$.

may not form a true *rewriting system* [10], but we borrow the notation and terminology for conciseness.

Figures 4 and 5 detail the partial evaluator's reduction rules for types and expressions respectively.

$$(\lambda\alpha :: \kappa.\tau_1)\ \tau_2 \rightsquigarrow \tau_1[\alpha \mapsto \tau_2]$$

Fig. 4. Reduction rules for partially evaluating types.

4.2 Elimination

Ultimately, the partial evaluator removes high-level features by applying the appropriate elimination rule. For example, higher-order functions are eliminated through β-reduction (β); polymorphic functions are eliminated through monomorphisation (*mono*). Almost all of the other rules are there to facilitate these eliminators by rewriting expressions into a form which is more amenable to further reduction. The most straightforward example of a "facilitating rule"

$$e_1 \rightsquigarrow \lambda x.e_1\ x \quad \text{if } e_1 : \tau_1 \to \tau_2,\ e_1 \text{ is not a } \lambda \text{ abstraction} \quad (\eta)$$
$$(\lambda x.e_1)e_2 \rightsquigarrow e_1[x \mapsto e_2] \quad (\beta)$$
$$(\texttt{if } e_1 \texttt{ then } e_2 \texttt{ else } e_3)\ e_4 \rightsquigarrow \texttt{if } e_1 \texttt{ then } e_2\ e_4 \texttt{ else } e_3\ e_4 \quad (\textit{if-distr})$$
$$\texttt{let } x \texttt{ = } e_1 \texttt{ in } e_2 \rightsquigarrow e_2[x \mapsto e_1] \quad \text{if } e_1 \text{ is higher-order} \quad (\textit{let-inline})$$
$$(\texttt{let } x \texttt{ = } e_1 \texttt{ in } e_2)\ e_3 \rightsquigarrow \texttt{let } x \texttt{ = } e_1 \texttt{ in } e_2\ e_3 \quad (\textit{let-distr})$$
$$(\texttt{let rec } x \texttt{ = } e_1 \texttt{ in } e_2)\ e_3 \rightsquigarrow \texttt{let rec } x \texttt{ = } e_1 \texttt{ in } e_2\ e_3 \quad (\textit{let-rec-distr})$$
$$(\texttt{let } \langle x, y\rangle \texttt{ = } e_1 \texttt{ in } e_2)\ e_3 \rightsquigarrow \texttt{let } \langle x, y\rangle \texttt{ = } e_1 \texttt{ in } e_2\ e_3 \quad (\textit{let-prod-distr})$$
$$(\Lambda\alpha.e)\tau \rightsquigarrow e[\alpha \mapsto \tau] \quad (\textit{mono})$$

Fig. 5. Reduction rules for partially evaluating expressions.

is let-inlining (*let-inline*). Consider the following expression (assume g is a free variable of the appropriate type):

$$\begin{aligned}&\texttt{let } \textit{twice} \texttt{ = } \lambda f : \texttt{ Int } \to \texttt{ Int. } \lambda x : \texttt{ Int. } f\ (f\ x)\\ &\texttt{in } \textit{twice}\ g\ n\end{aligned}$$

At the moment there are no possible β-reductions, yet a higher-order function remains. We must therefore inline the higher-order function bound by `let` so that β-reduction can take place. After running the above program through the partial evaluator we are left with a first-order residual program:

$$g\ (g\ n)$$

The same idea applies to polymorphic functions which quantify over type variables – they must be inlined and monomorphised. This process is closely related to approaches which specialize higher-order functions to their functional arguments [6]. A deeper comparison with specialisation is given in Sect. 7.2.

4.3 Distribution

We must be careful that other constructs in the core language do not interfere with the elimination of high-level features such as higher-order functions and polymorphism. For constructs which are around at run-time but also allow higher-order functions as a sub-expression, we must introduce an extra rule to *distribute* function applications inside the construct.

If-Expressions. If-expressions allow any type of data in their branches as long as both branches have the same type. We therefore should consider what happens if both branches contain higher-order functions, like in the following expression:

$$(\texttt{if } e_1 \texttt{ then } e_2 \texttt{ else } e_3)\ (\lambda x.e_4)$$

With just β-reduction, there is no way to make progress, yet higher-order functions still remain (e_2 and e_3) in the residual program! One might try adding extra reduction rules for `if`:

$$\texttt{if true then } e_t \texttt{ else } e_f \rightsquigarrow e_t$$
$$\texttt{if false then } e_t \texttt{ else } e_f \rightsquigarrow e_f$$

However, if e_1 is a free variable (whose value may not be known until run-time), then we are still stuck. Instead, we add the rule *if-distr* which distributes applications into the branches of the `if`. This allows us to progress with reductions even if we do not know the value of e_1 ahead of time. After applying this rule, we are left with the following residual expression:

$$\texttt{if } e_1 \texttt{ then } e_2\ (\lambda x.e_4) \texttt{ else } e_3\ (\lambda x.e_4)$$

Let Bindings. Our rule for inlining let-bindings covers the case when the bound expression is a higher-order function, but what about when the body of the `let` is a higher-order function? The following expression shows that there is a similar problem as with if-expressions:

$$(\texttt{let } n = 0 \texttt{ in } e_1)\ (\lambda x.e_2)$$

The partial evaluator will not inline the `let` as it does not bind a higher-order term. We are once again stuck, with no way to β-reduce the higher-order function bound in the body of the `let`. The solution is analogous to the one for if-expressions: introduce a rule which distributes applications inside the `let`'s body. The rules *let-distr*, *let-rec-distr* and *let-prod-distr* implement this behaviour for the various types of let-bindings.

4.4 Recursion

Practical functional programming languages almost always support general recursion, usually in the form of recursive definitions. General recursion is a particularly interesting feature as it makes the language turing-complete, and means that the language is no longer strongly-normalising. This can cause problems for a partial evaluator, as we can no longer blindly reduce expressions without risking non-termination (this is true even if the input program is total).

In general, any rule which indiscriminantly unfolds recursion (i.e. `let rec` bindings) will be problematic. However, if we do not unfold recursion, then we run into problems when recursion is used in combination with higher-order functions. If we define a function which is both higher-order and recursive, then it will remain in the residual program (which should be first-order). Unlike non-recursive higher-order functions, we cannot inline and reduce the definition due to the `let rec` blocking further evaluation.

To resolve this, we introduce the following simple restriction: *recursive functions must not be higher-order or use universal quantification in their type.* This is realised through the kind system, where the typing rule TYPE-LET-REC requires that the type of recursive definitions must have kind $\star_2$. This ensures that recursive definitions are first-order (modulo currying) in the residual program. The reason why we use the kind system to enforce this rather than a syntactic check is explained in Sect. 4.5.

With this set up, no problematic reduction rules are needed for unfolding recursion, as we can only bind first-order functions with `let rec` (which are easy to compile). However, this restrction does seem impractical: plenty of useful functions are both higher-order and recursive! Fortunately, we can easily rewrite the majority of these functions in an equivalent way which is accepted by the type system. More precisely, we can try to extract out the recursive part of the function into a local definition which is first-order. As an example, suppose we wanted to write the following function:

```
nTimes :: Int -> (Int -> Int) -> (Int -> Int)
nTimes 0 f x = x
nTimes n f x = f (nTimes (n - 1) f x)
```

In its current form, the function is both higher order and recursive, and so would not be permitted by our type system. However, we can refactor it into the following equivalent definition which would be permitted:

```
nTimes :: Int -> (Int -> Int) -> (Int -> Int)
nTimes n f = go n
  where
    go :: Int -> Int -> Int
    go 0 x = x
    go m x = f (go (m - 1) x)
```

The local definition `go` is recursive but not higher-order, while the exposed outer definition `nTimes` is higher-order but not recursive. To achieve this, the function `go` captures the function `f`, but does not have it as a parameter – when used, the function `nTimes` will be inlined, and the function *f* also inlined into the body of `go`. The result is a first-order program.

It is possible to do this refactoring for the majority of higher-order functions. Precisely, as long as the functional argument (in this case, `f :: a -> b`) remains constant throughout all recursive calls, the refactoring is possible and straightforward[4].

4.5 Polymorphism

Another trademark feature of modern functional programming languages is *polymorphism.* So that one function can operate on many different types of data,

[4] A practical compiler might choose to perform this refactoring automatically.

most functional languages use a uniform representation for all data – a pointer to a heap allocated cell. Polymorphic functions can then indiscriminantly treat all inputs in the same way, regardless of type. Since this is not an option without a heap, we use a variant of the other predominant method: *monomoprhisation* [19]. This is realised through the *mono* rule in the partial evaluator.

Recursive Functions. Like higher-order functions, we are relying on polymorphism being eliminated at compile-time by the partial evaluator. However, once again, recursive function definitions can cause issues when used in conjunction with polymorphism. As already discussed, recursive functions cannot be unfolded due to issues with termination. Unfortunately, this means that any function that is both recursive and polymorphic will remain in the residual program, as the partial evaluator cannot monomorphise without inlining first. Similar to higher-order functions, the typing rule TYPE-LET-REC prevents this from happening as the kind of any type which uses universal quantification will be $\star_3$.

To implement standard functions which are both polymorphic and recursive we can employ a similar trick to the one for higher-order functions: abstract out the recursive part into an inner auxiliary definition. This is always possible provided recursive calls are made with the same type variables to what the function was given originally (i.e. no *polymorphic recursion*). For example, we can improve our earlier example `nTimes` by making it polymorphic:

```
nTimes :: forall (a :: Type1). Int -> (a -> a) -> (a -> a)
nTimes n f = go n
  where
    go :: Int -> a -> a
    go 0 x = x
    go m x = f (go (m - 1) x)
```

Note how, even though the function `go` uses type variables, because it does not use universal quantification, it is still considered a first-order function (i.e. it has kind $\star_2$). This is because the type variable `a` is bound with kind $\star_1$.

Kind System. In addition to the direct interaction between polymorphism and recursion, there is a more subtle nuance. When the typing rule for `let rec` was introduced, you may have wondered why a kind system is used to ensure the function is first-order (modulo currying), as opposed to a syntactic condition. There are a few reasons for this.

Primarily, the problem with a syntactic check relates to polymorphic type variables. It raises the question – should a type variable be considered a first-order or higher-order type? Consider a recursive function which takes an argument whose type is a type variable[5]:

[5] Note that in its current form, the function `choose` is invalid as it does not give a kind for the type variable `a`. This is done intentionally to demonstrate the necessity of the kind system.

```
choose :: forall a. Int -> a -> a -> a
choose = go
  where
    go :: Int -> a -> a -> a
    go 0 x y = x
    go n x y = go (n - 1) y x
```

Depending on whether the variable a is later instantiated with a basic type or function type, the type of the monomorphised function may be either first-order (modulo currying) or higher-order. Because of this, we cannot treat all type variables as being basic types: doing so would allow the programmer to circumvent the restrictions on higher-order functions by hiding functions types behind a type variable. By separating type variables based on whether they represent functions or not, we can reason about whether a polymorphic function definition is truly first-order for every possible type instantiation. This idea of encoding information in kinds rather than types to handle polymorphism has been explored previously [8].

4.6 Semantic Preservation

An obvious consequence of introducing general recursion is that input programs are no longer guaranteed to always terminate. Not only does this cause issues with the termination of the partial evaluator itself, but it can also pose problems related to the preservation of program semantics. In general, we would expect the program resulting from partial evaluation to have the same semantics as the input program. However, since general recursion introduces the implicit side effect of non-termination, this is not always the case. Consider the following program:

$$\begin{array}{l}\texttt{let rec } f : \texttt{Int} \rightarrow \texttt{Int} = f\\ \texttt{in 0}\end{array}$$

Before any transformation, this program would not terminate as we we would get stuck trying to evaluate f (recall we are following strict semantics). Applying the partial evaluator would produce the following residual program:

$$\begin{array}{l}\texttt{let rec } f : \texttt{Int} \rightarrow \texttt{Int} = \lambda x.fx\\ \texttt{in 0}\end{array}$$

The program semantics have changed! Now, this program will terminate with a value of 0. The only difference between the two programs is that the right-hand side of f has been η-expanded by the partial evaluator. This means that now, we would only run into an infinite loop if f was applied to an argument, which is not the case.

The root of the problem is that non-termination is an untracked side effect, making the language impure. We propose two ways of handling this problem:

- Modify the language so it is pure and total by introducing a termination checker.
- Only provide the guarantee of semantics preservation for programs that terminate.

For the purpose of this paper we choose the latter, though a practical implementation may prefer to use a termination checker so that the compiler is more predictable. If the programmer wishes to intentionally perform an infinite loop, then this is still possible by using an `IO` primitive.

4.7 Further Optimisation

In addition to eliminating high-level constructs, partial evaluation can also be used as a general optimisation method. The partial evaluator presented in this paper uses only the minimal rules necessary to eliminate high-level constructs, but a practical implementation may wish to add additional rules for optimisation purposes.

A simple example is to add rules which implement *constant folding*, a process which reduces primitive operations at compile-time if all operands are known. For example, $3 * (2 + 2)$ should be reduced to 12 at compile-time. Integrating this optimisation into the partial evaluator could remove the need for a separate pass later on in the compilation process.

The inlining of non-essential definitions (i.e. those which are first-order) could also be easily implemented as an optimisation. Currently, the partial evaluator never inlines anything which isn't necessary (with the idea of avoiding code duplication), but if the bound expression is small then inlining may yield a performance benefit.

5 Implementation

5.1 Partial Evaluator

The most straightforward way to implement the partial evaluator is to continuously traverse the input expression, identifying and reducing expressions which match a reduction rule. For β-redexes, reduction will involve substitution, which is another traversal of the expression. It is well-known that this method of implementing normalisers/partial evaluators is inefficient due to the repeated term traversals, even if optimisations such as De-Bruijn indices [3] are used to speed up substitution.

A modern approach to implementing normalisers is *normalisation by evaluation* (NbE), where expressions are first evaluated into semantic values and then later *reified* back into syntactic terms [1,2]. Expensive substitutions are avoided entirely, with environments and variable lookups being used instead. NbE has been widely employed in the implementation of type checkers for dependently typed languages such as Idris and Agda. Since normalisers and partial evaluators are fundamentally very similar, it is relatively straightforward to adapt NbE algorithms to implement our partial evaluator efficiently – this is the approach we use in our sample implementation.

There are a few ways in which our implementation differs from a conventional NbE algorithm. First, the definition of our normal and neutral terms is more lenient than usual, as redexes like let-bindings should be permitted in the result (provided the let-binding does not bind a higher-order function of course). Second, because we are working in a language based on System F_ω, we must perform both term-level and type-level reductions. This requires two distinct evaluation environments. Third, core language terms must carry thorough typing annotations as we are compiling to a typed language backend – the algorithm must ensure that these typing annotations are preserved during evaluation. The complete algorithm is verbose and relatively uninteresting, and so we refer the reader to our sample implementation for the details.

5.2 Uncurrying

The goal of this step in the compilation pipeline is to remove curried functions by transforming them to ones which operate on tuples instead. Due to the η rule in our partial evaluator, functions will always be maximally η-expanded and maximally applied. This makes this process extremely trivial, and we implement this as two simple syntactic transformations (Fig. 6):

$$f t_1 t_2 \ldots t_n \rightsquigarrow f(t_1, t_2, \ldots t_n)$$
$$\lambda x_1.\lambda x_2.\ldots \lambda x_n.t \rightsquigarrow \lambda(x_1, x_2, \ldots x_n).t$$

Fig. 6. Reduction rules for uncurrying.

5.3 Lambda Lifting

At this stage the program may still have local function definitions. We remove these using the standard method of lambda lifting. This has been discussed in detail in existing literature [7,22], and so we do not repeat the details here.

5.4 Backend

At this point in the compilation pipeline, we have a relatively simple first-order language. We offload the remainder of the compilation process to a backend – there are many possible choices, but in our sample implementation we generate Rust code[6]. This would be an unusual choice for a production language as the

[6] Note that we do not depend on any code in the standard library which uses the heap.

Rust compiler will also perform type checking, which is unnecessary and inefficient. However, it is well suited to a prototype implementation as Rust supports first class tuples and nested let-bindings, of which both are utilized in $\mathcal{C}$. Compared to an alternative backend like LLVM [18], this simplifies the compilation process significantly as we do not need extra passes to handle these features.

6 Elaboration

Rather than continuously extend our partial evaluator with new features, we use a common architectural pattern: keep the core language small, but have a more expressive surface language which *elaborates* down to the core language. This section details several common features which can be implemented this way which cumulatively form a Haskell-like language.

6.1 Implicit Polymorphism

An easy extension to our core language which significantly improves practical usability is *implicit polymorphism*, where type applications and abstractions may be omitted and left to be inferred by the compiler. This is a well understood idea and so we do not discuss this in detail. One concrete approach is to use a modification of the Hindley-Milner algorithm [20] which produces type annotated terms (elaboration).

6.2 Algebraic Data Types

Non-recursive. Non-recursive algebraic datatypes are trivial to implement via a simple sum-of-products representation. Record and product types can be represented by nested product types, and sum types may be implemented using tagged unions.

Recursive. Implementing recursive algebraic datatypes is significantly more challenging. Clearly, it is not possible to represent these types at runtime as they have no fixed size and we do not have access to a heap[7]. However, like many other features such as higher-order functions, we can permit recursive datatypes in the surface language provided we can guarantee that they will be eliminated at compile time. A remarkably simple way of achieving this is to use Church-encoding to represent recursive datatypes as functions (à la System F), transformed during the elaboration step. We already know how to deal with higher-order functions in the core language, and so this can be implemented with little complexity. For example, after elaboration, the standard definition of a linked list would be represented by the following type:

$\quad List \equiv \lambda(A{::}\star_3).\forall X.X \to (A \to X \to X) \to X$

[7] The lack of a heap means that we cannot use the conventional linked representation.

There are a few important technical details. First, in the surface language any recursive algebraic data type must have kind $\star_3$, as it will eventually be elaborated into a polymorphic higher-order function. Second, elimination of recursive algebraic datatypes through recursive functions should be disallowed, and instead a primitive `fold` operator should be introduced. The fold operator can be elaborated down into a simple application of the church-encoded function.

This idea of elaborating data types into their church encoding so that they will be eliminated at compile time is essentially a form of *deforestation* [24]. Our approach is much more simplistic than many existing approaches to deforestation, mainly because we do not allow arbitrary recursive definitions (instead exposing a primitive `fold`).

6.3 Typeclasses

Typeclasses are another common feature in surface-level languages which we can support via elaboration. Typeclass constraints can be viewed as implicit function arguments, where the typeclass's functions are stored as a record – this technique is commonly referred to as "dictionary passing". For example, suppose we had a `Number` class:

```
class Number (a :: Type1) where
  add :: a -> a -> a
  sub :: a -> a -> a
```

This could be elaborated to the following record type:
`Number` $\equiv \lambda(a{::}\star_1).(a \to a \to a) \times (a \to a \to a)$

As with all features introduced via elaboration, we must be careful to ensure that the elaborated code is always valid with respect to the core language's typing rules. Since a typeclass constraint may eventually be elaborated into a higher-order type, then it means that in the surface language types using typeclasses should live in $\star_3$. To write a recursive function which uses typeclasses, we must apply our classic transformation of factoring out the recursive part of the function into a local definition.

6.4 Monadic Example

We now culminate these features into a simple high-level example program. Suppose we want to write a program which reads in two numbers from the command line, n and k, and then prints out k for n repetitions. Since this program heavily interacts with IO, it would make sense to write our program within the IO monad. Fortunately, despite not being a primitive in the language, we can still use the IO monad by building it in userspace:

```
newtype IO (a :: Type1) = IO { runIO :: World -> (World, a) }
```

The IO type has trivial instances for `Functor`, `Applicative` and `Monad`. There is some nuance in choosing the right kind for these typeclasses – we discuss this in more detail in Sect. 8.1, but for now we take a pragmatic approach and assume that all monads have kind $\star_1 \to \star_2$. See the appendix for the complete example code, including the definitions for the typeclasses and their instances.

```
instance Functor IO where ...
instance Applicative IO where ...
instance Monad IO where ...
```

Primitive functions should be wrapped in a format which is compatible with the IO monad.

```
readInt :: IO Int
readInt = IO $ \w -> primReadInt w

printInt :: Int -> IO ()
printInt n = IO $ \w -> (primPrintInt n w, ())
```

We can define the familiar `replicateM`, despite it being both higher-order and recursive:

```
replicateM_ :: forall m a. Monad m => Int -> m a -> m ()
replicateM_ n x = go n
  where
    go :: Int -> m ()
    go 0 = pure ()
    go m = do
      x
      go (m - 1)
```

Finally, we can write our program in idiomatic functional style, with no worries that it will be using the heap at runtime. Note that up until now, all of the code that we have written would likely be part of a standard library, and so the programmer would directly skip to this last step. Our program looks identical to regular Haskell code, which we believe is a large benefit of our approach.

```
printK :: IO ()
printK = do
  n <- readInt
  k <- readInt
  replicateM_ n (printInt k)
```

7 Related Work

7.1 Multi-stage Programming

Partial evaluators and multi-stage languages have always been closely related. While the former lets the compiler automatically manipulate the program [11], the latter gives full control to the programmer and allows them to choose which reductions will happen at compile-time [23]. Kovács's recent work [17] has shown how a heterogenous multi-stage language can be used to generate programs which contain no closures, a goal shared by this paper. We believe there are advantages to both Kovács's and our approaches, inherited from the fundamental differences between multi-stage programming and partial evaluation respectively – our approach has less syntactic overhead as we do not require extra staging annotations, but the programmer no longer has full control over the reductions that happen at compile-time.

7.2 Higher-Order Removal

The removal of higher-order functions by translating to a first-order representation has been very well-studied [5,6,21]. The usual motivation is to simplify the compilation process as first-order programs are much simpler to compile to machine-code. Unfortunately, existing methods for removing higher-order functions are not applicable to our use-case of heapless programming, as in the process of removing higher-order functions they introduce other language constructs which also require the heap at run-time.

Defunctionalisation. Defunctionalisation observes that there are only a finite amount of lambda abstractions in a program, and so to represent a function we can enumerate all of the possibilities encoded in an algebraic data type. If a lambda abstraction captures variables from the surrounding scope, parameters should be added to the corresponding ADT constructor representing the captured data.

For example, if a program contained two lambda abstractions:

$$\Gamma \vdash \lambda x : \texttt{Int}.x + x \tag{1}$$

$$\Gamma, y : \texttt{Int} \vdash \lambda x : \texttt{Int}.x + y \tag{2}$$

Then we encode functions by the following ADT:

```
data Func
  = Lam1     -- captures nothing
  | Lam2 Int -- captures y : Int
```

The problem with this method for our use-case occurs when one function captures another function from the surrouding scope. The captured function must be added as a parameter to the data type, making the data type recursive. This would require a heap at runtime. More recent work such as *lambda set specialisation* [5] does not change anything in this regard.

Closure Conversion. The predominant method for compiling higher-order functions is closure conversion, where functions are represented by a function pointer and values for any captured variables [21]. Since different functions (with the same type) may capture different amounts of variables, closures are variably sized, and so the usual approach is to allocate them on the heap behind a uniformly sized pointer.

While heap-allocated closures are obviously not an option without a heap, some low-level languages like Rust and C++ support stack-allocated closures instead. The basic idea is to allocate closures on the stack when they are created, and then pass them by reference so that they have a uniform representation. There are a few undesirable complications introduced with this method:

- When one closure captures another, the first closure is stored by reference in the second. This means that the second closure must not outlive the first, or we will access a dangling reference. Rust solves this with its signature "lifetimes", but we believe such an approach would be quite unwieldy given the ubiquity of closures in functional programming.
- Since different closures of the same type may be different sizes, every closure is assumed to have a unique (mutually incompatible) type. For example, an if-expression which returns different closures in different branches will be rejected by the type checker, since the types of branches will be different too. The approach in this paper does not suffer from this problem due to distribution rules (Sect. 4.3).

Specialisation. Our approach is closely related to *specialisation*, which generates new definitions for higher-order functions every time they are used with a new higher-order argument [6]. Unlike existing approaches to specialisation, our type system ensures complete removal of higher-order functions, rather than a "best effort" approach which aims to remove as much as possible. Specialising methods are better at avoiding duplication of code, as they do not require inlining of every higher-order definition. This difference becomes important when the same function is called with the same higher-order argument in many different places: our approach will inline the definition many times, while specialisation will produce a single top-level definition which is re-used. While this may seem like a significant disadvantage, in practice most non-recursive higher-order functions are only a few operations long, and so are prime candidates for inlining anyway.

On the other hand, there are other areas in which our approach appears to improve over specialising approaches. For example, our method can eliminate higher-order functions which appear in data structures such as products, which is vital for implementing typeclasses in a surface language (Sect. 6.3). We also cover how to handle other language features that may usually use the heap, such as the IO monad. We believe our approach is simpler to implement than most specialising algorithms, as it is a simple modification of normalisation rather than an entirely bespoke algorithm.

8 Future Work

8.1 Order Polymorphism

In the current formalisation of the core language, a polymorphic term must fix a specific kind for the type variables it quantifies over (e.g. $\star_1$, $\star_2$ etc.). This can be undesirable as often we want to use the same function or datatype for many different kinds. For example, consider the reader monad:

$\mathit{Reader} \equiv \lambda R.\lambda A.R \to A$

What kind should we give this type? There are many different possibilities: $\star_1 \to \star_1 \to \star_2$ and $\star_2 \to \star_2 \to \star_3$ are just two examples. It is undesirable to repeat ourselves and write multiple versions of the same type that only differ by kind, and so it would be better if the core language provided a way to write a single polymorphic definition.

Looking at the typing rules for the $\to$ type constructor, the most general kind for this would be polymorphic over *orders* (i.e. the number that the kind $\star$ is indexed by). We propose a system very similar to the universe level polymorphism [16] we see in dependently type languages like Agda. Constructs such as $\uparrow$ (increment order) and $\sqcup$ (maximum of two orders) could be exposed in the syntax for orders, along with type constructors which quantify orders. The kind for the reader monad could then be specified as $\forall ij.\star_i \to \star_j \to \star_{(\uparrow i)\sqcup j}$, which is maximally general. The details of such a system are yet to be worked out, however given the stark similarity to universe levels, we believe that such a system is feasible.

8.2 Heap Effect

So far we have discussed the design of a language which avoids using the heap entirely, so that it can be ran in environments where a heap would be inefficient or impractical. However, real-world applications are unlikely to be so clear-cut, and sometimes we may actually have (partial) access to the heap. To better support this use-case, we could allow finer grained control over what parts of the program use the heap.

Rather than banning heap usage across the entire program, a monad or algebraic effect [13] could be used to track heap usage in the type system. Functions which are disallowed in our core language (i.e. recursive and higher-order definitions) could be allowed on the condition that their type indicates that they use the heap. A handler for the heap effect could be implemented in different ways depending on the run-time environment, potentially after some stack-based initialisation code. For example, an operating system might first query the system memory map, identify a free location, set up a heap, and finally handle the heap effect so that subsequent code can use the heap. This is only possible in a language which supports modularity over where the heap is used.

9 Conclusion

We have introduced a novel approach for designing pure functional languages which do not require the heap at runtime. We have shown how, supported by an appropriate type system, partial evaluation can be used to entirely eliminate the high-level features of a language at compile time. We hope that this work will help facilitate more research into functional languages suitable for systems programming.

Acknowledgements. We would like to thank the reviewers of this paper for their time and their invaluable feedback.

Appendix

```
newtype IO (a :: Type1) = IO { runIO :: World -> (World, a) }

class Functor (f :: Type1 -> Type2) where
  fmap :: (a -> b) -> f a -> f b

class Functor f => Applicative (f :: Type1 -> Type2) where
  pure :: a -> f a
  (<*>) :: f (a -> b) -> f a -> f b

class Applicative f => Monad (f :: Type1 -> Type2) where
  (>>=) :: f a -> (a -> f b) -> f b

instance Functor IO where
  fmap f (IO g) = IO $ \w -> let (w', x) = g w in (w', f x)

instance Applicative IO where
  pure x = IO $ \w -> (w, x)
  IO f <*> IO x = IO $ \w ->
    let (w', f') = f w
        (w'', x') = x w'
    in (w'', f' x')

instance Monad IO where
  (IO g) >>= f = IO $ \w -> let (w', x) = g w in runIO (f x) w'

readInt :: IO Int
readInt = IO $ \w -> primReadInt w

printInt :: Int -> IO ()
printInt n = IO $ \w -> (primPrintInt n w, ())
```

```
replicateM_ :: forall m a. Monad m => Int -> m a -> m ()
replicateM_ n x = go n
  where
    go :: Int -> m ()
    go 0 = pure ()
    go m = do
      x
      go (m - 1)

printK :: IO ()
printK = do
  n <- readInt
  k <- readInt
  replicateM_ n (printInt k)

main :: World -> World
main w = let (w', ()) = runIO printK w in w'
```

References

1. Abel, A., Chapman, J.: Normalization by Evaluation in the Delay Monad: A Case Study for Coinduction via Copatterns and Sized Types. arXiv preprint arXiv:1406.2059 (2014)
2. Berger, U., Eberl, M., Schwichtenberg, H.: Normalization by evaluation. Prospects for Hardware Foundations: ESPRIT Working Group 8533 NADA—New Hardware Design Methods Survey Chapters, pp. 117–137 (1998)
3. Berghofer, S., Urban, C.: A head-to-head comparison of de Bruijn indices and names. Electron. Notes Theoret. Comput. Sci. **174**(5), 53–67 (2007)
4. Bernardy, J.P., Boespflug, M., Newton, R.R., Peyton Jones, S., Spiwack, A.: Linear Haskell: practical linearity in a higher-order polymorphic language. Proc. ACM Programm. Lang. **2**(POPL), 1–29 (2017)
5. Brandon, W., Driscoll, B., Dai, F., Berkow, W., Milano, M.: Better defunctionalization through lambda set specialization. Proc. ACM Programm. Lang. **7**(PLDI), 977–1000 (2023)
6. Chin, W.N., Darlington, J.: A higher-order removal method. LISP Symb. Comput. **9**, 287–322 (1996)
7. Danvy, O., Schultz, U.P.: Lambda-lifting in quadratic time. In: International Symposium on Functional and Logic Programming, pp. 134–151. Springer (2002)
8. Downen, P., Ariola, Z.M., Peyton Jones, S., Eisenberg, R.A.: Kinds are calling conventions. Proc. ACM Programm. Lang. **4**(ICFP), 1–29 (2020)
9. Hannan, J., Hicks, P.: Higher-Order UnCurrying. In: Proceedings of the 25th ACM SIGPLAN-SIGACT Symposium on Principles of Programming Languages, pp. 1–11 (1998)
10. Jay, C.B.: Long Bn Normal Forms and Confluence. Tech. rep., Tech. Rep. LFCS-91-183 (and its revised version) (1991)
11. Jones, N.D.: An introduction to partial evaluation. ACM Comput. Surv. (CSUR) **28**(3), 480–503 (1996)

12. Jones, N.D., Gomard, C.K., Sestoft, P.: Partial Evaluation and Automatic Program Generation. Peter Sestoft (1993)
13. Karachalias, G., Koprivec, F., Pretnar, M., Schrijvers, T.: Efficient compilation of algebraic effect handlers. Proc. ACM Programm. Lang. **5**(OOPSLA), 1–28 (2021)
14. Klabnik, S., Nichols, C.: The Rust Programming Language. No Starch Press (2023)
15. Koopman, P., Plasmeijer, R., van Eekelen, M., Smetsers, S.: Functional Programming in Clean (2002)
16. Kovács, A.: Generalized Universe Hierarchies and First-Class Universe Levels. arXiv preprint arXiv:2103.00223 (2021)
17. Kovács, A.: Closure-free functional programming in a two-level type theory. Proc. ACM Programm. Lang. **8**(ICFP), 659–692 (2024)
18. Lattner, C., Adve, V.: LLVM: a compilation framework for lifelong program analysis & transformation. In: International Symposium on Code Generation and Optimization, 2004. CGO 2004, pp. 75–86. IEEE (2004)
19. Lutze, M., Schuster, P., Brachthäuser, J.I.: The Simple Essence of Monomorphization. Proc. ACM Programm. Lang. **9**(OOPSLA1), 1015–1041 (2025)
20. Milner, R.: A theory of type polymorphism in programming. J. Comput. Syst. Sci. **17**(3), 348–375 (1978)
21. Minamide, Y., Morrisett, G., Harper, R.: Typed closure conversion. In: Proceedings of the 23rd ACM SIGPLAN-SIGACT Symposium on Principles of Programming Languages, pp. 271–283 (1996)
22. Morazán, M.T., Schultz, U.P.: Optimal lambda lifting in quadratic time. In: Implementation and Application of Functional Languages: 19th International Workshop, IFL 2007, Freiburg, Germany, September 27-29, 2007. Revised Selected Papers 19, pp. 37–56. Springer (2008)
23. Taha, W.: A gentle introduction to multi-stage programming. In: Domain-Specific Program Generation: International Seminar, Dagstuhl Castle, Germany, March 23-28, 2003. Revised Papers, pp. 30–50. Springer (2004)
24. Wadler, P.: Deforestation: transforming programs to eliminate trees. In: European Symposium on Programming, pp. 344–358. Springer (1988)

Functional Reactive GUI Programming with Modal Types

Jean-Claude Disch, Asger Heegaard, and Patrick Bahr(✉)

IT University of Copenhagen, Copenhagen, Denmark
jeanclaudedisch@live.dk, asgerheegaard@gmail.com, paba@itu.dk

Abstract. *Functional reactive programming* (FRP) is a programming paradigm for implementing reactive systems, i.e. programs that continuously interact with their environments. While FRP allows for a functional, high-level programming style, FRP programs are prone to undesirable operational behaviours such as *space leaks*. To ensure favourable operational properties of FRP programs, *modal type systems* have been introduced, which – among other things – make it impossible to write FRP programs with implicit space leaks. In a recent development, several modal FRP languages have been introduced that are able to accommodate *asynchronous* events and behaviours – motivated by the goal to use such languages for GUI programming.

This paper explores the suitability of one such asynchronous modal FRP language – called Async Rattus – for GUI programming in *practice*. To this end, we have implemented a mild extension of the Async Rattus language and used it to implement a small GUI framework. We demonstrate the language and its GUI framework by a number of case studies.

1 Introduction

Interactive applications, especially those with *graphical user interfaces* (GUIs), form a cornerstone of contemporary software systems. Most modern GUI frameworks use an imperative programming model that is based on shared mutable state that is read and updated via callback functions. While computationally efficient, this model combines features that are notoriously difficult to reason about, namely mutable state, higher-order functions, and concurrency. This often leads to error-prone code that is difficult to maintain and debug.

Functional reactive programming (FRP) has arisen as an alternative high-level programming paradigm to implement such interactive systems [27]. The fundamental idea is to represent dynamic behaviours using a type of time varying values, called *signals* or *behaviours*. Using Haskell syntax, we can express this idea by defining a type of signals as follows:

$$\textbf{type}\ Sig\ a = Time \rightarrow a$$

The original version of the chapter has been revised. A correction to this chapter can be found at https://doi.org/10.1007/978-3-031-99751-8_23

J. Gibbons (Ed.): TFP 2025, LNCS 15652, pp. 93–114, 2026.
https://doi.org/10.1007/978-3-031-99751-8_5

We can then implement combinators that manipulate such signals, which allows us to describe complex dynamic behaviours. For example, we can implement a mapping function $map :: (a \to b) \to Sig\ a \to Sig\ b$ to apply a function to a signal, or a switching function $switch :: Sig\ a \to Event\ (Sig\ a) \to Sig\ a$, which constructs a signal that behaves as the first argument but switches its behaviour to another signal as soon as it arrives as an event at a later time.

However, while conceptually simple and relatively easy to reason about, functional reactive programs directly based on this (denotational) notion of signals are impossible to implement efficiently in general – with early implementations suffering from space and time leaks. This deficiency has led to two prominent lines of work on devising FRP languages that carefully reign in the expressive power of the language in order to avoid such pathologic performance behaviour: One based on identifying a carefully restricted set of combinators that is made available to programmers to construct signals [25,26], and one based on modal type systems to keep track of temporal dependencies [17,18,21,23].

In this paper, we focus on the latter approach, which retains more of the expressive power of the denotational notion of signals – they can still be manipulated directly – at the cost of a more complicated type system. To this end, these modal FRP languages feature a modal type operator $\bigcirc$, so that a value of type $\bigcirc A$ is the promise of a value of type A that is available in the next time step. Using this *later modality*, (discrete) signals can be captured by the following recursive type definition in Haskell notation:

$$\textbf{data}\ Sig\ a = Cons\ a\ (\bigcirc\ (Sig\ a))$$

That is, a signal of type $Sig\ a$ consists of a value of type a and the promise of a new signal of type $Sig\ a$ in the next time step.

However, these early modal FRP languages are inherently *synchronous* in nature, i.e. each delayed value of type $\bigcirc A$ arrives at the same time, namely *the* next time step according to some global clock. This is an unrealistic and fundamentally inefficient notion of time for GUI applications where different signals may receive updates at different, independent times. In response to this, the asynchronous modal FRP calculi $\lambda_{\mathsf{Widget}}$ [15] and Async RaTT [8] have been proposed recently.

In this paper, we present *Widget Rattus*, an FRP language based on the Async RaTT calculus and implemented as an embedded language in Haskell for the purpose of GUI programming. Widget Rattus consists of a small extension of the Async Rattus language [7], which implements Async RaTT as an embedded language in Haskell, along with a small GUI framework.

In short, this paper makes the following contributions:

- We extend the Async Rattus language with a first-class notion of *channels* and a generalised notion of output channels (Sect. 2).
- We present a purely functional GUI framework implemented in Widget Rattus and demonstrate its use on two extended examples (Sect. 3).
- We give an overview of the implementation of the GUI framework based on the principles of FRP (Sect. 4).

- We compare Widget Rattus to $\lambda_{\mathsf{Widget}}$ and other related work (Sect. 5).

The Widget Rattus language and GUI framework is available as a Haskell package [16], which also contains further examples beyond those presented in Sect. 3. Throughout this paper, we use Haskell syntax.

2 From Async Rattus to Widget Rattus

In this section, we give a brief introduction to the Async Rattus language [7] (Sects. 2.1 to 2.5) and then present two extensions to the language that will enable GUI programming (Sect. 2.6).

$$\frac{\Gamma, \checkmark_{\mathsf{cl}(t)} \vdash t :: A}{\Gamma \vdash \mathsf{delay}_{\mathsf{cl}(t)}\, t :: \bigcirc A} \qquad \frac{\checkmark \notin \Gamma' \text{ or } A \text{ stable}}{\Gamma, x :: A, \Gamma' \vdash x :: A} \qquad \frac{\Gamma \vdash t :: \Box A}{\Gamma \vdash \mathsf{unbox}\, t :: A} \qquad \frac{\Gamma^{\Box} \vdash t :: A}{\Gamma \vdash \mathsf{box}\, t :: \Box A}$$

$$\frac{\Gamma \vdash s :: \bigcirc A \quad \Gamma \vdash t :: \bigcirc B \quad \checkmark \notin \Gamma'}{\Gamma, \checkmark_{\mathsf{cl}(s) \sqcup \mathsf{cl}(t)}, \Gamma' \vdash \mathsf{select}\, s\, t :: \mathit{Select}\, A\, B} \qquad \frac{\Gamma \vdash t :: \bigcirc A \quad \checkmark \notin \Gamma'}{\Gamma, \checkmark_{\mathsf{cl}(t)}, \Gamma' \vdash \mathsf{adv}\, t :: A} \qquad \frac{}{\Gamma \vdash \mathsf{never} :: \bigcirc A}$$

$$\frac{}{\Gamma \vdash \mathsf{chan} :: C(\mathsf{Chan}\, A)}\,\dagger \qquad \frac{\Gamma \vdash t :: \mathsf{Chan}\, A}{\Gamma \vdash \mathsf{wait}\, t :: \bigcirc A}\,\dagger \qquad \frac{\Gamma \vdash t :: A \quad A \text{ continuous}}{\Gamma \vdash \mathsf{promote}\, t :: \Box A}\,\dagger$$

$$\text{where} \qquad \begin{aligned} \cdot^{\Box} &= \cdot \\ (\Gamma, \checkmark_\theta)^{\Box} &= \Gamma^{\Box} \end{aligned} \qquad (\Gamma, x :: A)^{\Box} = \begin{cases} \Gamma^{\Box}, x :: A & \text{if } A \text{ stable} \\ \Gamma^{\Box} & \text{otherwise} \end{cases}$$

Fig. 1. Select typing rules for Async Rattus and its extension Widget Rattus. New typing rules introduced by Widget Rattus are marked by †.

2.1 Introduction to Async Rattus

The purpose of Async Rattus is to provide a language that allows us to implement the type of signals, *Sig*, along with a rich library of signal combinators such as *map* and *switch* from Sect. 1, while maintaining crucial operational properties such as avoiding space leaks and ensuring causality.

Async Rattus is an implementation of the *Async RaTT* calculus [8] as a shallowly embedded language in Haskell. By virtue of being shallowly embedded, Async Rattus has access to Haskell's extensive library ecosystem. However, Async Rattus differs from Haskell in two major ways.

The first difference is that Async Rattus is eagerly evaluated while Haskell uses lazy evaluation by default. The choice of eager evaluation is an important part of how Async Rattus prevents space leaks while still allowing the programmer to manipulate signals directly [8]. In a nutshell, the eager evaluation semantics of Async Rattus ensures that computations that wait for future inputs will be performed as soon as these future inputs arrive. As a consequence these inputs do not need to be kept in memory since they are consumed immediately.

The second fundamental difference introduced by Async Rattus is an extension of the type system. Async Rattus introduces two type modalities, $\bigcirc$ and $\Box$, called the *later* and *box* modalities, and written in ASCII syntax as `O` and `Box`, respectively. The later modality $\bigcirc$ represents values that will be available in the future, whereas the box modality $\Box$ is used for computations that remain stable across time and thus can be executed at any time. Figure 1 presents the most important typing rules of Async Rattus and its extension Widget Rattus (indicated by †). We describe the type modalities and the type system that enables them in more detail below.

To account for these fundamental differences in semantics and type system, Async Rattus is implemented by a combination of a Haskell library, which implements the basic primitives and types of the language, and a compiler plugin. This compiler plugin transforms the code so that it matches the eager evaluation semantics of Async Rattus, and it performs an additional typechecking pass to enforce the stricter typing rules of the language as described by Bahr et al. [7].

2.2 Later Modality and Clocks

The later modality $\bigcirc$ indicates values that are not immediately available but expected in the future, contingent on the occurrence of some event. A value of type $\bigcirc A$ represents a delayed computation that will produce a value of type A in the future. The timing of when the value will become available is determined by a *clock*, which is a record of data dependencies: An Async Rattus program may receive data from several input channels such as the keyboard or a button on a GUI. A clock θ is a set of such input channels, e.g. $\theta = \{c_{keyboard}, c_{ok\_button}\}$, and a *tick* on θ means that data has been received on some input channel $c \in \theta$.

Any value of type $\bigcirc A$ is effectively a pair (θ, f) consisting of a clock θ and a computation f that will produce a value of type A when executed. The computation f remains dormant until the clock θ *ticks*, which signals the occurrence of the anticipated event. This mechanism ensures that delayed computations respect temporal causality. That is, delayed computations are performed only when their time comes, according to the ticking of their associated clocks.

Conceptually, we can think of the two components θ and f of a delayed computation of type $\bigcirc A$ to be accessible via two functions $\mathsf{cl} :: \bigcirc A \to \text{Clock}$ and $\mathsf{adv} :: \bigcirc A \to A$, respectively. However, as we shall see, cl is not directly accessible to the programmer, and adv is subject to the typing rule in Fig. 1, which we discuss shortly. Conversely, to construct a delayed computation, one can use delay, which for now we can think of as having type $\mathsf{delay} :: \text{Clock} \to A \to \bigcirc A$. That is, it takes a clock θ and a computation f producing A and returns a delayed computation (θ, f) that will yield the value of type A once θ ticks. This conceptual representation suffices for the moment, but we will refine this oversimplification when presenting the typing rules for adv and delay. Also note that while Async Rattus is eagerly evaluated by default, delay does not evaluate its argument of type A eagerly, since it represents a delayed computation that may only be performed once the associated clock θ ticks.

An illustrative example of the interplay between the later modality and clocks is the following increment function:

$$
\begin{aligned}
&incr :: \bigcirc\, Int \rightarrow \bigcirc\, Int \\
&incr\ x = \mathsf{delay}_{\mathsf{cl}(x)}(\mathsf{adv}\ x + 1)
\end{aligned}
$$

The function *incr* delays the increment operation until the clock $\mathsf{cl}(x)$ associated with x ticks. This schedules the increment to happen when the underlying value of x becomes available, thereby enforcing causality of the system.

To keep track of temporal dependencies at compile time, typing contexts contain tokens of the form $\checkmark_\theta$ to indicate that a tick on a clock θ has occurred. These tokens $\checkmark_\theta$ are also called *ticks*. An example context in Async Rattus could look like this:

$$x :: Int, \checkmark_\theta, y :: Int, z :: Text, \checkmark_{\theta'}$$

Here the ticks represent the passage of time according to the clocks θ and θ'. Intuitively speaking, this context expresses the fact that the value assigned to variable x is available one time step (on clock θ) before the values assigned to y and z, which in turn are one time step (on clock θ') old. With this understanding in mind, we can see from the typing rules in Fig. 1 that adv can only be used to advance a delayed computation $t :: \bigcirc A$ if a tick on the clock of t has occurred, indicated by the token $\checkmark_{\mathsf{cl}(t)}$. Moreover, this tick must be the most recent tick, i.e. there are no other ticks occurring to the right of it, which is indicated by the condition $\checkmark \notin \Gamma'$. And finally, t itself must be typeable using only the part of the context to the left of the tick $\checkmark_{\mathsf{cl}(t)}$, i.e. t must come from the time before its clock ticked. This typing rule encodes the intuition that the presence of the tick $\checkmark_{\mathsf{cl}(t)}$ in the typing context indicates that the clock $\mathsf{cl}(t)$ has ticked in response to an event making the value computed by t available *now*.

Consider the following example of a function for eliminating the later modality that is not causal and indeed does not typecheck:

$$
\begin{aligned}
&advBad :: \bigcirc\, Int \rightarrow Int \\
&advBad\ x = \mathsf{adv}\ x
\end{aligned}
$$

The *advBad* function tries to use adv to extract a future value of the delayed computation x without waiting for its clock $\mathsf{cl}(x)$ to tick. In other words, *advBad* is not causal as it tries to look up data now that is only available later.

While adv is used for eliminating the later modality and executing delayed computations in response to events, delay is used to construct delayed computations. To safely construct a delayed computation one needs to associate it with a clock to indicate when it can be executed. The delay function allows us to delay a computation $t :: A$ until the time at which a certain clock θ ticks. The type system keeps track of that by making sure that t type checks in a context that includes $\checkmark_\theta$. The new context $\Gamma, \checkmark_\theta$ not only indicates that θ has ticked by the time t gets evaluated, but also that all variables that were previously available in Γ, are now one time step older according to the clock θ.

As an example, consider the following ill-typed definition using delay:

$$\begin{aligned}&\mathit{delayBad} :: \mathit{Int} \to \bigcirc\, \mathit{Int}\\&\mathit{delayBad}\ x = \mathsf{delay}_\theta\ x \quad \text{-- no clock } \theta \text{ available}\end{aligned}$$

In this example, *delayBad* tries to delay an integer x, but in order to do so it needs to specify a clock θ. Clocks cannot be constructed directly, but can only be extracted from other delayed computations. Since no such delayed computation is in context, we cannot use delay here.

Together, adv and delay enable precise control over when computations are carried out in Async Rattus. This ensures that values and delayed computations are only accessed at appropriate times, often in response to user generated input. The following is a typical example of how adv and delay interact:

$$\begin{aligned}&\mathit{doubleLater} :: \bigcirc\, \mathit{Int} \to \bigcirc\, \mathit{Int}\\&\mathit{doubleLater}\ x = \mathsf{delay}_{\mathsf{cl}(x)}\ (2 * \mathsf{adv}\ x)\end{aligned}$$

In this example, *doubleLater* takes a delayed integer and returns a new delayed integer that is twice the original value. To this end, the new delayed computation has the same clock as the incoming delayed computation x. That means, the term $2 * \mathsf{adv}\ x$ is type checked in the context $x :: \bigcirc \mathit{Int}, \checkmark_{\mathsf{cl}(x)}$.

The clock argument to delay can typically be inferred from the context in which it appears. In the above example, the clock has to be $\mathsf{cl}(x)$, as we need the tick $\checkmark_{\mathsf{cl}(x)}$ in context so that we can advance x. We therefore elide the clock argument from now on, and indeed the Async Rattus type checker will infer the clock argument. In practice, the above example would thus be written as follows in Async Rattus:

$$\begin{aligned}&\mathit{doubleLater} :: \bigcirc\, \mathit{Int} \to \bigcirc\, \mathit{Int}\\&\mathit{doubleLater}\ x = \mathsf{delay}\ (2 * \mathsf{adv}\ x)\end{aligned}$$

2.3 The Box Modality and Stable Types

Computations in Async Rattus may contain references to time-dependent data as for example the reference to x in the computation performed by $2*\mathsf{adv}\,x$ in the definition of *doubleLater* above. Such references to time-dependent values may cause space leaks in FRP programs as these values have to be kept in memory until the computation that references it is performed. To prevent this, Async Rattus does not allow programmers to move arbitrary data across time steps. Only data of certain types can be moved across time. We call such types *stable types*, and they include all types that cannot carry any temporal dependency. Types of the form $\bigcirc A$ and $A \to B$ are not stable, since delayed computations are by definition time-dependent and since functions may contain references to arbitrary data in their closure – including time-dependent data. Stable types include all base types like *Int* and *Bool* as well as all algebraic data types and record types that in turn only contain stable types, e.g. lists of integers.

The typing rule for variables enforces that only values of stable types can be moved across time: A variable that occurs to the left of a tick – and is thus from the past – can only be used if it is of a stable type. The following example illustrates this:

$$mapLaterBad :: (a \rightarrow b) \rightarrow \bigcirc\, a \rightarrow \bigcirc\, b$$
$$mapLaterBad\ f\ x = \mathsf{delay}_{\mathsf{cl}(x)}\ (f\ (\mathsf{adv}\ x)) \quad \text{-- f is out of scope}$$

This definition does not typecheck since f is no longer in scope when it is used under delay. The typing context to typecheck $f\ (\mathsf{adv}\ x)$ is $f :: a \rightarrow b, x :: \bigcirc a, \checkmark_{\mathsf{cl}(x)}$ and according to the typing rule for variables, we can see that f typechecks in this context only if its type $a \rightarrow b$ was stable, which it is not.

To safely and efficiently move values of such non-stable types across time, Async Rattus provides the box modality $\Box$, which turns any type A into a stable type $\Box A$. However, when constructing values of type $\Box A$ using the box primitive, the type system enforces restrictions that makes sure that such boxed values are indeed time-independent. The typing rule for box requires that its argument t typecheck in a context $\Gamma^{\Box}$, which is obtained from Γ by removing all ticks and all variable bindings $x :: A$ where A is not stable. This ensures that $\mathsf{box}\, t$ is time-independent and can thus be moved across time. Similarly to delay, also box evaluates its argument lazily. That is, the argument t is only evaluated when the boxed value is forced using unbox.

Using the box modality, we can revise the *mapLaterBad* function so that it takes a boxed function instead:

$$mapLater :: \Box\ (a \rightarrow b) \rightarrow \bigcirc\, a \rightarrow \bigcirc\, b$$
$$mapLater\ f\ x = \mathsf{delay}_{\mathsf{cl}(x)}\ (\mathsf{unbox}\, f\ (\mathsf{adv}\ x))$$

Now f is in scope because, while it is still occurring to the left of a tick, it is of a stable type, namely $\Box\,(a \rightarrow b)$.

2.4 Signals

Signals can be defined in Async Rattus by the following definition, which uses infix operator ::: as the constructor:

$$\textbf{data}\ Sig\ a = a ::: \bigcirc\ (Sig\ a)$$

That is, a signal of type $Sig\, a$ consists of a current value of type a and a future update to the signal of type $\bigcirc(Sig\, a)$. Such signals can be easily manipulated using pattern matching and recursion. For example, we can define a *map* function for signals, but similarly to the *mapLater* function on the $\bigcirc$ modality, the function argument has to be boxed:

$$map :: \Box\ (a \rightarrow b) \rightarrow Sig\ a \rightarrow Sig\ b$$
$$map\ f\ (x ::: xs) = \mathsf{unbox}\, f\ x ::: \mathsf{delay}\ (map\ f\ (\mathsf{adv}\ xs))$$

In order to ensure *productivity* of recursive function definitions, Async Rattus requires that recursive function calls, such as $map\, f\ (\mathsf{adv}\, xs)$ above, are guarded by a delay. More precisely, such a recursive occurrence may only occur in a context Γ that contains a $\checkmark_\theta$.

Similarly to *mapLater*, the type system of Async Rattus prevents us from implementing a *map* function that takes an unboxed function of type $a \rightarrow b$ as argument. Such an unboxed function would no longer be in scope under the delay, where it is needed for the recursive call. This restriction, enforced by the type system, is crucial for avoiding space leaks. A function f of type $a \rightarrow b$ is allowed to have values of non-stable types such as signals in its closure. Such values would need to be kept in memory indefinitely so that we can apply the function f at any point in time in the future as required by the *map* function.

Finally, the following example shows the use of never to introduce delayed computations that will never be triggered:

$$\begin{aligned}&\mathit{const} :: a \rightarrow \mathit{Sig}\ a\\&\mathit{const}\ x = x ::: \mathsf{never}\end{aligned}$$

This function allows us to construct signals whose update component will never be triggered and thus maintain a constant value.

2.5 Asynchronous Computations

Unlike synchronous modal FRP languages, each delayed computation in Async Rattus comes with its own local clock. That means we cannot easily combine two delayed computations since they may not be triggered simultaneously. For example, we cannot implement a function like this:

$$\begin{aligned}&\mathit{addBad} :: \bigcirc\ \mathit{Int} \rightarrow \bigcirc\ \mathit{Int} \rightarrow \bigcirc\ \mathit{Int}\\&\mathit{addBad}\ x\ y = \mathsf{delay}\ (\mathsf{adv}\ x + \mathsf{adv}\ y)\end{aligned}$$

The problem is that we cannot annotate delay with a single clock θ that will allow us to advance on both x and y since they may have different clocks.

To process more than one delayed computation, Async Rattus allows us to form the union $\theta \sqcup \theta'$ of two clocks θ and θ', which ticks whenever θ or θ' ticks. We can use such union clocks via the select primitive, which takes two delayed computations $s :: \bigcirc A$ and $t :: \bigcirc B$ as arguments and requires that a tick on the clock $\mathsf{cl}(s) \sqcup \mathsf{cl}(t)$ is in the context. In return, select produces a value of type *Select A B* defined as follows:

$$\textbf{data}\ \mathit{Select}\ a\ b = \mathit{Fst}\ a\ (\bigcirc\ b) \mid \mathit{Snd}\ (\bigcirc\ a)\ b \mid \mathit{Both}\ a\ b$$

A term select s t produces a value with constructor *Fst*, *Snd*, or *Both* if $\mathsf{cl}(s)$ ticks before, after, or at the same time as $\mathsf{cl}(t)$, respectively. Using select, we can implement a combinator that allows us to dynamically switch from one signal to another one:

$$\begin{aligned}&\mathit{switch} :: \mathit{Sig}\ a \rightarrow \bigcirc\ (\mathit{Sig}\ a) \rightarrow \mathit{Sig}\ a\\&\mathit{switch}\ (x ::: xs)\ d = x ::: \mathsf{delay}\ (\textbf{case}\ \mathsf{select}\ xs\ d\ \textbf{of}\end{aligned}$$

$$\begin{aligned}&Fst\ \ xs'\ d' \rightarrow switch\ xs'\ d'\\&Snd\ \ \_\ \ d' \rightarrow d'\\&Both\ \_\ \ d' \rightarrow d')\end{aligned}$$

The signal *switch xs ys*, first behaves like the signal *xs*, but it will start behaving like the delayed signal *ys* as soon as it arrives, i.e. when $\mathsf{cl}(ys)$ ticks.

2.6 Widget Rattus

Widget Rattus is a small extension of the Async Rattus language with two features that enable GUI programming: first-class channels and continuous types.

First-Class Channels. To implement GUIs we need to be able to dynamically create GUI components, or *widgets*, which in turn must be able to produce data obtained from user interaction, e.g. button press events or keyboard inputs from a text field. To this end, Widget Rattus introduces two primitives – shown in Fig. 1 – to construct and interact with channels, which can then be used by widgets to send their data: chan creates a new channel of type Chan A, which can send data of type A, and wait turns such a channel into a delayed computation that produces a value of type A as soon as such a value is sent on the channel. Since chan is an effectful operation – it allocates a fresh channel – it uses a monad C to indicate its effectful nature.

Below we use a channel to construct a simple button that consists of a signal that describes its text and a channel of type Chan () that is intended to produce a unit value whenever it is pressed:

```
data SimpleButton = SimpleButton (Sig Text) (Chan ())
simpleButton :: C SimpleButton
simpleButton = do c ← chan
                  return (Button (const "OK") c)
```

Here the button just displays a constant signal of the text “OK”. In the example below we make a more dynamic button that changes its text from “OK” to “Clicked” as soon as the button is clicked:

```
respond :: C SimpleButton
respond = do
  c ← chan
  let sig = switch (const "OK")
                   (mapLater (box (λ() → const "Clicked")) (wait c))
  return (Button sig c)
```

The dynamic behaviour is achieved by the *switch* function from Sect. 2.5. In turn, *mapLater* is used to turn the delayed computation wait c :: $\bigcirc()$ into a delayed signal of type $\bigcirc(Sig\ Text)$.

The channel type Chan a is stable and can thus be moved across time, which allows us to implement the following combinator to turn channels into signals:

$$chanSig :: \mathsf{Chan}\ a \rightarrow \bigcirc\ (Sig\ a)$$
$$chanSig\ c = \mathsf{delay}\ (\mathsf{adv}\ (\mathsf{wait}\ c) ::: chanSig\ c)$$

Since the channel c is of a stable type, we can move it across the tick introduced by delay and then pass it to the recursive call of *chanSig*.

Continuous Types. The second extension provided by Widget Rattus generalises the outputs that a reactive program can produce. An Async Rattus program can produce output in the form of signals of type *Sig A* for basic types A. A value of type *Sig A* is of the form $v_0 ::: (\theta_0, f_0)$, where $v_0 :: A$ and f is a delayed computation that produces a new signal $v_1 ::: (\theta_1, f_1)$ as soon as θ_0 ticks. That is, a signal produces a sequence of values $v_0, v_1, \ldots$, each triggered by a corresponding clock.

The output produced by GUI programs does not have this linear structure but is instead tree-shaped. We can imagine a GUI being represented as a signal of type *Sig Widget*, where *Widget* is a type that describes the top-level widget of the GUI, e.g. a container widget that contains other widgets, which in turn may consist of other widgets. That is, GUIs are described by a tree structure. For example, we may define a widget that consists of several buttons:

$$\textbf{data}\ Buttons = Buttons\ (Sig\ Color)\ (Sig\ (List\ SimpleButton))$$

This container widget consists of a colour signal but also of a signal of a list of buttons. Since buttons themselves consist of signals, the output mechanism of the language needs to handle nested signals.

To this end, Widget Rattus introduces the notion of continuous types. These are types whose values may dynamically change over time. For each continuous type A, the runtime system of Widget Rattus has a clock function $\mathsf{clock} :: A \rightarrow \mathsf{Clock}$ and an update function $\mathsf{update} :: \mathsf{InputValue} \rightarrow A \rightarrow A$. If we have a value v of a continuous type A, and we receive an input i on a channel $c \in \mathsf{clock}(v)$, the value v is updated to $\mathsf{update}\ i\ v :: A$. For example, *Sig Int* is a continuous type: An integer signal value $v_0 ::: (\theta_0, f_0)$ has the clock θ_0 and is updated once an input i is received on a channel $c \in \theta_0$ by performing the delayed computation f_0 which yields a new signal $v_1 ::: (\theta_1, f_1)$.

Continuous types allow us to deal with signals of type *Sig A* where A is not a basic type but may in general be a continuous type. In that case, the clock of a signal $v_0 ::: (\theta_0, f_0)$ is the union of the clock of v_0 and θ_0, i.e. $\mathsf{clock}(v_0) \sqcup \theta_0$. If we receive input i on channel $c \in \mathsf{clock}(v_0) \sqcup \theta_0$, there are two possible outcomes for the updated signal. If $c \in \theta_0$, then the new signal is produced by performing the delayed computation f_0, which produces a new signal $v_1 ::: (\theta_1, f_1)$. Otherwise, if $c \notin \theta_0$ (and thus $c \in \mathsf{clock}(v_0)$), then the new signal is $\mathsf{update}\ i\ v_0 ::: (\theta_0, f_0)$.

Any basic type is a continuous type, and – like stable types – continuous types are closed under product, sum and recursive types. However, unlike stable types, continuous types are closed under forming signal types, i.e. if A is a continuous type, then so is *Sig A*. Since continuous types can be updated over time, Widget Rattus comes with a primitive promote that promotes a continuous type to a boxed type as shown in Fig. 1. In particular, any widget type that we implement in Widget Rattus is a continuous type. That means, it can be used by Widget Rattus' runtime system to render it as a GUI on screen and update it in response to GUI events. Moreover, we can promote any widget so that we can safely move it into the future. So a button that is constructed at some point in time can safely be moved into the future by promoting it to a boxed type. The semantics of promote makes sure that the boxed widget is updated in response to events that make its clock tick, e.g. if it is the *respond* button defined above, it will change its label when it is clicked.

3 GUIs in Widget Rattus

To demonstrate the expressiveness of Widget Rattus, we have implemented the first four tasks from Kiss's *7GUIs* benchmark [20] as well as a simple calculator. The full implementation of these example GUIs can be found in the Widget Rattus package [16]. In this section, we take a closer look at two of these examples: a counter and a timer. The GUIs are constructed using the Widget Rattus libraries shown in Fig. 2 and Fig. 5. Figure 2 shows a selection of combinators to construct and manipulate signals, and Fig. 5 contains functions to construct widgets. Most of the signal combinators shown in Fig. 2 are taken from the original Async Rattus work [7]. But we have added a few combinators that have become handy for implementing the GUI examples, and we discuss their implementation in this section. The implementation of widgets and their constructor functions will be covered in more detail in Sect. 4.

Since Widget Rattus uses eager evaluation, it also uses strict variants of common data types, e.g. strict pair types $A \times B$ instead of the non-strict version (A, B) and the strict list type $\mathit{List}\,A$ instead of the non-strict version $[B]$ normally used in Haskell. We will encounter these types in the examples below.

3.1 Counter

We begin with an example of a simple counter GUI depicted in Fig. 3a. It contains a button that increments a label whenever it is pressed [20]. The implementation of this GUI in Widget Rattus is shown in Fig. 4.

To start a GUI application using Widget Rattus, we have to pass the (compound) widget that is to be rendered in the application to the *runApplication* function. Widget Rattus provides a number of functions to create widgets. For the widgets relevant to the examples in this section, the type signatures can be seen in Fig. 5.

For the counter GUI it is necessary to make a button and a label. The *mkButtons* function takes a signal that determines what text to display on the button. The signal may be of any type *a* that implements the *Displayable* type class, which includes *Text* and *Int*. For the counter we simply give our button a constant signal with the *Text* value "Increment".

$$
\begin{aligned}
&\mathit{map} :: \Box\,(a \to b) \to \mathit{Sig}\ a \to \mathit{Sig}\ b\\
&\mathit{mkSig} :: \Box\,(\bigcirc\ a) \to \bigcirc\,(\mathit{Sig}\ a)\\
&\mathit{const} :: a \to \mathit{Sig}\ a\\
&\mathit{scan} :: (\mathit{Stable}\ b) \Rightarrow \Box\,(b \to a \to b) \to b \to \mathit{Sig}\ a \to \mathit{Sig}\ b\\
&\mathit{scanAwait} :: (\mathit{Stable}\ b) \Rightarrow \Box\,(b \to a \to b) \to b \to \bigcirc\,(\mathit{Sig}\ a) \to \mathit{Sig}\ b\\
&\mathit{switch} :: \mathit{Sig}\ a \to \bigcirc\,(\mathit{Sig}\ a) \to \mathit{Sig}\ a\\
&\mathit{switchS} :: \mathit{Stable}\ a \Rightarrow \mathit{Sig}\ a \to \bigcirc\,(a \to \mathit{Sig}\ a) \to \mathit{Sig}\ a\\
&\mathit{switchR} :: \mathit{Stable}\ a \Rightarrow \mathit{Sig}\ a \to \bigcirc\,(\mathit{Sig}\ (a \to \mathit{Sig}\ a)) \to \mathit{Sig}\ a\\
&\mathit{interleave} :: \Box\,(a \to a \to a) \to \bigcirc\,(\mathit{Sig}\ a) \to \bigcirc\,(\mathit{Sig}\ a) \to \bigcirc\,(\mathit{Sig}\ a)\\
&\mathit{zipWith} :: (\mathit{Stable}\ a, \mathit{Stable}\ b) \Rightarrow \Box\,(a \to b \to c) \to \mathit{Sig}\ a \to \mathit{Sig}\ b \to \mathit{Sig}\ c\\
&\mathit{stop} :: \Box\,(a \to \mathit{Bool}) \to \mathit{Sig}\ a \to \mathit{Sig}\ a\\
&\mathit{timer} :: \mathit{Int} \to \Box\,(\bigcirc\ ())\\
&\mathit{mkSig} :: \Box\,(\bigcirc\ a) \to \bigcirc\,(\mathit{Sig}\ a)
\end{aligned}
$$

Fig. 2. Signal combinator library.

(a) Counter. (b) Timer.

Fig. 3. Example GUIs.

To add functionality to a button, we use the *btnOnClickSig* function. This function takes as input a button and returns a signal that ticks – producing a unit value – whenever the button is pressed. This signal can be turned into an integer signal that produces the intended value of the counter. To this end, we use the *scanAwait* combinator, which similarly to Haskell's *scanl* combinator on lists applies a given function f to a signal. An input signal that produces values $v_1, v_2, \ldots$ is thus transformed into a signal producing values $x, f\ x\ v_1, f\ (f\ x\ v_1)\ v_2, \ldots$, where x is the starting value provided to *scanAwait*. In this case, we start with 0 and increment the previous value by one at each tick of the input signal *clicks*. The resulting signal *counts* is then used to create a label that always displays the current value of *counts*, which is exactly the number of times that the button has been pressed.

Finally, *runApplication* only takes as input a single widget, but in most GUIs it is necessary to display multiple widgets. For this purpose Widget Rattus provides horizontal and vertical stacks. Stacks are widgets that take as input a list of other widgets, allowing users of Widget Rattus to create their GUI as a tree

$$
\begin{aligned}
&\mathit{counter} :: C\ \mathit{VStack}\\
&\mathit{counter} = \mathbf{do}\\
&\quad \mathit{btn} \leftarrow \mathit{mkButton}\ (\mathit{const}\ \texttt{"Increment"})\\
&\quad \mathbf{let}\ \mathit{clicks} = \mathit{btnOnClickSig}\ \mathit{btn}\\
&\quad \mathbf{let}\ \mathit{counts} = \mathit{scanAwait}\ (\mathsf{box}\ (\lambda n\ ()\rightarrow n+1))\ 0\ \mathit{clicks}\\
&\quad \mathit{lbl} \leftarrow \mathit{mkLabel}\ \mathit{counts}\\
&\quad \mathit{mkVStack}\ (\mathit{const}\ [\mathit{mkWidget}\ \mathit{lbl}, \mathit{mkWidget}\ \mathit{btn}])\\
&\mathit{main} :: \mathit{IO}\ ()\\
&\mathit{main} = \mathit{runApplication}\ \mathit{counter}
\end{aligned}
$$

Fig. 4. Counter GUI Implementation

$$
\begin{aligned}
&\mathit{mkButton} :: \mathit{Displayable}\ a \Rightarrow \mathit{Sig}\ a \rightarrow C\ \mathit{Button}\\
&\mathit{btnOnClickSig} :: \mathit{Button} \rightarrow \bigcirc\ (\mathit{Sig}\ ())\\
&\mathit{mkTextField} :: \mathit{Text} \rightarrow C\ \mathit{TextField}\\
&\mathit{textFieldOnInputSig} :: \mathit{TextField} \rightarrow \bigcirc\ (\mathit{Sig}\ \mathit{Text})\\
&\mathit{mkLabel} :: \mathit{Displayable}\ a \Rightarrow \mathit{Sig}\ a \rightarrow C\ \mathit{Label}\\
&\mathit{mkVStack} :: \mathit{IsWidget}\ a \Rightarrow \mathit{Sig}\ (\mathit{List}\ a) \rightarrow C\ \mathit{VStack}\\
&\mathit{mkConstVStack} :: \mathit{Widgets}\ \mathit{ws} \Rightarrow \mathit{ws} \rightarrow C\ \mathit{VStack}\\
&\mathit{mkSlider} :: \mathit{Int} \rightarrow \mathit{Sig}\ \mathit{Int} \rightarrow \mathit{Sig}\ \mathit{Int} \rightarrow C\ \mathit{Slider}\\
&\mathit{sldCurr} :: \mathit{Slider} \rightarrow \mathit{Sig}\ \mathit{Int}\\
&\mathit{mkProgressBar} :: \mathit{Sig}\ \mathit{Int} \rightarrow \mathit{Sig}\ \mathit{Int} \rightarrow \mathit{Sig}\ \mathit{Int} \rightarrow C\ \mathit{Slider}\\
&\mathit{mkWidget} :: \mathit{IsWidget}\ a \Rightarrow a \rightarrow \mathit{Widget}\\
&\mathit{runApplication} :: \mathit{IsWidget}\ a \Rightarrow C\ a \rightarrow \mathit{IO}\ ()
\end{aligned}
$$

Fig. 5. GUI combinator Library

structure composed of widgets. In the counter GUI a single vertical stack is made using the *mkVStack* function to contain both the button and label.

Note that *lbl* and *btn* are of two different types, namely *Label* and *Button*, but we have to construct a list of a single widget type in order to pass it to *mkVStack*. To this end, the library provides the *mkWidget* function to turn any widget type into the type *Widget*. Since we often find ourselves passing a constant signal of a list of differently-typed widgets, the library also provides a *mkConstVStack* function that takes any tuple consisting of widget types, e.g. $\mathit{Label} \times \mathit{Button}$. That means, the last line of *counter* can be more compactly written as $\mathit{mkConstVStack}\ (\mathit{lbl} \times \mathit{btn})$ instead.

3.2 Timer

As a second example, we consider an interactive timer that ticks up every second and whose value is displayed in both a progress bar and numerically on a label [20]. User input comes in the form of a slider that determines the maximum value of the timer, as well as a button that resets the timer. Figure 3b shows our Widget Rattus implementation of this GUI application: The grey bar is the progress bar which – like the text label above it – increments towards the maximum value determined by the blue slider at the top. However, the progress bar also changes in response to inputs to the slider, since changing the maximum timer value changes the percentage of how much time has passed relative to the maximum. Pressing the reset button sets the timer (and thus both the label and the progress bar) to zero. The primary challenge of the timer GUI is concurrency, since user input competes with the state of the timer.

```
everySecondSig :: ○ (Sig ())
everySecondSig = mkSig (timer 1000000)

mkTimerSig :: Int × Int → Sig (Int × Int)
mkTimerSig startState = stop (box (λ(n × nMax) → n ⩾ nMax)) timerSig
  where timerSig :: Sig (Int × Int)
        timerSig = scanAwait (box (λ(n × nMax) () → (n + 1) × nMax))
                               startState everySecondSig

reset :: () → (Int × Int) → (Int × Int)
reset () (n × nMax) = (0 × nMax)

setMax :: Int → (Int × Int) → (Int × Int)
setMax nMax' (n × nMax) = min n nMax' × nMax'

window :: C VStack
window = do
  slider ← mkSlider 50 (const 1) (const 100)
  resetBtn ← mkButton (const ("Reset" :: Text))
  let resetSig = mapAwait (box reset) (btnOnClickSig resetBtn)
  let setMaxSig = mapAwait (box setMax) (future (sldCurr slider))
  let inputSig :: ○ (Sig (Int × Int → Int × Int))
      = interleave (box (∘)) resetSig setMaxSig
  let inputSig' :: ○ (Sig (Int × Int → Sig (Int × Int)))
      = mapAwait (box (λf → mkTimerSig ∘ f)) inputSig
  let currentMax = current (sldCurr slider)
  let counterSig = switchR (mkTimerSig (0 × currentMax)) inputSig'
  let currentSig = map (box fst') counterSig
  let maxSig = map (box snd') counterSig
  label ← mkLabel currentSig
  pb ← mkProgressBar (const 0) maxSig currentSig
  mkConstVStack (slider × resetBtn × label × pb)
```

Fig. 6. Timer GUI implementation

The full Widget Rattus code for the timer GUI is shown in Fig. 6. At the top, *mkTimerSig* defines the base signal that increments the timer value until we reach the end of the timer. The state of the timer consists of two integer values: the number of seconds elapsed since the start of the timer and the maximum value of the timer, i.e. the number of seconds at which the timer will stop. This state is represented by the type $Int \times Int$.

The *mkTimerSig* function takes the initial state as input and produces a new timer signal that starts with that state. To this end, we use *timer* and *mkSig* from Fig. 2 to produce a signal of type $\bigcirc(\mathit{Sig}\ ())$ that ticks every second ($= 1000000$ microseconds). Using *scanAwait* we turn this into a signal that advances the state of the timer, by incrementing the first component (elapsed seconds) but leaving the second component (the maximum timer value) untouched. To stop the timer when the maximum value is reached, we finally apply the *stop* combinator. This combinator takes a predicate and a signal as argument, and produces a new signal that behaves as the old signal, but stops as soon as the predicate is satisfied. We can implement *stop* as follows:

$$
\begin{aligned}
&\mathit{stop} :: \Box\,(a \to \mathit{Bool}) \to \mathit{Sig}\ a \to \mathit{Sig}\ a\\
&\mathit{stop}\ f\ (x ::: xs) = \textbf{if}\ \mathsf{unbox}\ f\ x\ \textbf{then}\ \mathit{const}\ x\\
&\qquad\qquad\qquad\qquad\ \textbf{else}\ x ::: \mathsf{delay}\ (\mathit{stop}\ f\ (\mathsf{adv}\ xs))
\end{aligned}
$$

The below example shows how the *stop* function works:

$$
\begin{aligned}
xs &: 1\ 2\ 3\ 4\ 5\ 6\ldots\\
\mathit{stop}\ (\mathsf{box}\ (\geqslant 3))\ xs &: 1\ 2\ 3
\end{aligned}
$$

To illustrate a modular programming style, we have used two separate combinators – *scanAwait* and *stop* – to first define a signal and then modify it so that it stops at a certain point. Of course, we could have also used a combinator that combines the functionality of *scanAwait* and *stop*.

The GUI constructed by *window* in Fig. 6 first constructs the slider to adjust the timer and the reset button. The *mkSlider* function constructs a slider with 50 as its initial value and two constant signals that determine the minimum and maximum value of the slider to be 0 and 100, respectively.

Both the reset button and the slider change the state of the timer as described by the *reset* and *setMax* functions defined above *window*. These two functions are applied to the two signals produced by the reset button and the slider using *mapAwait*, to obtain the signals *resetSig* and *setMaxSig*, both of type $\bigcirc(\mathit{Sig}((\mathit{Int} \times \mathit{Int}) \to (\mathit{Int} \times \mathit{Int})))$. Both signals produce functions that are meant to manipulate the timer state, and we combine the two with the *interleave* combinator to create a signal that responds to both types of user input. The resulting signal *inputSig* ticks whenever either input signal ticks. When both signals tick, then the values of the two signals are combined – in this case using function composition $\circ$, so that both functions are applied – one after the other.

As an example of how *interleave* works consider the following integer signals xs and ys and how their interleaving looks like with the addition operator.

$$
\begin{aligned}
xs &: 1\ 3\ \ \ \ 5\ 3\ 1\ 3\ldots\\
ys &: \ \ \ 0\ 2\ \ \ 4\ \ \ \ \ \ \ \ldots\\
\mathit{interleave}\ (\mathsf{box}\ (+))\ xs\ ys &: 1\ 3\ 2\ 5\ 7\ 1\ 3\ldots
\end{aligned}
$$

Next, we need to combine the *inputSig* signal with the timer signal produced by *mkTimerSig*. To do so, we make use of a *switch* combinator. The signal combinator library in Fig. 2 has three such combinators: The simplest, *switch*, we have already seen in Sect. 2.5. It takes a signal *xs* and a delayed signal *ys* as arguments and produces a signal that first behaves like *xs* and switches to behaving like *ys* as soon as it arrives. The stateful version, *switchS*, works similarly but *ys* is now a delayed function that produces a signal depending on the previous value of the signal, rather than just a signal that is independent of the previous value of the signal. Finally, *switchR* is a repeating version of *switchS*. Instead of a single delayed function *ys*, it takes a delayed signal of such functions, and each time this signal produces a new function, that function is used to change the behaviour of the signal. We can implement it by repeatedly calling *switchS*:

$$
\begin{aligned}
&\mathit{switchR} :: \mathit{Stable}\ a \Rightarrow \mathit{Sig}\ a \to \bigcirc\,(\mathit{Sig}\ (a \to \mathit{Sig}\ a)) \to \mathit{Sig}\ a\\
&\mathit{switchR}\ \mathit{xs}\ \mathit{ys} = \mathit{switchS}\ \mathit{xs}\\
&\quad (\mathsf{delay}\ (\mathbf{let}\ \mathit{step} ::: \mathit{ys}' = \mathsf{adv}\ \mathit{ys}\ \mathbf{in} \lambda x \to \mathit{switchR}\ (\mathit{step}\ x)\ \mathit{ys}'))
\end{aligned}
$$

We use *switchS* to construct a signal that first behaves like *sig*. We further give *switchS* a delayed function that takes as argument the previous value x of the signal and produces a new signal. As soon as a function $\mathit{step} :: a \to \mathit{Sig}\ a$ is received on the *steps* signal, our delayed function will apply *step* to x to obtain a new signal on which to recursively continue.

Table 1. Example table for *counterSig*

Events		1 s	Max set to 10	1 s	Reset pressed
inputSig			setMax 10		reset
counterSig	(0,50)	(1,50)	(1,10)	(2,10)	(0,10)

In the case of the timer GUI, *switchR* is used to create *counterSig*, a signal representing a capped timer, whose maximum and current value can be affected by user input. The signal first starts as *mkTimerSig* ($0 \times \mathit{currentMax}$), i.e. it simply ticks up every second. This signal then dynamically switches according to the signal *inputSig′*, which takes the functions of *inputSig* and composes them with *mkTimerSig*. In other words, for every user input, which produces a function f on *inputSig*, we apply that function f to the current timer state, and then we pass the resulting new state to *mkTimerSig* to resume the timer with this new state.

Table 1 illustrates an example of how *counterSig* behaves for a given sequence of user input: *counterSig* initially behaves like *mkTimerSig* applied to (0×50). After every second the first part of *counterSig* increments. When the user sets the maximum value to 10 by dragging the slider, *setMax 10* is applied to the current value of *counterSig*. This returns (1×10) and *counterSig* switches its behaviour to reflect *mkTimerSig* (1×10). This increments to (2×10) after another second. Once the reset button is pressed the *reset* function is called with the current value of *counterSig*. This returns (0×10) and *counterSig* now behaves like *mkTimerSig* (0×10).

Finally, *counterSig* is split into its two components with the help of the two projection functions $fst' :: a \times b \to a$ and $snd' :: a \times b \to b$ of the strict pair type. The resulting signals are passed on to the label and the progress bar, which along with the other widgets are grouped into a vertical stack.

4 GUI Library Implementation

After demonstrating the use of the Widget Rattus GUI library in the previous section, we turn to the implementation of the GUI library in this section. To simplify the implementation of the GUI library, we have built it on top of *Monomer* [28], a Haskell library for writing GUI applications using pure functional code in a style pioneered by Elm [11].

GUI elements in Widget Rattus GUIs are called *widgets* and the GUI is represented as a tree structure. Conceptually speaking, widgets are simply GUI elements that are defined as unique data structures. A button, for example, consists of two fields: a signal of displayable content and an input channel:

```
data Button where
  Button :: Displayable a
    ⇒ { btnContent :: Sig a, btnClick :: Chan () } → Button
```

The *btnContent* field represents the value displayed on the button. Any widget that takes user input needs to instantiate a channel of the corresponding type as described in Sect. 2.6. In the case of a button this is a channel of type (), since the click event does not carry any data.

The *Displayable* type class is a variant of the standard type class *Show*:

```
class Stable a ⇒ Displayable a where
  display :: a → Text
```

It provides a method to render a value as text. The difference to *Show* is that: (1) it is a subclass of *Stable*, (2) it produces text of type *Text*, which unlike *String* is a strict type, and (3) its instance for *Text* implements *display* as the identity function rather than embedding the text in quotation marks.

To render widgets using Monomer, we need a way to turn them into corresponding data structures in Monomer, called *widget nodes*. This is achieved by the *IsWidget* type class:

```
class Continuous a ⇒ IsWidget a where
  mkWidgetNode :: a → Monomer.WidgetNode AppModel AppEvent
```

The *mkWidgetNode* method translates a Wiget Rattus widget of type *a* into a widget node in Monomer, which can then be rendered by the monomer library.

Every widget node in monomer has a model and event type. We will return to the definition of these types shortly.

Note that *IsWidget* is a subclass of *Continuous*, which we introduced in Sect. 2.6. This ensures that we can use widgets in a way that is similar to signals: Widgets have a current state, which is rendered on screen, and they can be updated in response to events. Recall that any stable type is continuous, and that continuous types are closed under forming product types, sum types, recursive types, and signals. Widget Rattus provides Template Haskell code that automatically generates *Continuous* instance declarations for such types, so we can focus on defining instances of *IsWidget*. For buttons, the instance declaration looks as follows:

```
instance IsWidget Button where
  mkWidgetNode Button {btnContent = val ::: _, btnClick = click} =
    Monomer.button (display val) (AppEvent click ())
```

The Monomer button constructor takes as input the text to be shown on the button and the event that should be produced when clicking the button. For the first argument, we use the current value of the *btnContent* signal and render it as text. For the second argument, we want the event to contain both the channel associated with the button, and the value it produces when clicking the button – in this case (). To this end, we define an *AppEvent* data type to contain exactly this data:

```
data AppEvent where
  AppEvent :: Chan a → a → AppEvent
```

This data type consists of an input a channel of type *a* and a value of type *a*. Button click events are of type (), since they do not contain any information.

As shown in Fig. 5, Widget Rattus provides functions to make the process of constructing GUI elements simpler. The *mkButton* function is implemented as follows:

```
mkButton :: Displayable a ⇒ Sig a → C Button
mkButton t = do c ← chan
                return Button {btnContent = t, btnClick = c}
```

The *mkButton* function only takes a signal as input. The input channel required for *btnClick* is allocated by the call to *chan*. This simple widget only consists of a single signal and a single channel. A more full-featured library would include additional signals (e.g. signals describing colour, styling etc.) and channels (e.g. a channel to indicate that the button received focus).

Widgets can be nested so that they form a tree structure. Vertical stacks provide the simplest example of this nested structure:

```
data VStack where
  VStack :: IsWidget a ⇒ Sig (List a) → VStack
```

As observed before, the list of widgets that the signal of a stack produces only allows lists of the *same* widget type (e.g. only a list of buttons). To allow widgets of different types, we also have a wrapper type *Widget*, so that we can turn a widget of any type into a widget of type *Widget*:

$$\begin{array}{l}\textbf{data}\ \mathit{Widget}\ \textbf{where}\\ \quad \mathit{Widget} :: \mathit{IsWidget}\ a \Rightarrow a \rightarrow \mathit{Sig}\ \mathit{Bool} \rightarrow \mathit{Widget}\end{array}$$

Such a wrapper widget type can contain any additional data that applies to all widgets. For our simple library, we include a signal of type *Bool* that is used to determine whether the widget is enabled at any given time. If a *Widget* never needs to be disabled, one can use the *mkWidget* function:

$$\begin{array}{l}\mathit{mkWidget} :: \mathit{IsWidget}\ a \Rightarrow a \rightarrow \mathit{Widget}\\ \mathit{mkWidget}\ w = \mathit{Widget}\ w\ (\mathit{const}\ \mathit{True})\end{array}$$

Finally, we turn to the implementation of *runApplication*, which takes a computation of type $C\,w$ that produces a widget of type w and runs an application that renders this widget. To this end, *runApplication* uses Monomer's *startApp* function, which requires four components, which we present here in simplified form. First, we have the event type *AppEvent*, which we have introduced above. Second, we have the *AppModel* type, which describes the current state of the application:

$$\begin{array}{l}\textbf{data}\ \mathit{AppModel}\ \textbf{where}\\ \quad \mathit{AppModel} :: \mathit{IsWidget}\ a \Rightarrow a \rightarrow \mathit{Clock} \rightarrow \mathit{AppModel}\end{array}$$

That is, the state of a Widget Rattus application is solely described by the widget that is to be rendered and a clock. The latter is simply the clock that represents all timers that are currently running, i.e. delayed computations produced by *timer* from Fig. 2. The *runApplication* function initialises the *AppModel* data structure with the widget it takes as argument and with the empty clock.

The last two components for Monomer's *startApp* are functions that interact with the state and event types. The first is a function that constructs a new widget node from the current state of the GUI application:

$$\begin{array}{l}\mathit{build} :: \mathit{AppModel} \rightarrow \mathit{WidgetNode}\ \mathit{AppModel}\ \mathit{AppEvent}\\ \mathit{build}\ (\mathit{AppModel}\ w\ \mathit{cl}) = \mathit{mkWidgetNode}\ w\end{array}$$

The second function is an event handler that updates the model. Below we present a simplified version that ignores timers (the *cl* component of the model):

$$\begin{array}{l}\mathit{handle} :: \mathit{AppModel} \rightarrow \mathit{AppEvent} \rightarrow \mathit{AppModel}\\ \mathit{handle}\ (\mathit{AppModel}\ w\ \mathit{cl})\ (\mathit{AppEvent}\ c\ i) =\\ \quad \textbf{if}\ c \in \mathsf{clock}\ w\ \textbf{then}\ \mathit{AppModel}\ (\mathsf{update}\ i\ w)\ \mathit{cl}\ \textbf{else}\ \mathit{AppModel}\ w\ \mathit{cl}\end{array}$$

Since the widget w is of a continuous type, it can be updated using the clock and update functions as described in Sect. 2.6.

5 Related Work

There is a long history of using the FRP paradigm to implement GUI frameworks in a functional programming language: Notable examples are the Haskell libraries *FranTk* [27] (based on the original *Functional Reactive Animation* framework *Fran* [12]), *Fruit* [10] (based on the arrowized FRP library *Yampa* [25]), and *Threepenny GUI* [2] (based on *Reactive Banana* [1], a traditional FRP library with a carefully selected set of combinators to avoid time leaks). The prominent *Elm* language [11] was initially also implemented as an embedded language in Haskell designed for FRP-based GUI programming but has later abandoned the FRP paradigm in favour of the *Elm Architecture.*

More recently, FRP languages have emerged that use modal types with the goal of avoiding issues of traditional FRP [5,6,8,9,15,17–19,21,23,24], namely space/time leaks and causality, while still maintaining its conceptual simplicity, i.e. manipulation of first-class signals using functional programming. The first foray into modal FRP for GUI programming was undertaken by Krishnaswami & Benton [22] using linear types to describe dynamically updating GUIs. However, this language is synchronous, which is at odds with the asynchronous nature of GUI applications and thus leads to inefficiencies. Graulund et al. [15] introduced the $\lambda_{\mathsf{Widget}}$ calculus which also combines modal types and linear types, but its temporal modalities are asynchronous. A crucial difference between Widget Rattus and $\lambda_{\mathsf{Widget}}$ is that the latter uses destructive updates to dynamically change GUI components, e.g. via a `setColor` function. By contrast Widget Rattus uses the core FRP idea of signals to *declaratively describe* the dynamic behaviour of GUI elements. Moreover, to our knowledge Widget Rattus is the first *implementation* of an asynchronous modal FRP language for GUI programming.

To date, most mainstream GUI frameworks are still based on an object-oriented model with a shared mutable state at its core. Nonetheless, recent developments strive towards APIs that encourage a more declarative programming style that reduces the reliance on callbacks to manipulate the state such as in Apple's *SwiftUI* [4] and Google's *Jackpack Compose* [14] libraries. However, the ideas of FRP have been adopted by Apple's *Combine* [3] library, which allows programmers to construct and manipulate signals for SwiftUI GUIs using higher-order functions, not unlike the *Sig* type we presented in this paper.

6 Conclusions and Future Work

We have demonstrated how the modal FRP language Async Rattus can support purely functional GUI programming with two mild extensions to the language: first-class channels and continuous types. We consider this work as a proof of concept that demonstrates the language's expressiveness for GUI programming. There are several avenues for future research to make it easier to implement GUIs (e.g. by devising a more expressive signal library that incorporates ideas from push-pull FRP [13]) and to further improve runtime efficiency (e.g. by updating nested widgets in-place rather than producing a new full widget tree). Finally, we conjecture that the type soundness result of the Async RaTT calculus [8], which undergirds Async Rattus, can be extended to account for the two language extensions presented here, so that we can formally establish the same operational guarantees: productivity, causality, and absence of implicit space leaks.

References

1. Apfelmus, H.: Reactive Banana (2011). https://wiki.haskell.org/Reactive-banana
2. Apfelmus, H.: Threepenny GUI (2013). https://wiki.haskell.org/Threepenny-gui
3. Apple Inc.: Combine. https://developer.apple.com/documentation/Combine
4. Apple Inc.: SwiftUI. https://developer.apple.com/documentation/SwiftUI
5. Bahr, P., Graulund, C.U., Møgelberg, R.E.: Simply RaTT: a fitch-style modal calculus for reactive programming without space leaks. Proc. ACM Program. Lang. **3**(ICFP), 109:1–109:27 (2019). https://doi.org/10.1145/3341713
6. Bahr, P., Graulund, C.U., Møgelberg, R.E.: Diamonds are not forever: liveness in reactive programming with guarded recursion. Proc. ACM Program. Lang. **5**(POPL), 2:1–2:28 (2021). https://doi.org/10.1145/3434283
7. Bahr, P., Houlborg, E., Rørdam, G.T.S.: Asynchronous reactive programming with modal types in Haskell. In: Gebser, M., Sergey, I. (eds.) Practical Aspects of Declarative Languages (2024)
8. Bahr, P., Møgelberg, R.E.: Asynchronous modal FRP. Proc. ACM Program. Lang. **7**(ICFP), 205:476–205:510 (2023). https://doi.org/10.1145/3607847
9. Cave, A., Ferreira, F., Panangaden, P., Pientka, B.: Fair reactive programming. In: Proceedings of the 41st ACM SIGPLAN-SIGACT Symposium on Principles of Programming Languages, pp. 361–372. ACM (2014). https://doi.org/10.1145/2535838.2535881
10. Courtney, A., Elliott, C.: Genuinely functional user interfaces. In: Haskell Workshop (2001)
11. Czaplicki, E., Chong, S.: Asynchronous functional reactive programming for GUIs. ACM SIGPLAN Not. **48**(6), 411–422 (2013). https://doi.org/10.1145/2499370.2462161
12. Elliott, C., Hudak, P.: Functional reactive animation. In: Proceedings of the second ACM SIGPLAN International Conference on Functional Programming, pp. 263–273. Association for Computing Machinery (1997). https://doi.org/10.1145/258948.258973
13. Elliott, C.M.: Push-pull functional reactive programming. In: Proceedings of the 2nd ACM SIGPLAN Symposium on Haskell, pp. 25–36. ACM (2009). https://doi.org/10.1145/1596638.1596643
14. Google: Jetpack Compose. https://developer.android.com/compose
15. Graulund, C.U., Szamozvancev, D., Krishnaswami, N.: Adjoint reactive GUI programming. In: FOSSACS 2021. LNCS, vol. 12650, pp. 289–309. Springer, Cham (2021). https://doi.org/10.1007/978-3-030-71995-1_15
16. Houlborg, E., Rørdam, G., Bahr, P., Disch, J.C., Heegaard, A.: WidgetRattus (2024). https://hackage.haskell.org/package/WidgetRattus. https://hackage.haskell.org/package/WidgetRattus
17. Jeffrey, A.: LTL types FRP: linear-time temporal logic propositions as types, proofs as functional reactive programs. In: Proceedings of the Sixth Workshop on Programming Languages Meets Program Verification. ACM (2012). https://doi.org/10.1145/2103776.2103783

18. Jeltsch, W.: Towards a common categorical semantics for linear-time temporal logic and functional reactive programming. Electron. Notes Theor. Comput. Sci. **286**, 229–242 (2012). https://doi.org/10.1016/j.entcs.2012.08.015. https://www.sciencedirect.com/science/article/pii/S157106611200045X
19. Jeltsch, W.: Temporal logic with "Until", functional reactive programming with processes, and concrete process categories. In: Proceedings of the 7th Workshop on Programming Languages Meets Program Verification, pp. 69–78. Association for Computing Machinery (2013). https://doi.org/10.1145/2428116.2428128
20. Kiss, E.: 7GUIs: A GUI programming benchmark (2014). https://eugenkiss.github.io/7guis/tasks
21. Krishnaswami, N.R.: Higher-order functional reactive programming without space-time leaks. In: Proceedings of the 18th ACM SIGPLAN International Conference on Functional Programming, pp. 221–232. ACM (2013). https://doi.org/10.1145/2500365.2500588
22. Krishnaswami, N.R., Benton, N.: A semantic model for graphical user interfaces. In: Proceedings of the 16th ACM SIGPLAN International Conference on Functional Programming, pp. 45–57. Association for Computing Machinery (2011). https://doi.org/10.1145/2034773.2034782
23. Krishnaswami, N.R., Benton, N., Hoffmann, J.: Higher-order functional reactive programming in bounded space. In: Proceedings of the 39th Annual ACM SIGPLAN-SIGACT Symposium on Principles of Programming Languages, pp. 45–58. ACM (2012). https://doi.org/10.1145/2103656.2103665
24. Krishnaswami, N., Benton, N.: Ultrametric semantics of reactive programs. In: 26th Annual IEEE Symposium on Logic in Computer Science (LICS), pp. 257–266 (2011). https://doi.org/10.1109/LICS.2011.38
25. Nilsson, H., Courtney, A., Peterson, J.: Functional reactive programming, continued. In: Proceedings of the 2002 ACM SIGPLAN Workshop on Haskell, pp. 51–64. ACM (2002). https://doi.org/10.1145/581690.581695
26. Ploeg, A.V.D., Claessen, K.: Practical principled FRP: forget the past, change the future, FRPNow! In: Proceedings of the 20th ACM SIGPLAN International Conference on Functional Programming, pp. 302–314. Association for Computing Machinery (2015). https://doi.org/10.1145/2784731.2784752
27. Sage, M.: FranTk - a declarative GUI language for Haskell. SIGPLAN Not. **35**(9), 106–117 (2000). https://doi.org/10.1145/357766.351250
28. Vallarino, F.: Monomer (2018). https://hackage.haskell.org/package/monomer

Compilation

Multi-GPU Code Generation for Out-of-Core Problems

Patrick van Beurden, Thomas Koopman(✉), and Sven-Bodo Scholz

Radboud University, Nijmegen, Netherlands
{patrick.vanbeurden,thomas.koopman,svenbodo.scholz}@ru.nl

Abstract. We propose a light-weight solution for generating code that can use multiple GPUs from purely declarative program specifications. Building on code generation for a single GPU, we show how CUDA's unified memory can be leveraged to use multiple GPUs to collaboratively compute data-parallel tasks, and to handle computations on data that does not fit any of the GPU's memories. We describe the key ideas and implement them in SaC. We provide initial performance evaluations on two different GPU architectures for three different benchmarks: matrix multiplication, N-body simulation, and stencil computations. If allocation costs can be amortized, these experiments show parallel efficiencies between 80% and 100% on up to four GPUs when using an explicitly memory-orchestrated CUDA version as baseline.

1 Introduction

Graphics processing units (GPUs) are processors that have higher peak compute rate and bandwidth compared to CPUs of comparable price and power consumption. This makes them attractive for a range of domains requiring extensive computation, such as physics simulations, financial applications and deep learning [12,21,27].

Obtaining the theoretic peak performance is challenging. The reason for this is that GPUs are not stand-alone systems but accelerators that are specialized to specific workloads. They need to be programmed differently, and have their own memory which needs to be coordinated with the CPU and RAM (also called the *host*). A straightforward way to increase the theoretic computational power of a system is to add multiple GPUs. However, realising this performance becomes difficult as the different GPUs need to be coordinated. An especially complicated class of problems are those that do not fit in the memory of a single GPU. We refer to these problems as being *out-of-core*. For an out-of-core problem we need to coordinate memories of different GPUs as well, making this a form of distributed computing, with all its associated challenges.

Making effective use of multiple GPUs requires the programmer to have extensive knowledge of the hardware in addition to the problem domain. A large body of research tries to shift this burden from the application programmer to compiler writers by generating low-level GPU code from a high-level language.

J. Gibbons (Ed.): TFP 2025, LNCS 15652, pp. 117–138, 2026.
https://doi.org/10.1007/978-3-031-99751-8_6

In particular, functional approaches through languages such as Accelerate [7], Futhark [16] or SaC [14] or other array languages such as APL [19] show GPU performance that is competitive with hand-written counterparts [2,15,18,26]. The related work uses extensive static analysis, sometimes in combination with language extensions, to coordinate the GPUs.

The main idea behind this paper is that we can shift the burden even further, by making the runtime instead of the compiler responsible for data-movement. This way only minimal changes to the compiler are necessary to support using multiple GPUs on out-of-core problems.

The mechanism that makes this possible is *unified memory*: one virtual address space that can be accessed by all GPUs and the CPU. The GPU driver and hardware are then responsible for maintaining a coherent view of memory between GPUs and the host. This approach is typically associated with bad performance. A reason for this is that the runtime needs to be advised on access patterns to work efficiently. In many languages this is hard to do, but by working with a functional language we have the strong semantic guarantees necessary to generate this advice.

Our paper makes the following contributions.

- We propose a code generation scheme that can use multiple GPUs and handle out-of-core problems. It constitutes a light-weight extension of a pre-existing code generation scheme for unified memory [31];
- We show the effectiveness of our approach by implementing this scheme in the language Single-Assignment C;
- We show how memory advice can overcome performance challenges typically associated with unified memory.

2 Background

Single-Assignment C (SaC) [14] generates CUDA code, a language for programming GPUs. We use this language to explain some GPU programming concepts, and briefly explain how SaC generates code.

2.1 GPU Programming

Computations are done through special functions called *kernels*. These contain a small computation such as "compute $t + 1$ and store it in index t", similar to a loop-body in C (Listing 1.1).

```
void f(int *x, int n) {
    for (int t = 0; t < n; t++) {
        x[t] = t + 1;
    }
}
```

Listing 1.1. Array initalisation in C

The programmer specifies for which t this is computed at the call site. For example, to compute the set $X = \{t + 1 \mid 0 \leq t < n\}$, the kernel could be as follows.

```
__global__ void f(int *x) {
    int t = blockIdx.x * blockDim.x +
            threadIdx.x;
    x[t] = t + 1;
}
```

The initalisation of `t` (the *thread*) is complicated because there is not one canonical way to map computations to the hardware. Instructions are always executed in groups of threads, typically 32, similar to SIMD instructions on a CPU. Execution units on a GPU are grouped into *streaming multiprocessors* (SMs), which also includes cache and control logic. The threads are divided into groups called *blocks* of `blockDim.x` threads, and then divided over the SMs. The index local to one such block is stored in `threadIdx.x`, and the block index by `blockIdx.x`. Increasing the number of threads per block may help to hide latency, similar to hyperthreading in CPUs. However, it also decreases the number of blocks which can have a negative effect on scaling and load balancing. There is no choice that is optimal for all problems. The number of threads per block is limited by the hardware, typically 1024.

We can specify the mapping to hardware—so the number of threads per block `blockDim.x` and the total number of threads—between triple angular brackets at the call site. As a concrete example, suppose we want to use 1024 threads per block. Then we need $n/1024$ blocks, and call `f` as follows

```
f$<<<$n / 1024, 1024$>>>$(x);
```

We use *thread space* for referring to the shape $[n/1024, 1024]$.

The variables end with `.x` because they are actually three-dimensional structs with also `.y` and `.z` members. In this case all `.y` and `.z` members are 1, but for indexing higher-dimensional arrays it may be convenient to arrange the threads in a higher-dimensional grid. For example, 1024 threads may also be arranged in a 32×32 or $16 \times 16 \times 4$ grid.

2.2 Unified Memory

Managing multiple address spaces requires extra work for the application programmer. Systems from personal computers to the world's largest supercomputer (Frontier, as of 2024) support abstractions that provide the programmer with a single virtual address space that can be accessed by the CPU and GPU. Depending on the vendor and exact implementation, these systems are called *unified memory*, *managed memory*, or *unified virtual addressing*. We will be using the term unified memory.

The implementation of unified memory in CUDA is not publicly accessible, but it seems that by default a page of memory can be accessed by only one processor—either a GPU or the CPU—at a time, and if a page is accessed that is not present in the respective processor's memory, a page fault occurs [9]. These page faults result in on-demand page migration, which can lead to mixed results [23,24,31]. This behaviour can be changed by giving the runtime *memory advice* on how the memory is used. For example the CUDA option *cudaMemAdviseSetReadMostly* has the device create a local copy.

2.3 Single-Assignment C

SaC is a functional array language for numeric programming. It tries to be as close to the mathematics as possible. For example, the array $X = \{t + 1 \mid 0 \leq t < n\}$ is specified as `X = {[t] -> t + 1 | [0] <= [t] < [n]}`. These array specifications, called *tensor comprehensions*, expose concurrency: each element can be computed independently from the others. The user can specify a compilation target, which the compiler `sac2c` will use to generate parallel code. For a GPU target, `sac2c` will generate a kernel from this specification. This kernel associates the *index set* `[n]` to the thread space `[n / 1024, 1024]`, in some way we can view as a black box for the purpose of this paper [20].

We can specify different expressions on different subsets of this index set, as illustrated in Fig. 1 and Listing 1.2. In the related work such a subset is also called a partition. In Sect. 3 we will talk about a different mathematical notion of a partition, so to avoid confusion we will use subset in this paper.

The compiler has two GPU related targets. The first, `cuda`, explicitly defines arrays on the GPU and host. The necessary transfers between the two are then done explicitly. The second, `cuda_man`, uses unified memory instead (also called *man*aged memory). This makes memory transfers implicit: pages will be migrated over when they are touched. The `cuda` target has been observed to be more performant [31].

$f(0)$	$f(1)$	$g(2)$	$g(3)$	$f(4)$	$f(5)$	$g(6)$	$g(7)$

Fig. 1. Array specified by Listing 1.2

```
{[i] -> f(i) | [0] <= [i] $<$ [8]
               width [2] step [4];
 [i] -> g(i) | [2] <= [i] $<$ [8]
               width [2] step [4]}
```

Listing 1.2. Array specified by two index sets

3 Design

To keep the implementation lean, we only make minor modifications to the existing target using unified memory and one GPU [31]. We need to implement a way to divide the work, and appropriately instruct the CUDA runtime on the memory access patterns.

3.1 Work Distribution

In SaC, the index subsets may overlap, which requires us to process them sequentially. For this reason we do not distribute the subsets over the GPUs, but split up each subset individually.

We need to split up such an index set into non-overlapping pieces that together make up the original set (also called a *partition*). We do this by splitting along the first dimension, as illustrated in Fig. 2. To be more precise, for the simple case where the index set is of the form $[n]$, we give GPU g rows $g \cdot b$ (inclusive) to $\max((g+1) \cdot b, n)$ (exclusive), where $b = \lceil \frac{n}{G} \rceil$, the smallest integer b such that $n \leq Gb$. This choice minimizes the maximum number of rows per GPU, so for regular computations this gives optimal load balance.

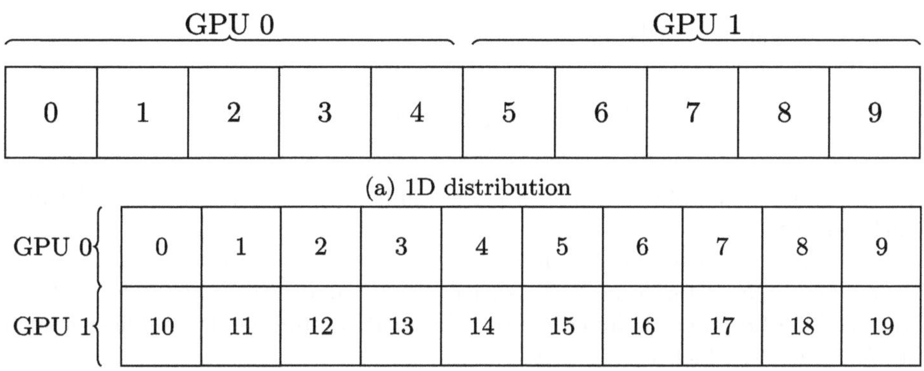

(a) 1D distribution

(b) 2D distribution

Fig. 2. Distribution of arrays over two GPUs

General Index Subsets. The most general way of specifying an index set in SaC is with a step and width. We need only minor modifications to the previous scheme. In set notation, an index set `[l] <= [i] < [u] step [s] width [w]` is equal to $[l, u) \cap S_{slw}$ where $S_{slw} = \{l + is + j \mid i \in \mathbb{Z},\ 0 \leq j < w\}$.

By distributing the intersection over the union, it becomes clear that a partition without strides over G GPUs, say

$$[l, u) = \bigcup_{g=1}^{G} [l_g, u_g),$$

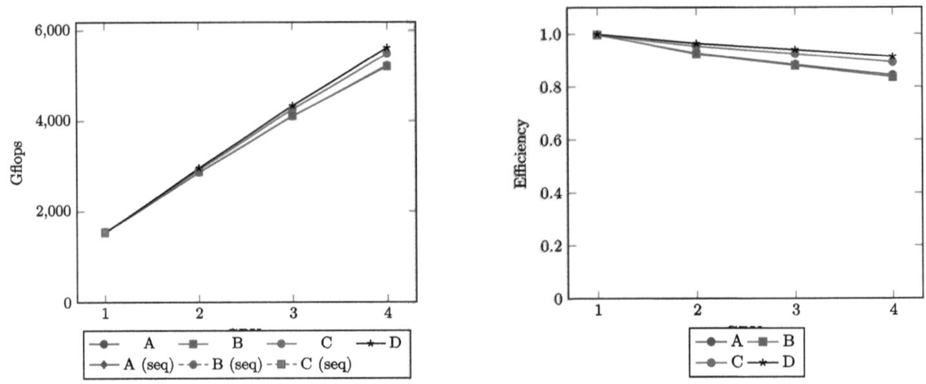

(a) Compute rate

(b) Efficiency

Fig. 3. Matrix Multiplication on Snellius.

also gives a strided partition

$$[l, u) \cap S_{slw} = \bigcup_{g=1}^{G} ([l_g, u_g) \cap S_{slw}).$$

For $l_g \equiv l \bmod s$, we have $S_{sl_gw} = S_{slw}$. So under this restriction the strides and widths are the same.

In a similar vein to the simple case $[l, u) = [0, n)$, we set $l_g = l + gb$, $u_g = \min(l + (g+1)b, u)$ for some b. To satisfy $l_g \equiv l \bmod s$, we must take b of the form sk. The best load balance is now obtained by finding the smallest b such that $bG \geq u - l$, which is $\lceil \frac{u-l}{sG} \rceil \cdot s$.

Example 1. For index set `[2] <= [i] < [1000] step [6] width [2]` and two GPUs, we have $b = 504$. The resulting index sets are `[2] <= [i] < [506] step [6] width [2]` for the first GPU, and `[506] <= [i] < [1000] step [6] width [2]` for the second.

Implementation of Work Distribution. The partition of Fig. 2a corresponds to rewriting the SaC code

```
{[i] -$>$ i | [0] $<$= [i] $<$ [10]}
```

to

```
{[i] -$>$ i | [0] $<$= [i] $<$ [5];
 [i] -$>$ i | [5] $<$= [i] $<$ [10]}
```

It is therefore tempting to also do this in the implementation. However, this leads to unnecessary code duplication as one kernel per GPU would be generated. Furthermore, the number of GPUs would need to be known at compile-time.

To avoid this, we reuse the thread space mechanism. This mechanism must know what the index subset is, so parameters describing the subset must be passed into the kernel (at the very least for cases where these parameters are not known at compile-time). This means we can restrict the execution of the kernel to the subsets defined above by only manipulating the call site, which allows us to treat the kernel generation, thread space mechanism included, as a black box.

We manipulate the call site by inserting some code around the kernel call at the very end of the compilation process, when we generate the CUDA code, which we sketch in Listing 1.3. The variables `l0`, `u0` correspond to the lower and upper bound in the first dimension. In the loop we replace these by l_g and u_g. To execute a kernel on a different GPU, we first call `cudaSetDevice(g)` where `g` is an index for that GPU. Then we call the kernel the same way as if we had one GPU. While the CPU will immediately continue after calling the kernel, the GPU has only finished computing after a call to `cudaDeviceSynchronize()`.

```
int old_l0 = l0;
int old_u0 = u0;

for (int g = 0; g < NUM_GPUS; g++) {
  /* Set l0, u0 to lg and ug */
  l0 = ...
  u0 = ...
  cudaSetDevice(g);
  /* The following three lines are
     unmodified from the
     cuda_man target. */
  grid = ...
  block = ...
  kernel<<<grid, block>>>(l0, u0, ...);
}

for (int g = 0; g < NUM_GPUS; g++) {
  cudaSetDevice(g);
  cudaDeviceSynchronize();
}

l0 = old_l0;
u0 = old_u0;
```

Listing 1.3. Kernel call distributed over `NUM_GPUS` GPUs

3.2 Memory Advice

An initial implementation of this code generation scheme gave poor results. For example, distributing the work of Listing 1.4 over two GPUs naively leads to a 6× slowdown compared to using a single GPU.

```
double[m, k] matmul(double[m, k] A,
                    double[k, n] B)
{
    C = {[i, j] -> sum({[p] ->
              A[i, p] * B[p, j]})};
    return C;
}
```

Listing 1.4. Matrix Multiplication in SaC

The entire jth column of B is needed to compute the jth element of a row of C. As discussed in Subsect. 2.2, the memory of B can only be on one GPU at a time by default. Whatever GPU accesses the memory first will get the memory page, and the other GPU will have to wait until it can be migrated back. This serializes the computation between the two GPUs. Instead, it would be better if both GPUs created a copy of this page. This eliminates contention on reads, at the cost of making writes to the same page by multiple GPUs more expensive. This never happens in the code we generate because we only read from B. We can instruct the runtime to use this copy-on-read scheme by giving the `cudaMemAdviseSetReadMostly` memory advice.

This is not necessary for A. To compute row i of C, only row i of A is needed. As both C and A have m rows, the distribution over GPUs is the same. The data that has to be accessed is already present on that GPU, so there is no contention between accesses.

Unfortunately, adding memory-advice has overhead, so we cannot insert it everywhere. In the example Nine-Point Stencil, whose most important computation is in Listing 1.5 adding memory-advice leads to a 2 - 5× slowdown compared to not inserting the memory advice.

```
{[i, j] -> w[0, 0] * x[i - 1, j - 1] +
           w[1, 0] * x[i    , j - 1] +
           w[2, 0] * x[i + 1, j - 1] +
           ...
           w[2, 2] * x[i + 1, j + 1];
   | [1, 1] <= [i, j] < [m - 1, n - 1];
 ...}
```

Listing 1.5. Sketch of the most computationally intensive part of a nine-point stencil.

This case is slightly more complicated than the access of A in Listing 1.4.The last row of GPU 0, which is the first row of GPU 1 is accessed by both GPUs. By GPU 0 as `x[i + 1, ...]` and by GPU 1 as `x[i - 1, ...]`. Except for the first and last row, all required data is already present on that GPU. We call this a *local* selection. The contention on these two rows is not enough to offset the cost of inserting the memory advice.

We can generalize this by looking at how the selection vector (for instance `[p, j]` in the case of B in Listing 1.4relates to the index vector of the parallel tensor comprehension (`[i, j]` in both examples).

Let us write `[iv1, ..., ivd]` for the selection vector, and `[jv1, ..., jvd]` for the index vector. If `jv1` is equal to `iv1`, the selections are all local, and we do not have to insert the advice. Suppose our GPU has rows l to u. If `iv1` is equal to `jv1 + c` for some constant `c`, then the accesses are local for rows $l + c$ to $u - c$. This is most accesses for small `c`. For this reason, we mark accesses for which `iv1` is of the form `jv1 + c`. Given the functional nature of SaC we can then check for all relatively-free variables of tensor comprehensions whether all accesses are marked. If that is the case, we do not give memory advice. Otherwise, we mark them as read-mostly.

4 Performance Evaluation

We evaluate our approach in the style of distributed computing: we look at how much faster our code gets when adding more GPUs. The runtime of using one GPU divided by the runtime of using multiple GPUs is called the *speedup*. We expect at most a $G\times$ speedup when using G GPUs. To measure how close we get to this, we also compute the *efficiency*: speedup divided by the number of GPUs. The closer this is to one, the better our system scales.

4.1 Evaluation Platform

Scientific computations typically use double precision, but this is poorly supported in consumer-grade GPUs. To capture this, we use two different evaluation platforms. The first node (`icis`) has a similar double precision to bandwidth ratio as a consumer-grade GPU. The second node (`snellius`) has first-rate support for double precision. The hardware and software specifications are given in Table 1.

We use the SaC compiler at commit `f5890fa` with flags `-gpu_mapping_strategy jings_method_ext` for all benchmarks. Additional flags for a specific benchmarks are mentioned in their description. We used the standard library at commit `78c74b2`.

4.2 Methodology

We consider three benchmarks, two with a high ratio of computations to array size (Matrix Multiplication and N-Body Simulation), and one with a low ratio (Nine-Point Stencil). We use floating point operations per second (*flops*) as a measure of performance for those with a high ratio, and bandwidth for the benchmark with a low ratio.

We evaluate the performance on a range of problem sizes, shown in Table 2. Class D of Matrix-Multiplication is out-of-core on both systems, the rest of the experiments are in-core. The reason for the small number of out-of-core examples is that SaC uses 32-bit integers for shapes, which limits the problem sizes.

We measure the costs inherent to the computation, that is the kernel-execution time, allocation of the result, and any inter-GPU communication. We

Table 1. Overview of the test systems, hardware and software.

	icis	snellius
GPU	RTX A6000 (2x)	A100 (4x)
VRAM (GB)	48	40
Peak Bandwidth (GB/s)	768	1560
Peak FP64 (GFLOP/s)	604.8	9746
C compiler	gcc 11.3.0	gcc 12.3.0
NVCC	12.0.14	12.1.105
NVLink bandwidth (GB/s)	14	25
Number of NVLinks	4	4

do not measure any CPU-GPU transfer time of input and output because this may not be needed, for instance when the data is created and consumed on the GPU. The exact implementation and instructions for reproducibility are available [5]. We have used `pragmas` to manually reduce the number of threads per block for N-Body.

Table 2. Overview of the memory footprints in GB.

Class	Matrix Multiplication	N-Body	Stencil
A	10.1	0.010	4.29
B	19.7	0.021	9.66
C	38.3	0.042	17.2
D	51.0	0.084	34.0

We compute and efficiency compared to the performance of our fastest, manually orchestrated target *cuda*. The efficiency for an out-of-core run is compared to the performance of the *cuda* target of the closest in-core class.

4.3 Matrix Multiplication

A matrix multiplication computes the composition of linear maps, making it a fundamental operation in linear algebra with applications in many areas. A few examples are linear programming, cryptography and deep learning [8,10]. The implementation, Listing 1.4is straightforwardly translated from the mathematical definition

$$C_{ij} = \sum_{p=1}^{k} A_{ip} \cdot B_{pj}$$

for $m \times k$ matrix A and $k \times n$ matrix B.

Data from A and B are reused k times. It is well-known that algorithmic changes that improve the temporal locality of accessing `A` and `B` can speed up the computation, but we refer this to future work.

This computation takes $2mn(k-1)$ flops. The matrices A and C are perfectly distributed over the GPUs, but all GPUs need to access B. That means we need $O(n^2)$ data-movement and $O(n^3/G)$ computation for multiplying two $n \times n$ matrices on G GPUs. The communication does not scale, but for large n this term is dominated by the computation. So we expect better efficiencies for large n.

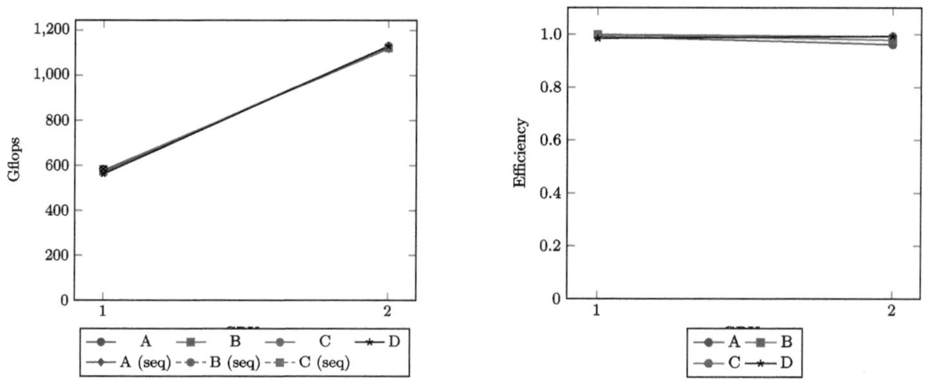

(a) Compute rate (b) Efficiency

Fig. 4. Matrix Multiplication on Icis.

This is supported by the results of Fig. 3, where we see efficiencies ranging from 84% for classes A and B, to 91% for class D on four GPUs. The efficiencies are even higher in Fig. 4, where they range from 95% to 98%. The A6000 has a much higher bandwidth to FP64 ratio than the A100, so data-movement contributes even less to the compute rate.

It is interesting that class D does not seem to suffer from being out-of-core. This is likely caused by the unified memory overlapping this extra communication with computation [6].

4.4 N-Body Simulation

The all-pairs N-body algorithm computes how the position and velocities of a system of bodies affect each other through gravity. In larger applications this exact algorithm is typically used to compute the forces between bodies that are near each other, and is combined with an approximate algorithm for bodies further away [4].

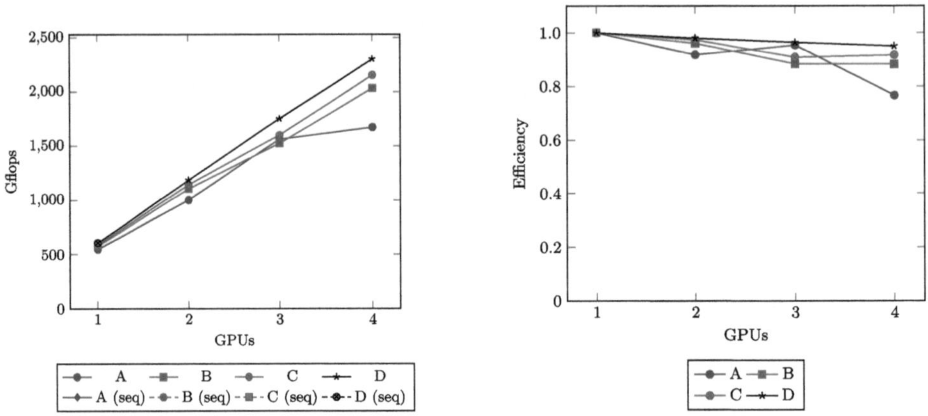

(a) Absolute performance (b) Efficiency

Fig. 5. N-Body simulation on Snellius.

The main structure of this algorithm is described in Listing 1.6. We have $[N, 3]$ arrays `pos`, `accel`, and `velocity` to represent vectors in three-dimensional space, and an array of shape $[N]$ for the masses.

```
accel = {[i] -> sum{[j] ->
                acc(pos[i], pos[j], mass[j]}};
velocity = velocity + accel * dt;
pos = pos + velocity;
```

Listing 1.6. Structure of nbody-simulation in SaC. The function acc computes the acceleration caused by the force of particle j on particle i.

Most time is spent in the $O(N^2)$ computation of `accel`. The total cost is $20N^2 + 12N$ flops per iteration.

The performance characteristics are very similar to Matrix Multiplication, but even more pronounced. The computation is evenly distributed: for G in total, each GPU does $O(N^2/G)$ computation per iteration. All bodies need to be replicated on each GPU, so that is $O(N)$ communication per iteration. In contrast to matrix-multiplication, this computation is typically in-core.

As expected, we see high efficiencies in Fig. 6, from 95% to 103%. This is the only benchmark where we see the efficiency exceeding 100%. This cannot be explained by variability in the measurements as the standard deviation is about 0.3%. The A6000 has 6 MB of L2 cache. Class A does not fit in the L2 cache of one GPU, but does fit in the combined cache of both. We suspect this is the cause.

In Fig. 5 we have a high efficiency of 95% for the largest problem class D. For the smallest problem class A this drops sharply for four GPUs, to 77%. The A100 has 6912 execution units per GPU, so 24768 in total. As problem class A has 20480 bodies, we can keep only 83% of these units busy.

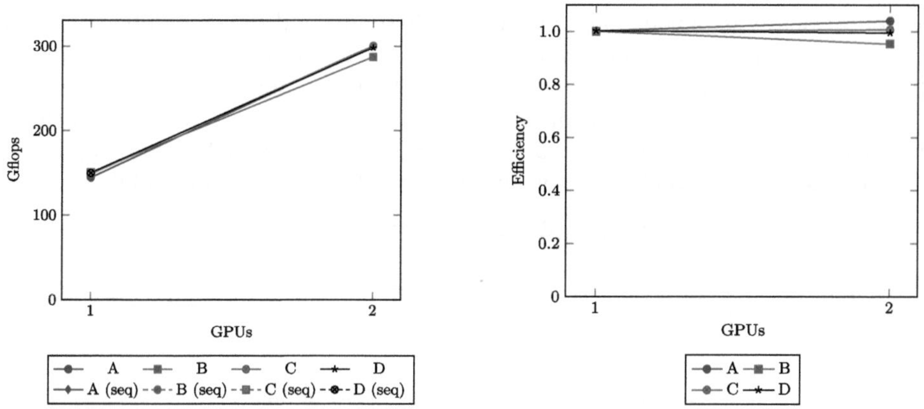

(a) Absolute performance (b) Efficiency

Fig. 6. N-Body simulation on Snellius.

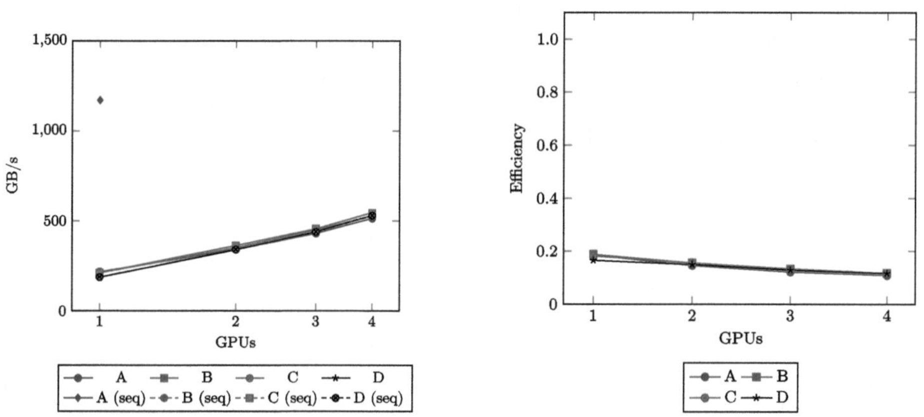

(a) Bandwidth (b) Efficiency

Fig. 7. Stencil on Snellius, 10 iterations

4.5 Nine-Point Stencil

The final algorithm we benchmark is a 2D iterative nine-point stencil computation. This updates each point in a 2D grid with a weighted averages of its nine neighbours, where we wrap around the edges. This is a common pattern in finite-difference methods for solving partial differential equations [3].

More recently, it has found application in convolutional neural networks [29, 32]. In contrast to the other two algorithms, each iteration does a small number of computations on each input element.

This tensor comprehension has nine index subsets because of the wrapping around the edges. In Listing 1.5 have shown the generated code for the most computationally expensive one. Specifying these nine subsets is cumbersome, so we have used the more generic code of Listing 1.7. is can handle analogues in any dimension `d`, and also any shape `wshp` of weights. For example, if we want to take a weighted average of points at most two removed (Manhattan-distance) in three dimensions, we would have `d = 3` and `wshp = [5, 5, 5]` [1]. The compiler is able to recognize the `mod` operator and generate the index subsets [30].

```
double[d:shp] relax(double[d:shp] x, double[d:wshp] w)
{
  return {iv -> sum({jv -> w[jv] * x[mod(iv + jv - wshp / 2, shp)]})
              | iv < shp};
}
```

Listing 1.7. Stencil computation in SaC.

We use the flag `-maxwlur 9` to ensure the weighted average of nine points in the inner computation is unrolled. This takes $17n^2$ flops per iteration for an $n \times n$ array, but it is more common to measure bandwidth as data-movement is the limiting factor. This is $16n^2$ bytes per iteration.

For G GPUs, we need to do $O(n^2/G)$ data-movement within a GPU, and $O(n)$ data movement between GPUs. Therefore, we expect good results, similar to Matrix Multiplication and N-Body. However, Fig. 7 and Fig. 8 show no improvements over the `cuda`-baseline.

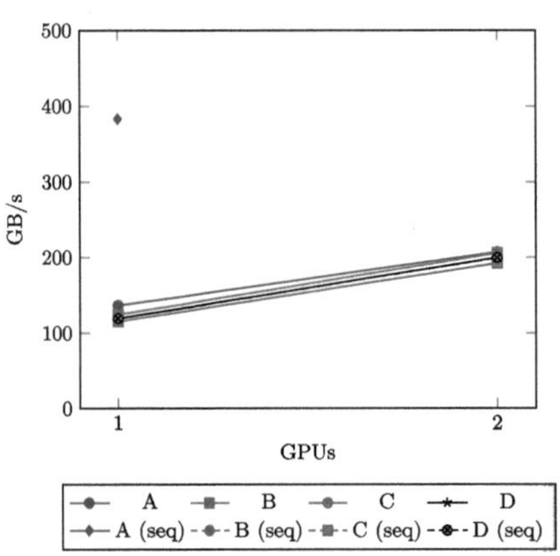

(a) Bandwidth

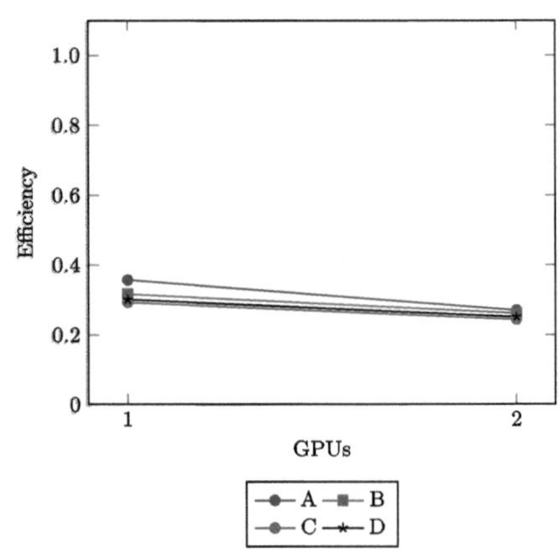

(b) Efficiency

Fig. 8. Stencil on Icis, 10 iterations

This is caused by a high cost for the first write to unified memory. When increasing the number of iterations, in Fig. 9 and Fig. 10, we do see speedups.

We can model the execution time for T iterations as $Tx + c$, where x is the cost per iteration, and c the cost for allocation, deallocation and constant overheads. From the measurements for $T = 100$ and $T = 10$, we can solve for x.

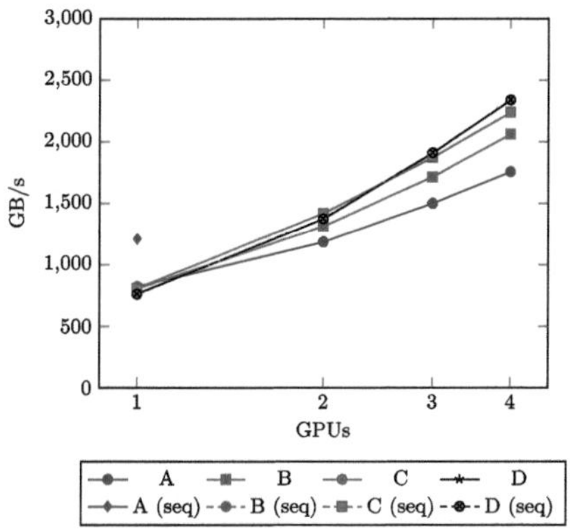

(a) Bandwidth

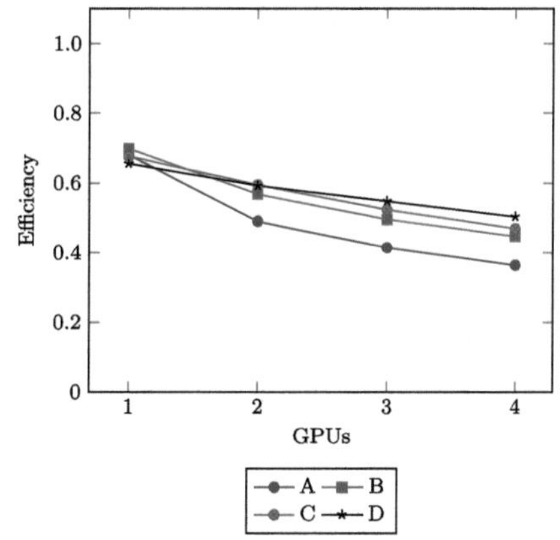

(b) Efficiency

Fig. 9. Stencil on Snellius, 100 iterations

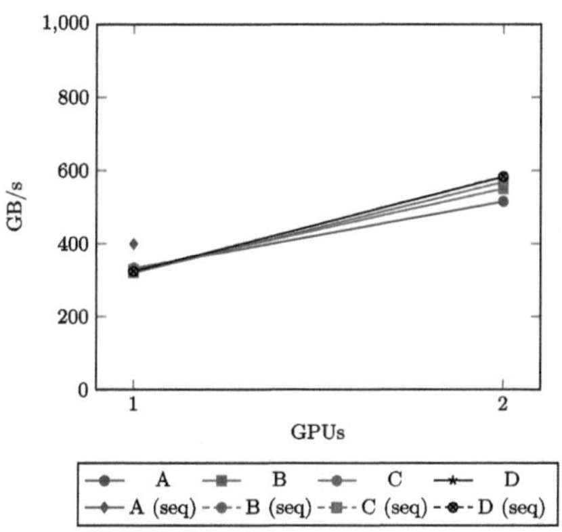

(a) Bandwidth

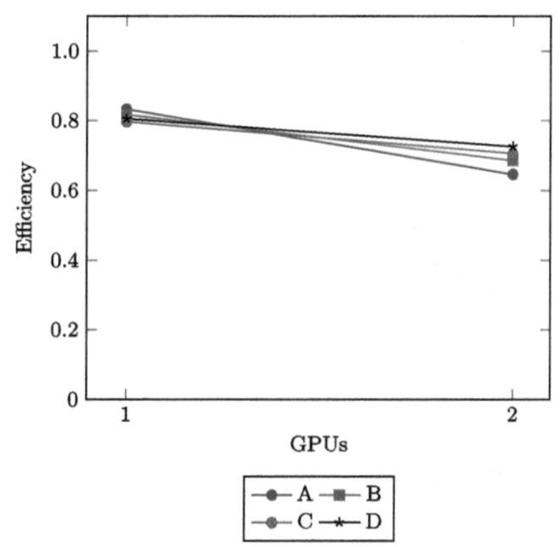

(b) Efficiency

Fig. 10. Stencil on Icis, 100 iterations

The bandwidth based on this number is graphed in Fig. 11 and Fig. 12. Here we have efficiencies between 48% and 81%. The efficiencies are lower than the other two benchmarks, especially for the smaller problem classes. This is because the synchronisation cost is not negligible in this benchmark. Each iteration takes 0.009 seconds for problem class D on Snellius. For comparison, in Matrix Multiplication we have one synchronisation every 35 seconds, and in N-Body one synchronisation every 96 seconds.

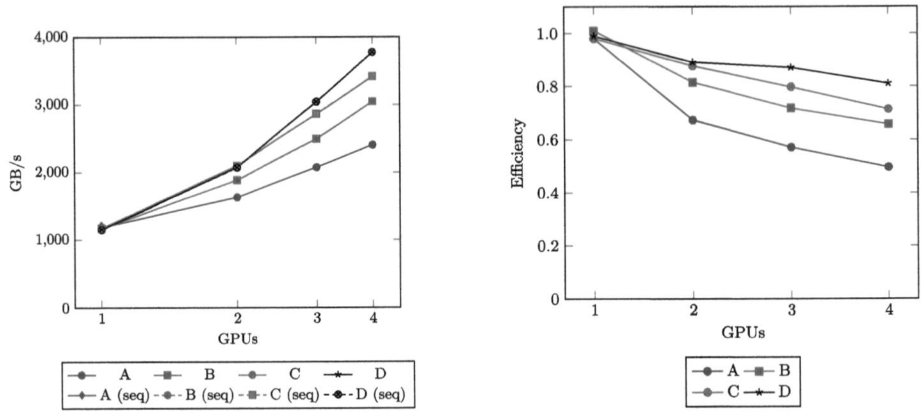

(a) Bandwidth (b) Efficiency

Fig. 11. Stencil on Snellius, without allocation and deallocation

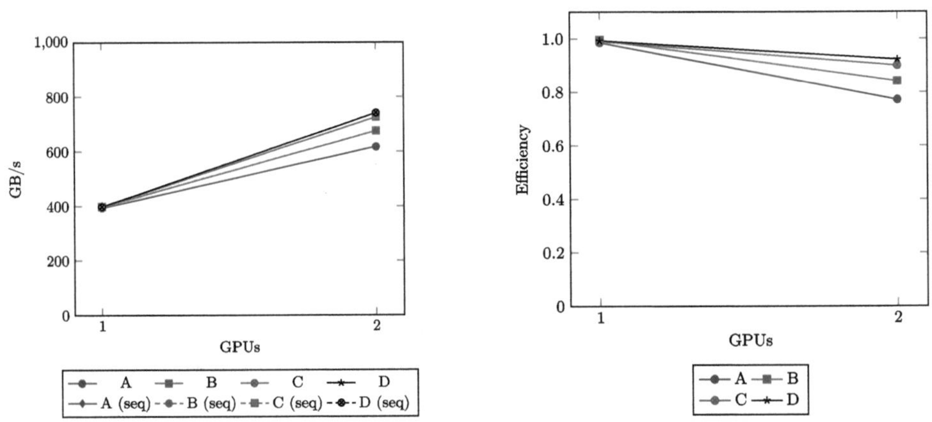

(a) Bandwidth (b) Efficiency

Fig. 12. Stencil on Icis, without allocation and deallocation

4.6 Effect of Memory Advice

We can only investigate the result of memory advice on small problems and few GPUs because we quickly run into time limits. We have done measurements on Snellius for two GPUs. For Matrix Multiplication we take three 1024×1024 matrices, for N-Body we take 32768 bodies and 10 iterations, for Stencil we take a grid of size 1024×1024 and 100 iterations. We divide the performance of either always inserting memory advice or never inserting memory advice by the runtime of our optimisation in Table 3.

We see that always inserting advice gives good results for Matrix Multiplication and N-Body, but poor results for Stencil. If we never insert advice, the

Table 3. Speedup of always giving advice, never giving advice compared to our memory advice optimisation.

	Matrix Multiplication	N-Body	Stencil
Always	0.93	0.94	0.20
Never	0.09	0.72	1.00

situation is reversed. Our optimisation makes the best choice in all three benchmarks. It is even a little bit faster in Matrix Multiplication and N-Body because we do not insert the advice for arrays where we do not need to.

5 Related Work

Several studies have investigated compiling high-level specifications in functional array languages to multi-GPU code with manually-allocated data. One work presents envisioned compiler and runtime systems extensions for SaC for leveraging multiple multi-core CPUs and multiple GPUs without requiring additional programmer effort [11]. A new distributed-variable type is proposed to enable partial transfers of manually-allocated arrays between host and device. Furthermore, control structures are suggested to keep track of which parts of an array are present where, essentially implementing a cache coherency protocol. The authors evaluate a hand-coded prototype on a two-dimensional five-point stencil computations with two different combinations of parameters using GTX 580 GPUs. Their experimental results find that assigning almost all the workload to the GPU leads to the best results, and achieve a nearly two-fold speedup with two GPUs, but run into significantly less improvement with three or more GPUs.

The next study extends the Futhark compiler with a new internal streaming operator called the *husk* operator [17]. The author introduces a new type and semantics to further present transformations for the map and reduce second order array combinators of Futhark, essentially allowing an intermediate Futhark program to expose opportunities for distributable data and operations. The study then also extends Futhark's CUDA C backend, leveraging the husk operator for multi-GPU execution and introducing a worker-thread runtime environment for concatenation or reduction of the results on multiple devices. Next, the entire implementation is tested on Futhark's benchmark suite, investigating both the effect of the husk operator in single and double GPU scenarios. In the multi-GPU case, their results vary from near-linear speedups to limited improvements, depending on the amount of data that has to be transferred between the two GPUs. In single GPU scenarios the overhead of the husk operator is generally negligible, except for some outlier applications—ranging from an improvement of roughly $1.7\times$ to significant slowdowns of $2.5\times$.

Accelerate [28] adds multi-GPU support by adding a fissioning program transformation during the compilation process, essentially converting intra-kernel data parallelism to inter-kernel task parallelism. Furthermore, a runtime multi-GPU scheduler is added, which decides what task is executed on which device. This scheduler resembles a typical approach, introducing a worker thread for each CUDA device. These worker threads are handling both kernel launches and copying dependencies to the GPU they represent. The authors evaluate their implementation against three benchmarks on a two-GPU system, where two of those three benchmarks are Matrix Multiplication and N-Body. For the N-Body, they achieve linear speedups and even a 2.4× speedup when the bodies fit in the cache of a single GPU. Their matrix multiplication benchmark achieves more modest speedups (around 1.3×), which the authors attribute to needing to communicate larger partial results and more expensive combination steps compared to their other benchmarks.

Another class of related work consists of more specialised transpilers and frameworks that tend to either implement a custom unified-memory protocol or extend CUDA's unified-memory driver [22,25]. One such example is the framework SnuRHAC, which automatically and transparently distributes workloads to multiple GPUs across multiple nodes [22]. The authors extend CUDA unified memory with an additional Linux kernel module to achieve scaling beyond a single node of multiple GPUs. Within a node, kernel workloads are distributed by dividing the thread blocks in CUDA grids among multiple GPUs. Page faulting is also reduced by implementing both static and dynamic page-prefetching techniques. The implementation also includes heuristics to decide whether to execute on a single GPU instead if the workload *e.g.* contains too many shared-write accesses.

Finally, we take a look at related work that conducts manual experimentation with CUDA unified memory. One study evaluated the effect of CUDA performance hints for both in-core and out-of-core single-GPU scenarios on two platforms across six different applications [9]. On one platform, they find that memory advice only lead to benefits in in-core scenarios, whereas on the other platform exclusively in out-of-core situations. When it comes to page prefetching, they find that it leads to significant improvements for one system, but no benefits on the other. Overall, the authors conclude that unified memory is a promising technology and point out that more research into optimal advice placement would benefit programmer productivity.

Another study investigates a manual multi-GPU implementation using unified memory [13]. The authors analyse both programmability and performance, focussing on the effect of performance hints. Their study considers two types of memory advice: access patterns and placement of memory, and experiments are also conducted with prefetching. The authors observe speedups ranging from 1.10× to 1.85× on their selected benchmarks. They find that programmability is generally much improved due to not needing to do manual allocations nor add explicit memory transfers, but at the same time performance hints are necessary to achieve good performance. When it comes to performance, unified memory can introduce communication optimisations due to only initiating transfers that are strictly necessary for a given computation.

6 Conclusions and Future Work

We have implemented multi-GPU support for the language SaC extending its existing unified memory compilation target. This extension is light-weight as we can reuse the existing mechanism of specifying subsets. Inserting memory advice is crucial to obtain good performance on multiple GPUs. We can generate accurate advice due to the functional semantics of SaC.

Our benchmarks show promising results for both the N-Body and Matrix Multiply algorithms. With large enough problem sizes, we see efficiencies above 90% with respect to SaC's manually-allocated *cuda* target. For a nine-point stencil we can obtain efficiencies in excess of 80%, but only when we do not count allocation time. If the compiler cannot sufficiently reuse allocations, our approach yields efficiencies as low as 12%, even for large problem sizes.

Future work is needed to address the efficient support of reductions or fold on multiple GPUs. We use a basic device-wide synchronisation with expensive context switches between GPUs. This does not stop us from obtaining high efficiency on large problem sets, but fine-tuning this with event-based synchronization may lead to performance benefits on smaller problem sizes.

Acknowledgments. We thank Jordy Aaldering and Peter van Achten for their helpful comments. We also thank SURF in Amsterdam, the Netherlands, for giving us access to the supercomputer Snellius. We also thank the Dutch Research Council (NWO) for funding the computing time we used, under project EINF-10769.

References

1. Aaldering, J., Scholz, S.B., Gastel, B.v.: Type patterns: pattern matching on shape-carrying array types. In: Proceedings of the 35th Symposium on Implementation and Application of Functional Languages. IFL '23, Association for Computing Machinery, New York, NY, USA (2024). https://doi.org/10.1145/3652561.3652572
2. Andreetta, C., et al.: FinPar: a Parallel Financial Benchmark. ACM Trans. Archit. Code Optim. **13**(2) (2016). https://doi.org/10.1145/2898354
3. Barkley Rosser, J.: Nine-point difference solutions for Poisson's equation. Comput. Math. Appl. **1**(3), 351–360 (1975). https://doi.org/10.1016/0898-1221(75)90035-8
4. Barnes, J., Hut, P.: A hierarchical O (N log N) force-calculation algorithm. nature **324**(6096), pp.446–449 (1986)
5. van Beurden, P., Koopman, T., Scholz, S.B.: Multi GPU Ifl2024 (2024). https://gitlab.sac-home.org/sac-group/artefact-ifl2024-multi-gpu , commit 123528eb3080a1e5f244efc43079f7047c8cee77
6. van Beurden, P., Scholz, S.B.: On generating out-of-core GPU code for multi-dimensional array operations. In: Proceedings of the 34th Symposium on Implementation and Application of Functional Languages. IFL '22, Association for Computing Machinery, New York, NY, USA (2023). https://doi.org/10.1145/3587216.3587223

7. Chakravarty, M.M., Keller, G., Lee, S., McDonell, T.L., Grover, V.: Accelerating haskell array codes with multicore GPUs. In: Proceedings of the Sixth Workshop on Declarative Aspects of Multicore Programming, pp. 3–14. DAMP '11, Association for Computing Machinery, New York, NY, USA (2011). https://doi.org/10.1145/1926354.1926358
8. Chen, H., Kim, M., Razenshteyn, I., Rotaru, D., Song, Y., Wagh, S.: Maliciously secure matrix multiplication with applications to private deep learning. In: Moriai, S., Wang, H. (eds.) ASIACRYPT 2020. LNCS, vol. 12493, pp. 31–59. Springer, Cham (2020). https://doi.org/10.1007/978-3-030-64840-4_2
9. Chien, S., Peng, I., Markidis, S.: Performance evaluation of advanced features in CUDA unified memory. In: 2019 IEEE/ACM Workshop on Memory Centric High Performance Computing (MCHPC), pp. 50–57 (2019). https://doi.org/10.1109/MCHPC49590.2019.00014
10. Cohen, M.B., Lee, Y.T., Song, Z.: Solving linear programs in the current matrix multiplication time. J. ACM **68**(1) (2021). https://doi.org/10.1145/3424305
11. Diogo, M., Grelck, C.: Towards heterogeneous computing without heterogeneous programming. In: Loidl, H.W., Peña, R. (eds.) Trends in Functional Programming, pp. 279–294. Springer, Berlin Heidelberg, Berlin, Heidelberg (2013)
12. Glaser, J., et al.: Strong scaling of general-purpose molecular dynamics simulations on GPUs. Comput. Phys. Commun. **192**, 97–107 (2015).https://doi.org/10.1016/j.cpc.2015.02.028, https://www.sciencedirect.com/science/article/pii/S0010465515000867
13. González, M., Morancho, E.: Multi-GPU systems and Unified Virtual Memory for scientific applications: the case of the NAS multi-zone parallel benchmarks. J. Parallel Distrib. Comput. **158**, 138–150 (2021).https://doi.org/10.1016/j.jpdc.2021.08.001, https://www.sciencedirect.com/science/article/pii/S0743731521001672
14. Grelck, C., Scholz, S.B.: SAC–A functional array language for efficient multi-threaded execution. Int. J. Parallel Prog. **34**, 383–427 (2006)
15. Guo, J., Thiyagalingam, J., Scholz, S.B.: Breaking the GPU programming barrier with the auto-parallelising SAC compiler. In: Proceedings of the Sixth Workshop on Declarative Aspects of Multicore Programming, pp. 15–24. DAMP '11, Association for Computing Machinery, New York, NY, USA (2011). https://doi.org/10.1145/1926354.1926359
16. Henriksen, T., Serup, N.G., Elsman, M., Henglein, F., Oancea, C.E.: Futhark: purely functional GPU-programming with nested parallelism and in-place array updates. In: Proceedings of the 38th ACM SIGPLAN Conference on Programming Language Design and Implementation, pp. 556–571 (2017)
17. Holst Larsen, S.: Multi-GPU futhark using parallel streams. Master's thesis, University of Copenhagen (2019). https://futhark-lang.org/student-projects/steffen-msc-thesis.pdf
18. Hsu, A.W.: Accelerating information experts through compiler design. In: Proceedings of the 2nd ACM SIGPLAN International Workshop on Libraries, Languages, and Compilers for Array Programming, pp. 37–42. ARRAY 2015, Association for Computing Machinery, New York, NY, USA (2015). https://doi.org/10.1145/2774959.2774968
19. Iverson, K.E.: A programming language. In: Proceedings of the May 1-3, 1962, spring joint computer conference, pp. 345–351 (1962)
20. Janssen, N., Scholz, S.B.: On mapping n-dimensional data-parallelism efficiently into GPU-thread-spaces. In: Proceedings of the 33rd Symposium on Implementation and Application of Functional Languages. p. 54–66. IFL '21, Association

for Computing Machinery, New York, NY, USA (2022). https://doi.org/10.1145/3544885.3544894
21. Jeon, W., Ko, G., Lee, J., Lee, H., Ha, D., Ro, W.W.: Chapter Six - Deep learning with GPUs. In: Kim, S., Deka, G.C. (eds.) Hardware Accelerator Systems for Artificial Intelligence and Machine Learning, Advances in Computers, vol. 122, pp. 167–215. Elsevier (2021). https://doi.org/10.1016/bs.adcom.2020.11.003, https://www.sciencedirect.com/science/article/pii/S0065245820300905
22. Jung, J., Park, D., Jo, G., Park, J., Lee, J.: SnuRHAC: A runtime for heterogeneous accelerator clusters with CUDA unified memory. In: Proceedings of the 30th International Symposium on High-Performance Parallel and Distributed Computing, pp. 107–120. HPDC '21, Association for Computing Machinery, New York, NY, USA (2021). https://doi.org/10.1145/3431379.3460647
23. Knap, M., Czarnul, P.: Performance evaluation of unified memory with prefetching and oversubscription for selected parallel CUDA applications on NVIDIA Pascal and Volta GPUs. J. Supercomput. **75**(11), 7625–7645 (2019)
24. Landaverde, R., Zhang, T., Coskun, A.K., Herbordt, M.: An investigation of unified memory access performance in CUDA. In: 2014 IEEE High Performance Extreme Computing Conference (HPEC), pp. 1–6 (2014). https://doi.org/10.1109/HPEC.2014.7040988
25. Matsumura, K., Sato, M., Boku, T., Podobas, A., Matsuoka, S.: MACC: an OpenACC transpiler for automatic multi-GPU use. In: Yokota, R., Wu, W. (eds.) SCFA 2018. LNCS, vol. 10776, pp. 109–127. Springer, Cham (2018). https://doi.org/10.1007/978-3-319-69953-0_7
26. McDonell, T.L., Chakravarty, M.M., Keller, G., Lippmeier, B.: Optimising purely functional GPU programs. In: Proceedings of the 18th ACM SIGPLAN International Conference on Functional Programming, pp. 49–60. ICFP '13, Association for Computing Machinery, New York, NY, USA (2013). https://doi.org/10.1145/2500365.2500595
27. Prades, J., Varghese, B., Reaño, C., Silla, F.: Multi-tenant virtual GPUs for optimising performance of a financial risk application. J. Parallel Distrib. Comput. **108**, 28–44 (2017).https://doi.org/10.1016/j.jpdc.2016.06.002, https://www.sciencedirect.com/science/article/pii/S0743731516300673, special Issue on Scalable Computing Systems for Big Data Applications
28. Svensson, B.J., Vollmer, M., Holk, E., McDonell, T.L., Newton, R.R.: Converting data-parallelism to task-parallelism by rewrites: purely functional programs across multiple GPUs. In: Proceedings of the 4th ACM SIGPLAN Workshop on Functional High-Performance Computing, pp. 12–22 (2015)
29. Vedaldi, A., Lenc, K.: MatConvNet: Convolutional Neural Networks for MATLAB. In: Proceedings of the 23rd ACM International Conference on Multimedia, pp. 689–692. MM '15, Association for Computing Machinery, New York, NY, USA (2015). https://doi.org/10.1145/2733373.2807412
30. Verloop, M., Koopman, T., Scholz, S.B.: Modulo in high-performance code: strength reduction for modulo-based array indexing in loops. In: Proceedings of the 35th Symposium on Implementation and Application of Functional Languages. IFL '23, Association for Computing Machinery, New York, NY, USA (2024). https://doi.org/10.1145/3652561.3652573
31. Vießmann, H.N., Scholz, S.B.: Effective host-GPU memory management through code generation. In: Proceedings of the 32nd Symposium on Implementation and Application of Functional Languages, pp. 138–149. IFL '20, Association for Computing Machinery, New York, NY, USA (2021). https://doi.org/10.1145/3462172.3462199

32. Šinkarovs, A., Vießmann, H.N., Scholz, S.B.: Array languages make neural networks fast. In: Proceedings of the 7th ACM SIGPLAN International Workshop on Libraries, Languages and Compilers for Array Programming, pp. 39–50. ARRAY 2021, Association for Computing Machinery, New York, NY, USA (2021). https://doi.org/10.1145/3460944.3464312

From Haskell to a New Structured Combinator Processor

Yukang Xie, Craig Ramsay, Robert Stewart(✉), and Hans-Wolfgang Loidl

Mathematical and Computer Sciences, Heriot-Watt University, Edinburgh, UK
{yx3007,Craig.Ramsay,R.Stewart,H.W.Loidl}@hw.ac.uk

Abstract. This paper presents KappaMutor, a new graph reduction processor, along with its Haskell compiler. KappaMutor is based on structured combinators, a recently proposed combinator encoding, which is more flexible and efficient than fine-grained SKI combinators. The processor exploits parallel memories to enable single-cycle reduction of structured combinators while maintaining good compactness, utilising less than 1% of the logical resources on a modern FPGA. Its Haskell compiler implements novel code generation strategies designed to minimise combinator usage and achieve full laziness—the first such implementation for structured combinators, to the best of our knowledge. Based on our measurements, structured combinators can reduce runtimes by 9% to 58%, compared to running equivalent SKI combinator programs on KappaMutor.

Keywords: Graph reduction · Structured combinators · Hardware design · Haskell

1 Introduction

The main research direction for functional language implementation in the 1980s was custom hardware development. In the 1990s, the community shifted its research focus to executing functional languages on von-Neumann processors through compiler techniques [12], driven by the growing dominance of stock CPUs[1]. Recent projects (e.g., Reduceron [14], PilGRIM [7], Cephalopode [17] and Heron [18]) have re-explored the original architectural ideas in light of stagnant single-core performance in modern CPUs, compounded by continued advances in hardware design methodologies and tooling. In particular, modern hardware designs leverage substantial increases in available memory bandwidth and logic resources, enabling the exploitation of parallelism in graph reduction. Furthermore, the evolution of FPGAs makes the exploration of custom architecture designs increasingly feasible.

[1] The authors provide a curated history of functional architectures at: https://haflang.github.io/history.html.

J. Gibbons (Ed.): TFP 2025, LNCS 15652, pp. 139–164, 2026.
https://doi.org/10.1007/978-3-031-99751-8_7

Early graph reduction systems translated lambda terms into *fixed* SKI combinators, whereas later systems supported larger *user-defined* supercombinators allowing more efficient execution (Sect. 6).

The tension between the simplicity of SKI combinators and the efficiency of supercombinators persists in custom processor designs for functional languages. Accetti *et al.* recently proposed *structured combinators* [2] to get the benefits of both approaches: (1) a *minimal runtime system* similar to that of a fixed combinator set; (2) *efficient generated programs* enabled by deriving the shape of combinators directly from user functions.

Accetti *et al.* developed the *Fun* instruction-set architecture (ISA) to encode structured combinators, and the *Blackbird-II* processor to execute Fun programs [1,2]. Its compilation process translates lambda terms into combinator graphs expressed in the Fun ISA. The compiler converts lambda expressions first to fixed-set combinators, followed by a traversal of the combinator graph, merging small combinators into larger structured combinators.

In this paper, we further explore the application of structured combinators in hardware graph reduction by presenting *KappaMutor*, a new FPGA-validated structured combinator processor and its accompanying compiler. They differ from Accetti *et al.*'s work in three ways:

Language: KappaMutor's compiler supports Haskell 2010 [13] as input language, providing the user modern functional language features. This is thanks to the MicroHs [5] compiler, which we have extended with a structured combinator backend.

Compiler: A new approach to building structured combinators from lambda terms is proposed in KappaMutor's compiler. Beyond minimising combinator usage, we have also achieved full laziness with structured combinators, a capability not explored in Accetti *et al.*'s work.

Architecture: Differing from the RISC-style ISA design proposed by Accetti *et al.*, KappaMutor is purely built for graph reduction. Our processor exploits more aggressive memory parallelism to achieve one-combinator-per-cycle reductions.

This paper makes the following **contributions**:

- A structured combinators compiler for Haskell 2010. Two optimisation strategies with different goals are implemented: (1) minimising the combinator count in generated programs and (2) achieving full laziness with structured combinators (Sect. 3).
- KappaMutor, an efficient structured combinator processor that preserves the non-strict semantics of Haskell. Implementation results show the compactness of our design, utilising less than 1% of the logical resources on a modern FPGA (Sect. 4).
- Evaluation demonstrates that programs generated by our compiler contain 5% to 10% fewer combinators than Accetti *et al.*'s scheme. Experimental comparisons are also provided to showcase the importance of supporting full laziness (Sect. 5).

2 Structured Combinators

2.1 Background

Combinators are symbols that represent simple primitive functions. Early hardware architectures used SKI combinators as an intermediary between user code and hardware execution [8, 20], due to their simplicity and established approaches to convert the λ-calculus to combinators [22]. These systems typically support a limited set of combinators, often numbering in the low tens. While custom hardware enables efficient execution of each combinator reduction, the fine-grained nature of these small combinator sets resulted in numerous reduction steps and consequently, slow runtime performance. Derived from user functions, the coarser-grained supercombinators [10] have proven more efficient for software implementations of functional languages (Sect. 6). However, the complex runtime system required by supercombinators poses challenges for hardware implementation.

Accetti *et al.*'s recent work on structured combinators [1, 2] addresses this tension. By encoding millions of combinators in a compact 27-bit format, structured combinators can efficiently represent user code while retaining a simple runtime system. The overhead of this approach is primarily limited to a 6-bit decoder in hardware (Sect. 2.2), a relatively inexpensive component. Structured combinators enable compiling functional programs to a smaller number of combinators, leading to fewer reduction steps and improved runtime performance compared to SKI architectures. We validate this claim in Sect. 5.2 with 13 Haskell benchmarks.

2.2 Definition and Encoding

Structured combinators are machine-friendly encodings for combinators, where the structure of their graph-reduction semantics is explicit. They are predefined graph transformations that capture the arity, the reduction pattern, and the contents of the new graph nodes. We follow [2] to present the definition of structured combinators.

Definition 1. *A structured combinator* $C^{p}_{a\,i}$ *is a 3-tuple:*

- ***Arity*** a*: The number of arguments the combinator expects.*
- ***Pattern*** p*: The shape of the lambda abstraction's body, independent of specific variable names.*
- ***Index list*** i*: A list of de Bruijn indices indicating the order of argument usage in the pattern.*

This 3-tuple representation is equivalent to the corresponding λ-form, providing sufficient information to guide the reduction. For instance, the expression $C^{\mathrm{XX(X(XX))}}_{4[0,3,2,1,2]} e_1 e_2 e_3 e_4$ will be reduced to $e_1 e_4 (e_3 (e_2 e_3))$. Table 1 is borrowed from [2] to show how the common SKI combinators can be represented as structured combinators.

Table 1. Common SKI combinators and their structured combinator representation

SKI combinator	λ-form	Pattern	Structured form
S	$\lambda abc.ac(bc)$	XX(XX)	$C^{\mathrm{XX(XX)}}_{3[0,2,1,2]}$
K	$\lambda ab.a$	X	$C^{\mathrm{X}}_{2[0]}$
I	$\lambda a.a$	X	$C^{\mathrm{X}}_{1[0]}$
B	$\lambda abc.a(bc)$	X(XX)	$C^{\mathrm{X(XX)}}_{3[0,1,2]}$
C	$\lambda abc.acb$	XXX	$C^{\mathrm{XXX}}_{3[0,2,1]}$

We employ the same encoding scheme as [2] to represent structured combinators in our KappaMutor processor, as depicted in Fig. 1. Each combinator requires 27 bits: 6 bits for 64 possible reduction patterns (with 1 to 6 holes), 3 bits for arity (up to 7), and 3 bits for each de Bruijn index in the index list.

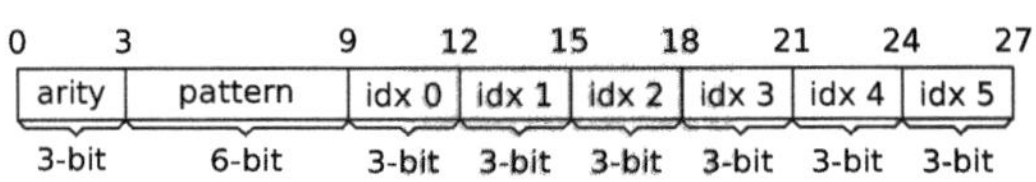

Fig. 1. The 27-bit structured combinator encoding.

Figure 2 illustrates how the Fibonacci function can be represented using both classic SKI combinators and structured combinators. Notably, the SKI representation requires 8 combinators, while the structured combinator representation needs only 3.

To calculate the number of possible structured combinators, we first define $h(n)$ as the number of reduction patterns with n holes. This function can be recursively defined as:

$$h(n) = \begin{cases} 1, & \text{if } n = 1 \\ \sum_{i=1}^{n-1} h(i) \times h(n-i), & \text{otherwise} \end{cases}$$

Using this definition, the total number of combinators supported by KappaMutor can be calculated:

$$\sum_{i=1}^{7}(\sum_{j=1}^{6} h(j) \times i^j) = 8,193,668$$

Therefore, with a 27-bit encoding, KappaMutor can support over 8 million unique combinators.

Haskell source

```
fib n = if n <= 1
        then 1
        else fib (n - 2) + fib (n - 1)
```

SKI combinators

$$fib : \mathbf{C}(\mathbf{S}(\mathbf{P}(\leq)1)(\mathbf{S}(\mathbf{C}' fib(\mathbf{P}(-)2)(+))(\mathbf{B} fib(\mathbf{P}(-)1))))1$$

Structured combinators

$$fib : C^{\mathrm{XXX(XX)X}}_{5[4,0,1,2,4,3]}(\leq)1(C^{\mathrm{XX(X(XXX))}}_{5[0,4,1,4,2,3]}(C^{\mathrm{X(XXX)X}}_{5[0,4,1,2,3]} fib(-)2(+)) fib(-)1)1$$

Fig. 2. The Fibonacci function, compiled to classic SKI combinators and structured combinators (combinator $\mathbf{P} = \lambda xyz.zxy$, and combinator $\mathbf{C}' = \lambda xyzw.x(yw)z$).

3 Compiler Design

3.1 Overview

Augustsson's MicroHs compiler [5] compiles Haskell 2010 to a set of 19 combinators. Our compiler extends MicroHs to support over 8 million structured combinators (Fig. 3). KappaMutor's compiler accepts Haskell 2010 as its input language, leveraging the MicroHs frontend to transform Haskell code to an intermediate representation, which is essentially the λ-calculus with literals and primitive operators. The compiler then removes all bound variables from the λ-calculus representation to construct a structured combinator graph for KappaMutor. As KappaMutor currently lacks support for floating-point operations and I/O (Sect. 4), we employ a limited prelude that includes only `Int` and `Bool` as primitive types. Apart from this limitation, other Haskell 2010 language features are well preserved by the MicroHs frontend.

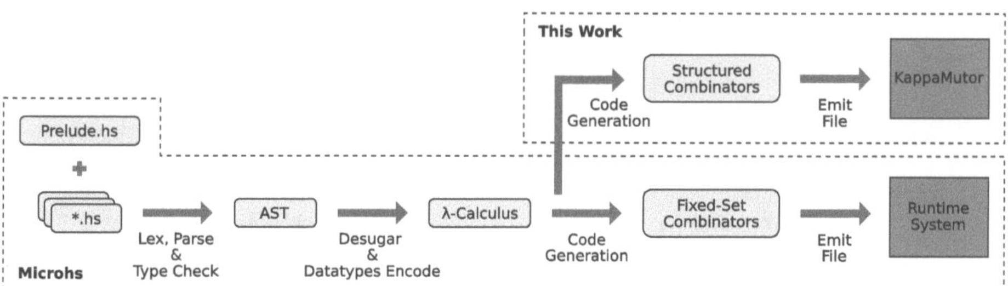

Fig. 3. Compilation workflow for KappaMutor.

The rest of this section focuses on our work that translates the λ-calculus to structured combinators. We implement two optimisation strategies of code generation—one for minimising the combinator counts; one for achieving full laziness. We first present the basic scheme and optimisation rewrites which apply to both strategies (Sect. 3.2), then explain the two strategies respectively (Sect. 3.3 and Sect. 3.4).

3.2 Basic Code Generation and Optimisation Rewrites

In [2], Accetti *et al.* proposed a compilation scheme to transform the λ-calculus to structured combinators. The scheme first attempts pattern matching on the shape of lambda bodies. If the pattern is supported by structured combinators, the lambda abstraction can be directly converted to a combinator. If pattern matching fails, the compiler transforms the lambda abstraction to fixed-set combinators using standard methods (e.g., bracket abstraction [15]), then walks through the combinator graph to merge small combinators into bigger structured combinators.

We propose a different approach in this paper. Our scheme resembles bracket abstraction [22], building the combinator graph bottom-up in one go. We also show how classic SKI combinator optimisation rewrites can be generalised and applied to structured combinators.

Bracket Abstraction Styled Algorithm. Fig. 4 is an extension of Fig. 16.2 in [15] to contrast the classic bracket abstraction algorithm with our code generation scheme. The compilation function, $\mathcal{C}[e]$, recursively removes all lambdas inside e. When a lambda abstraction is encountered, $\mathcal{A}\,x[e]$ is used to abstract out bound variable x from e. For basic bracket abstraction, we use the notation $\mathcal{A}_\text{b}$. In contrast, our scheme employs $\mathcal{A}_\text{s}$. We annotate variables and primitives, including combinators, as c. Notably, the input expression in $\mathcal{A}\,x[e]$ does not contain any lambdas, since $\mathcal{C}$ is first applied to the lambda body.

$\mathcal{C}[e]$ compiles e to combinators

$$\mathcal{C}[e_1\ e_2] = \mathcal{C}[e_1]\ \mathcal{C}[e_2]$$
$$\mathcal{C}[\lambda x.e] = \mathcal{A}\,x[\mathcal{C}[e]]$$
$$\mathcal{C}[c] = c$$

$\mathcal{A}_\text{b}\,x[e]$ abstracts x from e	$\mathcal{A}_\text{s}\,x[e]$ abstracts x from e
$\mathcal{A}_\text{b}\,x[e_1\ e_2] = \mathbf{S}\ (\mathcal{A}_\text{b}\,x[e_1])\,(\mathcal{A}_\text{b}\,x[e_2])$	$\mathcal{A}_\text{s}\,x[e_1\ e_2] = \mathcal{M}[\mathcal{A}_\text{s}\,x[e_1]]\,[\mathcal{A}_\text{s}\,x[e_2]]$
$\mathcal{A}_\text{b}\,x[x] = \mathbf{I}$	$\mathcal{A}_\text{s}\,x[x] = C^{\mathsf{X}}_{1[0]}$
$\mathcal{A}_\text{b}\,x[c] = \mathbf{K}\ c$, if $c \neq x$	$\mathcal{A}_\text{s}\,x[c] = C^{\mathsf{X}}_{2[0]}\ c$, if $c \neq x$

Fig. 4. Compilation $\mathcal{C}$, basic bracket abstraction $\mathcal{A}_\text{b}$ and our abstraction $\mathcal{A}_\text{s}$.

The MicroHs compiler generates code using bracket abstraction with optimisation rewrites, producing a fixed set of combinators. Our code generation follows the similar structure of this algorithm to build structured combinators. We adopt the same main translation as $\mathcal{C}$. For the two base cases of the abstraction function, structured combinators $C^{\mathrm{X}}_{1[0]}$ and $C^{\mathrm{X}}_{2[0]}$ are produced, equivalent to the **I** and **K** combinators. For the compound case, we require more delicately designed rules, written as $\mathcal{M}[e_1][e_2]$, to merge sub-expressions on-the-fly while combining combinators into bigger ones.

Sub-expression Combination. The combination function $\mathcal{M}$ employs three rules to merge sub-expressions, namely *absorption*, *extension* and *addition*. *Absorption* is the ideal rule because it merges two structured combinators into one, thus the reduction of an expression takes a single step rather than two. It combines the leading combinators of the two sub-expressions by merging their reduction patterns and index lists. It can only be applied when the resulting arity and reduction pattern are within the constraints of KappaMutor's architecture. Specifically, a structured combinator's arity should not exceed 7, and its pattern can contain up to 6 holes (Sect. 2.2). If absorption fails, the compiler attempts to apply the *extension* rule, which preserves one input expression, and extends the other's leading combinator to "send" the abstracted variable to the preserved expression. This also requires the generated combinator to fit within KappaMutor's architectural constraints. If extension also fails then the compiler falls back to the *addition* rule, which is equivalent to bracket abstraction. A $C^{\mathrm{XX(XX)}}_{3[0,2,1,2]}$ (i.e., the **S** combinator) is added on top of the input expressions.

$$\mathcal{M}\,[C^{\mathrm{XXX}}_{3[2,0,1]}e_1e_2]\,[C^{\mathrm{X(XX)}}_{3[1,2,0]}e_3e_4] \;\overset{\text{Absorption}}{\rightsquigarrow}\; C^{\mathrm{XXX(X(XX))}}_{5[4,0,1,3,4,2]}e_1e_2e_3e_4$$

$$\mathcal{M}\,[C^{\mathrm{XX}}_{2[1,0]}e_1]\,[C^{\mathrm{X(XXX)X}}_{4[0,2,3,0,1]}e_2e_3e_4] \;\overset{\text{Extension}}{\rightsquigarrow}\; C^{\mathrm{XX}(\mathbf{XX})}_{\mathbf{3}[2,0,\mathbf{1},\mathbf{2}]}e_1(C^{\mathrm{X(XXX)X}}_{4[0,2,3,0,1]}e_2e_3e_4)$$

$$\mathcal{M}\,[C^{\mathrm{X(XXX)X}}_{4[0,2,3,0,1]}e_1e_2e_3]\,[C^{\mathrm{XX}}_{2[1,0]}e_4] \;\overset{\text{Extension}}{\rightsquigarrow}\; C^{\mathbf{XX}\mathrm{(XX)}}_{\mathbf{3}[\mathbf{0},\mathbf{2},2,1]}(C^{\mathrm{X(XXX)X}}_{4[0,2,3,0,1]}e_1e_2e_3)e_4$$

$$\mathcal{M}\,[C^{\mathrm{X(XXX)X}}_{4[0,2,3,0,1]}e_1e_2e_3]\,[C^{\mathrm{XXX(XX)}}_{5[0,1,3,4,2]}e_4e_5e_6e_7] \;\overset{\text{Addition}}{\rightsquigarrow}\; C^{\mathbf{XX(XX)}}_{\mathbf{3[0,2,1,2]}}\,(C^{\mathrm{X(XXX)X}}_{4[0,2,3,0,1]}e_1e_2e_3)\,(C^{\mathrm{XXX(XX)}}_{5[0,1,3,4,2]}e_4e_5e_6e_7)$$

Fig. 5. Examples of expression merging $\mathcal{M}$: the absorption, extension and addition rules.

Figure 5 illustrates examples of the three rules, showing how absorption reduces combinators, extension preserves them, and addition increases them. Note that the extension rule can be applied to either the left or the right input expression. Additionally, the absorption and extension rules assume their input expressions are partially applied combinators that each expects precisely *one more* argument. We refer to such expressions as being in *unary form*.

Definition 2. *Expression* $e_0e_1\cdots e_n$ *is in unary form if* e_0 *is a structured combinator of arity* $n+1$.

Note that the result of $\mathcal{A}_s\, x[e]$ is always a unary-form expression. This guarantees that input expressions to the absorption rule are in unary-form.

Generic Optimisation Rewrites. Classic SKI compilation schemes rely on predefined rewrite rules to optimise code by reducing the usage of combinators. We propose a similar approach for structured combinator compilers, but instead of hardcoding rewrite rules, we use a more generic optimisation strategy.

Classic SKI rewrites	Addition rule with rewrites
$\mathbf{S}\,(\mathbf{K}\,e_1)\,(\mathbf{K}\,e_2) = \mathbf{K}\,(e_1 e_2)$	$\mathcal{M}\,[C^{XX(XX)X}_{4[0,2,3,2,0]}\,e_1][C^{XXXXX}_{4[1,3,0,1,0]}\,e_2e_3]$ ⇝ Addition $\boldsymbol{C}^{\mathbf{X}}_{\mathbf{2[0]}}\,((C^{XX(XX)X}_{3[0,1,2,1,0]}\,e_1)(C^{XXXXX}_{3[1,2,0,1,0]}\,e_2e_3))$
$\mathbf{S}\,(\mathbf{K}\,e_1)\,e_2 = \mathbf{B}\,e_1 e_2$	$\mathcal{M}\,[C^{XX(XX)X}_{4[0,2,3,2,0]}\,e_1][C^{XXXXX}_{4[1,3,2,1,2]}\,e_2e_3]$ ⇝ Addition $\boldsymbol{C}^{\mathbf{X(XX)}}_{\mathbf{3[0,1,2]}}\,(C^{XX(XX)X}_{3[0,1,2,1,0]}\,e_1)\,(C^{XXXXX}_{4[1,3,2,1,2]}\,e_2e_3)$
$\mathbf{S}\,e_1\,(\mathbf{K}\,e_2) = \mathbf{C}\,e_1 e_2$	$\mathcal{M}\,[C^{XX(XX)X}_{4[0,2,3,1,0]}\,e_1][C^{XXXXX}_{4[1,3,0,1,0]}\,e_2e_3]$ ⇝ Addition $\boldsymbol{C}^{\mathbf{XXX}}_{\mathbf{3[0,2,1]}}\,(C^{XX(XX)X}_{4[0,2,3,1,0]}\,e_1)\,(C^{XXXXX}_{3[1,2,0,1,0]}\,e_2e_3)$

Fig. 6. Classic SKI optimisation rewrites and examples of corresponding improved addition rule.

Among the numerous SKI rewrite rules, three are fundamental, as illustrated in Fig. 6. These rewrites occur during the compound case of bracket abstraction. The underlying principle of these rules is to avoid unnecessary transmission of the abstracted bound variable when it is not used in a sub-expression [15]. Traditional rewrites achieve this by examining the structure of the sub-expression: the bound variable is deemed unused if the sub-expression takes the form ($\mathbf{K}\ e$). The three SKI rewrites in Fig. 6 correspond to the following scenarios:

- **Mutual disuse**: If the bound variable is not used in either sub-expression, it is omitted from both.
- **Right-side usage**: If the bound variable is only used in the right sub-expression, the **B** combinator is employed to transmit the variable.
- **Left-side usage**: If the bound variable is only used in the left sub-expression, the **C** combinator is used to transmit the variable.

With structured combinators, we can more generically determine whether a bound variable is unused within a sub-expression: for an expression $C^{p}_{a\,i}\ e_1 \cdots e_n$, where $n < a$, the bound variable is unused if n is absent from i. Figure 6 illustrates how similar rewrites can be applied to the addition rule in our compiler. Note that they also work on non-unary formed expressions (Sect. 3.3).

When executing the addition rule, the compiler prioritises these rewrites over the introduction of the $C^{\mathrm{XX(XX)}}_{3[0,2,1,2]}$ combinator. Similar optimisations can be applied to the extension rule. For instance, $\mathcal{M}$ $[C^{\mathrm{XX}}_{2[1,0]} e_1]$ $[C^{\mathrm{X(XXX)X}}_{4[0,3,1,0,1]} e_2 e_3]$ will yield $C^{\mathrm{XXX}}_{2[2,0,1]} e_1 (C^{\mathrm{X(XXX)X}}_{3[0,2,1,0,1]} e_2 e_3)$, where the extension rule is enhanced by the SKI-styled rewrites.

Another category of generic rewrites applicable to structured combinators is based on η-reduction (i.e., $\lambda x.(f\ x) = f$). For a combinator $C^{p}_{a\,i}$, η-reduction is possible if index $a-1$ appears solely as the final element of i, and p conforms to the pattern p'X, where p' represents an arbitrary pattern. In the extension and addition rules, the compiler consistently attempts the η-reduction styled rewrites on preserved input sub-expressions. Note that η-reduction can reduce the arity of combinators, potentially revealing new reducible expressions. A combinator can be reduced at compile time if it is (1) fully applied and (2) its index list contains no duplicates. For example, $\mathcal{M}$ $[C^{\mathrm{XXX}}_{3[1,2,0]} e_1 e_2]$ $[C^{\mathrm{X(XX)X}}_{4[0,2,1,3]} e_3 e_4 e_5]$ will produce $C^{\mathrm{XXX(XX)}}_{4[1,3,0,2,3]} e_1 e_2 (e_3 (e_5 e_4))$.

3.3 Optimisation Strategy 1: Minimising Combinator Counts

Building on the basic scheme in Sect. 3.2, different strategies can be applied to further improve the generated code. The goal of our first optimisation strategy is to minimise combinator usage. This strategy improves nested calls to $\mathcal{A}_{\mathrm{s}}$, which are commonly introduced by curried functions and inner lambda abstractions. By reducing combinator counts, programs generated by this strategy generally have a faster runtime (Sect. 5.2).

Combining Non-unary Formed Expressions. The scheme described in Sect. 3.2 generates functionally correct code. However, it can be inefficient when applied to curried functions or functions with inner lambda abstractions, which lead to nested calls to $\mathcal{A}_{\mathrm{s}}$. For instance, consider the example in Fig. 7a (η-reduction is omitted here for clarity). The basic compilation produces three successively applied combinators which require three reduction steps. An obviously more efficient representation would be $C^{\mathrm{XXXXX}}_{5[2,0,3,1,4]}(+)(-)$, which can be reduced in a single step.

To improve the scheme, we first need to give combinators special treatment in the base case of $\mathcal{A}_{\mathrm{s}}\, x[e]$. Specifically:

- For $\mathcal{A}_{\mathrm{s}}\, x[C^{p}_{a\,i}]$, attempt to create $C^{p}_{a'\,i'}$ as result, where $a' = a+1$, and $i' = \mathrm{map}\,(+1)\,i$.
- If the new arity exceeds the architectural constraints, revert to the less efficient $C^{\mathrm{X}}_{2[0]}\ C^{p}_{n\,i}$.

The revised base cases for $\mathcal{A}_{\mathrm{s}}\, x[e]$ may yield non-unary expressions, which contradicts the underlying assumption of the absorption and extension rules presented in Sect. 3.2. Consequently, $\mathcal{M}$ requires changes to accommodate these

$$\lambda x.\,(\lambda y.\,(\lambda z.\,(x + y - z)))$$
$$\rightsquigarrow$$
$$\lambda x.\,(\lambda y.\,(C^{\mathrm{XXXXX}}_{5[0,1,2,3,4]}\,x(+)y(-)))$$
$$\rightsquigarrow$$
$$\lambda x.\,(C^{\mathrm{XXXXX}}_{5[0,1,2,4,3]}\,C^{\mathrm{XXXXX}}_{5[0,1,2,3,4]}\,x(+)(-))$$
$$\rightsquigarrow$$
$$C^{\mathrm{XXXXX}}_{5[0,1,4,2,3]}\,C^{\mathrm{XXXXX}}_{5[0,1,2,4,3]}\,C^{\mathrm{XXXXX}}_{5[0,1,2,3,4]}\,(+)(-)$$

(a) Basic code generation

$$\lambda x.\,(\lambda y.\,(\lambda z.\,(x + y - z)))$$
$$\rightsquigarrow$$
$$\lambda x.\,(\lambda y.\,(C^{\mathrm{XXXXX}}_{5[0,1,2,3,4]}\,x(+)y(-)))$$
$$\rightsquigarrow$$
$$\lambda x.\,(C^{\mathrm{XXXXX}}_{5[0,1,3,2,4]}\,x(+)(-))$$
$$\rightsquigarrow$$
$$C^{\mathrm{XXXXX}}_{5[2,0,3,1,4]}\,(+)(-)$$

(b) Supporting non-unary forms

Fig. 7. Abstracting bound variables from curried functions.

non-unary expressions. Figure 8 provides examples illustrating the non-unary versions of these two rules. The compiler checks the unary nature of input expressions and selects appropriate rules accordingly. The non-unary version of the absorption rule is applicable when the left input expression is non-unary and the right input expression is unary. Otherwise, the extension rule is employed. These enhancements effectively remove the unnecessary combinators resulting from nested calls to $\mathcal{A}_s$. Figure 7b shows how the improved code generation handles the same example.

$$\mathcal{M}\ [C^{\mathrm{XXX}}_{3[2,0,1]}e_1]\ [C^{\mathrm{XX}}_{2[1,0]}e_2]\ \overset{\text{Absorption}}{\rightsquigarrow}\ C^{\mathrm{(XX)XX}}_{3[2,1,0,2]}e_1e_2$$

$$\mathcal{M}\ [C^{\mathrm{XXX}}_{3[2,0,1]}e_1]\ [C^{\mathrm{XX(XXX)}}_{5[1,0,3,4,2]}e_2e_3]\ \overset{\text{Extension}}{\rightsquigarrow}\ C^{\mathbf{(XX)XX}}_{\mathbf{4[1,2,0,2]}}e_1(C^{\mathrm{XX(XXX)}}_{5[1,0,3,4,2]}e_2e_3)$$

Fig. 8. Absorption and extension rules, applied to non-unary-form expressions.

3.4 Optimisation Strategy 2: Full Laziness

Although Haskell's non-strict semantics is preserved by KappaMutor's graph reduction model (Sect. 4), certain forms of sharing, essential for achieving *full laziness*, are not inherently guaranteed. Full laziness requires *all* expressions to be evaluated *at most once* during execution, after their free variables been bound [15]. For example, in the following definition:

```
> f x y = y + (fib x)
> g = f 10
```

The partially applied function `f` in `g` can be reduced. The expression `(fib 10)` will be evaluated in the first call of `g` during runtime, and the result should be shared by the subsequent calls of `g`. Turner [22] highlighted that such property is particularly beneficial when the source code is in a combinatory programming style, as seen in functions built from simpler components like `foldr` [22].

Augustsson [5] further emphasised the importance of this property for handling overloaded functions in Haskell type classes.

SKI combinators naturally guarantee this property, and are described as supporting "self-optimising" by Turner. Here we present our second optimisation strategy, which aims to achieve full laziness. To the best of our knowledge, this is the first implementation of full laziness with structured combinators.

Lifting Free Expressions. Our scheme is inspired by Hughes's idea for realising full laziness with supercombinators [10]. When abstracting bound variables from the lambda body, instead of lifting each free variable as an argument to the combinator, we try to lift the maximal free expressions (i.e., the largest expression that does not contain the bound variable) so that the computation can be shared. In Fig. 9b, the maximal free expression `(fib x)` is lifted when abstracting `y`. With this strategy, `(fib x)` will be constructed and shared when the function is partially applied with `x`.

$$\lambda x.\,(\lambda y.\,(y + (\textit{fib}\ x))) \rightsquigarrow \lambda x.\,(C^{XX(XX)}_{4[3,0,1,2]}(+)\,\textit{fib}\,x) \rightsquigarrow C^{XX(XX)}_{4[3,0,1,2]}(+)\,\textit{fib}$$

(a) Lifting free variables

$$\lambda x.\,(\lambda y.\,(y + (\textit{fib}\ x))) \rightsquigarrow \lambda x.\,(C^{XXX}_{3[2,0,1]}(+)(\textit{fib}\,x)) \rightsquigarrow C^{XX(XX)}_{4[0,1,2,3]}C^{XXX}_{3[2,0,1]}(+)\,\textit{fib}$$

(b) Lifting free expressions

Fig. 9. Achieving full laziness by lifting free expressions.

It is surprisingly simple to identify and lift maximal free expressions with bracket abstraction. The rewrite rule $\mathbf{S}(\mathbf{K}e_1)(\mathbf{K}e_2) = \mathbf{K}(e_1e_2)$ essentially constructs the free expressions until it reaches its largest form. For structured combinators, we can easily adopt this rule, and prioritise it over the absorption rule. We also implement Hughes's technique of reordering combinator arguments to increase opportunities for η-reduction [10]. Note that in order to preserve full laziness, the optimisation we made in Sect. 3.3 that combines non-unary formed expressions, cannot be applied.

Avoiding Redundant Full Laziness. In the example of Fig. 9, the fully lazy strategy introduces an extra combinator. When sharing is not abundant in a program, the fully lazy strategy might damage the performance, comparing to the minimising combinator count strategy. As suggested in [15], it is important to eliminate redundant full laziness to mitigate the performance penalty.

Our solution is to avoid lifting irreducible expressions. With structured combinators, an irreducible expression is typically constructed by a partially applied combinator or primitive operator. Since evaluation cannot proceed under this situation, sharing such expressions does not save us reduction steps.

When abstracting bound variables, our compiler preserves all the maximal free expressions at the beginning. Between nested calls to the abstraction function $\mathcal{A}_s$, the compiler examines whether the abstraction result contains any *useful* free expressions. We say an expression $e_0 e_1 \cdots e_n$ is useful if (1) e_0 is a structured combinator of arity $a \leq n$, or (2) e_0 is not a structured combinator, or (3) at least one of e_1 to e_n is useful. If useful free expressions exist, the compiler keeps preserving all the free expressions, otherwise it will fallback to the minimising combinator strategy, which destructs redundant free expressions to provide better runtime performance.

In Sect. 5.2, we show that our fully lazy strategy can generally provide comparable running time to the minimising combinator strategy, even when there is not much sharing in a program.

4 The KappaMutor Processor

KappaMutor combines the foundation of Reduceron's [14] hardware architecture with a graph reduction model based on structured combinators [2]. The combination facilitates parallel memory access across dedicated memory units, bypassing costly node searching and allocation operations inherent in heap-centric architectures. KappaMutor performs normal order reduction, maintaining Haskell's non-strict semantics. This name plays on the relationship between the λ-calculus and combinators. Kappa (κ) and mu (μ), the Greek letters immediately preceding and following λ, are combined to suggest the absence of lambdas in our processor.

We implement KappaMutor in Chisel [6], a Scala-embedded hardware description language. The implementation currently supports the 27-bit structured combinator encoding (Sect. 2.2), integers, and basic arithmetic primitives. This section details KappaMutor's design, covering its program representation, reduction model, key features and optimizations. FPGA implementation results on resource utilisation and timing are also presented.

4.1 Program Representation

In KappaMutor, the source program is compiled into a sequence of top-level functions, each represented as a list of applications. This list comprises the spine application and nested applications of the function. The compiled program is a concatenation of these top-level function lists, forming a single list of applications. Whilst KappaMutor is implemented in Chisel, we adopt the style of [14] to present the program representation, using Haskell for clarity.

```
> type Prog = [App]
> type Func = [App]
```

This definition diverges from template instantiation-based designs like Reduceron and Heron [18], which define functions as 3-tuples comprising arity, spine application, and a list of nested applications.

Applications in the architecture are flattened, meaning they have no nested applications and can be represented as a list of atomic elements.

```
> type App = [Atom]
> data Atom =
>       PTR Int                   -- Pointer to an application
>     | COM Arity Pat [Idx]       -- Structured combinator
>     | INT Int                   -- Integer literal
>     | PRM Int                   -- Primitive operator with an opcode
>     | Y                         -- Y-combinator
```

Our definition of `Atom` deviates from Reduceron's, omitting function and argument pointers since β-reduction is not used in KappaMutor. In our design, a `PTR` pointing to the spine application of a top-level function effectively serves as a function pointer. Additionally, we exclude data constructors and pattern matching case tables, as they are eliminated by MicroHs's Scott encoding scheme. We introduce structured combinators as a new atomic category. A structured combinator is a 3-tuple comprising arity, reduction pattern (encoded as a 6-bit field in hardware), and a list of de Bruijn indices, as described in Sect. 2.2.

```
> type Arity = Int
> data Pat = X | At Pat Pat
> type Idx = Int
```

In KappaMutor, each `Atom` is represented using 32 bits, including its tag. For `COM`, the maximum arity is 7, and the pattern field supports reduction patterns with up to 6 holes (see Sect. 2.2). We limit the maximum application length to 7, as a combinator consumes at most 7 arguments, and compiled applications are typically under-applied. The compiler splits larger applications into multiple smaller in-sized ones.

4.2 Reduction Model

KappaMutor performs normal order reduction. Its execution centers on a reduction stack and its associated control logic. Figure 10 illustrates the processor's datapath. The system incorporates three specialised memory units: a dual-port heap for storing `App` structures, an update stack for handling `UpdateRecords` (Sect. 4.3), and the reduction stack for storing `Atom` elements.

We adopt Reduceron's stack implementation, enabling asynchronous reads and synchronous writes to the top 8 stack elements. Additionally, we employ Reduceron's infix primitive application scheme to maintain strict evaluation semantics for primitive operators.

At startup, the pointer to the entry function is placed on the top of the reduction stack. In each clock cycle, the type of the top `Atom` on the stack determines the next reduction rule to be applied. Execution terminates when

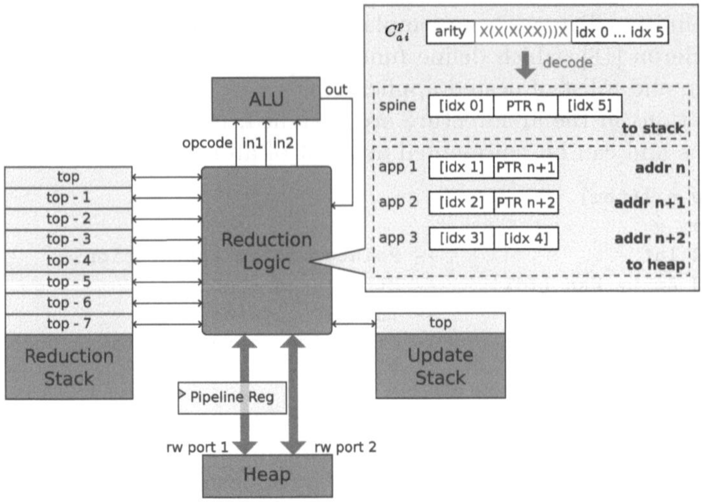

Fig. 10. Datapath diagram of KappaMutor and its combinator reduction example (`[a]` refers to the reduction stack element at position `(top-a-1)`).

the stack depth falls below the required number of arguments for a reduction rule. The reduction rules of KappaMutor include:

- `PTR`: The pointed application is fetched from the heap and pushed onto the reduction stack.
- `COM`: The combinator and its arguments, as specified by the arity field, are popped from the reduction stack. The combinator's pattern guides the reduction logic in modifying the stack and creating nested applications on the heap.
- `INT`: The type of the `Atom` at position `(top-2)` will be checked. If it's an `INT`, the ALU result is pushed onto the reduction stack; otherwise, a swap operation is performed to evaluate the second ALU input.
- `PRM`: The top two elements of the reduction stack are swapped to preserve the infix order of primitive operators.
- `Y`: Following the reduction rule $\mathbf{Y}R = R(\mathbf{Y}R)$, the second-top element of the reduction stack is consumed to create a self-referential application on the heap.

Most reduction rules are similar to those for Reduceron, with the exception of structured combinator (`COM`) reduction. Figure 10 illustrates an example of structured combinator application. The 6-bit reduction pattern is decoded to guide the construction of the spine and nested applications of the result, while the index list selects the appropriate arguments from the reduction stack. Note that the 6-bit decoder is the main price we pay for structured combinators. This cost is minimal—for comparison, an SKI architecture with 20 supported combinators would already require a 5-bit decoder.

4.3 Architecture Features

We now present three novel features of the KappaMutor processor that differentiate it from template instantiation based architectures like Reduceron and Heron [18]. Our improvements involve the heap writing and updating schemes for structured combinators. We also show how top-level functions can be automatically optimised during runtime.

Pipelined Heap Writes. Reduceron enforces a one-reduction-per-clock-cycle constraint by requiring functions with more than two nested applications in the body to be split into multiple ones. KappaMutor faces a similar challenge: certain supported reduction patterns (e.g., the one in Fig. 10) can generate up to three nested applications within a single reduction, which exceed the capabilities of a dual-port heap to process in one clock cycle.

Instead of splitting the combinator itself, we relax the one-reduction-per-clock-cycle requirement, allowing an additional cycle for heap writing when necessary. To mitigate potential performance impacts, we implement a pipelined heap writing mechanism by introducing a pipeline register to the architecture (Fig. 10). Execution stalls only when there is direct contention for heap access between consecutive reductions. With this design, combinators with at most three nested applications are supported.

Hiding Heap Updates. Heap updates are necessary to avoid duplicated computation in graph reduction. When an application is loaded from the heap onto the reduction stack, its evaluation progress is tracked. Upon reaching weak head normal form (WHNF) [15], the application is written back to the same heap address.

Reduceron has an efficient heap update mechanism which uses an update stack (Fig. 10) to manage heap updates. When a `PTR` is dereferenced during reduction, an `UpdateRecord` is pushed onto the update stack, recording the address and current stack depth.

```
> type StackDepth = Int
> type HeapAddr = Int
> type UpdateRecord = (StackDepth, HeapAddr)
```

Before applying any reduction rule, the architecture checks the update condition based on the current stack depth and the top `UpdateRecord`. If a heap update is necessary, the update is performed, and the top `UpdateRecord` is removed from the stack at that cycle.

KappaMutor adopts Reduceron's heap update mechanism but introduces an optimisation. Instead of dedicating separate clock cycles for heap updates, it is possible to perform heap updates and reductions in parallel, provided the reduction doesn't require heap access. This optimisation is possible for specific `Atom` types:

- `PTR`: Never appears as the top element in WHNF.

- COM: If the combinator does not create any nested applications (e.g., $C^{\mathrm{XXXX}}_{4[3,0,1,2]}$), it can be reduced in parallel with a heap update.
- INT and PRM: These atom types can always be reduced in parallel with a heap update.
- Y: The **Y** combinator cannot be reduced in parallel with a heap update, as it requires heap access.

Self-optimisation Through Heap Updates. To enable full laziness, which also known as self-optimisation [22] in the context of combinators, the underlying hardware must replace function definitions with their WHNF once it is reached (see Sect. 3.4). In KappaMutor, both top-level functions and runtime applications reside within the same heap, which inherently enables self-optimising through heap updates. Recall the example from Sect. 3.4:

```
> f x y = y + (fib x)
> g = f 10
```

Fig. 11 illustrates the first call to function g. After this initial call, g is updated to its WHNF. Note that the free expression (fib 10) is created at heap address n, and can be shared by all the subsequent calls to g, thus full laziness is fulfilled.

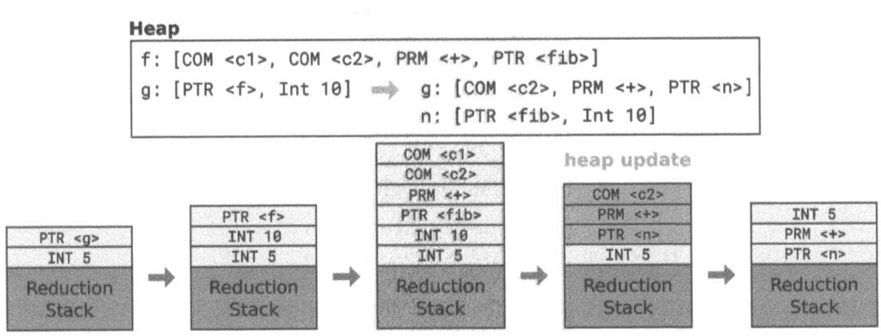

Fig. 11. Self-optimisation through heap updates, where <c1> is $C^{\mathrm{XX(XX)}}_{4[0,1,2,3]}$ and <c2> is $C^{\mathrm{XXX}}_{3[2,0,1]}$.

Turner suggested that self-optimisation should also be achievable in other types of graph reduction systems [22], such as a template instantiation machine. However, since Reduceron places programs in a separate memory, and all the argument pointers are replaced by actual arguments during template instantiation, it is less straightforward to achieve this self-optimising property.

4.4 Implementation on FPGA

We implement the KappaMutor processor on an Alveo U280 [3] UltraScale+ FPGA to demonstrate the feasibility of our design. While KappaMutor is not specifically tailored for FPGAs, the resource utilisation and timing results are encouraging. Table 2 outlines the parameter settings for the FPGA implementation. The reduction and update stacks are mapped to BlockRAM resources, while the dual-port heap is mapped to UltraRAM resources provided by the UltraScale+ device.

Table 2. Memory type and size of the implemented KappaMutor instance.

Memory unit	Element	Width	Depth
Heap	`App`	224-bit	64 K
Reduction stack	`Atom`	32-bit	4 K
Update stack	`UpdateRecord`	42-bit	512

Table 3 summarises the resource utilisation of KappaMutor on the FPGA. Logical components, including look-up tables (LUTs) and registers, are primarily used by the rotation logic within the reduction stack and the overall control logic, occupying less than 1% of the FPGA's resources. BlockRAM and UltraRAM utilization is 0.25% and 5%, respectively, also representing a small fraction of the available capacity. The compactness of KappaMutor suggests the potential for future scaling to a larger parallel design with tens of cores on a single FPGA. The design achieves a maximum clock frequency of 165 MHz, a respectable result for an FPGA implementation. These results demonstrate the hardware-friendly nature of structured combinators.

Table 3. KappaMutor resource utilisation on Alveo U280.

Resource type	Consumption	Available	Utilisation%
LUTs	7,224	1,303,680	0.55
Registers	965	2,607,360	0.04
BlockRAMs	5	2,016	0.25
UltraRAMs	48	960	5.00

5 Evaluation

Our evaluation focuses on the comparison of code generation schemes for structured combinators, encompassing an analysis of generated code, runtime performance, and the effectiveness of optimisation strategies for different scenarios.

5.1 Generated Code Analysis

Two metrics are employed for the analysis of compiler-generated programs: combinator count and application count. While not a direct indicator of runtime, combinator count approximates the potential reduction steps within a program,

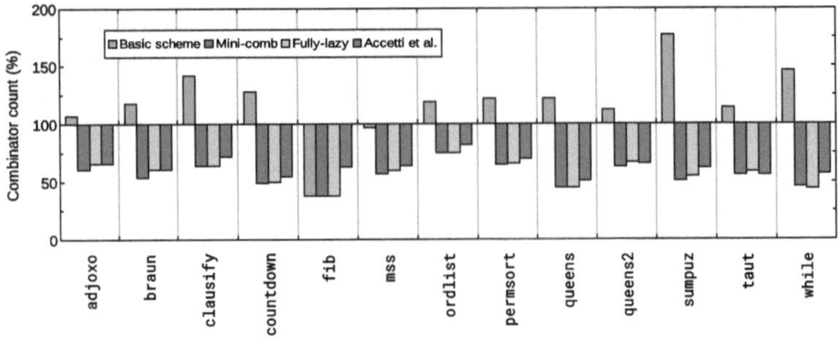

(a) Combinator count, normalised by MicroHs SKI code generation

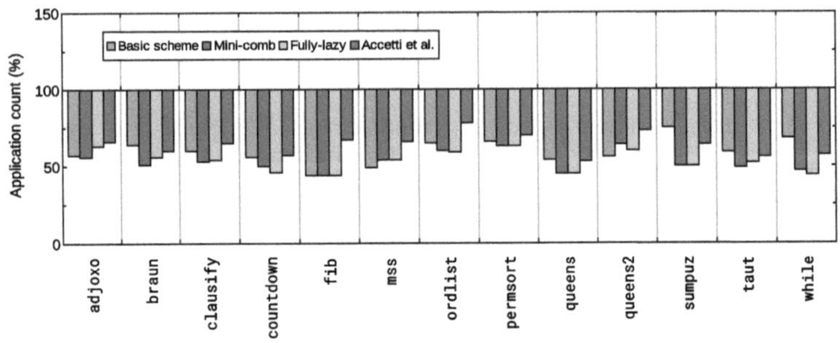

(b) Application count, normalised by MicroHs SKI code generation

Fig. 12. Static code comparison among code generation schemes.

which links to the runtime. Application count, on the other hand, is equivalent to program size given KappaMutor's program representation (Sect. 4.1).

The comparison includes our basic structured combinator compilation from Sect. 3.2 and the two optimisation strategies from Sect. 3.3 and 3.4. We further integrate Accetti *et al.*'s code generation [2] into MicroHs as a backend for comparison, and use a post-processing pass to the original MicroHs workflow, encoding its 19 combinators into structured combinators so that the SKI scheme can also be compared. The benchmark programs used in [14] and [18] for hardware graph reduction evaluation are adopted. We translate the f-lite [14] source code to Haskell, as expected by the MicroHs frontend, and use a minimal prelude file for simplicity [24].

Figures 12a and 12b show the combinator and application counts for programs generated by the four structured combinator schemes, normalised against the MicroHs SKI scheme. They show that our optimised schemes can reduce combinator and application counts by 25% (83 vs 62 combinators in `ordlist`) to 56% (404 vs 179 combinators in `while`) compared to the SKI scheme. Considering MicroHs already applies extensive optimisation rewrites to its SKI code generation, this significant reduction underscores the power of structured combinators, supporting the claims in [2].

Compared to Accetti *et al.*'s method, our two optimisation strategies both reduce combinator and application counts by 5% to 10% in most benchmarks. It is unsurprising that the basic scheme performs the worst. This is due to the prevalence of curried functions and inner lambda abstractions which can significantly degrade code efficiency of the basic scheme as discussed in Sect. 3.3. The results also validate the necessity of the optimisations we implemented. An interesting exception is the `fib` benchmark, where all our schemes yield identical results. This is because `fib` lacks curried functions and is the smallest benchmark, with the compiled code consisting of only three combinators. In terms of application count (i.e., program size), one might argue that the SKI scheme's use of 19 combinators could potentially reduce the required bits for encoding, thus it is unfair to compare program sizes in terms of application count. However, other atomic elements, such as integers and pointers, necessitate wider bit widths. Thus, it is challenging to exclusively optimise the bit width for combinators in a hardware implementation of the SKI approach.

5.2 Runtime Performance Analysis

For runtime performance, we focus on clock cycles and total heap allocations during program execution on KappaMutor. The comparison is still made among the four structured combinator schemes and MicroHs's SKI code generation. The same benchmark programs are compiled using different code generation implementations and executed on our KappaMutor processor within Chisel's simulation framework for runtime statistics collection.

Given the exact same underlying hardware architecture, clock cycles directly correspond to wall-clock execution time. Additionally, heap allocation numbers provide insights into memory consumption and potential garbage collection overhead, although at present we have not yet implemented a garbage collector for KappaMutor.

Figure 13a and 13b present the clock cycle and heap allocation results for programs generated by the four structured combinator schemes, normalised against the MicroHs SKI results. The data indicates that our minimising combinator strategy can reduce runtime by 9% (208k vs 189k cycles in `mss`) to 58% (363k vs 152k cycles in `while`) compared to the SKI scheme. It also gives a less than 5% improvement against Accetti *et al.*'s method. The result of the full laziness strategy is more interesting—we observe a consistent performance degradation (around 10% slower than minimising combinator strategy) in most benchmarks. This is because the benchmark programs contain little sharing that can only be exploited by full laziness, as discussed in Sect. 3.4. However, we believe this penalty is in an acceptable range. In Sect. 5.3 we show that the fully lazy scheme can be much more efficient when more subtle sharing occurs in a program.

Heap allocation results share a similar pattern to clock cycles, with two exceptions. First, the `fib` benchmark shows identical heap allocation results

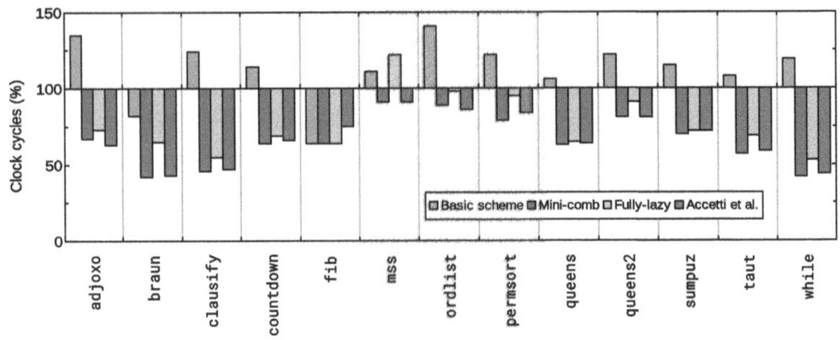

(a) Clock cycles, normalised by MicroHs SKI code generation

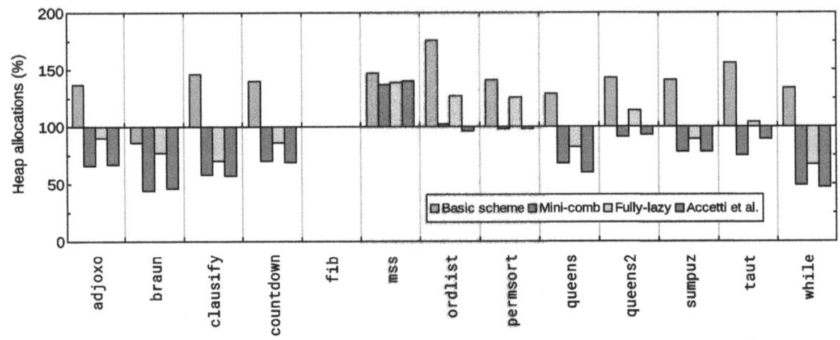

(b) Heap allocations, normalised by MicroHs SKI code generation

Fig. 13. Runtime performance comparison among code generation schemes

for all five schemes, likely due to its simplicity. Second, all structured combinator schemes generate more (around 35%) heap allocations in `mss` compared to the SKI scheme. This is because the SKI scheme behaves even more lazily, where irreducible free expressions are also lifted. Though this does not reduce running cycles, heap allocations might be avoided (Sect. 15.6 of [15] provides a more detailed discussion on this). Such small differences can be significant in some extreme cases, as seen in `mss`.

The distribution of arities, the number of holes, and nested applications for each combinator reduction during the benchmark runs is shown in Fig. 14. These results provide insight into how effectively our code generation leverages KappaMutor's capabilities. The significant proportion of high arity and hole usage validates our investment in hardware resources. In future work, this profile could inform hardware bound selection or the choice of supported combinators. We also observe that, in the absence of significant sharing, programs generated by the fully lazy strategy exhibit behavior similar to those generated by the minimising combinator strategy. This is an encouraging sign, as it suggests that we managed to mitigate the performance penalty of supporting full laziness (Sect. 3.4), given that the minimising combinator strategy can be considered ideal in such cases.

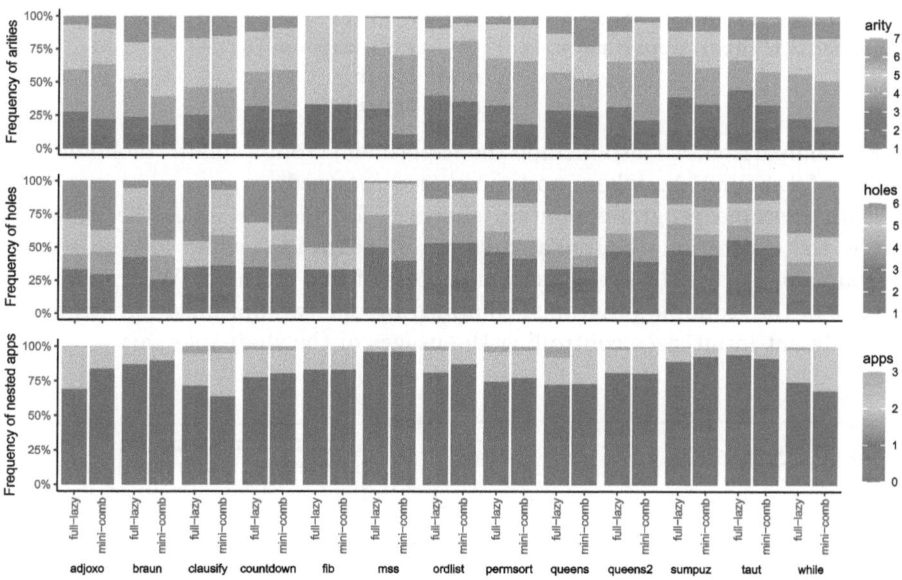

Fig. 14. Combinator characteristic distribution, collected from runtime.

5.3 The Importance of Full Laziness

Our full laziness strategy does not show clear advantages against the minimising combinator strategy in the benchmarks of Sect. 5.2, because of the lack of exploitable sharing. Here we further compare our two code generation strategies in more cases, to show that sometimes full laziness can bring significant influence to the runtime efficiency.

We explore two examples. The first one is the `sumTotient` function, which calculates the sum of Euler totients (the count of relatively prime integers to the given number) within a range:

```
> sumTotient :: (Int, Int) -> Int
> sumTotient (lower, upper) = sum (map euler [lower, lower+1 .. upper])

> euler :: Int -> Int
> euler n = length (filter (relprime n) [1 .. n-1])

> relprime :: Int -> Int -> Bool
> relprime x y = null (intersect (primeFactors x) (primeFactors y))
```

The `relprime` function determines whether two `Int`s are relatively prime by checking their factors. The definition of the trivial `intersect` and `primeFactors` are omitted here but full sources available at [24]. The second example uses the `Ord` class for the ad-hoc polymorphic `inboundIdx` function, which yields the indices of list elements within a given range:

```
> inboundIdx :: Ord a => a -> a -> [a] -> [Int]
> inboundIdx lower upper ns = [i | (n, i) <- zip ns [0..]
>                                , n >= lower
>                                , n <= upper]
```

For comparison, we also include the experiment from a "plain" monomorphic version of `inboundIdx`, where no type classes are used.

Both example programs contain sharing—for the first one, the shareable part is the expression `(primeFactors x)` in `relprime`, while for the second, the shareable part is the specialisation process of `Ord` methods. We compare the runtime of the example programs, compiled by our two optimisation strategies, with different input sizes controlling the usages of the shareable part.

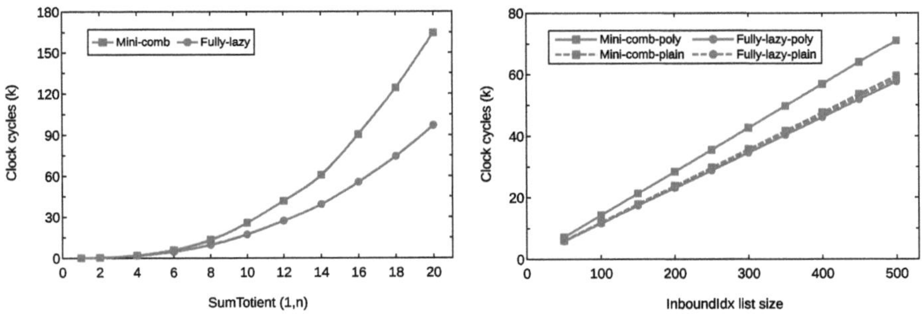

(a) Example 1: shareable computation (b) Example 2: ad-hoc polymorphism

Fig. 15. Runtime comparison between the two optimisation strategies.

Figure 15a shows that the fully lazy strategy generated program has a significantly lower runtime in our first example (41% lower in `sumTotient(1,20)`). This is because the computation of `(primeFactors x)` is shared, while the minimising combinator strategy generated code recomputes the expression on each call site of `relprime`. This example highlights the performance benefits of full laziness when a program contains substantial shareable computations. Figure 15b demonstrates that introducing ad-hoc polymorphism can penalise the runtime of programs generated by the minimising combinator strategy, whereas the penalty is negligible for fully lazy code generation. The fully lazy strategy achieves a 19% reduction in runtime compared to the minimising combinator strategy as a result of sharing type class specialisations. Given the simplicity of this example, we anticipate that full laziness would offer a more substantial performance advantage in real-world programs where the use of type classes is ubiquitous.

6 Related Work

Turner demonstrated that combinators [21] had a practical application for implementing functional languages [22]. This insight led to the development of early hardware architectures (e.g., SKIM [8] and NORMA [20]) that supported SKI combinators, a small fixed set of fine-grained operations. Due to hardware capacity at the time, these architectures adhered to a conservative *atom-based* memory layout. While this approach maintains a low memory bandwidth requirement, it requires additional graph traversal steps to locate redexes, ultimately reducing overall performance. Nevertheless, these systems demonstrated the viability of combinator architectures with simple runtime systems, even inspiring recent hardware [17] and software (MicroHs) [5] implementations over 40 years later.

Diverging from the minimalism of fixed combinator sets, Hughes showed how user applications could instead be compiled into coarser-grained supercombinators [10]. This insight led to supercombinator architectures (e.g., Tim [9] and Flagship [23]). Because they supported *user defined* supercombinators derived directly from user functions, fewer combinators are executed, often resulting in much shorter runtimes [23]. Similar to supercombinator hardware, recent architectures Reduceron [14] and Heron [18] support a near direct execution of user-defined functions using template instantiation, without the compiler doing too much heavy lifting, i.e. their compilers do not split user functions into fine-grained SKI combinators. Both projects also demonstrate that simple, non-pipelined, stack-based architectures can be sufficient for competitive graph reduction performance. *Structured* combinators, as implemented in Fun [2] and KappaMutor (this paper), enjoy the benefits of both fixed set SKI combinators *and* user-defined supercombinators, because they evaluate supercombinator-like structures, while retaining much of the runtime simplicity and self-optimisation properties of fixed set combinators.

The abstract G-machine [11] showed how to specialise user functions by compiling supercombinators to instructions for ISA-based processors, both special-purpose architectures (e.g., GRIP [16] and PilGRIM [7]), and general purpose CPUs (e.g., GHC). Each top-level function is compiled to a sequence of G-machine instructions. Although the G-machine began to move the research community's focus from hardware to compilers, Augustsson proposed the Big Word Machine (BWM) [4] architecture during this shift. Augustsson identified memory bandwidth as the primary bottleneck in graph reduction and proposed the BWM to leverage wider memory capabilities. However, due to the technical challenges of hardware implementation at the time, the BWM remained a design and was never physically realised. Recent hardware designs are influenced by the large memory words of the BWM and have been made possible by the growth in hardware capacity. Namely Reduceron, Heron and KappaMutor take advantage of the wide and parallel memory available on FPGAs by adopting an *application-based* memory layout, which eliminates the performance overheads of slow graph traversal incurred by atom-based layouts. It is worth noting however, that when energy efficiency—rather than raw performance—is the primary goal, the atom-based memory layout remains a compelling choice [17] given the energy cost of memory use.

Multiple recent projects (Reduceron, Heron, Cephalopode, PilGRIM, Fun, and KappaMutor) share the same overarching goal of moving runtime systems from software to hardware, to improve the efficiency and performance of functional languages. This renewed research interest in hardware-based graph reduction suggests that (functional) hardware description languages and digital prototyping platforms are now strong enough to re-explore the design space of specialised architectures in pursuit of dedicated functional programming chips.

7 Conclusion

This paper extends the application of structured combinators in specialised processor design for functional languages. KappaMutor, an efficient graph reduction processor is presented. Its parallel memories allow single-cycle reduction of structured combinators. Implementation results on an Alveo U280 UltraScale+ FPGA shows the design's compactness, with less than 1% logical resources utilisation. The accompanying compiler of KappaMutor supports Haskell 2010 as input language. New code generation schemes for structured combinators are implemented, aiming to minimise combinator usage and achieve full laziness. Future work will explore multi-core architectural designs and the integration of garbage collection. Our recent work [19] gives us confidence that the latency of hardware-based concurrent collection on modern FPGAs can be almost entirely hidden. The implementation of KappaMutor is open-source, as are the compiler and benchmark programs. An open access archive of these, and the datasets presented in this paper, is available at [24].

Acknowledgments. This work is supported by the HAFLANG project, funded by the Engineering and Physical Sciences Research Council (EP/W009447/1). We thank Cecil Accetti for discussions on structured combinators, Lennart Augustsson for identifying the full laziness issue in an earlier draft of this paper, and Phil Trinder for all the feedback on our draft.

References

1. Accetti, C., Liu, P.: Architectural support for functional programming. In: 30th IFIP/IEEE 30th International Conference on Very Large Scale Integration, VLSI-SoC 2022, Patras, Greece, October 3-5, 2022, pp. 1–2. IEEE (2022). https://doi.org/10.1109/VLSI-SOC54400.2022.9939644
2. Accetti, C., Ying, R., Liu, P.: Structured combinators for efficient graph reduction. IEEE Comput. Archit. Lett. **21**(2), 73–76 (2022). https://doi.org/10.1109/LCA.2022.3198844
3. AMD: Alveo U280 data center accelerator card data sheet (ds963) (2023). https://docs.amd.com/r/en-US/ds963-u280
4. Augustsson, L.: BWM: a concrete machine for graph reduction. In: Heldal, R., Holst, C.K., Wadler, P. (eds.) Functional Programming, Glasgow 1991, Proceedings of the 1991 Glasgow Workshop on Functional Programming, Portree, Isle of Skye, UK, 12-14 August 1991, pp. 36–50. Workshops in Computing, Springer (1991). https://doi.org/10.1007/978-1-4471-3196-0_3

5. Augustsson, L.: MicroHs: a small compiler for haskell. In: Vazou, N., Morris, J.G. (eds.) Proceedings of the 17th ACM SIGPLAN International Haskell Symposium, Haskell 2024, Milan, Italy, September 6-7, 2024, pp. 120–124. ACM (2024). https://doi.org/10.1145/3677999.3678280
6. Bachrach, J., et al.: Chisel: constructing hardware in a Scala embedded language. In: Groeneveld, P., Sciuto, D., Hassoun, S. (eds.) The 49th Annual Design Automation Conference 2012, DAC '12, San Francisco, CA, USA, June 3-7, 2012, pp. 1216–1225. ACM (2012). https://doi.org/10.1145/2228360.2228584
7. Boeijink, A., Hölzenspies, P.K.F., Kuper, J.: Introducing the PilGRIM: A Processor for Executing Lazy Functional Languages. In: Hage, J., Morazán, M.T. (eds.) Implementation and Application of Functional Languages - 22nd International Symposium, IFL 2010, Alphen aan den Rijn, The Netherlands, September 1-3, 2010, Revised Selected Papers. Lecture Notes in Computer Science, vol. 6647, pp. 54–71. Springer (2010). https://doi.org/10.1007/978-3-642-24276-2_4
8. Clarke, T.J.W., Gladstone, P., MacLean, C., Norman, A.C.: SKIM - The S, K, I Reduction Machine. In: Proceedings of the 1980 LISP Conference, Stanford, California, USA, August 25-27, 1980, pp. 128–135. ACM (1980). https://doi.org/10.1145/800087.802798
9. Fairbairn, J., Wray, S.: TIM: A simple, lazy abstract machine to execute supercombinatorics. In: Kahn, G. (ed.) Functional Programming Languages and Computer Architecture, Portland, Oregon, USA, September 14-16, 1987, Proceedings. Lecture Notes in Computer Science, vol. 274, pp. 34–45. Springer (1987). https://doi.org/10.1007/3-540-18317-5_3
10. Hughes, R.J.M.: Super-Combinators: a new implementation method for applicative languages. In: Park, D.M.R., Friedman, D.P., Wise, D.S., Jr., G.L.S. (eds.) Proceedings of the 1982 ACM Symposium on LISP and Functional Programming, LFP 1980, Pittsburgh, PA, USA, August 15-18, 1982, pp. 1–10. ACM (1982). https://doi.org/10.1145/800068.802129
11. Johnsson, T.: Efficient compilation of lazy evaluation. In: Deusen, M.S.V., Graham, S.L. (eds.) Proceedings of the 1984 SIGPLAN Symposium on Compiler Construction, Montreal, Canada, June 17-22, 1984, pp. 58–69. ACM (1984). https://doi.org/10.1145/502874.502880
12. Loidl, H.W., Hammond, K.: GRAPHing the future. In: International Workshop on the Implementation of Functional Languages. Norwich, England (1994)
13. Marlow, S.: Haskell 2010 Language Report (2010). https://www.haskell.org/onlinereport/haskell2010/
14. Naylor, M., Runciman, C.: The reduceron reconfigured and re-evaluated. J. Funct. Program. **22**(4–5), 574–613 (2012). https://doi.org/10.1017/S0956796812000214
15. Peyton Jones, S.L.: The Implementation of Functional Programming Languages. Prentice-Hall (1987)
16. Peyton Jones, S.L., Clack, C.D., Salkild, J., Hardie, M.: GRIP - A high-performance architecture for parallel graph reduction. In: Kahn, G. (ed.) Functional Programming Languages and Computer Architecture, Portland, Oregon, USA, September 14-16, 1987, Proceedings. Lecture Notes in Computer Science, vol. 274, pp. 98–112. Springer (1987). https://doi.org/10.1007/3-540-18317-5_7
17. Pope, J., Seger, C.H., Valter, H.: Higher-order hardware: implementation and evaluation of the Cephalopode Graph Reduction Processor. In: 22nd ACM-IEEE International Symposium on Formal Methods and Models for System Design, MEMOCODE 2024, Raleigh, NC, USA, October 3-4, 2024, pp. 87–97. IEEE (2024). https://doi.org/10.1109/MEMOCODE63347.2024.00015

18. Ramsay, C., Stewart, R.J.: Heron: modern hardware graph reduction. In: The 35th Symposium on Implementation and Application of Functional Languages, IFL 2023, Braga, Portugal, August 29-31, 2023, pp. 3:1–3:12. ACM (2023). https://doi.org/10.1145/3652561.3652564
19. Ramsay, C., Stewart, R.J.: Cloaca: a concurrent hardware garbage collector for non-strict functional languages. In: Vazou, N., Morris, J.G. (eds.) Proceedings of the 17th ACM SIGPLAN International Haskell Symposium, Haskell 2024, Milan, September 6-7, 2024, pp. 41–54. ACM (2024). https://doi.org/10.1145/3677999.3678277
20. Scheevel, M.: NORMA: a graph reduction processor. In: Scherlis, W.L., Williams, J.H., Gabriel, R.P. (eds.) Proceedings of the 1986 ACM Conference on LISP and Functional Programming, LFP 1986, Cambridge, Massachusetts, August 4-6, 1986, pp. 212–219. ACM (1986). https://doi.org/10.1145/319838.319864
21. Schönfinkel, M.: Über die Bausteine der mathematischen Logik. Mathematische Annalen **92**, 305–316 (1924). http://eudml.org/doc/159074
22. Turner, D.A.: A new implementation technique for applicative languages. Softw. Pract. Exp. **9**(1), 31–49 (1979). https://doi.org/10.1002/SPE.4380090105
23. Watson, P., Watson, I.: Evaluating functional programs on the FLAGSHIP machine. In: Kahn, G. (ed.) Functional Programming Languages and Computer Architecture, Portland, Oregon, USA, September 14-16, 1987, Proceedings. Lecture Notes in Computer Science, vol. 274, pp. 80–97. Springer (1987). https://doi.org/10.1007/3-540-18317-5_6
24. Xie, Y., Ramsay, C., Stewart, R.J., Loidl, H.W.: Dataset and source code archive for TFP 2025 paper: from Haskell to a new structured combinator processor (2025) . https://doi.org/10.17861/aa1d9f11-cdc9-406d-8ac8-d05719e7d955

Self-aware Program Analysis in stableKanren

Xiangyu Guo(✉) and Ajay Bansal

Arizona State University, Tempe, AZ 85281, USA
{Xiangyu.Guo,Ajay.Bansal}@asu.edu

Abstract. This paper presents two improvements to the compatibility and performance of stableKanren on monotonic programs. miniKanren supports monotonic reasoning, in which one program produces exactly one model. stableKanren extends miniKanren to nonmonotonic reasoning, where a program can have zero to multiple models. stableKanren handles loops and negations, the main elements of nonmonotonic reasoning, through an extended nonmonotonic resolution in its "run" interface. The current nonmonotonic resolution in the stableKanren also applies to monotonic programs and creates two issues. Firstly, a monotonic program with infinite answers could not produce an answer under stableKanren. Secondly, a monotonic program runs slower under stableKanren due to the additional nonmonotonic resolution. The nonmonotonic resolution is unnecessary for these monotonic programs. We construct a "run-partial" interface in stableKanren without nonmonotonic resolution. Using "run-partial" resolves the above two issues; however, expert knowledge is required to identify whether the program is monotonic or nonmonotonic and to choose the corresponding interface by the users. We further introduce two program analyses to the stableKanren "run" interface to identify the monotonic program implicitly. We use a macro to handle the first issue at the syntax level, so the "run" interface does not apply nonmonotonic resolution on monotonic programs without any negations. Furthermore, we present four syntax-level macros to construct two smaller twins of the input program. Each twin has different semantics on loops over negations, so we resolve the second issue by running these two twins. The twins of the monotonic programs produce identical outcomes, but the nonmonotonic programs do not. Our updated "run" interface can identify monotonic programs at the syntax level; there is still more work to identify such programs during execution.

Keywords: logic programming · miniKanren · stableKanren · macros

1 Introduction

Friedman et al. build miniKanren to show a natural way to extend functional programming to relational programming [2]. The core miniKanren implementation introduces only a few operators to users: == for *unification*, *fresh* for *existential quantification*, *conde* for *disjunction*, and a *run* interface for executing the query.

The reasoning capability provided by miniKanren is monotonic reasoning. Therefore, miniKanren programs always have and only have one model. To support nonmonotonic reasoning, Guo et al. extend miniKanren to stableKanren

J. Gibbons (Ed.): TFP 2025, LNCS 15652, pp. 165–181, 2026.
https://doi.org/10.1007/978-3-031-99751-8_8

[3], stableKanren adds two more operators *noto* for *negation* and *defineo* for *goal function* definition. In contrast to the programs under monotonic reasoning, nonmonotonic reasoning programs can have zero to multiple models. For example, the following stableKanren program has no model because of its contradiction.

Listing 1.1. A contradiction program in stableKanren

```
(defineo (cut_hair) (noto (cut_hair)))
```

The program defines one simple goal function *cut_hair*. To make such a goal succeed, the body of the goal function requires *cut_hair* to fail, which is a contradiction. It is impossible to make *cut_hair* succeed and fail simultaneously, so there is no model for such a program.

The missing *optimal substructure property* in nonmonotonic reasoning means the partial result obtained during the resolution may not be part of the final result. In stableKanren, the nonmonotonic resolution in the *run* interface continues to check other goal functions using the partial result to ensure nonmonotonicity [3]. However, this nonmonotonic resolution is unnecessary for monotonic programs and creates two issues.

We present these issues in detail in Sect. 3. Firstly, monotonic programs with infinite answers could not produce an answer under stableKanren (Listing 1.6). Secondly, monotonic programs run slower under stableKanren (Listing 1.7). We introduce *run-partial* to bypass the nonmonotonic resolution for monotonic programs. The *run-partial* interface resolves the issues but requires expert knowledge to identify the monotonic programs to choose the corresponding interface. We want the *run* interface in stableKanren to detect monotonic programs automatically and decide to check nonmonotonicity implicitly.

This paper adds two program syntax analyses to stableKanren to identify monotonic programs. In Sect. 2.1, we show that the input programs can be categorized as definite programs (Definition 2), stratified programs (Definition 6), and normal programs (Definition 4). The definite programs and the stratified programs are monotonic; hence, there is no need for nonmonotonic resolution. We focus on the syntax elements in stableKanren when creating syntax analysis macros. The definite programs have no negation (*noto*) in them. In Sect. 4.1, we design a new macro *has-negation?* (Listing 1.8) to distinguish definite programs. The stratified programs have negations, but the negations do not show up in the loop (Definition 5). In Sect. 4.2, we construct smaller executable twins (Listing 1.10, 1.11, 1.12, 1.13) from the input program to analyze the relationship between negations and loops. We run the executable twins internally and compare the outcomes in $O(N * E)$ time complexity, where N is the number of nodes, and E is the number of edges in the input program's dependency graph. The twins of the monotonic programs produce identical outcomes, but the twins of the nonmonotonic programs do not. As a result, we can identify stratified programs. In Sect. 4.3, we show that the updated *run* interface can identify monotonic programs to avoid nonmonotonic resolution. In Sect. 5, we propose future work to identify monotonicity during execution.

2 Preliminaries

In this section, we review a few definitions, including definite programs (Definition 2), normal programs (Definition 4), and stratified programs (Definition 6). Then, we show a high-level overview of miniKanren, its nonmonotonic extension stableKanren, and nonmonotonic resolution in stableKanren. Lastly, we present the issues in stableKanren's nonmonotonic resolution on monotonic programs.

2.1 Normal Programs

Lloyd defines *definite program* and *normal program* as follows [5].

Definition 1 (definite program clause). *A definite program clause is a clause of the form,*

$$A \leftarrow B_1, \cdots, B_n$$

where $A, B_1, \ldots, B_n$ *are atoms*[1].

A definite program clause contains precisely *one atom* A in its consequent. A is called the *head* and $B_1, \ldots, B_n$ is called the *body* of the program clause.

Definition 2 (definite program). *A definite program is a finite set of definite program clauses.*

Based on the definition of the definite program clause, we have the definition of *normal program clause* and *normal program*.

Definition 3 (normal program clause). *A normal program clause is a clause of the form,*

$$A \leftarrow B_1, \cdots, B_n, not\ B_{n+1}, \cdots, not\ B_m$$

For a normal program clause, the body of a program clause is a conjunction of literals instead of atoms; $B_1, \cdots, B_n$ are *positive literals* and $not\ B_{n+1}, \cdots, not\ B_m$ are *negative literals*[2].

Definition 4 (normal program). *A normal program is a finite set of normal program clauses.*

According to Gelder et al., there are sets of atoms named *unfounded sets* in a normal program that can help us categorize the normal programs [7].

Definition 5 (unfounded set). *Given a normal program, the unfounded set is a set of atoms that only cyclically support each other, forming a loop.*

Considering the combinations of negations and unfounded sets (loops) in normal programs, we have informal definitions of *stratified program*.

Definition 6 (stratified program). *Given a normal program, it is stratified if all unfounded sets (loops) do not contain any negation.*

[1] Atom is evaluated to be true or false.

[2] A positive literal is just an atom, a negative literal is the negation of an atom.

2.2 miniKanren

miniKanren provides three operators: == for *unification*, *conde* for *disjunction*, and *fresh* for *existential* to encode definite programs (Definition 2) [2]. For example, in Listing 1.2, the Scheme's *null?* function turns into a relation *nullo* in miniKanren.

Listing 1.2. A "nullo" to verify if the relation between a list and an empty list hold

```
(define (nullo x) (== '() x))
```

The *nullo* relation holds when the logic variable x is successfully unified with an empty list. A relation can be evaluated and have two outcomes: success means the relation holds, or failure means the relation does not hold. To evaluate a relation like *nullo*, miniKanren uses a *run* interface to query.

```
(run 1 (q) (nullo '(42)))
(run 1 (q) (nullo '()))
```

The *run* interface takes three parameters. The first is the number of answers expected from the query. The second is a logic variable to store the answer from the query. The third is a conjunction of relations to evaluate. The output of *run* is a list of values with which the logic variable in the second parameter can be bound or unified. When the evaluation fails, the logic variable binds to nothing, *run* returns an empty list. When the evaluation succeeds, the logic variable binds to something, *run* returns a non-empty list. In the above examples, the *nullo* works as *null?*, the first query returns an empty list, and the second query returns a non-empty list.

```
(run 1 (q) (nullo '(42)))
()
(run 1 (q) (nullo '()))
(_.0)
```

The non-empty list contains one element, "_.0" representing anything that the logic variable can be bound with. Moreover, the *nullo* relation can be evaluated with an unbound variable, which *null?* can not. For example, a logic variable l introduced by *fresh* is an unbound variable, and *nullo* tries to bind a value to l.

```
(run 1 (q) (fresh (l) (nullo l)))
(_.0)
```

The query returns a non-empty list, which means l successfully binds with a value. The local variable l can be unified with q to store the result in the output.

```
(run 1 (q) (fresh (l) (nullo l) (== l q)))
(())
```

The non-empty list returned from the query indicates that *nullo* binds l to an empty list. In this case, the query can be simplified by removing the intermediate local variable l.

```
(run 1 (q) (nullo q))
```

Similarly, in Listing 1.3, the Scheme's *cons* function turns into a relation *conso* in miniKanren.

Listing 1.3. A "conso" to relate an element and two lists

```
(define (conso a d p) (== (cons a d) p))
```

A function can return anything; *null?* returns a boolean value true or false; *cons* returns a list. Conversely, a relation only returns a success (true) or failure (false). Therefore, the number of parameters is the same for *null?* and *nullo* as they both return a boolean value. However, *conso* needs a third parameter to represent the returning list in *cons*. The same *run* interface can evaluate *cons* relation through queries.

```
> (run 1 (q) (conso 'a '(b c) q))
((a b c))
> (run 1 (q) (conso 'a '(b c) '(a b d)))
()
> (run 1 (q) (conso q '(b d) '(c b d)))
(c)
```

In the first query, *conso* works as *cons*, combining a given element and a list. The last two queries show the capability of *conso* that *cons* lacks. The second query says that the relationship between an element and two lists does not hold. The third query finds that the element to satisfy the relationship is *c*. A more complicated example *revo* in Listing 1.4 uses *nullo* and *conso* to determine that two lists are reversed to each other.

Listing 1.4. A revo relation to determine two lists are reversed to each other

```
(define (revo xs sx)
  (fresh (empty)
    (nullo empty)
    (rev-acco xs empty sx)))

(define (rev-acco xs acc sx)
  (conde [(nullo xs) (== sx acc)]
         [(fresh (h t acc1)
            (conso h t xs)
            (conso h acc acc1)
            (rev-acco t acc1 sx))]))
```

A set of queries to evaluate *revo* is as follows.

```
> (run 1 (q) (revo '(1 2) '(1 2)))
()
> (run 1 (q) (revo q '(a b c d)))
((d c b a))
> (run 4 (q) (revo q q))
(() (_.0) (_.0 _.0) (_.0 _.1 _.0))
> (run* (q) (revo q q))
; Infinite loop
```

The first two queries work as a verifier and a solver, respectively, as we have seen similar queries in previous examples. The latter two queries work as producers, where all parameters passed to the relation are unbound logic variables. These logic variables are bound to the value that satisfies the relation *revo*. The relation *(revo q q)* in the third query binds the palindrome string to the logic variable *q*. The query produces four palindromes. There is an infinite number of palindromes; therefore, the fourth query tries to find all the palindromes trapped in an infinite loop.

2.3 stableKanren

stableKanren extends miniKanren to support nonmonotonic reasoning by adding two more operators: *defineo* for goal definition, *noto* for negation to encode normal programs (Definition 4) [3]. For example, Emden et al. introduce a two-person game [6]. The game is given a directed connected graph (Fig. 1), a peg on a starting node, and two players. Each player takes a turn to move the peg to the adjacency node; the winning move in this game is defined as there is a move that will make it so that the opponent has no move.

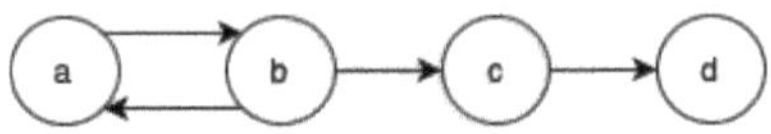

Fig. 1. A playboard in two-person game

The stableKanren program in Listing 1.5 is used to find the winning positions.

Listing 1.5. Two person game in stableKanren

```
(defineo (move x y)
  (conde [(== x 'b) (== y 'c)] [(== x 'a) (== y 'b)]
         [(== x 'b) (== y 'a)] [(== x 'c) (== y 'd)]))

(defineo (win x) (fresh (y) (move x y) (noto (win y))))
```

In this example, the variable x of *win* unifies with values representing the winning positions. A set of queries and outputs through *run* is shown below.

```
> (run 3 (q) (win q))
(c b a)
> (run 1 (q) (win 'c) (win 'a))
(_.0)
> (run 1 (q) (win 'b) (win 'a))
()
```

The first query generates possible winning positions. The second query asks "Can node c and node a both be the winning position?" It succeeds. So, a and c can both be the winning position. The last query asks: "Can node b and node a both be the winning position?" It fails. Therefore, a and b can not be the winning position simultaneously.

In miniKanren, each head in the definite program clause (Definition 1) creates a *goal function* [2]. It is sufficient to have one goal function for each head for definite programs (Definition 2), and this goal function is a *positive goal function*. However, for normal programs (Definition 4), there is a need for a *negative goal function* implicitly created internally corresponding to the *positive goal function* due to the new negation operator. In stableKanren, *defineo* creates the *negative goal function* from the *positive goal function* and wraps the two under the same name [3]. The *negation counter (n)* counts the number of negations (*noto* in stableKanren) and decides to use a positive or negative goal during resolution. The loops in normal programs (Definition 5) are also handled in *defineo*. Figure 2 gives a high-level overview of *defineo* and a set of internal macros and functions in stableKanren.

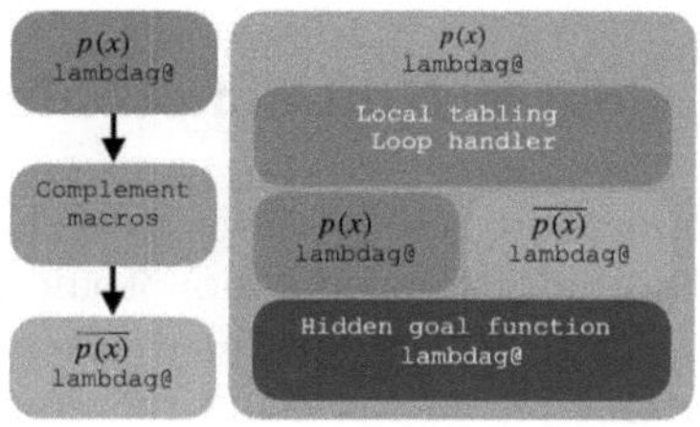

Fig. 2. A high-level overview of defineo

On the left-hand side, a positive goal function $p(x)$ is internally transformed to a negative goal function $\overline{p(x)}$. On the right-hand side, both positive and negative goal functions are wrapped inside a unique goal function along with other helpers.

A monotonic reasoning program produces exactly one model, and the partial model is guaranteed to be part of the final model since it has *optimal substructure property*. However, the partial model of a nonmonotonic reasoning program may not be the final model. It depends on how the negations and loops are formed inside the normal program (Definition 4). As Guo et al. mentioned, a normal program can lose the *optimal substructure property* if it has an odd number of negations in the loop, and the partial model cannot avoid it [3]. Therefore, the resolution in stableKanren continues to check other goal functions using the partial result to ensure nonmonotonicity. During the creation of the goal function, stableKanren collects the signature of the goal function, which can be used in nonmonotonic resolution. Figure 3 shows a high-level overview of signature collecting and the extended nonmonotonic resolution.

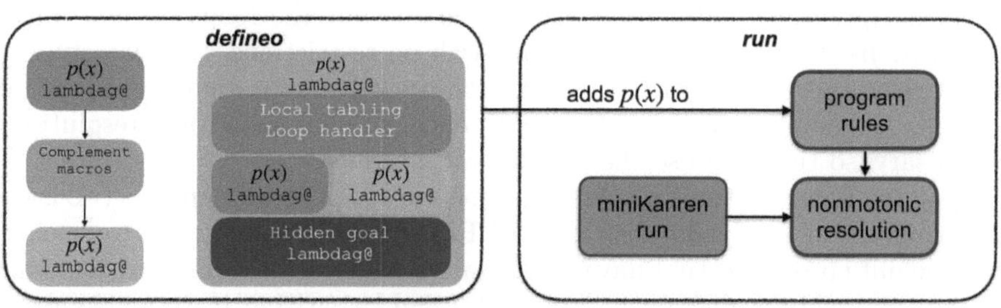

Fig. 3. Collecting signatures for extended resolution

In *defineo*, the signature of the goal function adds to a checking set (*program-rules*) for future nonmonotonicity resolution in the *run* interface. The traditional resolution in miniKanren *run* finds a partial model, and the nonmonotonic resolution added in stableKanren ensures that the partial model is also part of the final model.

3 Problems with Coarse Nonmonotonic Resolution

We notice that the nonmonotonic resolution in stableKanren is coarse, and not all normal programs require additional nonmonotonic resolution. For a special type of normal program, such as the stratified program (Definition 6), it is monotonic, and nonmonotonic resolution is not required. In particular, applying nonmonotonic resolution to monotonic programs creates two issues, which we discuss later in this section. We introduce a new interface *run-partial* without nonmonotonic resolution to run queries on monotonic programs. This *run-partial* interface temporarily resolves the issues, but it requires expert knowledge to categorize normal programs into monotonic or nonmonotonic.

Figure 4 shows the expert knowledge to categorize normal programs and the corresponding reasoning capabilities, either monotonic or nonmonotonic.

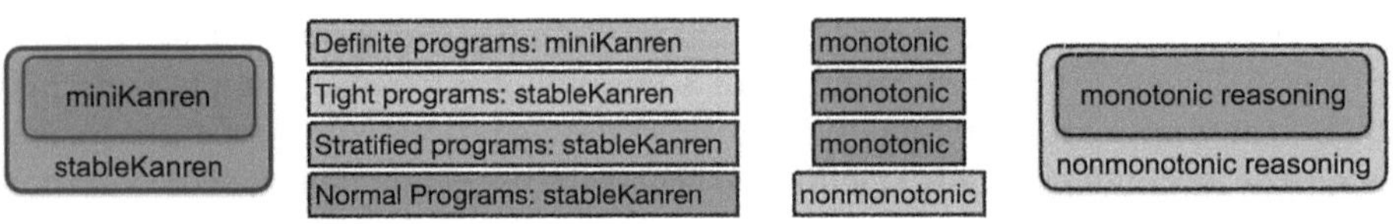

Fig. 4. Categories of normal programs and reasoning capabilities

The definite programs (Definition 2) are supported by miniKanren and stableKanren. Normal programs are categorized according to combinations of negations and loops (Definition 5). Firstly, tight programs are normal programs that have negations but without loops. Secondly, stratified programs (Definition 6) are normal programs with negations and loops, but the loops do not contain any negations. Lastly, normal programs with no restrictions. All three types of normal programs are supported by stableKanren. Definite, tight, and stratified programs are monotonic reasoning, and hence, the nonmonotonic resolution is unnecessary, so they can use the *run-partial* interface.

Applying nonmonotonic resolution to monotonic programs creates two issues, which can also be resolved by *run-partial.* Firstly, applying nonmonotonic checking on definite programs that have infinite answers does not terminate. For example, the *revo* relation defined in Listing 1.4 can be written in stableKanren by replacing *define* with *defineo* in Listing 1.6.

Listing 1.6. A revo relation to determine two lists are reversed to each other

```
(defineo (revo xs sx)
  (fresh (empty) (nullo empty) (rev-acco xs empty sx)))
```

```
(defineo (rev-acco xs acc sx)
  (conde [(nullo xs) (== sx acc)]
         [(fresh (h t acc1)
            (conso h t xs)
            (conso h acc acc1)
            (rev-acco t acc1 sx))]))
```

A simple query using *run* on the two empty lists does not terminate.

```
> (run 1 (q) (revo '() '()))
; infinite loop
```

The same query using *run-partial* can produce the answer.

```
> (run-partial 1 (q) (revo '() '()))
(_.0)
```

Secondly, applying nonmonotonic resolution to stratified programs slows the running speed. For example, consider the strongly connected components (SCCs) in Fig. 5.

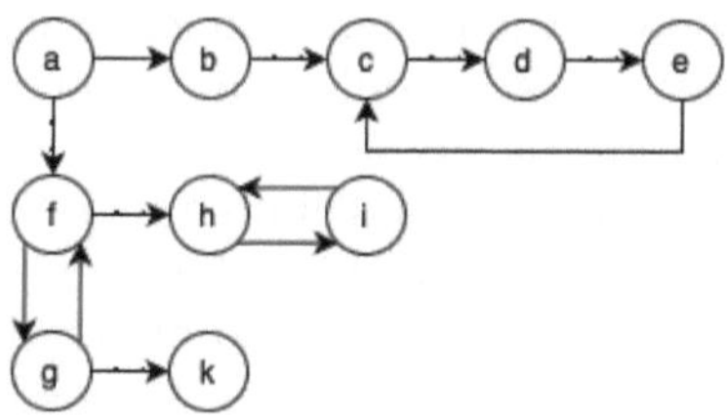

Fig. 5. A directed graph that contains multiple SCCs

We will call an SCC a *final SCC* if the only nodes reachable from nodes in that SCC are others in that SCC [8]. Given a node, we want to find all the nodes that can be reached from that node in the final SCCs. The solution in stableKanren is as follows.

Listing 1.7. An encoding of final-SCC problem in stableKanren

```
(defineo (edge x y)
  (conde [(== x 'a) (== y 'b)] [(== x 'b) (== y 'c)]
         [(== x 'c) (== y 'd)] [(== x 'd) (== y 'e)]
         [(== x 'e) (== y 'c)] [(== x 'a) (== y 'f)]
         [(== x 'f) (== y 'h)] [(== x 'f) (== y 'g)]
         [(== x 'g) (== y 'f)] [(== x 'g) (== y 'k)]
         [(== x 'h) (== y 'i)] [(== x 'i) (== y 'h)]))

(defineo (reachable x y)
  (conde [(edge x y)]
         [(fresh (z) (edge x z) (reachable z y))]))

(defineo (reducible x)
  (fresh (y) (reachable x y) (noto (reachable y x))))

(defineo (fullyReduce x y)
  (reachable x y) (noto (reducible y)))
```

Running a query on *fullyReduce* will produce all final SCC pairs for us.

```
> (time (length (run* (q) (fresh (x y)
                          (fullyReduce x y) (== q `(,x ,y))))))
100
```

Getting 100 final SCC pairs takes 32.81 s using the *run* interface. The same query using the *run-partial* only takes 0.01 s.

Although the *run-partial* interface resolves these two issues, it requires expert knowledge to identify whether a program is monotonic. The user has to make the right decision on which interface to run the query. We want to incorporate expert knowledge into the *run* interface so that it can implicitly identify monotonic programs and decide to avoid nonmonotonic resolution.

4 Identify Monotonic Programs in stableKanren

Identifying monotonic programs is decidable and has polynomial-time algorithms. The key idea is to identify negations and loops in stableKanren programs. The syntax of stableKanren consists of only four elements: *fresh*, *conde*, *noto*, *goal functions*. Identifying negations is simple; a syntax analysis using a macro can achieve this. A stableKanren clause is a definite program clause (Definition 1) as long as there is no negation (*noto*) in it. Identifying loops requires more analysis of the relation between goal functions. Instead of creating a dependency graph representation for the input program and then having a stand-alone algorithm to analyze the graph, we use four macros to construct smaller executable twins (Listing 1.10, 1.12, 1.13) from the input program. These smaller twins are variants of stableKanren programs with different semantics on loops over negations. Therefore, we can run the twins internally and compare the outcomes. The twins of the monotonic programs produce identical outcomes, but the nonmonotonic programs do not.

4.1 No Negation, No Problem

The stableKanren programs without using any *noto* (negation) operator, like the one we see in Listing 1.6, are definite programs (Definition 2). This section introduces a compilation time syntax analysis macro *has-negation?* to identify definite programs.

Listing 1.8. A syntax analysis to identify negation in the program

```
(define-syntax has-negation?
  (syntax-rules (noto conde fresh)
    ((_ (noto g)) #t)
    ((_ (conde (g0 g ...) (g1 g^ ...) ...))
        (or (has-negation? g0 g ...)
            (has-negation? g1 g^ ...)
            ...))
    ((_ (fresh (x ...) g0 g ...))
        (has-negation? g0 g ...))
```

```
((_ g) #f)
((_ g0 g1 ...)
   (or (has-negation? g0)
       (has-negation? g1)
       ...))))
```

The syntax of stableKanren consists of only four elements: *fresh*, *conde*, *noto*, *goal functions*. So, a macro needs to consider all the syntax elements. The *has-negation?* focuses on whether the program contains negation (*noto*). It iterates through nested *conde*, *fresh*, and conjunction until it reaches the goal function level. If there is a negative goal function, it returns true, and vice versa. We apply this syntax analysis to improve the *defineo* macro. Figure 6 shows the updated process for collecting signatures.

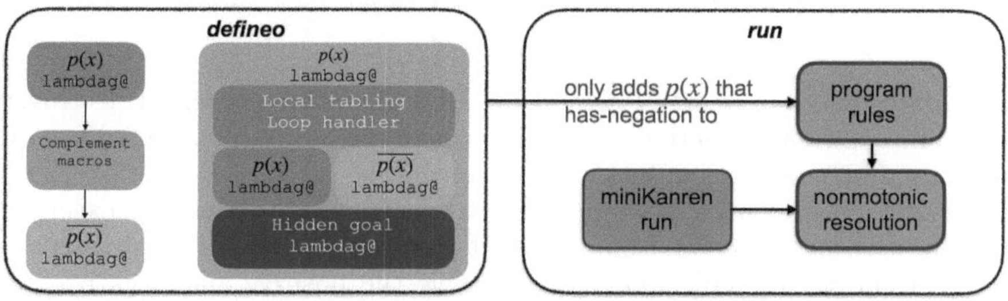

Fig. 6. Updated signature collecting process

In the improved *defineo*, only a goal function with negation will be added to the *program rules* set for nonmonotonic resolution. The nonmonotonic resolution can be avoided if the negations are stratified. We will handle the stratified negations in the next section.

4.2 Positive and Negative Twins

Identifying stratified negations requires more analysis of the relationship between goal functions. A loop can be a self-loop involving only one goal function. A loop can also contain more than one goal function. Traditionally, a logic programming solver creates a dependency graph for such a purpose [1]. To create a dependency graph, each goal function represents a node, and each invocation from the head goal function to the body function represents a directed edge. The edge is positive if there is no negation (*noto*), and vice versa. For example, Fig. 7 shows the dependency graph of the final SCC program in Listing 1.7.

There are two negations in the program: one from *fullyReduce* to *reducible* and the other from *reducible* to *reachable*. So, the dependency graph has two negative edges, respectively. The dependency graph also shows a self-loop formed by *reachable*, and this loop does not contain any negation. Therefore, the final SCC program is stratified. This non-functional approach is to create a dependency

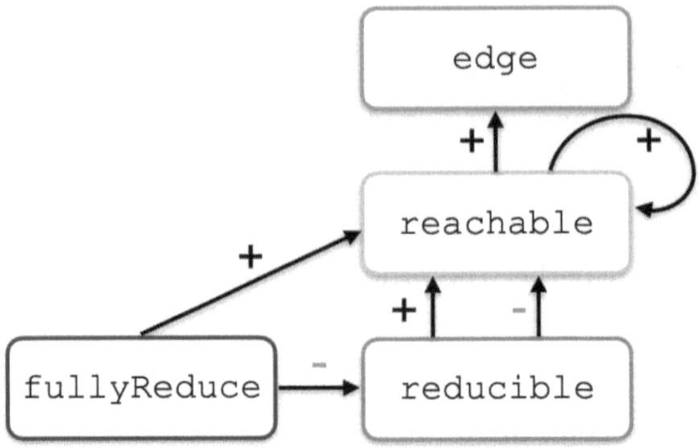

Fig. 7. Dependency graph of the final SCC program

graph (data) and have a stand-alone DFS/BFS algorithm (program) to traverse the graph. We want a functional approach where the graph constructed from the input program is self-executable.

This section presents a new approach to constructing two smaller executable twins, positive and negative, from the input program. We reuse the infrastructure in stableKanren to handle loops, but we give the positive and negative twins different semantics. So, we identify stratified programs by running positive and negative twins and comparing the results.

The smaller twins are created from the user input with the suffix + or −. For example, Listing 1.9 shows the negative twin of the final SCC program in Listing 1.7.

Listing 1.9. A negative twin of the final SCC program

```
(define (edge-)
  succeed)

(define (reachable-)
  (conde [(edge-)]
         [(fresh ()
            (edge-) (reachable-))]))

(define (reducible-)
  (fresh ()
    (reachable-) (noto (reachable-))))

(define (fullyReduce-)
  (reachable-) (noto (reducible-)))
```

A smaller twin only captures the dependency between the goals, so it has no variables in the program. For any unification (==) in the program, it is a special goal function (base case goal function) and is replaced by *succeed*. The positive twin is in the same structure, but replace the suffix − with +. This code snippet only captures the negations (*noto*) operator and the loops in the syntax; the semantics of handling these loops will be added later.

Macro *negative-twin* in Listing 1.10 shows how to create the body of a negative twin.

Listing 1.10. Macro to transform the input program to a negative twin

```
(define-syntax negative-twin
  (syntax-rules (conde fresh noto == succeed fail)
    ((_ (conde [(== a ...) ...] [(== b ...) ...] ...))
        succeed)
    ((_ (fresh (x ...) g g0 ...))
        (fresh () (negative-twin g) (negative-twin g0) ...))
    ((_ (conde [g g0 ...] [g1 g^ ...] ...))
        (conde
          [(negative-twin g) (negative-twin g0) ...]
          [(negative-twin g1) (negative-twin g^) ...] ...))
    ((_ (noto g))
        (noto (negative-twin g)))
    ((_ (== u v))
        succeed)
    ((_ succeed) succeed)
    ((_ fail) fail)
    ((_ (p ...))
        (eval `(,(sym-append-str (car `(p ...)) ``-''))))
    ((_ g g0 ...)
        (fresh ()
          (negative-twin g) (negative-twin g0) ...))))
```

The *negative-twin* iterates through nested *conde*, *fresh*, and conjunction until it reaches the goal function level. Then, it appends a − to each goal function. It also removes any variables introduced in the goal function or *fresh*. Therefore, all unifications (== operators) are converted to *succeed*. The *positive-twin* does the same transformation, except that it appends a + to each goal function.

The *negative-twin* and *positive-twin* construct the body of the twins. Macro *define-negative-twin* in Listing 1.11 shows how to define a negative twin.

Listing 1.11. Macro to create an executable negative twin

```
(define-syntax define-negative-twin
(syntax-rules ()
((_ name exp ...)
  (eval
    `(define (,(sym-append-str 'name ``-''))
        (negative-twin exp ...))))))
```

The *name* and *exp*... are the input goal function definition. To create a smaller negative twin, *define-negative-twin* appends a − after the *name*, and *negative-twin* transforms the *exp*.... So, *define-negative-twin* and *negative-twin* take an input program in Listing 1.7, create a negative twin as shown in Listing 1.9. The *define-positive-twin* does the same transformation, except that it appends a + to each goal function.

We wrap *define-negative-twin* and *define-positive-twin* with loop handling under different semantics. Listing 1.12 shows the semantics for loops under negative twin.

Listing 1.12. Macro to create an executable negative twin

```
1  (define-syntax define-negative-twin
2  (syntax-rules ()
3  ((_ name exp ...)
4    (eval
5      ‘(define (,(sym-append-str ‘name ‘‘-’’))
6         (lambdag@ (n cfs c : S P L)
7         (let* ([name- (sym-append-str ‘name ‘‘-’’)]
8                [signature (list name- ‘())]
9                [result (element-of-set? signature P)]
10               [record (element-of-set? signature cfs)])
11          (if (or (and result #t) (and record #t))
12            (unit c)
13            ((fresh ()
14               (negative-twin exp ...) (ext-p name- ‘()))
15              n (expand-cfs signature n cfs) c)))))))))
```

The local tabling and loop handling are infrastructures in stableKanren (lines 6 to 10, 13 to 15). Local tabulation is recorded on P and extended by *ext-p*, and the loop is tracked on *cfs* and updated by *expand-cfs*. If a loop is detected during runtime, *record* will be the loop point. Using the value stored in *record* and the current value, stableKanren is able to distinguish the positive loop, a loop without negation, and the negative loop, a loop with negations. The semantics is for the goal function to decide what to do when it encounters a loop. The semantics for *define-negative-twin* is that it always succeeds on any loops. Therefore, it always returns success, represented as *(unit c)* in stableKanren, in lines 12.

Similarly, Listing 1.13 shows the semantics for loops under positive twin.

Listing 1.13. Macro to create an executable positive twin

```
(define-syntax define-positive-twin
(syntax-rules ()
((_ name exp ...)
  (eval
    ‘(define (,(sym-append-str ‘name ‘‘+’’))
       (lambdag@ (n cfs c : S P L)
       (let* ([name+ (sym-append-str ‘name ‘‘+’’)]
              [signature (list name+ ‘())]
              [result (element-of-set? signature P)]
              [record (element-of-set? signature cfs)])
        (if (and result #t)
          (unit c)
          (if (and record #t)
            (let ([diff (- n (get-value record))])
              (if (= 0 diff)
                ; Positive loop (stratified negation)
                (unit c)
                ; Negative loop (normal program)
                (mzero)))
            ((fresh ()
                (positive-twin exp ...) (ext-p name+ ‘()))
              n (expand-cfs signature n cfs) c))))))))))
```

It also reuses the loop handling infrastructures in stableKanren (lines 6 to 10, 20 to 22). The only semantics difference between *define-negative-twin* and *define-positive-twin* is that the *define-positive-twin* terminates on the negative loops; therefore, it returns fails, represented as *(mzero)* in stableKanren, in line 19.

Both *define-negative-twin* and *define-positive-twin* are created in *defineo* as shown in Fig. 8.

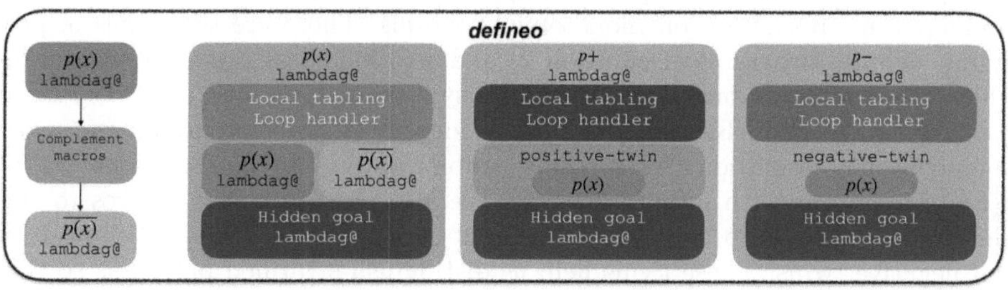

Fig. 8. A high-level overview of positive and negative twins in defineo

In addition to implicitly creating a negative goal and combining the positive and negative goals into one, the extended *defineo* creates positive and negative twins from the user input during compilation.

To identify stratified programs, we create a function *stratified?* and run the twins internally using *run-partial* and compare the results. The time complexity for running the twins is $O(N * E)$, where N is the number of nodes, and E is the number of edges in the input program's dependency graph. The semantics between the positive twin and the negative twin are slightly different. Therefore, the twins of the monotonic programs produce identical outcomes, but the nonmonotonic programs do not.

4.3 Enhanced Run

This section uses our improvements to make the *run* interface automatically identify monotonic programs. The enhanced *run* is as follows:

```
(define-syntax run
  (syntax-rules ()
    ((_ n (x) g0 g ...)
     (take n
       (lambdaf@ ()
         ((fresh (x) g0 g ...
          (lambdag@ (negation-counter cfs c : S P L)
            (if (and (not (stratified?))
                     (null? (nonmonotonic-resolution)))
              (mzero)
              (cons (reify x S) '()))))
          negation-counter call-frame-stack empty-c))))))
```

It uses *stratified?* to avoid nonmonotonic resolution on monotonic programs. As a result, using our updated *defineo* and *run*, the query on Listing 1.6 can produce an answer, and the query on Listing 1.7 produces 100 pairs of final SCCs in 0.03 s.

5 Conclusion and Future Work

This paper presents two improvements to stableKanren, so it will not apply nonmonotonic resolution on monotonic programs. There are two types of programs, definite programs (Definition 2) and stratified programs (Definition 6), which are monotonic programs. We add a syntax analysis macro *has-negation?* (Listing 1.8) to stableKanren's *defineo* to identify definite programs and avoid nonmonotonic resolution. As a result, stableKanren can produce answers for definite programs with infinite answers. We also introduce four macros to stableKanren's *defineo* to transform the input program into two smaller positive and negative twins. These twins help us distinguish stratified programs so that stableKanren saves running time by avoiding nonmonotonic resolution.

For future work, the nonmonotonic resolution can be bypassed when a normal program behaves like a stratified program during execution time. For example, from the syntax perspective, the two-person game in Listing 1.5 is a normal program since the negation appears in the loop. If a playboard is a cyclic graph like Fig. 1, it requires nonmonotonic resolution. However, if the playboard is a directed acyclic graph (DAG), which turns the negation in the normal program in Listing 1.5 into a stratified negation, the nonmonotonic resolution should be bypassed. Currently, our smaller twins cannot capture this execution time behavior, as the variables are discarded during the twin creation. Another issue is when a contradiction in Listing 1.1 coexists with other programs in the same environment, and the *run* interface cannot produce an answer even if the query did not touch the contradiction part. We can still use *run-partial* to produce the answers, but ideally, we want to improve *run* to isolate the contradiction implicitly. Lastly, our twin construction is heavily based on the Scheme macro, which is not provided in many other functional languages. Hemann et al. show a macro-free microKanren [4] that enables the implementation of miniKanren in functional languages without macros. Constructing twins without using macros will allow the porting of our work to other languages.

References

1. Apt, K.R., Blair, H.A., Walker, A.: Towards a Theory of Declarative Knowledge, pp. 89–148. Morgan Kaufmann Publishers Inc., San Francisco, CA, USA (1988). https://dl.acm.org/doi/10.5555/61352.61354
2. Friedman, D.P., Byrd, W.E., Kiselyov, O.: The Reasoned Schemer. The MIT Press, MIT Press (2005). https://doi.org/10.7551/mitpress/5801.001.0001
3. Guo, X., Smith, J., Bansal, A.: StableKanren: integrating stable model semantics with miniKanren. In: Proceedings of the 25th International Symposium on Principles and Practice of Declarative Programming. PPDP '23, Association for Computing Machinery, New York (2023). https://doi.org/10.1145/3610612.3610617

4. Hemann, J., Friedman, D.P.: Nearly macro-free MicroKanren. In: Trends in Functional Programming: 24th International Symposium, TFP 2023, Boston, MA, USA, January 13–15, 2023, Revised Selected Papers, pp. 72–91. Springer-Verlag, Berlin, Heidelberg (2023). https://doi.org/10.1007/978-3-031-38938-2_5
5. Lloyd, J.W.: Foundations of Logic Programming, 2nd Edn. Springer (1987). https://doi.org/10.1007/978-3-642-83189-8
6. Van Emden, M.H., Clark, K.L.: The Logic of Two-Person Games, chap. 12, pp. 320–340. Prentice-Hall, Inc., USA (1984)
7. Van Gelder, A., Ross, K.A., Schlipf, J.S.: The well-founded semantics for general logic programs. J. ACM **38**(3), 619–649 (1991). https://doi.org/10.1145/116825.116838
8. Warren, D.S.: Programming in tabled prolog (very) draft. Unfinished book on XSB programming (1999). https://www.swi-prolog.org/download/publications/tabling-book.pdf

Semantics

Reconstructing Continuation-Passing Semantics for WebAssembly

Guannan Wei[1,2(✉)], Alexander Y. Bai[2,3], Dinghong Zhong[4], and Jiatai Zhang[2]

[1] INRIA/ENS-PSL, Paris, France
guannan.wei@inria.fr
[2] Tufts University, Medford, USA
alexander.bai@tufts.edu , jiatai.zhang@tufts.edu
[3] MPI-SWS, Saarbrücken, Germany
[4] Paris, France

Abstract. WebAssembly is a popular low-level intermediate representation (IR) and compilation target. The official specification of WebAssembly provides a small-step reduction semantics. Unlike other common low-level IRs, WebAssembly provides structured control-flow constructs, whose reduction rules are complicated by additional administrative instructions in the reference semantics. This paper develops an alternative semantics in continuation-passing style (CPS), which can be implemented as a concise, compositional, and tail-recursive interpreter or CPS transformer. Using continuations from the meta-language eliminates the need for administrative instructions. We further demonstrate that the CPS semantics can be extended to support other forms of control abstractions, such as effect handlers.

Keywords: WebAssembly · Continuation-passing style · Big-step semantics

1 Introduction

Motivation. WebAssembly (Wasm) is a low-level intermediate representation aiming to be portable, compact, and efficient for the web. Unlike similar languages (e.g. LLVM's IR), Wasm provides structured control-flow constructs whose behaviors are regulated by a static type system. Another notable advancement with Wasm is that its semantics has been formally specified [13] from the outset and has evolved [34] in tandem with the language development.

The co-developed formal specification facilitates not only the development of language tools, but also the design and prototyping of new extensions for Wasm. For example, there are a number of proposals for adding richer control abstractions to Wasm, such as exception handling [30], continuations [32], effect handlers [19], and more, all building on top of the reference semantics.

The specification of Wasm describes a small-step reduction semantics [20], which is a standard approach and straightforward to implement as an inter-

J. Gibbons (Ed.): TFP 2025, LNCS 15652, pp. 185–204, 2026.
https://doi.org/10.1007/978-3-031-99751-8_9

preter. However, the reduction semantics [13,34] is complicated by the additional *administrative instructions*, which are extensions to handle control constructs (e.g., loops and breaks) at runtime but do not appear in source programs. These administrative instructions are inserted on-the-fly during the evaluation of the program, essentially serving as the representation of evaluation contexts. Another choice of the design is that the reference semantics conflates the control stack and the value stack [29], arguably adding cognitive overhead to understand the semantics. Since control transfer needs to search over the stack, these redundancies lead to inefficiency if just naively implementing the reference interpreter [27].

Moreover, the reference small-step semantics is *not compositional*, making it unsuitable to apply mechanical program transformations (e.g. partial evaluation, staging, or unfolding) to the interpreter [16], which are useful to derive other tools or optimizations based on the semantics. The lack of compositionality adds complication both in reasoning about the semantics and in developing tools that adhere to the semantics.

This Work. Following Reynolds' seminal work of definitional interpreters [23], an alternative is to leverage the control mechanisms from the meta-language to define the semantics of the object language, rather than using first-order representations of control. We can give meanings to the control constructs of the object language by using continuations from the higher-order meta-language.

This paper reconstructs a continuation-passing style (CPS) semantics for Wasm. The key contribution is a high-level, compositional, and tail-recursive semantics in CPS that captures the essence of Wasm's control-flow semantics. By employing CPS in the meta-language, our approach eliminates the need for administrative instructions, disentangles the control stack and the operand value stack, makes the semantics more concise and streamlined compared to the reference reduction semantics [13,34]. Such a CPS semantics can be straightforwardly implemented as a big-step interpreter or CPS transformer in a functional language.

Unlike a typical CPS interpreter with a single continuation, the interpreter uses a list (or, a trail) of continuations to handle lexically induced breaks, inspired by double-barrelled CPS [25] and the CPS semantics of dynamic continuations [2]. We further demonstrate that the CPS semantics serves as a flexible foundation that can be extended to define a wide range of control abstractions, which are not (yet) in the current WebAssembly standard, such as high-level for-loop [24], tail calls [31], exceptions [24,30], and effect handlers [19,21,22]. Since our CPS semantics is compositional, it facilitates equational reasoning of Wasm programs, for which we demonstrate the calculation of tail call semantics.

Contributions. This work makes the following contributions:

- We examine WebAssembly's control-flow semantics by developing a CPS-based semantics à la definitional interpreters, marking the first compositional and tail-recursive CPS semantics for WebAssembly.
- We extend the CPS semantics to support control abstractions such as structured loops, tail calls, try/catch, and effect handlers.

– We implement an WebAssembly interpreter based on the proposed semantics, validating its consistency with the reference interpreter.

The paper is organized as follows: Sect. 2 introduces μWasm, a minimal language following the essence of Wasm. Section 3 presents the core CPS semantics for μWasm. Section 4 discusses several control extensions and their CPS semantics. Section 5 describes the implementation of our CPS interpreter. Section 6 discusses related work and Sect. 7 concludes with remarks on future work.

2 μWasm: A Minimal Language à la WASM

In this section, we introduce a minimal language μWasm, including interesting control flow constructs as a proper subset of WebAssembly. We first present the abstract syntax, followed by an example informally explaining the control-flow semantics.

2.1 Syntax

$$
\begin{array}{rll}
\ell \in \mathsf{Label} & = \mathbb{N} \\
x \in \mathsf{Identifier} & = \mathbb{N} \\
t \in \mathsf{ValueType} & ::= \mathsf{i32} \mid \mathsf{i64} \mid \ldots \\
ft \in \mathsf{FunctionType} & ::= t^* \rightarrow t^* \\
e \in \mathsf{Instruction} & ::= \mathsf{nop} \mid t.\mathsf{const}\ c \mid t.\{\mathsf{add}, \mathsf{sub}, \mathsf{eq}, \ldots\} \\
& \quad \mid \mathsf{local.get}\ x \mid \mathsf{local.set}\ x \\
& \quad \mid \mathsf{block}\ ft\ es \mid \mathsf{loop}\ ft\ es \mid \mathsf{if}\ ft\ es\ es \\
& \quad \mid \mathsf{br}\ \ell \mid \mathsf{call}\ x \mid \mathsf{return} \\
es \in \mathsf{Instructions} & = \mathsf{List}[\mathsf{Instruction}] \\
f \in \mathsf{Function} & ::= \mathsf{func}\ x\ \{\mathsf{type} : ft, \mathsf{locals} : t^*, \mathsf{body} : es\} \\
m \in \mathsf{Module} & ::= \mathsf{module}\ f^*
\end{array}
$$

Fig. 1. The abstract syntax of μWasm.

Figure 1 presents the abstract syntax of μWasm. A μWasm module consists of a sequence of function definitions. Each function defines its type, identifier, a list of types for local variables, and a block of instructions.

WebAssembly assumes a stack-based computation model (instead of using named registers), thus most instructions do not take explicit operands. For example, i32.const 42 pushes the constant 42 onto the stack, and a numeric instruction such as i32.add consumes two values from the stack and pushes the result back. Instructions for local variables, e.g., local.get and local.set, accesses and updates local variables with an implicit stack too, respectively.

Control flow constructs in Wasm are structured and can be nested. For example, block-like constructs (block, loop, if) contain sequences of instructions. They also take a function type regulating the shape of the stack before and after the block. Block-like constructs introduce an implicit numeric label à la de Bruijn indices, which can be referred by br within the block. Break instruction (br) takes a label, referring to the jump target.

Compared to the full-fledged Wasm language, we have omitted many features, e.g., memory operations, globals, imports/exports, tables, etc. However, these features are largely orthogonal to the control flow semantics of Wasm, and can be added back in a straightforward manner. Labels (for blocks) and identifiers (for local variables and functions) are restricted to numerics compared to standard Wasm, in which can be symbols. Symbolic labels/identifiers can be mapped to their numeric correspondences as a semantics-preserving preprocessing step. In this work, we are interested in the dynamic semantics of Wasm, therefore we assume the same validation semantics for μWasm as in standard WebAssembly. We also assume that our definitional interpreter takes well-typed WebAssembly programs as input.

2.2 Example

Although WebAssembly looks like a standard stack-based low-level language, one of the uncommon features of WebAssembly is that the semantics of a break contextually depends on its target enclosing block. For example, the following code snippet defines a loop block containing a regular block, labeled ℓ_1 and ℓ_2 respectively

```
loop ℓ1
  ...
  block ℓ2
    ...
    br ℓ2
    ...
    br ℓ1
    ...
  end
  ...
  br ℓ1
  ...
end
```

There are three br instructions in this code snippet. Within the inner block, the first br instruction jumps to the end of the block, while the second br instruction jumps to the beginning of the enclosing loop block. Similarly, the br instruction at the end of the loop block jumps back to the beginning of the loop block. If there is no br back to the loop head, the loop finishes. Our CPS semantics will capture this contextual control-flow behavior.

$$
\begin{aligned}
v &\in \mathsf{Value} = \mathbb{Z} \\
\sigma &\in \mathsf{Stack} = \mathsf{List}[\mathsf{Value}] \\
\rho &\in \mathsf{Env} \ \ = \mathsf{List}[\mathsf{Value}] \\
\kappa &\in \mathsf{Cont} \ = \mathsf{Stack} \times \mathsf{Env} \to \mathsf{Ans} \\
\theta &\in \mathsf{Trail} \ = \mathsf{List}[\mathsf{Cont}]
\end{aligned}
$$

Fig. 2. Semantic domains and auxiliary functions.

3 A CPS Semantics for μWasm

We now present a continuation-passing semantics for μWasm. The semantics $[\![\cdot]\!]$ is defined as a recursive function mapping a *list of instructions* to functions with continuations:

$$[\![\cdot]\!] : \mathsf{List}[\mathsf{Inst}] \to (\mathsf{Stack} \times \mathsf{Env} \times \mathsf{Cont} \times \mathsf{Trail}) \to \mathsf{Ans}$$

In the following, we first explain the domain definitions and notations, then present the definition of $[\![\cdot]\!]$ in Fig. 3. We also discuss an alternative formulation and future work that bridges the gap between our core CPS semantics and the full Wasm language.

3.1 Preliminaries

Domains. Figure 2 shows the definitions of semantic domains. We represent values as integers, and the stack as a list of values. An environment (i.e. frames in Wasm reference semantics) ρ is represented as a list of values, mapping numeric-represented local variables as indices to values. We represent continuations κ as functions that take a stack and an environment, and return an answer. We deliberately leave the definition of the answer type Ans abstract, as it depends on the specific instantiation of the semantics. One possible choice is to define it as the Stack type, representing the side effects of instructions. A trail θ is a list (or stack) of continuations, which is used to represent lexical control structures.

Notations. Before explaining the details of the semantics, we introduce some notations used in Fig. 3.

For a list θ (representing Stack, Env, or Trail), $\theta(\ell)$ accesses the ℓ-th element in the list θ. $\sigma_1 +\!\!+ \sigma_2$ concatenates two stacks σ_1 and σ_2. $\rho[x \mapsto v]$ updates the environment ρ with x mapping to v, producing a new environment.

We write a function type $t^m \to t^n$ to denote that there are m argument types, and n result types. Given a type t^m and a stack σ, $\lfloor \sigma \rfloor_m$ takes the top m elements from the stack σ, which are of type t^m guaranteed by Wasm's type system. This is useful, e.g., for truncating the stack only taking the necessary arguments.

To the left of the equations in Fig. 3, we use a few notations to match the program syntax and the shape of the operand stack. For example, :: is the usual

Evaluation function: $[\![\cdot]\!] : \mathsf{List[Inst]} \to (\mathsf{Stack} \times \mathsf{Env} \times \mathsf{Cont} \times \mathsf{Trail}) \to \mathsf{Ans}$

$$
\begin{array}{ll}
[\![nil]\!](\sigma, \rho, \kappa, \theta) & = \kappa(\sigma, \rho) \\
[\![\mathsf{nop} :: rest]\!](\sigma, \rho, \kappa, \theta) & = [\![rest]\!](\sigma, \rho, \kappa, \theta) \\
[\![t.\mathsf{const}\ c :: rest]\!](\sigma, \rho, \kappa, \theta) & = [\![rest]\!](c :: \sigma, \rho, \kappa, \theta) \\
[\![t.\mathsf{add} :: rest]\!](v_1 :: v_2 :: \sigma, \rho, \kappa, \theta) & = [\![rest]\!](v_1 + v_2 :: \sigma, \rho, \kappa, \theta) \\
[\![\mathsf{local.get}\ x :: rest]\!](\sigma, \rho, \kappa, \theta) & = [\![rest]\!](\rho(x) :: \sigma, \rho, \kappa, \theta) \\
[\![\mathsf{local.set}\ x :: rest]\!](v :: \sigma, \rho, \kappa, \theta) & = [\![rest]\!](\sigma, \rho[x \mapsto v], \kappa, \theta) \\
[\![\mathsf{block}\ (t^m \to t^n)\ es :: rest]\!](\sigma_{arg}\ {}_m\!\!+\!\!\!+\ \sigma, \rho, \kappa, \theta) & = \\
\quad \mathsf{let}\ \kappa_1 := \lambda(\sigma_1, \rho_1).[\![rest]\!](\lfloor \sigma_1 \rfloor_n +\!\!\!+\ \sigma, \rho_1, \kappa, \theta)\ \mathsf{in} & \\
\quad [\![es]\!](\sigma_{arg}, \rho, \kappa_1, \kappa_1 :: \theta) & \\
[\![\mathsf{loop}\ (t^m \to t^n)\ es :: rest]\!](\sigma_{arg}\ {}_m\!\!+\!\!\!+\ \sigma, \rho, \kappa, \theta) & = \\
\quad \mathsf{let}\ \kappa_1 := \lambda(\sigma_1, \rho_1).[\![rest]\!](\lfloor \sigma_1 \rfloor_n +\!\!\!+\ \sigma, \rho_1, \kappa, \theta)\ \mathsf{in} & \\
\quad \mathsf{fix}\ \kappa_2 := \lambda(\sigma_2, \rho_2).[\![es]\!](\lfloor \sigma_2 \rfloor_m, \rho_2, \kappa_1, \kappa_2 :: \theta)\ \mathsf{in} & \\
\quad \kappa_2(\sigma_{arg}, \rho) & \\
[\![\mathsf{if}\ (t^m \to t^n)\ es_1\ es_2 :: rest]\!](v :: \sigma_{arg}\ {}_m\!\!+\!\!\!+\ \sigma, \rho, \kappa, \theta) & = \\
\quad \mathsf{let}\ es := \mathsf{if}\ v \equiv 0\ \mathsf{then}\ es_2\ \mathsf{else}\ es_1\ \mathsf{in} & \\
\quad \mathsf{let}\ \kappa_1 := \lambda(\sigma_1, \rho_1).[\![rest]\!](\lfloor \sigma_1 \rfloor_n +\!\!\!+\ \sigma, \rho_1, \kappa, \theta)\ \mathsf{in} & \\
\quad [\![es]\!](\sigma_{arg}, \rho, \kappa_1, \kappa_1 :: \theta) & \\
[\![\mathsf{br}\ \ell :: rest]\!](\sigma, \rho, \kappa, \theta) & = \theta(\ell)(\sigma, \rho) \\
[\![\mathsf{call}\ x :: rest]\!](\sigma_{arg}\ {}_m\!\!+\!\!\!+\ \sigma, \rho, \kappa, \theta) & = \\
\quad \mathsf{let}\ \{\mathsf{type} : t^m \to t^n, \mathsf{locals} : ts, \mathsf{body} : es\} := \mathsf{lookupFunc}(x)\ \mathsf{in} & \\
\quad \mathsf{let}\ \rho_1 := \mathsf{buildEnv}(\sigma_{arg}, ts) & \\
\quad \mathsf{let}\ \kappa_1 := \lambda(\sigma_1, \rho_1).[\![rest]\!](\lfloor \sigma_1 \rfloor_n +\!\!\!+ \sigma, \rho, \kappa, \theta)\ \mathsf{in} & \\
\quad [\![es]\!]([], \rho_1, \kappa_1, [\kappa_1]) & \\
[\![\mathsf{return} :: rest]\!](\sigma, \rho, \kappa, \theta) & = \theta.\mathsf{last}(\sigma, \rho)
\end{array}
$$

Fig. 3. The continuation-passing style semantics of μWasm.

cons operator used to destruct the stack into the top element and the rest of the stack. We also use $\sigma_1\ {}_m\!\!+\!\!\!+\ \sigma_2$ to split the stack into two parts, where the first part σ_1 has m values, and the second part σ_2 contains the rest of the stack.

3.2 CPS Semantics

Figure 3 presents the CPS semantics of μWasm, which structurally recurs over the list of instructions. The interpretation of instructions manipulating the stack and environment is straightforward to define. For example, const pushes a constant onto the stack, add pops two values from the stack, adds them, and pushes the result back. Then, they recursively evaluate the *rest* of the instructions with the new stack. Similarly, local.get and local.set access and update local variables with the environment.

Besides storage arguments such as the stack and environment to the interpreter, our semantics takes additional control arguments. In WebAssembly, there are three different ways to leave a block-like scope, namely by (1) falling through the immediately enclosing block, (2) breaking out of a block, and (3) returning from the current function. Therefore, to accommodate such control flow, $[\![\cdot]\!]$ takes the following additional control arguments:

- a continuation function κ representing the control-flow after consuming the current list of instructions (i.e. the case for $[\![nil]\!]$, yielding to the enclosing block), and
- a trail of continuations θ representing the control-flow for breaking (informed by the lexical structure of the program) or returning.

In the following, we explain how they play different roles for different control constructs.

Block, Loop, and Break. For control-flow instructions, μWasm models three kinds of block-like structures (block, loop, and if) which introduce labels that can be used by br. Within a block-like construct, a break instruction br consisting of a label, which indicates the number of blocks to skip. For example, br 0 targets the immediately enclosing block, and br 1 targets the next outer block, and so on. However, it is important to note that brs to a loop and to a block behave differently: the former jumps back to the beginning of the loop (as continue in C), while the latter escapes to the end of the block (recall the illustration in Sect. 2.2). In other words, the meaning of br depends on its enclosing constructs. Our semantics uses a trail θ to keep track of the lexical control-flow structure, then labels of brs are interpreted as the index of the trail to invoke the corresponding continuation.

Now we explain the rules defined in Fig. 3. For a block instruction, we prepare a new continuation κ_1 that evaluates the rest of the instructions after the block. This continuation is shared by falling through the block and breaking out of the block (appended to the trail θ). Similarly, for a if instruction, we prepare the same kind of continuation, but choose to evaluate the inner instructions based on the condition on the top of the stack.

However, for a loop instruction, we define two different continuations: (1) κ_1 represents the fall-through continuation that evaluates the rest of the instructions syntactically after the loop, and (2) κ_2 represents the break-out continuation that jumps back to the beginning of the loop. Note that κ_2 is defined as a fixed-point, so that it can be recursively pushed onto the trail θ within its definition. Lastly, we initiate the evaluation of the loop body by invoking κ_2.

Block-like structures are also annotated with a function type, indicating the stack values consumed and produced by the block. In Fig. 3, we use $\sigma_{arg\ m} +\!\!+\ \sigma$ to split the input stack for the argument values, and use $\lfloor \sigma_1 \rfloor_n$ to truncate the output stack for the return values.

Call and Return. For function calls, we use an auxiliary function lookupFunc to find the definition (i.e., its function type, local variable types, and body) by the function index. Our presentation omits the definition of lookupFunc, as it is straightforward to implement and not the focus of this paper. Another auxiliary function buildEnv (Appendix A shows its definition) constructs a new environment ρ_1 containing the arguments. The environment has also pre-allocated default values for local variables. The continuation κ_1 evaluates the rest of the instructions after the call, with the returned values appended with the previous stack (without the arguments to the callee), the caller's environment, continuation, and trail.

When we enter the function body *es*, we use an empty stack, the new environment ρ_1, and the return continuation κ_1. Since a function introduces a *fresh* block scope too, the trail θ is a just singleton list containing the return continuation κ_1, discarding all other jump targets that are non-local to the function. Within a function body, this continuation κ_1 will always be the last one in the trail, and will be invoked when encountering a return instruction, since it is the maximal number of blocks to skip.

Remarks. The presented semantics (Fig. 3) as a definitional interpreter is compositional. We apply the $[\![\cdot]\!]$ function only to the syntactic sub-constructs of the current term from the left-hand side. The interpreter is also tail-recursive – every call of $[\![\cdot]\!]$ and the continuations are in tail position. In a meta-language with proper tail-call optimization, the interpreter executes without stack overflow. In Sect. 4.2, we discuss the extension to support tail calls in the object language μWasm.

Single-Instruction Semantics. Notice that our evaluation function takes a list of instructions as an argument. Alternatively, we could define it as only taking a single instruction instead of a list of instructions:

$$[\![\cdot]\!]_{\mathbb{1}} : \mathsf{Inst} \rightarrow (\mathsf{Stack} \times \mathsf{Env} \times \mathsf{Cont} \times \mathsf{Trail}) \rightarrow \mathsf{Ans}$$

For example, the semantics for add would be

$$[\![t.\mathsf{add}]\!]_{\mathbb{1}}(v_1 :: v_2 :: \sigma, \rho, \kappa, \theta) = \kappa(v_1 + v_2 :: \sigma, \rho).$$

In this alternative semantics, we would need to define an auxiliary function (e.g. foldl) that iterates the evaluation over the list of instructions, so that the evaluation of *rest* becomes part of the continuation κ of the current instruction.

The evaluation function presented in Fig. 3 can be considered as the fused version of the single-instruction evaluation and the iterating driver. Or, inversely, we can mechanically derive the single-instruction evaluation from the fused version by equational reasoning, i.e., unfolding the evaluation of an *singleton* instruction list:

$$[\![e :: nil]\!](\sigma, \rho, \kappa, \theta) = [\![e]\!]_{\mathbb{1}}(\sigma, \rho, \kappa, \theta)$$

We choose to only present the fused evaluation function in Fig. 3, since it suits well the recursive structures of the language, such as block and loop.

Scaling to Full WebAssembly. Many features of WebAssembly, such as memory, global variables, and tables for function references, are orthogonal to control flow semantics. They are omitted in our semantics but nevertheless can be added on top of it, following the official reference interpreter. Our presented semantics have not dealt with errors, which are represented by the dedicated administrative instruction trap in WebAssembly. In our semantics, the interpretation of trap can be represented by errors in the host language.

4 Extensions

We have shown the CPS semantics for μWasm. In this section, we study how the CPS semantics can be extended to support additional control abstractions. Some of the simple constructs can be directly added to the language without global changes, while others such as exception/effect handling require additional facilities. We start from the simple constructs and gradually move to more complex ones.

4.1 Structured Loops

We first show how to add structured for-loop in μWasm. The for-loop resembles the behavior of similar looping constructs in other high-level languages, such as C. This extension is inspired by one of the assignment problems in Stanford's CS242 course [24].

Syntax and Statics. The syntax of μWasm is extended with the following construct:

$$e \in \mathsf{Instruction} ::= \cdots \mid \mathsf{for}\ (es_{\mathsf{init}};\ es_{\mathsf{cond}};\ es_{\mathsf{post}})\ es$$

The initialization instructions es_{init} run only once before the loop begins. The condition es_{cond} produces a single boolean (represented as i32) value on the stack. If the condition is true, then the loop body es is executed otherwise the loop terminates. The post-instructions es_{post} are executed (every time) after the loop body es. As for typing, only the condition es_{cond} has type $[] \rightarrow [\mathsf{i32}]$; all other constructs take no arguments and produce no results on the stack.

CPS Semantics. We formalize the CPS semantics for for-loop, following the same style presented in Fig. 3:

$$\begin{aligned}
&[\![\mathsf{for}\ (es_{\mathsf{init}};\ es_{\mathsf{cond}};\ es_{\mathsf{post}})\ es :: rest]\!](\sigma, \rho, \kappa, \theta) = \\
&\quad \mathsf{fix}\ \kappa_1 := \lambda(\sigma_1, \rho_1).[\![es_{\mathsf{cond}}]\!]([], \rho_1, \lambda(v :: \sigma_2, \rho_2). \\
&\qquad\qquad \mathsf{if}\ v \equiv 0\ \mathsf{then}\ [\![rest]\!](\sigma_2, \rho_2, \kappa, \theta) \\
&\qquad\qquad \mathsf{else}\ [\![es]\!]([], \rho_2, \lambda(\sigma_3, \rho_3).[\![es_{\mathsf{post}}]\!]([], \rho_3, \kappa_1, \theta), \theta))\ \mathsf{in} \\
&\quad [\![es_{\mathsf{init}}]\!]([], \rho, \kappa_1, \theta)
\end{aligned}$$

Similar to the semantics of loop-block, we use a fixed-point to define continuation κ_1 that evaluates the condition and possibly the loop body followed by the post-instructions. This continuation κ_1 is used as the continuation when recursively applying the semantic function to es_{post}.

Note that in the above definition, we have deliberately left out the branch semantics in for-loop, i.e. a br 0 instruction in the loop body would target the outer enclosing block, not the loop itself. However, the use of continuations in our semantics allows us to flexibly recover behaviors of br either as C-style continue or break. For example, we can append κ_1 to the trail continuation θ when evaluating the loop body es, and use it as the target for a br 0. Similarly, to implement a break behavior, we can append the evaluation of *rest* to the trail θ. Appendix B shows the full semantics of the for-loop with both variants of break semantics.

4.2 Tail Calls

Standard WebAssembly's call instruction prohibits tail-call optimization, which is useful particularly for recursive functions since tail calls ensure constant stack space consumption. A recent proposal [31] extends WebAssembly with tail calls, and has been experimentally supported by major implementations. Although our CPS semantics does not operationally describe every detail of a low-level virtual machine or implementation, it can help clarify the behavior of tail calls, especially from the perspective of continuations. Essentially, it becomes unnecessary to create a new frame/continuation for a tail call, as we can directly reuse the current one that returns.

Syntax and Statics. The proposal [31] adds several new call instructions that are the tail version of the regular ones. For brevity, we only demonstrate the return_call instruction with the following syntax:

$$e \in \mathsf{Instruction} ::= \cdots \mid \mathsf{return\_call}\ x$$

Here, return_call x represents a tail call to the function at index x. We omit the typing rules, which follows the proposal [31].

CPS Semantics. As its name suggests, the instruction return_call combines the semantics of return and call, performing them in a single step. In the CPS semantics for standard call/return, we do not need to return explicitly; instead, to return is to call the last continuation in the trail. And the caller prepares a new continuation for the callee to return. Combining these two steps into one eliminates the need to prepare a new continuation for the callee, as shown in the following definition:

$$\begin{aligned}
&[\![\mathsf{return_call}\ x :: rest]\!](\sigma_{arg\ m} +\!\!+\, \sigma, \rho, \kappa, \theta) = \\
&\quad \mathsf{let}\ \{\mathsf{type} : t^m \to t^n, \mathsf{locals} : ts, \mathsf{body} : es\} := \mathsf{lookupFunc}(x)\ \mathsf{in} \\
&\quad \mathsf{let}\ \rho_1 := \mathsf{buildEnv}(\sigma_{arg}, ts) \\
&\quad [\![es]\!]([], \rho_1, \theta.\mathsf{last}, [\theta.\mathsf{last}])
\end{aligned}$$

The definition is nearly identical to the semantics of the regular function call, except that we do not need to create a new continuation for the rest of instructions after the call. Since now we are at a tail position, es does not need to return to the current context (i.e. continue to $rest$), but instead can be optimized to return to the caller of the current context. Therefore, when evaluating the body of the callee, we directly use the return continuation $\theta.\mathsf{last}$.

Calculation. Although it is straightforward to directly define the semantics of tail calls in CPS, we show an alternative way to *derive* the semantics of return_call by calculation. The derivation is possible because the semantics is compositional, and justified by equational reasoning.

Since the semantics of return_call is a synthesis of return and call, our starting point is their syntactic combination. We syntactically construct a call at a tail position, and calculate the semantics by unfolding $[\![\cdot]\!]$ on call and return:

$$
\begin{aligned}
& [\![\mathsf{call}\ x :: \mathsf{return} :: rest]\!](\sigma_{arg\ m} +\!\!+\ \sigma, \rho, \kappa, \theta) \\
=&\{\textit{unfold}\ \mathsf{call}\} \\
& \mathsf{let}\ \{\mathsf{type} : t^m \to t^n, \mathsf{locals} : ts, \mathsf{body} : es\} := \mathsf{lookupFunc}(x)\ \mathsf{in} \\
& \mathsf{let}\ \rho_1 := \mathsf{buildEnv}(\sigma_{arg}, ts) \\
& \mathsf{let}\ \kappa_1 := \lambda(\sigma_1, \rho_1).[\![\mathsf{return} :: rest]\!](\lfloor \sigma_1 \rfloor_n +\!\!+ \sigma, \rho, \kappa, \theta)\ \mathsf{in} \\
& [\![es]\!]([], \rho_1, \kappa_1, [\kappa_1]) \\
=&\{\textit{unfold}\ \mathsf{return}\} \\
& \mathsf{let}\ \{\mathsf{type} : t^m \to t^n, \mathsf{locals} : ts, \mathsf{body} : es\} := \mathsf{lookupFunc}(x)\ \mathsf{in} \\
& \mathsf{let}\ \rho_1 := \mathsf{buildEnv}(\sigma_{arg}, ts) \\
& \mathsf{let}\ \kappa_1 := \lambda(\sigma_1, \rho_1).\theta.\mathsf{last}(\lfloor \sigma_1 \rfloor_n +\!\!+ \sigma, \rho)\ \mathsf{in} \\
& [\![es]\!]([], \rho_1, \kappa_1, [\kappa_1]) \\
=&\{\kappa_1\ \textit{is}\ \eta\textit{-equivalent to}\ \theta.\mathsf{last},\ \textit{inlining}\ \kappa_1\} \\
& \mathsf{let}\ \{\mathsf{type} : t^m \to t^n, \mathsf{locals} : ts, \mathsf{body} : es\} := \mathsf{lookupFunc}(x)\ \mathsf{in} \\
& \mathsf{let}\ \rho_1 := \mathsf{buildEnv}(\sigma_{arg}, ts)\ \mathsf{in} \\
& [\![es]\!]([], \rho_1, \theta.\mathsf{last}, [\theta.\mathsf{last}]) \\
=&\{\textit{definition of}\ \mathsf{return\_call}\} \\
& [\![\mathsf{return\_call}\ x :: rest]\!](\sigma_{arg\ m} +\!\!+\ \sigma, \rho, \kappa, \theta)
\end{aligned}
$$

In the third step, the replacement of κ_1 with $\theta.\mathsf{last}$ needs additional justification. It amounts to show that $\lambda(\sigma_1, \rho_1).\theta.\mathsf{last}(\lfloor \sigma_1 \rfloor_n +\!\!+ \sigma, \rho)$ is behaviorally equivalent to $\theta.\mathsf{last}$. First notice that the return type t^n must be the same for function x and the current function that returns to $\theta.\mathsf{last}$, therefore the caller-provided $\theta.\mathsf{last}$ itself will truncate the stack $\lfloor \sigma_1 \rfloor_n +\!\!+ \sigma$ by the top n elements too. In other words, $\lfloor \lfloor \sigma_1 \rfloor_n +\!\!+ \sigma \rfloor_n$ is equivalent to $\lfloor \sigma_1 \rfloor_n$, so we can safely replace it with σ_1. Second, the caller-provided $\theta.\mathsf{last}$ uses the environment from its own caller frame (recall Fig. 3), therefore it does not matter whether we pass ρ or ρ_1 here. After these reasoning steps, we can show that κ_1 is indeed behaviorally equivalent to θ.last, thus can be η-reduced and inlined.

Finally, we derive the same semantics for return_call as we have defined in the previous section.

4.3 Exceptions

In standard WebAssembly and μWasm, the jump target ℓ in a break instruction br ℓ is entirely static and local within a function. It is not possible to jump out of nested functions via br or similar break instructions. Now we demonstrate our semantics can be extended to support exception handling, a simple form of dynamic, non-local control flow.

There is already a work-in-progress proposal for exception handling in WebAssembly [30]. Without introducing heavy mechanisms (e.g. a table describing multiple handlers as in the proposal), we choose to demonstrate a higher-level, hypothetical try/catch construct, which is close to the description in one of the assignment problems in Stanford's CS242 course [24]. In the next section, we will further generalize it to more flexible effect handlers.

Syntax and Statics. The following shows the syntax for the new instructions:

$$e \in \mathsf{Instruction} ::= \cdots \mid \mathsf{try}\ es_1\ \mathsf{catch}\ es_2 \mid \mathsf{throw}$$

Instructions es_1 is the body that warrants to throw an exception, and es_2 is the handler that catches the exception. As for typing their stack behavior, es_1 takes no stack argument and returns no argument. The throw instruction expects an error code on the top of the stack, which becomes the input to es_2. Unlike a full-blown exception handling mechanism, we omit "exception tags" that can be used to differentiate the types of exceptions.

CPS Semantics. When we encounter a try-catch block, the instructions in es_1 are evaluated first. If an exception is thrown during the dynamic extent of es_1, control is transferred to es_2 (provided no other handler is installed within). Otherwise, execution continues with the instruction following the try-catch block. To model such a behavior, we extend the semantics $[\![\cdot]\!]$ with an additional failure continuation [25] (or, handler), denoted as γ argument of type Cont:

$$\begin{aligned}
&[\![\mathsf{try}\ es_1\ \mathsf{catch}\ es_2 :: rest]\!](\sigma, \rho, \kappa, \theta, \gamma) = \\
&\quad \mathsf{let}\ \kappa_1 := \lambda(\sigma_1, \rho_1).[\![rest]\!](\sigma, \rho_1, \kappa, \theta, \gamma)\ \mathsf{in} \\
&\quad \mathsf{let}\ \gamma_1 := \lambda(\sigma_2, \rho_2).[\![es_2]\!](\sigma_2, \rho_2, \kappa_1, \theta, \gamma)\ \mathsf{in} \\
&\quad [\![es_1]\!]([], \rho, \kappa_1, \theta, \gamma_1) \\
&[\![\mathsf{throw} :: rest]\!](v :: \sigma, \rho, \kappa, \theta, \gamma) \qquad = \gamma([v], \rho)
\end{aligned}$$

The success continuation κ_1 is prepared to evaluate the rest of the instructions after the try-catch block. The failure continuation γ_1 is prepared as the handler for es_2. When es_1 is evaluated, both the success and failure continuation are installed. If an exception is thrown, the control is transferred to the failure continuation by invoking γ with the error code on the stack. Similar to the base semantics of for-loop, we deliberately leave no interaction with breaks. It is also possible to recover a normal break behavior within es_1 or es_2 by appending the continuation κ_1 to the trail θ.

The interpretation of other constructs retains the failure continuation γ. For example, in contrast to local trail continuations, which are discarded for function calls, the failure continuation is preserved across function calls, enabling non-local control transfers. Note that the es_2 does not have the ability to resume execution at the point where the exception was thrown, which we will generalize in the next section.

4.4 Resumable Exceptions

Effect handlers [21,22] are known to be a generalization of exception handling. They enable handlers to access the (delimited) continuation at the point where the effectful operation is invoked. In this section, we demonstrate a flavor of effect handlers as an extension to WebAssembly, which is higher-level than the existing WasmFX proposal [19]. Based on the development of the previous section, we further introduce a new instruction resume, which allows the handler to invoke the resumption. To informally explain the semantics, let us consider the following code snippet:

```
1   try
2     i32.const 1
3     call print
4     i32.const -1 ;; error code
5     throw
6     i32.const 2
7     call print
8   catch
9     ;; stack: [-1, resumption]
10    call print
11    resume ;; back to line 6
12  end
```

The program outputs `1` first, followed by a `throw` instruction, which transfers the control to the `catch` block. When entering the `catch` block (i.e., the handler), the stack contains the error code `-1` and the resumption. The `catch` block prints the error code `-1`, and then resumes the execution back into the `try` block (line 6), printing `2`. Therefore, the whole output of this program is `1 -1 2`.

In the following, we discuss the extension and its CPS semantics under our framework.

Syntax and Statics. On top of Sect. 4.3, we add the new resume instruction:

$$e \in \mathsf{Instruction} ::= \cdots \mid \mathsf{try}\ es_1\ \mathsf{catch}\ es_2 \mid \mathsf{throw} \mid \mathsf{resume}$$

The resume instruction assumes that the top element of the stack is a resumable continuation. In essence, our extension is equivalent to unlabelled effect handlers (e.g. as in [5]), where handlers only handle a single kind of effects. One can readily read $\textsf{try}\ es_1\ \textsf{catch}\ es_2$ as $\textsf{handle}\ es_1\ \textsf{with}\ \{x, k \mapsto es_2\}$, where x is the error code and k is the resumption.

We do not intend to develop a type system for this extension, but one can borrow some ideas from from WasmFX [19]. One caveat is that we disallow using br in the try/catch block, since invoking br in the (possibly escaped) delimited continuation is ill-defined.

CPS Semantics. Following Danvy and Filinski [7], we extend our semantics with a meta-continuation, which conceptually is the continuation of continuations Cont. The notion of meta-continuations is useful for delimiting the context when evaluating the try block, since when suspended by a throw instruction only the continuation within the try block should be captured. Below we show the changes in the semantic domain definitions:

$$\begin{aligned}
\kappa \in \textsf{Cont} &= \textsf{Stack} \times \textsf{Env} \times \textsf{MCont} \to \textsf{Ans}\\
m \in \textsf{MCont} &= \textsf{Stack} \times \textsf{Env} \to \textsf{Ans}\\
\gamma \in \textsf{Handler} &= \textsf{Stack} \times \textsf{Env} \times \textsf{Cont} \times \textsf{MCont} \to \textsf{Ans}\\
v, r \in \textsf{Value} &::= \cdots \mid \textsf{Stack} \times \textsf{Env} \times \textsf{MCont} \times \textsf{Handler} \to \textsf{Ans}
\end{aligned}$$

We also extend the value domain to include resumable continuation values (denoted by r), in the sense that they are first-class values[1] that can be stored on the stack or in local variables. The resume instruction expects such a continuation value on the stack. With the changes in the domain definitions, the signature of the semantic function is the following:

$$[\![\cdot]\!] : \textsf{List}[\textsf{Inst}] \to (\textsf{Stack} \times \textsf{Env} \times \textsf{Cont} \times \textsf{Trail} \times \textsf{MCont} \times \textsf{Handler}) \to \textsf{Ans}$$

$$\begin{aligned}
&[\![\textsf{try}\ es_1\ \textsf{catch}\ es_2 :: \mathit{rest}]\!](\sigma, \rho, \kappa, \theta, m, \gamma) =\\
&\quad \textsf{let}\ m_1 := \lambda.(\sigma_1, \rho_1).[\![\mathit{rest}]\!](\sigma_1, \rho_1, \kappa, \theta, m, \gamma)\\
&\quad \textsf{let}\ \gamma_1 := \lambda(\sigma_1, \rho_1, \kappa_1, m_1).[\![es_2]\!](\sigma_1, \rho_1, \kappa_1, [], m_1, \gamma)\ \textsf{in}\\
&\quad [\![es_1]\!]([], \rho, \kappa_0, [], m_1, \gamma_1)\\
&[\![\textsf{throw} :: \mathit{rest}]\!](v :: \sigma, \rho, \kappa, \theta, m, \gamma) \qquad =\\
&\quad \textsf{let}\ r := \lambda(\sigma_1, \rho_1, m_1, \gamma_1).[\![\mathit{rest}]\!](\sigma_1, \rho_1, \kappa, \theta, m_1, \gamma)\ \textsf{in}\\
&\quad \gamma([v, r], \rho, \kappa_0, m)\\
&[\![\textsf{resume} :: \mathit{rest}]\!](r :: \sigma, \rho, \kappa, \theta, m, \gamma) \qquad =\\
&\quad \textsf{let}\ m_1 := \lambda.(\sigma_1, \rho_1).[\![\mathit{rest}]\!](\sigma_1, \rho_1, \kappa, \theta, m, \gamma)\\
&\quad r([], \rho, m_1, \gamma)
\end{aligned}$$

Fig. 4. CPS semantics (excerpt) for resumable exceptions.

Figure 4 shows the CPS semantics for resumable exceptions. When evaluating a try-catch instruction, *rest* along with its continuation κ is delayed as a meta-continuation m_1. This meta-continuation serves as the join point for both the

[1] Supporting first-class functions is already an ongoing proposal to WebAssembly [33].

success control flow (i.e., no exception is thrown during the dynamic extent of es_1) and the failure control flow via the handler es_2. The handler γ_1 evaluates es_2 with the latest continuation and meta-continuation, but with the current handler γ. Finally, the evaluation of es_1 is delimited by the identity continuation κ_0 (defined as $\lambda(\sigma, \rho, m).m(\sigma, \rho)$), with the new meta-continuation and handler.

When throwing an exception, we define the resumption continuation r to evaluate *rest* and its continuation κ, parameterized by the new meta-continuation m_1. The same handler γ is installed for the resumption of *rest*, reflecting the deep handler semantics. This resumption continuation r is reified as a proper first-class value (but opaque to the user) and pushed onto the stack, along with the error code v. Lastly, we call the handler with that stack and the identity continuation κ_0.

The program can choose to resume to the point where the exception was thrown via the `resume` instruction in the `catch` block[2]. The `resume` instruction expects that a continuation value r is also on top of the stack. To invoke the resumption, we provide an empty stack (which is nonetheless irrelevant since r will not use it), the current environment, and a new meta-continuation m_1.

Towards WasmFX-Style Effect Handlers. Our presentation of effect handlers to μWasm is both simpler and higher-level compared to the existing WasmFX proposal [19], as we only support unlabelled effects. Tags in WasmFX also allows more values to be passed to the handler instead of an error code. The handler clauses in WasmFX are specified by block labels instead of a single block of instructions as in our extension. WasmFX's design combines handling and resumption, leading to a combination of deep handler and shallow handler: the same handler is not reinstalled for the resumption, but any invocation of resumptions/continuations must be wrapped within some handler. In contrast, our CPS semantics simply follows the deep handler semantics. Different from WasmFX that is designed for one-shot continuations, we do not restrict the number of times a resumption can be invoked.

Implementing WasmFX-style effect handlers in our framework is possible, but would require a trail of continuations (instead of a meta-continuation), which supports more flexible manipulation of the context. We leave the full formalization of this as future work.

5 Implementation

The core CPS semantics presented in Fig. 3 can be viewed as either a big-step definitional interpreter for μWasm, or a translation from μWasm to λ-calculus with some functional data structures (e.g. lists).

We have implemented a big-step interpreter in Scala for standard WebAssembly[3]. A textual WebAssembly file (`.wat`) is parsed to a module using ANTLR, and then fed to the interpreter for evaluation. The following code snippet shows the core definitions and the main structure of the evaluation function:

[2] Although the resumption can escape via assignments.

[3] Available at https://github.com/Generative-Program-Analysis/wasm-cps.

```
type Stack = List[Value]
type Env = Map[Int, Value]
type Cont[A] = List[Value] ⇒ A
type Trail = List[Cont[Ans]]

def eval[Ans](insts: List[Inst], stack: Stack, env: Env,
              k: Cont[Ans], trail: Trail): Ans =
  insts match
    case Nil ⇒ k(stack, env)
    case Binary(op) ⇒
      val v2 :: v1 :: newStack = stack
      val result = evalBinOp(op, v1, v2)
      eval(rest, result :: newStack, env, k, trail)
    ... // more instructions
```

Compared to the minimal model language μWasm, our interpreter supports more top-level definitions (e.g. type definitions, tables, etc.) and instructions (e.g. memory operations, global variables, etc.). We have also experimentally implemented the extensions discussed in Sect. 4.1, Sect. 4.2, Sect. 4.4.

Although we have not yet implemented the full set of WebAssembly instructions, we have validated the control-flow semantics of the core instructions, ensuring that they behave consistently with other Wasm runtimes (e.g., Wasmtime, Wizard). In the future, we would like to further extend the interpreter with a larger set of instructions and validate its full semantics against the official WebAssembly specification test suite [35].

6 Related Work

Semantics of WebAssembly. The WebAssembly specification [13,34] defines a reference small-step reduction semantics, which has been used as the basis for various extensions and new developments. Besides the presented work, there are a few other works on defining big-step semantics for WebAssembly. Watt et al. [26] develop a big-step evaluation relation used in the soundness proof for Wasm Logic. Instead of using continuations, the big-step evaluation relation still makes use of first-order representations for the evaluation of block and loop (e.g., a list of labels as the evaluation context). Watt et al. [27] further develop a monadic interpreter as the oracle for fuzzing WebAssembly programs. The monadic interpreter (along with an intermediate interpreter) is written in Isabelle/HOL, and similarly uses a first-order representation of evaluation context. Following the abstracting definitional interpreter approach [11], Brandl et al. [4] develop a big-step abstract definitional interpreter for WebAssembly, which by using different monads can be instantiated for different purposes, such as concrete interpretation or taint analysis. Unlike ours that uses a list of continuations, Brandl et al. [4]'s definitional interpreter uses exceptions in Scala to encode breaks and return. To the best of our knowledge, our work is the first to reconstruct a big-step, compositional, semantics for WebAssembly using continuations.

Control Abstractions. Phipps-Costin et al. [19] proposed WasmFX, an extension for WebAssembly with typed delimited continuations and effect handlers. As an active proposal, the formal reduction semantics of WasmFX [28] is specified in the same style as the official WebAssembly specification, both of which make use of administrative instructions to handle control flow. In Sect. 4.4, we have discussed the major design difference between our extension and WasmFX. Our semantics of effect handlers is inspired by the CPS semantics of shift/reset [7]. Similar to our account of effect handlers, Hillerström et al. [14,15] have studied the CPS translation of effect handlers for a fine-grained call-by-value λ-calculus.

The extensions of for-loop (Sect. 4.1) and non-resumable exceptions (Sect. 4.3) are inspired by the Stanford CS242 course [24]. Although relatively straightforward, we believe these examples are pedagogically valuable in demonstrating their CPS semantics.

7 Conclusion and Future Work

We have presented a compositional, tail-recursive, and continuation-passing semantics for WebAssembly and demonstrated its application to several control abstraction extensions. We hope that the CPS semantics will serve as a useful reference for developing additional tools for WebAssembly, such as interpreters (as we showed in this paper), partial evaluators [3,17], compiler optimizations [1], and program analyses [36] informed by concrete semantics.

While we use a test suite to validate the correctness of our CPS semantics, formally proving its correctness or establishing its equivalence to the reference semantics remains a task for future work. One could conjecture that the reference reduction semantics can be transformed into a CPS semantics through refunctionalization [9] – and conversely, from the CPS semantics to its original form via defunctionalization [10,12]. Additionally, it would be interesting to transform the CPS semantics back to direct style [6,8,18], leveraging control operators in the meta-language. Given the correspondence between different formalizations of semantics, it is plausible that the CPS semantics could be mechanically derived from a single source of truth, such as SpecTec [37]. We leave these explorations for future work.

Acknowledgments. We would like to thank the reviewers of TFP for their insightful and constructive feedback, some of which has been incorporated into this revision of the paper. We also extend our gratitude to Andreas Rossberg, Elizabeth Gilbert, Ben Titzer, and Tiark Rompf for their valuable discussions, and to Mikail Khan for his contributions to the earlier implementations. Additionally, we thank the audiences at TFP and the WAW workshop for their questions and comments. The first author would like to thank Caterina Urban and the ANTIQUE team at INRIA for their support of this work.

A Auxiliary Definitions

We provide the definition of buildEnv that builds the initial environment for a function call according to the stack arguments and the types of local variables.

$$\begin{aligned}
&\mathsf{buildEnv} : (\mathsf{Stack} \times \mathsf{List}[\mathsf{ValueType}]) \to \mathsf{Env}\\
&\mathsf{buildEnv}(\sigma, ts) = \mathsf{reverse}(\sigma) +\!\!+ \mathsf{default}(ts)\\
&\mathsf{default} : \mathsf{List}[\mathsf{ValueType}] \to \mathsf{List}[\mathsf{Value}]\\
&\mathsf{default}([]) = []\\
&\mathsf{default}(t :: ts) = 0_t :: \mathsf{default}(ts)
\end{aligned}$$

B Recovering Break and Continue Semantics of br in for-Loop

Section 4.1 discussed the semantics of the structured for-loop, which has no interaction with br instructions. Here, we show how to recover C-style "continue" and "break" semantics of br in the loop body. Important changes compared to Sect. 4.1 are highlighted in red.

br as Continue in for-Loop:

$$\begin{aligned}
&[\![\mathsf{for}\ (es_{\mathsf{init}}; es_{\mathsf{cond}}; es_{\mathsf{post}})\ es :: rest]\!](\sigma, \rho, \kappa, \theta) =\\
&\quad \mathsf{fix}\ \kappa_1 := \lambda(\sigma_1, \rho_1).[\![es_{\mathsf{cond}}]\!]([], \rho_1, \lambda(v :: \sigma_2, \rho_2).\\
&\qquad\qquad \mathsf{if}\ v \equiv 0\ \mathsf{then}\ [\![rest]\!](\sigma, \rho_2, \kappa, \theta)\\
&\qquad\qquad \mathsf{else}\ [\![es]\!]([], \rho_2, \lambda(\sigma_3, \rho_3).[\![es_{\mathsf{post}}]\!]([], \rho_3, \kappa_1, \theta), \kappa_1 :: \theta))\ \mathsf{in}\\
&\quad [\![es_{\mathsf{init}}]\!]([], \rho, \kappa_1, \theta)
\end{aligned}$$

br as Break in for-Loop:

$$\begin{aligned}
&[\![\mathsf{for}\ (es_{\mathsf{init}}; es_{\mathsf{cond}}; es_{\mathsf{post}})\ es :: rest]\!](\sigma, \rho, \kappa, \theta) =\\
&\quad \mathsf{let}\ \kappa_0 := \lambda(\sigma_1, \rho_1).[\![rest]\!](\sigma, \rho_1, \kappa, \theta)\ \mathsf{in}\\
&\quad \mathsf{fix}\ \kappa_1 := \lambda(\sigma_2, \rho_2).[\![es_{\mathsf{cond}}]\!]([], \rho_2, \lambda(v :: \sigma_3, \rho_3).\\
&\qquad\qquad \mathsf{if}\ v \equiv 0\ \mathsf{then}\ \kappa_0(\sigma, \rho_3)\\
&\qquad\qquad \mathsf{else}\ [\![es]\!]([], \rho_3, \lambda(\sigma_4, \rho_4).[\![es_{\mathsf{post}}]\!]([], \rho_4, \kappa_1, \theta), \kappa_0 :: \theta))\ \mathsf{in}\\
&\quad [\![es_{\mathsf{init}}]\!]([], \rho, \kappa_1, \theta)
\end{aligned}$$

References

1. Appel, A.W.: Compiling with Continuations. Cambridge University Press (1992)
2. Biernacki, D., Danvy, O., Millikin, K.: A dynamic continuation-passing style for dynamic delimited continuations. ACM Trans. Program. Lang. Syst. **38**(1), 2:1–2:25 (2015)

3. Bondorf, A.: Improving binding times without explicit cps-conversion. In: LISP and Functional Programming, pp. 1–10. ACM (1992)
4. Brandl, K., Erdweg, S., Keidel, S., Hansen, N.: Modular abstract definitional interpreters for webassembly. In: ECOOP, LIPIcs, vol. 263, pp. 5:1–5:28, Schloss Dagstuhl - Leibniz-Zentrum für Informatik (2023)
5. Cong, Y., Asai, K.: Understanding algebraic effect handlers via delimited control operators. In: TFP. Lecture Notes in Computer Science, vol. 13401, pp. 59–79. Springer (2022)
6. Danvy, O.: Back to direct style. In: ESOP. Lecture Notes in Computer Science, vol. 582, pp. 130–150, Springer (1992)
7. Danvy, O., Filinski, A.: Abstracting control. In: LISP and Functional Programming, pp. 151–160. ACM (1990)
8. Danvy, O., Lawall, J.L.: Back to direct style II: first-class continuations. In: LISP and Functional Programming, pp. 299–310. ACM (1992)
9. Danvy, O., Millikin, K.: Refunctionalization at work. Sci. Comput. Program. **74**(8), 534–549 (2009)
10. Danvy, O., Nielsen, L.R.: Defunctionalization at work. In: PPDP, pp. 162–174. ACM (2001)
11. Darais, D., Labich, N., Nguyen, P.C., Horn, D.V.: Abstracting definitional interpreters (functional pearl). Proc. ACM Program. Lang. **1**(ICFP), 12:1–12:25 (2017)
12. Gibbons, J.: Continuation-passing style, defunctionalization, accumulations, and associativity. Art Sci. Eng. Program. **6**(2), 7 (2022)
13. Haas, A., et al.: Bringing the web up to speed with webassembly. In: PLDI, pp. 185–200. ACM (2017)
14. Hillerström, D., Lindley, S., Atkey, R.: Effect handlers via generalised continuations. J. Funct. Program. **30**, e5 (2020)
15. Hillerström, D., Lindley, S., Atkey, R., Sivaramakrishnan, K.C.: Continuation passing style for effect handlers. In: FSCD, LIPIcs, vol. 84, pp. 18:1–18:19. Schloss Dagstuhl - Leibniz-Zentrum für Informatik (2017)
16. Jones, N.D.: What not to do when writing an interpreter for specialisation. In: Dagstuhl Seminar on Partial Evaluation. Lecture Notes in Computer Science, vol. 1110, pp. 216–237. Springer (1996)
17. Lawall, J.L., Danvy, O.: Continuation-based partial evaluation. In: LISP and Functional Programming, pp. 227–238. ACM (1994)
18. Müller, M., Schuster, P., Brachthäuser, J.I., Ostermann, K.: Back to direct style: typed and tight. Proc. ACM Program. Lang. **7**(OOPSLA1), 848–875 (2023)
19. Phipps-Costin, L., et al.: Continuing WebAssembly with effect handlers. Proc. ACM Program. Lang. **7**(OOPSLA2), 460–485 (2023)
20. Plotkin, G.D.: A structural approach to operational semantics. J. Log. Algebraic Methods Program. **60–61**, 17–139 (2004)
21. Plotkin, G.D., Pretnar, M.: Handlers of algebraic effects. In: ESOP. Lecture Notes in Computer Science, vol. 5502, pp. 80–94. Springer (2009)
22. Plotkin, G.D., Pretnar, M.: Handling algebraic effects. Log. Methods Comput. Sci. **9**(4) (2013)
23. Reynolds, J.C.: Definitional interpreters for higher-order programming languages. In: ACM Annual Conference (2), pp. 717–740. ACM (1972)
24. Stanford University: CS242: Programming Languages (Fall 2019, Will Crichton) - Assignment 5 (2019). https://stanford-cs242.github.io/f19/assignments/assign5/. Accessed 28 Oct 2024
25. Thielecke, H.: Comparing control constructs by double-barrelled CPS. High. Order Symb. Comput. **15**(2–3), 141–160 (2002)

26. Watt, C., Maksimović, P., Krishnaswami, N.R., Gardner, P.: A program logic for first-order encapsulated WebAssembly. In: 33rd European Conference on Object-Oriented Programming (ECOOP 2019), Leibniz International Proceedings in Informatics (LIPIcs), vol. 134, pp. 9:1–9:30. Schloss Dagstuhl – Leibniz-Zentrum für Informatik (2019)
27. Watt, C., Trela, M., Lammich, P., Märkl, F.: WasmRef-Isabelle: a verified monadic interpreter and industrial fuzzing oracle for webassembly. Proc. ACM Program. Lang. **7**(PLDI), 100–123 (2023)
28. WebAssembly Contributors: WasmFX Specification (2024). https://wasmfx.dev/specs/core/. Accessed 11 Nov 2024
29. WebAssembly Contributors: Webassembly core specification: Runtime stack (2024). https://webassembly.github.io/spec/core/exec/runtime.html#stack. Accessed 17 Oct 2024
30. WebAssembly Contributors: WebAssembly Proposal: Exceptions (2024). https://github.com/WebAssembly/exception-handling/blob/main/proposals/exception-handling/Exceptions.md. Accessed 25 Sept 2024
31. WebAssembly Contributors: WebAssembly Proposal: Tail-Call (2024). https://github.com/WebAssembly/tail-call. Accessed 24 Oct 2024
32. WebAssembly Contributors: WebAssembly Proposal: Type Continuations (2024). https://github.com/WebAssembly/stack-switching/blob/main/proposals/continuations/Explainer.md. Accessed 25 Sept 2024
33. WebAssembly Contributors: WebAssembly Proposal: Typed Function References (2024). https://github.com/WebAssembly/function-references. Accessed 24 Oct 2024
34. WebAssembly Contributors: WebAssembly Specification (2024). https://webassembly.github.io/spec/core/. Accessed 25 Sept 2024
35. WebAssembly Contributors: Webassembly specification testsuite (2024). https://github.com/WebAssembly/spec/tree/main/test/core. Accessed 11 Nov 2024
36. Wei, G., et al.: Compiling parallel symbolic execution with continuations. In: ICSE, pp. 1316–1328. IEEE (2023)
37. Youn, D., et al.: Bringing the webassembly standard up to speed with spectec. Proc. ACM Program. Lang. **8**(PLDI), 1559–1584 (2024)

CoScheme: Compositional Copatterns in Scheme

Paul Downen(✉) and Adriano Corbelino II

University of Massachusetts Lowell, Lowell, MA 01854, USA
{Paul_Downen,Adriano_VilargaCorbelino}@uml.edu

Abstract. Since their introduction, copatterns have promised to extend functional languages—with their familiar pattern matching facilities—to synthesize and work with infinite objects through a finite set of observations. Thus far, their adoption in practice has been limited and primarily associated with specific tools like proof assistants. With that in mind, we aim to make copattern matching usable for ordinary functional programmers by implementing them as macros in the Scheme and Racket programming languages. Our approach focuses on composable copatterns, which can be combined in multiple directions and offer a new solution to the expression problem through novel forms of extensibility. To check the correctness of the implementation and to reason equationally about copattern-matching code, we describe an equational theory for copatterns with a sound, selective translation into λ-calculus.

Keywords: Codata · Copatterns · Scheme · Macros · Composition · Expression Problem

1 Introduction

Composition is one of the great promises of functional programming to combat complexity. As opposed to monolothic solutions, functional programming languages encourage us to decompose large problems into small, reusable, and reliable parts and then to recompose them back into a whole solution [13]. This practice is encouraged through tools like higher-order functions to abstract out common patterns and laziness to separate generation, selection, and consumption of information. Rather than implementing a complex algorithm as a single special-purpose loop, functional programming lets us express the same solution as the composition of simple domain-specific operations and generic combinators: maps, filters, folds, and unfolds.

However, the *expression problem* [29] is a familiar foe that still resists this (de)compositional approach. It captures the common problem that arises when we want to maintain code—such as an evaluator for the syntax trees of an expression language—by extending it in two different directions: adding new forms of data (*i.e.* classes of objects) and new operations (*i.e.* methods) on them. Traditionally, functional languages can easily add new operations over

J. Gibbons (Ed.): TFP 2025, LNCS 15652, pp. 205–258, 2026.
https://doi.org/10.1007/978-3-031-99751-8_10

any given data type, but adding a new constructor requires a major rewrite that can potentially alter the rest of the code. Conversely, object-oriented languages make it easy to add a new class of object, but extending a base class with a new method again requires major rewriting. Being a common obstacle in the way of maintaining, extending, and decomposing code, the expression problem has garnered many solutions in the object-oriented [19,30] and functional [16,24] worlds, and especially hybrid languages that mix both [3,11].

This work presents a novel solution to the expression problem: composable copatterns. Copatterns [2] are often associated with codata types for expressing infinite objects, but their use is not limited to just that. Their composition, in particular, allows us to define programs by performing equational reasoning in the evaluation context. Performing the "substitution of equals for equals" [28] enhances the predictability and composability of our programs since we can analyze our part code in isolation.

Previous implementations of copatterns can be found in strongly typed languages which impose prescribed restrictions on their use. For example, Agda gives the most full-fledged implementation of copatterns in a real system [6]. However, Agda is primarily a proof assistant rather than a general-purpose programming language, and as such, has different concerns than an ordinary functional programmer. There is also some support for copatterns in OCaml [18], but as an unofficial extension that has not been merged into the main compiler.

The copatterns implemented here are also implemented as macros like [18]; however, we present a different encoding that focuses on providing new methods of extensibility that were not available before, and can be desugared without any static typing information. To achieve that, and to fully integrate it into a practical general-purpose programming language, we choose a programmable programming language [10] and provide a new language extension as a library [27]. We focus, in particular, on Scheme and Racket, which offers a robust macro system for seamlessly implementing new language features.

Our extension presents three different composition flavors, allowing us to capture some "design patterns" used by functional programmers as first-class abstractions. First, we have *vertical* composition, which permits us to gather a collection of alternative options with failure handling. Second, we have *horizontal* composition, which permits us to compose a sequence of steps, parameters, matching, or guards. Third, we have *circular* composition, which allows us to recurse back on the entire composition itself.

Our primary contributions are organized as follows:

- Section 2 shows examples of programming with copattern equations in Scheme-like languages, including new forms of program composition—vertical and horizontal—that allows us to solve familiar examples of the expression problem [29] through a fusion of functional and object-oriented techniques.
- Section 3 exposes the challenges related to implementing copatterns in this scenario, introduces our library API, shows how we can desugar our abstractions into a set of primitives and how the implementations differ between Racket and a standard R^6RS-compliant Scheme.

- Section 4 presents a theory for how to translate copatterns into a small core target language—untyped λ-calculus with recursion and patterns—with a local double-barrel transformation reminiscent of selective continuation-passing style transformation. Importantly, only the new language constructs are transformed, while existing ones in the target language are unchanged.
- Section 4.2 demonstrates correctness in terms of an equational theory for reasoning about copattern-matching code in the source language, which is a conservative extension of the target language, and we prove that it is sound with respect to translation.

2 Programming with Composable Copatterns in Scheme

All examples shown below are executable Scheme and Racket code. You can follow along and interact with the code using the supporting library found online at https://github.com/pdownen/CoScheme.

2.1 Infinite Streams

For decades, functional programmers have had a reliable and versatile method for representing tree-shaped structures: inductive data types. These can model data of any size—for example, lists of an arbitrary length—but each instance must be *finite*. But how does a program handle infinite amounts of information, that cannot possibly occupy a finite memory space?

One method of modeling infinite information is through laziness, as in the Haskell programming language. For example, consider the usual infinite list of Fibonacci numbers in Haskell:

```
fibs :: [Int]
fibs = 0 : 1 : zipWith (+) fibs (tail fibs)
```

`fibs` cannot be fully evaluated because it has no base case—it would eventually expand out to `0 : 1 : 1 : 2 : 3 : 5 : 8 : ...` forever—but this is no problem in a non-strict language that only evaluates as much as needed. But what if we are working within a strict language without laziness built in? Must we give up on the approach entirely, or is there an alternate solution that works just as well with eager and lazy evaluation?

In contrast, *codata* describes types defined by primitive *destructors* that *use* values of the codata type—as opposed to the primitive constructors that define how to build values of a data type—and lets us easily model infinite data in eager languages, too. For example, the usual `Stream a` codata type of infinite `a`'s is defined by two destructors: `Head : Stream a -> a` extracts the first element and `Tail : Stream a -> Stream a` discards the first element and returns the rest. To define new streams, we can describe how they react to different combinations of `Head` and `Tail` destructors using *copatterns* [2]. Borrowing Agda's syntax, a possible copattern-based definition of the same `fibs` function above is:

```
fibs : Stream Nat
Head fibs = 0
Head (Tail fibs) = 1
Tail (Tail fibs) = zipWith _+_ fibs (Tail fibs)
```

However, at the moment, Agda currently does not understand if `fibs` is well-founded—it is—and so `fibs` is rejected. As a proof assistant, Agda has demanding requirements on all definitions to ensure well-foundedness: they must never have unproductive infinite loops, and they must cover every possible case (when matching on arguments or copatterns, as in `fibs`). But for a general-purpose programming language, we expect to be able to write arbitrary loops that may or may not terminate. Copattern-based definitions need to gracefully handle cases that fail to return—either due to an infinite loop or an exception, like an unhandled case, which are semantically similar [22]—and should generate code based on whatever is given. In this kind of setting, the language does not enforce—and indeed, our implementation does not check—coverage, which is instead up to the programmer to determine.

Let us now consider some examples of programming by equational reasoning to get familiar with copatterns and how we can use them in Scheme. For example, even in a dynamically-typed language like Scheme, linked lists can be thought of as an inductively-defined type combining two constructed forms: `List a = null | (cons a (List a))`. Likewise, infinite streams can be understood as the type of a procedure that exhibits two different behaviors at the same time: `Stream a ='head -> a &'tail -> Stream a`. In other words, any `Stream a` is a procedure that takes one argument, and its response depends on the exact value: given `'head` an `a` is returned, and given `'tail` another `Stream a` is returned.

In order to define new coinductive processes, one of the main entry points is the top-level, multi-line `define*` macro. This macro enables us to declare codata objects through a list of equations between a copattern on the left-hand side and an expression on the right-hand side. At the root of every copattern is a name for the object *itself*, which can be inside any number of applications—the applications may just list parameter names or more specific patterns, narrowing down the concrete arguments that match. Using `define*`, we can define the trivial `zeroes` stream—whose `'head` is `0` and whose `'tail` is more `zeroes`—as:

```
;; zeroes : Stream nat
(define* [(zeroes 'head) = 0]
         [(zeroes 'tail) = zeroes])
```

Streams like `zeroes` are black boxes that can only be observed by passing `'head` or `'tail` as arguments to get their response. Still, this is enough for many useful operations, like taking the first `n` elements, which can be `define*`d as:

```
;; takes : (Stream a, nat) -> List a
(define* [(takes s 0) = '()]
         [(takes s n) = (cons (s 'head) (takes (s 'tail) (- n 1)))])
```

A constant stream is not particularly useful; more interesting streams will change over time. For example, imagine a "stuttering" stream $(0, 0, 1, 1, 2, 2, 3, 3, \ldots)$

that repeats numbers twice before moving on. This stream can be defined by copattern matching equations:

```
;; stutter : nat -> Stream nat
(define* [ ((stutter n) 'head)         = n]
         [(((stutter n) 'tail) 'head) = n]
         [(((stutter n) 'tail) 'tail) = (stutter (+ n 1))])
```

So that `(takes (stutter 1) 10) ='(1 1 2 2 3 3 4 4 5 5)`,[1] because the first and second elements—`((stutter n)'head)` and `(((stutter n)'tail)'head)` respectively—return the same `n` before incrementing.

But why is `stutter` well-defined, and how can we understand its meaning? As in many functional languages, the `=` in code really implies equality between the two sides, and this equality still holds when we plug in real values for placeholder variables like `n`. So to determine the first `'head` element, of `(stutter 1)`, we match the left-hand side and replace it with the right to get `((stutter 1)'head) = 1`. Similarly, the second element is `(((stutter 1)'tail)'head) = 1` as well. The third element is accessed by two `'tail` projections and then a `'head` as the nested applications `((((stutter 1)'tail)'tail)'head)`, which doesn't exactly match any left-hand side. However, equality holds in any context, and the inner application `(((stutter 1)'tail)'tail)` *does* match the third equation. Thus, we can apply a few steps of equational reasoning to derive the expected answer 2:

```
((((stutter 1) 'tail) 'tail) 'head) = ((stutter (+ 1 1)) 'tail)  ; line 3
                                     = ((stutter 2) 'head)         ; +
                                     = 2                           ; line 1
```

So these three examples work, but is every case really covered? The `Stream Nat` interface that `stutter`'s output follows allows for any number of `'tail` projections followed by a final application to `'head` that returns a natural number. `stutter` works its way through these projections in groups of two, eliminating a pair of `'tail` projections at a time until it gets to the end case, which is either a `'head` (if the total number of `'tails` is even) or a `'tail` followed by `'head` (if the total number of `'tails` is odd). So, `stutter` behavior is defined no matter what is asked of it. Even with other observations like `takes`, which passes around partial applications of `stutter` as a first-class value, internally `stutter` only "sees" the `'head` and `'tail` applications from `takes`, and is dormant otherwise.

Reasoning about the coverage of our copatterns is important since our implementation does not provide coverage analysis. If we encounter an uncovered case, our implementation emits a runtime error, explaining that this is an uncovered copattern. Non-total configurations, akin to partial functions, are not always undesirable. They can simplify the development during a prototyping phase, and if the missing case does not make sense, they can be the most semantically meaningful.

With this practice under our belt, we can now directly translate the canonical Fibonacci example from Agda to Scheme like so:

[1] Try it! https://github.com/pdownen/CoScheme has implementations of `define*` and related macros used by these examples.

```
;; zips-with : ((a, b) -> c, Stream a, Stream b) -> Stream c
(define*
  [((zips-with f xs ys) 'head) = (f (xs 'head) (ys 'head))]
  [((zips-with f xs ys) 'tail) = (zips-with f (xs 'tail) (ys 'tail))])

;; fibs : Stream nat
(define*
  [ (fibs 'head)         = 0]
  [((fibs 'tail) 'head) = 1]
  [((fibs 'tail) 'tail) = (zips-with + fibs (fibs 'tail))])
```

so that `(takes fibs 10)` is `'(0 1 1 2 3 5 8 13 21 34)`.

2.2 Self-referential Objects

Codata can also be used to implement an abstract interface over regular finite data. As an alternate syntax for `define*`, we can explicitly give a top-level name to bind the definition to for external use, and on each equation give a hidden internal for self-reference and recursion. To illustrate this, consider the following queue example, which internally refers to itself by the name `self` for an object-oriented feel:

```
(define* queue
  [ (self 'new)                = (self '() '())]
  [((self in  out) 'enq x) = (self (cons x in) out)]
  [((self '() '()) 'deq)   = (error "Invalid dequeue: empty queue")]
  [((self in  '()) 'deq)   = ((self '() (reverse in)) 'deq)]
  [((self in  out) 'deq)   = (cons (car out) (self in (cdr out)))])
```

This reflects the purely functional queue implementation in using two lists (an inbox and an outbox) as internal states. We externally bound this declaration to the name `queue`, but the internal recursion is through the name `self`. This `queue` object responds to three methods: `'new` returns a new empty queue, `'enq x` puts the `x` to the end of the queue (*i.e.* the top of the inbox), and `'deq` returns the oldest enqueued element (from the top of the outbox or bottom of the inbox, as appropriate). Thus, `((((queue'new)'enq 1)'enq 2)'deq)` returns the oldest element `1` and a queue object containing only `2`.

Visualizing what we are defining through the lens of the object-oriented paradigm can give a new perspective here. With this metaphor, we can view our definitions as describing the protocols of objects, where the equations specify how an object should respond to a sequence of messages. Here, `queue` itself can only directly respond to one message—`'new`—that initializes the object with two empty lists for its private internal state. From there, the initialized `queue` object now only responds to the `'enq x` and `'deq` messages which can read and update the object's internal state. However, besides these two messages, there is no other way to manipulate the internal state of an initialized `queue` object; the `in` and `out` lists are completely hidden within an opaque procedural abstraction, enforcing an encapsulation of private state. Given an initialized `queue` object, it would not be possible, for instance, to break the first-in-first-out ordering by taking an element from the `in` list or to put an element on the `out` list.

Since we can already use encapsulation in copattern-based definitions, can we also use a functional model [1] of inheritance and dynamic dispatch? Our implementation of copattern matching in Scheme includes new facilities for composing code snippets compared to current functional (or object-oriented) languages. However, to avoid unwanted surprises, the programmer does have to ask for them. This is a small request, and can be done by replacing `define*` with `define-object`, as in the following file system example:

```
(define-object
  [((fs-object p . _) 'path) = p])

(define-object (<: (import-object fs-object))
  [((file p txt) 'text) = txt]
  [((file p txt) 'size) = (string-length ((file p txt) 'text))])

(define-object (directory <: (import-object fs-object))
  [((apply dir p cts) 'contents) = cts]
  [((apply dir p cts) 'overhead) = 8]
  [((apply dir p cts) 'size)
   = (apply + ((apply dir p cts) 'overhead)
              (map (λ(o) (o 'size)) ((apply dir p cts) 'contents)))])
```

This example emulates some functionality of a filesystem, specifically calculating various sizes. Every filesystem object has a path, which is captured by the `fs-object` object that only knows how to calculate its `'path` by returning the first piece of information it was given and ignoring the rest of the object's internal data. Filesystem objects all also have a size, but calculating it requires more object-specific information. This additional functionality is spelled out by more specific filesystem objects:

- A `file` contains some `'text` and its `'size` is the length of that text.
- A `directory` contains any number of additional filesystem objects, stored as its `'contents`, and its `'size` is the sum of it's `'contents` size plus an additional `'overhead` that defaults to 8.

Both `file` and `directory` objects inherit the code for calculating it's `'path` by importing `fs-object` with the extension clause `<: (import-object fs-object)`. Note that these three object definitions exercise three of the four possible definition forms, based on whether the external name is given explicitly or inferred, and on whether there is an extension clause is included:

- `fs-object`'s external name is inferred from the internal name in its copattern equation, and it has no listed extension clause,
- `file`'s external name is taken from its internal one and it extends `fs-object`,
- `directory`'s external name is given explicitly (and is different from its internal name) and it extends `fs-object`.

The last possibility is an explicit external name with no extensions, such as the following equivalent definition of `fs-object` that elaborates the naming inference:

```
(define-object fs-object
  [((fs-object p . _) 'path) = p])
```

While these definitions are functional, they contain some undesirable redundancy. In particular, we have to repeat the same initialization forms—`(file p txt)` and `(apply dir p cts)`—in front of every equational definition because the object must be initialized with parameters before it is used. What is worse, every time we want to ask a question about the object itself by recursively passing it a message, we have to repeat this same initialization again exactly as it occurred, leading to longer and more error-prone code. It would be better here to follow the common object-oriented factorization of steps: *first* the object is initialized with some internal data at the time of its construction, and *then* we get an object that can (recursively) respond to methods. This can be done by factoring out the common construction phase in the above definitions using a `construct` clause like so:

```
(define-object (<: (import-object fs-object))
  [(file p txt) (construct (list p txt))
   (object
    [(self 'text) = txt]
    [(self 'size) = (string-length (self 'text))])])

(define-object (directory* <: (import-object fs-object))
  [(apply dir p cts) (construct (cons p cts))
   (object
    [(self 'contents) = cts]
    [(self 'overhead) = 8]
    [(self 'size)
     = (apply + (self 'overhead)
              (map (λ(o) (o 'size)) (self 'contents)))])])
```

The `construct` operation lists its internal parameters given at the time of initialization. After this step, we describe a first-class anonymous `object` that knows how to refer to its fully-constructed form by an internal name (here we use the name `self`), so there is no need to re-construct `(file p txt)` or `(apply dir p cts)` to recursively call other methods. Factoring out the common copattern leads to shorter code, the definitions describe objects with exactly the same behavior as before.

So far, we have only shaved off small parts of shared code: the common `'path` method and the initial initialization copattern. Where this coding style starts to pay off is when we override some methods to automatically influence the result of others. For example, we might have a fancier type of directory structure that replicates the exact same behavior as a normal directory, but its `'overhead` is 128 instead of 8. Or we might have static links that act like a normal `file`, except that they only contain a path to the real place its text is stored, so it always has a fixed size (8). These specialized revisions of directories and files can be implemented by importing from the original definitions and modifying certain lines like so (where we omit the code for looking up the text for a static link):

```
(define-object (fancy-directory <: (import-object directory))
  [((fancy-dir p . cts) 'overhead) = 128])

(define-object (<: (import-object file))
  [(static-link p lnk) (construct (list p lnk))
   (object
    [(_ 'link) = lnk]
    [(_ 'text) = "..."]
    [(_ 'size) = 8])])
```

Although `fancy-directory` has only one defining equation about its `'overhead`, the implication is that its `'size` should be 120 larger than a regular `directory` due to the `'overhead` increase. We can test out this use of inheritance and dynamic dispatch by simulating a small directory structure:

```
(define ham (file "hamlet.md" "Words, words, words...."))
(define guide (file "Guide.md" "Don't Panic"))
(define books (directory* "Books" ham guide))
(define shortcut (static-link "Guide.md" "Books/Guide.md"))
(define docs (fancy-directory "Documents" shortcut books))
```

and calculating the sizes of each file system object:

```
(ham      'size) = 23  = (string-length "Words, words, words....")
(guide    'size) = 11  = (string-length "Don't Panic")
(books    'size) = 42  = (+ 8 23 11)
(shortcut 'size) = 8
(docs     'size) = 178 = (+ 128 8 42)
```

The question is: how were we able to inject new code in the middle of an object like `directory` to change its behavior? The key issue is that, within `directory`, recursive calls to `((apply dir p cts)'overhead)`—or just simply `(self'overhead)` in the second version—cannot be tied to *this* definition of `directory`. Instead, we employ *open recursion*: the internal references to the recursive object itself are left as unbound parameters that will only be bound to the full object value when the final definition is ready to use. This is why the internal and external names can be different—like in `queue` and `directory`—since the external name is bound to the final object value while the internal names are left (temporarily) open-ended and will be filled in later. In the same way, the internal names used in each clause are fully independent and can also differ from one another. This difference of using open recursion to leave internal names temporarily unbound also applies to definitions where the external name is inferred: although the external names `file` and `static-link` are inferred from the internal names in the copatterns, the internal variables are left unbound until the externally-visible name gets bound to the object value.

Thankfully, this whole framework is still built on purely functional idioms, which makes it easier to reason about code. How can we understand what inheritance should do? The answer should be familiar to functional programmers:

inheritance is composition and substitution! For example, the inheritance dependencies can be fully inlined as-is into `fancy-directory` to bring the full definition into one place by copying the inherited code into place like so:

```
(define-object fancy-directory
  [((fancy-dir p . cts) 'overhead) = 128]
  [((apply dir p cts)   'overhead) = 8]
  [((apply dir p cts)   'contents) = cts]
  [((apply dir p cts)   'size)
   = (apply + ((apply dir p cts) 'overhead)
              (map (λ(o) (o 'size)) ((apply dir p cts) 'contents)))]
  [((fs-object p . _)   'path)     = p])
```

After naïve inlining, there are some irrelevant differences: there are three different internal names (`fancy-dir`, `dir`, and `fs-object`) used in various clauses, and we use two equivalent syntaxes (`(fancy-dir p . cts)` and `(apply dir p cts)`) for copatterns that bind arbitrary-length argument sequences to `cts`. Cleaning up these differences by rewriting each initializing copattern to `(apply self p cts)` and renaming as necessary gives a more uniform code:

```
(define-object fancy-directory
  [((apply self p cts) 'overhead) = 128]
  [((apply self p cts) 'overhead) = 8]
  [((apply self p cts) 'contents) = cts]
  [((apply self p cts)   'size)
   = (apply + ((apply self p cts) 'overhead)
              (map (λ(o) (o 'size)) ((apply self p cts) 'contents)))]
  [((apply self p _)   'path)     = p])
```

From here, it becomes more obvious that the two different equations defining `(... 'overhead)` overlap, so the first one takes precedence and the second one is dead code that can be completely erased. Furthermore, when there are no more future extensions, we can inline the recursive calls at this point, to get the simpler closed definition that reveals exactly what each method will do:

```
(define* fancy-directory
  [((apply self p cts) 'overhead) = 128]
  [((apply self p cts) 'contents) = cts]
  [((apply self p cts) 'size)
   = (apply + 128 (map (λ(o) (o 'size)) cts))]
  [((apply self p _)   'path)     = p])
```

2.3 Decomposing the Expression Problem

Our notion of compositional copatterns can capture some object-oriented styles of code (de)composition with encapsulation, inheritance, and dynamic dispatch. How can this new capability for composition influence the kinds of functional programs we write? For example, consider the usual definition of a simple arithmetic expression evaluator in typed functional languages like Haskell and OCaml (we use Haskell syntax here):

```
data Expr = Num Int | Add Expr Expr

eval :: Expr -> Int
eval (Num n)   = n
eval (Add l r) = eval l + eval r
```

While Scheme does not have algebraic data types, we can encode complex constructor expressions as a list starting with the constructor name as a quoted symbol and the arguments as the remainder of the list, and when unambiguous, leave atomic data alone. So `Num 5` could just be represented as the plain number `5`, and `Add l r` would be represented as the *quasiquote* `` `(add ,l ,r) `` which plugs in the values bound to variables `l` and `r` as the second and third elements of the list (denoted by the "unquote" comma `,` before the variable names). We can then use the facilities of `define*` to write almost identical code in Scheme like so, using the *guard* `try-if` to test if the argument is a number:

```
;; eval : Expr -> Number
(define*
  [(eval n) (try-if (number? n)) = n]
  [(eval `(add ,l ,r))           = (+ (eval l) (eval r))])
```

Fantastic, it works! Both the Scheme and Haskell code have the same structure. And on the surface, they both share the same strengths and weaknesses. From the lens of the *expression problem* [29], it is easy to add new operations to existing expressions—such as listing the numeric literals in an expression

```
;; list-nums : Expr -> List num
(define*
  [(list-nums n)
   (try-if (number? n))      = (list n)]
  [(list-nums `(add ,l ,r)) = (append (list-nums l) (list-nums r))])
```

—but adding new classes of expressions is hard. For example, if we wanted to support multiplication, we could add a `Mult` constructor to the `Expr` data type, but this would require modifying *all* existing operations and case-splitting expressions over `Expr` values. Even worse, if we wanted to support both expression languages—with or without multiplication—we would have to copy the code and maintain both versions.

Thankfully, our implementation of copattern matching in Scheme includes new facilities for composing code snippets. As we previously saw with the object-oriented examples, we can turn ordinary functional code into a more extensional form by using `define-object` instead of `define*`.

```
;; list-nums* : Expr -> List num
(define-object
  [(list-nums* n)
   (try-if (number? n))       = (list n)]
  [(list-nums* `(add ,l ,r)) = (append (list-nums* l) (list-nums* r))])
```

The `list-nums*` object behaves exactly like `list-nums` in all the same contexts it works in, but in addition, it implicitly inherits additional functionality for composition defined elsewhere. This new composition lets us break existing multi-line definitions into individual parts, and recompose them later. For example, the evaluator can be composed in terms of separate objects for each line like so:

```
(define-object
  [(eval-num n) (try-if (number? n)) = n])

(define-object
  [(eval-add `(add ,l ,r)) = (+ (eval-add l) (eval-add r))])

;; eval* : Expr -> num
(define eval* (eval-num 'compose eval-add))
```

So `(eval expr)` is the same as `(eval* expr)` for any well-formed expression argument. Why program in this way? Now, if we want to extend the functionality of existing operations—like evaluation and listing literals—to support a new class of expression, we can define the new special cases separately as a patch and then *compose* them with the existing code as-is like so:

```
(define-object
  [(eval-mul `(mul ,l ,r)) = (* (eval-mul l) (eval-mul r))])
(define-object
  [(list-mul `(mul ,l ,r)) = (append (list-mul l) (list-mul r))])

;; eval-arith : Expr+Mul -> num
(define eval-arith (eval* 'compose eval-mul))

;; eval-arith : Expr+Mul -> List num
(define list-nums-arith (list-nums* 'compose list-mul))
```

So for an expression `(define expr1 '(add (mul 2 3) 4))`, the extended code correctly yields `(eval-arith expr1) = 10` and `(list-nums-arith expr1) = '(2 3 4)` whereas the original code fails at the `'mul` case.[2] Note that this composition automatically generates *new* functions and leaves the original code intact, which can still be used for the smaller expression language with only numbers and addition.

This example emphasizes our guiding principle: *composition*. We call combinations like `(eval-num 'compose eval-add eval-mul)` *vertical composition* since they behave as if we simply stacked their internal cases vertically, like in the original definition of `eval`.

Not all types of language extensions are this simple, though. Consider what happens if we want to support algebraic expressions which might have variables in them. To evaluate a variable, we need a given environment—mapping names to numbers—which we can use to look up the variable's value.

```
(define-object [(eval-var env `(var ,x)) = (lookup env x)])
```

[2] The astute reader might notice the open recursion at work here: the recursive calls to `eval-mul` cannot be specifically tied to this definition because it only says what to do with multiplication and fails to handle the other cases. Instead, recursive calls to `eval-mul` must *also* open to invoking the other code associated with `eval-num` and `eval-add` even though it is not known to be associated with them yet.

However, it is wrong to just vertically compose this variable evaluator with the previous code because the arithmetic evaluator only takes a single expression as an argument, whereas the variable evaluator needs *both* an environment and an expression. The manual way to perform this extension is routine for functional programmers: in addition to adding a new case, we have to add an extra parameter to each case, which gets passed along on all recursive calls.

It would be highly disappointing to have to rewrite our existing code in-place to do this extension. Fortunately, our copattern language allows for another type of composition—*horizontal composition*—which allows us to combine sequences of steps, one after another, and automatically fall through to the next case if something fails. For this example, we can define a general procedure `with-environment` to perform the above transformation, taking any extensible evaluator object expecting just an expression and threading an environment along each recursive call. This lets us patch our existing arithmetic evaluator with an environment and then compose it with variable evaluation like so:

```
(define (with-environment eval-ext)
  (object [(self env expr)
           (with-self (override-lambda* self
                        [(_ sub-expr) = (self env sub-expr)])
             (try-apply-forget eval-ext expr))]))

;; Env = List (Symbol . num)

;; eval-alg : (Env, Expr+Mul+Var) -> num
(define eval-alg
  ((with-environment (eval-arith 'unplug)) 'compose eval-var))
```

The `with-environment` function is the most complex code we have seen so far, but it just spells out the usual steps a functional programmer uses to modify existing code with an environment.

- Given the evaluator `eval-ext`, it returns a new first-class `object` (which is the same as `define-object` without assigning a name) that expects both an environment and expression to process.
- This new object then invokes `eval-ext` by passing just the expression, except that if `eval-ext` ever tries to recur with a sub-expression, the calls `(self sub-expr)` gets replaced with `(self env sub-expr)` just like the template transformation.
- This transformation of the evaluator's notion of self is done by the `with-self` operation, which can override the original recursive `self`.
- Finally, if none of the clauses of `eval-ext` succeed, then this updated evaluator also falls through as before, forgetting the application had ever happened via `try-apply-forget`.

The complete algebraic evaluator can then be made from an open-ended, extensible version of the arithmetic evaluator—retrieved from `(eval-arith 'unplug)`—horizontally composed to take an environment and vertically composed with the single-line `eval-var`. It can now successfully evaluate algebraic expressions, such as `(define expr2 '(add (var x) (mul 3 (var y))))`, so that running the evaluation `(eval-arith '((x . 10) (y . 20)) expr2)` returns 70 because the environment maps `x` to 10 and `y` to 20.

Another possible way to evaluate expressions with variables is *constant folding*, a common optimization where operations are simplified unless they are blocked by variables whose values are unknown. In other words, the evaluator might return a blocked expression if it cannot fully calculate the final number. Ideally, we would like to extend our existing evaluator as-is, with the additional cases when blocked expressions are encountered. However, as written, the equation handling ``(eval `(add ,l ,r))`` already commits to a real numeric addition, even if evaluating `l` or `r` does not give a numeric result.

To avoid over-committing before we know whether evaluation will successfully calculate a final number or not, we can—at first glance—rewrite the basic clauses of evaluation in a more defensive style. Essentially, this splits evaluation into two separate steps: (1) check which operation we are supposed to do and evaluate the two sub-expressions, (2) combine the two expressions according to that operation. For example, the steps for addition and multiplication look like:

```
(define-object eval-add-safe
  [(self 'eval ('add l r))
  = (self 'add (self 'eval l) (self 'eval r))]
  [(self 'add x y) (try-if (and (number? x) (number? y)))
  = (+ x y)])

(define-object eval-mul-safe
  [(self `(mul ,l ,r))
   = (self 'mul (self l) (self r))]
  [(self 'mul x y)
   (try-if (and (number? x) (number? y)))
   = (* x y)])
```

Here, the evaluation step is explicated by a `'eval` tag, to help distinguish from the other operation `'add` for adding the left and right results. Note that in this code, the `'add` clause only performs a numeric addition `+` if it knows for sure that *both* of the arguments are actually numbers. We can now compose the original base-case for evaluating numbers with this "safer" version of addition that fails to match cases where sub-expressions don't evaluate to numbers (multiplication could be added as well in a similar style):

```
;; eval-arith-safe : ('eval, Expr+Mul) -> num
;;                 & ('add, num, num) -> num
;;                 & ('mul, num, num) -> num
(define eval-arith-safe (eval-num 'compose eval-add-safe eval-mul-safe))
```

So `(eval-arith-safe expr1)` still evaluates to 70, but `(eval-arith-safe expr2)` fails when it finds a variable sub-expression.

If it finds a variable, constant folding will just leave it alone and return an unevaluated expression rather than a final number. Because the `'eval` operation might return a (partially) unevaluated expression, we now need to handle cases where the left or right (or both) sub-expressions do not evaluate to numbers. In each of those cases, we must reform the addition expression out of what we find, converting numbers `n` into a syntax tree of the form `` `(num ,n) ``.

```
(define-object
  [(leave-variables 'eval ('var x)) = (list 'var x)])

(define-object reform-operations
  [(reform 'add l r) = (list 'add l r)]
  [(reform 'mul l r) = (list 'mul l r)])
```

The final constant-folding algorithm can be composed from this "safe" version of evaluation, along with the cases for leaving variables alone and reforming partially-evaluated additions and multiplications.

```
;; constant-fold : ('eval, Expr+Mul+Var) -> Expr+Mul+Var
;;               & ('add, Expr+Mul+Var, Expr+Mul+Var) -> Expr+Mul+Var
;;               & ('mul, Expr+Mul+Var, Expr+Mul+Var) -> Expr+Mul+Var
(define constant-fold
  (eval-arith-safe 'compose leave-variables reform-operations))
```

So now `(constant-fold 'eval expr2)` successfully returns `expr2` itself (because there are no operations to perform without knowing the values of variables `x` and `y`). And running `(constant-fold 'eval expr3)` on the expression

```
(define expr3 '(add (add 1 1)
                    (mul (var x)
                         (mul 2 (add 2 3)))))
```

simplifies it down to `'(add 2 (mul (var x) 10))`. To add other operations, like subtraction, we can easily define similar `eval-sub-safe` and `reform-subtraction`, and `'compose` them with `constant-fold` without having to rewrite any code.

3 A Composable Copattern Macro Library

3.1 Challenges

Even though the behavior of small examples may be straightforward to understand, there are several challenges to correctly implementing copatterns in the general case. Some of these challenges are specific to Scheme—a dynamically-typed, call-by-value language—which forces us to carefully resolve the timing of when and which copatterns are matched. Other challenges are specific to our extensions to copatterns—the ability to compose copattern matching in two different directions—which also brings in the notion of the recursive "self."

Timing and the Order of Copattern Matching. Copatterns may have ambiguous cases where two different overlapping copattern equations match the same application. For example, this following function moves a number by `1` away from `0`—positives are incremented and negatives are decremented:

```
(define* [(away-from0 x) (try-if (>= x 0)) = (+ x 1)]
 [(away-from0 x) (try-if (<= x 0)) = (- x 1)])
```

Consequently, we must interpret the programmer's code as it is written since we cannot gain any information from a static type system. In the previous example, the two different equations overlap for `0` itself: either one matches the call `(away-from0 0)`. To disambiguate overlapping copatterns, the listed equations are always tried top-down, and the first full match "wins," as is typical in functional languages. In this case, the first line wins, so `(away-from0 0)` is `1`. Furthermore, guards like `try-if` and `try-match` are run left-to-right with shortcircuiting—the moment a copattern or a guard fails, everything to the right is skipped. This makes it possible to protect potentially-erroneous guards with another safety guard to its left, such as `(try-if (not (= y 0)))` followed by `(try-if (> (/ x y) z))`.

However, there are more timing issues besides these usual choices for disambiguation and short-circuiting. First of all, since we are in a call-by-value language, we have to handle cases where an object is used in a context that doesn't fully match a copattern *yet*, but could in the future—and possibly multiple different times. This can happen for instances like curried functions that take arguments in multiple different calls. Just like with ordinary curried functions, using such an object in a calling context passing only the first list of arguments—but not the second—builds a *value* which closes over the parameters so far. For example, consider this simple counter object that can add or get its current internal state.

```
(define* [((counter x) 'add y) = (counter (+ x y))]
         [((counter x) 'get)   = x])
```

The call `((counter 4) 'get)` matches the second equation, returning the answer `4`, but `(counter 4)` on its own is not enough information to definitively match either copattern, so it is just a value remembering that `x = 4` and waiting for another call. Similarly, the call `(counter (+ x y))` on the right-hand side is *also* incomplete in the same sense, so it, too, is a value. This definition gives us an object with the following behavior:

```
> (define c0 (counter 4))
> (define c1 (c0 'add 1))
> ((c1 'add 2) 'get)
7
> (c1 'get)
5
```

So far, what we have seen so far seems similar to pattern-matching functions in languages that are curried-by-default. One way in which copatterns generalize curried functions is that each equation can take a *different* number of arguments. For example, consider this reordering of the `stutter` stream from Sect. 2:

```
(define* [(((stutter n) 'tail) 'tail) = (stutter (+ n 1))]
         [(((stutter n) 'tail) 'head) = n]
         [ ((stutter n) 'head)        = n])
```

Since none of the copatterns overlap, its behavior is exactly the same as before. But notice the extra complication here: calling `((stutter 10) 'head)` with two arguments (`10` and `'head`) should immediately return `10`. However, the first equation is waiting for three arguments (an `n` and two `'tails` passed separately). That means that the underlying code implementing `stutter` *cannot* ask for three arguments in three different calls and then checks that the last two are `'tail`. Instead, it has to eagerly match the arguments that it is given against the patterns and try each of the guards to see if the current line fails—and only *after* that all succeed, it may ask for more arguments and continue the copattern match.

Composition and the Dimensions of Extensibility. The second set of challenges is due to the new notions of object composition that we develop here. In particular, we want to be able to combine objects in two different directions:

- *vertical composition* is an "either or" combination of two or more objects, such as `(o1 'compose o2 ...)` that acts like `o1` or `o2`, *etc.*[,] depending on which one knows how to respond to the context. Textually, the vertical composition of `(object line-a1 ...)` and `(object line-b1 ...)` behaves as if we copied all each line of copattern-matching equations internally used to define the two objects and pasted them vertically into the newly-composed object as:

```
(object line-a1
        ...
        line-b1
        ...)
```

- *horizontal composition* is an "and then" object combination in a copattern-matching line, such as `[(self 'method1) (o1 'unplug)]` defining a `'method1` that continues to act like `o1` when `o1` knows how to respond to the surrounding context, and otherwise tries the next line. Textually, the horizontal composition of a `'method1` followed by trying another object with its own copattern-matching contexts `Q1 Q2 ...` acts as if the two copatterns are combined, and the inner object is inlined into the outer one like so:

```
(object [(self 'method1) ((object [Q1 = response1]
                                  [Q2 = response2]
                                  ...) 'unplug)]
        ...)
=
(object [(self 'method1) (comatch Q1) = response1]
        [(self 'method1) (comatch Q2) = response2]
        ...)
```

Even though we can visually understand the two directions of composition by the textual manipulations above, in reality, both of these compositions are done at run-time (*i.e.* with arbitrary procedural values), as opposed to "compile-time" transformation (*i.e.* macro-expansion time manipulations of code). This means we need an extensible representation of run-time object values that allows for automatically switching from one object to another in the case of copattern-match failure, as well as correctly keeping track of what to try next.

The basic idea of this representation can be understood as an extension of an idiom in ordinary functional programming. In order to define an open-ended, pattern-matching function, we can give the cases we know how to handle now by matching on the arguments and include a default "catch-all" case at the end for the other behavior. In Haskell, this might look like

```
f next PatA1 PatA2 ... = expr1
f next PatB1 PatB2 ... = expr2
...
f next x1    x2    ... = next x1 x2 ...
```

For example, consider the single-line `eval-add` evaluator object from Sect. 2. In order to compose `eval-add` with another evaluator handling a different case, like `eval-mul`, its internal extensible code takes an extra hidden argument saying what to try `next` if its line does not match, analogous to:

```
(define (eval-add-ext1 next)
  (lambda*
    [(self 'eval `(add ,l ,r)) = (+ (self 'eval l) (self 'eval r))]
    [ self                     = (next self)]))
```

Note that, unlike the Haskell code above, the hidden `next` parameter also takes *another* hidden parameter: `self`. Why? Because if the `next` set of equations needs to recurse, it cannot actually jump to itself directly—that would skip the `eval-add` code entirely—but needs to jump back to the very first equation to try. This `self` parameter holds the value of the *whole* object after all compositions have been done, as it appeared in the original call site. Thus, the internal extensible code `eval-add-ext` *also* takes this second `self` parameter for the same reason: it may be the second component of a composition, and it is similar to the following Racket definition:

```
(define ((eval-add-ext2 next) self)
  (match-lambda*
    [(list 'eval `(add ,l ,r)) (+ (self 'eval l) (self 'eval r))]
    [args                      ((next self) args)]))
```

One final detail to note: unless otherwise stated, the `self` parameter—which is visible as the root of any copattern—is *always* the same view of the entire object. That means nesting multiple copatterns in sequence might not give the expected result because the `self` parameter in the hole of every copattern context will be bound to the same value. If we instead want the parameter in the hole of every copattern context to reflect the object at that point in time—that is, be assigned the value given by the partial applications given by the preceding copatterns—we can use the `nest` operation. For example, nesting copatterns in a sequence gives us a shorthand for the common functional idiom of a "local" loop that closes over some parameters that never change, such as this definition of mapping a function over a list:

```
(define* [(map* f xs) = ((map* f) xs)]
         [(map* f) (nest)
           (extension
            [(go null)         = null]
            [(go (cons x xs)) = (cons (f x) (go xs))])])
```

The map* function supports both curried and uncurried applications, and they are defined to be equal. Its real code is given in the curried case, where the function parameter f is bound first and never changes. Then, in a second step, we have the internal looping function go, which matches over its list parameter and recurses with a new list. The definition of go is given directly in the form of an extension—the result of 'unplugging an object—which is composed with the curried application (map* f). By using nest, we have go = (map* f), so that f is visible from the closure but does not need to be passed again at every step of the loop.

3.2 The Library API and Macro Desugaring

To meet all the implementation challenges listed above, the API of our compositional copattern library revolves around three groups of first-class values:

- *Objects* are ordinary values, typically functions, that can be used directly via application. Their exact interface varies based on their definition—such as a function from a list of numbers to a list of booleans, an evaluator from expression trees to numbers, or an object following the infinite stream interface—but they can be applied without any additional information.
- *Templates* represent openly-recursive, self-referential code without a fixed self. Instead, the "self" placeholder remains unbound for now, and it can be instantiated later via application to yield an *object* described above.
- *Extensions* represent extensible code that can be composed together both vertically and horizontally. Instead of failing on an unsuccessful match, will try an as-of-yet unspecified "next" option specified later via application to a template to produce a new template. This way, the "self" placeholder is also unbound for now—just like with templates—and can be bound later when the whole object is finished being composed.

Figure 1 describes a core API for forming or manipulating objects, templates, and extensions as first-class values. These individual operations can implement all of the examples seen thus far, which make heavy use of top-level definitional forms like define* and define-object. The grammar of syntax supported by these definitional forms, the operations which interpret copatterns, and multi-clause equations, is described in Fig. 2. Let us now look at how each layer of the abstractions—from top-level definitions, multi-equation first-class values, nested copatterns, and the small terminal operations—can be desugared to the next one, all the way down to basic, purely-functional Scheme.

Object formation:

```
(λ* TemplateStx)                          : Object
(object ExtensionStx)                     : Object
(object (<: Expr ...) ExtensionStx)       : Object
(plug Extension)                          : Object
(introspect Template)                     : Object
```

Template formation:

```
(template TemplateStx)     : Template
(continue x Expr)          : Template
(non-rec Expr)             : Template
(closed-cases Extension)   : Template
```

Extension formation:

```
(extension ExtensionStx)                 : Extension
(compose Extension ...)                  : Extension
(comatch Copattern Extension)            : Extension
(chain ResponseStx)                      : Extension
(always-is Expr)                         : Extension
(try x Template)                         : Extension
(try-if Expr Extension)                  : Extension
(try-match Expr Pattern Extension)       : Extension
(try-λ Params Extension)                 : Extension
(nest Extension)                         : Extension
```

Fig. 1. Compositional copattern API.

```
TemplateStx  ::= ExtensionStx | ExtensionStx (else Expr)
               | ExtensionStx (continue x Expr)
ExtensionStx ::= (Copattern ResponseStx) ...
ResponseStx  ::= (op ...) ResponseStx | = Expr | try x Template

Params    ::= x | (Pattern ...) | (Pattern ... . x)
Copattern ::= x | _
            | (Copattern Pattern ...)
            | (Copattern Pattern ... . x)
            | (apply Copattern Pattern ... x)
Pattern   ::= x | _ | 'Expr | `QQPat | ...
QQPat     ::= ,Pattern | (QQPat ...) | Expr
```

Definitional forms:

```
(define* x TemplateStx)
(define* TemplateStx)
(define-object (x <: Expr ...) ExtensionStx)
(define-object x ExtensionStx)
(define-object (<: Expr ...) ExtensionStx)
(define-object ExtensionStx)
```

Fig. 2. Grammar of syntax used by multi-clause definitions and multi-step operations.

Top-Level Definitions. There are two main styles of top-level definitions. The simplest one is when an explicit name is given to the definition in question, which directly expands to an ordinary definition bound to a first class object—described via `λ*` or `object`—like so:

```
(define* x TemplateStx)          = (define x (λ* TemplateStx))
(define-object x ExtensionStx) = (define x (object ExtensionStx))
```

This style can be used to evoke an object-oriented flavor of code, in which an object is externally named `x` to the outside world, but internally refers to itself by some other name like `self` or `this` for recursive calls.

In a more functional style of code, recursive function definitions use the same name for both external callers as well as internal recursive calls, so there is no need to declare the name another time. We support this style of definition, too, by looking for the "root" of the initial copattern on the left-hand side, which gives a name to the function itself in the context of some application. Following the syntax of `Copatterns` in Fig. 2, the root of the identifier `x` is just `x`, the anonymous wildcard `_` has no root, and the root of any other nested copattern is the root of its inner `Copattern`. Eliding the full details of digging into a copattern to reveal its root, if the name `x` is the root of first `Copattern` inside `TemplateStx` or `ExtensionStx`, then the implicitly-named definitional forms expand into the explicitly-named ones by copying that first recursive name:[3]

```
(define* TemplateStx)          = (define* x Template)
(define-object ExtensionStx) = (define-object x ExtensionStx)
```

Two more conspicuous cases introduce a *inheritance declaration* `<: Expr ...` to the definition. This implicitly incorporates additional code from a list of supertypes in `Expr ...` to an object that is not explicitly written in the definition itself, allowing for a form of object-oriented-like inheritance evoked by the sub-typing `<:` syntax. The generalized definition is implemented directly in terms of the support for inheritance in anonymous `objects`. A `define-object` with an explicit name is expanded to just:

```
(define-object (x <: Expr ...) ExtensionStx)
= (define x (object <: Expr ...) ExtensionStx)
```

For an implicitly-named `define-object`, we must look for the name as before; assuming `x` is the first root inside `ExtensionStx`, the two forms produce the same definition:

```
(define-object (<: Expr ...) ExtensionStx)
= (define-object (x <: Expr ...) ExtensionStx)
```

[3] Note that we only extract the root name in the *first* clause of the definition to be used for the external name. In its full generality, a different internal name can be used in each clause. Only good taste dictates that the names in each clause should be the same to fit within a standard functional style.

First-Class Objects, Templates, and Extensions. The most unassuming way to form a usable object—which does not introduce any implicit code not given in the object itself—is with the multi-clause `λ*` form. A `λ*` interprets the list of clauses as an openly-recursive `template`, and then closes off the recursive loop via `introspect` that binds the final object value in for the recursive parameter:

```
(λ* TemplateStx) = (introspect (template TemplateStx))
```

In contrast, an `object` is like a `λ*`, but enhanced with the ability to inherit code—given in a `(<: Expr ...)` constraint—which can extend or modify the clauses it contains. These modifiers are themselves transformations on extensions—first-class functions from old extensions to new extensions—which are applied to the given `extension` value before it is closed off with the `plug` operation on extensions analogous to `introspect` above:

```
(object ExtensionStx)
= (object (<:) ExtensionStx)
(object (<: Expr ...) ExtensionStx)
= (object (!<: meta Expr ...) ExtensionStx)
(object (!<: Expr ...) ExtensionStx)
= (plug ((compose Expr ...) (extension ExtensionStx)))
```

Note that the multiple extension modifiers are composed together using ordinary function composition, so the left-most one has precedence (being the final function in the chain). The empty inheritance `(<:)` is the same as if no inheritance constraint is given. Furthermore, the normal inheritance `(<: Expr ...)` is the same as a literal inheritance `(!<: meta Expr ...)` adding `meta` which is the implicit superclass of "all" objects.[4] Literal inheritance `(!<: Expr ...)` is instead interpreted exactly as-is, with no added defaults.

The default `meta` superclass provides the extra code for composition seen in the examples, including `'compose` and `'unplug`. How does it work? Since the superclasses used by the object inheritance mechanism are just extension transformers, we can implement `meta` directly as a function that composes the extension value making up an object with extra methods for manipulating it:

```
(define (meta ext)
  (compose ext
           (extension
             [(self 'unplug)     = ext]
             [(self 'adapt mod) = (plug (meta (mod (self 'unplug))))]
             [(self 'compose . os)
             = (plug (meta (apply compose
                                  (self 'unplug)
                                  (map (λ(o) (o 'unplug)) os))))])))
```

In other words, `(meta ext)` does everything that `ext` does, and in addition supports the methods:

[4] The library implementation stores this choice of the default superclass in a mutable parameter `default-superclass` that can be changed by the programmer.

- `(self 'unplug)` returns `ext` in its original state,
- `(self 'adapt mod)` is defined in terms of `(self 'unplug)` to retrieve the original extension value and apply some new transformation to it—plugging it back together with the same `meta` functionality—and
- `(self 'compose o ...)` will `'unplug` this object and each of `o ...` to get all the underlying extensions, composes them together vertically into one, and then plugs it back into a usable `meta` object again.

Now, what are these first-class extensions and templates, and how are they created? The `extension` macro—defined in terms of a list of clauses with an initial `Copattern` paired with some response (a combination of guards or other operations before a right-hand side)—interprets each line separately as its own horizontal composition `chain` before vertically composing them together with `compose` like so:

```
(extension [Copattern ResponseStx] ...)
= (compose [chain (comatch Copattern) ResponseStx] ...)
```

The main difference between a template and an extension is that a template is responsible for providing the final "catch-all" clause saying what to do if nothing matches. As such, the `template` macro first builds an `extension` out of the given syntax, and then applies it to one of three final clauses:

```
(template ExtensionStx [else Expr])
= ((extension ExtensionStx) (non-rec Expr))
(template ExtensionStx [continue x Expr])
= ((extension ExtensionStx) (continue x Expr))
(template ExtensionStx)
= (closed-cases (extension ExtensionStx))
```

The first case has an `[else Expr]` clause that evaluates some default expression if nothing else matches. The `[continue x Expr]` clause in the second case is similar but more general: `Expr` is evaluated if nothing else matches, and `x` is bound to the whole template itself, allowing for `Expr` to continue the recursive loop again if it uses `x`. The final case, providing no catch-all clause, uses `closed-cases` to instead raise an error if nothing matches.

Nested Copattern Matching and Chains. Nested copattern matching is now straightforward to desugar in terms of horizontally composing curried sequences of more basic, λ-like forms. More specifically, `try-λ` is a functional abstraction over extensions analogous to the normal functional abstraction over expressions, and mimics all three of Scheme's λ forms: `(try-λ (Pattern ...) Extension)` matches a sequence of arguments against the given sequence of parameter patterns, `(try-λ (Pattern ... . x) Extension)` does the same while binding any additional arguments as a list to `x`, and `(try-λ x Extension)` just binds any list of arguments to `x`. These three forms correspond to three application contexts in a copattern, which are desugared like so:

```
(comatch (Copattern . x) Extension)
= (comatch Copattern (try-λ x Extension))
(comatch (Copattern Pattern ...) Extension)
= (comatch Copattern (try-λ (Pattern ...) Extension))
(comatch (Copattern Pattern ... . x) Extension)
= (comatch Copattern (try-λ (Pattern ... . x) Extension))
```

Alternate copattern forms described using `apply`, like `(apply Copattern x y z)`, are defined similarly to the above.

An `extension` value is also created by chaining this initial `comatch` with some response. In practice, this chaining just involves reassociating the parentheses of intermediate operations and interpreting the right-hand side, so `chain` has the following behavior:

```
(chain (op ...) ResponseStx) = (op ... (chain ResponseStx))
(chain = Expr)               = (always-is Expr)
(chain try x Template)       = (try x Template)
```

Because reassociation does not depend on the operations `op` involved, extension chains automatically work with *any* new user-defined operations—macros or functions—which turn an extension (as their last argument) into another extension.

Terminal Operations and Combinators. Single-step operations and combinators are terminal forms, defined directly in terms of plain Scheme expressions. The simplest ones of these are also the most general: the `try` and `continue` macros let programmers write arbitrary extensions and templates (respectively) by abstracting over the next template to try or the object to continue recursion (respectively). In reality, both of these forms desugar directly into plain λ-abstractions.

```
(try x Template)   = (λ(x) Template)
(continue x Expr) = (λ(x) Expr)
```

Common special cases include the self-contained forms: the non-recursive template `(non-rec Expr)` and the fully-committed extension `(always-is Expr)` that evaluate and run `Expr` without failing to the next case or looping back to the beginning. Both forms are shorthand for the above abstractions that just never use the bound variable.

```
(non-rec Expr)    = (continue _ Expr)
(always-is Expr) = (try _ (non-rec Expr)) = (try _ (continue _ Expr))
```

The remaining basic combinators for adding guards and functional abstractions to extensions can be defined in terms of the above. A convenient shorthand for manually writing new extension combinators is to abstract over both the "next" case to try and the "self" reference at the same time, which is just a shorter notation for a curried function:

```
(try next self Expr) = (try next (continue self Expr))
                     = (λ(next) (λ(self) Expr))
```

The boolean `try-if` guard will check some boolean expression first: if it is true it continues to try the underlying extension (which may succeed or fail on its own accord), and otherwise skips it entirely.

```
(try-if Expr Extension)
= (try next self
       (if Expr
           ((Extension next) self)
           (next self)))
```

The pattern-matching guard `try-if` operates similarly, but generalizes the simple boolean check to matching the value of an expression against a given pattern.

```
(try-match Expr Pattern Extension)
= (try next self
       (match Expr
           [Pattern ((Extension next) self)]
           [_ (next self)]))
```

The most complicated single combinator is the `try-λ` functional abstraction over an extension. This form presents a functional interface that can pattern-match against its arguments: if the match succeeds then the variables in the pattern are bound while trying to execute the underlying extension, but if the match fails the extension is never tried at all. The pattern-matching component can be factored out of `try-λ` via horizontal composition by first just binding the arguments as is, and then matching them against the given patterns in a second step like so:[5]

```
(try-λ (Pattern ...) Extension)
= (try-λ (x ...) (chain (try-match x Pattern) ... Extension))
```

Now we only have to handle the simpler job of accepting a given number of arguments. This operation can still fail if applied to a different number of arguments, or if the underlying extension fails. We can efficiently define different cases for these two cases using a `case-λ` which combines functions of different numbers of arguments like so:[6]

```
(try-λ (x ...) Extension)
= (try next self
       (case-λ
         [(x ...) ((Extension (continue s ((next s) x ...))) self)]
         [args    (apply (next self) args)]))
```

Notice the most subtle part of `try-λ` : we must ensure that when we try the next case to handle failure, they must be copied and passed again whenever `next` is

[5] This equation is more of a specification than an efficient implementation. In practice, the `try-match` operations are only generated if the given pattern is non-trivial.

[6] Alternatively, some implementations like Racket have a built-in `match-λ` which effectively extends `case-λ` to pattern-match directly on the arguments. In these systems, we can use `match-λ` here to handle both pattern-matching and argument passing here at the same time.

invoked. If we forgot to wrap both applications of `next` with the given arguments, they would disappear forever if we handle to fall through to the next case.

Object-Manipulating Functions. The final operations remaining in the API are not even macros: they are just ordinary functions. For example, the `compose` that we have used twice now—to implement vertical composition of extensions as well as to combine multiple superclass constraints—is just ordinary function composition! Some of the other purely functional operations are similarly simple. For example, `closed-cases` closes off an extension by providing a final catch-all case that raises an error when run, and `plugging` an extension to get an object is just composition of `introspect` and `closed-cases`.

```
(closed-cases Extension) = (Extension (non-rec (error "...")))
(plug Extension)         = (introspect (closed-cases Extension))
```

The `introspect` function is a little tricker, because it needs to plug in the final form of an object while creating that object. Attempting to recursively tie the knot directly as

```
(introspect Template)
=/= (letrec ([self (Template self)])
      self)
```

will cause a run-time error: since Scheme is a call-by-value language, it will try to evaluate `self` before it is actually bound to a value yet. So instead, we have to delay the self-reference just by one step by η-expanding, since λ-abstractions return values without evaluating their bodies.

```
(introspect Template)
= (letrec ([self (Template (λ args (apply self args)))])
    self)
```

The `nest` operation does the same knot-tying as `introspect`, but also returns a new extension, rather than an object. To do so, it will recursively instantiate the view of the extension at this point in time—after some applications and guards have been evaluated—to provide the new self-referencing value. If at any point this extension fails and falls past its last case, the updated self-reference will be undone, and reverts back to its old form.

```
(nest Extension)
= (try next there
    (letrec ([here ((Extension (non-rec (next there)))
                    (λ args (apply here args)))])
      here))
```

Use Case: Defining New Custom Macros via the API. To demonstrate the flexibility of the API, we show how some other, more niche, operations can be defined in terms of the ones we already saw. In particular, the case studies on the object-oriented file system and the expression problem involved some complex meta-programming facilities.

First, we needed to override some of the behavior of multi-clause λ* s, which can be done by wrapping its value in a new λ* that handles the new behavior or else falls through to the original.

```
(override-λ* Expr ExtensionStx)
= (λ* ExtensionStx [else Expr])
```

Next, we needed to temporarily replace the self-reference in an extension with another, until we fall out of the scope of that extension. This can be done by capturing the old notion of the object itself—to be used if the extension ever falls through past its end—and passing a new one in its place like so:

```
(with-self new-self Extension)
= (try next old-self ((Extension (non-rec (next old-self))) new-self))
```

For the object-oriented examples, we needed a way to import the code of one object into another. We also used shorthand to construct an object in two steps (initialization and then recursive method definition). Both of these two operations are implemented as ordinary functions using the above library functionality that behave like so:

```
((import-object super-obj) sub-ext)
= (compose sub-ext (super-obj 'unplug))

(construct state obj)
= (extension
   [self try (with-self
               (λ args (apply (apply self state) args))
             (obj 'unplug))]))
```

Finally, to extend an evaluator with an environment, we needed a combinator to apply a functional extension to some argument(s) in the form of a new extension. The most direct way to do so is to apply those arguments after passing the `next` template and `self` object

```
(try-apply-remember Extension Expr ...)
= (try next self
      (((Extension next) self) Expr ...))
```

however, this does not give the desired behavior! This application looks "permanent" from the perspective of the next cases that follow this extension, which will be passed the arguments `Expr ...` as if they were in the original calling context. Instead, we want any alternatives that handle `Extension`'s failure to be evaluated in the same context, and so the extra arguments `Expr ...` need to be forgotten like so:

```
(try-apply-forget Extension Expr ...)
= (try next self
      (let ([forgetful (continue self (λ _ (next self)))])
        (((Extension forgetful) self) Expr ...)))
```

3.3 Practical Details of Macro Definitions

One concern for a real implementation is to consider what kind of pattern-matching facilities the host language already provides. Unfortunately, the answer is not standard across different languages in the Scheme family. For example, the R^6RS standard does not require any built-in support for pattern matching to be fully compliant, but specific languages like Racket may include a library for pattern matching by default. Thus, we provide two different implementations to illustrate how copatterns may be implemented depending on their host language:

- A Racket implementation that uses its standard pattern-matching constructs `match` and `match-lambda*`. Thus, the **match** from the target language in Fig. 3 is interpreted as Racket's `match`, and the translation of $E[\![\lambda P.O]\!]$ is implemented directly as `match-lambda*` instead of separating the λ from the pattern as in Fig. 5. This choice ensures the pattern language implemented is exactly the same as the pattern language already used in Racket programs.
- A general implementation intended for any R^6RS-compliant Scheme,[7] which internally implements its own pattern-matching macro, `try-match`, by expanding into other primitives like `if` and comparison predicates. Of note, due to only having to handle a single line of pattern-matching at a time, this implementation is 75 lines of Scheme and supports quasiquoting forms of patterns. This gives a sufficiently expressive intersection between Racket's pattern-matching syntax and the manually implemented R^6RS version.

4 A Core Copattern Calculus

4.1 Double-Barrel Translation

To help study the behavior and correctness of composable copattern matching, we model a simplified version of the library API in the form of an extended λ-calculus, and give a high-level translation into a conventional λ-calculus with recursion and pattern matching (given in Fig. 3). Our pattern language is modeled after a small common core found among various implementations of Scheme, which includes normal variable wildcards x that can match anything, quoted symbols $'x$, and lists of the form null or $(\text{cons}\, P\, P')$. Note that we assume all bound variables x in a pattern are distinct. As shorthand, we write a list of patterns $P_1\ P_2\ \dots\ P_n$ for $(\text{cons}\, P_1\ (\text{cons}\, P_2\ \dots (\text{cons}\, P_n\, \text{null})))$. To model the patterns found in typed functional languages like ML and Haskell, such as constructor applications $K\ P...$, we can represent the constructor as a quoted symbol $'K$ and the application as a list $'K\ P....$ The patterns' specifics are surprisingly not essential to the main copattern translation and could be extended with other features found in more specific implementations.

For simplicity, this translation begins from a smaller source language with copatterns (given in Fig. 4) separated into three main syntactic categories that reflect the different groups of values from the macro library:

[7] We have explicitly tested this implementation against Chez Scheme.

$$Term \ni M, N ::= x \mid M\ N \mid \lambda x.M \mid K \mid \mathbf{match}\, M\, \mathbf{with}\,\{\, P \to N ... \,\} \mid \mathbf{rec}\, x = M$$
$$Pattern \ni \quad P ::= x \mid \text{'}x \mid \text{null} \mid \text{cons}\, P\, P'$$

Fig. 3. Target language: pure λ-calculus with pattern-matching and recursion.

- (M, N) *Term* syntax represents all ordinary expressions of the host language as well as the new first-class *objects* of the library. The new forms of terms are $\lambda^* B$, which gives a self-referential copattern-matching object, along with **template** B and **extension** O which include the other two syntactic categories as first-class values that can be applied as functions to instantiate their open-ended recursion and composition.
- (B) *Template* syntax represents a simplified grammar supported by `template` and similar macros specified as `TemplateStx` in Fig. 2. Including some extension cases in a template is written as $O; B$, the catch-all clause which may continue the loop again via a recursive object bound to x is written as **continue** $x \to M$, and the closed case where the catch-all clause raises an error is the empty string ε. Since the simpler final **else** clause is a special case of **continue**, we treat it as syntactic sugar.
- (O) *Extension* syntax represents a simplified grammar supported by `extension` and similar macros specified as `ExtensionStx` in Fig. 2 with terser notation. Vertical composition is written as $O; O'$, similar to $O; B$, with the empty string ε as its neutral element. Copattern-matching is written as $Q[x]O$, where Q is a copattern context with x as the root identifier naming the recursive object itself. The more basic forms are written as $\lambda P.O$ for a functional abstraction over an extension, **match** $P \leftarrow M\ O$ for a pattern-matching guard, and **try** $x \to B$ for the statement which binds the following cases to x before running a template specified by B. We treat if-guards and the form $(= M)$ as syntactic sugar for special cases of the more general forms, and also sometimes use the alternative notation **do** M in place of $(= M)$ in contexts where the latter notation appears awkward.

The syntax in B and O directly reflects the core operations for forming and combining copattern-matching expressions of the library API. Here, the copattern syntax $Q[x]$ itself is expressed as a subset of contexts, Q, surrounding an object internally named x. Two lines separated by a semicolon $(O; O')$ represents a binary vertical composition `compose` that tries either O or O', and ε represents an empty extension `(extend)` with respect to vertical composition: it immediately refers to the next option. Prefixing with a copattern-matching expression $(Q[x]\ O)$ represents the `(comatch Q[x] O)` form that tries $Q[x]$ and then O. Smaller special cases of matching include pattern lambdas $(\lambda P.O)$ for `try-λ` , and pattern guards (**match** $P \leftarrow M\ O$) for `try-match`. Other operations use the same names as in Fig. 1.

$$\begin{aligned}
\mathit{Term} \ni M, N &::= \cdots \mid \lambda^* B \mid \mathbf{template}\, B \mid \mathbf{extension}\, O \\
\mathit{Template} \ni \quad B &::= \varepsilon \mid O; B \mid \mathbf{continue}\, x \to M \\
\mathit{Extension} \ni \quad O &::= \varepsilon \mid O; O' \mid Q[x]\ O \mid \lambda P.\ O \mid \mathbf{match}\, P \leftarrow M\ O \mid \mathbf{try}\, x \to B \\
\mathit{Copattern} \ni \quad Q &::= \Box \mid Q\ P \\
\mathit{Pattern} \ni \quad P &::= x \mid \text{'}x \mid \mathrm{null} \mid \mathrm{cons}\, P\, P'
\end{aligned}$$

Syntactic sugar:

$$\begin{aligned}
\mathbf{else}\, M &= \mathbf{continue}\ _ \to M & (= M) = \mathbf{do}\, M &= \mathbf{try}\ _ \to \mathbf{else}\, M \\
\mathbf{if}\, M\ O &= \mathbf{match}\, \mathrm{True} \leftarrow M\ O & (\mathbf{let}\, x = M\ O) &= \mathbf{match}\, x \leftarrow M\ O
\end{aligned}$$

Fig. 4. Source language: target extended with nested copatterns, self-referential objects, recursion templates, and composable extensions.

This simplified grammar makes it easier to define the full macro expansion as a translation from the source (Fig. 4) to target (Fig. 3) as given in Fig. 5. This translation shares many similarities to continuation-passing style (CPS) translations. However, we explicitly avoid converting the entire program to CPS. Notably, every syntactic form for the source language is unchanged; for example, $[\![M\ N]\!] = [\![M]\!]\ [\![N]\!]$. Instead, the only time we need to introduce an extra parameter is for the two new syntactic categories. All templates are translated to functions that take a value for the whole object itself to a new version of that object. Similarly, all extensions are translated to functions that take both a template as the "base case" to try next and a value for the whole object itself. Even though this is dynamically-typed, we can view the type of templates as object transformers and extensions as template transformers:

$$\begin{aligned}
\mathit{Object} &= \text{some type of function} \\
\mathit{Template} &= \mathit{Object} \to \mathit{Object}' \\
\mathit{Extension} &= \mathit{Template} \to \mathit{Template}' = \mathit{Template} \to \mathit{Object} \to \mathit{Object}'
\end{aligned}$$

The interesting cases for translating terms are the new forms. **template** B and **extension** O are just translated to their given forms as transformation functions. With $\lambda^* B$, we need to recursively plug its translation in for its self parameter. Note the one detail that the recursive *self* is η-expanded to in this application. This ensures that $\lambda x.\mathit{self}\ x$ is treated as a value in a real implementation, and is always safe assuming that B describes a function (non-functional cases of $\lambda^* B$ are undefined user error).

For templates and extensions, the terminators **continue** and **try** are translated to plain λ-abstractions that allow the programmer direct access to their implicit parameters. Complex copatterns ($x\ P_1 ... P_n\ O$) are reduced down to a simpler sequence of pattern lambdas ($x\ \lambda P_1 . \ldots \lambda P_n .\ O$), and pattern lambdas ($\lambda P.O$) are reduced down to a simpler non-matching lambda followed by an explicit match guard ($\lambda x.\mathbf{match}\ P \leftarrow x\ O$).

This leaves just the base cases of simple extension forms. Each time an extension (of form $\lambda b.\lambda s. \ldots$) "fails," it calls the given next template with the given

Translating new terms:

$$
\begin{aligned}
[\![\lambda^* B]\!] &= (\textbf{rec}\, \textit{self} = T[\![B]\!]\ (\lambda x.\textit{self}\ x)) \\
[\![\textbf{template}\, B]\!] &= T[\![B]\!] \\
[\![\textbf{extension}\, O]\!] &= E[\![O]\!] \\
[\![M]\!] &= \text{by induction} \qquad\qquad\qquad\qquad \text{(otherwise)}
\end{aligned}
$$

Translating templates:

$$
\begin{aligned}
T[\![\varepsilon]\!] &= \lambda s.\textit{fail}\ s \\
T[\![O; B]\!] &= \lambda s.E[\![O]\!]\ T[\![B]\!]\ s \\
T[\![\textbf{continue}\, x \to M]\!] &= \lambda x.[\![M]\!]
\end{aligned}
$$

Translating copattern-matching and pattern-matching functions:

$$
\begin{aligned}
E[\![(Q[x]\ P)\ O]\!] &= E[\![Q[x]\ (\lambda P.O)]\!] \\
E[\![x\ O]\!] &= \lambda b.\lambda x.E[\![O]\!]\ b\ x \\
E[\![\lambda P.O]\!] &= E[\![\lambda x.\,\textbf{match}\, P \leftarrow x\ O]\!] \qquad\qquad (\text{if } P \notin \textit{Variable})
\end{aligned}
$$

Translating other extensions:

$$
\begin{aligned}
E[\![\varepsilon]\!] &= \lambda b.\lambda s.b\ s \\
E[\![O; O']\!] &= \lambda b.\lambda s.E[\![O]\!]\ (E[\![O']\!]\ b)\ s \\
E[\![\lambda x.O]\!] &= \lambda b.\lambda s.(\lambda x.E[\![O]\!]\ (\lambda s'.b\ s'\ x)\ s) \\
E[\![\textbf{match}\, P \leftarrow M\ O]\!] &= \lambda b.\lambda s.\,\textbf{match}\ [\![M]\!]\ \textbf{with}\,\{\, P \to E[\![O]\!]\ b\ s;\ \_ \to b\ s\,\} \\
E[\![\textbf{try}\, x \to B]\!] &= \lambda x.T[\![B]\!]
\end{aligned}
$$

Fig. 5. Translating copattern-based source code to the target language.

self object ($b\ s$). A match guard $[\![\textbf{match}\ P \leftarrow M\ O]\!]$ will try to match the translation of M against the pattern P; the success case continues as $E[\![O]\!]$ with the same next template and self. A non-matching lambda $[\![\lambda x.O]\!]$ always succeeds (for now), but note that the next template to try on failure has to be changed to include the given argument. Why? Because the lambda has already consumed the next argument from its context, it would be gone if, later on, the following operations fail and move on to the next option. So instead of invoking the given b directly as $b\ s'$ (for a potentially different future s'), they need to invoke b applied to this argument x as $b\ s'\ x$.

In this translation, we also give the η-reduced forms on the right-hand side when available. This shows that the empty extension ε is just the identity function (given the next thing b to try, ε does nothing and immediately moves on to b), and horizontal composition $O; O'$ is just ordinary function composition.

$$\begin{aligned} \mathit{Value} \ni V, W &::= x \mid \lambda x.M \mid \mathrm{null} \mid \mathrm{cons}\, V\, W \mid \text{'}x \\ \mathit{EvalCxt} \ni \quad E &::= \Box \mid E\ M \mid V\ E \mid \mathbf{match}\, E\, \mathbf{with}\, \{\, P \to N ... \,\} \mid \mathbf{rec}\, x = E \end{aligned}$$

$$(\beta) \qquad (\lambda x.M)\ V = M[V/x]$$

$$(\mathit{match}) \qquad \mathbf{match}\, V\, \mathbf{with}\, \{\, P \to N;\ P' \to N' ... \,\} = N[W.../x...] \qquad (\text{if } P[W.../x...] = V)$$

$$(\mathit{apart}) \qquad \mathbf{match}\, V\, \mathbf{with}\, \{\, P \to N;\ P' \to N' ... \,\} = \mathbf{match}\, V\, \mathbf{with}\ \{\, P' \to N' ... \,\} \qquad (\text{if } P \# V)$$

$$(\mathit{rec}) \qquad (\mathbf{rec}\, x = V) = V[(\mathbf{rec}\, x = V)/x]$$

Apartness between patterns and values ($P \# V$):

$$\frac{V \notin \mathit{Variable} \cup \{\, \text{'}x \,\}}{\text{'}x \# V} \qquad \frac{V \notin \mathit{Variable} \cup \{\, \mathrm{null} \,\}}{\mathrm{null} \# V}$$

$$\frac{V \notin \mathit{Variable} \cup \{\, \mathrm{cons}\, W\ W' \mid W, W' \in \mathit{Value} \,\}}{\mathrm{cons}\, P\ P' \# V}$$

$$\frac{P \# W}{\mathrm{cons}\, P\ P' \# \mathrm{cons}\, W\ W'} \qquad \frac{P' \# W'}{\mathrm{cons}\, P\ P' \# \mathrm{cons}\, W\ W'}$$

Fig. 6. Untyped equational axioms of the target language.

4.2 Correctness

We already used the translation to a core λ-calculus as a specification for implementing compositional copatterns, but the translation is also useful for another purpose: checking the expected meaning of copattern-matching code. With that in mind, we now look for some laws that let us equationally reason about some programs to make sure they behave as expected.

First, the core target language—a standard call-by-value λ-calculus extended with pattern-matching and recursion—has the equational theory shown in Fig. 6, which is the *reflexive*, *symmetric*, *transitive*, and *compatible* (*i.e.* equalities can be applied in *any* context) closure of the listed rules. It has the usual β axiom (restricted to substituting value arguments), two axioms for handling pattern-match success (*match*) and failure (*apart*), and an axiom for unrolling recursive values (*rec*). Values (V, W) include the usual ones for call-by-value λ-calculus (x and $\lambda x.M$) as well as lists (null and $\mathrm{cons}\, V\ W$) and symbolic literals ($'x$). Matching a value V against a pattern P will succeed if the variables (x...) in the pattern can be replaced by other values (W...) to generate exactly that V: $P[W.../x...] = V$. In contrast, matching fails if the two are known to be *apart*, written $P \# V$ and defined in Fig. 6, which implies that all possible substitutions of P will *never* generate V. Note that while matching and apartness are mutually exclusive, there are some values that are neither matching nor apart from some patterns. For example, compare the variable x against the pattern null; x may indeed stand for null or another value like $\lambda y.M$.

The first usual property is that the translation specified in Fig. 5 is a *conservative extension*: any two terms that are equal by the target equational theory are still equal after translation. Because the translation is hygienic and compositional by definition, we can follow the proof strategy in [9].

Proposition 1 (Conservative Extension). *If $M = N$ in the equational theory of the target (Fig. 6), then so too does $[\![M]\!] = [\![N]\!]$.*

$$\begin{aligned} \mathit{ExtensionFunc} \ni F &::= Q[x\ P]\ O \mid \lambda P.O \\ \mathit{Value} \ni V &::= \cdots \mid \lambda^*(F; B) \mid \mathbf{template}\, B \mid \mathbf{extension}\, O \end{aligned}$$

Identity, associativity, and annihilation laws of composition:

$$\begin{array}{lll} \varepsilon; O = O & (O_1; O_2); O_3 = O_1; (O_2; O_3) & \mathbf{do}\, M; O = \mathbf{do}\, M \\ \varepsilon; B = B & (O_1; O_2); B = O_1; (O_2; B) & \mathbf{do}\, M; B = \mathbf{else}\, M \end{array}$$

Pattern and copattern matching:

$$\begin{array}{rll} \mathbf{match}\, P \leftarrow V\ O &= O[W.../x...] & (\text{if } P[W.../x...] = V) \\ \mathbf{match}\, P \leftarrow V\ O &= \varepsilon & (\text{if } P \# V) \\ (\mathbf{template}\,(\lambda P.\,\mathbf{do}\, M); B)\ V'\ V &= M[W.../x...] & (\text{if } P[W.../x...] = V) \\ (\mathbf{template}\,(\lambda P.O); B)\ V'\ V &= (\mathbf{template}\, B)\ V'\ V & (\text{if } P \# V) \\ C[(\mathbf{template}\,(Q[y] = M); B)\ V] &= M[V/y][W.../x...] & (\text{if } Q[W.../x...] = C) \\ C[(\mathbf{template}\,(Q[y]\ O); B)\ V] &= C[(\mathbf{template}\, B)\ V] & (\text{if } Q \# C) \\ C[\lambda^*(Q[y] = M); B] &= M[(\lambda^*(Q[y] = M); B)/y] & (\text{if } Q[W.../x...] = C) \\ & \quad [W.../x...] & \\ C[\lambda^*(Q[y]\ O); \mathbf{else}\, M] &= C[M] & (\text{if } Q \# C) \end{array}$$

Apartness between copatterns and contexts ($Q \# C$):

$$\frac{Q[W.../x...] = C \quad P \# V}{Q\ P \# C\ V} \qquad \frac{Q \# C}{Q\ P \# C} \qquad \frac{Q \# C}{Q \# C\ V}$$

Fig. 7. Some equalities of copattern extensions.

To reason about the new features in the source language—introduced by λ^*, **template**, and **extension**—we introduce additional axioms given in Fig. 7, so that the source equational theory is the *reflexive*, *symmetric*, *transitive*, and *compatible* closure of these rules in both Figs. 6 and 7. The purpose of these new equalities is to perform some reasoning about programs using copatterns, and in particular, to check that the syntactic use of = really means equality. For example, a special case is $Q[\lambda^*(Q[y] = M); B] = M[\lambda^*(Q[y] = M); B/y]$, which says a λ^* appearing in *exactly* the same context as the left-hand side of an equation will unroll (recursively) to the right-hand side. Other equations describe algebraic laws of copattern alternatives and how to fill in templates and extensions when applied. This source equational theory is *sound* with respect to translation.

Proposition 2 (Soundness). *The translation is* sound *w.r.t. the source and target equational theories (e.g. $M = N$ in Fig. 7 implies $[\![M]\!] = [\![N]\!]$ in Fig. 6).*

Proofs of these propositions are given in Appendix A of the appendix.

5 Related Work

While we use the expression problem as a motivating application of compositional copatterns, it has multiple previous solutions using various features and spreading on multiple paradigms. The Visitor pattern [19] is a classic solution in the object-oriented world. However, we have other options such as [30], which brings Java interfaces closer to Haskell's type classes, and [21], which presents the abstraction of object algebras that are easily integrated into OO languages, since they do not depend upon fancy features. On the other hand, on the functional paradigm side, we have solutions like [24] and [16]. The former utilizes Haskell's type system, specifically type classes, to provide a modular way to construct data types and functions. However, this approach relies on a type system. The latter is a compiler framework that provides tools to specify different languages for the compiler passes. The framework achieves this by automatically handling a portion of the mapping between two given entities.

Previously, copatterns have been developed exclusively from the perspective of statically-typed languages. Much of the work has been for dependently typed languages like Agda [6], which use a type-driven approach to elaborate copatterns [23,25]. The closest related works are about implementing copatterns using macros in OCaml [15,18]. As with the above work in dependently typed languages, [18] is also concerned with type system ramifications, and CoCaml [15] supports only a subset of coinductive data types, called *regular*, with periodic repetitions that allow for finite representation in memory using cyclic structures. Here, we show how to implement copatterns with no typing information or restrictions on cyclic structures, and focus instead on composition and equational reasoning. The literature also presents other examples of open recursion and inheritance in a functional setting; for instance, [4] implements memorization for monadic computations using inheritance and mixins.

The translation in Fig. 5 is reminiscent of "double-barreled CPS" [26] used to define control effects like delimited control [8] and exceptions [17]. In our case, rather than a "successful return path" continuation, there is a "resume recursion" continuation. Expressions that return successfully just return as normal, similar to a selective CPS [20], which makes it possible to implement as a macro expansion. A "next case" continuation—to handle copattern-matching failure—is introduced to make each line of a copattern-based definition a separate first-class value. From that point, the "recursive self" must be a parameter because no one sliver of a definition suffices to describe the whole.

Theories of object-oriented languages [1,7] also model the "self" keyword as a parameter later instantiated by recursion; either as an explicit recursive binding, or encoded as self-application. This is done to handle the implicit composition of code from inheritance, whereas here, we need to handle explicit composition of first-class extensible objects. The full connection between copatterns—as we describe here—and object-oriented languages remains to be seen. In terms of the Lisp family of languages, the approach here seems closest to a first-class generalization of *mixins* [3,11] with a simple dispatch mechanism (matching), in contrast to class-based frameworks focused on complex dispatch [5,12,14].

6 Conclusion

We have shown here how to implement a more extensible, compositional version of copatterns as a macro in standard Scheme as well as Racket. Our major focus involves new ways to compose (co)pattern matching code in multiple directions—vertically and horizontally—which can be used to solve the expression problem since it can encode certain functional and object-oriented design patterns. Despite the more general forms of program composition, we still support straightforward equational reasoning to understand code behavior, even when that code is assembled from multiple parts of the program. This equational reasoning is formalized in terms of an extended λ-calculus, which is soundly translated into a common core calculus familiar to functional programmers; we leave the definition of a *complete* and minimal equational theory for copatterns as future work.

Our work here does not include static types, inherited from Scheme's nature as a dynamically typed language. As future work, we intend to develop a type system for the copattern language described here; specific challenges include correctly specifying type types of (de)composed code as well as coverage analysis that ensures every case is handled after the composition is finished. The second direction of future work is to incorporate effects into copattern definitions and their equational reasoning, for example, subsuming (delimited) control operators into the copattern language as a way of expressing compositional effect handlers.

Acknowledgments. This material is based upon work supported by the National Science Foundation under Grant No. 2245516.

Disclosure of Interests. The authors have no competing interests to declare that are relevant to the content of this article.

A Proofs

A.1 Conservative extension of the target

Lemma 1. *The following instances of translation are all values up to the equational theory of the target language in Fig. 6:*

(a) $T[\![B]\!] = \lambda s.M$ *for some term* M*,*
(b) $E[\![O]\!] = \lambda b.\lambda s.M$ *for some term* M*,*
(c) $E[\![F]\!] = \lambda b.\lambda s.\lambda x.M$ *for some term* M*,*
(d) $[\![V]\!] = W$ *for some value* W*.*

Proof. By mutual induction on the syntax of templates B, extensions O, extension functions F, and values V.

(a) $T[\![B]\!] = \lambda s.M$ for some term M, as shown by the following cases:
  - ($B = \varepsilon$) $T[\![\varepsilon]\!] = \lambda s.\ \mathit{fail}\ s$, so $M = \mathit{fail}\ s$.
  - ($B = O; B'$) $T[\![O; B']\!] = \lambda s.\ [\![O]\!]\ [\![B']\!]\ s$, so $M = [\![O]\!]\ [\![B']\!]\ s$.
  - ($B = \mathbf{continue}\ x \to N$) $T[\![\mathbf{continue}\ x \to N]\!] = \lambda x.[\![N]\!]$, so $M = [\![N]\!]$.

(b) $E[\![O]\!] = \lambda b.\lambda s.M$ for some term M, as shown by the following cases:
  - ($O = \varepsilon$) $E[\![\varepsilon]\!] = \lambda b.\lambda s.\ b\ s$, so $M = b\ s$.
  - ($O = O_1; O_2$) $E[\![O_1; O_2]\!] = \lambda b.\lambda s.\ [\![O_1]\!]\ ([\![O_2]\!]\ b)\ s$, so $M = [\![O_1]\!]\ ([\![O_2]\!]\ b)\ s$.
  - ($O = Q[x]\ O$) follows by induction on Q (generalizing O):
    - ($Q = \Box$) for all O,

$$
\begin{aligned}
E[\![x\ O]\!] &= \lambda b.\lambda x.E[\![O]\!]\ b\ x \\
&= \lambda b.\lambda s.E[\![O]\!][s/x]\ b\ s \qquad (\alpha)
\end{aligned}
$$

      so $M = E[\![O]\!][s/x]\ b\ s$ for the given O.
    - ($Q = Q'\ P$) assuming the inductive hypothesis (IH) that, for all O, there is an N_O such that $E[\![Q[x]\ O]\!] = \lambda b.\lambda s.N_O$. For all O,

$$
\begin{aligned}
E[\![(Q'[x]\ P)O]\!] &= E[\![Q'[x]\ (\lambda P.O)]\!] \\
&= \lambda b.\lambda s.N_{(\lambda P.O)} \qquad (IH)
\end{aligned}
$$

      so $M = N_{(\lambda P.O)}$ given by the inductive hypothesis applied to $\lambda P.O$.
  - ($O = \lambda P.\ O$) follows by cases if P is a variable or another pattern:
    - ($P \in \mathit{Variable}$) $E[\![\lambda x.\ O]\!] = \lambda b.\lambda s.(\lambda x.E[\![O]\!]\ (\lambda s'.b\ s'\ x)\ s)$, so $M = \lambda x.E[\![O]\!]\ (\lambda s'.b\ s'\ x)\ s$.
    - ($P \notin \mathit{Variable}$) $E[\![\lambda P.\ O]\!] = E[\![\lambda x.\mathbf{match}\ P \leftarrow x\ O]\!]$, which follows by the above case.
  - ($O = \mathbf{match}\ P \leftarrow N\ O$)

$$
\begin{aligned}
E[\![\mathbf{match}\ P \leftarrow N\ O]\!] = \lambda b.\lambda s.\ &\mathbf{match}\ [\![N]\!]\mathbf{with} \\
&\{\ P \to E[\![O]\!]\ b\ s; \\
&\ \ \_ \to b\ s\ \}
\end{aligned}
$$

    so $M = \mathbf{match}\ [\![N]\!]\mathbf{with}\ \{P \to E[\![O]\!]\ b\ s;\ \_ \to b\ s\}$.
  - ($O = \mathbf{nest}\ O$) $E[\![\mathbf{nest}\ O]\!] = \lambda b.\lambda s.(\mathbf{rec}\ s' = E[\![O]\!]\ (\lambda\_.b\ s)\ (\lambda x.s'\ x))$, so $M = (\mathbf{rec}\ s' = E[\![O]\!]\ (\lambda\_.b\ s)\ (\lambda x.s'\ x))$
  - ($O = \mathbf{try}\ x \to B$) assuming the inductive hypothesis (IH) from part (a) that $T[\![B]\!] = \lambda s.N$ for some N,

$$
\begin{aligned}
E[\![\mathbf{try}\ x \to B]\!] &= \lambda x.T[\![B]\!] \\
&= \lambda x.(\lambda s.\ N) \qquad (IH) \\
&= \lambda b.(\lambda s.\ N)[b/x] \qquad (\alpha)
\end{aligned}
$$

    so $M = N[b/x]$

(c) $E[\![F]\!] = \lambda b.\lambda s.\lambda x.M$ for some term M, as shown by the following cases:

- ($F = \lambda P.\ O$) Following the same calculation in the matching special case of part (b) above, $E[\![\lambda P.O]\!] = \lambda b.\lambda s.(\lambda x.M)$ for some M.
- ($F = Q[x\ P]\ O$) follows by induction on Q (generalizing O):
  - ($Q = \square$) for all O,

$$E[\![(y\ P)\ O]\!] = E[\![y\ (\lambda P.O)]\!] = \lambda b.\lambda y.E[\![\lambda P.O]\!]\ b\ y$$

Following the same calculation in the previous case ($F = \lambda P.O$) gives us some N such that $E[\![\lambda P.O]\!] = \lambda b.\lambda s'.\lambda x.N$, so continuing we have

$$\begin{aligned} E[\![(y\ P)\ O]\!] &= \lambda b.\lambda y.(\lambda b.\lambda s'.\lambda x.N)\ b\ y \\ &= \lambda b.\lambda y.\lambda x.N[y/s'] && (\beta) \\ &= \lambda b.\lambda s.\lambda x.N[y/s'][s/y] && (\alpha) \end{aligned}$$

so $M = N[y/s'][s/y]$.
  - ($Q = Q'\ P'$) assuming the inductive hypothesis that, for all O, there is an N_O such that $E[\![Q'[y\ P]\ O]\!] = \lambda b.\lambda s.\lambda x.N_O$. For all O,

$$\begin{aligned} E[\![(Q'[y\ P]\ P')\ O]\!] &= E[\![Q'[y\ P]\ (\lambda P'.O)]\!] \\ &= \lambda b.\lambda s.\lambda x.N_{(\lambda P'.O)} && (IH) \end{aligned}$$

so $M = N_{(\lambda P'.O)}$ given by the inductive hypothesis applied to $\lambda P'.O$.

(d) $[\![V]\!] = W$ for some value W, as shown by the following cases:
- ($V = x$) $[\![x]\!] = x$, so $W = x$.
- ($V = \lambda x.M$) $[\![\lambda x.M]\!] = \lambda x.[\![M]\!]$, so $W = \lambda x.[\![M]\!]$.
- ($V = \text{null}$) $[\![\text{null}]\!] = \text{null}$, so $W = \text{null}$.
- ($V = \text{cons}\, V_1\ V_2$) $[\![\text{cons}\, V_1\ V_2]\!] = \text{cons}\, [\![V_1]\!]\ [\![V_2]\!]$, where $[\![V_1]\!] = W_1$ and $[\![V_2]\!] = W_2$ by the inductive hypotheses, so $W = \text{cons}\, W_1\ W_2$.
- ($V = \textbf{template}\ B$) $[\![\textbf{template}\ B]\!] = T[\![B]\!] = \lambda s.M$, for some M, by the inductive hypothesis part (a), so $W = \lambda s.M$.
- ($V = \textbf{extension}\ O$) $[\![\textbf{extension}\ O]\!] = E[\![O]\!] = \lambda b.\lambda s.M$, for some M, by the inductive hypothesis part (b), so $W = \lambda b.\lambda s.M$.
- ($V = \lambda^*(F; B)$) assuming the inductive hypotheses that
  IH_1 there is some N_1 such that $E[\![F]\!] = \lambda b.\lambda s.\lambda x.N_1$, and
  IH_2 there is some N_2 such that $T[\![B]\!] = \lambda s.N_2$,

$$\begin{aligned} [\![\lambda^*(F;B)]\!] &= (\textbf{rec}\ \mathit{self} = T[\![F;B]\!]\ (\lambda x.\mathit{self}\ x)) \\ &= (\textbf{rec}\ \mathit{self} = E[\![F]\!]\ T[\![B]\!]\ (\lambda x.\mathit{self}\ x)) && (\beta) \\ &= (\textbf{rec}\ \mathit{self} = (\lambda b.\lambda s.\lambda x.N_1)\ T[\![B]\!]\ (\lambda x.\mathit{self}\ x)) && (IH_1) \\ &= (\textbf{rec}\ \mathit{self} = (\lambda b.\lambda s.\lambda x.N_1)\ (\lambda s.N_2)\ (\lambda x.\mathit{self}\ x)) && (IH_2) \\ &= (\textbf{rec}\ \mathit{self} = \lambda x.N_1[(\lambda s.N_2)/b][(\lambda x.\mathit{self}\ x)/s]) && (\beta) \\ &= \lambda x.N_1[(\lambda s.N_2)/b] \\ &\qquad [(\lambda x.\mathit{self}\ x)/s] && (rec) \\ &\qquad [(\textbf{rec}\ \mathit{self} = \lambda x.N_1[(\lambda s.N_2)/b][(\lambda x.\mathit{self}\ x)/s])/\mathit{self}] \end{aligned}$$

Lemma 2 (Pattern Translation).
$[\![P]\!] = P$.

Proof. By induction on the syntax of P. □

Lemma 3 (Apartness Translation)
If $P \# V$ *then* $P \# [\![V]\!]$.

Proof. By induction on the derivation of apartness $P \# V$. □

Lemma 4 (Compositionality)
There exists a translation of contexts $[\![C]\!]$ *such that* $[\![C[M]]\!] = [\![C]\!][[\![M]\!]]$, *and similarly for contexts which surround templates* B *and extensions* O. *The same holds for* $T[\![C]\!]$ *and* $E[\![C]\!]$ *for contexts returning templates and extensions, respectively.*

Proof. By induction on the possible contexts C and the definition of the translation. □

Lemma 5 (Hygiene)
If x *is captured by* C *if and only if it is captured by* $[\![C]\!]$ *in* $[\![C]\!][x]$. *The same holds for* $T[\![C]\!]$ *and* $E[\![C]\!]$ *for contexts returning templates and extensions, respectively.*

Proof. By induction on the possible contexts C and the implicit side-conditions on the definition of translation where new binding forms introduced on the right-hand side must not capture free variables of sub-terms. □

Lemma 6 (Substitution). *For all values* V,

(a) $[\![M[V/x]]\!] = [\![M]\!][[\![V]\!]/x]$,
(b) $T[\![B[V/x]]\!] = T[\![B]\!][[\![V]\!]/x]$,
(c) $E[\![O[V/x]]\!] = E[\![O]\!][[\![V]\!]/x]$.

Proof. The proof strategy follows from proposition 2 of [9].

Suppose we have a free occurrence of x in a term M which is decomposed as $C[x]$, where C does not capture x. Because the translation is compositional (Lemma 4), we can decompose every occurrence of a variable from its surrounding context as $[\![C[x]]\!] = [\![C]\!][x]$. Then, because the translation is hygienic (Lemma 5), we know $[\![C]\!]$ does not capture x. Thus,

$$\begin{aligned} [\![C[x]]\!][[\![V]\!]/x] &= [\![C]\!][x][[\![V]\!]/x] && (\textit{Lemma } 4) \\ &= [\![C]\!][[\![V]\!]][[\![V]\!]/x] \\ &= [\![C[V]]\!][[\![V]\!]/x] && (\textit{Lemma } 4) \end{aligned}$$

This replacement can then be iterated for each free occurrence of x in the term, until x no longer appears free in the final term M', in which the substitution is $[\![M']\!][[\![V]\!]/x] = [\![M']\!]$.

The same procedure applies for free occurrences of variables in templates and extensions. □

Lemma 7 (Equivalence Relation)

The translation preserves the structure of an equivalence relation with respect to the equational theory of the target. Equalities between translated terms have the following properties:

(a) Reflexivity: $[\![M]\!] = [\![M]\!]$.
(b) Symmetry: *if* $[\![M]\!] = [\![N]\!]$ *then* $[\![N]\!] = [\![M]\!]$,
(c) Transitivity: *if* $[\![M_1]\!] = [\![M_2]\!]$ *and* $[\![M_2]\!] = [\![M_3]\!]$ *then* $[\![M_1]\!] = [\![M_3]\!]$.
(d) Congruence: *if* $[\![M]\!] = [\![M]\!]$ *then for all contexts* C, $[\![C[M]]\!] = [\![C[N]]\!]$.

and similarly for equalities between translated templates $T[\![B]\!]$ *and extensions* $E[\![O]\!]$.

Proof. The proof strategy follows from proposition 1 of [9].

Reflexivity, transitivity, and symmetry of the equational theory follows immediately.

Congruence—$M = N$ implies $C[M] = C[N]$ for all contexts C—follows from the fact that the translation is *compositional* (Lemma 4). An equation $C[M] = C[N]$, derived from congruence of $M = N$ inside C, can be derived by distributing the translation across contexts to apply the underlying equality $[\![M]\!] = [\![N]\!]$ gotten from soundness of $M = N$:

$$\begin{aligned} [\![C[M]]\!] &= [\![C]\!][[\![M]\!]] && (\textit{Lemma } 4) \\ &= [\![C]\!][[\![N]\!]] \\ &= [\![C[N]]\!] && (\textit{Lemma } 4) \end{aligned}$$

Proposition 1 (Conservative Extension). *If* $M = N$ *in the equational theory of the target (Fig. 6), then so too does* $[\![M]\!] = [\![N]\!]$.

Proof. The soundness of the inference rules defining the structure of the source equivalence relation follow from Lemma 7.

It then remains to show that each individual axiom (β, *rec*, *etc.*) from the target language is still equal after translation. Each one holds by the inductive hypothesis—because the definition of translation for these cases does not change syntax—along with Lemmas 1 and 6 for cases which substitute values. For example, with the β axiom, we have

$$\begin{aligned} [\![(\lambda x.M)\ V]\!] &= (\lambda x.[\![M]\!])\ [\![V]\!] \\ &= (\lambda x.[\![M]\!])\ W && (\textit{Lemma } 1) \\ &= [\![M]\!][W/x] && (\beta) \\ &= [\![M]\!][[\![V]\!]/x] && (\textit{Lemma } 1) \\ &= [\![M[V/x]]\!] && (\textit{Lemma } 6) \end{aligned}$$

since values are only translated to values, $[\![V]\!] = W$ up to the target equational theory (Lemma 1), which means that β-reduction still applies after translation. For the *match* and *apart* axioms, we need to know that patterns and apartness is not affected by translation, given by Lemmas 2 and 3.

$$\varepsilon; O = O \qquad (O_1; O_2); O_3 = O_1; (O_2; O_3) \qquad \mathbf{do}\, M; O = \mathbf{do}\, M$$
$$\varepsilon; B = B \qquad (O_1; O_2); B = O_1; (O_2; B) \qquad \mathbf{do}\, M; B = \mathbf{else}\, M$$

$$\begin{aligned}
\lambda^*(F; B) &= (\mathbf{template}\, F; B)\ (\lambda^*(F; B)) \\
\lambda x.(\lambda^*(F; B))\ x &= \lambda^*(F; B) \\
(\mathbf{template}\, O; B)\ V &= (\mathbf{extension}\, O)\ (\mathbf{template}\, B)\ V \\
(\mathbf{template}\, \varepsilon)\ V &= \mathit{fail}\ V \\
(\mathbf{template}\, \mathbf{continue}\, x \to M)\ V &= M[V/x] \\
(\mathbf{extension}\, \mathbf{try}\, x \to B)\ V &= \mathbf{template}\, B[V/x] \\
(\mathbf{template}\, (x\ O); B)\ V &= (\mathbf{template}\, O[V/x]; B)\ V \\
(\mathbf{template}\, (\lambda x.O); B)\ V\ W &= \begin{pmatrix} \mathbf{template} \\ \quad O[W/x]; \\ \quad \mathbf{continue}\, s' \to \\ \qquad (\mathbf{template}\, B)\ s'\ W \end{pmatrix} V
\end{aligned}$$

$$\begin{aligned}
&\mathbf{match}\, P \leftarrow V\ O = \varepsilon && (\text{if } P \# V) \\
&\mathbf{match}\, P \leftarrow V\ O = O[W.../x...] && (\text{if } P[W.../x...] = V) \\
&\lambda P.O = \lambda x.(\mathbf{match}\, P \leftarrow x)\ O \\
&(Q[x]\ P)\ O = Q[x]\ (\lambda P.O)
\end{aligned}$$

Fig. 8. Core axioms of the equational theory.

$$\begin{aligned}
(\mathbf{template}\, (\lambda P.O); B)\ V'\ V &= \begin{pmatrix} \mathbf{template} \\ \quad O[W/x]; \\ \quad \mathbf{continue}\, s' \to \\ \qquad (\mathbf{template}\, B)\ s'\ V \end{pmatrix} V' && (\text{if } P[W.../x...] = V) \\
(\mathbf{template}\, (\lambda P.\, \mathbf{do}\, M); B)\ V'\ V &= M[W.../x...] && (\text{if } P[W.../x...] = V) \\
(\mathbf{template}\, (\lambda P.O); B)\ V'\ V &= (\mathbf{template}\, B)\ V'\ V && (\text{if } P \# V) \\
C[(\mathbf{template}\, (Q[y]\ O); B)\ V] &= \begin{pmatrix} \mathbf{template} \\ \quad O[W/x]; \\ \quad \mathbf{continue}\, s' \to \\ \qquad C[(\mathbf{template}\, B)\ s'] \end{pmatrix} V && (\text{if } Q[W.../x...] = C) \\
C[(\mathbf{template}\, (Q[y] = M); B)\ V] &= M[V/y][W.../x...] && (\text{if } Q[W.../x...] = C) \\
C[(\mathbf{template}\, (Q[y]\ O); B)\ V] &= C[(\mathbf{template}\, B)\ V] && (\text{if } Q \# C) \\
C[\lambda^*(Q[y] = M); B] &= M[(\lambda^*(Q[y] = M); B)/y] && (\text{if } Q[W.../x...] = C) \\
&\quad [W.../x...] \\
C[\lambda^*(Q[y]\ O); \mathbf{else}\, M] &= C[M] && (\text{if } Q \# C)
\end{aligned}$$

Fig. 9. Other equalities derived from the core axioms.

A.2 Soundness of the source

Proposition 2 (Soundness). *The translation is* sound *w.r.t. the source and target equational theories (e.g. $M = N$ in Fig. 7 implies $[\![M]\!] = [\![N]\!]$ in Fig. 6).*

Proof. The reflexive, symmetric, transitive, and congruent structure of the equational theory is sound by Lemma 7, and the axioms of the target language are sound by Proposition 1.

It remains to show that each equality in Fig. 7 are sound as well. The proof of soundness is finished by the following lemmas, which are organized in two parts:

- The equalities in Fig. 8 are *core axioms*, whose soundness is shown by translating both sides into the target λ-calculus and deriving an equality in the target equational theory.
- The remaining equalities in Fig. 9 are *derived* only in terms of those core axioms directly in the source language, so their soundness follows from Lemma 7 in addition to the specific lemmas proving soundness of the core axioms.

Note that every equation listed in Fig. 7 can be found in either Fig. 8 or Fig. 9, however, there are some additional core axioms in Fig. 8 that do not appear in Fig. 7, but are useful for deriving other equations. □

Core Axioms

Lemma 8 (Extension Composition Identity Left). *In the target,*

$$E[\![\varepsilon; O]\!] = E[\![O]\!]$$

Proof.

$$\begin{aligned}
& E[\![\varepsilon; O]\!] \\
= \;& \lambda b.\lambda s.\ E[\![\varepsilon]\!]\ (E[\![O]\!]\ b)\ s \\
= \;& \lambda b.\lambda s.\ E[\![\varepsilon]\!]\ ((\lambda b.\lambda s.\ M_0)\ b)\ s && (\textit{Lemma}\ 1) \\
= \;& \lambda b.\lambda s.\ (\lambda b.\lambda s.\ b\ s)\ ((\lambda b.\lambda s.\ M_0)\ b)\ s \\
= \;& \lambda b.\lambda s.\ (\lambda b.\lambda s.\ b\ s)\ (\lambda s.\ M_0)\ s && (\beta) \\
= \;& \lambda b.\lambda s.\ (\lambda s.\ (\lambda s.\ M_0)\ s)\ s && (\beta) \\
= \;& \lambda b.\lambda s.\ (\lambda s.\ M_0)\ s && (\beta) \\
= \;& \lambda b.\lambda s.\ M_0 && (\beta) \\
= \;& E[\![O]\!] && (\textit{Lemma}\ 1)
\end{aligned}$$

□

Lemma 9 (Template Composition Identity Left). *In the target,*

$$T[\![\varepsilon; B]\!] = T[\![B]\!]$$

Proof.

$$\begin{aligned}
& T[\![\varepsilon; B]\!] \\
= \ & \lambda s.\ E[\![\varepsilon]\!]\ T[\![B]\!]\ s \\
= \ & \lambda s.\ (\lambda b.\lambda s.\ b\ s)\ T[\![B]\!]\ s \\
= \ & \lambda s.\ T[\![B]\!]\ s & (\beta, \textit{Lemma } 1) \\
= \ & T[\![B]\!] & (\alpha, \beta, \textit{Lemma } 1)
\end{aligned}$$

□

Lemma 10 (Extension Composition Associativity). *In the target,*

$$E[\![(O_1; O_2); O_3]\!] = E[\![O_1; (O_2; O_3)]\!]$$

Proof. The left-hand side simplifies as follows:

$$\begin{aligned}
& E[\![(O_1; O_2); O_3]\!] \\
= \ & \lambda b.\lambda s.\ E[\![O_1; O_2]\!]\ (E[\![O_3]\!]\ b)\ s \\
= \ & \lambda b.\lambda s.\ (\lambda b.\lambda s.\ E[\![O_1]\!]\ (E[\![O_2]\!]\ b)\ s)\ (E[\![O_3]\!]\ b)\ s \\
= \ & \lambda b.\lambda s.\ (\lambda b.\lambda s.\ (\lambda b.\lambda s.M_1)\ ((\lambda b.\lambda s.M_2)\ b)\ s)\ ((\lambda b.\lambda s.M_3)\ b)\ s & (\textit{Lemma } 1) \\
= \ & \lambda b.\lambda s.\ (\lambda b.\lambda s.\ (\lambda b.\lambda s.M_1)\ ((\lambda b.\lambda s.M_2)\ b)\ s)\ (\lambda s.M_3)\ s & (\beta) \\
= \ & \lambda b.\lambda s.\ (\lambda b.\lambda s.M_1)\ ((\lambda b.\lambda s.M_2)\ (\lambda s.M_3))\ s & (\beta) \\
= \ & \lambda b.\lambda s.\ (\lambda b.\lambda s.M_1)\ (\lambda s.M_2[(\lambda s.M_3)/b])\ s & (\beta) \\
= \ & \lambda b.\lambda s.\ M_1[(\lambda s.M_2[(\lambda s.M_3)/b])/b] & (\beta)
\end{aligned}$$

The right-hand side simplifies to the same term as follows:

$$\begin{aligned}
& E[\![O_1; (O_2; O_3)]\!] \\
= \ & \lambda b.\lambda s.\ E[\![O_1]\!]\ ([\![O_2; O_3]\!]\ b)\ s \\
= \ & \lambda b.\lambda s.\ E[\![O_1]\!]\ ((\lambda b.\lambda s.\ E[\![O_2]\!]\ (E[\![O_3]\!]\ b)\ s)\ b)\ s \\
= \ & \lambda b.\lambda s.\ E[\![O_1]\!]\ (\lambda s.\ E[\![O_2]\!]\ (E[\![O_3]\!]\ b)\ s)\ s & (\beta) \\
= \ & \lambda b.\lambda s.\ (\lambda b.\lambda s.M_1)\ (\lambda s.\ (\lambda b.\lambda s.M_2)\ ((\lambda b.\lambda s.M_3)\ b)\ s)\ s & (\textit{Lemma } 1) \\
= \ & \lambda b.\lambda s.\ (\lambda b.\lambda s.M_1)\ (\lambda s.\ (\lambda b.\lambda s.M_2)\ (\lambda s.M_3)\ s)\ s & (\beta) \\
= \ & \lambda b.\lambda s.\ (\lambda b.\lambda s.M_1)\ (\lambda s.M_2[(\lambda s.M_3)/b])\ s & (\beta) \\
= \ & \lambda b.\lambda s.\ M_1[(\lambda s.M_2[(\lambda s.M_3)/b])/b] & (\beta)
\end{aligned}$$

□

Lemma 11 (Template Composition Associativity). *In the target,*

$$T[\![(O_1; O_2); B]\!] = T[\![O_1; (O_2; B)]\!]$$

Proof. The left-hand side simplifies as follows:

$$
\begin{aligned}
& T[\![(O_1; O_2); B]\!] \\
= \; & \lambda s.\ E[\![O_1; O_2]\!]\ T[\![B]\!]\ s \\
= \; & \lambda s.\ (\lambda b.\lambda s.\ E[\![O_1]\!]\ (E[\![O_2]\!]\ b)\ s)\ T[\![B]\!]\ s \\
= \; & \lambda s.\ E[\![O_1]\!]\ (E[\![O_2]\!]\ T[\![B]\!])\ s && (\beta, \mathit{Lemma}\ 1) \\
= \; & \lambda s.\ (\lambda b.\lambda s.M_1)\ ((\lambda b.\lambda s.M_2)\ T[\![B]\!])\ s && (\mathit{Lemma}\ 1) \\
= \; & \lambda s.\ (\lambda b.\lambda s.M_1)\ (\lambda s.M_2[T[\![B]\!]/b])\ s && (\beta, \mathit{Lemma}\ 1) \\
= \; & \lambda s.\ M_1[(\lambda s.M_2[T[\![B]\!]/b])/b] && (\beta)
\end{aligned}
$$

The right-hand side simplifies to the same term as follows:

$$
\begin{aligned}
& T[\![O_1; (O_2; B)]\!] \\
= \; & \lambda s.\ E[\![O_1]\!]\ T[\![O_2; B]\!]\ s \\
= \; & \lambda s.\ E[\![O_1]\!]\ (\lambda s.\ E[\![O_2]\!]\ T[\![B]\!]\ s)\ s \\
= \; & \lambda s.\ (\lambda b.\lambda s.M_1)\ (\lambda s.\ (\lambda b.\lambda s.\ M_2)\ T[\![B]\!]\ s)\ s && (\mathit{Lemma}\ 1) \\
= \; & \lambda s.\ (\lambda b.\lambda s.M_1)\ (\lambda s.M_2[T[\![B]\!]/b])\ s && (\beta, \mathit{Lemma}\ 1) \\
= \; & \lambda s.\ M_1[(\lambda s.M_2[T[\![B]\!]/b])/b] && (\beta)
\end{aligned}
$$

□

Lemma 12 (Extension Commit). *In the target,*

$$E[\![\mathbf{do}\ M; O]\!] = E[\![\mathbf{do}\ M]\!]$$

Proof.

$$
\begin{aligned}
& E[\![\mathbf{do}\ M; O]\!] \\
= \; & \lambda b.\lambda s.\ E[\![\mathbf{do}\ M]\!]\ (E[\![O]\!]\ b)\ s \\
= \; & \lambda b.\lambda s.\ E[\![\mathbf{do}\ M]\!]\ ((\lambda b.\lambda s.\ M_O)\ b)\ s && (\mathit{Lemma}\ 1) \\
= \; & \lambda b.\lambda s.\ E[\![\mathbf{do}\ M]\!]\ (\lambda s.\ M_O)\ s && (\beta) \\
= \; & \lambda b.\lambda s.\ E[\![\mathbf{try}\ \_ \to \mathbf{continue}\ \_ \to M]\!]\ (\lambda s.\ M_O)\ s \\
= \; & \lambda b.\lambda s.\ (\lambda\_.\ T[\![\mathbf{continue}\ \_ \to M]\!])\ (\lambda s.\ M_O)\ s \\
= \; & \lambda\_.\lambda s.\ T[\![\mathbf{continue}\ \_ \to M]\!]\ s && (\beta, b \notin FV(M)) \\
= \; & \lambda\_.\lambda s.\ (\lambda\_.\ [\![M]\!])\ s \\
= \; & \lambda\_.\lambda\_.\ [\![M]\!] && (\beta, s \notin FV(M)) \\
= \; & \lambda\_.\ T[\![\mathbf{continue}\ \_ \to M]\!] \\
= \; & E[\![\mathbf{try}\ \_ \to \mathbf{continue}\ \_ \to M]\!] \\
= \; & E[\![\mathbf{do}\ M]\!]
\end{aligned}
$$

□

Lemma 13 (Template Commit). *In the target,*

$$T[\![\mathbf{do}\ M; B]\!] = T[\![\mathbf{else}\ M]\!]$$

Proof.

$$\begin{aligned}
& T[\![\mathbf{do}\ M; B]\!] \\
= \;& \lambda s.\ E[\![\mathbf{do}\ M]\!]\ T[\![B]\!]\ s \\
= \;& \lambda s.\ E[\![\mathbf{try}\ _ \to \mathbf{continue}\ _ \to M]\!]\ T[\![B]\!]\ s \\
= \;& \lambda s.\ (\lambda_.\ T[\![\mathbf{continue}\ _ \to M]\!])\ T[\![B]\!]\ s \\
= \;& \lambda s.\ (\lambda_.\ \lambda_.\ [\![M]\!])\ T[\![B]\!]\ s \\
= \;& \lambda s.\ (\lambda_.\ [\![M]\!])\ s && (\beta) \\
= \;& \lambda_.\ [\![M]\!] && (\beta, s \notin FV(M)) \\
= \;& T[\![\mathbf{continue}\ _ \to M]\!] \\
= \;& T[\![\mathbf{else}\ M]\!]
\end{aligned}$$

□

Lemma 14 ($\eta\lambda^*$). *In the target,*

$$E[\![\lambda x.\ (\lambda^*(F; B))\ x]\!] = E[\![\lambda^*(F; B)]\!]$$

Proof. From Lemma 1, we have $E[\![F]\!] = \lambda b.\lambda s.\lambda z.M$ for some term M. In the following, let $M' = M[T[\![B]\!]/b][(\lambda y.\mathit{self}\ y)/s]$,

$$\begin{aligned}
& E[\![\lambda x.\ (\lambda^*(F; B))\ x]\!] \\
= \;& \lambda x.E[\![(\lambda^*(F; B))]\!]\ x \\
= \;& \lambda x.(\mathbf{rec}\ \mathit{self} = (\lambda s.E[\![F]\!]\ T[\![B]\!]\ s)\ (\lambda y.\mathit{self}\ y))\ x \\
= \;& \lambda x.(\mathbf{rec}\ \mathit{self} = E[\![F]\!]\ T[\![B]\!]\ (\lambda y.\mathit{self}\ y))\ x && (\beta) \\
= \;& \lambda x.(\mathbf{rec}\ \mathit{self} = (\lambda b.\lambda s.\lambda z.M)\ T[\![B]\!]\ (\lambda y.\mathit{self}\ y))\ x && (\mathit{Lemma}\ 1) \\
= \;& \lambda x.(\mathbf{rec}\ \mathit{self} = \lambda z.M[T[\![B]\!]/b][(\lambda y.\mathit{self}\ y)/s])\ x \\
= \;& \lambda x.(\mathbf{rec}\ \mathit{self} = \lambda z.M')\ x && (\beta) \\
= \;& \lambda x.(\lambda z.M'[\mathbf{rec}\ \mathit{self} = \lambda z.M'/\mathit{self}])\ x && (\mathit{rec}) \\
= \;& \lambda x.M'[\mathbf{rec}\ \mathit{self} = \lambda z.M'/\mathit{self}][x/z] && (\beta) \\
= \;& \lambda z.M'[\mathbf{rec}\ \mathit{self} = \lambda z.M'/\mathit{self}] && (\alpha) \\
= \;& \mathbf{rec}\ \mathit{self} = \lambda z.M' && (\mathit{rec}) \\
= \;& \mathbf{rec}\ \mathit{self} = \lambda z.M[T[\![B]\!]/b][(\lambda y.\mathit{self}\ y)/s] \\
= \;& \mathbf{rec}\ \mathit{self} = (\lambda b.\lambda s.\lambda z.M)\ T[\![B]\!]\ (\lambda x.\mathit{self}\ x) && (\beta) \\
= \;& \mathbf{rec}\ \mathit{self} = E[\![F]\!]\ T[\![B]\!]\ (\lambda x.\mathit{self}\ x) && (\mathit{Lemma}\ 1) \\
= \;& \mathbf{rec}\ \mathit{self} = (\lambda s.E[\![F]\!]\ T[\![B]\!]\ s)\ (\lambda x.\mathit{self}\ x) && (\beta) \\
= \;& \mathbf{rec}\ \mathit{self} = T[\![F; B]\!]\ (\lambda x.\mathit{self}\ x) \\
= \;& E[\![\lambda^*(F; B)]\!]
\end{aligned}$$

□

Lemma 15 (Unfold λ^*). *In the target,*

$$E[\![\lambda^*(F;B)]\!] = [\![(\textbf{template } F;B)\ (\lambda^*(F;B))]\!]$$

Proof. Note, $T[\![F;B]\!]\ (\lambda x.\mathit{self}\ x) = E[\![F]\!]\ T[\![B]\!]\ (\lambda x.\mathit{self}\ x)$ is β-equal to some value of the form $\lambda z.M'$ because $T[\![F;B]\!] = \lambda b.\lambda s.\lambda z.M$ from Lemma 1. So $\textbf{rec}\ \mathit{self} = T[\![F;B]\!]\ (\lambda x.\mathit{self}\ x)$ unfolds via β and rec in the following,

$$\begin{aligned}
& E[\![\lambda^*(F;B)]\!] \\
=\ & (\textbf{rec}\ \mathit{self} = T[\![F;B]\!]\ (\lambda x.\mathit{self}\ x)) \\
=\ & T[\![F;B]\!]\ (\lambda x.(\textbf{rec}\ \mathit{self} = T[\![F;B]\!]\ (\lambda x.\mathit{self}\ x))\ x)) && (\beta, rec) \\
=\ & T[\![F;B]\!]\ (\lambda x.[\![\lambda^*(F;B)]\!]\ x) \\
=\ & T[\![F;B]\!]\ [\![\lambda^*(F;B)]\!] && (\mathit{Lemma}\ 14) \\
=\ & [\![\textbf{template}\ (F;B)]\!]\ [\![\lambda^*(F;B)]\!] \\
=\ & [\![(\textbf{template}\ (F;B))\ (\lambda^*(F;B))]\!]
\end{aligned}$$

□

Lemma 16 (Template Extension). *In the target,*

$$[\![(\textbf{template } O;B)\ V]\!] = [\![(\textbf{extension } O)\ (\textbf{template } B)\ V]\!]$$

Proof.

$$\begin{aligned}
& [\![(\textbf{template } O;B)\ V]\!] \\
=\ & [\![(\textbf{template } O;B)]\!]\ [\![V]\!] \\
=\ & (\lambda s.\ E[\![O]\!]\ T[\![B]\!]\ s)\ [\![V]\!] \\
=\ & E[\![O]\!]\ T[\![B]\!]\ [\![V]\!] && (\beta, \mathit{Lemma}\ 1) \\
=\ & E[\![\textbf{extension } O]\!]\ T[\![\textbf{template } B]\!]\ [\![V]\!] \\
=\ & E[\![(\textbf{extension } O)\ (\textbf{template } B)\ V]\!]
\end{aligned}$$

□

Lemma 17 (Template Failure). *In the target,*

$$[\![(\textbf{template } \varepsilon)\ V]\!] = [\![\mathit{fail}\ V]\!]$$

Proof.

$$\begin{aligned}
& [\![(\textbf{template } \varepsilon)\ V]\!] \\
=\ & [\![(\textbf{template } \varepsilon)]\!]\ [\![V]\!] \\
=\ & T[\![\varepsilon]\!]\ [\![V]\!] \\
=\ & (\lambda s.\mathit{fail}\ s)\ [\![V]\!] \\
=\ & \mathit{fail}\ [\![V]\!] && (\beta, \mathit{Lemma}\ 1) \\
=\ & [\![\mathit{fail}\ V]\!]
\end{aligned}$$

□

Lemma 18 (Template Continue). *In the target,*

$$[\![(\textbf{template continue}\ x \to M)\ V]\!] = [\![M[V/x]]\!]$$

Proof.

$$\begin{aligned}
& [\![(\textbf{template continue}\ x \to M)\ V]\!] \\
=\ & T[\![(\textbf{continue}\ x \to M)]\!]\ [\![V]\!] \\
=\ & (\lambda x.\ [\![M]\!])\ [\![V]\!] \\
=\ & [\![M]\!][[\![V]\!]/x] && (\beta, \textit{Lemma}\ 1) \\
=\ & [\![M[V/x]]\!] && (\textit{Lemma}\ 6)
\end{aligned}$$

□

Lemma 19 (Extension Try). *In the target,*

$$[\![(\textbf{extension try}\ x \to B)\ V]\!] = \textbf{template}\ B[V/x]$$

Proof.

$$\begin{aligned}
& [\![(\textbf{extension try}\ x \to B)\ V]\!] \\
=\ & [\![\textbf{extension try}\ x \to B]\!]\ [\![V]\!] \\
=\ & E[\![\textbf{try}\ x \to B]\!]\ [\![V]\!] \\
=\ & (\lambda x.\ T[\![B]\!])\ [\![V]\!] \\
=\ & T[\![B]\!][[\![V]\!]/x] && (\beta, \textit{Lemma}\ 1) \\
=\ & T[\![B[V/x]]\!] && (\textit{Lemma}\ 6) \\
=\ & [\![\textbf{template}\ B[V/x]]\!]
\end{aligned}$$

□

Lemma 20 (Template Self). *In the target,*

$$[\![(\textbf{template}\ (x\ O); B)\ V = (\textbf{template}\ O[V/x]; B)\ V]\!]$$

Proof.

$$\begin{aligned}
& [\![(\textbf{template}\ (x\ O); B)\ V]\!] \\
=\ & E[\![x\ O]\!]\ T[\![B]\!]\ [\![V]\!] && (\beta, \textit{Lemma}\ 1) \\
=\ & (\lambda b.\lambda x.E[\![O]\!]\ b\ x)\ T[\![B]\!]\ [\![V]\!] \\
=\ & E[\![O]\!][[\![V]\!]/x]\ T[\![B]\!]\ [\![V]\!] && (\beta, \textit{Lemma}\ 1) \\
=\ & E[\![O[V/x]]\!]\ T[\![B]\!]\ [\![V]\!] && (\textit{Lemma}\ 6) \\
=\ & [\![(\textbf{template}\ O[V/x]; B)\ V]\!] && (\beta, \textit{Lemma}\ 1)
\end{aligned}$$

□

Lemma 21 (Template Lambda). *In the target,*

$$[\![\textbf{template}\ (\lambda x.O; B)\ V\ W]\!] = \left[\!\!\left[\begin{pmatrix}\textbf{template} \\ \quad O[W/x]; \\ \quad \textbf{continue}\ s' \to (\textbf{template}\ B)\ s'\ W\end{pmatrix} V\right]\!\!\right]$$

Proof.

$$\begin{aligned}
& [\![(\textbf{template}\ (\lambda x.O); B)\ V\ W]\!] \\
= \; & (\lambda s.E[\![\lambda x.O]\!]\ T[\![B]\!]\ s)\ [\![V]\!]\ [\![W]\!] \\
= \; & E[\![\lambda x.O]\!]\ T[\![B]\!]\ [\![V]\!]\ [\![W]\!] && (\beta, \textit{Lemma}\ 1) \\
= \; & (\lambda b.\lambda s.\lambda x.E[\![O]\!]\ (\lambda s'.b\ s'\ x)\ s)\ T[\![B]\!]\ [\![V]\!]\ [\![W]\!] \\
= \; & E[\![O]\!][[\![W]\!]/x]\ (\lambda s'.T[\![B]\!]\ s'\ [\![W]\!])\ [\![V]\!] && (\beta, \textit{Lemma}\ 1) \\
= \; & E[\![O[W/x]]\!]\ (\lambda s'.T[\![B]\!]\ s'\ [\![W]\!])\ [\![V]\!] && (\textit{Lemma}\ 6) \\
= \; & \left[\!\!\left[\begin{pmatrix}\textbf{template} \\ \quad O[W/x]; \\ \quad \textbf{continue}\ s' \to (\textbf{template}\ B)\ s'\ W\end{pmatrix} V\right]\!\!\right] && (\beta, \textit{Lemma}\ 1)
\end{aligned}$$

□

Lemma 22 (Try Match). *In the target,*

$$[\![\textbf{match}\ P \leftarrow V\ O]\!] = [\![O[W.../x...]]\!] \qquad (\textit{if}\ P[W.../x...] = V)$$

Proof. By Lemmas 2 and 6, $[\![V]\!] = [\![P[W.../x...]]\!] = [\![P]\!][[\![W]\!].../x...] = P[[\![W]\!].../x...]$ in the following:

$$\begin{aligned}
& E[\![\textbf{match}\ P \leftarrow V\ O]\!] \\
= \; & \lambda b.\lambda s.\textbf{match}\ [\![V]\!]\textbf{with}\ \{P \to E[\![O]\!]\ b\ s; _ \to b\ s\} \\
= \; & \lambda b.\lambda s.\ E[\![O]\!][[\![W]\!].../x...]\ b\ s && (\textit{match}, \textit{Lemmas}\ 2\ \textit{and}\ 6) \\
= \; & \lambda b.\lambda s.\ E[\![O[W.../x...]]\!]\ b\ s && (\textit{Lemma}\ 6) \\
= \; & E[\![O[W.../x...]]\!] && (\alpha, \beta, \textit{Lemma}\ 1)
\end{aligned}$$

□

Lemma 23 (Try Match Apart). *In the target,*

$$[\![\textbf{match}\ P \leftarrow V\ O]\!] = [\![\varepsilon]\!] \qquad (\textit{if}\ P \# V)$$

Proof. By Lemma 3, $P \# [\![V]\!]$ in the following:

$$\begin{aligned}
& E[\![\textbf{match}\ P \leftarrow V\ O]\!] \\
= \; & \lambda b.\lambda s.\textbf{match}\ [\![V]\!]\textbf{with}\ \{P \to E[\![O]\!]\ b\ s; _ \to b\ s\} \\
= \; & \lambda b.\lambda s.\ b\ s && (\textit{apart}, \textit{Lemma}\ 3) \\
= \; & E[\![\varepsilon]\!]
\end{aligned}$$

□

Lemma 24 (Pattern Lambda). *In the target,*

$$E[\![\lambda P.O]\!] = E[\![\lambda x.(\mathbf{match}\ P \leftarrow x)\ O]\!]$$

Proof. By cases on whether P is a variable or another pattern:

- If $P = y$, then

$$\begin{aligned}
& E[\![\lambda x.(\mathbf{match}\ y \leftarrow x)\ O]\!] \\
= \ & \lambda b.\lambda s.\lambda x.\ E[\![\mathbf{match}\ y \leftarrow x\ O]\!]\ (\lambda s'.b\ s'\ x)\ s \\
= \ & \lambda b.\lambda s.\lambda x.\,\mathbf{match}\ x\mathbf{with}\ \{ && (\beta) \\
& \qquad\qquad y \to E[\![O]\!]\ (\lambda s'.b\ s'\ x)\ s; \\
& \qquad\qquad _ \to (\lambda s'.b\ s'\ x)\ s\ \} \\
= \ & \lambda b.\lambda s.\lambda x.E[\![O]\!][x/y]\ (\lambda s'.b\ s'\ x)\ s && (\mathit{match}) \\
= \ & \lambda b.\lambda s.\lambda y.E[\![O]\!]\ (\lambda s'.b\ s'\ y)\ s && (\alpha) \\
= \ & E[\![\lambda y.O]\!]
\end{aligned}$$

- Otherwise, when $P \notin \mathit{Variable}$, $E[\![\lambda P.O]\!] = E[\![\lambda x.(\mathbf{match}\ P \leftarrow x)\ O]\!]$ directly by definition of translation. □

Lemma 25 (Copattern Abstraction). *In the target,*

$$E[\![(Q[x]\ P)\ O]\!] = E[\![Q[x]\ (\lambda P.O)]\!]$$

Proof. $E[\![(Q[x]\ P)\ O]\!] = E[\![Q[x]\ (\lambda P.O)]\!]$ directly by definition of translation. □

Derived Equations

Lemma 26 (Template Match). *In the source,*

$$\mathbf{template}\ (\lambda P.O; B)\ V'\ V = \begin{pmatrix} \mathbf{template} \\ \quad O[W.../x...]; \\ \quad \mathbf{continue}\ s' \to (\mathbf{template}\ B)\ s'\ V \end{pmatrix} V'$$
$$(\mathit{if}\ P[W.../x...] = V)$$

Proof.

$$\begin{aligned}
& \mathbf{template}\ (\lambda P.O; B)\ V'\ V \\
= \ & \mathbf{template}\ (\lambda x.(\mathbf{match}\ P \leftarrow x)\ O; B)\ V'\ V && (\mathit{Lemma}\ 24) \\
= \ & \begin{pmatrix} \mathbf{template} \\ \quad (\mathbf{match}\ P \leftarrow V)\ O; \\ \quad \mathbf{continue}\ s' \to (\mathbf{template}\ B)\ s'\ V \end{pmatrix} V' && (\mathit{Lemma}\ 21) \\
= \ & \begin{pmatrix} \mathbf{template} \\ \quad O[W.../x...]; \\ \quad \mathbf{continue}\ s' \to (\mathbf{template}\ B)\ s'\ V \end{pmatrix} V' && (\mathit{Lemma}\ 22)
\end{aligned}$$

□

Lemma 27 (Template Do Match). *In the source,*

$$(\textbf{template } (\lambda P.\textbf{do } M); B)\ V'\ V = M[W.../x...] \qquad (\textit{if } P[W.../x...] = V)$$

Proof.

$$\begin{aligned}
&(\textbf{template } (\lambda P.\textbf{do } M); B)\ V'\ V \\
&= \begin{pmatrix}\textbf{template} \\ \quad \textbf{do } M[W.../x...]; \\ \quad \textbf{continue } s' \rightarrow (\textbf{template } B)\ s'\ V\end{pmatrix} V' && (\textit{Lemma } 26) \\
&= (\textbf{template else } M[W.../x...])\ V' && (\textit{Lemma } 13) \\
&= (\textbf{template continue } _ \rightarrow M[W.../x...])\ V' \\
&= M[W.../x...] && (\textit{Lemma } 18)
\end{aligned}$$

□

Lemma 28 (Template Apart). *In the source,*

$$(\textbf{template } (\lambda P.O); B)\ V'\ V = (\textbf{template } B)\ V'\ V \qquad (\textit{if } P \# V) \tag{1}$$

Proof.

$$\begin{aligned}
&(\textbf{template } (\lambda P.O); B)\ V'\ V \\
&= (\textbf{template } (\lambda x.(\textbf{match } P \leftarrow x)\ O); B)\ V'\ V && (\textit{Lemma } 24) \\
&= \begin{pmatrix}\textbf{template} \\ \quad (\textbf{match } P \leftarrow V)\ O; \\ \quad \textbf{continue } s' \rightarrow (\textbf{template } B)\ s'\ V\end{pmatrix} V' && (\textit{Lemma } 21) \\
&= \begin{pmatrix}\textbf{template} \\ \quad \varepsilon; \\ \quad \textbf{continue } s' \rightarrow (\textbf{template } B)\ s'\ V\end{pmatrix} V' && (\textit{Lemma } 23) \\
&= (\textbf{template continue } s' \rightarrow (\textbf{template } B)\ s'\ V)\ V' && (\textit{Lemma } 9) \\
&= (\textbf{template } B)\ V'\ V && (\textit{Lemma } 18)
\end{aligned}$$

□

Lemma 29 (Context Match). *In the source,*

$$C[(\textbf{template } (Q[y]\ O); B)\ V] = \begin{array}{l}\textbf{template} \\ \quad O[V/y][W.../x...]; \\ \quad \textbf{continue } s' \rightarrow C[(\textbf{template } B)\ s']\end{array}$$
$$(\textit{if } Q[W.../x...] = C \neq \square)$$

Proof. By induction on the syntax of Q.

- $Q = \Box$ is impossible due to the assumption $Q[W.../x...] = C \neq \Box$.
- If $Q = \Box\ P$ then $C = \Box\ V'$ such that $P[W.../x...] = V$, and so

$$
\begin{aligned}
& C[(\textbf{template}\ (Q[y]\ O); B)\ V] \\
=\ & (\textbf{template}\ ((y\ P)\ O); B)\ V\ V' \\
=\ & (\textbf{template}\ (y\ (\lambda P.O)); B)\ V\ V' && (\textit{Lemma}\ 25) \\
=\ & (\textbf{template}\ (\lambda P.O[V/y]); B)\ V\ V' && (\textit{Lemma}\ 20) \\
=\ & \begin{pmatrix} \textbf{template} \\ \quad O[V/y][W.../x...]; \\ \quad \textbf{continue}\ s' \to (\textbf{template}\ B)\ s'\ V' \end{pmatrix} V && (\textit{Lemma}\ 26)
\end{aligned}
$$

- If $Q = Q'\ P$ then $C = C'\ V'$ where $[W.../x...] = [W_1..., W_2.../x_1..., x_2...]$ such that $Q'[W_2.../x_1...] = C$ and $P[W_2.../x_2...] = V'$. Assume the inductive hypothesis

$$
C'[(\textbf{template}\ (Q'[y]\ O); B)\ V] = \begin{array}{l} \textbf{template} \\ \quad O[V/y][W.../x...]; \\ \quad \textbf{continue}\ s' \to C'[(\textbf{template}\ B)\ s'] \end{array}
$$

The equality holds by this inductive hypothesis and the following lemmas,

$$
\begin{aligned}
& C[(\textbf{template}\ (Q[y]\ O); B)\ V] \\
=\ & C'[(\textbf{template}\ ((Q'[y]\ P)\ O); B)\ V]\ V' \\
=\ & C'[(\textbf{template}\ (Q'[y]\ (\lambda P.O)); B)\ V]\ V' && (\textit{Lemma}\ 25) \\
=\ & \begin{pmatrix} \textbf{template} \\ \quad \lambda P.O[V/y][W_1.../x_1...]; \\ \quad \textbf{continue}\ s' \to C'[(\textbf{template}\ B)\ s'] \end{pmatrix} V\ V' && (\mathit{IH}) \\
=\ & \begin{pmatrix} \textbf{template} \\ \quad O[V/y][W_1.../x_1...][W_2.../x_2...]; \\ \quad \textbf{continue}\ s'' \to \\ \qquad \begin{pmatrix} \textbf{template} \\ \quad \textbf{continue}\ s' \to \\ \qquad C'[(\textbf{template}\ B)\ s'] \end{pmatrix} s''\ V' \end{pmatrix} V && (\textit{Lemma}\ 26) \\
=\ & \begin{pmatrix} \textbf{template} \\ \quad O[V/y][W_1.../x_1...][W_2.../x_2...]; \\ \quad \textbf{continue}\ s'' \to (C'[(\textbf{template}\ B)\ s''])\ V' \end{pmatrix} V && (\textit{Lemma}\ 18) \\
=\ & \begin{pmatrix} \textbf{template} \\ \quad O[V/y][W.../x...]; \\ \quad \textbf{continue}\ s' \to C[(\textbf{template}\ B)\ s'] \end{pmatrix} V && (\alpha)
\end{aligned}
$$

Lemma 30 (Context Exact Match). *In the source,*

$$C[(\textbf{template}\ (Q[y] = M); B)\ V] = M[V/y][W.../x...] \quad (\textit{if}\ Q[W.../x...] = C)$$

Proof.

$$\begin{aligned}
& C[(\textbf{template}\ (Q[y] = M); B)\ V] \\
= \;& C[(\textbf{template}\ (Q[y]\textbf{do}\ M); B)\ V] \\
= \;& \begin{pmatrix} \textbf{template} \\ \quad \textbf{do}\ M[V/y][W.../x...]; \\ \quad \textbf{continue}\ s' \to C[(\textbf{template}\ B)\ s'] \end{pmatrix} V & (\textit{Lemma}\ 29) \\
= \;& (\textbf{template else}\ M[V/y][W.../x...])\ V & (\textit{Lemma}\ 13) \\
= \;& (\textbf{template continue}\ _ \to M[V/y][W.../x...])\ V \\
= \;& M[V/y][W.../x...]
\end{aligned}$$

□

Lemma 31 (Context Apart). *In the source,*

$$[\![C[(\textbf{template}\ (Q[y]\ O); B)\ V]]\!] = [\![C[(\textbf{template}\ B)\ V]]\!] \quad (\textit{if}\ Q \# C)$$

Proof. By induction on the derivation of apartness $Q \# C$:

- Suppose $Q \# C$ because $Q = Q'\ P$ and $C = C'\ W'$ such that $P \# W$ and $Q'[W.../x...] = C'$.

$$\begin{aligned}
& C[(\textbf{template}\ (Q'[y]\ P)\ O; B)\ V] \\
= \;& C'[(\textbf{template}\ (Q'[y]\ P)\ O; B)\ V]\ W' \\
= \;& C'[(\textbf{template}\ Q'[y]\ (\lambda P.O); B)\ V]\ W' & (\textit{Lemma}\ 25) \\
= \;& \begin{pmatrix} \textbf{template} \\ \quad \lambda P.O[W.../x...]; \\ \quad \textbf{continue}\ s' \to C'[(\textbf{template}\ B)\ s'] \end{pmatrix} V\ W' & (\textit{Lemma}\ 29) \\
= \;& (\textbf{template continue}\ s' \to C'[(\textbf{template}\ B)\ s'])\ V\ W' & (\textit{Lemma}\ 28) \\
= \;& C'[(\textbf{template}\ B)\ V]\ W' & (\textit{Lemma}\ 18) \\
= \;& C[(\textbf{template}\ B)\ V]
\end{aligned}$$

- Suppose $Q \# C$ because $Q = Q'\ P$ and $Q' \# C$, and assume the inductive hypothesis $C[(\textbf{template}\ (Q'[y]\ O); B)\ V] = C[(\textbf{template}\ B)\ V]$.

$$\begin{aligned}
& C[(\textbf{template}\ (Q[y]\ O); B)\ V] \\
= \;& C[(\textbf{template}\ ((Q'[y]\ P)\ O); B)\ V] \\
= \;& C[(\textbf{template}\ (Q'[y]\ (\lambda P.\ O)); B)\ V] & (\textit{Lemma}\ 25) \\
= \;& C[(\textbf{template}\ B)\ V] & (\textit{IH})
\end{aligned}$$

– Suppose $Q \# C$ because $C = C'\ W$ and $Q \# C'$, and assume the inductive hypothesis $C'[(\textbf{template}\ (Q[y]\ O); B)\ V] = C'[(\textbf{template}\ B)\ V]$.

$$\begin{aligned} & C[(\textbf{template}\ (Q[y]\ O); B)\ V] \\ = {} & C'[(\textbf{template}\ (Q[y]\ O); B)\ V]\ W \\ = {} & C'[(\textbf{template}\ B)\ V]\ W && (IH) \\ = {} & C[(\textbf{template}\ B)\ V] \end{aligned}$$

□

Lemma 32 (Context λ^* Match). *In the source,*

$$C[\lambda^*(Q[y] = M); B] = M[(\lambda^*(Q[y] = M); B)/y][W.../x...] \quad (\textit{if } Q[W.../x...] = C)$$

Proof.

$$\begin{aligned} & C[\lambda^*(Q[y] = M); B] \\ = {} & C[(\textbf{template}\ (Q[y] = M); B)\ (\lambda^*(Q[y] = M); B)] && (\textit{Lemma } 15) \\ = {} & M[(\lambda^*(Q[y] = M); B)/y][W.../x...] && (\textit{Lemma } 30) \end{aligned}$$

□

Lemma 33 (Context λ^* Apart). *In the source,*

$$C[\lambda^*(Q[y]\ O); \textbf{else}\ M] = C[M] \qquad (\textit{if } Q \# C)$$

Proof.

$$\begin{aligned} & C[\lambda^*(Q[y]\ O); \textbf{else}\ M] \\ = {} & C[(\textbf{template}\ (Q[y]\ O); \textbf{else}\ M)\ (\lambda^*(Q[y]\ O); \textbf{else}\ M)] && (\textit{Lemma } 15) \\ = {} & C[(\textbf{template else}\ M)\ (\lambda^*(Q[y]\ O); \textbf{else}\ M)] && (\textit{Lemma } 31) \\ = {} & C[(\textbf{template continue}\ \_ \to M)\ (\lambda^*(Q[y]\ O); \textbf{else}\ M)] \\ = {} & C[M] && (\textit{Lemma } 18) \end{aligned}$$

□

References

1. Abadi, M., Cardelli, L.: A Theory of Objects. Springer, New York (1996). https://doi.org/10.1007/978-1-4419-8598-9
2. Abel, A., Pientka, B., Thibodeau, D., Setzer, A.: Copatterns: programming infinite structures by observations. In: Proceedings of the 40th Annual ACM SIGPLAN-SIGACT Symposium on Principles of Programming Languages, POPL 2013, pp. 27–38. ACM, New York (2013). https://doi.org/10.1145/2429069.2429075

3. Bracha, G., Cook, W.R.: Mixin-based inheritance. In: Conference on Object-Oriented Programming Systems, Languages, and Applications / European Conference on Object-Oriented Programming, OOPSLA/ECOOP 1990, Ottawa, Canada, 21–25 October 1990, Proceedings, pp. 303–311. ACM (1990). https://doi.org/10.1145/97945.97982
4. Brown, D.S., Cook, W.R.: Function inheritance: Monadic memoization mixins (2009)
5. Chambers, C.: Object-oriented multi-methods in Cecil. In: Madsen, O.L. (ed.) ECOOP 1992. LNCS, vol. 615, pp. 33–56. Springer, Heidelberg (1992). https://doi.org/10.1007/BFb0053029
6. Cockx, J., Abel, A.: Elaborating dependent (co)pattern matching. Proceedings of the ACM on Programming Languages **2**(ICFP) (2018). https://doi.org/10.1145/3236770
7. Cook, W.R., Palsberg, J.: A denotational semantics of inheritance and its correctness. Inf. Comput. **114**(2), 329–350 (1994). https://doi.org/10.1006/INCO.1994.1090
8. Danvy, O., Filinski, A.: Abstracting control. In: Proceedings of the 1990 ACM Conference on LISP and Functional Programming, LFP 1990, Nice, France, 27–29 June 1990, pp. 151–160. ACM (1990). https://doi.org/10.1145/91556.91622
9. Downen, P., Ariola, Z.M.: Compositional semantics for composable continuations: From abortive to delimited control. In: Proceedings of the 19th ACM SIGPLAN International Conference on Functional Programming, ICFP 2014, pp. 109–122. ACM, New York (2014). https://doi.org/10.1145/2628136.2628147
10. Felleisen, M., et al.: A programmable programming language. Commun. ACM **61**(3), 62–71 (2018). https://doi.org/10.1145/3127323
11. Flatt, M., Krishnamurthi, S., Felleisen, M.: Classes and mixins. In: Proceedings of the 25th ACM SIGPLAN-SIGACT Symposium on Principles of Programming Languages, pp. 171–183 (1998)
12. Gabriel, R., White, J., Bobrow, D.: CLOS: integrating object-oriented and functional programming. Commun. ACM **34**, 28–38 (1991). https://doi.org/10.1145/114669.114671
13. Hughes, J.: Why functional programming matters. Comput. J. **32**(2), 98–107 (1989). https://doi.org/10.1093/comjnl/32.2.98
14. Ingalls, D.H.H.: A simple technique for handling multiple polymorphism. In: Conference Proceedings on Object-Oriented Programming Systems, Languages and Applications, OOPSLA 1986, pp. 347–349. Association for Computing Machinery, New York (1986). https://doi.org/10.1145/28697.28732
15. Jeannin, J.B., Kozen, D., Silva, A.: CoCaml: functional programming with regular coinductive types. Fund. Inform. **150**(3), 347–377 (2017). https://doi.org/10.3233/FI-2017-1473
16. Keep, A.W., Dybvig, R.K.: A nanopass framework for commercial compiler development. In: Proceedings of the 18th ACM SIGPLAN International Conference on Functional Programming, ICFP 2013, pp. 343–350. Association for Computing Machinery (2013). https://doi.org/10.1145/2500365.2500618
17. Kim, J., Yi, K., Danvy, O.: Assessing the overhead of ML exceptions by selective CPS transformation. BRICS Rep. Ser. **5** (1998)
18. Laforgue, P., Régis-Gianas, Y.: Copattern matching and first-class observations in OCaml, with a macro. In: Proceedings of the 19th International Symposium on Principles and Practice of Declarative Programming, Namur, Belgium, 09–11 October 2017, pp. 97–108 (2017). https://doi.org/10.1145/3131851.3131869

19. Lasater, C.G.: Design Patterns. Wordware Publishing, Inc. (2006)
20. Nielsen, L.R.: A selective CPS transformation. In: Seventeenth Conference on the Mathematical Foundations of Programming Semantics, MFPS 2001, Aarhus, Denmark, 23–26 May 2001. Electronic Notes in Theoretical Computer Science, vol. 45, pp. 311–331. Elsevier (2001). https://doi.org/10.1016/S1571-0661(04)80969-1
21. Oliveira, B.C.S., Cook, W.R.: Extensibility for the masses. In: Noble, J. (ed.) ECOOP 2012. LNCS, vol. 7313, pp. 2–27. Springer, Heidelberg (2012). https://doi.org/10.1007/978-3-642-31057-7_2
22. Peyton Jones, S., Reid, A., Henderson, F., Hoare, T., Marlow, S.: A semantics for imprecise exceptions. In: Proceedings of the ACM SIGPLAN 1999 Conference on Programming Language Design and Implementation, PLDI 1999, pp. 25–36. Association for Computing Machinery, New York (1999). https://doi.org/10.1145/301618.301637
23. Setzer, A., Abel, A., Pientka, B., Thibodeau, D.: Unnesting of copatterns. In: Dowek, G. (ed.) RTA 2014. LNCS, vol. 8560, pp. 31–45. Springer, Cham (2014). https://doi.org/10.1007/978-3-319-08918-8_3
24. Swierstra, W.: Data types à la Carte. J. Funct. Program. **18**(4) (2008). https://doi.org/10.1017/S0956796808006758
25. Thibodeau, D.: Programming infinite structures using copatterns. Master's thesis. School of Computer Science, Mcgill University, Montreal (2015)
26. Thielecke, H.: Comparing control constructs by double-barrelled CPS. Higher-Order Symb. Comput. **15**, 141–160 (2002). https://doi.org/10.1023/A:1020887011500
27. Tobin-Hochstadt, S., St-Amour, V., Culpepper, R., Flatt, M., Felleisen, M.: Languages as libraries. In: Proceedings of the 32nd ACM SIGPLAN Conference on Programming Language Design and Implementation, PLDI 2011, pp. 132–141. Association for Computing Machinery, New York (2011). https://doi.org/10.1145/1993498.1993514
28. Wadler, P.: A critique of Abelson and Sussman or why calculating is better than scheming. SIGPLAN Not. **22**(3), 83–94 (1987). https://doi.org/10.1145/24697.24706
29. Wadler, P., et al.: The expression problem. Posted on the Java Genericity mailing list (1998)
30. Wehr, S., Thiemann, P.: JavaGI: the interaction of type classes with interfaces and inheritance. ACM Trans. Program. Lang. Syst. **33**(4), 1–83 (2011). https://doi.org/10.1145/1985342.1985343

Noninterference Through Bisimulation

April Tune(✉), Wendy Yang, and G. A. Kavvos

School of Computer Science, University of Bristol, Bristol, UK

Abstract. Noninterference properties state that data does not flow in an undesirable manner, e.g. from a high-security to a low-security setting. Within programming languages noninterference is often enforced through the use of modal type systems. Proving the property often requires non-trivial techniques, such as denotational semantics or logical relations. We show that a simple bisimulation technique (due to Choudhury, Eades, and Weirich) can be adapted to show noninterference for a variety of modal type systems.

Keywords: lambda calculus · modal type theory · information flow · noninterference · bisimulation

1 Introduction

This paper aims to showcase a simple technique for proving *information flow properties* of programming languages.

Information flow is a well-studied concept in computer science at large [13]. In programming languages, information flow can be readily controlled using type systems—in particular *modal type systems*. Such type systems are sometimes used to separate data into classified and unclassified; in this case, ensuring secure information flow implies an important security property, viz. that non-classified data cannot leak any information about classified data. Information flow properties can also be used to ensure referential transparency, e.g. in programming calculi with effects [35].

Information flow properties are usually proven by analysing the semantics of a language. Some approaches proceed through the use of a *denotational semantics* that mathematically reifies information flow properties. This entails a large amount of mathematical overhead, but it exposes the mathematical and conceptual reasons that enforce noninterference. For that reason, most noninterference properties are shown using *syntactic proofs over the operational semantics* of typed terms. Such proofs normally require a considerable amount of technical lemmata, many of which are subtle to formulate and tricky to prove.

In this paper we show that a much simpler technique, based on *bisimulation*, can be adapted to show noninterference for a wide range of modal type systems. This technique, which was first used to prove noninterference by Choudhury, Eades, and Weirich [8], appears just as powerful as denotational techniques, while

J. Gibbons (Ed.): TFP 2025, LNCS 15652, pp. 259–280, 2026.
https://doi.org/10.1007/978-3-031-99751-8_11

also being simple—much simpler than both logical relations and parametricity translations, which require tricky syntactic lemmas.

This technique boils down to a simple 'recipe' which we can use to prove a desired noninterference result:

1. Define the types and terms of a language with information flow control, as well as an operational semantics.
2. Define an *indistinguishability relation*, which relates terms that some observer should not be able to distinguish. This relation may also carry some typing information, or information about the *clearance* of the observer, i.e. the highest 'security level' of data they should be able to read.
3. Extend the indistinguishability relation to apply to substitutions. This is usually a pointwise definition, but may be more complicated.
4. Show, via induction on the relation, that *substitution preserves indistinguishability*. This shows that terms remain indistinguishable no matter what we substitute for their free variables.
5. Show, via induction on the transition relation, that the indistinguishability relation is a bisimulation for the operational semantics.
6. Deduce the noninterference property from this fact.

Because of its simple syntactic nature it is possible that this technique will struggle to prove properties of languages that are drastically more complex, e.g. languages with higher-order state. Still, this technique is effective, simple, and more intuitive than a standard proof through logical relations. To substantiate this claim we will prove noninterference theorems for two small programming languages with modal types, namely Moggi's *monadic metalanguage* [35] and Clouston's *Fitch-style modal λ-calculus* [10]. We will treat the first as a sort of "worked example" for those who want to apply it to their own languages; the latter will serve as a secondary example to demonstrate its wide applicability.

These two languages are very different. The former is the typed λ-calculus with a modal type constructor $T(A)$, corresponding to a strong monad. The latter is the simplest possible λ-calculus with a type constructor $\Box A$, corresponding to the minimal modal logic K under the Curry-Howard isomorphism. Categorically, the $\Box$ type constructor amounts to a right adjoint. While a noninterference theorem has been shown before for the monadic metalanguage [28], a noninterference result for the Fitch-style λ-calculus is presented here for the first time. Remarkably, the bisimulation technique applies to both with equal ease.

To show the power of the technique we augment both of these languages with (equi-)*recursive types*. The point is that the various techniques in the literature *cannot* easily handle this extension: the denotational models do not evidently admit recursive types; and defining logical relations over recursive types is non-trivial [6,11]. In contrast, the bisimulation technique we use here requires no sophistication, and works with recursive types directly out of the box. This simplicity means that is readily amenable to formalisation in a proof assistant To substantiate this we provide a short formalisation of our results in Agda.

2 The Monadic Metalanguage

The programming languages that are closest to mathematics, such as Haskell, are often called *purely functional.* It is difficult to precisely define what purity is; some researchers identify it with *referential transparency* [42, §3.2.1], which itself has many explications: the value of a program is determined by the value of its parts; calling a function on the same input always produces the same output; any term can be replaced by its value without changing the overall outcome. Of course, most programming languages are *not* of this sort, as they allow *effects*, such as a mutable store, nondeterminism, and exceptions.

Moggi [35] proposed that the semantics of languages with effects can be unified using the categorical abstraction of a *strong monad.* It is possible to present how this abstraction works entirely type-theoretically. Assume that we have a special type constructor $T(-)$. If A is a type of values, then $T(A)$ is the type of *computations* that return a value of type A. Only terms of $T(-)$ type are allowed to have effects. This allows us to encapsulate effects under a particular kind of type, keeping the rest of the language pure.

In this setting it is reasonable to have a function $: A \rightarrow T(A)$ that maps a value $a : A$ to a 'pure' computation $(a) : T(A)$ which performs no effects and returns $a : A$ immediately. However, it would be ill-advised to have a function $T(A) \rightarrow A$ that extracts the value returned by a computation. The reason is that this value could depend on effects, thereby causing impurity.

How can we then use the value returned by a computation $M : T(A)$? The answer is that we can bind this value to a free variable $x : A$, but only in a term $x : A \vdash N : T(B)$ which is also of $T(-)$ type. Thus, values produced by a potentially side-effectful computation can only influence terms of $T(-)$ type, i.e. other side-effectful computations. Under these conditions we can form a *sequencing* term

$$x \Leftarrow M \text{ in } N : T(B)$$

This program first runs the computation M, performing all its side-effects and obtaining a value V. It then substitutes this value into N to obtain $N[V/x]$, and continues by running that computation. The simply-typed λ-calculus equipped with these two primitives is known as the *monadic metalanguage* [35]. However, similar techniques can also be used as a kind of design pattern that models effectful computation within a purely functional language [5,47].

The discussion above has a strong flavour of information flow: the type constructor $T(-)$ is a *modality* that isolates a region of the language. Data can flow from the *pure region* into the *impure region* $(A \rightarrow T(A))$, but never backwards. We may call this the **Hotel California invariant**: 'you can check out any time you like, but you can never leave' [15].

However, this invariant is so far just a motto: all we have done is give some intuitions and some design criteria. While it may seem impossible for pure values to meaningfully depend on effectful computations, how can we ensure this? Our ultimate objective is to precisely *define* what it means to "meaningfully depend" on a term, and *prove* that the language with these typing rules abides by this desired information flow invariant.

The key property in this setting is that a term $c : T(A) \vdash M :$ of base type with a free computation variable $c : T(A)$ should evaluate the same value irrespective of which computation $M : T(A)$ we substitute for c. It should be clear that this requirement corresponds to our informal intuitions, since if one had access to a forbidden term of type $T(A) \to A$ (or, if they had any other way to extract information from a term of type $T(A)$), they could use it to branch based on the result of an impure computation.

More rigorously, the requisite property is that, for any closed $C_1, C_2 : T(A)$, the term $M[C_1/x]$ evaluates to the same value as the term $M[C_2/x]$—either or . A denotational proof of this property was given by Kavvos [28], based on the model of Abadi *et al.* [1]. In this section we will present a much simpler proof based on *bisimulation*.

2.1 Syntax and Semantics

The syntax of the monadic metalanguage is given in Fig. 1. This version of the metalanguage also includes *recursive types*, in the style of the fixed point calculus **FPC** [23, §7.4] [24, §20]. Such an extension of the monadic metalanguage has been previously considered by Filinski [16], who shows that it admits a straightforward domain-theoretic semantics.

The rules of the calculus itself are given in Fig. 1. Types may include a number of *type variables* α, with the recursive type constructor $\mathsf{rec}\alpha.A$ binding α inside A. We say that a type is *closed* if it has no free type variables ($\mathrm{FV}(A) = \varnothing$), i.e. if any type variable used was first bound via rec.

The recursive type is meant to be isomorphic to its *unfolding* $A[\mu\alpha.A/\alpha]$. Terms over a context are given using the typing judgement $\Gamma \vdash M : A$. Contexts are of the form $\Gamma = x_1 : A_1, \ldots, x_n : A_n$, where all the A_i are limited to closed types. The typing rules combine the usual rules for recursive types with the term constructors for the monadic metalanguage.

The combination of products, sums, and recursive types is rather expressive. For example, recursive types and function types suffice to define terms by recursion, in the style of PCF—see *loc. cit.* Furthermore, we can define a type of Booleans by defining the shorthands

$$\stackrel{\text{def}}{=} \mathbf{1} + \mathbf{1} \qquad\qquad \stackrel{\text{def}}{=} \quad {}_1(\langle\rangle) \qquad\qquad \stackrel{\text{def}}{=} \quad {}_2(\langle\rangle)$$

$$M \qquad P \qquad Q \stackrel{\text{def}}{=} \qquad (M; \_ . P; \_ . Q)$$

where _ is any fresh variable. The 'lazy' natural numbers can be defined in a similar manner [24, §20.2].

A small-step operational semantics is given in Fig. 2. This is essentially the standard small-step semantics of recursive types [24, §20.1], extended with the rule MM/OPSEM/BIND for the primitives of the monadic metalanguage. It evidently satisfies the expected progress and preservation results, and it is deterministic. Letting $\longmapsto^*$ denote the reflexive transitive closure, we define

$$M \Downarrow V \stackrel{\text{def}}{\equiv} M \longmapsto^* V \text{ and } V \ \mathsf{val}$$

to mean that a term M evaluates to a (necessarily unique) value V val.

$$\text{types } A, B ::= \alpha \mid \mathbf{1} \mid A \times B \mid A + B \mid A \to B \mid \mathsf{rec}\ \alpha.\ A \mid TA$$

$$\text{contexts } \Gamma ::= \cdot \mid \Gamma, x : A\ (\mathrm{FV}(A) = \varnothing)$$

MM/TERM/VAR
$$\frac{}{\Gamma, x : A, \Gamma' \vdash x : A}$$

MM/TERM/UNIT
$$\frac{}{\Gamma \vdash \langle\rangle : \mathbf{1}}$$

MM/TERM/IN
$$\frac{\Gamma \vdash M : A_i}{\Gamma \vdash \mathsf{in}_i(M) : A_1 + A_2}$$

MM/TERM/CASE
$$\frac{\Gamma \vdash M : A_1 + A_2 \qquad \Gamma, x : A_1 \vdash P : B \qquad \Gamma, y : A_2 \vdash Q : B}{\Gamma \vdash \mathsf{case}(M; x.\, P; y.\, Q) : B}$$

MM/TERM/TUPLE
$$\frac{\Gamma \vdash M : A_1 \qquad \Gamma \vdash N : A_2}{\Gamma \vdash \langle M, N\rangle : A_1 \times A_2}$$

MM/TERM/PROJ
$$\frac{\Gamma \vdash M : A_1 \times A_2}{\Gamma \vdash \pi_i(M) : A_i}$$

MM/TERM/LAM
$$\frac{\Gamma, x : A \vdash M : B}{\Gamma \vdash \lambda x.\, M : A \to B}$$

MM/TERM/APP
$$\frac{\Gamma \vdash M : A \to B \qquad \Gamma \vdash N : A}{\Gamma \vdash M(N) : B}$$

MM/TERM/RETURN
$$\frac{\Gamma \vdash M : A}{\Gamma \vdash \mathsf{return}(M) : TA}$$

MM/TERM/BIND
$$\frac{\Gamma \vdash M : TA \qquad \Gamma, x : A \vdash N : TB}{\Gamma \vdash \mathsf{let}\ x \Leftarrow M\ \mathsf{in}\ N : TB}$$

MM/TERM/FOLD
$$\frac{\Gamma \vdash M : A[\mathsf{rec}\ \alpha.\ A/\alpha]}{\Gamma \vdash \mathsf{fold}(M) : \mathsf{rec}\ \alpha.\ A}$$

MM/TERM/UNFOLD
$$\frac{\Gamma \vdash M : \mathsf{rec}\ \alpha.\ A}{\Gamma \vdash \mathsf{unfold}(M) : A[\mathsf{rec}\ \alpha.\ A/\alpha]}$$

Fig. 1. Types and terms of the monadic metalanguage.

$$\frac{}{\langle\rangle\ \texttt{val}}\ \textsc{MM/Val/Unit} \qquad \frac{V\ \texttt{val}}{\texttt{in}_i(V)\ \texttt{val}}\ \textsc{MM/Val/In} \qquad \frac{}{\langle M, N\rangle\ \texttt{val}}\ \textsc{MM/Val/Prod} \qquad \frac{}{\lambda x.\, M\ \texttt{val}}\ \textsc{MM/Val/Lam}$$

$$\frac{}{\texttt{fold}(M)\ \texttt{val}}\ \textsc{MM/Val/Fold} \qquad \frac{V\ \texttt{val}}{\texttt{return}(V)\ \texttt{val}}\ \textsc{MM/Val/Ret}$$

$$\frac{}{(\lambda x.\, M)(N) \longmapsto M[N/x]}\ \textsc{MM/OpSem/Beta} \qquad \frac{M \longmapsto M'}{M(N) \longmapsto M'(N)}\ \textsc{MM/OpSem/StepApp}$$

$$\frac{}{\texttt{unfold}(\texttt{fold}(M)) \longmapsto M}\ \textsc{MM/OpSem/Unfold} \qquad \frac{M \longmapsto M'}{\texttt{unfold}(M) \longmapsto \texttt{unfold}(M')}\ \textsc{MM/OpSem/StepUnfold}$$

$$\frac{}{\pi_i(\langle M_1, M_2\rangle) \longmapsto M_i}\ \textsc{MM/OpSem/Proj} \qquad \frac{M \longmapsto M'}{\pi_i(M) \longmapsto \pi_i(M')}\ \textsc{MM/OpSem/StepProj}$$

$$\frac{}{\texttt{case}(\texttt{in}_i(M); x_1.\, P_1; x_2.\, P_2) \longmapsto P_i[M/x_i]}\ \textsc{MM/OpSem/Case}$$

$$\frac{M \longmapsto M'}{\texttt{case}(M; x.\, P; y.\, Q) \longmapsto \texttt{case}(M'; x.\, P; y.\, Q)}\ \textsc{MM/OpSem/StepCase}$$

$$\frac{}{\texttt{let}\ x \Leftarrow \texttt{return}(M)\ \texttt{in}\ N \longmapsto N[M/x]}\ \textsc{MM/OpSem/Bind}$$

$$\frac{M \longmapsto M'}{\texttt{let}\ x \Leftarrow \texttt{return}(M)\ \texttt{in}\ N \longmapsto \texttt{let}\ x \Leftarrow \texttt{return}(M')\ \texttt{in}\ N}\ \textsc{MM/OpSem/StepBind}$$

Fig. 2. Small-step operational semantics for the monadic metalanguage.

2.2 Indistinguishability

The key step in our proof is to define a typed *indistinguishability relation*

$$\Gamma \vdash M \sim N : A$$

for terms of type A in context Γ. The meaning of this relation is that the terms M and N cannot be distinguished by an *unprivileged observer*. The meaning of 'privilege' will change depending on the information flow property of interest.

For the monadic metalanguage, the property of interest is that impure terms cannot effect pure terms. Therefore, to be privileged is to be impure, i.e. to have access to the values returned by effectful computations. Thus, an unprivileged observer is one who observes only the pure regions of the calculus.

MM/SIM/PROT
$$\frac{\Gamma \vdash M : TA \qquad \Gamma \vdash M' : TA}{\Gamma \vdash M \sim M' : TA}$$

MM/SIM/VAR
$$\frac{}{\Gamma, x : A, \Gamma' \vdash x \sim x : A}$$

MM/SIM/APP
$$\frac{\Gamma \vdash M \sim M' : A \rightarrow B \qquad \Gamma \vdash N \sim N' : A}{\Gamma \vdash M(N) \sim M'(N') : B}$$

MM/SIM/LAM
$$\frac{\Gamma, x : A \vdash M \sim M' : B}{\Gamma \vdash \lambda x.\, M \sim \lambda x.\, M' : A \rightarrow B}$$

MM/SIM/UNIT
$$\frac{}{\Gamma \vdash \langle\rangle \sim \langle\rangle : \mathbf{1}}$$

MM/SIM/IN
$$\frac{\Gamma \vdash M \sim M' : A_i}{\Gamma \vdash \mathsf{in}_i(M) \sim \mathsf{in}_i(M') : A_1 + A_2}$$

MM/SIM/CASE
$$\frac{\Gamma \vdash M \sim M' : A_1 + A_2 \qquad \Gamma, x : A_1 \vdash P \sim P' : B \qquad \Gamma, y : A_2 \vdash Q \sim Q' : B}{\Gamma \vdash \mathsf{case}(M; x.\, P; y.\, Q) \sim \mathsf{case}(M'; x.\, P'; y.\, Q') :}$$

MM/SIM/PROJ
$$\frac{\Gamma \vdash M \sim M' : A_1 \times A_2}{\Gamma \vdash \pi_i(M) \sim \pi_i(M') : A_i}$$

MM/SIM/TUPLE
$$\frac{\Gamma \vdash M \sim M' : A_1 \qquad \Gamma \vdash N \sim N' : A_2}{\Gamma \vdash \langle M, N\rangle \sim \langle M', N'\rangle : A_1 \times A_2}$$

MM/SIM/FOLD
$$\frac{\Gamma \vdash M \sim M' : A[\mathsf{rec}\ \alpha.\ A/\alpha]}{\Gamma \vdash \mathsf{fold}(M) \sim \mathsf{fold}(M') : \mathsf{rec}\ \alpha.\ A}$$

MM/SIM/UNFOLD
$$\frac{\Gamma \vdash M \sim M' : \mathsf{rec}\ \alpha.\ A}{\Gamma \vdash \mathsf{fold}(M) \sim \mathsf{fold}(M') : A[\mathsf{rec}\ \alpha.\ A/\alpha]}$$

Fig. 3. Indistinguishability relation $\sim$ for the monadic metalanguage.

These intuitions are reflected in Fig. 3, which gives the clauses defining the indistinguishability relation. The majority of the clauses are *congruence rules*, which ensure that the relation is preserved under all constructs of the language. The only non-trivial rule is MM/SIM/PROT which ensures that $M \sim N : TA$ for *any* two terms of monadic type. Thus, an observer that cannot distinguish terms up to $\sim$ sees pure terms as they are, but impure terms as opaque and cannot be distinguished.

The main desideratum is that the indistinguishability relation is a *bisimulation* [39]:

Definition 1 (Bisimulation). *A relation R is a bisimulation with respect to a transition system $\longmapsto$ just if the following conditions hold:*

1. *If xRy and $x \longmapsto x'$, then there exists a y' such that $y \longmapsto y'$ and $x'Ry'$.*
2. *If xRy and $y \longmapsto y'$, then there exists an x' such that $x \longmapsto x'$ and $x'Ry'$.*

Bisimulations specify equivalences between programs. States that are *bisimilar*, i.e. related by a bisimulation, are allowed to evaluate in 'lock-step,' with the relation being preserved by every step of reduction. We will use this property to infer something about the result of the evaluation of a term. Moreover, if we choose a bisimulation carefully, we should be able to learn something about the invariants of programs.

This discussion provides a blueprint for what this relation should look like for any given language, in order to obtain a bisimulation.

1. Terms containing privileged information must always be related.
2. Values of base types must be related only if they are syntactically equal.
3. All other rules must be simple congruences.

The proof that $\sim$ is a bisimulation is relatively simple, but requires some additional lemmata—a *reflexivity* lemma and a *presupposition* lemma:

Lemma 1. *If* $\Gamma \vdash M : A$ *then* $\Gamma \vdash M \sim M : A$.

Lemma 2. $\Gamma \vdash M \sim N : A$ *implies* $\Gamma \vdash M : A$ *and* $\Gamma \vdash N : A$.

In addition to these, we will also need to show that substitution preserves indistinguishability. To do this, we will extend the definition of indistinguishability pointwise to simultaneous substitutions.

A (simultaneous) *substitution* is a partial function γ from variables to terms. We write $\gamma(x) \downarrow$ to mean that the substitution is defined for variable x, and $M[\gamma]$ for the resulting from applying the substitution γ to M. The definition is the usual structural one, with base case $(x)[\gamma] \simeq \gamma(x)$ (if the right hand side is defined). We write $\gamma : \Delta \to \Gamma$ whenever γ is a substitution such that

$$\forall (x : A) \in \Gamma.\ \gamma(x) \downarrow \wedge\ \Delta \vdash \gamma(x) : A$$

The substitution lemma then amounts to the fact the following rule is admissible.

$$\frac{\Gamma \vdash M : A \qquad \gamma : \Delta \to \Gamma}{\Delta \vdash M[\gamma] : A}$$

We may similarly extend the definition of $\sim$ to substitutions:

$$\Delta \vdash \gamma_1 \sim \gamma_2 : \Gamma \overset{\text{def}}{\equiv} \forall (x : A) \in \Gamma.\ \gamma_1(x) \downarrow\ \wedge\ \gamma_2(x) \downarrow\ \wedge\ \Delta \vdash \gamma_1(x) \sim \gamma_2(x) : A$$

We can then prove that

Lemma 3. *The following rule is admissible:*

$$\frac{\Delta \vdash \gamma_1 \sim \gamma_2 : \Gamma \qquad \Gamma \vdash M_1 \sim M_2 : A}{\Delta \vdash M_1[\gamma_1] \sim M_2[\gamma_2] : A}$$

Proof. By induction on the evidence that $\Gamma \vdash M_1 \sim M_2 : A$. Note that if this holds via MM/Sim/Prot, then $M_i[\gamma_i]$ will also have a type TA and so the conclusion holds by the same rule.

We can now show that $\sim$ is a bisimulation for $\longmapsto$ on *non-monadic types*, i.e. types that are not of the form $T(-)$.

Theorem 1 (Bisimulation I). *If A is not a monadic type, $\Gamma \vdash M \sim N : A$ and $M \longmapsto M'$, then there exists a term $\Gamma \vdash N' : A$ such that $N \longmapsto N'$ and $\Gamma \vdash M' \sim N' : A$.*

Proof. By induction on the evidence that $M \longmapsto M'$. The cases for return and bind can immediately be discharged, as any reduction involving these terms must have monadic type. The other of β-reduction is a simple application of Lemma 3. All other cases are simple congruences.

One subtle point is that the result *does not hold* over monadic types: being unable to peer into the structure of their terms, the unprivileged observer cannot guarantee that impure terms reduce in lockstep. As a simple example, consider the two indistinguishable terms $(\lambda x.\, x)($ $(M))$ and (M) for some closed M. Clearly the left term can reduce, but we will be unable to show the same for the right term. However, this is no skin off our backs, as this restricted form of the lemma is all we need to prove for our main result:

Theorem 2 (Noninterference I). *If $x : TA \vdash M :$ and $\vdash N_1, N_2 : TA$ then $M[N_1/x] \Downarrow V$ if and only if $M[N_2/x] \Downarrow V$.*

Proof. We have that $\vdash N_1 \sim N_2 : T(A)$ via MM/Sim/Prot. Hence, by Lemmas 1 and 3 we have that $\vdash M[N_1/x] \sim M[N_2/x] :$.

If $M[N_1/x] \Downarrow V$ we obtain a sequence of reductions

$$M[N_1/x] = P_0 \longmapsto \ \dots \ \longmapsto P_k = V$$

Applying Theorem 1 to every step of this reduction we obtain a sequence of reductions

$$M[N_2/x] = P'_0 \longmapsto \ \dots \ \longmapsto P'_k$$

with $\vdash P_i \sim P'_i :$ for every $0 \leq i \leq k$. Hence $\vdash V \sim P'_k :$. But the only rule of Fig. 3 that could apply to the closed value V of $= \mathbf{1}{+}\mathbf{1}$ type is MM/Sim/In, followed by MM/Sim/Unit. Hence $V = {}_i(\langle\rangle) = P'_k$ for some $i \in \{1, 2\}$. Hence $M[N_2/x] \Downarrow V$. The other direction is entirely symmetric.

3 Fitch-Style λ-Calculus

Another class of calculi with modal types are the *Fitch-style calculi* [10]. These calculi have a type former $\Box A$, which has its origins in the Curry-Howard isomorphism for modal logic.

It is informally understood that the use of these modalities enforces some type of information flow control [28]. For modalities of $\Box$-type the resultant information control property says that *modal data may only depend on modal data.* This invariant is especially useful in settings that model intensionality (where source code must only depend on source code) [27,29,30], globality (where globally-available data must only depend on globally-available resources) [32], or metaprogramming (where constructed programs may only depend on statically-available data, and not dynamically-computed data) [12,25].

Most of the aforementioned applications use a calculus based on the dual-context syntax of Davies and Pfenning [12,26,36]. More recent work on modal type theory relies on the Fitch-style calculus of Clouston [10] [19–21]. While noninterference theorems have indeed been shown for variants of the dual-context systems [28,34], no noninterference results have been shown for the Fitch-style calculus so far.

In this section we show that the bisimulation proof of [8] directly adapts to yield a noninterference result for the Fitch-style λ-calculus.

3.1 Syntax and Semantics

While the monadic metalanguage was a simple variation on the simply-typed λ-calculus, the syntax of modal λ-calculi with a $\Box$-style modality is more complicated. The reason is that the monadic metalanguage models a *strong* monad, which makes the $T(-)$ type constructor interact pleasantly with the context. This is not so for calculi with a $\Box$ modality: expressing such modalities requires fundamental changes to the judgemental structure of the context [41, §4.1] [19].

λ-calculi with a $\Box$ modality have a type $\Box A$ for every type A. However, unlike the monadic metalanguage, the information flow invariant here is more restrictive: *data should not flow either into or out of a box.* Thus, it must not be possible to define neither a function of type $A \to \Box A$ nor a function of type $\Box A \to A$. In a sense, the $\Box$ separates the language into two strata: the data 'within the box,' and the data 'outside the box.'

To prohibit the definition of a function $A \to \Box A$ we must have a way to *protect* the context so that data cannot flow into a boxed type. This is achieved by introducing a *lock* (🔒) on contexts. This is an operation that forbids access to variables to its left. This limitation is encoded by the variable rule:

$$\frac{\text{🔒} \notin \Delta}{\Gamma, x : A, \Delta \vdash x : A}$$

Locks enable us to *introduce* a term of boxed type: if we have a term $\Gamma, \text{🔒} \vdash M : A$ in a locked context, then we can promote it to a term of boxed type:

$$\frac{\Gamma, \text{🔒} \vdash M : A}{\Gamma \vdash \quad (M) : \Box A}$$

It might appear that the lock prohibits access to *all* variables behind it. This is not true: the *elimination* rule for terms of boxed type allows us to 'unbox' a term of boxed type, at the price of introducing exactly one lock in the context:[1]

$$\frac{\Gamma \vdash M : \Box A \qquad 🔒 \notin \Delta}{\Gamma, 🔒, \Delta \vdash \qquad (M) : A}$$

Thus, if a variable is behind a lock, it can only be used if it is of modal type. This maintains the information flow invariant: things in the box can only be used within the box, while the box remains sealed. Inspired by the relevant piece of laboratory equipment, we may call this the **glovebox invariant**.

We can hence write

$$\vdash \lambda f.\, \lambda x. \quad (\qquad (f)(\qquad (x))) : \Box(A \to B) \to \Box A \to \Box B$$

which applies a function $A \to B$ (within the glovebox) to an argument A (within the glovebox) to obtain a result B (within the glovebox).

The syntax of the Fitch-style λ-calculus with recursive types is given in Fig. 4. Types have an almost identical structure to the monadic metalanguage, where $T(-)$ is replaced with $\Box(-)$. Contexts are similar, but they can now be extended in two ways: by binding a variable x to a closed type $\vdash A$ type; or by adding a new lock. The term typing rules are similar to the simply-typed λ-calculus and **FPC**, with the exception the variable rule (Fitch/Term/App) and the modal rules that we discussed above (Fitch/Term/Box, Fitch/Term/Unbox).

The small-step semantics is presented in Fig. 5. As before, this is the usual small-step semantics for recursive types, with the addition of the reduction $(\quad (M)) \longmapsto M$. Note that terms of the form $\quad (M)$ are values (by Fitch/Val/Prod). The usual progress and preservation theorems are satisfied.

3.2 Indistinguishability

Following our recipe, we define an indistinguishability relation in Fig. 6. In this setting the observer is *outside* the box, and cannot see inside.

As for the metalanguage, the relation will consist almost entirely of congruence rules. The exception of terms which have modal type, which will always be related. Thus, all $\quad (-)$ terms are related (Fitch/Term/Box). We do *not* have a congruence rule for $\quad (-)$, but instead have a rule that relates all well-typed terms of the form $\quad (M)$ with each other. Such a rule would be derivable from Fitch/Term/Box and a congruence rule. However, this choice is inessential for the noninterference result, but makes some of the proofs technically easier.

We can then show results analogous to Lemma 3 and Theorem 1. We say that a closed type A is *pure*, denoted A pure, just if it does not contain a $\Box$.

Lemma 4. *The following rule is admissible:*

$$\frac{🔒 \notin \Gamma \qquad A \qquad \Delta \vdash \gamma_1 \sim \gamma_2 : \Gamma \qquad \Gamma \vdash M_1 \sim M_2 : A}{\Delta \vdash M_1[\gamma_1] \sim M_2[\gamma_2] : A}$$

[1] The additional variables in Δ are required for weakening to be admissible.

$$
\begin{array}{llll}
\text{types } A, B ::= \alpha & & \text{contexts } \Gamma ::= \cdot \\
\quad \mid \mathbf{1} & & \quad \mid \Gamma, x : A \ (\mathrm{FV}(A) = \varnothing) \\
\quad \mid A \times B & & \quad \mid \Gamma, \text{🔒} \\
\quad \mid A + B & & \\
\quad \mid A \to B & & \\
\quad \mid \mathsf{rec}\ \alpha.\ A & & \\
\quad \mid \Box A & &
\end{array}
$$

$$
\textsc{Fitch/Term/Var}\quad \frac{\vdash \Gamma, x : A, \Gamma' \ \mathsf{ctx} \qquad \text{🔒} \notin \Gamma'}{\Gamma, x : A, \Gamma' \vdash x : A}
\qquad
\textsc{Fitch/Term/Unit}\quad \frac{\vdash \Gamma\ \mathsf{ctx}}{\Gamma \vdash \langle\rangle : \mathbf{1}}
\qquad
\textsc{Fitch/Term/In}\quad \frac{\Gamma \vdash M : A_i}{\Gamma \vdash \mathsf{in}_i(M) : A_1 + A_2}
$$

$$
\textsc{Fitch/Term/Case}\quad \frac{\Gamma \vdash M : A_1 + A_2 \qquad \Gamma, x : A_1 \vdash P : B \qquad \Gamma, y : A_2 \vdash Q, y : A_2 : B}{\Gamma \vdash \mathsf{case}(M; x.\, P; y.\, Q) : B}
$$

$$
\textsc{Fitch/Term/Tuple}\quad \frac{\Gamma \vdash M : A_1 \qquad \Gamma \vdash N : A_2}{\Gamma \vdash \langle M, N\rangle : A_1 \times A_2}
\qquad
\textsc{Fitch/Term/Proj}\quad \frac{\Gamma \vdash M : A_1 \times A_2}{\Gamma \vdash \pi_i(M) : A_i}
\qquad
\textsc{Fitch/Term/Lam}\quad \frac{\Gamma, x : A \vdash M : B}{\Gamma \vdash \lambda x.\, M : A \to B}
$$

$$
\textsc{Fitch/Term/App}\quad \frac{\Gamma \vdash M : A \to B \qquad \Gamma \vdash N : A}{\Gamma \vdash M(N) : B}
\qquad
\textsc{Fitch/Term/Box}\quad \frac{\Gamma, \text{🔒} \vdash M : A}{\Gamma \vdash \mathsf{box}(M) : \Box A}
\qquad
\textsc{Fitch/Term/Unbox}\quad \frac{\Gamma \vdash M : \Box A \qquad \text{🔒} \notin \Delta}{\Gamma, \text{🔒}, \Delta \vdash \mathsf{unbox}(M) : A}
$$

$$
\textsc{Fitch/Term/Fold}\quad \frac{\Gamma \vdash M : A[\mathsf{rec}\ \alpha.\ A/\alpha]}{\Gamma \vdash \mathsf{fold}(M) : \mathsf{rec}\ \alpha.\ A}
\qquad
\textsc{Fitch/Term/Unfold}\quad \frac{\Gamma \vdash M : \mathsf{rec}\ \alpha.\ A}{\Gamma \vdash \mathsf{unfold}(M) : A[\mathsf{rec}\ \alpha.\ A/\alpha]}
$$

Fig. 4. Types and terms of the Fitch calculus.

Theorem 3 (Bisimulation II). *Let* $\text{🔒} \notin \Gamma$ *and* A *pure. If* $\Gamma \vdash M \sim N : A$ *and* $M \longmapsto M'$*, then there exists a term* $\Gamma \vdash N' : A$ *such that* $N \longmapsto N'$ *and* $\Gamma \vdash M' \sim N' : A$.

The reason for restricting this result to contexts without a lock is similar to the restriction to non-monadic types in Theorem 1. As all $(-)$ terms are related we may have a term $((\lambda x.\, x)(M))$, which may take a reduction step. However, this term is related to (M), which may not be able to a match this reduction for an appropriate M. However, this situation can only occur in locked contexts, which we ultimately do not need to prove non-interference.

The main theorem is then proved in the same manner as Theorem 2.

Theorem 4 (Noninterference II). *If* $x : \Box A \vdash M :$ *and* $\vdash N_1, N_2 : \Box A$ *then* $M[N_1/x] \Downarrow V$ *if and only if* $M[N_2/x] \Downarrow V$.

$$\frac{}{\langle\rangle\ \mathtt{val}}\ \textsc{Fitch/Val/Unit} \qquad \frac{V\ \mathtt{val}}{\mathtt{in}_i(V)\ \mathtt{val}}\ \textsc{Fitch/Val/In} \qquad \frac{}{\langle M, N\rangle\ \mathtt{val}}\ \textsc{Fitch/Val/Prod}$$

$$\frac{}{\lambda x.\, M\ \mathtt{val}}\ \textsc{Fitch/Val/Lam} \qquad \frac{}{\mathtt{fold}(M)\ \mathtt{val}}\ \textsc{Fitch/Val/Fold} \qquad \frac{}{\mathtt{box}(M)\ \mathtt{val}}\ \textsc{Fitch/Val/Box}$$

$$\frac{}{(\lambda x.\, M)(N) \longmapsto M[N/x]}\ \textsc{Fitch/Opsem/Beta} \qquad \frac{M \longmapsto M'}{M(N) \longmapsto M'(N)}\ \textsc{Fitch/Opsem/StepApp}$$

$$\frac{}{\mathtt{unfold}(\mathtt{fold}(M)) \longmapsto M}\ \textsc{Fitch/Opsem/Unfold} \qquad \frac{M \longmapsto M'}{\mathtt{unfold}(M) \longmapsto \mathtt{unfold}(M')}\ \textsc{Fitch/Opsem/StepUnfold}$$

$$\frac{}{\pi_i(\langle M_1, M_2\rangle) \longmapsto M_i}\ \textsc{Fitch/Opsem/Proj} \qquad \frac{M \longmapsto M'}{\pi_i(M) \longmapsto \pi_i(M')}\ \textsc{Fitch/Opsem/StepProj}$$

$$\frac{}{\mathtt{case}(\mathtt{in}_i(M); x_1.\, P_1; x_2.\, P_2) \longmapsto P_i[M/x_i]}\ \textsc{Fitch/Opsem/Case}$$

$$\frac{M \longmapsto M'}{\mathtt{case}(M; x.\, P; y.\, Q) \longmapsto \mathtt{case}(M'; x.\, P; y.\, Q)}\ \textsc{Fitch/Opsem/StepCase}$$

$$\frac{}{\mathtt{unbox}(\mathtt{box}(M)) \longmapsto M}\ \textsc{Fitch/Opsem/Unbox} \qquad \frac{M \longmapsto M'}{\mathtt{unbox}(M) \longmapsto \mathtt{unbox}(M')}\ \textsc{Fitch/Opsem/StepUnbox}$$

Fig. 5. Small-step operational semantics for the Fitch-style calculus.

4 Agda Formalisation

We have argued that the technique above is simple and adaptable, and hence can be used in the setting of a proof assistant. To substantiate that we have formalised them in Agda. In this section we give a brief overview of our formalisation[2] [45] of the monadic metalanguage.

To encode the terms of the monadic metalanguage we use an intrinsically-typed deep embedding, with terms are indexed by both contexts and types [3]. For the monadic metalanguage this definition is given in Fig. 7, and looks essentially identical to our typing rules. The only deviation is that we parameterise

[2] Also avaliable on GitHub at https://github.com/april-pl/modal-agda.

$$\textsc{Fitch/Sim/Prot}\quad \frac{\Gamma \vdash M : \Box A \qquad \Gamma \vdash M' : \Box A}{\Gamma \vdash M \sim M' : \Box A}$$

$$\textsc{Fitch/Sim/Unbox}\quad \frac{\Gamma \vdash M : \Box A \qquad \Gamma \vdash M' : \Box A \qquad \text{🔒} \notin \Delta}{\Gamma, \text{🔒}, \Delta \vdash \mathsf{unbox}(M) \sim \mathsf{unbox}(M') : A}$$

$$\textsc{Fitch/Sim/Var}\quad \frac{\text{🔒} \notin \Gamma'}{\Gamma, x : A, \Gamma' \vdash x \sim x : A}$$

$$\textsc{Fitch/Sim/App}\quad \frac{\Gamma \vdash M \sim M' : A \to B \qquad \Gamma \vdash N \sim N' : A}{\Gamma \vdash M(N) \sim M'(N') : B}$$

$$\textsc{Fitch/Sim/Lam}\quad \frac{\Gamma, x : A \vdash M \sim M' : B}{\Gamma \vdash \lambda x.\, M \sim \lambda x.\, M' : A \to B}$$

$$\textsc{Fitch/Sim/Unit}\quad \frac{}{\Gamma \vdash \langle\rangle \sim \langle\rangle : \mathbf{1}}$$

$$\textsc{Fitch/Sim/In}\quad \frac{\Gamma \vdash M \sim M' : A_i}{\Gamma \vdash \mathsf{in}_i(M) \sim \mathsf{in}_i(M') : A_1 + A_2}$$

$$\textsc{Fitch/Sim/Case}\quad \frac{\Gamma \vdash M \sim M' : A_1 + A_2 \qquad \Gamma, x : A_1 \vdash P \sim P' : B \qquad \Gamma, y : A_2 \vdash Q \sim Q' : B}{\Gamma \vdash \mathsf{case}(M; x.\, P; y.\, Q) \sim \mathsf{case}(M'; x.\, P'; y.\, Q') : B}$$

$$\textsc{Fitch/Sim/Proj}\quad \frac{\Gamma \vdash M \sim M' : A_1 \times A_2}{\Gamma \vdash \pi_i(M) \sim \pi_i(M') : A_i}$$

$$\textsc{Fitch/Sim/Tuple}\quad \frac{\Gamma \vdash M \sim M' : A_1 \qquad \Gamma \vdash N \sim N' : A_2}{\Gamma \vdash \langle M, N \rangle \sim \langle M', N' \rangle : A_1 \times A_2}$$

$$\textsc{Fitch/Sim/Fold}\quad \frac{\Gamma \vdash M \sim M' : A[\mathsf{rec}\ \alpha.\ A/\alpha]}{\Gamma \vdash \mathsf{fold}(M) \sim \mathsf{fold}(M') : \mathsf{rec}\ \alpha.\ A}$$

$$\textsc{Fitch/Sim/Unfold}\quad \frac{\Gamma \vdash M \sim M' : \mathsf{rec}\ \alpha.\ A}{\Gamma \vdash \mathsf{unfold}(M) \sim \mathsf{unfold}(M') : A[\mathsf{rec}\ \alpha.\ A/\alpha]}$$

Fig. 6. Indistinguishability relation $\sim$ for the Fitch calculus.

the unfold constructor, which constructs a term of type B when given a proof of equality `B ≡ A [ Rec A ]`. We do this to avoid an instance of the *green slime*, a unification problem which arises when the type of a constructor mentions a defined function (in our case: substitution on types) [33, Principle 1].

We can then directly encode the transition relation (Fig. 8), as well as its indistinguishability relation. As terms are intrinsically typed, the relation must also be indexed by the type and context of the terms it relates; this allows us to project individual terms out of a proof of relation. It is then possible to show that the relation is a bisimulation:

```
data TyContext : Set where
  none : TyContext
  new  : TyContext → TyContext

data TypeIn : TyContext → Set where
  TyVar : α∈ θ → TypeIn θ
  Unit : TypeIn θ
  T    : TypeIn θ → TypeIn θ
  _⇒_ : TypeIn θ → TypeIn θ → TypeIn θ
  _×_  : TypeIn θ → TypeIn θ → TypeIn θ
  _+_  : TypeIn θ → TypeIn θ → TypeIn θ
  Rec : TypeIn (new θ) → TypeIn θ

Type : Set
Type = TypeIn none

Bool : Type
Bool = Unit + Unit

data Context : Set where
  ∅ : Context
  _,_ : Context → Type → Context

data _⊢_ : Context → Type → Set where
  ⋆ : Γ ⊢ Unit

  var : A ∈ Γ → Γ ⊢ A
  η_  : Γ ⊢ A → Γ ⊢ T A
  ƛ_  : Γ , A ⊢ B → Γ ⊢ A ⇒ B

  _•_ : Γ ⊢ A ⇒ B → Γ ⊢ A → Γ ⊢ B

  bind_of_ : Γ ⊢ T A → Γ , A ⊢ T B → Γ ⊢ T B

  case_of_,_ : Γ ⊢ A + B → Γ , A ⊢ C → Γ , B ⊢ C → Γ ⊢ C
  inl : Γ ⊢ A → Γ ⊢ A + B
  inr : Γ ⊢ B → Γ ⊢ A + B

  ⟨_,_⟩ : Γ ⊢ A → Γ ⊢ B → Γ ⊢ A × B
  π₁ : Γ ⊢ A × B → Γ ⊢ A
  π₂ : Γ ⊢ A × B → Γ ⊢ B

  fold : (A : TypeIn (new none)) → Γ ⊢ (A [ Rec A ]) → Γ ⊢ Rec A
  unfold : (A : TypeIn (new none)) → (B ≡ A [ Rec A ]) → Γ ⊢ Rec A → Γ ⊢ B
```

Fig. 7. Agda contexts, types and terms for the monadic metalanguage.

```
data _⇝_ : Γ ⊢ A → Γ ⊢ A → Set where
  βbind : bind (η t) of u ⇝ u [ t ]
  βƛ : (ƛ t) • r ⇝ t [ r ]

  βinl : case (inl t) of l , r ⇝ l [ t ]
  βinr : case (inr t) of l , r ⇝ r [ t ]

  βπ₁ : π₁ ⟨ t , u ⟩ ⇝ t
  βπ₂ : π₂ ⟨ t , u ⟩ ⇝ u

  βunfold : { B : TypeIn (new none)}
          → { t : Γ ⊢ B ⁅ Rec B ⁆ }
          → _⇝_ { A = B ⁅ Rec B ⁆ } (unfold B refl (fold B t)) t

  ξbind : t ⇝ t′ → bind t of u ⇝ bind t′ of u
  ξappl : l ⇝ l′ → l • r ⇝ l′ • r

  ξcase : t ⇝ t′ → case t of l , r ⇝ case t′ of l , r

  ξπ₁ : t ⇝ t′ → π₁ t ⇝ π₁ t′
  ξπ₂ : t ⇝ t′ → π₂ t ⇝ π₂ t′

  ξunfold : { B : TypeIn (new none)}
          → { t t′ : Γ ⊢ Rec B }
          → t ⇝ t′
          → (p : C ≡ B ⁅ Rec B ⁆)
          → _⇝_ { A = C } (unfold B p t) (unfold B p t′)


data _⇝*_ : Γ ⊢ A → Γ ⊢ A → Set where
  *refl : t ⇝* t
  *step : t ⇝ u → t ⇝* u
```

Fig. 8. Agda transition relation for the monadic metalanguage.

```
bisim : (t₁ t₂ : Γ ⊢ A)
      → pure A
      → Γ ⊢ t₁ ~ t₂ : A
      → t₁ ⇝ t₁′
      → Σ[ t₂′ ∈ Γ ⊢ A ] ((t₂ ⇝ t₂′) ×′ (Γ ⊢ t₁′ ~ t₂′ : A))

bisim* : pure A
       → Γ ⊢ t₁ ~ t₂ : A
       → t₁ ⇝* t₁′
       → Σ[ t₂′ ∈ Γ ⊢ A ] ((t₂ ⇝* t₂′) ×′ (Γ ⊢ t₁′ ~ t₂′ : A))
```

We may now prove Theorem 2:

```
non-interference : (v : ∅ ⊢ Bool)
                 → (M : ∅ , T A ⊢ Bool)
                 → (t : ∅ ⊢ T A)
                 → (u : ∅ ⊢ T A)
                 → M [ t ] ⇓ v
                 → M [ u ] ⇓ v
```

```
data Context : Set where
  ∅   : Context
  _,_ : Context → Type → Context
  _■ : Context → Context

data _⊢_ : Context → Type → Set where
  *   : Γ ⊢ Unit
  var : A ∈ Γ → Γ ⊢ A

  ƛ_  : Γ , A ⊢ B → Γ ⊢ A ⇒ B
  box : Γ ■ ⊢ A    → Γ ⊢ □ A
  unbox : {ext : Γ is Γ₁ ■ :: Γ₂} → Γ₁ ⊢ □ A → Γ ⊢ A

  _•_ : Γ ⊢ A ⇒ B → Γ ⊢ A → Γ ⊢ B

  case_of_,_ : Γ ⊢ A + B → Γ , A ⊢ C → Γ , B ⊢ C → Γ ⊢ C
  inl : Γ ⊢ A → Γ ⊢ A + B
  inr : Γ ⊢ B → Γ ⊢ A + B

  ⟨_,_⟩ : Γ ⊢ A → Γ ⊢ B → Γ ⊢ A × B
  π₁ : Γ ⊢ A × B → Γ ⊢ A
  π₂ : Γ ⊢ A × B → Γ ⊢ B

  fold : (A : TypeIn (new none)) → Γ ⊢ (A ⁅ Rec A ⁆) → Γ ⊢ Rec A
  unfold : (A : TypeIn (new none)) → (B ≡ A ⁅ Rec A ⁆) → Γ ⊢ Rec A → Γ ⊢ B
```

Fig. 9. Agda contexts and terms for the Fitch-style λ-calculus.

Extending this formalisation to other calculi should proceed in a similar manner: after providing a suitable embedding of terms, one can directly define the transition and indistinguishability relations, which should essentially be a direct translation of the type-theoretic rules. The proofs of ius and bisim then proceed by simple induction; the latter must take as an argument any necessary proofs of purity (in our case, a proof that the terms involved are all non-monadic). This is used to immediately discharge any cases involving impure terms, and in all other cases the proof is simply threaded through.

The same is true of the Fitch-style calculus, whose terms are given in Fig. 9. Note that the term constructor unbox builds in weakening by taking an (implicit) proof of type `Γ` is `Γ1 ■ :: Γ2`, which intuitively means that Γ is of the form Γ_1,🔒,Γ_2 where 🔒 $\notin \Gamma_2$. This trick, as well as our definition of substitution at `unbox`, is due to Valliappan, Ruch, and Tomé Cortiñas [46].[3]

After embedding the language inside Agda, the proof statement and proof terms themselves should be essentially identical to the ones given for monadic metalanguage. In our case, the only real difference is that in some cases we carry around an extra proof term showing that the context is free of locks; we can use this to immediately discharge any case including the `unbox` constructor.

5 Conclusions and Related Work

We have isolated, generalized, and applied a simple bisimulation-based technique for proving noninterference theorems for programming calculi. Unlike other work, the technique is purely syntactic and simple, requiring no complex mathematical models (as with techniques based on semantics), and only a few syntactic lemmas (stability under substitution). We have shown that the technique can be adapted across a variety of modal type systems that control information flow, and can handle advanced features like recursive types with no adjustments at all.

The technique seems to be applicable to virtually any 'pure' language with a small-step operational semantics; the only key requirement appears to be the ability to isolate which terms should be indistinguishable, given the clearance of the observer (pure/impure, or modal/non-modal in each of our case studies). However, it extends to languages with effects is difficult to answer. For example, it is well-known that bisimulation may interact in unexpected ways with advanced language features, such as a higher-order store [31]. Thus, the limits of this technique are yet to be determined.

Related Work. The property of noninterference goes back to Goguen and Meseguer [18]. It has always been challenging to prove that programs do not violate it.

One approach to proving this property goes through using a *denotational semantics* that encodes information flow [1,28]. A more common approach uses the technique of *logical relations* [22,38,43]. Finally, a third approach proceeds by an adequate translation to a parametric calculus [44], such as the simply-typed λ-calculus [40], System F_ω [7], or the Calculus of Constructions [2].

The denotational approach proceeds by constructing a model that encapsulates information flow properties, such as *classified sets* [1,28]. The model satisfies the noninterference property compositionally. If it is additionally proven to be *adequate* for the language in question, then the noninterference property can be lifted to the operational semantics of the language. It is currently unclear whether this technique adapts to more sophisticated programming constructs. For example, the model of classified sets does have domain-theoretic structure [1], but solving recursive domain equations over it appears non-trivial.

[3] We remark that their definition of substitution arises from the structure of a parametric right adjoint: see [19].

By far the most common approach is that of logical relations. As with properties like canonicity and normalization, it is impossible to prove noninterference by induction over the syntax or the operational semantics. In the case of normalization, the reason is well-known: normalization implies the consistency of Peano Arithmetic (PA), whose main axiom is induction; hence, if normalization were provable by induction, this would contradict Gödel's Second Incompleteness Theorem [17, §6]. The logical relations technique overcomes this barrier by allowing induction over *types*. To the best of our knowledge there is no comparable metamathematical argument about the logical complexity of proving noninterference. Perhaps something can be gleaned from the fact it is a *hyperproperty* [9].

While logical relations are an effective technique that has been used in a multitude of settings [22,38,43], it has some shortcomings. First, it requires substantial amounts of tricky technical lemmas, leading to very long proofs. The length and syntactic complexity of these proofs naturally invite formalization, which can be challenging and costly.

Second, logical relation proofs do not scale well to more advanced features of programming languages, such as recursive types, higher-order state, or parametric polymorphism. For example, the mere existence of a logical relation for recursive types is non-trivial to show, as types may get bigger when unfolded. One solution is to use ideas from Pitts' *minimal invariants* [37] to show that necessarily relations exist [6,11]. Another is to use *step-indexing* [4], perhaps by constructing the logical relation within a logic with guarded recursion [14]. The latter technique has recently been used to prove a noninterference result for a very expressive language with recursive types, a higher-order store, and parametric polymorphism [22]. Both of these solutions are surprisingly sophisticated and technically involved.

Acknowledgments. This work was supported by the UKRI Engineering and Physical Sciences Research Council (EPSRC) grants EP/Y000242/1 and EP/Y033418/1, the UKRI International Science Partnerships Fund (ISPF), a Royal Society Research Grant, and a grant from the Advanced Research + Invention Agency (ARIA).

References

1. Abadi, M., Banerjee, A., Heintze, N., Riecke, J.G.: A core calculus of dependency. In: Proceedings of the 26th ACM SIGPLAN-SIGACT Symposium on Principles of Programming Languages. POPL '99, pp. 147–160. Association for Computing Machinery, San Antonio, Texas, USA (1999). https://doi.org/10.1145/292540.292555
2. Algehed, M., Bernardy, J.-P.: Simple noninterference from parametricity. In: Proceedings of the ACM on Programming Languages 3(ICFP), pp. 1–22 (2019). https://doi.org/10.1145/3341693
3. Altenkirch, T., Reus, B.: Monadic presentations of lambda terms using generalized inductive types. In: Computer Science Logic, pp. 453–468. Springer, Heidelberg (1999)

4. Appel, A.W., McAllester, D.: An indexed model of recursive types for foundational proof-carrying code. ACM Trans. Program. Lang. Syst. **23**(5), 657–683 (2001). https://doi.org/10.1145/504709.504712
5. Benton, N., Hughes, J., Moggi, E.: Monads and effects. In: Barthe, G., Dybjer, P., Pinto, L., Saraiva, J. (eds.) Applied Semantics, pp. 42–122. Springer, Heidelberg (2002)
6. Birkedal, L., Harper, R.: Relational interpretations of recursive types in an operational setting. Inf. Comput. **155**(1), 3–63 (1999). https://doi.org/10.1006/inco.1999.2828
7. Bowman, W.J., Ahmed, A.: Noninterference for free. In: Proceedings of the 20th ACM SIGPLAN International Conference on Functional Programming - ICFP 2015, pp. 101–113. Association for Computing Machinery (2015). https://doi.org/10.1145/2784731.2784733
8. Choudhury, P., Eades, H., Weirich, S.: A dependent dependency calculus. In: I. Sergey. Programming Languages and Systems, pp. 403–430. Springer, Cham (2022)
9. Clarkson, M.R., Schneider, F.B.: Hyperproperties. J. Comput. Secur. **18**(6), 1157–1210 (2010). https://doi.org/10.3233/JCS-2009-0393
10. Clouston, R.: Fitch-Style Modal Lambda Calculi. In: Springer International Publishing, Apr. 2018, pp. 258–275. isbn: 978-3-319-89365-5. https://doi.org/10.1007/978-3-319-89366-2_14
11. Crary, K., Harper, R.: Syntactic logical relations for polymorphic and recursive types. Electron. Notes Theoretical Comput. Sci. **172**, 259–299 (2007). https://doi.org/10.1016/j.entcs.2007.02.010
12. Davies, R., Pfenning, F.: A modal analysis of staged computation. J. ACM **48**(3), 555–604 (2001). https://doi.org/10.1145/382780.382785
13. Denning, D.E.: A lattice model of secure information flow. Commun. ACM **19**(5), 236–243 (1976). https://doi.org/10.1145/360051.360056
14. Dreyer, D., Ahmed, A., Birkedal, L.: Logical step-indexed logical relations. Logical Methods Comput. Sci. **7**(2), 1–37 (2011). https://doi.org/10.2168/LMCS-7(2:16)2011
15. Eagles: Hotel California. Label number AS 53051, Asylum Records (1976)
16. Filinski, A.: On the relations between monadic semantics. Theoret. Comput. Sci. **375**(1–3), 41–75 (2007). https://doi.org/10.1016/j.tcs.2006.12.027
17. Girard, J.-Y., Lafont, Y., Taylor, P.: Proofs and Types. Cambridge University Press (1989)
18. Goguen, J.A., Meseguer, J.: Security policies and security models. In: 1982 IEEE Symposium on Security and Privacy, pp. 11–11 (1982). https://doi.org/10.1109/SP.1982.10014
19. Gratzer, D., Cavallo, E., Kavvos, G.A., Guatto, A., Birkedal, L.: Modalities and parametric adjoints. ACM Trans. Comput. Log. **23**(3), 1–29 (2022). https://doi.org/10.1145/3514241
20. Gratzer, D., Kavvos, G.A., Nuyts, A., Birkedal, L.: Multimodal dependent type theory. In: Proceedings of the 35th Annual ACM/IEEE Symposium on Logic in Computer Science, pp. 492–506. Association for Computing Machinery (2020). https://doi.org/10.1145/3373718.3394736
21. Gratzer, D., Kavvos, G.A., Nuyts, A., Birkedal, L.: Multimodal dependent type theory. Logical Methods Comput. Sci. **17**(3) (2021). https://doi.org/10.46298/lmcs-17(3:11)2021
22. Gregersen, S.O., Bay, J., Timany, A., Birkedal, L.: Mechanized logical relations for termination-insensitive noninterference. In: Proceedings of the ACM on Programming Languages 5(POPL) (2021). https://doi.org/10.1145/3434291

23. Gunter, C.A.: Semantics of Programming Languages: Structures and Techniques. MIT Press (1992)
24. Harper, R.: Practical Foundations for Programming Languages. Cambridge University Press (2016)
25. Jang, J., Gélineau, S., Monnier, S., Pientka, B.: Moebius: metaprogramming using contextual types: the stage where system F can pattern match on itself. In: Proceedings of the ACM on Programming Languages 6(POPL) (2022). https://doi.org/10.1145/3498700
26. Kavvos, G.A.: Dual-context calculi for modal logic. Logical Methods Comput. Sci. **16**(3) (2020). https://doi.org/10.23638/LMCS-16(3:10)2020
27. Kavvos, G.A.: Intensionality, Intensional Recursion, and the Gödel-Löb axiom. J. Appl. Logics - IfCoLog J. Logics Appl. **8**(8), 2287–2311 (2021)
28. G.A. Kavvos: Modalities, Cohesion, and Information Flow. Proceedings of the ACM on Programming Languages 3(POPL) (2019). https://doi.org/10.1145/3290333
29. Kavvos, G.A.: On the semantics of intensionality. In: Esparza, J., Murawski, A.S.: Foundations of software science and computation structures. LNCS, pp. 550–566. Springer, Heidelberg (2017). https://doi.org/10.1007/978-3-662-54458-7_32
30. Kavvos, G.A.: On the Semantics of Intensionality and Intensional Recursion. DPhil thesis, University of Oxford (2017)
31. Koutavas, V., Levy, P.B., Sumii, E.: From applicative to environmental bisimulation. Electron. Notes Theor. Comput. Sci. **276**, 215–235 (2011). https://doi.org/10.1016/j.entcs.2011.09.023
32. Licata, D.R., Orton, I., Pitts, A.M., Spitters, B.: Internal universes in models of homotopy type theory. In: Kirchner, H. (eds.) 3rd International Conference on Formal Structures for Computation and Deduction (FSCD 2018). Leibniz International Proceedings in Informatics (LIPIcs), pp. 22:1–22:17. Schloss Dagstuhl-Leibniz-Zentrum fuer Informatik (2018). https://doi.org/10.4230/LIPIcs.FSCD.2018.22
33. McBride, C.: A polynomial testing principle
34. Miyamoto, K., Igarashi, A.: A modal foundation for secure information flow. In: Proceedings of the Workshop on Foundations of Computer Security (FCS'04), pp. 187–203 (2004)
35. Moggi, E.: Notions of computation and monads. Inf. Comput. **93**(1), 55–92 (1991). https://doi.org/10.1016/0890-5401(91)90052-4
36. Pfenning, F., Davies, R.: A judgmental reconstruction of modal logic. Math. Struct. Comput. Sci. **11**(4), 511–540 (2001). https://doi.org/10.1017/S0960129501003322
37. Pitts, A.M.: Relational properties of domains. Inf. Comput. **127**(2), 66–90 (1996). https://doi.org/10.1006/inco.1996.0052
38. Rajani, V., Garg, D.: On the expressiveness and semantics of information flow types. J. Comput. Secur. **28**(1), 129–156 (2020). https://doi.org/10.3233/JCS-191382
39. Sangiorgi, D.: Introduction to Bisimulation and Coinduction. Cambridge University Press (2011)
40. Shikuma, N., Igarashi, A.: Proving noninterference by a fully complete translation to the simply typed lambda-calculus. Logical Methods Comput. Sci. **4**(3), 10 (2008). https://doi.org/10.2168/LMCS-4(3:10)2008
41. Shulman, M.: Brouwer's fixed-point theorem in real-cohesive homotopy type theory. Math. Struct. Comput. Sci. **28**(6), 856–941 (2018). https://doi.org/10.1017/S0960129517000147

42. Strachey, C.: Fundamental Concepts in Programming Languages. Higher-Order and Symbolic Computation **13**, 11–49 (2000). https://doi.org/10.1023/A:1010000313106
43. Sumii, E., Pierce, B.C.: Logical relations for encryption. J. Comput. Secur. **11**(4), 521–554 (2003). https://doi.org/10.3233/JCS-2003-11403
44. Tse, S., Zdancewic, S.: Translating dependency into parametricity. In: Proceedings of the ninth ACM SIGPLAN International Conference on Functional Programming - ICFP '04. Association for Computing Machinery (2004). https://doi.org/10.1145/1016850.1016868
45. MISC
46. Valliappan, N., Ruch, F., Tomé Cortiñas, C.: Normalization for fitch-style modal calculi. In: Proceedings of the ACM on Programming Languages 6(ICFP) (2022). https://doi.org/10.1145/3547649
47. Wadler, P.: The essence of functional programming. In: Proceedings of the 19th ACM SIGPLAN-SIGACT Symposium on Principles of Programming Languages - POPL '92. Association for Computing Machinery (1992). https://doi.org/10.1145/143165.143169

Types

A Type Theoretic Treatment of Context-Free Languages Without Mutual Recursion

Jaro Reinders[1](✉) and Casper Bach[2]

[1] Delft University of Technology, Delft, The Netherlands
j.s.reinders@tudelft.nl
[2] University of Southern Denmark, Odense, Denmark
casperbach@imada.sdu.dk

Abstract. Parsing is the process of recovering structure from strings, an essential part of implementing programming languages. Previous work has shown that formalizing languages and parsers using an idiomatic type theoretic approach can be simple and enlightening. Unfortunately, this approach has only been applied to regular languages, which are not expressive enough for many practical applications. We have extended the type theoretic formalization to context-free languages (without mutual recursion) which are substantially more expressive. We hope our formalization can serve as a foundation for reasoning about new disambiguation techniques and even more expressive formalisms such as data-dependent grammars.

Keywords: Parsing · Type Theory · Formal Languages

1 Introduction

Parsing—i.e., the process of recovering structure from strings—is an essential building block for many practical programming applications. While parsing has been extensively studied, it remains a relevant subject of research where new research questions continuously emerge. For example, how to compose grammars and parsers (e.g., [20]), dealing with ambiguous parse trees (e.g., [3,5,22]), and parsing grammar formalisms beyond context-free grammars (e.g., [1]). Research questions such as these serve a practical purpose, but answering them often requires a deep theoretical understanding of the semantics of parsing.

This theoretical understanding can be approached in different ways. Parsing is often studied using automata theory [15]. However, it is valuable to study more *denotational* approaches to parsing too. A main purpose of denotational semantics is to abstract away operational concerns, as such concerns tends to be a hindrance for equational reasoning. Such equational reasoning could be used to study and answer some of the open research questions in the parsers of today and tomorrow.

J. Gibbons (Ed.): TFP 2025, LNCS 15652, pp. 283–301, 2026.
https://doi.org/10.1007/978-3-031-99751-8_12

This paper studies the denotational semantics of parsing for context-free grammars. While the study is theoretical in nature, the motivation is to provide a foundation for practical future studies on proving the correctness of, e.g., parser optimizations and disambiguation techniques, as well as potentially providing a foundation for building and reasoning about parsers for more expressive grammar formalisms, such as data-dependent grammars [1].

We approach the question of giving a denotational semantics of parsing by building on existing work by Elliott [11]. In his recent work, Elliott demonstrated that regular grammars have a simple and direct denotational semantics. And that we can obtain parsers for such languages that are correct by construction, using *derivatives*. While it was well-known that we can parse regular grammars using Brzozowski derivatives [7], Elliott's work provides a simple and direct mechanization in Agda's type theory of the denotational semantics of these derivatives. This mechanization provides an implementation of parsing that is correct by construction, and that we can reason about without relying on (bi-)simulation arguments. While the parsers obtained in this manner are not designed to be performant, the denotational approach opens up the door to exploiting grammar structure to obtain optimized parsers.

Elliott leaves open the question of how the approach scales to more expressive grammar formalisms, such as context-free languages and beyond. However, the question of using derivatives to parse context-free grammars has been considered by others. Might et al. [18] demonstrate how to build parsers from context-free grammars using derivatives and optimizations applied to them, to obtain reasonable performance. Thiemann's work [21] uses lattice theory and powerset semantics to formalize a notion of partial derivative for a variant of context-free grammars. In this work, we build on the approach of Elliott and study how to build a simple and direct mechanization in Agda's type theory of the denotational semantics of derivatives for context-free grammars.

The main challenge for our mechanization is the question of how to deal with the recursive nature of context-free languages.

1.1 The Challenge with Parsing Context-Free Grammars

We give an overview of what it means to take the derivative of a grammar, how this provides an approach to parsing, and which challenges it poses.

To illustrate, consider the following context-free grammar of palindromic bit strings:

$$\langle pal \rangle ::= \epsilon \mid 0 \mid 1 \mid 0\,\langle pal \rangle\,0 \mid 1\,\langle pal \rangle\,1$$

Say we want to use this grammar to parse the string 0110. The idea of parsing with derivatives is to divide the problem into separate steps for each input symbol, each narrowing down the grammar. After all input symbols have been processed, we can simply check if the final grammar accepts the empty string to see if the whole input is accepted by the original grammar.

We call each of these transformation steps derivatives. Taking the derivative of a grammar with respect to an input symbol can be done naively by keeping only the productions which start with that symbol and then removing that symbol from the start of each of the productions. Empty productions (ϵ) are always removed when taking a derivative.

Using this naive derivation procedure on the $\langle pal \rangle$ grammar with respect to the bit 0 yields the following derived grammar:

$$\langle pal_0 \rangle ::= \epsilon \mid \langle pal \rangle\, 0$$

This grammar essentially represents the residual parsing obligations after parsing a 0 bit. The derived grammar contains fewer productions than the original grammar because we have pruned those productions that started with the terminal symbol 1.

For the next derivative step, we encounter a new special case: one of the productions starts with a nonterminal. A naive solution is to recursively unfold nonterminals until the production starts with a terminal symbol. For the $\langle pal \rangle$ grammar, we only have to unfold $\langle pal \rangle$ once which yields the following grammar:

$$\langle pal_0' \rangle ::= \epsilon \mid 0\,0 \mid 1\,0 \mid 0\,\langle pal \rangle\, 0\,0 \mid 1\,\langle pal \rangle\, 1\,0$$

By continuing this procedure, with additional recursive unfolding where needed, we eventually yield a grammar that contains the empty production ϵ, whereby we can conclude that 0110 is, in fact, a palindromic bit string.

However, naive recursive unfolding does not work for all grammars. Consider, for example, the infinitely recursive grammar:

$$\langle rec \rangle ::= \langle rec \rangle$$

Unfolding this grammar never reveals a starting nonterminal. While the $\langle rec \rangle$ grammar is contrived, the same issue arise for any *left-recursive* grammar, such as the following grammar of arithmetic expressions (left-recursive because of the $\langle expr \rangle$ non-terminal in the left-most position in the first production):

$$\langle expr \rangle ::= \langle expr \rangle \ + \ \langle expr \rangle \mid 0 \mid 1$$

Parsing context-free grammars, thus, requires more sophisticated techniques.

1.2 Contributions

This paper tackles the challenges discussed in the previous section by providing a mechanization in Agda of parsing a subset of context-free grammars with derivatives. We represent grammars using a restricted form of μ-regular expressions, which extend regular expressions with fixed points and which can express all context-free languages.

The subset of grammars that we consider corresponds to context-free grammars without mutually recursive nonterminals. In other words, the grammars can consist of multiple nonterminals which may refer to themselves and others, but there may not be a cycle which involves more than one nonterminal. For example, the following mutually recursive grammar does not fit into the subset of grammars we consider:

$$\langle expr \rangle ::= \langle expr \rangle + \langle expr \rangle \mid 0 \mid 1 \mid \langle stmt \rangle$$
$$\langle stmt \rangle ::= \langle expr \rangle \mid \langle stmt \rangle ; \langle stmt \rangle$$

The $\langle pal \rangle$, $\langle rec \rangle$, and $\langle expr \rangle$ grammars from the previous section are all examples of grammars that are in the subset. We conjecture that our approach can be extended to deal with all context-free grammars, at the cost of some additional bookkeeping. We leave verifying this conjecture as a challenge for future work.

We make the following technical contributions:

- We provide a semantics in Agda of context-free grammars without mutual recursion.
- We provide a derivative-based parser for this class of grammars, along with its simple and direct correctness proof.

The paper assumes basic familiarity with Agda. The rest of this paper is structured as follows. Section 2 recalls the essential definition from Elliott's work which we subsequently extend in Sect. 3 to context-free grammars. Section 4 discusses expressiveness, performance, and simplicity of our approach, whereas Sect. 5 discusses related work, and Sect. 6 concludes.

2 Finite Languages

In this section, we introduce background information, namely how we define languages, basic language combinators, and parsers. Our exposition follows Elliott [11]. In Sect. 3, we extend these concepts to context free languages.

2.1 Languages

We define languages as being functions from strings to types.[1]

```
Lang = String → Type
```

The result type can be thought of as the proposition that the input string is in the language. Equivalently, since our type theory is constructive, you can think of the result type as the type of concrete syntax trees which can result from parsing the input string.

Remark 1. Note that a language may admit multiple different proofs (or concrete syntax trees) for the same string. This is in constrast to the traditional set-theoretic definition which throws away the information about why the string is in the language and only leaves the single bit of information that the string is or is not in the language.

[1] We use Type as a synonym for Agda's Set to avoid confusion with set-theoretic sets.

The above definition of language is broad; it includes languages that are not context-free.

Example 1. The language $a^n b^n c^n$ can be specified as follows:

```
abc : Lang
abc w = Σ[ n ∈ ℕ ] w ≡ repeat n 'a' ++ repeat n 'b' ++ repeat n 'c'
```

We can show that the string *aabbcc* is in this language by choosing n to be 2, from which the required equality follows by reflexivity after normalization:

```
aabbcc : abc "aabbcc"
aabbcc = 2 , refl
```

Example 1 shows that it is possible to prove that certain strings are in a language manually, but for practical applications we do not want to be burdened with writing such proofs ourselves. In other words, we want a parser which can determine by itself whether a string is in the language or not.

Unfortunately, we cannot hope to write a parser for arbitrary languages defined in this way. A language could be defined, for example, such that the inclusion of a particular string is predicated on whether or not the Collatz conjecture holds. Therefore, we need to restrict ourselves to a subset of languages. We explore basic language combinators for this purpose in the next section.

2.2 Basic Language Combinators

Let's start with a simple example: POSIX file system permissions. These are usually summarized using the characters 'r', 'w', and 'x' if the permissions are granted, or '-' in place of the corresponding character if the permission is denied. For example the string "r-x" indicates that read and execute permissions are granted, but the write permission is denied. The full language can be expressed using the following grammar:

$$\begin{aligned}\langle \mathit{permissions} \rangle &::= \langle \mathit{read} \rangle\ \langle \mathit{write} \rangle\ \langle \mathit{execute} \rangle \\ \langle \mathit{read} \rangle &::= - \mid \mathrm{r} \\ \langle \mathit{write} \rangle &::= - \mid \mathrm{w} \\ \langle \mathit{execute} \rangle &::= - \mid \mathrm{x}\end{aligned}$$

This grammar uses three important features: sequencing, choice, and matching character literals. We can define these features as combinators on languages in Agda as shown in the left column of Fig. 1. Using these combinators we can define our permissions language as follows:

```
permissions = read * write * execute
read        = ‘ '-' ∪ ‘ 'r'
write       = ‘ '-' ∪ ‘ 'w'
execute     = ‘ '-' ∪ ‘ 'x'
```

The right column of Fig. 1 lists combinators whose purpose will become clear when we discuss how to write parsers for this simple language in the next section.

$$
\begin{array}{lll}
\text{`\_} : \mathsf{Char} \to \mathsf{Lang} & \emptyset : \mathsf{Lang} & \_\cdot\_ : \mathsf{Type} \to \mathsf{Lang} \to \mathsf{Lang} \\
(\text{`}\ c)\ w = w \equiv c :: [] & \emptyset\ \_ = \bot & (A\ \cdot\ P)\ w = A \times P\ w
\end{array}
$$

$$
\begin{array}{ll}
\_\cup\_ : \mathsf{Lang} \to \mathsf{Lang} \to \mathsf{Lang} & \epsilon : \mathsf{Lang} \\
(P \cup Q)\ w = P\ w \uplus Q\ w & \epsilon\ w = w \equiv []
\end{array}
$$

$$
\begin{array}{l}
\_*\_ : \mathsf{Lang} \to \mathsf{Lang} \to \mathsf{Lang} \\
(P * Q)\ w = \exists[\ u\ ]\ \exists[\ v\ ]\ w \equiv u +\!\!+\ v \times P\ u \times Q\ v
\end{array}
$$

Fig. 1. Basic language combinators.

2.3 Parsers

We want to write a program which can automatically prove for us whether or not a given string is in a language. What should this program return for strings that are not in the language? We want to make sure our program does find a proof if it exists, so if it does not exist then we want a proof that the string is not in the language. We can capture this using decidable types (Dec) from the Agda standard library. It can be defined as follows:

```
data Dec (A : Type) : Type where
  yes :    A → Dec A
  no  : ¬ A → Dec A
```

A value of type Dec A either witnesses that A is inhabited by constructing an inhabitant, or it proves that A is empty by showing how a hypothetical inhabitant of A leads to a contradiction.

We can prove the decidability of one type using the decidability of a related type if we have functions going both ways between the types. For this purpose, the Agda standard library provides the map : $A \Leftrightarrow B \to$ Dec $A \to$ Dec B function. The ⇔ type is an abstraction for having two functions going both way and can be constructed as such using the mk⇔ function.

A parser for a language, then, is a program which can tell us whether any given string is in the language or not.

```
Parser : Lang → Type
Parser P = (w : String) → Dec (P w)
```

Remark 2. Readers familiar with Haskell might notice the similarity between (w : String) → Dec (P w) and `String -> Maybe a` , which is a common way to implement parser combinators (although usually `Maybe (a, String)` is the return type, giving parsers the freedom to consume only a prefix of the input string and return the rest). The differences are that the result of our Parser type depends on the language specification and input string, and that a failure carries with it a proof that the string cannot be part of the language. This allows us to separate the specification of our language from the implementation while ensuring correctness.

Remark 3. Note that the Dec type only requires our parsers to produce a single result; it does not have to exhaustively list all possible ways to parse the input string. In Haskell, one might write `String -> [(a, String)]` following Hutton and Meijer [16], which allows a parser to return multiple results but does nothing to ensure that it correctly produces all possible results. If we wanted to capture all possible results in our Agda formalisation then we could replace Dec by a type which fixes the cardinality of the result type fully. However, we expect that would introduce many complications in our proofs. In practice, furthermore, we want our parsers to only give us a single result. Hence, our effort would be better spent in proving that our languages are unambiguous, meaning there is at most one valid way to parse each input string. Hence, we choose to use Dec in this paper.

To construct a parser for our permissions language, we start by defining parsers for each of the language combinators. Let us start by considering the character combinator. If the given string is empty or has more than one character, it can never be in a language formed by one character. If the string does consist of only one character, then it is in the language if that character is the same as from the language specification. In Agda, we can write such a parser for characters as follows:

```
'-parse_ : (x : Char) → Parser (' x)
('-parse _) [] = no λ ()
('-parse x) (c :: []) =
  Dec.map (mk⇔ (λ { refl → refl }) (λ { refl → refl })) (c ≟ x)
('-parse _) (_ :: _ :: _) = no λ ()
```

This is a correct implementation of a parser for languages that consist of a single character, but the implementation seems ad hoc and it is hard to read, especially considering this is one of the simpler combinators.

Following the approach of parsing with derivatives, we can factor this parser into two cases: the empty string case and the case with at least one character. Folowwing Elliott [11] and earlier work, we call the former nullability and denote it with the greek character ν (not to be confused with greatest fixed points), and we call the latter derivative and denote it with the greek character δ.

Crucially, nullability deals only with (decidable) types, and derivatives deal only with languages. This clearly separates the level of abstraction between both cases.

Returning to our character parser, a single character language is not nullable. On the level of types we express this as $\bot$, the uninhabited type, which is trivially decidable as no λ () .

The derivative of a single character language depends on whether the character of the derivative is the same as the character of the language. We might be tempted to define this condition externally in Agda, but that would break the abstraction of derivatives only dealing with languages. Instead, we are pushed toward defining a combinator, _ ‘ _, which allows us to express this conditional on the level of languages. If the condition holds then there is still a second condition which is that the remainder of the string needs to be empty. We use the epsilon language, ϵ, for that purpose. To conclude, the derivative of the character language $`\, c'$ with respect to the character c is $(c \stackrel{?}{=} c') \cdot \epsilon$ as shown in Fig. 2.

$$\nu\ P = P\ [] \qquad\qquad (\delta\ c\ P)\ w = P\ (c :: w)$$

$$A \Leftrightarrow B = (A \to B) \times (B \to A) \qquad\qquad P \Longleftrightarrow Q = \forall\ \{w\} \to P\ w \Leftrightarrow Q\ w$$

$$\begin{array}{lll}
\nu\emptyset & : \bot & \Leftrightarrow \nu\ \emptyset \\
\nu\epsilon & : \top & \Leftrightarrow \nu\ \epsilon \\
\nu\cdot & : (A \times \nu\ P) & \Leftrightarrow \nu\ (A\ \cdot\ P) \\
\nu` & : \bot & \Leftrightarrow \nu\ (`\ c') \\
\nu\cup & : (\nu\ P \uplus \nu\ Q) & \Leftrightarrow \nu\ (P \cup Q) \\
\nu* & : (\nu\ P \times \nu\ Q) & \Leftrightarrow \nu\ (P * Q)
\end{array}
\qquad
\begin{array}{lll}
\delta\emptyset & : \emptyset & \Longleftrightarrow \delta\ c\ \emptyset \\
\delta\epsilon & : \emptyset & \Longleftrightarrow \delta\ c\ \epsilon \\
\delta\cdot & : (A\ \cdot\ \delta\ c\ P) & \Longleftrightarrow \delta\ c\ (A\ \cdot\ P) \\
\delta` & : ((c \equiv c')\ \cdot\ \epsilon) & \Longleftrightarrow \delta\ c\ (`\ c') \\
\delta\cup & : (\delta\ c\ P \cup \delta\ c\ Q) & \Longleftrightarrow \delta\ c\ (P \cup Q) \\
\delta* & : (\nu\ P\ \cdot\ \delta\ c\ Q \cup \delta\ c\ P * Q) & \\
 & & \Longleftrightarrow \delta\ c\ (P * Q)
\end{array}$$

Fig. 2. Nullability, derivatives, and how they relate to the basic combinators.

Furthermore, Fig. 2 shows the nullability and derivatives of all basic combinators using simple and self-contained equivalances. The implementation of parsers for our basic combinators follow completely from the decomposition into nullability and derivatives and these equivalances. For example, we can rewrite our character parser as follows:

$$\begin{array}{ll}
\text{`-parse\_} : (c' : \mathsf{Char}) \to \mathsf{Parser}\ (`\ c') & \\
(\text{`-parse \_})\ [] & = \mathsf{Dec.map}\ \nu`\ \bot\text{-dec} \\
(\text{`-parse}\ c')\ (c :: w) & = \mathsf{Dec.map}\ \delta`\ (((c \stackrel{?}{=} c')\ \cdot\text{-parse}\ \epsilon\text{-parse})\ w)
\end{array}$$

Parsers for the other basic combinators are similarly straightforward.

The parser for our full permissions language can now be implemented by simply mapping each of the language combinators onto their respective parser combinators.

```
permissions-parse = read-parse *-parse (write-parse *-parse execute-parse)
read-parse        = (‘-parse '-') ∪-parse (‘-parse 'r')
write-parse       = (‘-parse '-') ∪-parse (‘-parse 'w')
execute-parse     = (‘-parse '-') ∪-parse (‘-parse 'x')
```

This allows us to generate a parser for any language that is defined using the basic combinators from Fig. 1. We mechanize this result later in Sect. 3.3, but we first consider extending the expressivity of our combinators.

2.4 Infinite Languages

This permissions language is very simple. In particular, it is finite. In practice, many languages are inifinite, for which the basic combinators will not suffice. For example, file paths can be arbitrarily long on most systems. Elliott [11] defines a Kleene star combinator which enables him to specify regular languages such as file paths.

However, we want to go one step further, specifying and parsing context-free languages. Most practical programming languages are at least context-free, if not even more complicated. An essential feature of many languages is the ability to recognize balanced brackets. A minimal example language with balanced brackets is the following:

$$\langle \mathit{brackets} \rangle ::= \epsilon \mid [\ \langle \mathit{brackets} \rangle\ ] \mid \langle \mathit{brackets} \rangle\ \langle \mathit{brackets} \rangle$$

This is the language of all strings which consist of balanced square brackets. It is common for programming languages to include some form of balanced brackets. Furthermore, this language is well known to be context-free and not regular. Thus, we need more powerful combinators.

We could try to naively transcribe the brackets grammar using our basic combinators, but Agda will justifiably complain that it is not terminating. Here we have added a NON_TERMINATING pragma to make Agda to accept it anyway, but this is obviously not the proper way to define our brackets language.

```
{-# NON_TERMINATING #-}
brackets = ϵ ∪ ` '[' * brackets * ` ']' ∪ brackets * brackets
```

We need to find a different way to encode this recursive relation. A fixed point combinator could resolve this issue as follows:

```
postulate μ : (Lang → Lang) → Lang
bracketsμ = μ (λ P → ϵ ∪ ` '[' * P * ` ']' ∪ P * P)
```

Unfortunately, such a fixed point combinator does not exists for arbitrary functions on languages. Luckily, we will see in the next section that we can define such a fixed point combinator if we restrict the class of functions of which we take the fixed point.

3 Context-Free Languages

3.1 Fixed Points

To be able to specify the recursive structure of context-free languages, we need a fixed point. From type theory we know that a fixed point of an endofunctor on types is well-defined if it is strictly positive. So we could restrict the argument of our fixed point combinator to only accept strictly positive functors. We are dealing with languages and not types directly, but luckily our definition of language is based on types and our basic combinators are strictly positive. One catch is that Agda currently has no way of directly expressing that a functor is strictly positive.[2] We can still make this evident to Agda by defining a data type of descriptions as shown by Chapman et al. [8]. In our case, the descriptions describe grammars rather than data types, but the technique is the same.

```
data Desc : Type₁ where
  ∅     : Desc
  ϵ     : Desc
  '_    : Char → Desc
  _∪_   : Desc → Desc → Desc
  _*_   : Desc → Desc → Desc
  _·_   : {A : Type} → Dec A → Desc → Desc
  var   : Desc
```

Remark 4. We have introduced **Desc** to be able to represent strictly positive functors, of which we know how to take a fixed point. That is not the only reason for choosing this representation, however. Having a concrete description data type as a representation of our grammars gives us the ability to symbolically manipulate the grammar. We use this later in Sect. 3.3 to define what it means to take the derivative of a grammar description.

We can give semantics to our descriptions in terms of languages that we defined in Sect. 2. We use the ◇ prefix to refer to the language combinators defined in Sect. 2.

```
⟦_⟧ₒ : Desc → Lang → Lang
⟦ ∅ ⟧ₒ               _ = ◇∅
⟦ ϵ ⟧ₒ               _ = ◇ϵ
⟦ ' c ⟧ₒ             _ = ◇' c
⟦ D₁ ∪ D₂ ⟧ₒ         P = ⟦ D₁ ⟧ₒ P ◇∪ ⟦ D₂ ⟧ₒ P
⟦ D₁ * D₂ ⟧ₒ         P = ⟦ D₁ ⟧ₒ P ◇* ⟦ D₂ ⟧ₒ P
⟦ _·_ {A} _ D ⟧ₒ     P = A ◇· ⟦ D ⟧ₒ P
⟦ var ⟧ₒ             P = P
```

Using these descriptions, we can define a fixed point as follows:

```
data ⟦_⟧ (D : Desc) : Lang where
  roll : ⟦ D ⟧ₒ ⟦ D ⟧ w → ⟦ D ⟧ w

unroll : ⟦ D ⟧ w → ⟦ D ⟧ₒ ⟦ D ⟧ w
unroll (roll x) = x
```

This fixed point is very similar to the usual fixed point on types, but this is a fixed point of languages so we need to propagate the input string parameter w.

Using this fixed point, we can finally define the brackets language.[3]

---

[2] Poiret et al. have implemented positivity annotations in a development version of Agda [19].

[3] We split this definition into two because we want to separately reuse the description later.

bracketsD = ϵ ∪ ' '[' ∗ var ∗ ' ']' ∪ var ∗ var
brackets = ⟦ bracketsD ⟧

This representation is not modular, however. We cannot nest fixed points in descriptions. For example, we could not create a new language which contains the brackets language as a subexpression, because the fixed point is only taken over the whole descriptor. This problem comes up naturally when considering derivatives, which we discuss next.

3.2 Derivatives by Example

As we have seen with finite languages in Sect. 2, when writing parsers it is useful to consider how a language changes after one character has been parsed. We will call this the *derivative* of the original language. For example, we could consider what happens to our brackets languages after one opening brackets has been parsed: δ '[' brackets. In this section, we search for a description of this reduced language.

We can systematically deduce the derivative language from the brackets definition by going over each of the disjuncts. The first disjunct, ϵ, does not play a role because we know the string contains at least the opening bracket. The second disjunct, brackets surrounding a self-reference, is trickier. The opening bracket clearly matches, but it would be a mistake to say the new disjunct should be a self-reference followed by a closing bracket: var ∗ ' ']'.

Note that the self-reference in the new language would refer to the derivative of the old language, not to the old language itself. We would like to refer to the original bracket language: brackets ∗ ' ']', but we cannot nest the brackets language into another description.

There are cases where we do want to use self-reference in the new language. Consider the third disjunct, var ∗ var. It is a sequence so we expect from the finite case of Sect. 2 that matching one character results in two new disjuncts: one where the first sequent matches the empty string and then we take the derivative of the second, and one where we take the derivative of the first and the second is unchanged. In this case both sequents are self-references, so we need to know three things:

1. Does the original language match the empty string?
2. What is the derivative of the language?
3. What does it mean for the language to remain the same?

At first glance, the last point seems obvious, but remember that we are taking the derivative of the language, so self-references will change meaning even if they remain unchanged. Similarly to the previous disjunct, we want to refer to the original brackets in this case. To resolve this issue of referring to the original brackets expression, we introduce a new combinator μ , which has the meaning of locally taking a fixed point of a subexpression.

```
data Desc : Type₁ where
  – ...
  μ : Desc → Desc

⟦_⟧ₒ : Desc → Lang → Lang
– ...
⟦ μ D ⟧ₒ _ = ⟦ D ⟧
```

The first question is easy to answer: yes, the first disjunct of brackets is ϵ which matches the empty string.

```
νbrackets : Dec (ν brackets)
νbrackets = yes (roll (inj₁ refl))
```

The second question is where having a self-reference in the new language is useful. We can refer to the derivative of brackets by using self-reference.

Using these answers, we can write the derivative of brackets with respect to the opening bracket.

```
bracketsD' = μ bracketsD * ' ']' ∪ νbrackets · var ∪ var * μ bracketsD
brackets'  = ⟦ bracketsD' ⟧
```

This example has illustrated three important points which we should keep in mind:

- We can reuse many of the results of finite languages (Sect. 2).
- We need a new μ combinator to nest fixed points in descriptions. This is necessary to refer back to the original language before derivation.
- Taking the derivative of a self-reference simply results in a self-reference again, because self-references in the derivative refer to the derivative.

Again, we do not want to have to manually construct these derivatives. Instead, we show how to do it in general for any description in the next section.

3.3 Parsing in General

Our goal is to define a parse function for every description fixed point.

```
parse : ∀ D → Parser ⟦ D ⟧
```

We approach this by decomposing parsing into computing nullability and derivatives separately as follows:

```
νD : ∀ D → Dec (ν ⟦ D ⟧)
δD : Char → Desc → Desc
```

The νD function can easily be written to be correct by construction, however δD must be proven correct separately as follows:

```
δD-correct : ⟦ δD c D ⟧ ⟺ δ c ⟦ D ⟧
```

The actual parsing can now be done character by character:

$\mathsf{parse}\ D\ []\ = \nu\mathsf{D}\ D$
$\mathsf{parse}\ D\ (c :: w) = \mathsf{Dec.map}\ \delta\mathsf{D\text{-}correct}\ (\mathsf{parse}\ (\delta\mathsf{D}\ c\ D)\ w)$

That is the main result of this paper. The remainder of the paper concerns the implementation of νD, δD, δD-correct.

3.4 Nullability

If we know the nullability of a language, P, then the nullability of a description functor applied to P is the same as the empty string parsers for our finite languages, but with the nullability of the variables given by the nullability of P. For the μ case we use the nullability of the fixed point, which we will implement shortly. The cases for the basic combinators are the same as in Fig. 2. We only use this explicitly in the sequencing case because the other cases are simple enough to implement directly.

$$
\begin{aligned}
&\nu_o : \mathsf{Dec}\ (\nu\ P) \to \forall\ D \to \mathsf{Dec}\ (\nu\ (\llbracket\ D\ \rrbracket_o\ P))\\
&\nu_o\ \_\ \emptyset && = \mathsf{no}\ \lambda\ ()\\
&\nu_o\ \_\ \epsilon && = \mathsf{yes\ refl}\\
&\nu_o\ \_\ (`\ c) && = \mathsf{no}\ \lambda\ ()\\
&\nu_o\ z\ (D \cup D_1) && = \nu_o\ z\ D \uplus\text{-}\mathsf{dec}\ \nu_o\ z\ D_1\\
&\nu_o\ z\ (D * D_1) && = \mathsf{Dec.map}\ \nu{*}\ (\nu_o\ z\ D \times\text{-}\mathsf{dec}\ \nu_o\ z\ D_1)\\
&\nu_o\ z\ (x\ \cdot\ D) && = x \times\text{-}\mathsf{dec}\ \nu_o\ z\ D\\
&\nu_o\ z\ \mathsf{var} && = z\\
&\nu_o\ \_\ (\mu\ D) && = \nu\mathsf{D}\ D
\end{aligned}
$$

Naively, we might try $\nu\mathsf{D}\ D = \nu_o\ (\nu\mathsf{D}\ D)$, but that will not terminate. Consider the language $\llbracket\ \mathsf{var}\ \rrbracket$, to determine the nullability of this language we would need to know the its nullability. Instead, we use the following lemma.

Lemma 1. *The nullability of a fixed point is determined completely by a single application of the underlying functor to the empty language.*

$$\nu D\emptyset{\Leftrightarrow}\nu D : \nu\ (\llbracket\ D\ \rrbracket_o\ \diamond\emptyset) \Leftrightarrow \nu\ \llbracket\ D\ \rrbracket$$

Proof. The forward direction is easily proven by noting that nullability and the semantics of a description are functors and that the empty language is initial. It is also straightforward to write the proof directly.

$$\nu\mathsf{D}\emptyset{\to}\nu\mathsf{D} : \forall\ D \to \nu\ (\llbracket\ D\ \rrbracket_o\ \diamond\emptyset) \to \nu\ (\llbracket\ D\ \rrbracket_o\ \llbracket\ D_0\ \rrbracket)$$

The backwards direction is more difficult. We prove a more general lemma from which our desired result follows. The generalized lemma states that, if the application of a descriptor functor to a fixed point of another descriptor is nullable, then either the fixed point plays no role and the descriptor functor is also nullable if applied to the empty language, or the other descriptor (that we took the fixed point of) is nullable when applied to the empty language.

$$\nu\mathsf{D}\emptyset{\leftarrow}\nu\mathsf{D} : \forall\ D \to \nu\ (\llbracket\ D\ \rrbracket_o\ \llbracket\ D_0\ \rrbracket) \to \nu\ (\llbracket\ D\ \rrbracket_o\ \diamond\emptyset) \uplus \nu\ (\llbracket\ D_0\ \rrbracket_o\ \diamond\emptyset)$$

If we choose $D_0 = D$ then both cases of the resulting disjoint union have the same type, so we can just pick whichever of the two we get as a result using the reduce : $A \uplus A \to A$ function. Modulo wrapping and unwrapping of the fixed point (using the roll constructor), we now have the two functions which prove the lemma:

$$\nu\mathsf{D}\emptyset{\Leftrightarrow}\nu\mathsf{D}\ \{D\} =$$
$$\quad \mathsf{mk}{\Leftrightarrow}\ (\mathsf{roll} \circ \nu\mathsf{D}\emptyset{\rightarrow}\nu\mathsf{D}\ D)\ (\mathsf{reduce} \circ \nu\mathsf{D}\emptyset{\leftarrow}\nu\mathsf{D}\ \{D_0 = D\}\ D \circ \mathsf{unroll})$$

From Lemma 1, we know that it is sufficient to only look one layer deep when determining the nullability of a fixed point. We can safely assume the argument is not nullable.

$$\nu\mathsf{D} = \mathsf{Dec.map}\ \nu\mathsf{D}\emptyset{\Leftrightarrow}\nu\mathsf{D} \circ \nu_o\ (\mathsf{no}\ \lambda\ ())$$

Remark 5. Lemma 1 does not define an isomorphism on types. In particular, the backwards direction is not injective. Consider the brackets language. It has the following null element, where we first choose the third disjunct, var $*$ var, and then the first disjunct ϵ for both branches.

$$\mathsf{brackets}_0 : \nu\ \mathsf{brackets}$$
$$\mathsf{brackets}_0 = \mathsf{roll}\ (\mathsf{inj}_2\ (\mathsf{inj}_2\ ([]\ ,\ []\ ,\ \mathsf{refl}\ ,\ \mathsf{roll}\ (\mathsf{inj}_1\ \mathsf{refl})\ ,\ \mathsf{roll}\ (\mathsf{inj}_1\ \mathsf{refl}))))$$

When we round-trip this through our lemma, we get a different result:

$$\mathsf{brackets}_0\text{'} : \nu\mathsf{D}\emptyset{\Leftrightarrow}\nu\mathsf{D}\ \{\mathsf{bracketsD}\}\ .\mathsf{to}\ (\nu\mathsf{D}\emptyset{\Leftrightarrow}\nu\mathsf{D}\ \{\mathsf{bracketsD}\}\ .\mathsf{from}\ \mathsf{brackets}_0)$$
$$\qquad \equiv \mathsf{roll}\ (\mathsf{inj}_1\ \mathsf{refl})$$
$$\mathsf{brackets}_0\text{'} = \mathsf{refl}$$

It now directly takes the first disjunct, ϵ.

In practice, such problems should be avoided by using unambiguous languages, ensuring that there is only one valid parse result for each string. In that case, only one of the two solutions are possible and we would have to specify exactly which one we intend to allow when defining the language.

3.5 Derivatives

The final piece of the puzzle are derivatives. They tell us how the language descriptions change after parsing each input character.

In Sect. 3.2, we established that the meaning of self-references changes and thus they need to be replaced by local fixed points of the original language. We define a function σD to perform this substitution. It is a simple recursive function which replaces the var constructor with a given D' description.

$$
\begin{array}{ll}
\sigma : \mathsf{Desc} \to \mathsf{Desc} \to \mathsf{Desc} & \\
\sigma\ \emptyset & D' = \emptyset \\
\sigma\ \epsilon & D' = \epsilon \\
\sigma\ (`\ c) & D' = `\ c \\
\sigma\ (D \cup D_1)\ D' = \sigma\ D\ D' \cup \sigma\ D_1\ D' & \\
\sigma\ (D * D_1)\ D' = \sigma\ D\ D' * \sigma\ D_1\ D' & \\
\sigma\ (x\ \cdot\ D) & D' = x\ \cdot\ \sigma\ D\ D' \\
\sigma\ \mathsf{var} & D' = D' \\
\sigma\ (\mu\ D) & D' = \mu\ D
\end{array}
$$

It turns out that the only the sequencing case, $*$ leaves the variables untouched, thus we only need to apply the substitution there. This substitution does mean we need to keep track of the original description, D_0, through the recursion. Most other cases follow the structure we uncovered in Fig. 2. For the self-reference case, var, we produce a self-reference again, which works because it now refers to the derivative. Finally, for the internal fixed point, μ, we can simply recursively call the derivative function. Thus, our derivative helper function is defined as follows:

$$
\begin{array}{ll}
\delta_o : \mathsf{Desc} \to \mathsf{Char} \to \mathsf{Desc} \to \mathsf{Desc} & \\
\delta_o\ D_0\ c\ \emptyset & = \emptyset \\
\delta_o\ D_0\ c\ \epsilon & = \emptyset \\
\delta_o\ D_0\ c\ (`\ c') & = (c \stackrel{?}{=} c')\ \cdot\ \epsilon \\
\delta_o\ D_0\ c\ (D \cup D_1) & = \delta_o\ D_0\ c\ D \cup \delta_o\ D_0\ c\ D_1 \\
\delta_o\ D_0\ c\ (D * D_1) & = \nu_o\ (\nu\mathsf{D}\ D_0)\ D\ \cdot\ \delta_o\ D_0\ c\ D_1 \cup \delta_o\ D_0\ c\ D * \sigma\ D_1\ (\mu\ D_0) \\
\delta_o\ D_0\ c\ (x\ \cdot\ D) & = x\ \cdot\ \delta_o\ D_0\ c\ D \\
\delta_o\ D_0\ c\ \mathsf{var} & = \mathsf{var} \\
\delta_o\ D_0\ c\ (\mu\ D) & = \mu\ (\delta\mathsf{D}\ c\ D)
\end{array}
$$

At the top level, we simply delegate to the helper by passing $D_0 = D$. $\delta\mathsf{D}\ c\ D = \delta_o\ D\ c\ D$

Lemma 2. *Substitution of a local fixed point into a description is the same as applying the corresponding functor to the semantic fixed point.*

$$\sigma\mu : \forall\ D \to [\![\ \sigma\ D\ (\mu\ D_0)\ ]\!]_o\ P\ w \equiv [\![\ D\ ]\!]_o\ [\![\ D_0\ ]\!]\ w$$

The proof follows directly by induction and computation.

To prove the correctness of the derivative, we consider both directions of the equivalence separately. Furthermore, it is important that we separate the top-level description, D_0 , from the current description, D, as they need to change independently throughout the induction.

$$\delta\mathsf{D\text{-}to} : \forall\ D \to [\![\ \delta_o\ D_0\ c\ D\ ]\!]_o\ [\![\ \delta\mathsf{D}\ c\ D_0\ ]\!]\ w \to \delta\ c\ ([\![\ D\ ]\!]_o\ [\![\ D_0\ ]\!])\ w$$

$$\delta\mathsf{D\text{-}from} : \forall\ D \to \delta\ c\ ([\![\ D\ ]\!]_o\ [\![\ D_0\ ]\!])\ w \to [\![\ \delta_o\ D_0\ c\ D\ ]\!]_o\ [\![\ \delta\mathsf{D}\ c\ D_0\ ]\!]\ w$$

The proofs follow from induction, the equivalances in Fig. 2, and Lemma 2. Finally, we combine these two direction into our desired equivalance:

δD-correct $\{D = D\}$ =
  mk⇔ (roll ∘ δD-to D ∘ unroll) (roll ∘ δD-from D ∘ unroll)

This completes our proof.

4 Discussion

Zooming back out, we want to discuss three aspects of our work: expressiveness, performance, and simplicity.

Expressiveness. Our language descriptions are similar to μ-regular expressions, which have been shown to be equivalent to context-free grammars [21]. The major difference is that we only have a single variable which always refers to the nearest enclosing fixed point and we cannot refer back to earlier fixed points. Each fixed point roughly corresponds to a nonterminal in the context-free grammar, so we conjecture this limitation means we only support context-free grammars without mutual recursion. We hope to expand our work to cover mutually recursive context-free grammars in future work, for example using indexed descriptions [9] where the index can be a set of multiple variables.

Furthermore, an anonymous reviewer of a draft of this paper has pointed out that simply showing an equivalence of expressive power does not mean μ-regular expressions are as easy to use as context-free grammars in practice. In future work, we hope to explore this further by specifying and parsing more representative and practical languages.

Going beyond context-free languages, many practical programming languages cannot be adequately described as context-free languages. For example, features such as associativity, precedence, and indentation sensitivity cannot be expressed directly using context-free grammars. Recent work by Afroozeh and Izmaylova [1] shows that all these advanced features can be supported if we extend our grammars with data-dependencies. In future work, we want to explore using our framework as a foundation for such extensions.

Performance. For a parser to practically useful, it must at least have linear asymptotic complexity for practical grammars. Might et al. [18] show that naively parsing using derivatives does not achieve that bound, but optimizations might make it possible. In particular, they argue that we could achieve $O(n|G|)$ time complexity (where $|G|$ is the grammar size) if the grammar size stays approximately constant after every derivative. By compacting the grammar, they conjecture it is possible to achieve this bound for all unambiguous grammars. In future work, we want to investigate if similar optimizations could be applied to our parser and if we can prove that we achieve this bound.

Simplicity. One of the main contributions of Elliott's type theoretic formalization of languages [11] is its simplicity of implementation and proof. To be able to extend his approach to context-free languages we have had to introduce language descriptors, which are a slight complication. For example, descriptors made it harder to parameterize the symbolic representation of a language with its semantics as Elliott does in his paper, allowing him to write a correct by construction derivative function. Instead, we have split the derivative function into a syntactic transformation and an external correctness proof. Nevertheless, we think our approach retains much of the simplicity of Elliott's work.

5 Related Work

Formal languages have a long history. We refer the interested reader to Hopcroft et al. [15] which is an overview of traditional formal language theory.

The main inspiration for our work is the work by Elliott on automatic and symbolic differentiation of languages [11]. As the title suggests, it shows a duality between two styles of implementing language derivatives in Agda. In this paper, we focus on the symbolic approach to differentiation, but we still benefit from Elliott's clear and concise presentation. Our work is an extension of Elliott's symbolic differentiation to a more expressive subset of context-free languages.

For the idea behind our derivative rule for fixed points of languages, we were inspired by Grenrus's blog post [14].

Previous work has implemented context-free (or similar) languages in Agda. For example, Danielsson [10] and Allais [2] show how to implement a form of parser combinators in Agda. Both ensure termination by requiring that parsers consume at least some input each recursion. In our work, we lift this restriction, freeing programmers from having to ensure their parsers consume input.

Another approach to parsing context-free grammars in Agda is to first convert arbitrary context-free grammars to a form more amenable to parsing. For example, Brink et al. [6] show how to formalize the left-corner transformation in Agda, which removes left-recursion from the grammar, thus allowing the use of a more naive parsing algorithm. Another example of this approach is by Bernardy and Jannson [4], who first transform the grammar into Chomsky Normal Form and subsequently formalize and the efficient Valiant's algorithm. Similarly, Firsov and Uustalu have implemented certified CYK parsing [12] and the necessary certified grammar normalization [13]. For the sake of simplicity, we avoid such syntactic transformations in our work.

Perhaps the closest related work to ours can be found outside of Agda formalizations, namely Thiemann's [21] work on partial derivatives for context-free languages. His work supports μ-regular expressions without single-variable restriction of our approach, which allows him to encode context free grammars with mutually recursive nonterminals. In Thiemann's approach, however, languages are sets of strings and parsing only determines whether a string is in the set or not, whereas our parsers conststruct a parse tree. Furthermore, our proofs are mechanized in Agda, which gives us confidence in the correctness, but also facilitates computer-aided experimentation.

Finally, there are some works which focus less on formalization and more on the practical implementation of parsing μ-regular expressions. Might et al. [18] show how to parse μ-regular expressions using derivatives. They use laziness and memoization to avoid nontermination. Krishnaswami and Yallop [17] propose an alternative approach to parsing μ-regular expressions. They introduce a type system which enforces their languages to be in LL(1), which they parse efficiently using staging.

6 Conclusion

In conclusion, we have formalized (non mutually recursive) context-free grammars using a type theoretic approach to provide fertile ground for further formalizations of disambiguation strategies and parsers that are both correct and performant.

References

1. Afroozeh, A., Izmaylova, A.: One parser to rule them all. In: 2015 ACM International Symposium on New Ideas, New Paradigms, and Reflections on Programming and Software (Onward!), Onward! 2015, pp. 151–170. Association for Computing Machinery, New York (2015). https://doi.org/10.1145/2814228.2814242
2. Allais, G.: Agdarsec - total parser combinators, pp. 45–59 (2018), publisher Copyright: JFLA 2018 - Journees Francophones des Langages Applicatifs. All rights reserved. Sylvie Boldo, Nicolas Magaud. Journées Francophones des Langages Applicatifs 2018. Sylvie Boldo; Nicolas Magaud. Journées Francophones des Langages Applicatifs 2018, Jan 2018, Banyuls-sur-Mer, France. publié par les auteurs, 2018. ⟨hal-01707376⟩; Vingt-neuviemes Journees Francophones des Langages Applicatifs, JFLA 2018 - 29th French-Speaking Conference on Applicative Languages, JFLA 2018 ; Conference date: 24-01-2018 Through 27-01-2018
3. Basten, B.: Ambiguity Detection for Programming Language Grammars. Theses, Universiteit van Amsterdam (2011). https://theses.hal.science/tel-00644079
4. Bernardy, J., Jansson, P.: Certified context-free parsing: a formalisation of valiant's algorithm in agda. Log. Methods Comput. Sci. **12**(2) (2016). https://doi.org/10.2168/LMCS-12(2:6)2016
5. Brabrand, C., Giegerich, R., Møller, A.: Analyzing ambiguity of context-free grammars. Sci. Comput. Program. **75**(3), 176–191 (2010). https://doi.org/10.1016/J.SCICO.2009.11.002
6. Middelkoop, A., Dijkstra, A., Swierstra, S.D.: Dependently typed attribute grammars. In: Hage, J., Morazán, M.T. (eds.) IFL 2010. LNCS, vol. 6647, pp. 105–120. Springer, Heidelberg (2011). https://doi.org/10.1007/978-3-642-24276-2_7
7. Brzozowski, J.A.: Derivatives of regular expressions. J. ACM **11**(4), 481–494 (1964). https://doi.org/10.1145/321239.321249
8. Chapman, J., Dagand, P.E., McBride, C., Morris, P.: The gentle art of levitation. In: Proceedings of the 15th ACM SIGPLAN International Conference on Functional Programming, ICFP '10, pp. 3–14. Association for Computing Machinery, New York (2010). https://doi.org/10.1145/1863543.1863547
9. Chapman, J., Dagand, P.E., McBride, C., Morris, P.: The gentle art of levitation. SIGPLAN Not. **45**(9), 3–14 (2010). https://doi.org/10.1145/1932681.1863547
10. Danielsson, N.A.: Total parser combinators. SIGPLAN Not. **45**(9), 285–296 (2010). https://doi.org/10.1145/1932681.1863585

11. Elliott, C.: Symbolic and automatic differentiation of languages. Proc. ACM Program. Lang. **5**(ICFP) (2021). https://doi.org/10.1145/3473583
12. Firsov, D., Uustalu, T.: Certified cyk parsing of context-free languages. J. Log. Algeb. Methods Program. **83**(5), 459–468 (2014). https://doi.org/10.1016/j.jlamp.2014.09.002. https://www.sciencedirect.com/science/article/pii/S2352220814000601
13. Firsov, D., Uustalu, T.: Certified normalization of context-free grammars. In: Proceedings of the 2015 Conference on Certified Programs and Proofs, CPP '15, pp. 167–174. Association for Computing Machinery, New York (2015). https://doi.org/10.1145/2676724.2693177
14. Grenrus, O.: Fix-ing regular expressions (2020). https://well-typed.com/blog/2020/06/fix-ing-regular-expressions/. Accessed 16 Apr 2025
15. Hopcroft, J.E., Motwani, R., Ullman, J.D.: Introduction to automata theory, languages, and computation, 3rd edn., Pearson international edition. Addison-Wesley (2007)
16. Hutton, G., Meijer, E.: Monadic parsing in haskell. J. Funct. Program. **8**(4), 437–444 (1998). https://doi.org/10.1017/S0956796898003050
17. Krishnaswami, N.R., Yallop, J.: A typed, algebraic approach to parsing. In: Proceedings of the 40th ACM SIGPLAN Conference on Programming Language Design and Implementation, PLDI 2019, pp. 379–393. Association for Computing Machinery, New York (2019). https://doi.org/10.1145/3314221.3314625
18. Might, M., Darais, D., Spiewak, D.: Parsing with derivatives: a functional pearl. In: Proceedings of the 16th ACM SIGPLAN International Conference on Functional Programming, ICFP '11, pp. 189–195. Association for Computing Machinery, New York (2011). https://doi.org/10.1145/2034773.2034801
19. Poiret, J., Escot, L., Ceulemans, J., Altenmüller, M., Nuyts, A.: Read the mode and stay positive. In: 29th International Conference on Types for Proofs and Programs, Valencia, Spain (2023)
20. Schwerdfeger, A., Van Wyk, E.: Verifiable parse table composition for deterministic parsing. In: van den Brand, M., Gašević, D., Gray, J. (eds.) SLE 2009. LNCS, vol. 5969, pp. 184–203. Springer, Heidelberg (2010). https://doi.org/10.1007/978-3-642-12107-4_15
21. Thiemann, P.: Partial derivatives for context-free languages. In: Esparza, J., Murawski, A.S. (eds.) FoSSaCS 2017. LNCS, vol. 10203, pp. 248–264. Springer, Heidelberg (2017). https://doi.org/10.1007/978-3-662-54458-7_15
22. Vinju, J.J.: Comparing bottom-up with top-down parsing architectures for the syntax definition formalism from a disambiguation standpoint. In: Lämmel, R., Mosses, P.D., Steimann, F. (eds.) Eelco Visser Commemorative Symposium (EVCS 2023). Open Access Series in Informatics (OASIcs), vol. 109, pp. 31:1–31:16. Schloss Dagstuhl – Leibniz-Zentrum für Informatik, Dagstuhl (2023). https://doi.org/10.4230/OASIcs.EVCS.2023.31

Custom Representations of Inductive Families

Constantine Theocharis(✉) and Edwin Brady

University of St Andrews, St Andrews, UK
{kt81,ecb10}@st-andrews.ac.uk

Abstract. Inductive families provide a convenient way of programming with dependent types. Yet, when it comes to compilation, their default linked-tree runtime representations, as well as the need to convert between different indexed views of the same data, can lead to unsatisfactory runtime performance. In this paper, we introduce a language with dependent types, and inductive families with customisable representations. Representations are a version of Wadler's views [25], refined to inductive families like in Epigram [23], but with compilation guarantees: a represented inductive family will not leave any runtime traces behind, without relying on heuristics such as deforestation. This way, we can build a library of convenient inductive families based on a minimal set of primitives, whose re-indexing and conversion functions are erased during compilation. We show how we can express optimisation techniques such as representing Nat-like types as GMP-style [28] big integers, without special casing in the compiler. With dependent types, reasoning about data representations is also possible through a provided modality. This yields computationally irrelevant isomorphisms between the original and represented data.

Keywords: Dependent types · Memory representation · Inductive families

1 Introduction

Inductive families are a generalisation of inductive data types found in programming languages with dependent types. An inductive definition is equipped with an eliminator that and enables structural recursion over the data, and captures the notion of mathematical induction. This is a powerful tool for programming as well as theorem proving. However, this abstraction has a cost when it comes to compilation: the standard runtime representation of inductive types is a linked tree structure. This representation is not always the most efficient and often forces users to rely on machine primitives to achieve desirable performance, at the cost of structural induction and dependent pattern matching.

Despite advances in the erasure of irrelevant indices in inductive families [12] and the use of theories with irrelevant fragments [8,24], there is still a need to convert between differently-indexed versions of the same data. For example, consider the function that converts from BinTreeOfHeight T n to BinTree T by forgetting the height index n. This is *not* erased by any current language

J. Gibbons (Ed.): TFP 2025, LNCS 15652, pp. 302–328, 2026.
https://doi.org/10.1007/978-3-031-99751-8_13

with dependent types, unless sized binary trees are defined as a refinement of binary trees with an erased height field, which hinders dependent pattern matching due to the presence of non-structural witnesses.

Wadler's views [25] provide a way to abstract over inductive interfaces, so that different views of the same data can be defined and converted between seamlessly. In the context of inductive families, views have been used in Epigram [23] that use the index refinement machinery of dependent pattern matching to avoid certain proof obligations with eliminator-like constructs. While Wadler's views exhibit a nice way to transport across a bijection between the original data and the viewed data, they do not *erase* the view from the final program.

In this paper, we propose an extension DATATT to Martin-Löf type theory [21] with which allows programmers to define inductive types with custom, correct-by-construction data representations. This is done through user-defined translations of the constructors and eliminators of an inductive type to a concrete implementation, which form a bijective view of the original data called a 'representation'. Representations are defined internally to the language, and require coherence properties that ensure a representation is faithful to its the original inductive family. We contribute the following:

- A formulation of common optimisations such as the 'Nat-hack', and similarly for other inductive types, as well as zero-cost data reuse when reindexing, using custom *representations* (Sect. 2).
- A dependent type system DATATT with data types formulated in terms of inductive algebras for signatures, along with a translation to MLTT that replaces all data types with their defined inductive algebras (Sect. 3). We have formalised this in Agda (Appendix A).
- A prototype implementation of this system in SUPERFLUID, a programming language with inductive families (Sect. 4).

2 A Tour of Data Representations

A common optimisation done by programming languages with dependent types such as Idris 2 [29], Agda [27], Rocq [31] and Lean [30] is to represent natural numbers more efficiently. The definition of natural numbers is

$$\textbf{data}\ \mathsf{Nat} \left\{ \begin{array}{l} \mathsf{zero} : \mathsf{Nat} \\ \mathsf{succ} : \mathsf{Nat} \to \mathsf{Nat} \end{array} \right\} \tag{1}$$

and generates a case analysis principle $\mathsf{case}_{\mathsf{Nat}}$ of type

$$(P : \mathsf{Nat} \to \mathcal{U}) \to P\ \mathsf{zero} \to ((n : \mathsf{Nat}) \to P\ (\mathsf{succ}\ n)) \to (s : \mathsf{Nat}) \to P\ s\,,$$

which powers pattern matching. This is a special case of the induction principle $\mathsf{elim}_{\mathsf{Nat}}$, where the inductive hypotheses are given in each method. Without further intervention, Nat is represented in unary, where each digit becomes a heap cell at runtime. This is inefficient for many basic operations on natural numbers, especially since computers are well-equipped to deal with numbers natively, so many real-world implementations will treat Nat specially, swapping the default inductive type representation with one based on GMP [28] integers. This is done with the replacements

$$
\begin{aligned}
&|\mathsf{zero}| = \mathsf{0},\\
&|\mathsf{succ}| = \texttt{\textbackslash x => x + 1},\\
&|\mathsf{case}_{\mathsf{Nat}}\ P\ m_{\mathsf{zero}}\ m_{\mathsf{succ}}\ s|\\
&\qquad = \texttt{let s = } |s| \texttt{ in if s == 0}\\
&\qquad\quad \texttt{then } |m_{\mathsf{zero}}|\\
&\qquad\quad \texttt{else } |m_{\mathsf{succ}}| \texttt{ (s - 1)},
\end{aligned}
$$

where $|\cdot|$ denotes a source translation into a compilation target language with appropriate big unsigned integer primitives. This is the 'Nat-hack'.[1]

In addition to the constructors and case analysis, the compiler might define translations for commonly used definitions which have a more efficient counterpart in the target, such as addition, multiplication, etc. The recursively-defined functions are well-suited to proofs and reasoning, while the primitives are more efficient for computation. This way, the surface program can take advantage of the structural properties of induction, while still benefiting from an efficient representation at runtime.

Unfortunately, this approach only works for the data types which the compiler recognises as 'special'. Particularly in the presence of dependent types, other data types might end up being equivalent to Nat or another 'nicely-representable' type, but in a non-trivial way that the compiler cannot recognise. It is also hard to know when such optimisations will fire and performance can become brittle upon refactoring. Hence, one of our goals is to extend this optimisation to work for any data type. To achieve this, our framework requires that representations are fully typed in a way that ensures the behaviour of the representation of a data type matches the behaviour of the data type itself.

2.1 The Well-Typed Nat-Hack

A representation definition looks like

$$
\textbf{repr}\ \mathsf{Nat}\ \textbf{as}\ \mathsf{UBig}\ \left\{
\begin{aligned}
&\mathsf{zero}\ \textbf{as}\ \mathsf{0}\\
&\mathsf{succ}\ n\ \textbf{as}\ 1 + n\\
&\mathsf{elim}_{\mathsf{Nat}}\ \textbf{as}\ \mathsf{ubig\text{-}elim}\\
&\qquad\quad \textbf{by}\ \mathsf{ubig\text{-}elim\text{-}zero\text{-}id},\\
&\qquad\qquad\ \mathsf{ubig\text{-}elim\text{-}add\text{-}one\text{-}id}
\end{aligned}
\right\}
$$

[1] Idris 2 will in fact look for any Nat-like types and apply this optimisation. A similar optimisation is also done with list-like and boolean-like types because they have a canonical representation in the target runtime, Chez Scheme.

The inductive type Nat is represented as the type UBig of big unsigned integers, with translations for the constructors zero and succ, and the eliminator $\mathsf{elim}_{\mathsf{Nat}}$ (now with the inductive hypotheses). Additionally, the eliminator must satisfy the computation rules of the Nat eliminator, which are postulated as propositional equalities. This representation is valid in a context containing the symbols

$$\begin{aligned} 0, 1 : \mathsf{UBig} \qquad + : \mathsf{UBig} \to \mathsf{UBig} \to \mathsf{UBig} \\ \mathsf{ubig\text{-}elim} : (P : \mathsf{UBig} \to \mathcal{U}) \to P\ 0 \to ((n : \mathsf{UBig}) \to \overline{P\ n} \to P\ (1+n)) \\ \to (s : \mathsf{UBig}) \to P\ s \end{aligned}$$

and propositional equalities

$$\begin{aligned} &\mathsf{ubig\text{-}elim\text{-}zero\text{-}id} :_{\forall P b r}\ \mathsf{ubig\text{-}elim}\ P\ b\ r\ 0 = b \\ &\mathsf{ubig\text{-}elim\text{-}add\text{-}one\text{-}id} :_{\forall P b r n}\ \mathsf{ubig\text{-}elim}\ P\ b\ r\ (1+n) = r\ n\ (\lambda\_.\ \mathsf{ubig\text{-}elim}\ P\ b\ r\ n)\,. \end{aligned}$$

For the remainder of the paper we will work with eliminators rather than case analysis but the approach can be specialised to the latter if the language has general recursion. Assuming call-by-value semantics, inductive hypotheses are labelled $\overline{P}$ which denotes lazy values, that is, functions $\mathsf{Unit} \to P$.

The compiler knows how to perform pattern matching on Nat, and produces invocations of $\mathsf{elim}_{\mathsf{Nat}}$ as a result. On the other hand, it does not know how to pattern match on UBig. With this representation, we get the best of both worlds: Nat is used for pattern matching, but is then replaced with UBig during compilation, generating more efficient code. We expect that the underlying implementation of UBig indeed satisfies these postulated properties, which is a separate concern from the correctness of the representation itself. However, such postulates are only needed when the representation target is a primitive; the next examples use defined types as targets, so that the coherence of the target eliminator follows from the coherence of other eliminators used in its implementation.

2.2 Vectors as a Refinement of Lists

In addition to representing inductive types as primitives, we can use representations to share the underlying data when converting between indexed views of the same data. For example, we can define a representation of Vec in terms of List, so that the conversion from one to the other is 'compiled away'. We can do this by representing the indexed type as a refinement of the unindexed type by an appropriate relation. For the case of Vec, we know intuitively that

$$\mathsf{Vec}\ T\ n \simeq \{l : \mathsf{List}\ T \mid \mathsf{length}\ l = n\}$$

which we shorthand as $\mathsf{List}'\ T\ n := \{l : \mathsf{List}\ T \mid \mathsf{length}\ l = n\}$. We will take the subset $\{x : A \mid P\ x\}$ to mean a Σ-type $(x : A) \times P\ x$ where the right component is irrelevant and erased at runtime. We also assume that Vec's n index is computationally irrelevant. We can thus choose List' T n as the representation of Vec T n. We are then tasked with providing terms that correspond to the constructors of Vec but for List'. These can be defined as

$$\begin{array}{ll} \mathsf{nil} : \mathsf{List'}\ T\ \mathsf{zero} & \mathsf{cons} : T \to \mathsf{List'}\ T\ n \to \mathsf{List'}\ T\ (\mathsf{succ}\ n) \\ \mathsf{nil} = (\mathsf{nil}, \mathsf{refl}) & \mathsf{cons}\ x\ (xs, p) = (\mathsf{cons}\ x\ xs, \mathsf{cong}\ (\mathsf{succ})\ p)\,. \end{array}$$

Next we need to define the eliminator for List', which should have the form

$$\begin{aligned} &\mathsf{elim\text{-}List'} : (E : (n : \mathsf{Nat}) \to \mathsf{List'}\ T\ n \to \mathsf{Type}) \\ &\quad \to E\ \mathsf{zero}\ \mathsf{nil} \\ &\quad \to ((x : T) \to (n : \mathsf{Nat}) \to (xs : \mathsf{List'}\ T\ n) \to \overline{E\ n\ xs} \to E\ (\mathsf{succ}\ n)\ (\mathsf{cons}\ x\ xs)) \\ &\quad \to (n : \mathsf{Nat}) \to (v : \mathsf{List'}\ T\ n) \to E\ n\ v\,. \end{aligned}$$

Dependent pattern matching does a lot of the heavy lifting by refining the length index and equality proof by matching on the underlying list. However we still need to substitute the lemma cong (succ) (succ-inj p) $= p$ in the recursive case.

$$\begin{aligned} &\mathsf{elim\text{-}List'}\ P\ b\ r\ \mathsf{zero}\ (\mathsf{nil}, \mathsf{refl}) = b \\ &\mathsf{elim\text{-}List'}\ P\ b\ r\ (\mathsf{succ}\ m)\ (\mathsf{cons}\ x\ xs, e) = \mathsf{subst}\ (\lambda p.\ P\ (\mathsf{succ}\ m)\ (\mathsf{cons}\ x\ xs, p)) \\ &\qquad\qquad (\mathsf{succ\text{-}cong\text{-}id}\ e)\ (r\ x\ (xs, \mathsf{succ\text{-}inj}\ e) \\ &\qquad\qquad (\lambda\_.\ \mathsf{elim\text{-}List'}\ P\ b\ r\ m\ (xs, \mathsf{succ\text{-}inj}\ e)))\,. \end{aligned}$$

Finally, we need to prove that the eliminator satisfies the expected computation rules propositionally. These are

$$\mathsf{elim\text{-}List'\text{-}nil\text{-}id} : \mathsf{elim\text{-}List'}\ P\ b\ r\ \mathsf{zero}\ (\mathsf{nil}, \mathsf{refl}) = b$$

$$\begin{aligned} \mathsf{elim\text{-}List'\text{-}cons\text{-}id} : {} & \mathsf{elim\text{-}List'}\ P\ b\ r\ (\mathsf{succ}\ m)\ (\mathsf{cons}\ x\ xs, \mathsf{cong}\ \mathsf{succ}\ p) \\ & = r\ x\ (xs, p)\ (\lambda\_.\ \mathsf{elim\text{-}List'}\ P\ b\ r\ m\ (xs, p))\,. \end{aligned}$$

The first holds definitionally, and the second requires a small amount of equality reasoning. This completes the definition of the representation of Vec as List', which would be written as

$$\textbf{repr}\ \mathsf{Vec}\ T\ n\ \textbf{as}\ \mathsf{List'}\ T\ n \left\{ \begin{array}{r l} \mathsf{nil}\ \textbf{as} & \mathsf{nil} \\ \mathsf{cons}\ \textbf{as} & \mathsf{cons} \\ \mathsf{elim}_{\mathsf{Vec}}\ \textbf{as} & \mathsf{elim\text{-}List'} \\ \textbf{by} & \mathsf{elim\text{-}List'\text{-}nil\text{-}id}, \\ & \mathsf{elim\text{-}List'\text{-}cons\text{-}id} \end{array} \right\}$$

Now the hard work is done. Every time we are working with a v : Vec T n, its form will be (l, p) at runtime, where l is the underlying list and p is the proof that the length of l is n. Under the assumption that the Σ-type's right component is irrelevant and erased at runtime, every vector is simply a list at runtime, where the length proof has been erased. In practice, this erasure is achieved in SUPERFLUID using quantitative type theory [8]. In Sect. 3.7 we show how to formally identify computationally irrelevant conversion functions.

We can utilise this representation to convert between Vec and List at zero runtime cost. We can do this using the repr and unrepr operators of the language (defined in Sect. 3). These allow us to convert between an inductive type and its representation. Specifically, we can define the functions

$$\begin{aligned}
&\text{forget-length} : \mathsf{Vec}\ T\ n \to \mathsf{List}\ T\\
&\text{forget-length}\ v = \mathsf{let}\ (l, _) = \mathsf{repr}\ v\ \mathsf{in}\ l\\[1em]
&\text{remember-length} : (l : \mathsf{List}\ T) \to \mathsf{Vec}\ T\ (\text{length}\ l)\\
&\text{remember-length}\ l = \mathsf{unrepr}\ (l, \mathsf{refl})\,.
\end{aligned}$$

In Sect. 3.7 we will show that such functions are inverses of one another and are computationally irrelevant. These operators are typed as

$$\mathsf{repr} : A \to \mathsf{Repr}\ A \qquad \mathsf{unrepr} : \mathsf{Repr}\ A \to A$$

where Repr A computes to the defined representation of A, if A is a data type. Repr is a kind of 'intensional' modality, with the property that Repr $A \simeq A$. It allows us to transport across equivalences introduced by representations in a computationally-irrelevant manner.

2.3 General Reindexing

The idea from the previous example can be generalised to any data type. In general, suppose that we have two inductive families

$$\mathsf{F} : P \to \mathcal{U} \qquad \mathsf{G} : (p : P) \to X\ p \to \mathcal{U}$$

for some index family $X : P \to \mathcal{U}$. If we hope to represent G as some refinement of F then we must provide a way to compute G's extra indices X from F, like we computed Vec's extra Nat index from List with length in the previous example. This means that we need to provide a function comp : $\forall p.\ \mathsf{F}\ p \to X\ p$ which can then be used to form the family

$$\mathsf{F}^{\mathsf{comp}}\ p\ x := \{f : \mathsf{F}\ p \mid \mathsf{comp}\ f = x\}.$$

If G is 'equivalent' to the algebraic ornament of F by the algebra defining comp (given by an isomorphism between the underlying polynomial functors), then it is also equivalent to the Σ-type above. The 'recomputation lemma' of algebraic ornaments [15] then arises from its projections. Our system allows us to *set* the representation of G as $\mathsf{F}^{\mathsf{comp}}$, so that the forgetful map from G to F as well as the recomputation map from F to G are erased, constructed with repr and unrepr. We formulate this pattern in the general setting in Sect. 3.7.

2.4 Zero-Copy Deserialisation

The machinery of representations can be used to implement zero-copy deserialisation of data formats into inductive types. Here we sketch how this could work. Consider the following record for a player in a game:

$$\textbf{data}\ \mathsf{Player}\ \left\{\begin{array}{l}\mathsf{player} : (\mathsf{position} : \mathsf{Position}) \\ \quad\rightarrow (\mathsf{direction} : \mathsf{Direction}) \\ \quad\rightarrow (\mathsf{items} : \mathsf{Fin}\ \mathsf{MAX\_INVENTORY}) \\ \quad\rightarrow (\mathsf{inventory} : \mathsf{Inventory}\ (\mathsf{fin\text{-}to\text{-}nat}\ \mathsf{items})) \rightarrow \mathsf{Player}\end{array}\right\}$$

We can use the Fin type to maintain the invariant that the inventory has a maximum size. Additionally, we can index the Inventory type by the number of items it contains, which might be defined similarly to Vec:

$$\textbf{data}\ \mathsf{Inventory}\ (n : \mathsf{Nat})\ \left\{\begin{array}{l}\mathsf{empty} : \mathsf{Inventory}\ \mathsf{zero} \\ \quad\mathsf{add} : \mathsf{Item} \rightarrow \mathsf{Inventory}\ n \rightarrow \mathsf{Inventory}\ (\mathsf{succ}\ n)\end{array}\right\}$$

We can use the full power of inductive families to model the domain of our problem in the way that is most convenient for us. If we were writing this in a lower-level language, we might choose to use the serialised format directly when manipulating the data, relying on the appropriate pointer arithmetic to access the fields of the serialised data, to avoid copying overhead. Representations allow us to do this while still being able to work with the high-level inductive type.

We can define a representation for Player as a pair of a byte buffer and a proof that the byte buffer contents correspond to a player record. Similarly, we can define a representation for Inventory as a pair of a byte buffer and a proof that the byte buffer contents correspond to an inventory record of a certain size. By the implementation of the eliminator in the representation, the projection $\mathsf{inventory} : (p : \mathsf{Player}) \rightarrow \mathsf{Inventory}\ p.\mathsf{items}$ is compiled into some code to slice into the inventory part of the player's byte buffer. We assume that the standard library already represents Fin in the same way as Nat, so that reading the items field is a constant-time operation (we do not need to build a unary numeral). We can thus define the representation of Player as

$$\textbf{repr}\ \mathsf{Player}\ \textbf{as}\ \{\mathsf{Buf} \mid \mathsf{IsPlayer}\}\ \left\{\begin{array}{r}\mathsf{player}\ \textbf{as}\ \mathsf{buf\text{-}is\text{-}player} \\ \mathsf{elim}_{\mathsf{Player}}\ \textbf{as}\ \mathsf{elim\text{-}buf\text{-}is\text{-}player} \\ \textbf{by}\ \mathsf{elim\text{-}buf\text{-}is\text{-}player\text{-}id}\end{array}\right\}$$

with an appropriate definition of IsPlayer which refines a byte buffer. The refinement would have to match the expected structure of the byte buffer, so that all the required fields can be extracted. Allais [5] explores how data descriptions that index into a flat buffer can be defined.

2.5 Transitivity

Representations are transitive, so in the previous example, the eventual representation of Vec at runtime is determined by the representation of List. It is possible to define a custom representation for List itself, for example a heap-backed array or a finger tree, and Vec would inherit this representation. However it will still be the case that Repr (Vec T n) $\equiv$ List T, which means the Repr modality only considers the immediate defined representation of a term. Regardless, we can construct predicates that find types which satisfy a certain eventual representation. For example, given a Buf type of byte buffers, we can consider the set of all types which are eventually represented as a Buf:

$$\textbf{data}\ \mathsf{ReprBuf}\ (T : \mathcal{U}) \left\{ \begin{array}{c} \mathsf{buf} : \mathsf{ReprBuf}\ \mathsf{Buf} \\ \mathsf{from} : \mathsf{ReprBuf}\ (\mathsf{Repr}\ T) \to \mathsf{ReprBuf}\ T \\ \mathsf{refined} : \mathsf{ReprBuf}\ T \to \mathsf{ReprBuf}\ \{t : T \mid P\ t\} \end{array} \right\}$$

Every such type comes with a projection function to the Buf type

$$\begin{aligned} &\mathsf{as\text{-}buf} : \{r : \mathsf{ReprBuf}\ T\} \to T \to \mathsf{Buf} \\ &\mathsf{as\text{-}buf}\ \{r = \mathsf{buf}\}\ x = x \\ &\mathsf{as\text{-}buf}\ \{r = \mathsf{from}\ t\}\ x = \mathsf{as\text{-}buf}\{t\}(\mathsf{repr}\ x) \\ &\mathsf{as\text{-}buf}\ \{r = \mathsf{refined}\ t\}\ (x, \_) = \mathsf{as\text{-}buf}\{t\}x \end{aligned}$$

which eventually computes to the identity function after applying repr the appropriate amount of times. Upon compilation, every type is converted to its eventual representation, and all repr calls are erased, so the as-buf function becomes the identity function at runtime, given that the r argument is known at compile-time and monomorphised.

3 A Type System for Data Representations

In this section, we develop an extension of dependent type theory with inductive families and custom data representations. We start in Sect. 3.2 by exploring the semantics of data representations in terms of inductive algebras for signatures. In Sect. 3.5 we define a core language DATATT with these features. The base theory is intensional Martin-Löf type theory (MLTT) [21] with a single universe $\mathcal{U} : \mathcal{U}$. We omit considerations of consistency and universe hierarchy, though these can be added if needed. In Sect. 3.5, we define the modality Repr that allows us to convert between inductive types and their representations. Finally, in Sect. 3.6 we define a translation from DATATT to *extensional* MLTT, which 'elaborates away' all inductive families to their representations. All of the examples in the paper so far have been written in a surface language that elaborates to DATATT.

The languages we work with are defined in an intrinsically well-formed manner [7] as a setoid over definitional equality, with de-Bruijn indices for variables. Weakening of terms is generally left implicit to reduce syntactic noise, and often named notation is used when indices are implied. We use $(a : A) \to B$ for dependent functions, $(a : A) \times B$ for dependent pairs, $a \equiv_A a'$ for propositional equality, and $a = a' : A$ for definitional equality. Substitution is denoted with square brackets: if $\Gamma, A \vdash B$ and $\Gamma \vdash a : A$ then $\Gamma \vdash B[a]$. We also notationally identify elements of the universe $A : \mathcal{U}$ with types A type. Besides the usual judgement forms of MLTT, we also have telescopic judgement forms

$\Gamma \vdash \Delta \ \mathsf{tel}$ $\quad \Delta$ is a telescope in Γ

$\Gamma \vdash \delta :: \Delta$ $\quad \delta$ is a spine (list of terms) matching telescope Δ

with accompanying rules shown in Fig. 1.

$$\textsc{Tel-Empty}\ \frac{}{\Gamma \vdash \bullet \ \mathsf{tel}} \qquad \textsc{Tel-Extend}\ \frac{\Gamma \vdash A \ \mathsf{type} \qquad \Gamma, A \vdash \Delta \ \mathsf{tel}}{\Gamma \vdash (A, \Delta) \ \mathsf{tel}}$$

$$\textsc{Spine-Empty}\ \frac{}{\Gamma \vdash () :: \bullet} \qquad \textsc{Spine-Extend}\ \frac{\Gamma \vdash a : A \qquad \Gamma \vdash \delta : \Delta[a]}{\Gamma \vdash (a, \delta) :: (A, \Delta)}$$

Fig. 1. Rules for forming telescopes and spines.

Extending contexts by telescopes (such as Γ, Δ) is defined by induction on telescopes. We write $\Delta \to X$ for an iterated function type with codomain $\Gamma, \Delta \vdash X$, and $(\delta :: \Delta) \to X[\delta]$ when names are highlighted. We will often use the notation $\delta.y$ to extract a certain index y from a spine δ. This is used when we define telescopes using named notation. For example, if $\delta :: (X : A \to \mathcal{U}, y : (a : A) \to X\ a)$, then $\delta.X : A \to \mathcal{U}$ and $\delta.y : (a : A) \to \delta.X\ a$.

3.1 Algebraic Signatures

A representation of a data type must be able to emulate the behaviour of the original data type. In turn, the behaviour of the original data type is determined by its elimination, or induction principle. This means that a representation of a data type should provide an implementation of induction of the same 'shape' as the original. Induction can be characterised in terms of algebras and displayed algebras of algebraic signatures [3,20]. Algebraic signatures consist of a list of operations, each with a specified arity. There are many flavours of algebraic signatures with varying degrees of expressiveness. For this paper, we are interested in the ones which can be used as a syntax for defining inductive families in a type theory. Thus, we define two new judgement forms

$\Gamma \vdash S \ \mathsf{sig}\ \Delta$ $\quad S$ is a signature with indices Δ in context Γ

$\Gamma \vdash O \ \mathsf{op}\ \Delta$ $\quad O$ is an operation with indices Δ in context Γ

with accompanying rules shown in Fig. 2. Signatures are lists of operations, and operations build up constructor types.

$$\frac{\Gamma \vdash \Delta \ \mathsf{tel}}{\Gamma \vdash \epsilon \ \mathsf{sig} \ \Delta}\ \textsc{Sig-Empty} \qquad \frac{\Gamma \vdash \Delta \ \mathsf{tel} \qquad \Gamma \vdash O \ \mathsf{op} \ \Delta \qquad \Gamma \vdash S \ \mathsf{sig} \ \Delta}{\Gamma \vdash (O \lhd S) \ \mathsf{sig} \ \Delta}\ \textsc{Sig-Extend}$$

$$\frac{\Gamma \vdash A \ \mathsf{type} \qquad \Gamma, A \vdash O \ \mathsf{op} \ \Delta}{\Gamma \vdash (A \ \rightarrow_{\mathsf{ext}} O) \ \mathsf{op} \ \Delta}\ \textsc{Op-Ext} \qquad \frac{\Gamma \vdash \delta :: \Delta \qquad \Gamma \vdash O \ \mathsf{op} \ \Delta}{\Gamma \vdash (\iota \ \delta \rightarrow_{\mathsf{int}} O) \ \mathsf{op} \ \Delta}\ \textsc{Op-Int} \qquad \frac{\Gamma \vdash \delta :: \Delta}{\Gamma \vdash (\iota \ \delta) \ \mathsf{op} \ \Delta}\ \textsc{Op-Ret}$$

Fig. 2. Rules for forming signatures and operations.

Each signature is described by an associated telescope of indices Δ, and a *finite list* of operations:

- $(x : A) \rightarrow_{\mathsf{ext}} O[x]$, a (dependent) abstraction over some external type A, of another operation O.
- $\iota \ \delta \ \rightarrow_{\mathsf{int}} \ O$, an abstraction over a recursive occurence of the object being defined, with indices δ, of another operation O.
- $\iota \ \delta$, a constructor of the object being defined, with indices δ.

Example 1 (Natural numbers). The signature for natural numbers is indexed by the empty telescope $\bullet$. It is defined as $\Gamma \vdash (\iota \ () \lhd \iota \ () \rightarrow_{\mathsf{int}} \iota \ () \lhd \epsilon) \ \mathsf{sig} \ \bullet$. We can add labels to aid readability, omit index spines if they are empty, and omit the final ϵ from signatures:

$$\Gamma \vdash (\mathit{zero} : \iota \lhd \mathit{succ} : \iota \ \rightarrow_{\mathsf{int}} \iota) \ \mathsf{sig} \ \bullet \ .$$

Example 2 (Vectors). The signature for vectors of elements of type T and length n is indexed by the telescope $(T : \mathcal{U}, n : \mathbb{N})$, defined as

$$\begin{aligned} \Gamma \vdash (&\mathit{nil} \colon (T : \mathcal{U}) \rightarrow_{\mathsf{ext}} \iota \ T \ \mathit{zero} \lhd \\ &\quad \mathit{cons} : (T : \mathcal{U}) \rightarrow_{\mathsf{ext}} (n' : \mathbb{N}) \rightarrow_{\mathsf{ext}} (t : T) \rightarrow_{\mathsf{ext}} \iota \ T \ n' \rightarrow_{\mathsf{int}} \iota \ T \ (\mathit{succ} \ n')) \\ &\quad \mathsf{sig} \ (T : \mathcal{U}, n : \mathbb{N}) \, . \end{aligned}$$

Later (Sect. 3.4) we will see how we can use the signature in Example 1 to define the type of natural numbers $\Gamma \vdash \mathbb{N} \ \mathsf{type}$.

Notice that this syntax only allows occurrences of ι in positive positions, which is a requirement for inductive types. Different classes of algebraic signatures, theories and quantification are explored in detail by Kovács [20]. We make no distinction between parameters and indices, though it is possible to add parameters by augmenting the syntax for signatures with an extra telescope that must be uniform across operations.

3.2 Interpreting Signatures in the Type Theory

In order to make use of our definition for algebraic signatures, we would like to be able to interpret their structure as types in the type theory we are working with.

Algebras. An *algebra* for a signature $\Gamma \vdash S \ \mathsf{sig} \ \Delta$ and carrier type $\Gamma, \Delta \vdash X \ \mathsf{type}$ interprets the structure of S in terms of the type X. Concretely, this produces a telescope which matches the structure of S but replaces each occurrence of $\iota \ \delta$ with $X[\delta]$. The function arrows $\to_{\mathsf{int}}$ and $\to_{\mathsf{ext}}$ in S are interpreted as the function arrow $\to$ of the type theory.

Example 3 (Natural numbers). An algebra for the signature of natural numbers (Example 1) over a carrier $\Gamma \vdash N \ \mathsf{type}$ is a spine matching the telescope

$$\Gamma \vdash (\mathit{zero} : N, \ \ \mathit{succ} : N \to N) \ \mathsf{tel}.$$

Example 4 (Vectors). An algebra for the signature of vectors (Example 4) over a carrier $\Gamma, T : \mathcal{U}, n : \mathbb{N} \vdash V \ \mathsf{type}$ is a spine matching the telescope

$$\begin{aligned}\Gamma \vdash (&\mathit{nil} : (T : \mathcal{U}) \to V[T, \mathit{zero}], \\ &\quad \mathit{cons} : (T : \mathcal{U}) \to (n' : \mathbb{N}) \to (t : T) \to (\mathit{ts} : V[T, n']) \to V[T, \mathit{succ}\ n']) \ \mathsf{tel}.\end{aligned}$$

Induction. The actual type of natural numbers $\Gamma \vdash \mathbb{N} \ \mathsf{type}$ is the carrier of an algebra over the signature of natural numbers. In particular, the 'best' such algebra: one whose operations do not forget any information. In the language of category theory, this is the initial algebra in the category of algebras over the signature of natural numbers. An equivalent formulation of initial algebras is algebras which support *induction*, which is more suitable for our (syntactic) purposes. An algebra $\alpha :: (\mathit{zero} : X, \ \mathit{succ} : X \to X)$ for natural numbers supports induction if:

> For any type family $X \vdash Y \ \mathsf{type}$, if we can construct a $\mathit{zero}_Y : Y[\alpha.\mathit{zero}]$ and a $\mathit{succ}_Y : (x : X) \to Y[x] \to Y[\alpha.\mathit{succ}\ x]$, then we can construct a $\sigma[x] : Y[x]$ for all $x : X$.

The type family Y is commonly called the *motive*, and $(\mathit{zero}_Y, \mathit{succ}_Y)$ are the *methods*. The produced term family $x : X \vdash \sigma : Y[x]$ is a *section* of the type family Y. Induction also requires that the section acquires its values from the provided methods. This means that

$$\sigma[\alpha.\mathit{zero}] = \mathit{zero}_Y \qquad \sigma[\alpha.\mathit{succ}\ x] = \mathit{succ}_Y\ x\ \sigma[x].$$

We call these *coherence conditions*. A section that satisfies these conditions is called a *coherent section*. These equations might or might not hold definitionally. In the former case, we have the definitional equalities

$$\begin{aligned}\Gamma &\vdash \sigma[\alpha.\mathit{zero}] = \mathit{zero}_Y : Y[\alpha.\mathit{zero}] \\ \Gamma, x : X &\vdash \sigma[\alpha.\mathit{succ}\ x] = \mathit{succ}_Y\ x\ \sigma[x] : Y[\alpha.\mathit{succ}\ x].\end{aligned}$$

In the latter case, we have a spine of propositional equality witnesses

$$\begin{aligned}\Gamma \vdash \sigma_{\mathsf{coh}} :: (&\mathit{zero}_{\mathsf{coh}} : \sigma[\alpha.\mathit{zero}] \equiv \mathit{zero}_Y, \\ &\quad \mathit{succ}_{\mathsf{coh}} : (x : X) \to \sigma[\alpha.\mathit{succ}\ x] \equiv \mathit{succ}_Y\ x\ \sigma[x]).\end{aligned}$$

Displayed Algebras. Notice that the methods $(zero_Y, succ_Y)$ look like an algebra for the signature of natural numbers too, but their carrier is now a type family over another algebra carrier X, and the types of the operations mention both X and Y, using α to go from Δ to X. These are *displayed algebras.* In general, a displayed algebra for a signature $\Gamma \vdash S \text{ sig } \Delta$, algebra α for S over carrier $\Gamma, \Delta \vdash X \text{ type}$, and carrier family $\Gamma, \Delta, X \vdash Y \text{ type}$, interprets the structure of S in terms of both X and Y. This produces a telescope which matches the structure of S but replaces each recursive occurrence $\iota\ \delta$ with an argument $x : X$ as well as an argument $y : Y[x]$. Each operation returns a Y with indices computed from α. Again, the function arrows in S are interpreted as function types in the type theory.

Example 5 (Vectors). A displayed algebra for an algebra (*nil*, *cons*) for vectors (Example 4) over a carrier family $\Gamma, T : \mathcal{U}, n : \mathbb{N}, v : V[T, n] \vdash W \text{ type}$ is a spine matching the telescope

$$\begin{aligned}\Gamma \vdash (&nil_W : (T : \mathcal{U}) \to W[T, zero, nil\ T],\\ &cons_W : (T : \mathcal{U}) \to (n' : \mathbb{N}) \to (t : T) \to (ts : V[T, n'])\\ &\quad \to (ts_W : W[T, n', ts]) \to W[T, succ\ n', cons\ T\ n'\ t\ ts]) \text{ tel}.\end{aligned}$$

In practice, in a call-by-value setting, it is desirable for the inductive hypotheses of a displayed algebra (ts_W above) to be *lazy* values. This improves performance when the inductive hypotheses are not needed. We leave this as an implementation detail.

Finally, we come to the central definition that classifies the algebras which support induction:

Definition 1. *An algebra is* inductive *if every displayed algebra over it has a coherent section.*

The elimination rule for inductive data types in programming languages is exactly this: given any motive and methods (a displayed algebra), we get a dependent function from the type of the scrutinee to the type of the motive (a section). Furthermore this function satisfies some appropriate computation rules: when we plug in a constructor, we get the result of the method corresponding to it (the coherence conditions). Usually in programming languages, these conditions hold definitionally, as they are the primary means of computation with data.

3.3 Defining Algebras and Friends

In order to utilise these constructions for our type system, we now explicitly define the following objects:

$\Gamma \vdash S^{\mathsf{alg}}\ X$ tel — Algebras for a signature $\Gamma \vdash S$ sig Δ over a carrier $\Gamma, \Delta \vdash X$ type.

$\Gamma \vdash \alpha^{\mathsf{dispAlg}}\ Y$ tel — Displayed algebras for an algebra $\Gamma \vdash \alpha :: S^{\mathsf{alg}}\ X$ over a motive $\Gamma, \Delta, X \vdash Y$ type.

$\Gamma \vdash \beta^{\mathsf{coh}}\ \sigma$ tel — Propositional coherence for a section $\Gamma, \Delta, X \vdash \sigma : Y$ of a displayed algebra $\Gamma \vdash \beta :: \alpha^{\mathsf{dispAlg}}\ Y$.

All constructions labelled with superscripts are not part of the syntax of the type system, but rather functions in the metatheory which compute syntactic objects such as telescopes.

The algebras for a signature are defined by case analysis on S:

$$\boxed{\Gamma \vdash S^{\mathsf{alg}}\ X\ \mathsf{tel}}$$

$$\epsilon^{\mathsf{alg}}\ X = \bullet \qquad (O \lhd S')^{\mathsf{alg}}\ X = ((\nu :: O^{\mathsf{in}}\ X) \to X[\nu^{\mathsf{out}}],\ S'^{\mathsf{alg}}\ X)\,.$$

An empty signature ϵ produces an empty telescope, while an extended signature $O \lhd S'$ produces a telescope extended with a function corresponding to O. This function goes from the inputs of O interpreted in X, to X evaluated at the output indices. The inputs and outputs of each operation O in an algebra are defined by case analysis on O:

$$\boxed{\Gamma \vdash O^{\mathsf{in}}\ X\ \mathsf{tel}} \qquad \boxed{\Gamma \vdash \{O\}\ \nu^{\mathsf{out}} :: \Delta}$$

$$\begin{aligned}
&(A \to_{\mathsf{ext}} O')^{\mathsf{in}}\ X = (a : A,\ O'[a]^{\mathsf{in}}\ X) && \{O = A \to_{\mathsf{ext}} O'\}\ (a, \nu')^{\mathsf{out}} = \nu'^{\mathsf{out}}\\
&(\iota\ \delta \to_{\mathsf{int}} O')^{\mathsf{in}}\ X = (x : X[\delta],\ O'^{\mathsf{in}}\ X) && \{O = \iota\ \delta \to_{\mathsf{int}} O'\}\ (x,\ \nu')^{\mathsf{out}} = \nu'^{\mathsf{out}}\\
&(\iota\ \delta)^{\mathsf{in}}\ X = \bullet && \{O = \iota\ \delta\}\ ()^{\mathsf{out}} = \delta\,.
\end{aligned}$$

A similar construction can be performed for displayed algebras over algebras. Displayed algebras are defined by case analysis on S, which is an implicit parameter of $-^{\mathsf{dispAlg}}$:

$$\boxed{\Gamma \vdash \{S\}\ \alpha^{\mathsf{dispAlg}}\ Y\ \mathsf{tel}}$$

$$\begin{aligned}
&\{S = \epsilon\}\ ()^{\mathsf{dispAlg}}\ Y = \bullet\\
&\{S = O \lhd S'\}\ (\alpha_O, \alpha')^{\mathsf{dispAlg}}\ Y = ((\mu :: \alpha_O^{\mathsf{dispIn}}\ Y) \to Y[\mu^{\mathsf{dispOut}}],\ \alpha'^{\mathsf{dispAlg}}\ Y)\,.
\end{aligned}$$

We omit the definitions of $\_^{\mathsf{dispIn}}$ and $\_^{\mathsf{dispOut}}$ and refer to the Agda formalisation, but they are similar to the definitions of $-^{\mathsf{in}}$ and $-^{\mathsf{out}}$.

Next we define the coherence conditions for a displayed algebra as a telescope

$$\boxed{\Gamma \vdash \{S\}\ \{\alpha\}\ \beta^{\mathsf{coh}}\ \sigma\ \mathsf{tel}}$$

$$\begin{aligned}
&\{S = \epsilon\}\ \{\alpha = ()\}\ ()^{\mathsf{coh}}\ \sigma = \bullet\\
&\{S = O \lhd S'\}\ \{\alpha = (\alpha_O, \alpha')\}\ (\beta_O, \beta')^{\mathsf{coh}}\ \sigma\\
&\qquad = ((\nu :: O^{\mathsf{in}}\ X) \to \sigma[\alpha_O\ \nu] \equiv \beta_O\ (\sigma \mathbin{\$} \nu),\ \beta'^{\mathsf{coh}}\ \sigma)\,.
\end{aligned}$$

The notation $\sigma \mathbin{\$} \nu$ applies the section σ to the input ν, yielding a displayed input by sampling the section to get the inductive hypotheses.

Now we can define induction for an algebra α as a type

$$\boxed{\Gamma \vdash \{S\}\ \alpha^{\mathsf{ind}}\ \mathsf{type}}$$

$$\begin{aligned}\{S\}\ \alpha^{\mathsf{ind}} = (Y : (\delta :: \Delta) \to X[\delta] \to \mathcal{U}) \to (\beta :: \alpha^{\mathsf{dispAlg}}\ (\delta.\ x.\ Y\ \delta\ x)) \\ \to (\sigma : (\delta :: \Delta) \to (x : X[\delta]) \to Y\ \delta\ x)) \times (\rho :: \beta^{\mathsf{coh}}\ (\delta.\ x.\ \sigma\ \delta\ x)),\end{aligned}$$

where Y is the motive, β are the methods, and σ is the output section which must satisfy the propositional coherence conditions ρ. Finally, we can package an inductive algebra over a signature as a telescope

$$\boxed{\Gamma \vdash S^{\mathsf{indAlg}}\ \mathsf{tel}}$$

$$S^{\mathsf{indAlg}} = (X : \Delta \to \mathcal{U},\ \alpha :: S^{\mathsf{alg}}\ (\delta.\ X\ \delta),\ \kappa : \alpha^{\mathsf{ind}}),$$

by collecting the carrier X, algebra α and induction κ all together.

3.4 Constructing Inductive Families

We now extend intensional MLTT with a type for inductive families, which we denote $\mathsf{data}_\Delta\ S\ \gamma$. This type defines an inductive family matching a signature S with indices Δ, together with an inductive algebra γ which 'implements' the signature S. Notice that this is different to the usual way that inductive families are defined in type theory, for example W-types [1], where all we need to provide is a signature.[2] Here, we must also implement the signature and prove the induction principle by providing γ, rather than it being 'built-in' to the type theory. For example, if the type theory has W-types, then we can construct γ using an appropriate W-type. In effect, this will later allow us to translate away inductive definitions to their defined representations. This leads to the formal definition of a representation:

Definition 2. *A* representation *of a signature S is an inductive algebra for S.*

In Fig. 3 we define the data type, and its corresponding introduction, elimination, and computation rules. Constructors form an algebra for the signature S over $\mathsf{data}_\Delta\ S\ \gamma$, denoted by $\mathsf{ctor}_S = (\mathsf{ctor}_{S.O})_{O \in S}$. Similarly, the eliminator forms a coherent section over the constructor algebra, which holds definitionally.

One might think, what do we gain by adding data to the theory? If we can provide an inductive algebra γ for a signature S ourselves, then why not use γ directly? The reason is that by having a primitive for inductive types, we can take advantage of their properties in an extensional way. For example, an induction principle suggests that the constructors corresponding to each method are

[2] Notice that the data defining a W-type $(A : \mathcal{U}, B : A \to \mathcal{U})$ can be viewed as a kind of signature, where A describes the operations and their non-recursive parameters, while B describes the arities of the recursive parameters.

$$\frac{\textsc{Data-Form}\quad \Gamma \vdash S\ \mathsf{sig}\ \Delta \qquad \Gamma \vdash \gamma :: S^{\mathsf{indAlg}} \qquad \Gamma \vdash \delta :: \Delta}{\Gamma \vdash \mathsf{data}_\Delta\ S\ \gamma\ \delta\ \mathsf{type}}$$

$$\frac{\textsc{Data-Intro}\quad O \in S \qquad \Gamma \vdash \nu :: O^{\mathsf{in}}\ (\mathsf{data}_\Delta\ S\ \gamma)}{\Gamma \vdash \mathsf{ctor}_{S.O}\ \nu : \mathsf{data}_\Delta\ S\ \gamma\ \nu^{\mathsf{out}}}$$

$$\frac{\textsc{Data-Elim}\quad \begin{array}{c}\Gamma,\ \delta :: \Delta,\ \mathsf{data}_\Delta\ S\ \gamma\ \delta \vdash M\ \mathsf{type}\\ \Gamma \vdash \beta :: \mathsf{ctor}_S^{\mathsf{dispAlg}}\ M \qquad \Gamma \vdash \delta :: \Delta \qquad \Gamma \vdash x : \mathsf{data}_\Delta\ S\ \gamma\ \delta\end{array}}{\Gamma \vdash \mathsf{elim}_S\ M\ \beta\ \delta\ x : M[\delta, x]}$$

$$\frac{\textsc{Data-Comp}\quad \begin{array}{c}O \in S \qquad \Gamma \vdash \nu :: O^{\mathsf{in}}\ (\mathsf{data}_\Delta\ S\ \gamma)\\ \Gamma,\ \delta :: \Delta,\ \mathsf{data}_\Delta\ S\ \gamma\ \delta \vdash M\ \mathsf{type} \qquad \Gamma \vdash \beta :: \mathsf{ctor}_S^{\mathsf{dispAlg}}\ M\end{array}}{\Gamma \vdash \mathsf{elim}_S\ M\ \beta\ \nu^{\mathsf{out}}\ (\mathsf{ctor}_{S.O}\ \nu) = \beta_O\ (\mathsf{elim}_S\ M\ \beta\ \$\ \nu) : M[\nu^{\mathsf{out}}, \mathsf{ctor}_{S.O}\ \nu]}$$

Fig. 3. Rules for data types, constructors and eliminators. We write $O \in S$ to indicate that O is an operation in the signature S. We write α_O to extract the telescope element corresponding to operation O from the algebra α for S.

disjoint. Since constructors ctor are primitive terms in the theory, we can make use of this when formulating a unification algorithm. Aside from disjointness, we can also rely on other properties such as injectivity, acyclicity, and 'no-confusion'. McBride [22] originally explored the properties which arise from the existence of induction principles, or equivalently, initiality.

For example, if we have an inductive algebra $(N, zero_N, succ_N, elim_N)$ for the natural numbers signature *NatSig* (Example 1), we can prove propositionally that for all $x : N$, $zero_N \neq succ_N\ x$, by invoking $elim_N$. However, the typechecker does not know this fact; it is not derivable as a definitional equality contradiction. However, it *is* derivable definitionally that for all $x : \mathbb{N}$, $\mathsf{ctor}_{zero} \neq \mathsf{ctor}_{succ}\ x$, where $\mathbb{N} = \mathsf{data}\ NatSig\ (N, zero_N, succ_N, elim_N)$ because the syntax does not equate ctor_i and ctor_j unless $i = j$.

Importantly, the existence of data enables the use of *dependent pattern matching* on its inhabitants. Nested pattern matching on $\mathbb{N}$, for example, can be elaborated to invocations of $\mathsf{elim}_{\mathbb{N}}$, which has the expected computation rules as shown in Fig. 3. Converting dependent pattern matching to eliminators has been explored in depth by Goguen, McBride and McKinna [17], as well as by Cockx and Devriese [14] in absence of Axiom K.

3.5 Reasoning About Representations

So far we are able to construct data types using the $\mathsf{data}_\Delta\ S\ \gamma$ type constructor. These data types are themselves implemented in terms of inductive algebras. However, the rules for data types do not utilise them. We would like to be able to relate data types to their underlying inductive algebras. One reason is to avoid unnecessary computation. If we have a type X that is the carrier of two inductive algebras (X, α, κ) and (X, α', κ') for signatures S and S' respectively, then we can form the data types $D = \mathsf{data}_\Delta\ S\ (X, \alpha, \kappa)$ and $D' = \mathsf{data}_\Delta\ S'\ (X, \alpha', \kappa')$ and make use of the structural properties of initiality. However, we would also like to be able to freely convert between X, D and D' without incurring any runtime cost. After all, D and D' are meant to be translated away to their underlying representation, X. This argument can also be made in the context of theorem proving: sometimes it is easier to prove a property about D or D', due to their structure, but we should be able to 'transport' the property to X.

To make use of these conversions in a computationally-irrelevant manner, while still retaining the fact that D, D' and X are distinct types, we introduce a modality

$$\mathsf{Repr} : \mathcal{U} \to \mathcal{U},$$

which takes types to their representations. It comes with two term formers repr and unrepr, which are definitional inverses of each other. We highlight the main rules of Repr in Fig. 4.

$$\textsc{Repr-Form}\ \frac{\Gamma \vdash A\ \mathsf{type}}{\Gamma \vdash \mathsf{Repr}\ A\ \mathsf{type}} \qquad \textsc{Repr-Intro}\ \frac{\Gamma \vdash a : A}{\Gamma \vdash \mathsf{repr}\ a : \mathsf{Repr}\ A} \qquad \textsc{Repr-Elim}\ \frac{\Gamma \vdash a : \mathsf{Repr}\ A}{\Gamma \vdash \mathsf{unrepr}\ a : A}$$

$$\textsc{Repr-Id}_1\ \frac{\Gamma \vdash a : \mathsf{Repr}\ A}{\Gamma \vdash \mathsf{repr}\ (\mathsf{unrepr}\ a) = a : \mathsf{Repr}\ A} \qquad \textsc{Repr-Id}_2\ \frac{\Gamma \vdash a : A}{\Gamma \vdash \mathsf{unrepr}\ (\mathsf{repr}\ a) = a : A}$$

$$\textsc{Repr-Data}\ \frac{\Gamma \vdash S\ \mathsf{sig}\ \Delta \qquad \Gamma \vdash \gamma :: S^{\mathsf{indAlg}} \qquad \Gamma \vdash \delta :: \Delta}{\Gamma \vdash \mathsf{Repr}\ (\mathsf{data}_\Delta\ S\ \gamma\ \delta) = \gamma.X\ \delta}$$

Fig. 4. Introduction and elimination forms, as well as computation rules for the Repr modality.

These rules allow us to go between a data type $D = \mathsf{data}_\Delta\ S\ \gamma\ \delta$ and its representation $\gamma.X\ \delta$. In the translation to extensional MLTT that we are yet to define, this modality is also translated away. Indeed, its purpose is purely intensional: we do not want to equate $\mathsf{data}_\Delta\ S\ \gamma$ with $\gamma.X$ because that would render conversion checking undecidable, but we still want to make use of the fact that these types are 'the same'. In other words, $\mathsf{Repr}\ A \simeq A$ but not $\mathsf{Repr}\ A = A$. All the contextual machinery of general modal type systems [18] is not necessary here because this modality is fibred over contexts so it presents as a type former.

One might hope for additional computation rules. For example, the representation of a constructor should be equal to the underlying algebra element of the constructor type's representation:[3]

$$\mathsf{repr}\ (\mathsf{ctor}_{S.O}\ \nu) = \gamma.\alpha_O\ (\mathsf{repr}\ \nu)\,.$$

Unfortunately, having this as a computation rule would render conversion checking undecidable, because if one applies unrepr to a term repr $(\mathsf{ctor}_{S.O}\ \nu)$ which has already been reduced to its representation, unrepr $(\gamma.\alpha_O\ (\mathsf{repr}\ \nu))$, there is no clear way to decide that this is convertible to $\mathsf{ctor}_{S.O}\ \nu$ even though the definitional equality rules would imply that it is (due to Repr-Id$_2$). Nevertheless, we can still postulate this equality propositionally, and it is justified by the translation step.

We can also ask for compatibility equations between Repr and the rest of the type formers of MLTT; for example $\mathsf{Repr}\ ((a : A) \times B[a]) = (\mathrm{a} : \mathsf{Repr}\ A) \times \mathsf{Repr}\ B[\mathsf{unrepr}\ a]$, which can hold definitionally without breaking conversion. These are given for $\mathcal{U}$, Π, Σ, unit and identity types in the Agda formalisation.

Subuniverse of Concrete Types. As described, the modality Repr is not idempotent: $\mathsf{Repr}\ (\mathsf{Repr}\ A) = \mathsf{Repr}\ A$ does not always hold. An inductive algebra used as a representation of a data type might itself be implemented in terms of another data type, which again reduces under the action of Repr. A more principled approach might be to view the image of Repr as a subuniverse of $\mathcal{U}$. The restriction

$$\mathsf{Repr} : \mathcal{U} \to \mathcal{U}_C$$

targets a universe of 'concrete' types $\mathcal{U}_C < \mathcal{U}$ closed under all standard type formers, but without any data types. We can then require that all inductive algebras γ used in the rule Data-Form must have a concrete carrier $X : \Delta \to \mathcal{U}_C$. This does not limit expressivity because we can always wrap any inductive algebra carrier with Repr to bring it down to $\mathcal{U}_C$. We do not assume this additional structure for simplicity, but it might be a useful feature in practice. For example, it would simplify the transitivity example in Sect. 2.5.

3.6 Translating to Extensional MLTT

We now define a type- and equality-preserving translation step $\mathcal{R}$ shown in Fig. 5 from DATATT to extensional MLTT, to be applied during the compilation process. The extensional flavour of MLTT involves adding the equality reflection rule

$$\frac{\textsc{Reflect}\ p \quad \Gamma \vdash p : a =_A a'}{\Gamma \vdash a \equiv a' : A}\,.$$

General undecidability of conversion is not a problem because type checking is decidable for DATATT[4] and we apply this transformation after type checking, on

[3] When we write repr ν we mean to apply repr to all recursive occurences (all places that ι appears in the domain of O).

[4] Not formalised in this paper.

fully-typed terms. The translation is defined over the syntax of DATATT [11] such that definitional equality is preserved, shown in Fig. 5. $\mathcal{R}$ replaces data types with their underlying inductive algebras. We use the notation Ty and Tm for types and terms respectively, with a subscript indicating the language.

$$\boxed{\mathcal{R} : \mathsf{Ty}_{\text{DATATT}}\ \Gamma \to \mathsf{Ty}_{\text{MLTT}}\ \mathcal{R}\Gamma}$$

$$\mathcal{R}(\mathsf{Repr}\ A) = \mathcal{R}A$$
$$\mathcal{R}(\mathsf{data}_\Delta\ S\ \gamma\ \delta) = \mathcal{R}(\gamma.X)\ \mathcal{R}\delta$$
(otherwise recurse with $\mathcal{R}$)

$$\boxed{\mathcal{R} : \mathsf{Tm}_{\text{DATATT}}\ \Gamma\ A \to \mathsf{Tm}_{\text{MLTT}}\ \mathcal{R}\Gamma\ \mathcal{R}A}$$

$$\mathcal{R}(\mathsf{repr}\ t) = \mathcal{R}t$$
$$\mathcal{R}(\mathsf{unrepr}\ t) = \mathcal{R}t$$
$$\mathcal{R}(\mathsf{ctor}_{S.O}\ \{\gamma\}\ \nu) = \mathcal{R}(\gamma.\alpha_O)\ \mathcal{R}\nu$$
$$\mathcal{R}(\mathsf{elim}_S\ \{\gamma\}\ M\ \beta\ \delta\ x) = (\mathcal{R}(\gamma.\kappa)\ \mathcal{R}M\ \mathcal{R}\beta).\sigma\ \mathcal{R}\delta\ \mathcal{R}x$$
(otherwise recurse with $\mathcal{R}$)

Fig. 5. Translation of DATATT to MLTT, replaces data types with their underlying inductive algebras, and eliminators by the induction principle provided by representations.

All the mappings above are structurally recursive, demonstrated by the construction of a *model* of DATATT in the Agda formalisation. The translation is extended to contexts, substitutions, telescopes and spines pointwise, and the rest of the syntax is preserved: $\mathcal{R}((a : A) \to B[a]) = (a : \mathcal{R}A) \to (\mathcal{R}B)[a]$ etc. All data types are translated to the carriers of their inductive algebras. Invocations of Repr are removed. One can view Repr as locally applying $\mathcal{R}$ to a part of the program. The definitional equality preservation by $\mathcal{R}$ is shown in Fig. 6. The isomorphism of repr/unrepr, as well as the rule REPR-DATA are preserved by metatheoretic reflexivity on the other side, since all representation operators are erased. Coherence rules for eliminators are preserved by reflecting the propositional coherence rules provided by their defined representations.

$$\boxed{\mathcal{R}_{\approx}^{\mathsf{Ty}\ \Gamma} : A \approx_{\text{DATATT}} A' \to \mathcal{R}A \approx_{\text{MLTT}} \mathcal{R}A'}$$

$$\mathcal{R}(\text{REPR-DATA}\ \{S, \gamma, \Delta\}) = \text{REFL}\ (\mathcal{R}(\gamma.X)\ \mathcal{R}\delta)$$
(otherwise recurse with $\mathcal{R}_{\approx}$)

$$\boxed{\mathcal{R}_{\approx}^{\mathsf{Tm}\ \Gamma\ A} : a \approx_{\text{DATATT}} a' \to \mathcal{R}a \approx_{\text{MLTT}} \mathcal{R}a'}$$

$$\mathcal{R}(\text{REPR-ID}_1\ \{a\}) = \text{REFL}\ \mathcal{R}a$$
$$\mathcal{R}(\text{REPR-ID}_2\ \{a\}) = \text{REFL}\ \mathcal{R}a$$
$$\mathcal{R}(\text{DATA-COMP}\ \{S, O, \gamma, M, \beta, \nu\}) = \text{REFLECT}\ (\mathcal{R}(\gamma.\kappa)\ \mathcal{R}M\ \mathcal{R}\beta).\rho_O\ \mathcal{R}\nu$$
(otherwise recurse with $\mathcal{R}_{\approx}$)

Fig. 6. Equality translation of DATATT to extensional MLTT. This amounts to an inductive proof that $\mathcal{R}$ preserves equality.

Theorem 1 (AGDA). *$\mathcal{R}$ preserves typing and definitional equality.*

Theorem 2 (AGDA). *$\mathcal{R}$ is a left-inverse of the inclusion i :* MLTT $\hookrightarrow$ DATATT*:*

$$\frac{\Gamma \vdash a : A}{\Gamma \vdash \mathcal{R}(i(a)) = a : A} \quad \textit{(in extensional MLTT).}$$

Inductive Types in an Empty Context. Basic MLTT with dependent functions, pairs and propositional equality as we have presented here is not sufficient to construct most inductive algebras in an empty context. Without W-types or fixpoints, we must postulate the induction principles we have access to, like the example with GMP integers in Sect. 2. In practice, we often want to be able to construct inductive types 'from scratch'. For this, we can extend the base theory with W-types or something similar. One convenient choice is to extend the syntax of both the source and target languages of $\mathcal{R}$ with a class of data types like in Fig. 3, but without requiring them to be implemented by inductive algebras. The advantage is that now we can opt-in when we want to represent inductive types specially, but otherwise fall back to some kind of default implementation. The downside is that now the target still contains inductive types, though this is okay for compilation purposes if we choose a 'sane default', usually tagged unions containing indirections. This is the approach we take in SUPERFLUID.

3.7 Computational Irrelevance

In a compiler, there will be an additional program extraction step from the target of $\mathcal{R}$ into some simply-typed or untyped language, to be handled by the code-generation backend. We call this language PROG, and the transformation by vertical bars $|x|$. As opposed to $\mathcal{R}$, it might not preserve the definitional equality of the syntax—we might want to compile two definitionally equal terms differently. For example, we might not always want to reduce function application redexes. We will use the `monospace` font for terms in PROG.

Definition 3. *A function $\Gamma \vdash f : (a : A) \to B$, is* computationally irrelevant *if $|\mathcal{R}A| = |\mathcal{R}B|$ and $|\mathcal{R}f| =$* `\x => x`*.*

Theorem 3 (AGDA). *The type former Repr is injective up to equivalence, i.e.*

$$\frac{\Gamma \vdash p : \mathsf{Repr}\ T =_{\mathcal{U}} \mathsf{Repr}\ T'}{\Gamma \vdash \mathit{conv}_p : T \simeq T'}, \tag{2}$$

and if $|-|$ erases internal equality reasoning, conv_p is computationally irrelevant.

Proof For the input proof p, for conv_p we have $\lambda x.\ \mathsf{unrepr}_{T'}\ (\mathsf{coe}\ (\mathsf{repr}\ x)\ p)$ and for conv_p^{-1} we have $\lambda x.\ \mathsf{unrepr}_T\ (\mathsf{coe}\ (\mathsf{repr}\ x)\ (\mathsf{sym}\ p))$. Both directions map to $\lambda x.\ \mathsf{coe}\ \_\ x$ by $\mathcal{R}$ which becomes `\x => x` by $|-|$.

In addition, we can reason about the computational irrelevance of refinements. Consider extending both source and target languages of $\mathcal{R}$ with usage-aware 'subset' dependent pairs

$$\frac{\Gamma \vdash A\ \mathsf{type} \qquad \Gamma, A \vdash B\ \mathsf{type}}{\Gamma \vdash \{A \mid B\}\ \mathsf{type}}$$

in such a way that Repr and $\mathcal{R}$ preserve them, but the extraction step erases the right component, i.e. $|\{A \mid B\}| = |A|$, $|(x, y)| = |x|$ and $|\pi_1 x| = |x|$. This can be implemented using quantitative type theory for example. Suppose we have an inductive family $G = \mathsf{data}_I\ S_G\ \gamma_G$ over some index type I, and an inductive type $F = \mathsf{data}\ S_F\ \gamma_F$ such that G is represented by a refinement $r : F \to I$, meaning

$$\gamma_G = (\lambda i.\ \{f : F \mid r\ f \equiv_I i\}, \alpha, \kappa)\,.$$

Then, we can construct computationally irrelevant functions

$$\begin{aligned} &\mathsf{forget}_i : G\ i \to F && \mathsf{remember} : (f : F) \to G\ (r\ f) \\ &\mathsf{forget}_i = \lambda g.\ \pi_1\ (\mathsf{repr}\ g) && \mathsf{remember} = \lambda x.\ \mathsf{unrepr}\ (x, \mathsf{refl})\,. \end{aligned}$$

By reasoning similar to Theorem 3, $|\mathcal{R}\ \mathsf{forget}_i| = |\mathcal{R}\ \mathsf{remember}| =$ `\x => x`.

4 Implementation

SUPERFLUID is a programming language with dependent types with quantities, inductive families and data representations. Its compiler is written in Haskell and the compilation target is JavaScript. After prior to code generation, the $\mathcal{R}$ transformation is applied to the elaborated core program, which erases all inductive constructs with defined representations. Then, a JavaScript program is extracted, erasing all irrelevant data by usage analysis similarly to Idris 2. As a result, with appropriate postulates in the prelude, we are able to represent Nat as JavaScript's `BigInt`, and List T/SnocList T/Vec T n as JavaScript's arrays with the appropriate index refinement, such that we can convert between them without any runtime overhead. The syntax of SUPERFLUID very closely mirrors the syntax given in the first half of this paper. It supports global definitions, inductive families, as well as postulates. Users are able to define custom representations for data types using **repr** – **as** – blocks.

Currently we do not require proofs of eliminator coherence, but they are straightforward to add. We also treat the rule for representing constructors ($\mathsf{repr}\ (\mathsf{ctor}_{S.O}\ \nu) = \gamma.\alpha_O\ (\mathsf{repr}\ \nu)$) as definitional in the implementation, at the cost of breaking decidability of equality, but with the benefit of fewer manual transports. SUPERFLUID also supports the definition of representations for global functions in addition to inductive families. This is a simple symbol-replacement mechanism (like Idris's `%transform` pragma) so that we can still take advantage of inductively defined functions—such as addition on natural numbers—for theorem proving, but use the optimised primitive addition when generating code.

We are currently working on adding dependent pattern matching that is elaborated to internal eliminators, so that we can take advantage of the structural unification rules for data types [22]. We have written some of the examples in this paper in SUPERFLUID, which can be found in the `examples` directory. Overall the implementation is a proof of concept, but we expect that our framework can be implemented in an existing language.

5 Related Work

Using inductive types as a form of abstraction was first explored by Wadler [25] through *views*. The extension to dependent types was developed by McBride and McKinna [23], as part of the Epigram project. Our system differs from views in the computational content of the abstraction; even with deforestation [26] views are not always zero-cost, but representations are. Atkey [9] shows how to generically derive inductive types which are refinements of other inductive types. This work could be integrated in our system to automatically generate representations for refined data types. Zero-cost data reuse when it comes to refinements of inductive types has been explored in the context of Church encoding in Cedille [16], but does not extend to custom representations.

Work by Allais [4,5] uses a combination of views, erasure by quantitative type theory, and universes of flattened data types to achieve performance improvements when working with serialised data in Idris 2. Our approach differs because we have access to 'native' data representations, so we do not need to rely on encodings. Additionally, they rely on partial evaluation to erase their views, which does not always fire. On the topic of memory layout optimisation, Baudon [10] develops Ribbit, a DSL for the specification of the memory representation of algebraic data types, which can specify techniques like struct packing and bit-stealing. To our knowledge however, this does not provide control over the indirection introduced by *inductive* types.

Dependently typed languages with extraction features, including Idris 2 [35], Rocq [34] and Agda [32], have some overlapping capabilities with our approach, but they do not provide any of the correctness guarantees. Optimisation tricks such as the Nat-hack, and its generalisation to other types, can emulate a part of our system but are unverified and special casing in the compiler. Since the extended abstract version of this paper, an optimisation was merged into Idris 2 [36] to erase the forgetful and recomputation functions for reindexing list/maybe/number-like types. There is also demand for this kind of optimisation in Agda [33].

6 Future Work

There are elements of our formalisation which should be developed further. We did not formulate normalisation and decidability of equality for DATATT, which is needed for typechecking. We have implemented a normalisation-by-evaluation [2] algorithm used in SUPERFLUID, but have only sketched that it has the desired properties. On the practical side, we have not explored examples of representations in great detail. Once the implementation of SUPERFLUID is more complete, we would like to explore more sophisticated and complete examples, along with compelling benchmarks. We would also like to describe SUPERFLUID's feature of representing global function definitions more formally in the future.

As a next step we aim to expand the class of theories we consider, in particular to include quotient-induction. Representations for quotient-inductive types in could give rise to ergonomic ways of computing with more 'traditional' data structures such as hash maps or binary search trees. We could program inductively over these structures but extract programs without redundancy in data representation. Additionally, quotient-inductive types could be a good candidate for improving typechecking ergonomics by deciding their equational theories, similar to Frex [6]. Such a system could apply certain representations during typechecking rather than code generation, to solve equations involving free variables through a normalisation-by-evaluation procedure.

We would like to further explore the relationship of the Repr modality with general systems for defining modalities, such as *multi-modal type theory* by Gratzer [18]. Additionally, we expect that metaprogramming with representations is most naturally done in the context of *two-level type theory* (2LTT) [19]. We would like to explore the embedding of DATATT in a two-level type theory, where signatures become types in the meta-fragment. Then we could develop various methods of generating representations internally, for example through algebraic ornaments, without needing to laboriously prove induction principles by hand. The translation step in Sect. 3.6 can already be viewed as a kind of staging procedure, and could be integrated with the one of 2LTT.

7 Conclusion

This paper addresses some of the inefficiencies of inductive families in dependently typed languages by introducing custom runtime representations that preserve logical guarantees and simplicity of the surface language while optimising performance and usability. These representations are formalised as inductive algebras, and come with a framework for reasoning about them: provably zero-cost conversions between original and represented data. The compilation process guarantees erasure of abstraction layers, translating high-level constructs to their defined implementations. Our hope is that by decoupling logical structure from runtime representation, type-driven correctness can be leveraged further without great sacrifices in performance.

Acknowledgements. We thank the anonymous reviewers for their feedback that improved the quality of this paper, Guillaume Allais for helpful comments on the extended abstract, as well as Nathan Corbyn, Ellis Kesterton, and Matthew Pickering for interesting discussions surrounding it.

A Appendix

Implementation. The implementation of SUPERFLUID can be found at https://github.com/kontheocharis/superfluid.

Formalisation. The Agda formalisation of the developments of this paper can be found at https://github.com/kontheocharis/rep-agda.

A.1 Definition of MLTT

For reference, we define Martin-Löf type theory with $\mathcal{U} : \mathcal{U}$, Π, Σ, propositional equality and unit. We omit the definition of the substitution calculus and equality coercions (see [13, 5.1.2]). We use de-Brujin indices, keeping weakening implicit, and abuse notation for substitutions of terms: $A[t]$ for $A[\mathsf{id}, t]$ (Figs. 7 and 8).

$$\textsc{Univ-Form}\ \frac{}{\Gamma \vdash \mathcal{U}\ \mathsf{type}} \qquad \textsc{El-Form}\ \frac{\Gamma \vdash a : \mathcal{U}}{\Gamma \vdash \mathsf{El}\ a\ \mathsf{type}} \qquad \textsc{Univ-Intro}\ \frac{\Gamma \vdash A\ \mathsf{type}}{\Gamma \vdash \mathsf{code}\ A : \mathcal{U}} \qquad \textsc{Pi-Form}\ \frac{\Gamma \vdash A\ \mathsf{type} \qquad \Gamma, x : A \vdash B\ \mathsf{type}}{\Gamma \vdash (x : A) \to B\ \mathsf{type}}$$

$$\textsc{Pi-Intro}\ \frac{\Gamma, x : A \vdash b : B}{\Gamma \vdash \lambda\ x.\ b : (x : A) \to B} \qquad \textsc{Pi-Elim}\ \frac{\Gamma \vdash f : (x : A) \to B \qquad \Gamma \vdash a : A}{\Gamma \vdash f\ a : B[a]}$$

$$\textsc{Eq-Form}\ \frac{\Gamma \vdash A\ \mathsf{type} \qquad \Gamma \vdash a : A \qquad \Gamma \vdash b : A}{\Gamma \vdash a \equiv_A b\ \mathsf{type}} \qquad \textsc{Eq-Intro}\ \frac{\Gamma \vdash a : A}{\Gamma \vdash \mathsf{refl}\ a : a \equiv_A a}$$

$$\textsc{Eq-Elim}\ \frac{\begin{array}{c}\Gamma \vdash A\ \mathsf{type} \qquad \Gamma, a : A, b : A, a \equiv_A b \vdash P\ \mathsf{type} \\ \Gamma, a : A \vdash r : P[a, a, \mathsf{refl}\ a] \qquad \Gamma \vdash a : A \qquad \Gamma \vdash b : A \qquad \Gamma \vdash p : a \equiv_A b\end{array}}{\Gamma \vdash \mathsf{J}\ P\ d\ p : P[a, b, p]}$$

$$\textsc{Unit-Form}\ \frac{}{\Gamma \vdash \top\ \mathsf{type}} \qquad \textsc{Unit-Intro}\ \frac{}{\Gamma \vdash \mathsf{tt} : \top} \qquad \textsc{Sigma-Form}\ \frac{\Gamma \vdash A\ \mathsf{type} \qquad \Gamma, x : A \vdash B\ \mathsf{type}}{\Gamma \vdash (x : A) \times B\ \mathsf{type}}$$

$$\textsc{Sigma-Intro}\ \frac{\Gamma \vdash a : A \qquad \Gamma \vdash b : B[a]}{\Gamma \vdash (a, b) : (x : A) \times B} \qquad \textsc{Sigma-Elim-Fst}\ \frac{\Gamma \vdash p : (x : A) \times B}{\Gamma \vdash \mathsf{fst}\ p : A} \qquad \textsc{Sigma-Elim-Snd}\ \frac{\Gamma \vdash p : (x : A) \times B}{\Gamma \vdash \mathsf{snd}\ p : B[\mathsf{fst}\ p]}$$

Fig. 7. Typing rules for MLTT.

A.2 Definition of DATATT

The language DATATT is the extension of MLTT. by the rules in Figs. 3 and 4. Below we present some additional definitional equality rules of Repr that make it commute with most of the syntax, as well as some propositional equalities that are justified by the translation $\mathcal{R}$ (Figs. 9 and 10).

Universes

$\mathsf{El}\ (\mathsf{code}\ A) = A$

$\mathsf{code}\ (\mathsf{El}\ t) = t$

Equality and unit

$\mathsf{J}\ P\ r\ (\mathsf{refl}\ a) = r\ a$

$x = \mathsf{tt}$

Π types

$(\lambda\ x.\ b)\ a = b[a]$

$\lambda\ x.\ (f\ x) = f$

Σ types

$\mathsf{fst}\ (a, b) = a$

$\mathsf{snd}\ (a, b) = b$

$(\mathsf{fst}\ p, \mathsf{snd}\ p) = p$

Fig. 8. Definitional equality rules for MLTT, omitting substitution rules such as $(\mathsf{El}\ a)[\sigma] = \mathsf{El}\ (a[\sigma])$.

η rules

$\mathsf{unrepr}\ (\mathsf{repr}\ t) = t$

$\mathsf{repr}\ (\mathsf{unrepr}\ t) = t$

Stability under substitution

$\mathsf{repr}\ (t[\sigma]) = (\mathsf{repr}\ t)[\sigma]$

$\mathsf{unrepr}\ (t[\sigma]) = (\mathsf{unrepr}\ t)[\sigma]$

$\mathsf{Repr}\ (T[\sigma]) = (\mathsf{Repr}\ T)[\sigma]$

Compatibility with Π types

$\mathsf{Repr}\ ((x : A) \to B) = (x : A) \to \mathsf{Repr}\ B$

$\mathsf{repr}\ (\lambda\ x.\ b) = \lambda\ x.\ (\mathsf{repr}\ b)$

$\mathsf{unrepr}\ (\lambda\ x.\ b) = \lambda\ x.\ (\mathsf{unrepr}\ b)$

$\mathsf{repr}\ (f\ a) = (\mathsf{repr}\ f)\ a$

$\mathsf{unrepr}\ (f\ a) = (\mathsf{unrepr}\ f)\ a$

Compatibility with universes

$\mathsf{Repr}\ \mathcal{U} = \mathcal{U}$

$\mathsf{repr}\ (\mathsf{code}\ A) = \mathsf{code}\ A$

$\mathsf{unrepr}\ (\mathsf{code}\ A) = \mathsf{code}\ A$

Compatibility with equality

$\mathsf{Repr}\ (a \equiv_A b) = \mathsf{repr}\ a \equiv_{\mathsf{Repr} A} \mathsf{repr}\ b$

$\mathsf{repr}\ (\mathsf{refl}\ a) = \mathsf{refl}\ (\mathsf{repr}\ a)$

$\mathsf{unrepr}\ (\mathsf{refl}\ a) = \mathsf{refl}\ (\mathsf{unrepr}\ a)$

$\mathsf{repr}\ (\mathsf{J}\ P\ d\ p) = \mathsf{J}\ (\mathsf{Repr}\ P)\ (\mathsf{repr}\ d)\ p$

$\mathsf{unrepr}\ (\mathsf{J}\ (\mathsf{Repr}\ P)\ d\ p) = \mathsf{J}\ P\ (\mathsf{unrepr}\ d)\ p$

Compatibility with eliminators

$\mathsf{repr}\ (\mathsf{elim}_S\ M\ \beta\ \delta\ x)$
$\quad = \mathsf{elim}_S\ (\mathsf{Repr}\ M)\ (\mathsf{repr}\ \beta)\ \delta\ x$

$\mathsf{unrepr}\ (\mathsf{elim}_S\ (\mathsf{Repr}\ M)\ \beta\ \delta\ x)$
$\quad = \mathsf{elim}_S\ M\ (\mathsf{unrepr}\ \beta)\ \delta\ x$

Fig. 9. (AGDA) Definitional compatibility rules for Repr. Similar rules are given for Σ and ⊤ in the formalisation. In this version, Repr only applies to codomains of functions which aligns with the substitution rule. However, it is also possible to formulate it as $\mathsf{Repr}\ ((x : A) \to B) = (x : \mathsf{Repr}\ A) \to \mathsf{Repr}\ B[\mathsf{unrepr}\ x]$.

$$\mathsf{repr\text{-}ctor}_{S.O}\ \{\gamma\}\ \nu :$$
$$\qquad \mathsf{repr}\ (\mathsf{ctor}_{S.O}\ \{\gamma\}\nu) \equiv \gamma.\alpha_O\ (\mathsf{repr}\ \nu)$$

$$\mathsf{elim\text{-}equiv}_S\ \{\gamma\}\ M\ \beta\ \delta\ x :$$
$$\qquad \mathsf{elim}_S\ \{\gamma\}\ M\ \beta\ \delta\ x \equiv \gamma.\kappa\ (\delta.\ x.\ M[\delta, \mathsf{unrepr}\ x])\ (\mathsf{repr}^*\ \beta)\ \delta\ (\mathsf{repr}\ x)$$

Fig. 10. Additional propositional equalities for Repr on constructors and eliminators. Here, repr^* applies Repr on all the recursive arguments of a displayed algebra. The rule $\mathsf{elim\text{-}equiv}_S\ \{\gamma\}\ M\ \beta\ \delta\ x$ is also derivable internally by case analysis on x.

References

1. Abbott, M., Altenkirch, T., Ghani, N.: Representing nested inductive types using W-types. In: Díaz, J., Karhumäki, J., Lepistö, A., Sannella, D. (eds.) ICALP 2004. LNCS, vol. 3142, pp. 59–71. Springer, Heidelberg (2004). https://doi.org/10.1007/978-3-540-27836-8_8
2. Abel, A.: Normalization by evaluation: Dependent types and impredicativity. Habilitation thesis, Ludwig-Maximilians-Universität München. https://www2.tcs.ifi.lmu.de/~abel/talkHabil2013.pdf
3. Adamek, J., Rosicky, J., Vitale, E.M.: Cambridge tracts in mathematics: algebraic theories: a categorical introduction to general algebra series number 184. Cambridge University Press, Cambridge, England (2010). https://www.cambridge.org/academic/subjects/mathematics/logic-categories-and-sets/algebraic-theories-categorical-introduction-general-algebra?format=HB&isbn=9780521119221
4. Allais, G.: Builtin types viewed as inductive families. In: Programming Languages and Systems, pp. 113–139. Springer (2023). https://doi.org/10.1007/978-3-031-30044-8_5
5. Allais, G.: Seamless, correct, and generic programming over serialised data. arXiv (2023). http://arxiv.org/abs/2310.13441
6. Allais, G., Brady, E., Corbyn, N., Kammar, O., Yallop, J.: Frex: dependently-typed algebraic simplification. arXiv (2023). https://doi.org/10.48550/ARXIV.2306.15375
7. Altenkirch, T., Kaposi, A.: Type theory in type theory using quotient inductive types. In: Proceedings of the 43rd Annual ACM SIGPLAN-SIGACT Symposium on Principles of Programming Languages, POPL 2016, pp. 18–29. Association for Computing Machinery, New York (2016). https://doi.org/10.1145/2837614.2837638
8. Atkey, R.: Syntax and semantics of quantitative type theory. In: Proceedings of the 33rd Annual ACM/IEEE Symposium on Logic in Computer Science, LICS 2018, pp. 56–65. Association for Computing Machinery, New York (2018). https://doi.org/10.1145/3209108.3209189
9. Atkey, R., Johann, P., Ghani, N.: When is a type refinement an inductive type? In: Foundations of Software Science and Computational Structures. Lecture Notes in Computer Science, pp. 72–87. Springer, Heidelberg (2011). https://bentnib.org/inductive-refinement.pdf
10. Baudon, T., Radanne, G., Gonnord, L.: Bit-stealing made legal: compilation for custom memory representations of algebraic data types. Proc. ACM Program. Lang. **7**(ICFP), 813–846 (2023). https://doi.org/10.1145/3607858

11. Boulier, S., Pédrot, P.M., Tabareau, N.: The next 700 syntactical models of type theory. In: Proceedings of the 6th ACM SIGPLAN Conference on Certified Programs and Proofs, CPP 2017, pp. 182–194. Association for Computing Machinery, New York (2017). https://doi.org/10.1145/3018610.3018620
12. Brady, E., McBride, C., McKinna, J.: Inductive families need not store their indices. In: Berardi, S., Coppo, M., Damiani, F. (eds.) TYPES 2003. LNCS, vol. 3085, pp. 115–129. Springer, Heidelberg (2004). https://doi.org/10.1007/978-3-540-24849-1_8
13. Castellan, S., Clairambault, P., Dybjer, P.: Categories with families: unityped, simply typed, and dependently typed. arXiv (2019). http://arxiv.org/abs/1904.00827
14. Cockx, J., Devriese, D.: Proof-relevant unification: dependent pattern matching with only the axioms of your type theory. J. Funct. Prog. **28**(e12), e12 (2018). https://www.cambridge.org/core/services/aop-cambridge-core/content/view/E54D56DC3F5D5361CCDECA824030C38E/S095679681800014Xa.pdf/div-class-title-proof-relevant-unification-dependent-pattern-matching-with-only-the-axioms-of-your-type-theory-div.pdf
15. Dagand, P.E., McBride, C.: A categorical treatment of ornaments. In: 2013 28th Annual ACM/IEEE Symposium on Logic in Computer Science. IEEE (2013). https://doi.org/10.5555/2591370.2591396
16. Diehl, L., Firsov, D., Stump, A.: Generic zero-cost reuse for dependent types. Proc. ACM Program. Lang. **2**(ICFP), 1–30 (2018). https://doi.org/10.1145/3236799
17. Goguen, H., McBride, C., McKinna, J.: Eliminating dependent pattern matching. In: Algebra, Meaning, and Computation. Lecture Notes in Computer Science, pp. 521–540. Springer, Heidelberg (2006). https://research.google.com/pubs/archive/99.pdf
18. Gratzer, D., Kavvos, G.A., Nuyts, A., Birkedal, L.: Multimodal dependent type theory. In: Proceedings of the 35th Annual ACM/IEEE Symposium on Logic in Computer Science. ACM, New York (2020). https://doi.org/10.1145/3373718.3394736
19. Kovács, A.: Staged compilation with two-level type theory. Proc. ACM Program. Lang. **6**(ICFP), 540–569 (2022). https://dl.acm.org/doi/10.1145/3547641
20. Kovács, A.: Type-theoretic signatures for algebraic theories and inductive types. Ph.D. thesis, Eötvös Loránd University (2023). https://andraskovacs.github.io/pdfs/phdthesis_compact.pdf
21. Martin-Löf, P.: Intuitionistic type theory **1**, 1–91 (1984). https://intuitionistic.wordpress.com/wp-content/uploads/2010/07/martin-lof-tt.pdf
22. McBride, C., Goguen, H., McKinna, J.: A few constructions on constructors. In: Lecture Notes in Computer Science, pp. 186–200. Springer, Heidelberg (2006). http://www.e-pig.org/downloads/concon.pdf
23. McBride, C., McKinna, J.: The view from the left. J. Funct. Programming **14**(1), 69–111 (2004). https://www.cambridge.org/core/services/aop-cambridge-core/content/view/F8A44CAC27CCA178AF69DD84BC585A2D/S0956796803004829a.pdf/div-class-title-the-view-from-the-left-div.pdf
24. Moon, B., Eades III, H., Orchard, D.: Graded modal dependent type theory. In: ESOP 2021. LNCS, vol. 12648, pp. 462–490. Springer, Cham (2021). https://doi.org/10.1007/978-3-030-72019-3_17
25. Wadler, P.: Views: a way for pattern matching to cohabit with data abstraction. In: Proceedings of the 14th ACM SIGACT-SIGPLAN Symposium on Principles of Programming Languages, POPL 1987, pp. 307–313. Association for Computing Machinery, New York (1987). https://doi.org/10.1145/41625.41653

26. Wadler, P.: Deforestation: transforming programs to eliminate trees. Theor. Comput. Sci. **73**(2), 231–248 (1990). https://www.sciencedirect.com/science/article/pii/030439759090147A
27. The Agda Wiki. https://wiki.portal.chalmers.se/agda/pmwiki.php. Accessed 3 May 2024
28. The GNU MP Bignum Library. https://gmplib.org/. Accessed 8 Dec 2024
29. Idris: A Language for Type-Driven Development. https://www.idris-lang.org/. Accessed 3 May 2024
30. Lean: Programming Language and Theorem Prover. https://lean-lang.org/. Accessed 3 May 2024
31. Welcome to a World of Rocq. https://rocq-prover.org/. Accessed 16 Apr 2025
32. agda2hs Documentation — agda2hs documentation. https://agda.github.io/agda2hs/. Accessed 19 Feb 2025
33. Should Agda optimise away the erasure from Vec to List? Issue #7701. https://github.com/idris-lang/Idris2/pull/3486. Accessed 19 Feb 2025
34. Program extraction — Coq 8.13.2 documentation. https://coq.inria.fr/doc/v8.13/refman/addendum/extraction.html. Accessed 19 Feb 2025
35. Pragmas — Idris2 0.0 documentation. https://idris2.readthedocs.io/en/latest/reference/pragmas.html#transform. Accessed 19 Feb 2025
36. Make 'CONS', 'NIL', 'JUST' and 'NOTHING' constructors have uniform names by Z-snails. Pull Request #3486. https://github.com/idris-lang/Idris2/pull/3486. Accessed 19 Feb 2025

Two-Dimensional Numerical Representations
An Adventure with Block Matrices

Michael Youssef(✉)

University of Kaiserslautern-Landau (RPTU), Kaiserslautern, Germany
youssef@rptu.de

Abstract. Numerical representation is a technique for modelling datastructures after number systems. Typically, the method has been used to derive one-dimensional datastructures. This paper explores utilizing the technique for modelling two-dimensional datastructures instead, with insights into multi-dimensional ones. The aim of this paper is to devise datastructures for modelling block matrices. We look into the different derivations and highlight some roadblocks that would otherwise not be an issue in the one-dimensional case. The points under consideration include dimensional bias, ease of defining functions and proving properties about them as well as the difficulty of understanding the derived datastructure.

Keywords: Block Matrices · Numerical Representations · Agda

1 Introduction

Numerical representations are a well-established concept that has been around for quite a while. The main idea is that some datastructures can be modelled after number systems, and hence, inherit the systems' properties. For example, when it comes to lists, the increment, decrement and addition operations correspond to the cons, tail and append operations respectively.

Over the last three decades, there has been a lot of work done to derive one-dimensional datastructures. Most notably, Okasaki [9] introduced a number of datastructures that are based on various number systems. What has not been explored much is the use of the same techniques for two-dimensional datastructures. In fact, and as we show later on in the paper, some of these datastructures are subtly hidden in both recent and well-established works.

The aim of this paper is to highlight the different challenges faced when transitioning to two-dimensional structures that would otherwise not be an issue when dealing with their one-dimensional counterparts, as well as deriving a suitable datastructure for modelling block matrices which is ideally easy to understand, work with and reason about.

As we will see later on, some number systems give rise to datastructures that are easy to understand, however, they are not necessarily the most convenient ones to work with. For example, for some of these derivations, it is in fact fairly tedious to prove even a basic property such as associativity of matrix multiplication.

J. Gibbons (Ed.): TFP 2025, LNCS 15652, pp. 329–355, 2026.
https://doi.org/10.1007/978-3-031-99751-8_14

Contributions. This paper makes the following contributions.

- Explores the design space of two-dimensional numerical representations in the context of block matrices.
- Highlights the relevant design decisions when it comes to transitioning from one-dimensional to two-dimensional structures.
- Reasons about a suitable implementation of block matrices with regard to difficulty of proving properties and programming with the corresponding structure in the context of semiring frameworks.

2 Numerical Representations

To start off, we briefly recap one-dimensional numerical representations. Deriving the datastructures can be done in multiple ways. For example, Okasaki [9] does it in an ad-hoc fashion, while some of the works that followed have done it more rigorously. Hinze [1] used functor equations to derive numerical representations. While more recently, Hinze and Swierstra [2] used isomorphic equational reasoning to derive them using the laws of exponents in Agda [7]. They also proposed that this method can be used for deriving two or multi-dimensional representations. This paper focuses on extending their work in that direction, and as such, we use their framework. To that end, we recap the main idea of the framework. The starting point is defining a finite map from some finite set to an arbitrary type A.

$$\mathit{sequence} : \mathit{Index}\ n \rightarrow A$$

Index is some representation of a finite set, and the entire function type represents a finite sequence type of length n. The main idea is to vary the representation of the *Index* type such that different number systems yield different representations of the sequence type itself.

For example, if we use Agda's standard library finite sets *Fin*, we get vanilla lists indexed by length (a.k.a vectors) as the corresponding sequence type by solving the isomorphism equation $(\mathit{Fin}\ n \rightarrow \mathit{elem}) \cong \mathit{Array}\ n\ \mathit{elem}$.

```
data Fin : Peano → Set where
  izero :                Fin (succ n)
  isucc : (i : Fin n) → Fin (succ n)

data Array : Peano → Set → Set where
  nil  :                              Array zero     elem
  cons : elem → Array n elem → Array (succ n) elem
```

2.1 From One to Two-Dimensional Representations

The idea behind a two or multi-dimensional derivation is to use a multi-dimensional finite map instead. For example, if we solve the equation $(\mathit{Fin}\ n \rightarrow \mathit{Fin}\ n \rightarrow \mathit{elem}) \cong \mathit{PMatrix}\ n\ \mathit{elem}$. We can obtain a two-dimensional numerical representation based on the same index type modelling square matrices.

$$
\begin{aligned}
&\textit{data } \textit{PMatrix} : \textit{Peano} \to \textit{Set} \to \textit{Set} \textit{ where}\\
&\quad \textit{empty} : \textit{PMatrix zero } A\\
&\quad \textit{block} : A \to \textit{Array } n\ A \to \textit{Array } n\ A\\
&\qquad\qquad \to \textit{PMatrix } n\ A\\
&\qquad\qquad \to \textit{PMatrix } (\textit{succ } n)\ A
\end{aligned}
$$

For the detailed derivation, see Appendix A.1.

For the remainder of the paper we explore varying the index type based on number systems, and inspecting the corresponding datastructures that we can derive from them. We occasionally steer the choice of the number system based on its desired properties depending on context.

3 Exploration of The Design Space

In this section, we explore some of the common, and likewise, less common number systems with regards to two-dimensional numerical representations. We highlight some considerations and how they affect the resulting datastructures. Moreover, since we intend to use the matrices within semiring frameworks, the main focus will be on square matrices, however, most of the time, it is necessary to drop that restriction in the sense that it becomes necessary to model the general case of rectangular matrices to be able to model the square ones.

3.1 Row vs Column-Major vs Neutral

One immediate method of approaching two-dimensional representations is to model them as one-dimensional ones with their element types again being one-dimensional datastructures. In other words, we can solve the equations as follows.

$$
\begin{aligned}
&(\textit{Index } m \to (\textit{Index } n \to \textit{elem}))\\
\cong&\\
&(\textit{Index } m \to \textit{Sequence } n\ \textit{elem})\\
\cong&\\
&\textit{Sequence } m\ (\textit{Sequence } n\ \textit{elem})
\end{aligned}
$$

Although this approach always works for any number system, this is essentially the naive approach which still exists in some mainstream programming languages that model matrices as sequences of sequences. The fundamental issue with this approach is the dimensional bias. In essence, row or column-major operations could be substantially more difficult depending on which dimension we favor.

To make matters worse, some operations do not benefit from either of the choices. One such operation is the matrix *transpose* since it operates along the diagonal.

Moreover, if we intend to respect dimensional constraints, we would need to rely on some mechanism such as dependent types to maintain type invariants on the length of the inner sequences.

It is worth mentioning that it is possible to respect matrix dimensions without explicitly encoding them in the types, but for that, we would need to resort to non-trivial measures such as using nested datatypes as Okasaki achieved with top-down and bottom-up matrices [8].

3.2 Empty Row or Column Size

Yet another roadblock is the empty sequence. In the one dimensional case, that is not an issue, since there is a single numerical value representing the size of the datastructure, however, for the case of two dimensions, considering some type of matrices indexed by their row and column dimensions, the types $\mathit{Matrix}\ \mathbf{0}\ n\ \mathit{elem}$ and $\mathit{Matrix}\ n\ \mathbf{0}\ \mathit{elem}$ are different, yet model the same thing, the empty matrix.

Furthermore, this duplicity is not always an issue as we have briefly mentioned before that we are primarily interested in square matrices, however, as we demonstrate later on, some representations of square block matrices require rectangular sub-matrices.

Another way to tackle the emptiness issue is to use number systems that don't admit a zero representation. This would typically work in most applications since the base case of a block matrix is usually assumed to be a scalar.

Another similar idea is to use an adjusted index type that models a zeroless sequence type. For example, an adjusted index based on the Peano numerals vs the original index would be the following.

$$\begin{array}{l} \mathit{data}\ \mathit{Fin}\ :\ \mathit{Peano} \to \mathit{Set}\ \mathit{where} \\ \quad \mathit{izero}\ :\ \mathit{Fin}\ (\mathit{succ}\ n) \\ \quad \mathit{isucc}\ :\ (i\ :\ \mathit{Fin}\ n) \to \mathit{Fin}\ (\mathit{succ}\ n) \end{array}$$

$$\begin{array}{l} \mathit{data}\ \mathit{AtMost}\ :\ \mathit{Peano} \to \mathit{Set}\ \mathit{where} \\ \quad \mathit{izero}\ :\ \mathit{AtMost}\ n \\ \quad \mathit{isucc}\ :\ \mathit{AtMost}\ n \to \mathit{AtMost}\ (\mathit{succ}\ n) \end{array}$$

The idea here is that $\mathit{Fin}\ \mathbf{0}$ is uninhabited, while $\mathit{AtMost}\ \mathbf{0}$ has exactly one inhabitant. Using this indexing scheme allows for non-empty numerical representations. We will stick to non-emptiness for the remainder of the paper unless otherwise stated.

3.3 Common Number Systems

Peano Numerals. First off, we start with Peano numerals. The one-dimensional structure we get using the index scheme described in Sect. 3.2 is simply a non-empty vanilla list. Similarly, the two-dimensional counterpart is not so different, we essentially get two constructors for representing a scalar value as well as $\mathbf{2} + n \times \mathbf{2} + n$ matrices. The corresponding equation to solve for deriving this datastructure is $(\mathit{AtMost}\ m \to \mathit{AtMost}\ m \to \mathit{elem}) \cong \mathit{AMatrix}\ m\ \mathit{elem}$.

$$
\begin{array}{lll}
\textit{data}\ \textit{AMatrix} & : & \textit{Peano} \to \textit{Set} \to \textit{Set}\ \textit{where} \\
\quad \textit{scalar} & : & \textit{elem} \to \textit{AMatrix}\ \mathbf{0}\ \ \textit{elem} \\
\quad \textit{block} & : & \textit{elem} \to \textit{Array}\ \quad m\ \textit{elem} \to \textit{Array}\ \quad m \qquad\quad \textit{elem} \\
 & & \quad \to \textit{AMatrix}\ m\ \textit{elem} \to \textit{AMatrix}\ (\textit{succ}\ m)\ \textit{elem}
\end{array}
$$

This simple and easy to work with datastructure suffices for a lot of applications. A few points, however, are in order:

- The datastructure is an example of why modelling square matrices almost always requires non-square sub-matrices. In this case, we only need to have row and column vectors, and opt to represent them using *Arrays*, otherwise we would need to have two indices for both dimensions and model the sub-matrices using *AMatrix* $\mathbf{0}$ n and *AMatrix* n $\mathbf{0}$.
- Even though the datastructure is simple and suffices for a lot of applications, this is quite a simplistic view of block matrices. We would ideally like to split the matrix in a less discriminating way between all sub-blocks.

Leibniz Numerals. Leibniz numerals are essentially a unique binary representation as opposed to standard binary numerals that allow for leading zeros and suffer from a non-unique representation.

$$
\begin{array}{lll}
\textit{data}\ \textit{Leibniz} & : & \textit{Set}\ \textit{where} \\
\quad \mathbb{0}b & : & \textit{Leibniz} \\
\quad \_\mathbb{1} & : & \textit{Leibniz} \to \textit{Leibniz} \\
\quad \_\mathbb{2} & : & \textit{Leibniz} \to \textit{Leibniz}
\end{array}
$$

A corresponding non-zero index type based in Leibniz numerals would be.

$$
\begin{array}{lllll}
\textit{data}\ \textit{LIndex} & : & \textit{Leibniz} \to \textit{Set}\ \textit{where} & & \\
\quad \textit{I0} & : & \textit{LIndex}\ \mathbb{0}b & & \\
\quad \_\textit{I1}_1 & : & \textit{LIndex}\ l & \to & \textit{LIndex}\ (l\ \mathbb{1}) \\
\quad \_\textit{I1}_2 & : & \textit{LIndex}\ l & \to & \textit{LIndex}\ (l\ \mathbb{1}) \\
\quad \_\textit{I2}_1 & : & \textit{LIndex}\ (\textit{lsucc}\ l) & \to & \textit{LIndex}\ (l\ \mathbb{2}) \\
\quad \_\textit{I2}_2 & : & \textit{LIndex}\ l & \to & \textit{LIndex}\ (l\ \mathbb{2})
\end{array}
$$

As Hinze and Swierstra have shown in [2], the one-dimensional derivations of Leibniz numerals yield Braun trees or one-two trees (a.k.a. lazy Braun trees) depending on the index derivations. In principle, Leibniz numerals distinguish between even and odd lengths, this translates to a duplicity of constructors in the corresponding datastructure. For example, for Braun trees, we get three constructors. Likewise, if we derive arbitrary sized Braun matrices or one-two matrices, we get nine constructors. We show the one-two trees here but include the Braun matrices in the Appendix A.2.

```
data LM   : Leibniz → Leibniz → Set → Set where
  scalar  : elem → LM 0b 0b elem
  column₁ : LM l 0b elem → LM l 0b elem → LM (l 1) 0b   elem
  row₁    : LM 0b l elem → LM 0b l elem → LM 0b   (l 1) elem
  column₂ : LM l 0b elem → LM 0b 0b elem → LM l 0b elem
    →       LM (l 2) 0b elem
  row₂    : LM 0b l elem → LM 0b 0b elem → LM 0b l elem
    →       LM 0b   (l 2)   elem
  block₂₁ : LM l₁ l₂       elem → LM l₁ l₂   elem
    →       LM 0b (l₂ 1)   elem
    →       LM l₁ l₂       elem → LM l₁ l₂   elem
    →       LM (l₁ 2) (l₂ 1) elem
  block₁₂ : LM l₁ l₂ elem → LM l₁ l₂ elem
    →       LM (l₁ 1) 0b elem
    →       LM l₁ l₂ elem → LM l₁ l₂ elem
    →       LM (l₁ 1) (l₂ 2) elem
  block₂₂ : LM l₁ l₂ elem → LM l₁ l₂ elem
    →       LM 0b l₂ elem → LM l₁ 0b elem
    →       LM 0b 0b elem
    →       LM l₁ 0b elem → LM 0b l₂ elem
    →       LM l₁ l₂ elem → LM l₁ l₂ elem
    →       LM (l₁ 2) (l₂ 2) elem
  block₁₁ : LM l₁ l₂ elem → LM l₁ l₂ elem
    →       LM l₁ l₂ elem → LM l₁ l₂ elem
    →       LM (l₁ 1) (l₂ 1) elem
```

Similarly to the *AMatrix*, we can not opt to have square matrices only since some of the sub-matrices have differing row and column sizes.

Furthermore, unfortunately when it comes to Leibniz numerals, the duplicity scales up as we add more dimensions. For example, scaling up to a third dimension or more would cause an explosion in the number of cases.

Moreover, implementing matrix multiplication for Braun or one-two matrices, which is arguably the most important matrix operation, would require a whopping 27 cases to tackle.

One way to address this issue is instead of having a single datastructure with all possibilities of splitting rows and columns, we can have two mutually recursive data structures instead. This approach typically yields more constructors in total, but less per each datastructure. This sometimes comes in handy if we just want square matrices, since we don't necessarily need to have all possible combinations of row and column sizes such as the case with the *AMatrix*, where we only needed row and column vectors for the non-matching dimensions. We will demonstrate the approach with one of the examples that follow.

3.4 Implementations Based on Leaf Trees

Perhaps a less obvious numerical representation is the usage of leaf tree number systems, particularly, binary leaf trees. A basic implementation of such datastructure is described using two constructors, one for the leaf itself and another for a binary split. We model that as follows.

$$
\begin{array}{l}
\textit{data Shape} : \textit{Set where} \\
\quad O : \textit{Shape} \\
\quad B : \textit{Shape} \to \textit{Shape} \to \textit{Shape} \\
\textit{fromShape} : \textit{Shape} \to \textit{Peano} \\
\textit{fromShape } O \qquad\quad = \textit{succ zero} \\
\textit{fromShape } (B\ x\ y) = \textit{fromShape } x + \textit{fromShape } y
\end{array}
$$

This datastructure suffers from non-uniqueness. This is, however, not necessarily a major issue as the point here is to have flexibility when splitting a matrix into blocks. A non-unique representation allows for such flexibility. On the other hand, the resulting data structures are typically not easy to work with or reason about as the resulting types are not very restrictive. Furthermore, we may run into issues depending on how different dimensions are manipulated across different functions over them. This is simply due to the fact that two matrices of the same size and elements may have different splitting schemes, i.e. propositional equality is not sufficient in the general case.

The index type corresponding to this number system is the following.

$$
\begin{array}{l}
\textit{data SIndex} : \textit{Shape} \to \textit{Set where} \\
\quad \textit{one} \;\; : \textit{SIndex } O \\
\quad \textit{left} \;\; : \textit{SIndex } l \to \textit{SIndex } (B\ l\ r) \\
\quad \textit{right} : \textit{SIndex } r \to \textit{SIndex } (B\ l\ r)
\end{array}
$$

Surprisingly, this is the most common two-dimensional numerical base for already existing block matrix implementations. We cover some possible derivations below.

M Trees. Eriksson and Jansson [10] used a representation of block matrices based on leaf trees to model the transitive closure operation using closed semirings and other similar algebraic structures. The datastructure they used can be obtained by solving the equation. $(\textit{SIndex } r \to \textit{SIndex } c \to \textit{elem}) \cong M\ r\ c\ \textit{elem}$

$$
\begin{array}{lll}
\multicolumn{3}{l}{\textit{data } M : \textit{Shape} \to \textit{Shape} \to \textit{Set} \to \textit{Set where}} \\
\quad \textit{scalar} & : \textit{elem} & \to M\ O\ \ O\ \ \textit{elem} \\
\quad \textit{row} & : M\ O\ c_1\ \textit{elem} \to M\ O\ c_2\ \textit{elem} & \to M\ O\ \ (B\ c_1\ c_2)\ \textit{elem} \\
\quad \textit{column} & : M\ r_1\ O\ \textit{elem} \to M\ r_2\ O\ \textit{elem} & \to M\ (B\ r_1\ r_2)\ O\ \ \textit{elem} \\
\quad \textit{block} & : M\ r_1\ c_1\ \textit{elem} \to M\ r_1\ c_2\ \textit{elem} \to & \\
 & \quad M\ r_2\ c_1\ \textit{elem} \to M\ r_2\ c_2\ \textit{elem} & \to M\ (B\ r_1\ r_2)\ (B\ c_1\ c_2)\ \textit{elem}
\end{array}
$$

This implementation is quite flexible, row-column neutral and easy to understand, however, since the underlying number system is not unique, defining functions and proving properties about them can sometimes be slightly difficult as we stated before. For example, we could have two matrices of types $M\ O\ (B\ O\ (B\ O\ O))$ and $M\ O\ (B\ (B\ O\ O)\ O)$ that contain the same elements, yet are not propositionally equal. We have to maintain some invariants about manipulating the matrices for each function definition in an ad-hoc fashion. This is not necessarily an issue, but it can be a bit cumbersome if we define a lot of functions over the datastructure.

KD-Trees. We have previously noted that in the two-dimensional case, the number of constructors can increase substantially and pointed out that one way to tackle this is to use mutual recursion. If we apply this idea to leaf trees, we get a datastructure similar to KD-trees, or 2D-trees in the two-dimension case.

$$(\mathit{SIndex}\ r \rightarrow \mathit{SIndex}\ c \rightarrow \mathit{elem}) \cong \mathit{KDTreeR}\ r\ c\ \mathit{elem}$$
$$(\mathit{SIndex}\ r \rightarrow \mathit{SIndex}\ c \rightarrow \mathit{elem}) \cong \mathit{KDTreeC}\ r\ c\ \mathit{elem}$$

```
data KDTreeR : Shape → Shape → Set → Set
data KDTreeC : Shape → Shape → Set → Set

data KDTreeR where
  single    : elem                            → KDTreeR O O elem
  split-col : KDTreeR O c1          elem → KDTreeR O c2 elem
    →         KDTreeR O (B c1 c2) elem
  split-row : KDTreeC r1          c elem → KDTreeC r2 c elem
    →         KDTreeR (B r1 r2) c elem

data KDTreeC where
  single    : elem                            → KDTreeC O O elem
  split-row : KDTreeC r1          O elem → KDTreeC r2 O elem
    →         KDTreeC (B r1 r2) O elem
  split-col : KDTreeR r c1          elem → KDTreeR r c2 elem
    →         KDTreeC r (B c1 c2) elem
```

Note: Of course, the main idea of KD-Trees is to have sparsity. We can address this by adding additional constructors. For example, we can augment the row-biased KD-Tree by a sparse constructor *sparse* : *KDTreeR m n elem* and similarly, *sparse* : *KDTreeC m n elem* for the column-biased one. We can moreover mark the sparse constructors with additional information. For example, we could wish to have an identity sparse matrix as well as a zero sparse matrix *zero* : *KDTreeR m n elem* and *id* : *KDTreeR m m elem* and similarly, *zero* : *KDTreeC m n elem* and *id* : *KDTreeC m m elem*. This scheme for modelling sparsity in a datastructure by adding dedicated constructors is straightforward and always works, however, we quickly stumble upon a major issue. Propositional equality no longer works since the same matrix can be represented in multiple ways. For example a *KDTreeR O O elem* can be represented as *single* 0 or *sparse*.

In some applications, this can be an issue. For many of the KD-Tree applications, however, one uses labelled sparse matrices where the required equality between the sparse representations and the dense ones is not actually needed, and hence, propositional equality is once again usable in this case.

Multiway Split. The underlying leaf trees we have chosen here are binary leaf trees. Generally speaking, nothing prevents us from having ternary or even a multi-way split instead. If we opt for a multi-way split, we can derive a datastructure which allows for an arbitrary splitting scheme. This is perhaps as flexible as it gets. We can split a matrix into an arbitrary number of sub-matrices with arbitrary sizes.

For example, we can model a number system using multiway leaf trees using vanilla lists and derive a corresponding index type as follows.

```
data Array (A : Set) : Peano → Set where
  nil  : Array A zero
  cons : A → Array A n → Array A (succ n)
data Shape : Set where
  M : Array Shape n → Shape

data SIndex : Shape → Set where
  leaf : SIndex (M nil)
  here : SIndex x         → SIndex (M (cons x xs))
  next : SIndex (M xs) → SIndex (M (cons x xs))
```

The corresponding one-dimensional datastructure would be the following

```
data SArr : Shape → Set → Set where
  leaf   : elem
     →     SArr (M nil) elem
  cons   : SArr x elem → SArr (M xs) elem
     →     SArr (M (cons x xs)) elem
mwayex : SArr
  (M (cons (M (cons (M nil) (cons (M nil) nil))) nil)) Peano
mwayex = cons (cons (leaf zero) (cons (leaf zero) (leaf zero)))
              (leaf zero)
```

In general, the leaf tree scheme allows us to model the datastructure by its structural shape. The multi-way leaf tree scheme is the least restrictive where the shape itself is some sequence type based on how we instantiate the *Array* type used in the split.

3.5 Skew Binary

We turn our attention back to canonical number systems.

To balance off the properties of both Peano and Leibniz numerals, we can use skew binary numbers as the underlying number system. The idea is that we obtain a non-discriminating representation of sub-blocks, while allowing for ease of appending rows and columns to the matrix.

Skew binary based numerical representations are considerably more difficult than the ones based on the number systems we mentioned before, and as such, we consider multiple ways of exploring the design space.

To start off, we define canonical skew binary numbers as described by Myers [6].

$$
\begin{array}{l}
2\,\hat{}\,\_ \dot{-} 2 \;:\; Peano \rightarrow Peano \\
2 \uparrow zero \quad \dot{-} 2 = zero \\
2 \uparrow 1 \quad \dot{-} 2 = zero \\
2 \uparrow (succ\; n) \quad \dot{-} 2 = succ\,(succ\,((2 \uparrow n \dot{-} 2) \cdot 2)) \\
2\,\hat{}\,\_ \dot{-} 1 \;:\; Peano \rightarrow Peano \\
2 \uparrow zero \quad \dot{-} 1 = zero \\
2 \uparrow (succ\; n) \quad \dot{-} 1 = succ\,(2 \uparrow (succ\; n) \dot{-} 2)
\end{array}
$$

$$
\begin{array}{l}
\mathbf{data}\; Skew^1 \;:\; Set\; \mathbf{where} \\
\quad 0\,b \;:\; Skew^1 \\
\quad \_\mathbb{1}\_\mathbb{0}s \;:\; Skew^1 \rightarrow Peano \rightarrow Skew^1 \\
\mathbf{data}\; Skew \;:\; Set\; \mathbf{where} \\
\quad 0\,b\mathbb{0} \;:\; Skew \\
\quad \_\mathbb{1}\_\mathbb{0}s \;:\; Skew^1 \rightarrow Peano \rightarrow Skew \\
\quad \_\mathbb{2}\_\mathbb{0}s \;:\; Skew^1 \rightarrow Peano \rightarrow Skew
\end{array}
$$

$$
\begin{array}{l}
\mathbb{N}[\![\_,\_]\!]^1 \;:\; Skew^1 \rightarrow Peano \rightarrow Peano \\
\mathbb{N}[\![\; 0\,b \;,\; n \;]\!]^1 = zero \\
\mathbb{N}[\![\; x\,\mathbb{1}\,m\,\mathbb{0}s \;,\; n \;]\!]^1 = 2 \uparrow (n + m) \dot{-} 1 + \mathbb{N}[\![\, x \,,\, succ\,(n + m) \,]\!]^1 \\
\mathbb{N}[\![\_]\!] \;:\; Skew \rightarrow Peano \\
\mathbb{N}[\![\; 0\,b\mathbb{0} \;]\!] = zero \\
\mathbb{N}[\![\; x\,\mathbb{1}\,m\,\mathbb{0}s \;]\!] = 2 \uparrow (1 + m) \dot{-} 1 + \mathbb{N}[\![\, x \,,\, 2 + m \,]\!]^1 \\
\mathbb{N}[\![\; x\,\mathbb{2}\,m\,\mathbb{0}s \;]\!] = 2 \uparrow (2 + m) \dot{-} 2 + \mathbb{N}[\![\, x \,,\, 2 + m \,]\!]^1
\end{array}
$$

The corresponding index type we get is the following.

$$
\begin{array}{l}
\mathbf{data}\; TreeIndex \;:\; Peano \rightarrow Set\; \mathbf{where} \\
\quad Node \;:\; TreeIndex\; h \\
\quad L \;:\; TreeIndex\; h \rightarrow TreeIndex\,(succ\; h) \\
\quad R \;:\; TreeIndex\; h \rightarrow TreeIndex\,(succ\; h) \\
\mathbf{data}\; SkewIndex^1 \;:\; Skew^1 \rightarrow Peano \rightarrow Set\; \mathbf{where} \\
\quad single \;:\; SkewIndex^1\; 0\,b\; n \\
\quad node \;:\; TreeIndex\; (succ\,(n + x)) \rightarrow SkewIndex^1\; (l\; \mathbb{1}\; x\; \mathbb{0}s)\; n \\
\quad rest \;:\; SkewIndex^1\; l\,(succ\,(n + x)) \rightarrow SkewIndex^1\; (l\; \mathbb{1}\; x\; \mathbb{0}s)\; n \\
\mathbf{data}\; SkewIndex \;:\; Skew \rightarrow Set\; \mathbf{where} \\
\quad scalar \;:\; SkewIndex\; 0\; b\mathbb{0} \\
\quad T_1 \;:\; TreeIndex\; n \rightarrow SkewIndex\; (l\; \mathbb{1}\; n\; \mathbb{0}s) \\
\quad Ts_1 \;:\; SkewIndex^1\; l\; n \rightarrow SkewIndex\; (l\; \mathbb{1}\; n\; \mathbb{0}s) \\
\quad T_2 \;:\; TreeIndex\; n \rightarrow SkewIndex\; (l\; \mathbb{2}\; n\; \mathbb{0}s) \\
\quad T_3 \;:\; TreeIndex\; n \rightarrow SkewIndex\; (l\; \mathbb{2}\; n\; \mathbb{0}s) \\
\quad Ts_2 \;:\; SkewIndex^1\; l\; n \rightarrow SkewIndex\; (l\; \mathbb{2}\; n\; \mathbb{0}s)
\end{array}
$$

This is quite a lengthy index type, however, it clearly highlights Okasaki's description of a one-dimensional sequence type based on skew binary numbers: a sequence of trees where the possible sole 2 numeral might introduce two trees instead of 1, hence the duplicity in *SkewIndex* and $SkewIndex^1$.

The one-dimensional numerical representation we get is the following.

```
data Tree : Peano → Set → Set where
  scalar  :   elem                                   → Tree zero     elem
  Node    :   Tree h elem → elem → Tree h elem → Tree (succ h) elem
data SRAL¹ : Skew¹ → Peano → Set → Set where
  scalar  :   elem
    →         SRAL¹ 0 b          n elem
  Node-𝟙  :   Tree (succ (n + m)) elem → SRAL¹ l (succ (n + m)) elem
    →         SRAL¹ (l 𝟙 m 𝟘s) n elem
data SRAL : Skew → Set → Set where
  scalar  : elem
          → SRAL 0 b𝟘        elem
  Node-𝟙  : Tree n elem →                     SRAL¹ l n elem
          → SRAL (l 𝟙 n 𝟘s) elem
  Node-𝟚  : Tree n elem →  Tree n elem → SRAL¹ l n elem
          → SRAL (l 𝟚 n 𝟘s) elem
```

The two-dimensional square representation is the following.

```
data QT : Peano → Set → Set where
  scalar : e → QT zero e
  block : e
    → Tree m e → Tree m e → Tree m e → Tree m e
    → QT m e → QT m e → QT m e → QT m e
      → QT (succ m) e
data SM¹ : Skew¹ → Peano → Set → Set where
  scalar : e → SM¹ 0 b m e
  block : QT (succ (m + x)) e
        → SRAL¹ l (succ (m + x)) (Tree (succ (m + x)) e)
        → SRAL¹ l (succ (m + x)) (Tree (succ (m + x)) e)
        → SM¹ l (succ (m + x)) e → SM¹ (l 𝟙 x 𝟘s) m e
data SM : Skew → Set → Set where
  scalar  : e → SM 0 b𝟘 e
  block𝟙  : QT m e
      → SRAL¹ l m (Tree m e) → SRAL¹ l m (Tree m e)
      → SM¹ l m e → SM (l 𝟙 m 𝟘s) e
  block𝟚  : QT m e → QT m e → QT m e → QT m e
      → SRAL¹ l m (Tree m e) → SRAL¹ l m (Tree m e)
      → SRAL¹ l m (Tree m e) → SRAL¹ l m (Tree m e)
      → SM¹ l m e → SM (l 𝟚 m 𝟘s) e
```

We can once again resort to using one-dimensional sequences to model the sub-blocks.

We introduced an additional datastructure for the trees themselves. This complicates things as we have too many interfaces to deal with. Notice how some constructors require lists of trees such as *SRAL¹ l m (Tree m e)* for example. We would need to define an additional datastructure that combines both tree indices and list indices to tackle finite maps of the following shape.

$$SkewIndex^1\ l \to TreeIndex\ n \to elem$$

It is arguably justifiable to do away with trees in this case, since the skew binary lists can themselves model trees. After all, lists are just a special case of trees where the left sub-tree is empty.

To unify the interface, we modify the number system and do some extensive amends to the index type calculations.

First, the number system. We do away with the additional argument to ℕ⟦_,_⟧¹ and introduce some patterns for ease of readability.

```
data Skew¹ : Set where
  0 b      : Skew¹
  _𝟙_𝟘s    : Skew¹ → Peano → Skew¹
data Skew : Set where
  _‵       : Skew¹ → Skew
  _2_𝟘s    : Skew¹ → Peano → Skew
pattern _𝟙 l = l 𝟙 zero 𝟘s
pattern 𝟘 = 0 b ‵
pattern _2 s = s 2 zero 𝟘s
 {-# TERMINATING #-}
ℕ⟦_⟧¹ : Skew¹ → Peano
ℕ⟦ 0 b               ⟧¹ = zero
ℕ⟦ 0 b 𝟙 n 𝟘s        ⟧¹ = 2 ↑ (succ n) ∸ 1
ℕ⟦ (l 𝟙 n 𝟘s) 𝟙 m 𝟘s ⟧¹ = 2 ↑ (succ m) ∸ 1 + ℕ⟦ l 𝟙 (1 + m + n) 𝟘s ⟧¹
ℕ⟦_⟧ : Skew → Peano
ℕ⟦ s ‵               ⟧ = ℕ⟦ s ⟧¹
ℕ⟦ 0 b 2 m 𝟘s        ⟧ = 2 ↑ (2 + m) ∸ 2
ℕ⟦ (l 𝟙 x 𝟘s) 2 m 𝟘s ⟧ = 2 ↑ (2 + m) ∸ 2 + ℕ⟦ (l 𝟙 (1 + m + x) 𝟘s) ⟧¹
inc : Skew → Skew
inc (0 b               ‵ ) = 0 b 𝟙 ‵
inc ((x 𝟙)             ‵ ) = x 2
inc ((x 𝟙 succ m 𝟘s)   ‵ ) = (x 𝟙 m 𝟘s) 𝟙 ‵
inc (0 b 2 m 𝟘s          ) = 0 b 𝟙 (succ m) 𝟘s ‵
inc ((x 𝟙) 2 n 𝟘s        ) = x 2 (succ n) 𝟘s
inc ((x 𝟙 succ m 𝟘s) 2 n 𝟘s) = (x 𝟙 m 𝟘s) 𝟙 (succ n) 𝟘s ‵
```

Unfortunately, Agda's termination checker is not able to tell that ℕ⟦_⟧¹ terminates. However, it is easy to see that it in fact does terminate, since the number of 𝟙 constructors decreases.

For the indices, we only show the resulting types here, the lengthy derivations can be found in the Appendix A.3. The one thing to point out about the derivations is the fact that we use both zeroless and zeroful indices for the derivation i.e. both *Fin* and *AtMost*.

```
data SkewIndex¹ : Skew¹ → Set where
  c1 : SkewIndex¹ (0 b 𝟙)
  c2 : SkewIndex¹ (0 b 𝟙 succ m 𝟘s)
  c3 : SkewIndex¹ (0 b 𝟙 m 𝟘s)             → SkewIndex¹ (0 b 𝟙 succ m 𝟘s)
  c4 : SkewIndex¹ (0 b 𝟙 m 𝟘s)             → SkewIndex¹ (0 b 𝟙 succ m 𝟘s)
  c5 : SkewIndex¹ (0 b 𝟙 m 𝟘s)             → SkewIndex¹ ((l 𝟙 x 𝟘s) 𝟙 m 𝟘s)
  c6 : SkewIndex¹ (l 𝟙 succ (m + x) 𝟘s)    → SkewIndex¹ ((l 𝟙 x 𝟘s) 𝟙 m 𝟘s)
data SkewIndex : Skew → Set where
  T1 : SkewIndex¹ (0 b 𝟙)                  → SkewIndex 𝟘
  T2 : SkewIndex¹ (0 b 𝟙)                  → SkewIndex ((l 𝟙 n 𝟘s) ')
  T3 : SkewIndex¹ (l 𝟙 n 𝟘s)               → SkewIndex ((l 𝟙 n 𝟘s) ')
  T4 : SkewIndex¹ (0 b 𝟙 succ n 𝟘s)        → SkewIndex (0 b 𝟚 n 𝟘s)
  T5 : SkewIndex¹ (0 b 𝟙 succ n 𝟘s)        → SkewIndex ((l 𝟙 m 𝟘s) 𝟚 n 𝟘s)
  lL : SkewIndex¹ (l 𝟙 succ (n + m) 𝟘s)    → SkewIndex ((l 𝟙 m 𝟘s) 𝟚 n 𝟘s)
```

We can then use this index to unify the interfaces. In the one-dimensional case, we get the following skew binary tree.

```
data SRAL¹ : Skew¹ → Set → Set where
  single  : elem → SRAL¹ (0 b 𝟙) elem
  Node-0𝟙 : SRAL¹ (0 b 𝟙) elem
     →      SRAL¹ (0 b 𝟙 m 𝟘s) elem →  SRAL¹ (0 b 𝟙 m 𝟘s) elem
     →      SRAL¹ (0 b 𝟙 succ m 𝟘s) elem
  Node-l𝟙 : SRAL¹ (0 b 𝟙 n 𝟘s) elem
     →      SRAL¹ (l 𝟙 succ (n + m) 𝟘s) elem
     →      SRAL¹ ((l 𝟙 m 𝟘s) 𝟙 n 𝟘s) elem
data SRAL : Skew → Set → Set where
  Node-0' : SRAL¹ (0 b 𝟙) elem → SRAL 𝟘 elem
  Node-𝟙' : SRAL¹ (0 b 𝟙) elem → SRAL¹ (l 𝟙 n 𝟘s) elem
    → SRAL (l 𝟙 n 𝟘s ') elem
  Node-0𝟚 : SRAL¹ (0 b 𝟙 succ n 𝟘s) elem → SRAL (0 b 𝟚 n 𝟘s) elem
  Node-l𝟚 : SRAL¹ (0 b 𝟙 succ n 𝟘s) elem
    → SRAL¹ (l 𝟙 succ (n + m) 𝟘s) elem
    → SRAL ((l 𝟙 m 𝟘s) 𝟚 n 𝟘s) elem
```

We also still maintain a constant time append operation of course.

```
cons : elem → SRAL s elem → SRAL (inc s) elem
cons x (Node-0' (single x1))
  = Node-𝟙' (single x) (single x1)
cons x (Node-𝟙' (single x1) (single x2))
  = Node-0𝟚 (Node-0𝟙 (single x) (single x1) (single x2))
cons x (Node-𝟙' (single x1) (Node-0𝟙 x2 x3 x4))
  = Node-𝟙' (single x) (Node-l𝟙 (single x1) (Node-0𝟙 x2 x3 x4))
cons x (Node-𝟙' (single x1) (Node-l𝟙 (single x2) x3))
  = Node-l𝟚 (Node-0𝟙 (single x) (single x1) (single x2)) x3
cons x (Node-𝟙' (single x1) (Node-l𝟙 (Node-0𝟙 x2 x4 x5) x3))
  = Node-𝟙' (single x) (Node-l𝟙 (single x1) (Node-l𝟙 (Node-0𝟙 x2 x4 x5) x3))
cons x (Node-0𝟚 (Node-0𝟙 x1 xs xs1))
  = Node-𝟙' (single x) (Node-0𝟙 x1 xs xs1)
cons x (Node-l𝟚 {m = zero} x1 (Node-0𝟙 x2 x5 x6))
  = Node-0𝟚 (Node-0𝟙 (single x) x1 (Node-0𝟙 x2 x5 x6))
cons x (Node-l𝟚 {m = zero} x1 (Node-l𝟙 x2 x5))
  = Node-l𝟚 (Node-0𝟙 (single x) x1 x2) x5
cons x (Node-l𝟚 {m = succ m} x1 (Node-0𝟙 x2 x3 x4))
  = Node-𝟙' (single x) (Node-l𝟙 x1 (Node-0𝟙 x2 x3 x4))
cons x (Node-l𝟚 {m = succ m} x1 (Node-l𝟙 x2 x3))
  = Node-𝟙' (single x) (Node-l𝟙 x1 (Node-l𝟙 x2 x3))
```

This function seems like it is difficult to define, but since we are using a canonical skew binary number system, and the increment operation itself is a constant time operation, we can almost fully rely on Agda's automatic proof search to define it. The only thing we have to do ourselves in resolve conflicts when two subtrees of the same size are in context. For example, agsy's solution for the second case would be *Node-0𝟚 (Node-0𝟙 (single x) (single* x_2*) (single* x_2*))* .

We can also define a lengthy two-dimensional skew square block matrix which is included in the Appendix A.4

Skew binary based matrices are substantially more difficult to understand than the previously discussed ones. However, on an interface level, they are similar to Braun matrices, we also get 9 constructors for the core part of the datastructure, and defining the matrix multiplication still requires 27 cases. The additional benefit we get is that appending rows and columns can be done in constant time.

This might seem like an unnecessarily complex datastructure due to the number of constructors and the non-trivial arrangement of the indices, however, we will discuss a potential use for it in the following section.

4 Minimizing Proof Effort

We have demonstrated several representations of block matrices. Furthermore, as we have already hinted towards, doing proofs with block matrices are usually very tedious in terms of the technical details related to the structure of the matrix, rather than the core logic of the proof due to the sheer number of cases that need to be considered. For example, even proving something as mundane as associativity of matrix multiplication would require a few hundred lines of code with some of the implementations mentioned above.

We have previously pointed out that even if we are to model square matrices, we end up requiring matrices of arbitrary row and column sizes, however, if we only consider matrices of shape $\mathbf{2}^{n} \times \mathbf{2}^{n}$, it is always possible to model them using square matrices only. Such matrices can either be a single element, or four sub-matrices of equal size if we are using a four-way split. Obviously, these matrices do not model matrices of all possible sizes in general, nevertheless, they are, by far, the easiest to work with. We try to exploit this property in this section.

Intuitively, if we are using an underlying idempotent semiring S, we can interpret the matrix as a graph, or perhaps an automaton. In that case, most properties that we would want to prove in this setting would still hold regardless of the fact that we could add a vertex without any edges in graph terms, or an unreachable node in automata terms.

What we are really trying to demonstrate here, in part, is that adding a row and a column composed of neutral elements preserves matrix addition and multiplication.

In other words, we can embed matrices of any size into larger ones. We first lay down the foundations of this approach, and then demonstrate it using the Peano shaped matrices.

To achieve embedding of matrices, we require a few prerequisites.

$$
\begin{array}{ll}
B{\to}A & : B \to A \\
A{\to}B & : A \to B \\
\textit{iso-fro} & : A{\to}B\,(B{\to}A\ a) \equiv a \\
\textit{embed-I} & : B{\to}A\ I^{B} \equiv I \\
\textit{embed-+} & : B{\to}A\,(a +^{B} b) \equiv (B{\to}A\ a + B{\to}A\ b) \\
\textit{embed-}\bullet & : B{\to}A\,(a \bullet^{B} b) \equiv (B{\to}A\ a \bullet B{\to}A\ b)
\end{array}
$$

A and B can be any type in general as long as they satisfy the requirements, however, for the task at hand, $\mathbf{1} + n$ is the type of square matrices of size $1 + n$, and B is the type of matrices of size n. We can then prove that the reverse morphism $B{\to}A$ is an algebra homomorphism over the following expression signature.

$$
\begin{array}{l}
\textit{data Expr (Carrier : Set) : Set where} \\
\quad \_^{a} \quad : (a : Carrier) \rightarrow Expr\ Carrier \\
\quad I^{s} \quad : Expr\ Carrier \\
\quad \_+^{s}\_ \ : Expr\ Carrier \rightarrow Expr\ Carrier \rightarrow Expr\ Carrier \\
\quad \_\bullet^{s}\_ \ : Expr\ Carrier \rightarrow Expr\ Carrier \rightarrow Expr\ Carrier
\end{array}
$$

$$
\begin{array}{l}
B{\rightarrow}A\text{-}homo : \forall\ x \rightarrow B{\rightarrow}A\ (algB\ x) \equiv algA\ (fmap\ B{\rightarrow}A\ x) \\
B{\rightarrow}A\text{-}homo\ (atom\ a) \quad = refl \\
B{\rightarrow}A\text{-}homo\ (I^{s} \quad) \quad = embed\text{-}I \\
B{\rightarrow}A\text{-}homo\ (e_1 +^{s} e_2) = trans\ embed\text{-}+ \\
\quad (+\text{-}congruent\ (B{\rightarrow}A\text{-}homo\ e_1)\ (B{\rightarrow}A\text{-}homo\ e_2)) \\
B{\rightarrow}A\text{-}homo\ (e_1 \bullet^{s} e_2) \ = trans\ embed\text{-}\bullet \\
\quad (\bullet\text{-}congruent\ (B{\rightarrow}A\text{-}homo\ e_1)\ (B{\rightarrow}A\text{-}homo\ e_2))
\end{array}
$$

$$
\begin{array}{l}
algA : KExpr\ A \rightarrow A \\
algA\ (a\ ^{a}) \quad = a \\
algA\ (I^{s}\ ) \quad = I \\
algA\ (a +^{s} b) = algA\ a + algA\ b \\
algA\ (a \bullet^{s} b) = algA\ a \bullet algA\ b
\end{array}
$$

It can be shown that *Expr* is a functor and *algA* and *algB* are evaluation functions over *Expr* functioning similarly for both types. The following proposition transfers equational proofs over the two types.

$$
\begin{array}{l}
\uparrow^{AB} : \forall\ s_1\ s_2 \rightarrow algA\ (fmap\ B{\rightarrow}A\ s_1) \equiv algA\ (fmap\ B{\rightarrow}A\ s_2) \\
\quad \rightarrow algB\ s_1 \equiv algB\ s_2 \\
\uparrow^{AB}\ a\ b\ algA[fmap\_B \rightarrow A\_a] \equiv algA[fmap\_B \rightarrow A\_a] \ = \\
\quad algB\ a \\
\quad \equiv\langle\ sym\ iso\text{-}fro \ \rangle \\
\quad A{\rightarrow}B\ (B{\rightarrow}A\ (algB\ a)) \\
\quad \equiv\langle\ cong\ A{\rightarrow}B\ (B{\rightarrow}A\text{-}homo\ a) \ \rangle \\
\quad A{\rightarrow}B\ (algA\ (fmap\ B{\rightarrow}A\ a)) \\
\quad \equiv\langle\ cong\ A{\rightarrow}B\ algA[fmap\_B \rightarrow A\_a] \equiv algA[fmap\_B \rightarrow A\_a]\ \rangle \\
\quad A{\rightarrow}B\ (algA\ (fmap\ B{\rightarrow}A\ b)) \\
\quad \equiv\langle\ cong\ A{\rightarrow}B\ (sym\ (B{\rightarrow}A\text{-}homo\ b))\ \rangle \\
\quad A{\rightarrow}B\ (B{\rightarrow}A\ (algB\ b)) \\
\quad \equiv\langle\ iso\text{-}fro \ \rangle \\
\quad algB\ b \\
\quad \blacksquare
\end{array}
$$

For the application we use Peano indexed matrices as we pointed out earlier. We use the general variant of *AMatrix* which admits arbitrary row and column sizes.

$$
\begin{array}{lll}
\textit{data}\ M & : & \textit{Peano} \rightarrow \textit{Peano} \rightarrow \textit{Set} \rightarrow \textit{Set}\ \textit{where} \\
\quad \textit{single} & : & \textit{elem} \rightarrow M\ 0\ 0\ \textit{elem} \\
\quad \textit{row} & : & M\ 0\ 0\ \textit{elem} \rightarrow M\ 0\ n\ \textit{elem} \rightarrow M\ 0\ (\textit{succ}\ n)\ \textit{elem} \\
\quad \textit{column} & : & M\ 0\ 0\ \textit{elem} \rightarrow M\ m\ 0\ \textit{elem} \rightarrow M\ (\textit{succ}\ m)\ 0\ \textit{elem} \\
\quad \textit{block} & : & M\ 0\ 0\ \textit{elem} \rightarrow M\ 0\ n\ \textit{elem} \rightarrow M\ m\ 0\ \textit{elem} \\
\quad\quad \rightarrow & & M\ m\ n\ \textit{elem} \rightarrow M\ (\textit{succ}\ m)\ (\textit{succ}\ n)\ \textit{elem}
\end{array}
$$

What remains is to instantiate this framework accordingly. We instantiate A, B and the two morphisms as follows.

$$
\begin{array}{l}
\textit{cons}^2\ :\ \textit{Matrix}\ 0\ 0\ S \rightarrow \textit{Matrix}\ 0\ m\ S \\
\quad \rightarrow \quad \textit{Matrix}\ n\ 0\ S \rightarrow \textit{Matrix}\ n\ m\ S \rightarrow \textit{Matrix}\ (\textit{succ}\ n)\ (\textit{succ}\ m)\ S \\
\textit{cons}^2\ x\ r\ c\ m\ =\ \textit{block}\ x\ r\ c\ m \\
\textit{tail}_2\ :\ \textit{Matrix}\ (\textit{succ}\ n)\ (\textit{succ}\ m)\ S \rightarrow \textit{Matrix}\ n\ m\ S \\
\textit{tail}_2\ (\textit{block}\ x\ r\ c\ m)\ =\ m \\
\textit{pad}\ m\ =\ \textit{cons}^2\ 1^{M}\ 0^{M}\ 0^{M}\ m
\end{array}
$$

$$
\begin{array}{lll}
A & = & M\ (\textit{succ}\ s)\ \textit{elem} \\
B & = & M\ s\ \textit{elem} \\
B{\rightarrow}A & = & \textit{pad} \\
A{\rightarrow}B & = & \textit{tail} \\
I & = & 1^{M}
\end{array}
$$

We use the two-dimensional variants of *cons* and *tail*. For cons, we pad the matrix by the identity of multiplication precisely at M_{00} and the identity of addition at M_{0i} and M_{i0} for any index i.

To instantiate the rest of the requirements, we require proving four of the semiring axioms for matrices of arbitrary sizes. This is due to the fact that we actually use them to construct the embedding. Note how there is no case for the identity of addition in *Expr* after all. The four required semiring axioms for the matrix type at hand are the following.

$$
\begin{array}{lll}
+^{M}\textit{-left-id} & : & 0^{M} +^{M} M \equiv M \\
+^{M}\textit{-right-id} & : & M +^{M} 0^{M} \equiv M \\
\bot^{M}\textit{-left-absorb-}\bullet & : & M \bullet^{M} 0^{M} \equiv 0^{M} \\
\bot^{M}\textit{-right-absorb-}\bullet & : & 0^{M} \bullet^{M} M \equiv 0^{M}
\end{array}
$$

The implementation for matrix addition is trivial, while the one for multiplication is omitted since we only construct matrices using sub-matrices, and can define it using the textbook rows by columns algorithm.

The detailed proof of the rest of the requirements is included in the Appendix A.5. We only show the concrete types in the following code block. The proof itself is quite lengthy, but is nothing but a mechanical process of applying the semiring axioms. In fact, we can perhaps define a specialized solver using only the four axioms provided to automate the proof.

Note that the proof seems to use the axiom for the identity of the multiplication, but this is only for the case of the zero matrix, which follows from the underlying semiring S of the element type.

$$\begin{aligned}
&\textit{iso-fro} &&: \textit{tail}_2\,(\textit{pad}\ M) &&\equiv M\\
&\textit{embed-I} &&: \textit{pad}\ 1^{\ M} &&\equiv 1^{\ M}\\
&\textit{embed-+} &&: \textit{pad}\ (M_1 +^M M_2) &&\equiv (\textit{pad}\ M_1 +^M \textit{pad}\ M_2)\\
&\textit{embed-}\bullet &&: \textit{pad}\ (M_1 \bullet^M M_2) &&\equiv (\textit{pad}\ M_1 \bullet^M \textit{pad}\ M_2)
\end{aligned}$$

Using this setup, we can for example transfer a proof of associativity as follows.

$$\begin{aligned}
&\bullet^M\textit{-associative} : \forall \{m_1\ m_2\ m_3\ :\ M\ (\textit{succ}\ r)\ (\textit{succ}\ r)\ S\}\\
&\quad \rightarrow (m_1 \bullet^M m_2) \bullet^M m_3 \equiv m_1 \bullet^M (m_2 \bullet^M m_3)\\
&p : \forall \{m_1\ m_2\ m_3\ :\ M\ r\ r\ S\} \rightarrow (m_1 \bullet^M m_2) \bullet^M m_3 \equiv m_1 \bullet^M (m_2 \bullet^M m_3)\\
&p = \uparrow^{AB} ((a^{\ a} \bullet^s b^{\ a}) \bullet^s c^{\ a})\,(a^{\ a} \bullet^s (b^{\ a} \bullet^s c^{\ a}))\ \bullet^M\textit{-associative}
\end{aligned}$$

What this expression gives is a proof of multiplication associativity for matrices of size $n \times n$, given a proof of it for matrices of size $n+1 \times n+1$. We can do the same for any expression which can be constructed from *Expr*. This method can then be inductively extended for a larger matrix of arbitrary size, i.e. transferring the proofs from matrices of dimensions $n+m \times n+m$ to ones of dimensions $n \times n$.

This is essentially a proof of concept that it suffices to prove properties for matrices of the convenient size of $2^{\ n} \times 2^{\ n}$ only, which in principle means that we don't need to tackle the messy details of the rectangular sub-matrices, and can instead focus on the perfectly balanced ones instead. Of course, we would need to prove the properties themselves for the matrices of size $2^{\ n} \times 2^{\ n}$, however, this is a one-time effort.

Unfortunately, the Peano indexed matrices are not the most convenient when it comes to capturing the perfectly balanced matrices. We ideally require a binary number system.

We can attempt using the one-two matrices, but the definition of *cons* and *tail* are no longer as convenient which complicates the proof steps. The definitions are included in the Appendix A.6 for reference. While the proof is doable, it is not nearly as easy as its counterpart for the Peano indexed matrices.

At this point we can opt to use skew binary matrices, however, the way we set them up does not allow constructing the convenient perfectly balanced matrices. This is evident in the *Node-𝟘𝟙* constructor of $SRAL^1$, and is to be expected as skew binary numbers are meant to model lists of perfect trees of size $2^{\ n} - 1$, not $2^{\ n}$. While this is suboptimal, we would still dramatically reduce the required proof effort by using this method since we would have to deal with matrices that have any combination of row and column sizes of $\mathbf{0}\ b\ \mathbb{1}$ and $\mathbf{0}\ b\ \mathbb{1}\ m\ \mathbb{0}s$ only.

Alternatively, we can still amend the skew binary calculations using some ad-hoc steps that don't necessarily respect the underlying number system such that we obtain a perfect sub-division, however, this would yield a datastructure which no longer has constant time increment and decrement operations. For example, we can construct the following mutually recursive sequence type.

```
data SRAL¹ : Skew¹ → Set → Set
data SRAL  : Skew → Set → Set

data SRAL¹ where
  single : elem
           → SRAL¹ 0 b elem
  double : SRAL¹ 0 b elem          → SRAL¹ 0 b elem
           → SRAL¹ (0 b 𝟙) elem
  split  : SRAL¹ (0 b 𝟙 m 𝟘s) elem → SRAL¹ (0 b 𝟙 m 𝟘s) elem
           → SRAL¹ (0 b 𝟙 succ m 𝟘s) elem
  T₁     : SRAL¹ 0 b elem          → SRAL¹ (l 𝟙 succ m 𝟘s) elem
           → SRAL¹ ((l 𝟙 m 𝟘s) 𝟙) elem
  T₂     : SRAL (0 b 𝟚 n 𝟘s) elem  → SRAL¹ (l 𝟙 2 + n + m 𝟘s) elem
           → SRAL¹ ((l 𝟙 m 𝟘s) 𝟙 succ n 𝟘s) elem

data SRAL where
  Node-‵  : SRAL¹ l elem
            → SRAL (l ‵) elem
  Node-𝟚  : SRAL 𝟘 elem                    → SRAL¹ (0 b 𝟙) elem
            → SRAL (0 b 𝟚) elem
  Node-s𝟚 : SRAL¹ (0 b 𝟙 succ m 𝟘s) elem → SRAL (0 b 𝟚 m 𝟘s) elem
            → SRAL (0 b 𝟚 succ m 𝟘s) elem
  Node-𝟙𝟚 : SRAL¹ (0 b 𝟙) elem           → SRAL¹ (l 𝟙 succ m 𝟘s) elem
            → SRAL ((l 𝟙 m 𝟘s) 𝟚) elem
  Node    : SRAL (0 b 𝟚 n 𝟘s) elem → SRAL (0 b 𝟚 n 𝟘s) elem
            → SRAL¹ (l 𝟙 2 + n + m 𝟘s) elem
            → SRAL ((l 𝟙 m 𝟘s) 𝟚 (succ n) 𝟘s) elem
```

This *split* constructor paired with the *Node-‵* constructor allow for modelling a perfectly balanced binary split, if we move to a two-dimensional datastructure based on this scheme, we get perfectly balanced four sub-matrices.

We could overlook the fact that the increment and decrement operations are no longer constant time, since this only applies to the case of the perfectly balanced constructor *split*. This is still better than using the Leibniz based matrices, but certainly not as convenient as the Peano based ones.

Note that maintaining constant time operations allows us to construct a simple solver for doing the otherwise highly mechanical proofs.

The ideal matrix type for this scheme would allow for a trivial implementation of the *cons* and *tail* operations, while still allowing for a perfect subdivision of the $\mathbf{2}^{\,n} \times \mathbf{2}^{\,n}$ sized matrices.

5 Conclusion and Future Work

We have demonstrated various two-dimensional numerical representations and discussed them in the context of semiring frameworks. We set out to find an implementation that is ideally easy to understand and work with, as well as being easy to reason about. Furthermore, we minimized proof effort by exploiting a few axioms of idempotent semirings.

As was pointed out, perfectly balanced matrices are the most convenient to work with in the context of square matrices since they can be modelled without having to deal with rectangular sub-matrices. The go-to way for modelling such matrices typically uses leaf trees, but then again, as we have shown, this is suboptimal for embedding since the underlying number system in this case would typically not allow for trivial implementations of the increment and decrement operations.

In general, it is not necessary to embed the matrices into larger-by-one counterparts, any matrix of larger size suffices, but it is not entirely clear if there is a more convenient setup. It remains to be seen if there is a more convenient datastructure that balances all the requirements.

We mostly focused on constructions based on canonical number systems, however, it is not necessarily required that we take that approach. While such systems yield datastructures that are very easy to define functions over, the datastructures themselves typically have a lot of constructors. Perhaps a balance between a number system which is canonical, and another which does not exhibit much overlap would be ideal in some situations.

Leaf trees were only briefly discussed, however, there has been a lot of focused work done in that area. For example, Kaldewaij and Dielissen [3] have presented various leaf tree variants and their applications. It would be interesting to see how their work could be applied in a similar context as the one here.

Sparse matrices were only briefly mentioned, however, they are a very important topic in the context of block matrices. Perhaps a more detailed discussion on that topic in the context of two-dimensional numerical representations would be beneficial.

We have only considered semirings, however, it is possible to apply the ideas presented here to more complex structures such as closed semirings [5], or Kleene algebras [4].

A Additional Derivations and Proofs

A.1 Deriving PMatrix

```
trieifyPMatrix : ∀ elem → ∀ n → (Fin n → Fin n → elem) ≅ PMatrix n elem
trieifyPMatrix elem zero =
  (Index zero → Fin zero → elem)
  ≅⟨ (Fin-zero ≅→≅ ≅-reflexive) ⟩
  (⊥ → Fin zero → elem)
  ≅⟨ law-of-exponents-⊥ ⟩
  ⊤
  ≅⟨ use-as-definition-empty ⟩
  PMatrix zero elem
  ∎
trieifyPMatrix elem (succ n) =
  (Fin (succ n) → Fin (succ n) → elem)
  ≅⟨ (Fin-succ ≅→≅ (Fin-succ ≅→≅ ≅-reflexive)) ⟩
  (⊤ ⊎ Fin n → ⊤ ⊎ Fin n → elem)
  ≅⟨ (≅-reflexive ≅→≅ law-of-exponents-⊎) ⟩
  (⊤ ⊎ Fin n → (⊤ → elem) × (Fin n → elem))
  ≅⟨ law-of-exponents-⊎ ⟩
  (⊤ → (⊤ → elem) × (Fin n → elem)) × (Fin n → (⊤ → elem) × (Fin n → elem))
  ≅⟨ (→-distributes-× ≅×≅ →-distributes-×) ⟩
  ((⊤ → ⊤ → elem) × (⊤ → Fin n → elem)) ×
  ((Fin n → ⊤ → elem) × (Fin n → Fin n → elem))
  ≅⟨ [A×B]×[C×D]≅A×B×C×D ⟩
    (⊤ → ⊤ → elem) × (⊤ → Fin n → elem)
  × (Fin n → ⊤ → elem) × (Fin n → Fin n → elem)
  ≅⟨ (law-of-exponents-⊤ → ⊤ ≅×≅ (law-of-exponents-⊤
  ≅×≅ ((≅-reflexive ≅→≅ law-of-exponents-⊤) ≅×≅ ≅-reflexive))) ⟩
  elem × (Fin n → elem) × (Fin n → elem) × (Fin n → Fin n → elem)
  ≅⟨ (≅-reflexive ≅×≅
     (trieify elem n ≅×≅ (trieify elem n ≅×≅ trieifyPMatrix elem n))) ⟩
  elem × Array n elem × Array n elem × PMatrix n elem
  ≅⟨ use-as-definition-block ⟩
  PMatrix (succ n) elem
  ∎
```

A.2 Braun Matrices

```
data BM : Leibniz → Leibniz → Set → Set where
  scalar  : e → BM 0b 0b e
  column1 : BM l 0b e → BM l 0b e → BM (l 1) 0b e
  column2 : BM (lsucc l) 0b e → BM l 0b e → BM (l 2) 0b e
  row1    : BM 0b l e → BM 0b l e → BM 0b (l 1) e
  row2    : BM 0b (lsucc l) e → BM 0b l e → BM 0b (l 2) e
  block21 : BM (lsucc l1) l2 e → BM (lsucc l1) l2 e
   →        BM l1 l2 e → BM l1 l2 e
   →        BM (l1 2) (l2 1) e
  block12 : BM l1 (lsucc l2) e → BM l1 l2 e
   →        BM l1 (lsucc l2) e → BM l1 l2 e
   →        BM (l1 1) (l2 2) e
  block22 : BM (lsucc l1) (lsucc l2) e → BM (lsucc l1) l2 e
   →        BM l1 (lsucc l2) e → BM l1 l2 e
   →        BM (l1 2) (l2 2) e
  block11 : BM l1 l2 e → BM l1 l2 e
   →        BM l1 l2 e → BM l1 l2 e
   →        BM (l1 1) (l2 1) e
```

A.3 Skew Binary Index Derivations

```
{-# TERMINATING #-}
re-index¹ : ∀ l m → Fin (ℕ⟦ l 𝟙 m 0s ⟧¹) ≅ SkewIndex¹ (l 𝟙 m 0s)
re-index¹ 0 b zero =
  Fin 1
  ≅⟨ Fin − 1 ⟩
  ⊤
  ≅⟨ use − as − definition − 0b𝟙 ⟩
  SkewIndex¹ (0 b 𝟙)
  ∎
re-index¹ 0 b (succ m) =
  Fin (succ (succ (succ (2 ↑ succ m ∸ 2 · 2))))
  ≅⟨ ≅ −symmetric (Fin − m + n ≅ Fin − n + Fin − m 3 (2 ↑ succ m ∸ 2 · 2)) ⟩
  Fin 3 ⊎ Fin (2 ↑ succ m ∸ 2 · 2)
  ≅⟨ ≅ −reflexive ≅ ⊎ ≅ Fin − 2 · n ≅ Fin − n ⊎ Fin − n ⟩
  Fin 3 ⊎ Fin 2 ↑ succ m ∸ 2 ⊎ Fin 2 ↑ succ m ∸ 2
  ≅⟨ rebalance − fin ⟩
  ⊤ ⊎ Fin 2 ↑ succ m ∸ 1 ⊎ Fin 2 ↑ succ m ∸ 1
  ≅⟨ ≅ −reflexive ≅ ⊎ ≅ re-index¹ 0 b m ≅ ⊎ ≅ re-index¹ 0 b m ⟩
  ⊤ ⊎ SkewIndex¹ (0 b 𝟙 m 0s) ⊎ SkewIndex¹ (0 b 𝟙 m 0s)
  ≅⟨ use − as − definition − 0b𝟙sm0s ⟩
  SkewIndex¹ (0 b 𝟙 succ m 0s)
  ∎
re-index¹ (l 𝟙 x 0s) m =
  Fin (2 ↑ succ m ∸ 1 + ℕ⟦ l 𝟙 succ (m + x) 0s ⟧¹)
  ≅⟨ ≅ −symmetric
      (Fin − m + n ≅ Fin − n + Fin − m 2 ↑ succ m ∸ 1 ℕ⟦ l 𝟙 succ (m + x) 0s ⟧¹) ⟩
  Fin 2 ↑ succ m ∸ 1 ⊎ Fin ℕ⟦ l 𝟙 succ (m + x) 0s ⟧¹
  ≅⟨ re-index¹ 0 b m ≅ ⊎ ≅ re-index¹ l (succ (m + x)) ⟩
  SkewIndex¹ (0 b 𝟙 m 0s) ⊎ SkewIndex¹ (l 𝟙 succ (m + x) 0s)
  ≅⟨ use − as − definition − l𝟙𝟙 ⟩
  SkewIndex¹ ((l 𝟙 x 0s) 𝟙 m 0s)
  ∎


re-index : ∀ s → AtMost ℕ⟦ s ⟧ ≅ SkewIndex s
re-index 𝟘 =
  AtMost zero
  ≅⟨ AtMost − n ≅ ⊤ ⊎ Fin − n ⟩
  Fin 1
  ≅⟨ re-index¹ 0 b zero ⟩
  SkewIndex¹ (0 b 𝟙)
  ≅⟨ use − as − definition − 0 ⟩
  SkewIndex 𝟘
  ∎
re-index ((l 𝟙 n 0s) ⁾) =
  AtMost ℕ⟦ l 𝟙 n 0s ⟧¹
  ≅⟨ AtMost − n ≅ ⊤ ⊎ Fin − n ⟩
```

```
  Fin (succ ℕ⟦ l 𝟙 n 0s ⟧^1)
  ≅⟨ Fin-succ ⟩
  ⊤ ⊎ Fin ℕ⟦ l 𝟙 n 0s ⟧^1
  ≅⟨ ≅ −reflexive ≅ ⊎ ≅ re-index^1 l n ⟩
  ⊤ ⊎ SkewIndex^1 (l 𝟙 n 0s)
  ≅⟨ ≅ −symmetric Fin − 1 ≅ ⊎ ≅ ≅ −reflexive ⟩
  Fin 1 ⊎ SkewIndex^1 (l 𝟙 n 0s)
  ≅⟨ re-index^1 0 b zero ≅ ⊎ ≅ ≅ −reflexive ⟩
  SkewIndex^1 (0 b 𝟙) ⊎ SkewIndex^1 (l 𝟙 n 0s)
  ≅⟨ use − as − definition − 𝟙' ⟩
  SkewIndex ((l 𝟙 n 0s) ')
  ∎
re-index (0 b 2 n 0s) =
  AtMost (succ (succ (2 ↑ succ n ∸ 2 · 2)))
  ≅⟨ AtMost − n ≅ ⊤ ⊎ Fin − n ⟩
  Fin (succ (succ (succ (2 ↑ succ n ∸ 2 · 2))))
  ≅⟨ re-index^1 0 b (succ n) ⟩
  SkewIndex^1 (0 b 𝟙 succ n 0s)
  ≅⟨ use − as − definition − 0b2 ⟩
  SkewIndex (0 b 2 n 0s)
  ∎
re-index ((l 𝟙 x 0s) 2 n 0s) =
  AtMost (succ (succ ((2 ↑ succ n ∸ 2 · 2) + ℕ⟦ l 𝟙 succ (n + x) 0s ⟧^1)))
  ≅⟨ AtMost − n ≅ ⊤ ⊎ Fin − n ⟩
  Fin (succ (succ (succ ((2 ↑ succ n ∸ 2 · 2) + ℕ⟦ l 𝟙 succ (n + x) 0s ⟧^1))))
  ≅⟨ ≅ −symmetric
     (Fin − m + n ≅ Fin − n + Fin − m 3 ((2 ↑ succ n ∸ 2 · 2) + ℕ⟦ l 𝟙 succ (n + x) 0s ⟧^1)) ⟩
  Fin 3 ⊎ Fin ((2 ↑ succ n ∸ 2 · 2) + ℕ⟦ l 𝟙 succ (n + x) 0s ⟧^1)
  ≅⟨ ≅ −reflexive ≅ ⊎ ≅ ≅ −symmetric
     (Fin − m + n ≅ Fin − n + Fin − m (2 ↑ succ n ∸ 2 · 2) ℕ⟦ l 𝟙 succ (n + x) 0s ⟧^1) ⟩
  Fin 3 ⊎ Fin (2 ↑ succ n ∸ 2 · 2) ⊎ Fin ℕ⟦ l 𝟙 succ (n + x) 0s ⟧^1
  ≅⟨ ≅ −reflexive ≅ ⊎ ≅ Fin − 2 · n ≅ Fin − n ⊎ Fin − n ≅ ⊎ ≅ ≅ −reflexive ⟩
  Fin 3 ⊎ (Fin 2 ↑ succ n ∸ 2 ⊎ Fin 2 ↑ succ n ∸ 2) ⊎ Fin ℕ⟦ l 𝟙 succ (n + x) 0s ⟧^1
  ≅⟨ rebalance − fin ⟩
  Fin 1 ⊎ (Fin 2 ↑ succ n ∸ 1 ⊎ Fin 2 ↑ succ n ∸ 1) ⊎ Fin ℕ⟦ l 𝟙 succ (n + x) 0s ⟧^1
  ≅⟨ Fin − 1 ≅ ⊎ ≅ ≅ −symmetric Fin − 2^sn ∸ 2 ≅ Fin − 2^n ∸ 1 ⊎ Fin − 2^n ∸ 1
     ≅ ⊎ ≅ ≅ −reflexive ⟩
  ⊤ ⊎ Fin 2 ↑ succ (succ n) ∸ 2 ⊎ Fin ℕ⟦ l 𝟙 succ (n + x) 0s ⟧^1
  ≅⟨ ≅ −symmetric ⊎ − associative ⟩
  (⊤ ⊎ Fin 2 ↑ succ (succ n) ∸ 2) ⊎ Fin ℕ⟦ l 𝟙 succ (n + x) 0s ⟧^1
  ≅⟨ (≅ −symmetric Fin-succ) ≅ ⊎ ≅ ≅ −reflexive ⟩
  Fin (2 ↑ succ (succ n) ∸ 1) ⊎ Fin ℕ⟦ l 𝟙 succ (n + x) 0s ⟧^1
  ≅⟨ re-index^1 0 b (1 + n) ≅ ⊎ ≅ re-index^1 l (1 + n + x) ⟩
  SkewIndex^1 (0 b 𝟙 1 + n 0s) ⊎ SkewIndex^1 (l 𝟙 1 + n + x 0s)
  ≅⟨ use − as − definition − l𝟙2 ⟩
  SkewIndex ((l 𝟙 x 0s) 2 n 0s)
  ∎
```

A.4 Skew Binary Matrix

```
data SRAL¹2D : Skew¹ → Skew¹ → Set → Set where
  scalar : elem → SRAL¹2D (0 b 1) (0 b 1) elem
  row1 : SRAL¹2D (0 b 1) (0 b 1) elem          → SRAL¹2D (0 b 1) (0 b 1 m 0s) elem
    →    SRAL¹2D (0 b 1) (0 b 1 m 0s) elem → SRAL¹2D (0 b 1) (0 b 1 succ m 0s) elem
  col1 : SRAL¹2D (0 b 1) (0 b 1) elem          → SRAL¹2D (0 b 1 m 0s) (0 b 1) elem
    →    SRAL¹2D (0 b 1 m 0s) (0 b 1) elem → SRAL¹2D (0 b 1 succ m 0s) (0 b 1) elem
  row2 : SRAL¹2D (0 b 1) (0 b 1 n 0s) elem
    →    SRAL¹2D (0 b 1) (l 1 succ (n + m) 0s) elem
    →    SRAL¹2D (0 b 1) ((l 1 m 0s) 1 n 0s) elem
  col2 : SRAL¹2D (0 b 1 n 0s) (0 b 1) elem
    →    SRAL¹2D (l 1 succ (n + m) 0s) (0 b 1) elem
    →    SRAL¹2D ((l 1 m 0s) 1 n 0s) (0 b 1) elem
  block0 : SRAL¹2D (0 b 1) (0 b 1) elem
    →      SRAL¹2D (0 b 1) (0 b 1 n 0s) elem
    →      SRAL¹2D (0 b 1) (0 b 1 n 0s) elem
    →      SRAL¹2D (0 b 1 m 0s) (0 b 1) elem
    →      SRAL¹2D (0 b 1 m 0s) (0 b 1 n 0s) elem
    →      SRAL¹2D (0 b 1 m 0s) (0 b 1 n 0s) elem
    →      SRAL¹2D (0 b 1 m 0s) (0 b 1) elem
    →      SRAL¹2D (0 b 1 m 0s) (0 b 1 n 0s) elem
    →      SRAL¹2D (0 b 1 m 0s) (0 b 1 n 0s) elem
    →      SRAL¹2D (0 b 1 succ m 0s) (0 b 1 succ n 0s) elem
  block1 : SRAL¹2D (0 b 1) (0 b 1 n 0s) elem
    →      SRAL¹2D (0 b 1) (l 1 succ (n + m) 0s) elem
    →      SRAL¹2D (0 b 1 k 0s) (0 b 1 n 0s) elem
    →      SRAL¹2D (0 b 1 k 0s) (l 1 succ (n + m) 0s) elem
    →      SRAL¹2D (0 b 1 k 0s) (0 b 1 n 0s) elem
    →      SRAL¹2D (0 b 1 k 0s) (l 1 succ (n + m) 0s) elem
    →      SRAL¹2D (0 b 1 succ k 0s) ((l 1 m 0s) 1 n 0s) elem
  block2 : SRAL¹2D (0 b 1 n 0s) (0 b 1) elem
    →      SRAL¹2D (0 b 1 n 0s) (0 b 1 k 0s) elem
    →      SRAL¹2D (0 b 1 n 0s) (0 b 1 k 0s) elem
    →      SRAL¹2D (l 1 succ (n + m) 0s) (0 b 1) elem
    →      SRAL¹2D (l 1 succ (n + m) 0s) (0 b 1 k 0s) elem
    →      SRAL¹2D (l 1 succ (n + m) 0s) (0 b 1 k 0s) elem
    →      SRAL¹2D ((l 1 m 0s) 1 n 0s) (0 b 1 succ k 0s) elem
  block3 : SRAL¹2D (0 b 1 n 0s) (0 b 1 k 0s) elem
    →      SRAL¹2D (0 b 1 n 0s) (l2 1 succ (k + h) 0s) elem
    →      SRAL¹2D (l1 1 succ (n + m) 0s) (0 b 1 k 0s) elem
    →      SRAL¹2D (l1 1 succ (n + m) 0s) (l2 1 succ (k + h) 0s) elem
    →      SRAL¹2D ((l1 1 m 0s) 1 n 0s) ((l2 1 h 0s) 1 k 0s) elem
data SRAL2D : Skew → Set → Set where
  Node-0' : SRAL¹2D (0 b 1) (0 b 1) elem     → SRAL2D 0 elem
  Node-1' : SRAL¹2D (0 b 1) (0 b 1) elem     → SRAL¹2D (0 b 1) (l 1 n 0s) elem
    →       SRAL¹2D (l 1 n 0s) (0 b 1) elem → SRAL¹2D (l 1 n 0s) (l 1 n 0s) elem
    →       SRAL2D (l 1 n 0s ') elem
  Node-02 : SRAL¹2D (0 b 1 succ n 0s) (0 b 1 succ n 0s) elem → SRAL2D (0 b 2 n 0s) elem
  Node-12 : SRAL¹2D (0 b 1 succ n 0s) (0 b 1 succ n 0s) elem
    →       SRAL¹2D (0 b 1 succ n 0s) (l 1 succ (n + m) 0s) elem
    →       SRAL¹2D (l 1 succ (n + m) 0s) (0 b 1 succ n 0s) elem
    →       SRAL¹2D (l 1 succ (n + m) 0s) (l 1 succ (n + m) 0s) elem
    →       SRAL2D ((l 1 m 0s) 2 n 0s) elem
```

A.5 Proof of Embedding

```
iso-fro : tail2 (pad M) ≡ M
iso-fro = refl
embed-I : pad 1^M ≡ 1^M
embed-I {zero} = refl
embed-I {succ m} = refl
embed-+ : pad (M1 +^M M2) ≡ (pad M1 +^M pad M2)
embed-+ {M1 = single x} {M2 = single y}
  = block − cong (cong single (sym +-idempotent))
    (cong single (sym +-idempotent))
    (cong single (sym +-idempotent))
    refl
embed-+ {M1 = block x a1 a2 m1} {M2 = block y b1 b2 m2}
  = block − cong (cong single (sym +-idempotent))
    (cong2 row (cong single (sym +-idempotent)) (sym +^M-left-id))
    (cong2 column (cong single (sym +-idempotent)) (sym +^M-left-id))
    refl
embed-• : pad (M1 •^M M2) ≡ (pad M1 •^M pad M2)
embed-• {M1 = single x} {single y}
  = block − cong
    (cong single (sym (trans
        (cong2 _+_ •-left-id ⊥−left−absorb−•) +-right-id)))
    (cong single (sym (trans
        (cong2 _+_ ⊥−left−absorb−• ⊥−right−absorb−•) +-left-id)))
    (cong single (sym (trans
        (cong2 _+_ ⊥−right−absorb−• ⊥−left−absorb−•) +-left-id)))
    (cong single (sym (trans
        (cong2 _+_ ⊥−left−absorb−• refl) +-left-id)))
embed-• {M1 = block x a1 a2 m1} {M2 = block y b1 b2 m2}
  = block − cong
    (sym (trans (cong2 _+^M_ (cong single •-left-id)
      (trans (cong2 _+^M_ (cong single ⊥−left−absorb−•)
      (⊥^M-left-absorb-•)) +^M-left-id)) (cong single +-right-id)))
    (sym (trans (cong2 row (cong2 _+^M_ (cong single ⊥−left−absorb−•)
      (trans (cong2 _+^M_ (⊥^M-right-absorb-• zero y)
        (⊥^M-right-absorb-• n b2)) +^M-right-id))
      (cong2 _+^M_ (⊥^M-left-absorb-• 0 1^M)
        (cong2 _+^M_ (⊥^M-right-absorb-• 0 b1) (⊥^M-right-absorb-• n m2))))
        (cong2 row (cong single +-left-id) (trans +^M-left-id +^M-left-id))))
    (sym (trans (cong2 _+^M_ (cong2 column (cong single ⊥−right−absorb−•)
      (⊥^M-right-absorb-• 0 1^M))
      (cong2 column (cong2 _+^M_ (⊥^M-left-absorb-• 0 x)
        (⊥^M-left-absorb-• n a1))
        (cong2 _+^M_ (⊥^M-left-absorb-• 0 a2) (⊥^M-left-absorb-• n m1))))
        (cong2 column (trans +^M-left-id +^M-left-id)
          (trans +^M-left-id +^M-left-id))))
    (block-congruent
      (sym (trans (cong2 _+^M_
        (cong single ⊥−right−absorb−•) refl) +^M-left-id))
      (sym (trans (cong2 _+^M_
        (⊥^M-left-absorb-• 0 0^M) refl) +^M-left-id))
      (sym (trans (cong2 _+^M_
        (⊥^M-left-absorb-• 0 0^M) refl) +^M-left-id))
      (sym (trans (cong2 _+^M_
        (⊥^M-left-absorb-• 0 0^M) refl) +^M-left-id)))
```

A.6 Cons and Tail for One-Two Matrices

```
data Pack (l : Leibniz) (A : Set) : Set where
  p : Matrix 0b 0b A →      Matrix 0b l A
    → Matrix l  0b A →      Matrix l  l A → Pack l A
↓ : Pack l A → Matrix l l A
↓ (p _ _ _ m) = m

ex : Matrix (lsucc r) (lsucc r) KS → Pack r KS
ex {0b} (block11 (scalar a) (scalar b) (scalar c) (scalar d))
  = p (scalar a) (scalar b) (scalar c) (scalar d)
ex {r 1} (block22 m1 m2 a1 b1 x b2 a2 m3 m4)
  = p x (row1 a1 a2) (column1 b1 b2) (block11 m1 m2 m3 m4)
ex {r 2} (block11 a b c d) with ex a | ex b | ex c | ex d
... | p x arr3 arr1 m1 | p x2 arr4 m4 m2 | p x1 m3 arr2 m7 | p x3 m6 m5 m8
  = p x (row2 arr3 x2 arr4)
        (column2 arr1 x1 arr2)
        (block22 m1 m2 m3 m4 x3 m5 m6 m7 m8)

cons2 : Pack r KS → Matrix (lsucc r) (lsucc r) KS
cons2 (p (scalar a) (scalar b) (scalar c) (scalar d))
  = block11 (scalar a) (scalar b) (scalar c) (scalar d)
cons2 (p x (row1 arr3 arr4)
           (column1 arr1 arr2)
           (block11 m1 m2 m3 m4))
  = block22 m1 m2 arr3 arr1 x arr2 arr4 m3 m4
cons2 (p x (row2 arr3 x2 arr4) (column2 arr1 x1 arr2)
  (block22 m1 m2 m3 m4 x3 m5 m6 m7 m8))
  = block11 (cons2 (p x arr3 arr1 m1))
            (cons2 (p x2 arr4 m4 m2))
            (cons2 (p x1 m3 arr2 m7))
            (cons2 (p x3 m6 m5  m8))

pad : Matrix r r KS → Matrix (lsucc r) (lsucc r) KS
pad a = cons2 (p (scalar I) ⊥M ⊥M a)

tail2 : Matrix (lsucc r) (lsucc r) KS → Matrix r r KS
tail2 p = ↓ (ex p)
```

References

1. Hinze, R.: Manufacturing datatypes. J. Funct. Program. **11**, 493–524 (2001). https://doi.org/10.1017/S095679680100404X
2. Hinze, R., Swierstra, W.: Calculating datastructures. In: Mathematics of Program Construction: 14th International Conference, MPC 2022, Tbilisi, Georgia, September 26–28, 2022, Proceedings, pp. 62–101. Springer, Heidelberg (2022). https://doi.org/10.1007/978-3-031-16912-0_3
3. Kaldewaij, A., Dielissen, V.J.: Leaf trees. Sci. Comput. Program. **26**(1–3), 149–165 (1996). https://doi.org/10.1016/0167-6423(95)00026-7
4. Kozen, D.: A completeness theorem for Kleene algebras and the algebra of regular events. Inf. Comput. **110**, 214–225 (1991). https://doi.org/10.1109/LICS.1991.151646
5. Lehmann, D.J.: Algebraic structures for transitive closure. Theoretical Comput. Sci. **4**(1), 59–76 (1977). https://doi.org/10.1016/0304-3975(77)90056-1
6. Myers, E.W.: An applicative random-access stack. Inf. Process. Lett. **17**(5), 241–248 (1983). https://doi.org/10.1016/0020-0190(83)90106-0
7. Norell, U.: Towards a practical programming language based on dependent type theory. Ph.D. thesis, Chalmers University of Technology and Göteborg University (2007). https://research.chalmers.se/en/publication/46311

8. Okasaki, C.: From fast exponentiation to square matrices: an adventure in types. In: Proceedings of the Fourth ACM SIGPLAN International Conference on Functional Programming, ICFP '99, pp. 28–35. Association for Computing Machinery, New York (1999). https://doi.org/10.1145/317636.317781
9. Okasaki, C.: Purely Functional Data Structures. Cambridge University Press, USA (1999). https://doi.org/10.1017/CBO9780511530104
10. Sandberg Eriksson, A., Jansson, P.: An Agda formalisation of the transitive closure of block matrices (extended abstract). In: Proceedings of the 1st International Workshop on Type-Driven Development, TyDe 2016, pp. 60–61. Association for Computing Machinery, New York (2016). https://doi.org/10.1145/2976022.2976025

Program Synthesis

Synthesizing Accumulative Functions Via Program Transformation

Junyu Lin(✉) and Akimasa Morihata

The University of Tokyo, Komaba 3-8-1, Meguro, Tokyo, Japan
lin-junyu108@g.ecc.u-tokyo.ac.jp, morihata@graco.c.u-tokyo.ac.jp

Abstract. Accumulative functions, such as tail-recursive functions, employ accumulation parameters to carry and update the intermediate results. Despite their ubiquity and importance for efficient implementations, the automatic synthesis of accumulative functions remains challenging. The presence of accumulative parameters not only expands the search space but also unfastens the input-output examples from the traces of recursive calls, leading existing program synthesis methods to either fail in generating nontrivial accumulative functions or rely on pre-provided skeletons of recursive calls with accumulations. In this paper, we investigate an alternative approach to synthesizing accumulative functions. Our strategy integrates an off-the-shelf synthesizer, which may not inherently produce accumulative functions, and a program transformation that derives accumulative functions from non-accumulative ones. We specifically focus on the transformation introduced by Kühnemann et al. (RTA 2001), which effectively derives accumulative functions if the non-accumulative ones consist of substitution operators. By guiding the synthesizer to use substitution operators, we aim to obtain functions suitable for the transformation. We demonstrate the ability of our approach with examples from existing benchmarks.

Keywords: Program synthesis · Accumulative function · Program transformation

1 Introduction

Accumulative functions refer to a type of function that uses an accumulator to keep track of and update the intermediate results as part of a computation. A typical example is the tail-recursive function. For instance, the following *tail_reverse* serves as a tail-recursive, linear-time variant of the non-accumulative

J. Gibbons (Ed.): TFP 2025, LNCS 15652, pp. 359–377, 2026.
https://doi.org/10.1007/978-3-031-99751-8_15

quadratic-time *reverse* function, using the list concatenation function *append*.

$$\begin{aligned} reverse\ [] &= [] \\ reverse\ (x :: xs) &= append\ (reverse\ xs)\ (x :: []) \\ append\ []\ y &= y \\ append\ (x :: xs)\ y &= x :: append\ xs\ y \end{aligned}$$

$$\begin{aligned} tail\_reverse\ x &= tail\_reverse_1\ x\ [] \\ tail\_reverse_1\ []\ y &= y \\ tail\_reverse_1\ (x :: xs)\ y &= tail\_reverse_1\ xs\ (x :: y) \end{aligned}$$

In recent years, recursive function synthesis has become a significant research area [1,6,8,11,13–16,21]. Some methods leverage the programming-by-example (PBE) paradigm due to the simplicity and accessibility of input-output examples for specifying program behavior. These methods generally depend on recursive traces, and some of them [1,16] even require *trace-complete* examples, consisting of all input-output pairs in a recursion trace. For example, consider a set of input-output examples for the *reverse* function, $\{[1,2] \to [2,1], [2] \to [2], [] \to []\}$, where $x \to y$ denotes inputting x to the function must result in y. This is complete for the recursion trace of *reverse* $[1,2]$ and hence allows candidate expressions to be searched directly. We cannot only immediately know *reverse* $[] = []$ but also easily guess the right-hand side for *reverse* $[1,2]$ to be an expression to calculate $[2,1]$ from 1 and $[2]$, since the subcomputation, *reverse* $[2]$ results in $[2]$. Other methods [13,21] do not explicitly use trace-complete examples, but they attempt to reconstruct complete traces during synthesis.

Unfortunately, the trace-based approach mentioned above hardly applies to accumulative functions. For example, the *tail_reverse* function involves the auxiliary recursive function, $tail\_reverse_1$, whose synthesis may necessitate its trace-complete examples with the accumulator y, say $\{([1,2],[]) \to [2,1], ([2],[1]) \to [2,1], ([],[2,1]) \to [2,1]\}$. However, it is difficult to infer such input-output examples for the auxiliary function from those for the top-level function, namely *tail_reverse*.

Some synthesizers [6,8,14] can produce accumulative functions with a user-provide recursion pattern, which is either a recursion skeleton [6], or a partial implementation with holes, called program sketching [8,14]. For example, the following is a sketch for synthesizing *tail_reverse*, in which ?? denotes holes.

$$\begin{aligned} tail\_reverse\ x &= tail\_reverse_1\ x\ ?? \\ tail\_reverse_1\ []\ y &= ?? \\ tail\_reverse_1\ (x :: xs)\ y &= tail\_reverse_1\ xs\ ?? \end{aligned}$$

However, preparing an appropriate sketch is in general non-trivial. A sketch with a too-large hole will fail in the synthesis, whereas one specifying a too-detailed computation structure inhibits the benefit of automatic synthesis. We can hardly know in advance what level of detail is necessary for a successful synthesis.

In this paper, we address the synthesis of accumulative functions, considering an alternate approach via program transformation. We focus on the method by Kühnemann et al. [12], which can automatically derive an accumulative function by eliminating a special kind of operator, called substitution operator. We begin the synthesis process with preparing a set of substitution operators. Next, we instruct the synthesizer to construct a non-accumulative recursive function consisting of the substitution operator. Finally, we transform the obtained function into accumulative versions. In our approach, the synthesizer avoids the complexity of introducing accumulative auxiliary function and does not rely on a pre-provided program skeleton.

To evaluate the promise of our approach, we collected benchmark examples from a state-of-the-art synthesis approach PARA [8] and conducted an experiment. We employed TRIO [13], which is a state-of-the-art PBE-based synthesizer, and SMYTH [14], a famous sketch-based synthesizer, as the underlying synthesizer. Our approach could synthesize 8 out of 10 accumulative versions of the benchmark functions, whereas existing synthesizers without the transformation were less successful. For example, SMYTH succeeded in only 2 cases if provided modest sketches and 6 even when sketches contained fairly detailed information.

In summary, our paper makes the following contributions.

- We investigate an approach that synthesizes an accumulative function via program transformation. The approach consists of a synthesis of a non-accumulative program and a transformation into an accumulative one.
- We take examples from existing benchmark programs to demonstrate the ability of our approach. The result shows our approach can synthesize natural accumulative functions for several examples.

The rest of the paper is organized as follows. Section 2 provides the background, including substitution operators and the transformation method by Kühnemann et al. Section 3 details the experiments conducted. Section 4 discusses related work. Finally, Sect. 5 serves as the conclusion and outlines directions for future work.

2 Background

In this section, we present the approach proposed by Kühnemann et al. We begin by introducing modular tree transducers, on which their method is formalized. We then turn to two key components used in the algorithm: substitution modules and the *Yield* module. Finally, we describe the transformation algorithm step by step.

2.1 Modular Tree Transducer

Kühnemann et al. introduced a transformation method based on modular tree transducers (ModT) [5]. Modular tree transducer is an extension of macro tree transducer (MTT) [4]. A macro tree transducer can be considered as a recursive first-order functional program over trees. We can define an MTT as below. We assume that f is a function name, c is a tree constructor, x_i, y_i are variables and r is the right-hand side. We only consider total deterministic MTTs.

$$
\begin{aligned}
\mathit{prog} &:= \mathit{decl} \cdots \mathit{decl} \\
\mathit{decl} &:= f\ (c\ x_1 \cdots x_n)\ y_1 \cdots y_m = r \\
r &:= x_i \mid y_i \mid c\ r \cdots r \mid f\ x_i\ r \cdots r
\end{aligned}
$$

An n-modular tree transducer (n-ModT) is a hierarchy $(m_1, \dots, m_n)$ of modules. Each module m_i $(i \leq n)$ forms an MTT except that its function may call functions defined in the modules $m_{i+1}, \dots, m_n$ as if they are constructors.

From the definition, 1-ModT is an MTT, and *reverse* is a 2-ModT since it contains 2 modules: *reverse* and *append*. And *tail_reverse* is an MTT because it consists of only a single module containing both *tail_reverse* and *tail_reverse₁*.

2.2 Substitution Module and *Yield* Module

The transformation by Kühnemann et al. automatically composes the two modules of a 2-ModT (m_1, m_2) to an MTT if m_2 is a special module, called a *substitution module*, and m_1 is non-accumulative. The resulting MTT is accumulative, and hence, we can use the transformation to obtain accumulative functions.

A substitution module consists of substitution functions and provides a mechanism for substituting accumulation parameters with some leaves. Let $\pi_1, \dots, \pi_n$ be a series of distinct constructors. Given $i, j \in \mathbb{N}$ and $j \leq i \leq n$, sub_i is a substitution function defined below, where c is a constructor other than $\pi_1, \dots, \pi_i$.

$$
\mathit{sub}_i\ \pi_j\ y_1\ \cdots\ y_i = y_j \tag{1}
$$

$$
\mathit{sub}_i (c\ r_1\ \cdots\ r_k)\ y_1\ \cdots\ y_i = c\ (\mathit{sub}_i\ r_1\ y_1\ \cdots\ y_i)\ \cdots\ (\mathit{sub}_i\ r_k\ y_1\ \cdots\ y_i) \tag{2}
$$

For example, recall the *append* module defined below.

$$
\begin{aligned}
\mathit{append}\ []\ y &= y \\
\mathit{append}\ (x :: xs)\ y &= x :: \mathit{append}\ xs\ y
\end{aligned}
$$

It forms a substitution module, where $\mathit{append} = \mathit{sub}_1$ and $\pi_1 = []$[1].

A *Yield* module translates an expression in which the tree substitution operations are symbolically represented, into the tree it denotes. The following is the

[1] Strictly speaking, we must regard $(x ::)$ as a constructor; otherwise *append* must traverse x as well, which looks like containing a type error. We disregard this kind of minor adjustment between ModTs and functional programs.

definition of each function, $Yield_n$ ($n \in \mathbb{N}$), in a *Yield* module. We use sub_i to denote the symbolic representation of the substitution as well so as to make its connection to substitution functions obvious.

$$Yield_n\ \pi_i\ y_i \cdots y_n = y_i \tag{3}$$

$$\begin{aligned} Yield_n\ (c\ x_1 \cdots x_k)\ y_1\ \cdots\ y_n &= \\ &c\ (Yield_n\ x_1\ y_1 \cdots y_n) \cdots (Yield_n\ x_k\ y_1 \cdots y_n) \end{aligned} \tag{4}$$

$$\begin{aligned} Yield_n\ (sub_m\ x\ y_1 \cdots y_m)\ y'_1 \cdots y'_n &= \\ &Yield_m\ x\ (Yield_n\ y_1\ y'_1 \cdots y'_n) \cdots (Yield_n\ y_m\ y'_1 \cdots y'_n) \end{aligned} \tag{5}$$

2.3 Transformation Algorithm

We explain the transformation by Künemann et al. with taking *reverse* defined below as an example.

$$\begin{aligned} reverse\ [] &= [] \\ reverse\ (x :: xs) &= append\ (reverse\ xs)\ (x :: []) \end{aligned}$$

Freezing. The first step is preparing a new function f' (here, $reverse'$) by substituting the substitution functions (here, *append*) with new constructors sub_1. We call this step freezing and the new constructors frozen functions.

$$\begin{aligned} reverse'\ [] &= [] \\ reverse'\ (x :: xs) &= sub_1\ (reverse'\ xs)\ (x :: []) \end{aligned}$$

Introducing *Yield* Module. After freezing, $reverse'$ becomes an MTT but sub_1 does not perform the "append" operation. To recover the original computation, we introduce the *Yield* module defined as follows.

$$\begin{aligned} Yield_0\ [] &= [] \\ Yield_0\ (sub_1\ xs\ y) &= Yield_1\ xs\ y \\ Yield_1\ []\ y &= y \\ Yield_1\ (sub_1\ xs\ y)\ y' &= Yield_1\ xs\ (Yield_1\ y\ y') \end{aligned}$$

Note $reverse\ xs = Yield_0\ (reverse'\ xs)$ holds from the construction of $reverse'$.

Deforestation. $Yield_0\ (reverse'\ xs)$ is still inefficient because the *Yield* module recursively traverses and reconstructs the tree generated by $reverse'$. We eliminate this inefficiency by applying deforestation [20] that eliminates intermediate lists and trees.

For example, we compose the second line of $reverse'$ and $Yield_i$ functions via the unfolding-folding approach [3]. Assume composing $reverse'$ and $Yield_i$ is

$reverse_i$.

$$\begin{aligned} reverse_1\ (x :: xs)\ y &= Yield_1\ (reverse'\ (x :: xs)\ y) \\ &= Yield_1\ (sub_1\ (reverse'\ xs)\ (x :: []))\ y \\ &= Yield_1\ (reverse'\ xs)\ (Yield_1\ (x :: [])\ y) \\ &= reverse_1\ xs\ (x :: y) \end{aligned}$$

Other parts are obtained similarly. Eventually, we get the following accumulative function.

$$\begin{aligned} reverse_0\ [] &= [] \\ reverse_0\ (x :: xs) &= reverse_1\ xs\ (x :: []) \end{aligned}$$

$$\begin{aligned} reverse_1\ []\ y &= y \\ reverse_1 (x :: xs)\ y &= reverse_1\ xs\ (x :: y) \end{aligned}$$

Compared with the original function, this function has a linear time complexity. Hence, we successfully derive an efficient accumulative variant of *reverse*.

3 Accumulative Function Synthesis via Transformation

3.1 Experiment Setup

We implemented our approach as follows. We first inputted the definitions of substitution operators and input-output examples (10 pairs) to TRIO [13] to obtain a non-accumulative recursive function. Then, we manually applied the transformation described in Sect. 2 if possible.

Since TRIO is not template-based, we do not expect TRIO alone to successfully synthesize accumulative programs with some exceptions discussed in Sect. 3.4. Hence, we did not conduct a detailed experiment in this direction.

For comparison, we select SMYTH [14], which is one of the most famous template-based synthesizers. It can generate accumulative programs if an accumulative partial program (sketch) is given. We inputted the same substitution operators and input-output examples as the case of TRIO as well as three different types of sketches. The first type contains the top definition of the function without any detailed sketches (Fig. 1, left). The second contains the top definition of the function and initialization of the accumulator as the new program sketch (Fig. 1, middle). The third additionally contains the base-case expressions (Fig. 1, right). In addition, we also experimented with the ability to synthesize non-accumulative functions.

In either case, the synthesis is regarded as a failure when the synthesizer executes time out (max 300 s) or outputs wrong answers.

```
let f0 x y =
  let rec
     f1 x y a = ??
  in f1 x ??
```

```
let f0 x y =
  let rec
     f1 x y a = ??
  in f1 x Z
```

```
let f0 x y =
  let rec
     f1 x y a =
        match x with
          | Z ->
             a
          | S n ->
              ??
  in f1 x Z
```

Fig. 1. Three types of sketches for `nat_mul`

3.2 Benchmark Examples

We exhaustively picked up examples for which accumulative implementations are natural and efficient from the benchmark used in the state-of-the-art study [8] and obtained 10 functions. Detailed definitions of the functions experimented are provided in Appendix A. They can be divided into three categories: three natural number functions (`nat_mul`, `nat_exp`, and `nat_factorial`), two list functions (`list_sum` and `list_reverse`), and five tree functions (`tree_preorder`, `tree_inorder`, `tree_postorder`, `tree_count_leaves`, and `tree_count_nodes`).

3.3 Experimental Results

Table 1 summarizes the results of our experiments. The "operator" column shows the substitution operators we inputted. Our approach is denoted by "non-acc", in which we instruct the synthesizer to generate a recursive function that uses substitution operators. For this case, we regard successful only when the transformation applies to the obtained function. "w/ base case" and "w/o base case" respectively use the third and second types of sketches mentioned in Sect. 3.1. We omitted the case using the first, simplest type of sketches because this approach failed for all examples. The mark ✓ denotes the method successfully synthesizes an accumulative version of the target function. The mark ✓✗ means the method fails to synthesize with the original setup but succeeds after increasing the number of input-output examples to 20 pairs.

Regardless of the underlying synthesizer, our approach could synthesize 8 out of 10 benchmark functions but timed out in `nat_exp` and `nat_factorial` with the original setup. SMYTH successfully generated 6 benchmark functions when the base-case expression was specified and only succeeded 2 functions without the base-case expression.

In what follows, we pick one example for each category and analyze it in detail. For our approach, we show the non-accumulative output from TRIO and then the result after transformation. For comparison, we show sketches (where ?? denotes the hole) inputted to SMYTH. For better readability, we avoid showing cryptic programs obtained from the synthesizers and omit the input-output examples.

Table 1. Result of experiments

function (operator)	**TRIO**	**SMYTH** (non-acc)	**SMYTH** (w/ base case)	**SMYTH** (w/o base case)
`nat_mul` (add)	✓	✓	✓	
`nat_exp` (add, mul)				
`nat_factorial` (add, mul)	✓✗			
`list_sum` (add)	✓	✓	✓	✓
`list_reverse` (append)	✓	✓	✓	✓
`tree_preorder` (append)	✓	✓	✓	
`tree_inorder` (append)	✓	✓	✓	
`tree_postorder` (append)	✓	✓	✓	
`tree_count_leaves` (add)	✓	✓		
`tree_count_nodes` (add)	✓	✓		

Natural Number Functions: Here we pick `nat_mul`, whose objective is to multiply two natural numbers. The substitution operator `add` below is supplied to the synthesizers.

```
let rec add m n =
    match m with
    | Z -> n
    | S m1 -> S (add m1 n)
```

TRIO could generate the following program.

```
let rec f x y =
    match x with
    | Z -> y
    | S x1 -> add (f x1 y) y
```

Then eliminating `add` makes it accumulative. In this function, `a` is the accumulator, increasing `y` in every recursive call.

```
let rec f0 x y =
  match x with
    | Z -> x
    | S n -> f1 n y y

and f1 x y a =
  match x with
    | Z -> a
    | S n -> f1 n y (add y a)
```

The three sketches for SMYTH have been shown in Fig. 1. SMYTH could generate accumulative `nat_mul` only for the third, most detailed sketch.

List Functions. To synthesize the list_reverse function, we specified append as a substitution operator.

Then TRIO outputted the non-accumulative list_reverse.

```
let rec f x =
    match x with
    | [] -> x
    | Cons (x, xs) -> append (f xs) (Cons(x, []))
```

After applying the transformation, we obtain the accumulative version of list_reverse, in which y is the accumulator.

```
let rec f0 x =
  match x with
    | [] -> []
    | Cons (x, xs) -> f1 xs (Cons(x, []))
and
f1 x y =
  match x with
    | [] -> y
    | Cons (x, xs) -> f1 xs (Cons(x, y))
```

SMYTH failed to synthesize accumulative list_reverse from the abstract sketch that only consists of function top definition.

```
let f0 x =
  let rec f1 x y = ??
  in f1 x ??
```

SMYTH synthesized accumulative list_reverse successfully after specifying the initial accumulation value.

```
let f0 x =
  let rec f1 x y = ??
  in f1 x []
```

Tree Functions. We take tree_preorder function as an example on tree functions. We inputted the specification with a substitution operator append as the same as the case of reverse.

TRIO outputted the following program.

```
let rec f x =
    match x with
    | Leaf -> []
    | Node(l, v, r) -> append (Cons(v, (f l))) (f r)
```

Then, we eliminate append to obtain accumulative tree_preorder, in which y is the accumulator.

```
let rec f0 x =
  match x with
  | Leaf -> []
  | Node(l, v, r) -> Cons (v, (f1 l (f0 r)))

and f1 x y =
  match x with
  | Leaf -> y
  | Node(l, v, r) -> Cons (v, (f1 l (f1 r y)))
```

SMYTH failed to synthesize accumulative `tree_preorder` from the following sketch that contains only the top definition of the function.

```
let f0 x =
  let rec f1 x y = ??
  in f1 x ??
```

Specifying the initial accumulation was still insufficient for synthesizing accumulative `tree_preorder`.

```
let f0 x =
  let rec f1 x y = ??
  in f1 x []
```

SMYTH could fill the hole when the sketch contains the base-case expression in addition to the initial accumulation value. Also, this is the simplest sketch for SMYTH to output the accumulative `tree_preorder`.

```
let f0 x =
  let rec f1 x y =
    match x with
      | Leaf -> y
      | Node(l, v, r)-> ??
  in f1 x []
```

3.4 Discussions

In our approach, SMYTH and TRIO exhibited similar performance. This performance was better than that of SMYTH to synthesize accumulative functions from sketches. The key to success is the full use of the algebraic property of the substitution operators via the program transformation. Moreover, substitution operators are shared in most examples, being only three in total. The sharing is natural because each datatype involves only a few substitution operators. In total, our approach is a promising alternative method for synthesizing accumulative functions.

SMYTH failed in most examples if the sketch did not contain the base-case; moreover, even when using the sketch with a base-case, it was less successful than our approach. This result suggests the inherent difficulty of synthesizing accumulative functions in the template-based approach. Preparing an appropriate sketch is generally nontrivial. For example, even though `count_tree_nodes` and `count_tree_leaves` are similar computations, their base cases are different. Detailed sketches tend to be more problem-specific, and we need to prepare one for each problem.

We can sometimes obtain accumulative functions by supplying the synthesizer with higher-order functions that specify the recursion pattern. For instance, supplying `fold` (a.k.a., `fold_left` or `foldl`) enables TRIO or SMYTH to synthesize `list_sum` = `fold add Z`. However, this approach does not seem to scale to nontrivial functions. First, there are many such higher-order functions, including those for left-to-right, right-to-left, top-down, etc. Second, synthesizing appropriate parameters for such a higher-order function tends to be nontrivial. For instance, consider `list_reverse` = `fold (fun r a -> append r (a :: [])) []`, in which the first parameter for `fold` must be a new function. Synthesizers generally do not prefer to introduce new functions (or, equivalently, lambda abstractions) to avoid the endless expansion of the search space. In short, this higher-order-function-based approach seems less effective than template-based approaches.

The `nat_exp` and `nat_factorial` functions rely on the multiplication operator, `mul`. Unfortunately, `mul` is not the substitution operator on natural numbers because $\texttt{mul}\ x\ (\texttt{S}\ y) \neq \texttt{S}\ (\texttt{mul}\ x\ y)$. Hence, naively applying the transformation eliminates only `add`, which is the subcomputation of `mul`, and makes only `mul`, i.e., neither `nat_exp` nor `nat_factorial`, accumulative. To synthesize accumulative `nat_exp` and `nat_factorial`, we must regard `mul` as a substitution operator. In fact we can, as `mul` satisfies the following equations.

$$\begin{aligned} \texttt{mul}\ (\texttt{S Z})\ z &= z \\ \texttt{mul}\ (\texttt{add}\ x\ y)\ z &= \texttt{add}\ (\texttt{mul}\ x\ z)\ (\texttt{mul}\ y\ z) \end{aligned}$$

That is, `mul` is a substitution operator if `add` and `S Z` are the constructors. This observation reminds us of the study by Voigtländer [18]. He proposed a method of eliminating `reverse` and `map` in addition to `append`. Further study, including characterization of eliminatable operators and integration to the program synthesis, is a future work.

4 Related Work

4.1 Recursive Program Synthesis

Recently, many approaches for recursive program synthesis have been proposed. TRIO [13] proposes two techniques for synthesizing recursive programs. The block-based pruning enables us to reject imperfect candidates of the recursive program by checking consistency with blocks (non-recursive expressions). The library sampling accelerates synthesis using library functions (i.e. user-provided external operators) by sampling their behaviors. SYRUP [21] uses recursion traces to build a trace-indexed version space algebra and select candidates by trace-based ranking function. BURST [15] firstly uses angelic semantics to enable bottom-up synthesis of recursive functions. Despite these impressive developments, they cannot synthesize accumulative recursive functions unless an accumulative recursion pattern is explicitly specified.

Among others, we selected TRIO as the underlying synthesizer of our approach mainly because of its excellent capability of user-defined external operators, which our approach must instruct the synthesizer to use. TRIO naturally accepts even complicated external operators, including those defined as recursive functions, as a part of the specification of the synthesis. Moreover, its library-sampling approach may reduce the cost of dealing with complex external operators. In addition, we anticipate that search-based synthesizers (including TRIO) might be preferable to constraint-solving-based ones. In the former, defining an appropriate search precedence may enable us to prioritize the use of substitution operators. In contrast, in the latter, the synthesis process is usually hidden behind the constraint solver, making it more difficult to control. We leave detailed analysis and experiments on this issue as future work.

Nevertheless, our approach is not specialized in TRIO. We have already observed that SMYTH performs similarly to TRIO and hence anticipate the suitability of other synthesizers including BURST and SYRUP. However, adopting SYRUP is not very straightforward because SYRUP requires defining the external operator as a logical formula understandable by the underlying SMT solver.

CYPRESS [11] synthesizes recursive programs by cyclic program synthesis approach, which can discover recursive auxiliaries based on cyclic proofs. Auxiliaries, such as `tail_reverse1` for `tail_reverse`, are often essential for developing accumulative programs. However, because the main specification of CYPRESS limits auxiliary recursive procedures without extra parameters, CYPRESS is unable to synthesize programs with accumulator parameters.

SYNDUCE [6] synthesizes a recursive function from a reference implementation that works on different data types. SYNDUCE uses a recursion template to limit the recursion strategy. It can generate accumulative functions by supplying an appropriate template. SMYTH [14] is also a template-based program synthesizer. Given a partial program with holes, i.e. a *template*, it finds the program fragment to fill the holes with iterative forward-backward abstract interpretation obtained by computing possible output (input) with corresponding input (output).

PARA [8] is another sketch-based synthesizer that uses paramorphisms. Paramorphism is a recursive pattern that allows you to not only fold a data structure but also access the rest of the original data structure during the recursion. Similar to SMYTH, it finds program fragments to fill holes in the pre-provided template. Paramorphisms and accumulation appear to be orthogonal: the former enables extracting information from remaining unprocessed elements, whereas the latter focuses on maintaining additional information about elements already processed. Detailed comparison and cooperation is future work.

4.2 Accumulation

Transformational developments of accumulative functions, called *accumulation*, have been studied for a long time. They may be categorized into two approaches.

One approach [9,17] aims at manually (or semi-automatically) driving non-trivial programs and algorithms, including the pioneering work by Bird [2]. This approach is generally difficult to coordinate with program synthesizers because it provides less feedback on what kind of programs the accumulation is more likely to succeed.

The other approach, sometimes called *deforestation* [20], eliminates intermediate data structures passed between functions. It is known that deforestation concerning some kinds of functions, the list concatenation operator in particular, leads to accumulative programs [7,10,19]. The transformation by Kühnemann et al. [12], which we have employed, generalizes the observation to arbitrary substitution operators. The key is the algebraic property of substitution operators similar to the associativity, which is known to be useful for accumulation. The transformation is better suited for cooperation with program synthesizers because prioritizing substitution operators will likely lead to successful accumulation. It is worth noting that we can use a further generalization developed by Voigtländer [18], which can eliminate the reverse and map functions in addition to the substitution operators.

5 Conclusion and Future Works

In this paper, we present an alternative approach to synthesizing accumulative recursive programs using the transformation developed by Kühnemann et al. Our method avoids the complexities inherent in directly synthesizing accumulative programs. The experiment demonstrates the strong probability of our approach to outperform template-based approaches to obtain accumulative functions.

The scalability of our approach depends on the transformation's capability to deal with substitution operators and the synthesizer's ability of non-accumulative function synthesis. For further improvement, it seems important to guide the synthesizer to generate the function that is suitable for transformation (for example, prioritize the use of substitution operators). We plan to investigate a system for supporting the integration of program synthesis and transformations.

Acknowledgements. We appreciate instructive comments from reviewers and attendees of TFP 2025 and PPL 2024. This research was supported by JSPS Kakenhi Grant Number 23K11044.

A Benchmark Functions

This appendix provides the details of the benchmark functions used in our experiments.

A.1 Operators

In the experiments, we used **add**, **mul**, **append** as the external operator to synthesize functions. Their definition is as follows.

```
let rec add m n =
    match m with
    | Z -> n
    | S m1 -> S (add m1 n)
```

```
let rec mul x y =
    match x with
    | Z -> y
    | S x1 -> add (mul x1 y) y
```

```
let rec append l1 l2 =
    match l1 with
    | [] -> l2
    | Cons (h,t) -> Cons(h, append t l2)
```

A.2 nat_mul function

The non-accumulative nat_mul function is defined as follows.

```
let rec f x y =
    match x with
    | Z -> y
    | S x1 -> add (f x1 y) y
```

The accumulative nat_mul function is defined as follows.

```
let f0 x y =
  let rec f1 x y a =
    match x with
      | Z -> a
      | S n -> f1 n y (add y a)
   in f1 x Z
```

A.3 nat_exp function

The non-accumulative nat_exp function is defined as follows.

```
let rec f x y =
    match y with
    | Z -> S Z
    | S y1 -> mul x (f x y1)
```

The accumulative nat_exp function is defined as follows.

```
let f0 x y =
  let rec f1 x y a =
    match y with
      | Z -> a
      | S n -> f1 x n (mul x a)
   in f1 x y (S Z)
```

A.4 nat_factorial function

The non-accumulative nat_factorial function is defined as follows.

```
let rec f x =
    match x with
    | Z -> S Z
    | S x1 -> mul x (f x1)
```

The accumulative nat_factorial function is defined as follows.

```
let f0 x =
  let rec f1 x a =
    match x with
      | Z -> a
      | S n -> f1 n (mul x a)
   in f1 x (S Z)
```

A.5 list_sum function

The non-accumulative list_sum function is defined as follows.

```
let rec f x =
    match x with
    | [] -> Z
    | Cons(x, xs) -> add x (f xs)
```

The accumulative list_sum function is defined as follows.

```
let f0 x =
  let rec f1 x a =
    match x with
      | [] -> a
      | Cons(x, xs) -> f1 xs (add x a)
   in f1 x Z
```

A.6 list_reverse function

The non-accumulative list_reverse function is defined as follows.

```
let rec f x =
    match x with
    | [] -> x
    | Cons(x, xs) -> append (f xs) (Cons(x, []))
```

The accumulative list_reverse function is defined as follows.

```
let f0 x =
  let rec f1 x a =
    match x with
    | [] -> a
    | Cons (x, xs) -> f1 xs (Cons(x, a))
  in f1 x []
```

A.7 tree_preorder function

The non-accumulative tree_preorder function is defined as follows.

```
let rec f x =
    match x with
    | Leaf -> []
    | Node(l, v, r) -> append (Cons(v, (f l))) (f r)
```

The accumulative tree_preorder function is defined as follows.

```
let f0 x =
  let rec f1 x y =
    match x with
      | Leaf -> a
      | Node(l, v, r)-> Cons (v, (f1 l (f1 r a)))
  in f1 x []
```

A.8 tree_inorder function

The non-accumulative tree_inorder function is defined as follows.

```
let rec f x =
    match x with
    | Leaf -> []
    | Node(l, v, r) -> append (f l) (Cons(v, (f r)))
```

The accumulative tree_inorder function is defined as follows.

```
let f0 x =
  let rec f1 x a =
    match x with
      | Leaf -> a
      | Node(l, v, r)-> f1 r (Cons(v, (f1 l a)))
  in f1 x []
```

A.9 tree_postorder function

The non-accumulative tree_postorder function is defined as follows.

```
let rec f x =
    match x with
    | Leaf -> []
    | Node(l, v, r) -> append (f l) (Cons((f r), v))
```

The accumulative tree_postorder function is defined as follows.

```
let f0 x =
  let rec f1 x a =
    match x with
      | Leaf -> a
      | Node(l, v, r)-> Cons(v, f1 r (f1 l a)))
  in f1 x []
```

A.10 tree_count_leaves function

The non-accumulative tree_count_leaves function is defined as follows.

```
let rec f x =
    match x with
    | Leaf -> S Z
    | Node(l, v, r) -> add (f l) (f r)
```

The accumulative tree_count_leaves function is defined as follows.

```
let f0 x =
  let rec f1 x a =
    match x with
      | Leaf -> a
      | Node(l, v, r)-> f1 l (add (f1 r) a)
  in f1 x (S Z)
```

A.11 tree_count_nodes function

The non-accumulative tree_count_nodes function is defined as follows.

```
let rec f x =
    match x with
    | Leaf -> Z
    | Node(l, v, r) -> S (add (f l) (f r))
```

The accumulative tree_count_nodes function is defined as follows.

```
let f0 x =
  let rec f1 x a =
    match x with
      | Leaf -> a
      | Node(l, v, r)-> S (f1 l (add (f1 r) a))
  in f1 x Z
```

References

1. Albarghouthi, A., Gulwani, S., Kincaid, Z.: Recursive program synthesis. In: Sharygina, N., Veith, H. (eds.) Computer Aided Verification: 25th International Conference, pp. 934–950. CAV 2013, Saint Petersburg, Russia (2013). https://doi.org/10.1007/978-3-642-39799-8_67
2. Bird, R.S.: The promotion and accumulation strategies in transformational programming. ACM Trans. Program. Lang. Syst. **6**(4), 487–504 (1984). https://doi.org/10.1145/1780.1781
3. Burstall, R.M., Darlington, J.: A transformation system for developing recursive programs. J. ACM **24**(1), 44–67 (1977). https://doi.org/10.1145/321992.321996
4. Engelfriet, J., Vogler, H.: Macro tree transducers. J. Comput. Syst. Sci. **31**(1), 71–146 (1985). https://doi.org/10.1016/0022-0000(85)90066-2
5. Engelfriet, J., Vogler, H.: Modular tree transducers. Theoret. Comput. Sci. **78**(2), 267–303 (1991). https://doi.org/10.1016/0304-3975(91)90353-4
6. Farzan, A., Nicolet, V.: Counterexample-guided partial bounding for recursive function synthesis. In: Silva, A., Leino, K.R.M. (eds.) Computer Aided Verification: 33rd International Conference. CAV 2021, vol. 12759, pp. 832–855. Virtual Event (2021). https://doi.org/10.1007/978-3-030-81685-8_39
7. Gill, A.J.: Cheap deforestation for non-strict functional languages. Ph.D. thesis, University of Glasgow (1996)
8. Hong, Q., Aiken, A.: Recursive Program Synthesis using Paramorphisms. In: Proceedings of the ACM on Programming Languages. PLDI, vol. 8, pp. 102–125 (2024). https://doi.org/10.1145/3656381
9. Hu, Z., Iwasaki, H., Takeichi, M.: Calculating Accumulations. New Gener. Comput. **17**(2), 153–173 (1999). https://doi.org/10.1007/BF03037434
10. Hughes, R.J.M.: A novel representation of lists and its application to the function "reverse." Inf. Process. Lett. **22**(3), 141–144 (1986). https://doi.org/10.1016/0020-0190(86)90059-1
11. Itzhaky, S., Peleg, H., Polikarpova, N., Rowe, R.N.S., Sergey, I.: Cyclic program synthesis. In: Proceedings of the 42nd ACM SIGPLAN International Conference on Programming Language Design and Implementation, pp. 944–959 (2021). https://doi.org/10.1145/3453483.3454087

12. Kühnemann, A., Glück, R., Kakehi, K.: Relating accumulative and non-accumulative functional programs. In: Middeldorp, A. (ed.) RTA 2001. LNCS, vol. 2051, pp. 154–168. Springer, Heidelberg (2001). https://doi.org/10.1007/3-540-45127-7_13
13. Lee, W., Cho, H.: Inductive synthesis of structurally recursive functional programs from non-recursive expressions. In: Proceedings of the ACM on Programming Languages. POPL, vol. 7, pp. 2048–2078 (2023). https://doi.org/10.1145/3571263
14. Lubin, J., Collins, N., Omar, C., Chugh, R.: Program sketching with live bidirectional evaluation. In: Proceedings of the ACM on Programming Languages. ICFP, vol. 4, pp. 1–29 (2020). https://doi.org/10.1145/3408991
15. Miltner, A., Nuñez, A.T., Brendel, A., Chaudhuri, S., Dillig, I.: Bottom-up synthesis of recursive functional programs using angelic execution. In: Proceedings of the ACM on Programming Languages. POPL, vol. 6, pp. 1–29 (2022). https://doi.org/10.1145/3498682
16. Osera, P.M., Zdancewic, S.: Type-and-example-directed program synthesis. In: Proceedings of the 36th ACM SIGPLAN Conference on Programming Language Design and Implementation, pp. 619–630 (2015). https://doi.org/10.1145/2737924.2738007
17. Pettorossi, A., Proietti, M.: Rules and strategies for transforming functional and logic programs. ACM Comput. Surv. **28**(2), 360–414 (1996). https://doi.org/10.1145/234528.234529
18. Voigtländer, J.: Concatenate, reverse and map vanish for free. In: Wand, M., Jones, S.L.P. (eds.) Proceedings of the Seventh ACM SIGPLAN International Conference on Functional Programming, pp. 14–25. ICFP (2002). https://doi.org/10.1145/581478.581481
19. Wadler, P.: The Concatenate Vanishes. Glasgow University, Dept of Computer Science (1987)
20. Wadler, P.: Deforestation: transforming programs to eliminate trees. Theor. Comput. Sci. **73**(2), 231–248 (1990). https://doi.org/10.1016/0304-3975(90)90147-A
21. Yuan, Y., Radhakrishna, A., Samanta, R.: Trace-guided inductive synthesis of recursive functional programs. In: Proceedings of the ACM on Programming Languages. PLDI, vol. 7, pp. 860–883 (2023). https://doi.org/10.1145/3591255

Alpha Beta Pruning with the Selection Monad

Johannes Hartmann(✉)

Department of Computer Science, University of Oxford, Oxford, UK
Johannes.Hartmann@cs.ox.ac.uk

Abstract. In this paper, we explore how the selection monad, widely studied in the context of sequential games, can be extended to support the alpha-beta pruning algorithm. The selection monad provides an elegant implementation of the minimax algorithm, commonly used to determine the best move in two-player games with perfect information. However, the minimax algorithm becomes inefficient for large game trees due to computational complexity. Alpha-beta pruning is a well-known optimization that reduces the number of nodes evaluated in the minimax algorithm. We present a general implementation of the alpha-beta pruning algorithm utilizing the selection monad and demonstrate its application on a simple example tree. Additionally, we show how the alpha-beta pruning algorithm can be implemented using the generalized selection monad, enhancing the efficiency of game tree evaluations.

Keywords: Selection monad · Functional programming · Algorithm design · Performance Optimisation · Monads · Alpha Beta Pruning

1 Introduction

In this paper, we investigate how the selection monad can be extended to support the alpha-beta pruning optimization for the minimax algorithm. The selection monad has been widely studied in the context of sequential games [1–4, 7, 9], offering an elegant way to model algorithms that explore search trees. In its simplest form, it performs a depth-first traversal, evaluating every node independently before selecting the optimal path. However, this naive approach does not take advantage of contextual information that could improve efficiency.

To provide the necessary background, we begin with a brief introduction to the selection monad. A more detailed exploration can be found in prior work [2,5]. The core concept underlying this monad is the notion of selection functions that are functions of type $(A \to R) \to A$. Given a function that evaluates elements of type A according to some criterion R , a selection function returns the optimal A value based on that criterion. These selection functions form a monad, allowing them to be composed using the standard sequencing operation for monads.

J. Gibbons (Ed.): TFP 2025, LNCS 15652, pp. 378–391, 2026.
https://doi.org/10.1007/978-3-031-99751-8_16

In the context of sequential 2-player games, we can represent a playthrough as a sequence of moves, with the outcome of the game expressed as an integer: higher values favor player 1, while lower values favor player 2. The minimax algorithm provides a method for determining an optimal playthrough by recursively evaluating the game tree. Player 1 aims to maximize the outcome, while player 2 seeks to minimize it. This process follows a depth-first exploration, alternating between selecting the maximum and minimum values at each level of the tree.

However, evaluating every possible move and countermove is computationally expensive, especially for large game trees. The alpha-beta pruning algorithm optimizes minimax by eliminating branches that cannot influence the final result, significantly reducing the number of nodes explored while still guaranteeing an optimal outcome.

The remainder of this paper is structured as follows: we first introduce the alpha-beta pruning algorithm and its mechanics. We then demonstrate how the selection monad can be extended to incorporate alpha-beta pruning, providing a general implementation and applying it to a simple example tree. Through this approach, we aim to bridge the gap between functional representations of game-tree exploration and efficient game-solving techniques.

2 Alpha Beta Pruning

To understand alpha-beta pruning, consider the following game tree:

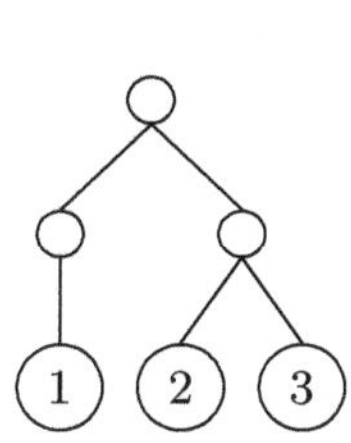

Suppose we have alternating minimizing and maximizing functions exploring a tree in a depth-first manner, starting at the root node as the minimizing function. When evaluating the left child of the root (a maximizer), we examine its children and return the maximum value—1 in this case. Returning to the root, we then explore the right child. A naive minimax algorithm would evaluate all children, but after evaluating the first child with a value of 2, we know that the minimizing parent already has a better option. Thus, the remainder of the branch is pruned. This is the fundamental idea behind alpha-beta pruning.

Expanding on this example, alpha-beta pruning operates by maintaining two values, alpha and beta, which represent the best values encountered so far by the maximizing and minimizing functions, respectively. If the maximizing function encounters a value greater than beta, it can stop evaluating further children, as the minimizing function above would never choose this branch. Similarly, if the minimizing function encounters a value lower than alpha, it can prune the remaining children, as the maximizing function above would never select this part of the tree.

Pruning the search tree in this manner can significantly reduce the number of nodes evaluated, particularly in large game trees, leading to a more efficient search algorithm while still guaranteeing an optimal result.

Although alpha-beta pruning is a well-established optimization of the minimax algorithm, it has not been studied in the context of the selection monad. In the following section, we demonstrate how the selection monad can be extended to support the alpha-beta pruning algorithm.

3 Alpha Beta Pruning with the Selection Monad

In this section, we demonstrate how the selection monad can be extended to support the alpha-beta pruning algorithm. We provide a general implementation of the alpha-beta pruning algorithm using the selection monad and illustrate its application to a simple example tree.

First, we show how the selection monad J can be used to implement a basic minimax algorithm.

3.1 General J Setup

A selection function J is a function with the following type signature:

```
type J r a = (a -> r) -> a
```

Selection functions form a monad in the following way:

```
(>>=) :: J r a -> (a -> J r b) -> J r b
(>>=) e f p = f (e (p . flip f p)) p

return :: a -> J r a
return x p = x
```

The Haskell standard library provides a *sequence* function for monads, which, given a list of monadic values, returns a monadic list of these values. In the case of the selection function J, the sequence function can be defined as follows:

```
sequence :: [J r a] -> J r [a]
sequence [] = return []
sequence (e:es) = e >>=
                  \x -> sequence es >>=
                  \xs -> return (x:xs)
```

In the context of sequential games, we can interpret a selection function as a function that chooses the best move based on a given predicate. Furthermore, since we often track a history of previously played moves, we can use this history to determine the available options and select the optimal one. To accommodate this, we extend the *sequence* function to take a history as an additional argument:

```
hSequenceJ :: [a] -> [[a] -> J r a] -> J r [a]
hSequenceJ h []       = return []
hSequenceJ h (ma:mas) = ma h >>=
                        \x -> hSequenceJ (h ++ [x]) mas >>=
                        \xs -> return (x:xs)
```

It is important to note that the monadic behavior of selection functions is only relevant for the sequence function; we do not utilize their monadic properties beyond this context.

Next, consider the following two selection functions, which choose the optimal value from a list according to a given evaluation function:

```
maxWithJ :: Ord r => [a] -> J r a
maxWithJ xs f = foldr1 (\x y -> if f x >= f y then x else y) xs

minWithJ :: Ord r => [a] -> J r a
minWithJ xs f = foldr1 (\x y -> if f x < f y then x else y) xs
```

Using these selection functions, we can implement a minimax algorithm as a sequence of alternating *minWithJ* and *maxWithJ* selections:

```
optimalGame = hSequenceJ [] (take 5 all) p
  where
    all :: Ord r => [[a] -> J r a]
    all = (minWithJ . nextMoves) : (maxWithJ . nextMoves) : all
```

where *nextMoves* is a function that returns the possible moves based on the history of previously played moves:

```
nextMoves :: [a] -> [a]
nextMoves = undefined
```

This approach effectively performs a brute-force search of the game tree, selecting the path that represents an optimal strategy.

However, due to the exhaustive nature of brute-force search—evaluating every possible move and counter-move—the minimax algorithm is computationally expensive for large game trees, exhibiting exponential time complexity. The alpha-beta pruning algorithm is a well-known optimization that significantly reduces the search space, improving efficiency while maintaining optimality.

3.2 Alpha Beta Pruning Min and Max functions:

We begin with the implementation of a simple maximum function. The function updates the alpha bound as it traverses the list and short-circuits if the maximum meets the beta bound.

```
maxAB :: Ord a => (a, a) -> a -> [a] -> a
maxAB (a,b) v []     = v
maxAB (a,b) v (x:xs) = if x >= b
                       then x
                       else maxAB (max a x, b) (max v x) xs
```

This function takes initial values for alpha and beta, the current best value, and a list of candidate values. It returns the best value while respecting the alpha-beta bounds.

We can now extend this function into a selection function by introducing a predicate function to evaluate the values:

```
maxWithAB :: Ord r => (r, r) -> a -> [a] -> J r a
maxWithAB (a,b) v [] p     = v
maxWithAB (a,b) v (x:xs) p = let v' = if p x > p v then x else v
                                in if p x >= b
                                   then v'
                                   else maxWithAB (max a (p x),b) v' xs p
```

However, this function does not conform to the established pattern of the selection monad. Additionally, it applies the predicate function twice per iteration, increasing computational complexity.

To implement alpha-beta pruning within the selection monad, we must carry the alpha and beta values alongside the current value. Since selection functions have limited access to external values, we attach the alpha and beta values directly to each candidate value.

We thus define maxWithABJ, a function that takes a list of values, each paired with their corresponding alpha and beta bounds, and a predicate function p of type $(R, R, A) \rightarrow R$ which evaluates each candidate. The alpha-beta pruning behavior is incorporated by checking whether each candidate's corresponding R value falls within the alpha-beta bounds. If a value exceeds the beta bound, the search is terminated early, returning the best value found so far. Additionally, the alpha and beta values are updated accordingly throughout the search process.

```
maxWithABJ :: Ord r => [(r, r, a)] -> J r (r, r, a)
maxWithABJ ((a, b, x) : xs) p = let r = p (a, b, x) in
           if r >= b then (a,b,x) else go (max a r, b) (r, (a, b, x)) xs
  where
   go _ best [] = snd best
   go (a, b) (rBest, best) ((_, _, x') : xs) =
     let r                = p (a, b, x')
         (rNew, newBest) = if rBest >= r
                            then (rBest, best)
                            else (r, (a, b, x'))
     in if r >= b then newBest else go (max a r, b) (rNew, newBest) xs

minWithABJ :: Ord r => [(r, r, a)] -> J r (r, r, a)
minWithABJ ((a, b, x) : xs) p = let r = p (a, b, x) in
           if r <= a then (a,b,x) else go (a, min b r) (r, (a, b, x)) xs
  where
   go _ best [] = snd best
   go (a, b) (rBest, best) ((_, _, x') : xs) =
     let r                = p (a, b, x')
         (rNew, newBest) = if rBest < r
                            then (rBest, best)
                            else (r, (a, b, x'))
     in if r < b then newBest else go (a,min r b) (rNew, newBest) xs
```

The second part of the alpha-beta pruning process involves ensuring that the correct alpha and beta values are passed to the next selection function. To understand how this is achieved, we now consider a basic example.

4 Example

In this example, we construct a simple game tree without incorporating any specific game logic. The tree is defined as follows:

4.1 Tree Setup

```
data Tree a = B a [Tree a] | L a deriving Show
```

A tree is either a branch (B) with a label and a list of child trees or a leaf (L) containing a value. While labels are not strictly necessary, we include them to later identify paths through the tree.

To apply the minimax algorithm, we need a function that determines the possible next moves based on a given path through the tree. Given a sequence of moves from the start of the game, the function nextNodes returns the possible next moves from the current position.

```
nextNodes :: Eq a => Tree a -> [a] -> [a]
nextNodes (L x) []           = [x]
nextNodes (L x) _            = []
nextNodes (B a cs) []        = [a]
nextNodes (B a cs) [x]       = if x == a then values cs else []
nextNodes (B a cs) (x:y:xs) = if x /= a
                               then []
                               else nextNodes (findNode y cs) (y:xs)
```

Additionally, we need a function that, given a label and a list of trees, finds and returns the tree corresponding to that label:

```
findNode :: Eq a => a -> [Tree a] -> Tree a
findNode a ((L x):xs)     | a == x     = L x
                          | otherwise = findNode a xs
findNode a ((B x cs):xs) | a == x     = B x cs
                          | otherwise = findNode a xs
```

To extract the values of all leaves in a list of trees, we define:

```
values :: [Tree a] -> [a]
values []            = []
values ((B x _):xs) = x : values xs
values ((L x ):xs)  = x : values xs
```

Now, let us consider an example tree:

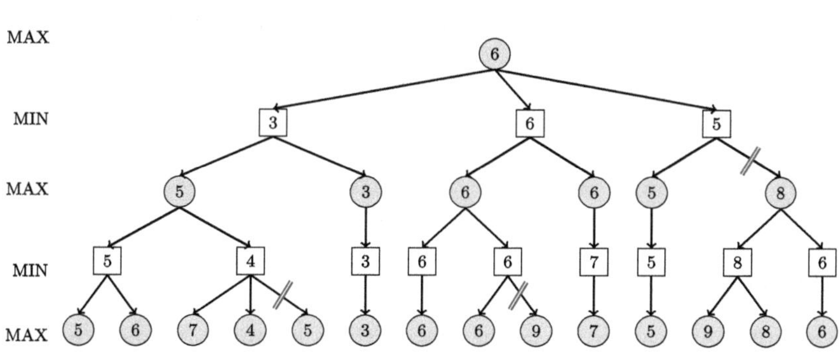

Fig. 1. Example tree [10]

Which can be represented in Haskell as follows:

```
x :: Tree Int
x = B 1 [
      B 2 [
        B 3 [
          B 4 [L 5, L 6],
```

```
      B 5 [L 7, L 4, L 5]],
    B 6 [
      B 7 [L 3]]],
  B 8 [
    B 9 [
      B 10 [L 6],
      B 11 [L 6, L 9]],
    B 12 [
      B 13 [L 7]]],
  B 14 [
    B 15 [
      B 16 [L 5]],
    B 17 [
      B 18 [L 9, L 8],
      B 19 [L 6]
    ]
  ]]
```

4.2 Finding Best Path Without Alpha-Beta Pruning

We begin by examining how the selection monad can be used to determine the optimal path through the tree. The objective is to identify the best outcome under the assumption that player 1 seeks to maximize the result while player 2 aims to minimize it.

To achieve this, we first define a predicate function that, given a path through the tree, returns the value of the leaf at the end of that path:

```
p ::  [Int] -> Int
p = last
```

Using this predicate, we construct a sequence of alternating minimum and maximum selection functions. The length of this sequence corresponds to the depth of the tree. By applying the *hSequenceJ* function, we compute the optimal path through the tree. Finally, we apply *p* to this path to obtain the resulting outcome.

```
exampleComp :: Int
exampleComp = p $ hSequenceJ [] (take 5 all) p
  where
    all :: Ord r => [[Int] -> J r Int]
    all = (minWithJ . nextNodes x) : (maxWithJ . nextNodes x) : all
```

4.3 Alpha Beta Pruning

Following the same approach as in the previous example, we now incorporate alpha-beta pruning by utilizing the functions *maxWithABJ* and *minWithABJ* to determine the optimal path. The key distinction is that we must now attach alpha and beta values to the current state.

Our predicate function requires a minor adjustment to accommodate the attached alpha and beta values. However, since these values do not affect the final outcome, we can simply ignore them in the computation.

```
p' :: [(Int, Int, Int)] -> Int
p' x = let (_ , _ , r) = last x in r
```

Similar to the previous example, we can construct a list of alternating minimum and maximum functions and utilize the *hSequenceJ* function to find the best path through the tree. It is essential to ensure that the alpha and beta values are correctly passed to the subsequent selection function. This is achieved by extending the *f* function to return all possible moves along with their corresponding alpha and beta values.

At the start of the game, with an empty history, we initialize the alpha and beta values to the minimum and maximum possible values, respectively, and attach them to all possible moves at that stage. In cases where a history of moves already exists, we will attach the alpha and beta values from the last move to the current possible moves.

```
f :: Bounded r => Tree Int -> [(r, r, Int)] -> [(r, r, Int)]
f x [] = map (minBound,maxBound,) (nextNodes x [])
f x h  = map (((\(a,_,_) -> a) . last) h,((\(_,b,_) -> b) . last) h,)
       (nextNodes x (map (\(_,_,x) -> x) h))
```

With this extended function *f*, we can now utilize the minWithABJ and maxWithABJ selection functions, optimized for alpha-beta pruning, to find the best path through the tree.

```
exampleComp' :: Int
exampleComp' = p' $ hSequenceJ [] (take 5 all) p'
  where
    all :: [[(Int, Int, Int)] -> J Int (Int, Int, Int)]
    all = (minWithABJ . f x) : (maxWithABJ . f x) : all
```

Using the Haskell debug trace tool, we verified that this implementation effectively prunes the search space as anticipated, ensuring that the predicate function is never evaluated for nodes expected to be pruned.

However, due to other performance issues inherent in the design of the selection monad, there remain numerous unnecessary calls to the predicate function. These issues are discussed in more detail in "Towards a More Efficient Selection Function" [6].

5 Alpha Beta Pruning with the Generalized Selection Monad

The previously presented implementation of alpha-beta pruning can be easily extended to utilize the more general type for selection functions, denoted as *GK*, to further benefit from the performance optimizations that arise from this generalization [6]. The performance improvements coming from the generalized selection monad are coming from an optimized sequence function that avoids unnecessary applications of the predicate function. I wont cover this in detail here, but the interested reader can find more information in the paper "Towards a More Efficient Selection Function" [6].

The type for selection functions *GK* is defined as follows:

```
type GK r a = forall b. (a -> (r,b)) -> (r,b)
```

5.1 MinWith and MaxWith Functions

For reference, we will begin with the unoptimized implementation of the minimax algorithm for the generalized selection function *GK*. The equivalent history-dependent sequence function for *GK* is defined as follows:

```
hSequenceGK :: [a] -> [[a] -> GK r a] -> GK r [a]
hSequenceGK h [] p      = p []
hSequenceGK h (e:es) p = e h (\x -> hSequenceGK (h ++ [x]) es
                             (\xs -> p (x:xs)))
```

The corresponding *minWithGK* and *maxWithGK* functions can be defined as:

```
minWithGK :: Ord r => [x] -> GK r x
minWithGK xs f = foldr1 (\(r,x) (s,y) -> if r <= s then (r,x) else (s,y))
                    (map f xs)

maxWithGK :: Ord r => [x] -> GK r x
maxWithGK xs f = foldr1 (\(r,x) (s,y) -> if r >= s then (r,x) else (s,y))
                    (map f xs)
```

We can define a predicate function that accounts for the new type of *GK*:

```
pGK ::  [Int] -> (Int, [Int])
pGK [x]    = (x, [x])
pGK (x:xs) = let (r,v) = pGK xs in (r,x:v)
```

With this setup, computing an optimal path through the tree becomes straightforward:

```
exampleCompGK :: (Int, [Int])
exampleCompGK = hSequenceGK [] (take 5 all) pGK
  where
    all :: Ord r => [[Int] -> GK r Int]
    all = (minWithGK . nextNodes x) : (maxWithGK . nextNodes x) : all
```

5.2 Alpha Beta Pruning With GK

We can now adjust the previously defined alpha-beta pruning functions to work with the generalized selection function *GK*:

```
alphaMaxWith :: Ord r => [(r, r, x)] -> ((r, r, x) -> (r, y)) -> (r, y)
alphaMaxWith ((a, b, x) : xs) p = let (r,y) = p (a, b, x) in
             if r >= b then (r,y) else go (max a r, b) (r,y) xs
  where
    go _ best [] = best
    go (a, b) (r, y) ((_, _, x) : xs) =
      let (r', y') = p (a, b, x)
          newBest  = if r >= r' then (r, y) else (r', y')
      in if r >= b || r' >= ↩
b then newBest else go (max r' a, b) newBest xs

betaMinWith :: Ord r => [(r, r, x)] -> ((r, r, x) -> (r, y)) -> (r, y)
betaMinWith ((a, b, x) : xs) p = let (r,y) = p (a, b, x) in
            if r <= a then (r,y) else go (a, min b r) (r,y) xs
  where
    go _ best [] = best
    go (a, b) (r, y) ((_, _, x) : xs) =
     let (r', y') = p (a, b, x)
         newBest = if r <= r' then (r, y) else (r', y')
      in if r <= a || r' <= a
          then newBest
          else go (min r' a, b) newBest xs
```

We also need to adjust the predicate function for the new type of GK:

```
pGK' :: [(Int, Int, Int)] -> (Int, [Int])
pGK' [(a, b ,x)]    = (x,[x])
pGK' ((a, b, x):xs) = let (r,v) = pGK' xs in (r,x:v)
```

The optimal path through the tree can now be computed as follows:

```
exampleCompGK' :: (Int, [Int])
exampleCompGK' = hSequenceGK [] (take 5 all) pGK'
  where
        es :: [(Int,Int,Int)] -> GK Int (Int, Int, Int)
        es h = alphaMaxWith (f x h)
        es' :: [(Int,Int,Int)] -> GK Int (Int, Int, Int)
        es' h = betaMinWith (f x h)
        all :: [[(Int,Int,Int)] -> GK Int (Int, Int, Int)]
        all = es' : es : all
```

A quick analysis using the Haskell debug trace tool confirms that this implementation prunes the search space as expected. By attaching the debug tool to the leaf nodes, we observe that the unoptimized implementation visits every leaf, resulting in a total of 14 calls to the predicate function for the given example tree. In contrast, the optimized implementation only visits 9 leaf nodes, demonstrating the effectiveness of alpha-beta pruning with the generalized selection monad.

6 Performance Analysis

To quantify the benefits of alpha-beta pruning utilizing both the selection monad J and its generalized variant GK, we conducted a series of experiments comparing runtime across various game tree sizes and branching factors.

6.1 Experimental Setup

First, we modified the $minWith$ and $maxWith$ functions to ensure that the reference implementation utilizing the selection monad J behaves similarly to our alpha-beta pruning implementation. This modification allows the predicate function to be applied only once for each element.

```
minWithJ' :: Ord r => [a] -> J r a
minWithJ' xs f = snd $ foldr1 (\(fx, x) (fy, y) -> if fx < fy
                                                     then (fx, x)
                                                     else (fy, y))
                              [(f x, x) | x <- xs]

maxWithJ' :: Ord r => [a] -> J r a
maxWithJ' xs f = snd $ foldr1 (\(fx, x) (fy, y) -> if fx > fy
                                                     then (fx, x)
                                                     else (fy, y))
                              [(f x, x) | x <- xs]
```

We further parameterized our definitions with a given tree t and search depth d:

```
test :: Tree Int -> Int -> Int
test t d = p $ hSequenceJ [] (take d all) p
  where
    all :: Ord r => [[Int] -> J r Int]
    all = (minWithJ' . nextNodes t) : (maxWithJ' . nextNodes t) : all
```

```
testAB :: Tree Int -> Int -> Int
testAB t d = p' $ hSequenceJ [] (take d all) p'
  where
    all :: [[(Int, Int, Int)] -> J Int (Int, Int, Int)]
    all = (minWithABJ . f t) : (maxWithABJ . f t) : all

testGK :: Tree Int -> Int -> (Int, [Int])
testGK t d = hSequenceGK [] (take d all) pGK
  where
    all :: Ord r => [[Int] -> GK r Int]
    all = (minWithGK . nextNodes t) : (maxWithGK . nextNodes t) : all

testABGK :: Tree Int -> Int -> (Int, [Int])
testABGK t d = hSequenceGK [] (take d all) pGK'
  where
        es :: [(Int,Int,Int)] -> GK Int (Int, Int, Int)
        es h = alphaMaxWith (f t h)
        es' :: [(Int,Int,Int)] -> GK Int (Int, Int, Int)
        es' h = betaMinWith (f t h)
        all :: [[(Int,Int,Int)] -> GK Int (Int, Int, Int)]
        all = es' : es : all
```

We also employed the following generator function to create game trees of various sizes and complexities:

```
gameTree :: Int -> Int -> (Int -> a) -> Int -> Tree a
gameTree 0 _ f c = L (f c)
gameTree d b f c = B (f c)
        [gameTree (d - 1) b f (c * b + i)| i <- [0..(b - 1)]]
```

Given a depth d, a branching factor b, a function f that labels the leaf nodes, and a counter c, the gameTree function constructs a game tree.

Two Sets of Experiments Were Conducted

1. Increasing Depth with Maximum Pruning Potential: In this experiment, the leaf nodes are labeled with increasing integers to maximize pruning efficiency. The tests conducted are as follows:

```
test1 d = test (gameTree d 4 id 0) d
test2 d = testAB (gameTree d 4 id 0) d
test3 d = testGK (gameTree d 4 id 0) d
test4 d = testABGK (gameTree d 4 id 0) d
```

The runtime graphs (see Fig. 2) illustrate that both alpha-beta pruned implementations (test2 and test4) exhibit significantly better scalability with increasing depth compared to their unpruned counterparts.

2. Constant Leaf Label

In this scenario, all leaves are labeled with a constant value, allowing for even greater pruning opportunities:

```
testC1 d = test (gameTree d 4 (const 0) 0) d
testC2 d = testAB (gameTree d 4 (const 0) 0) d
testC3 d = testGK (gameTree d 4 (const 0) 0) d
testC4 d = testABGK (gameTree d 4 (const 0) 0) d
```

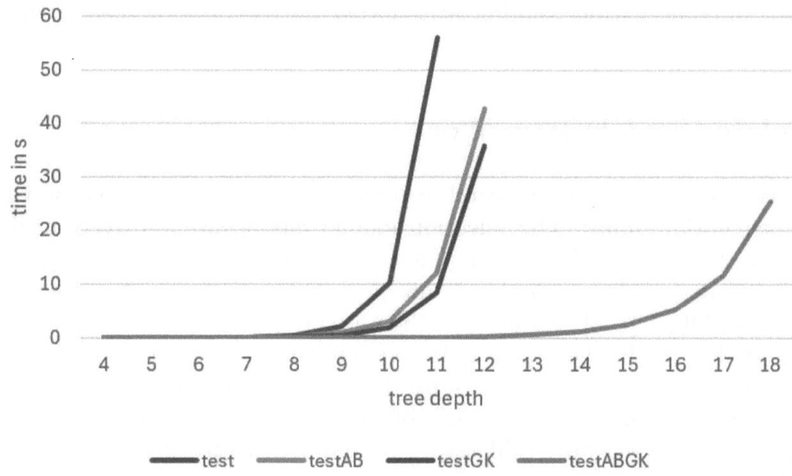

Fig. 2. Runtime in seconds for different tree depths

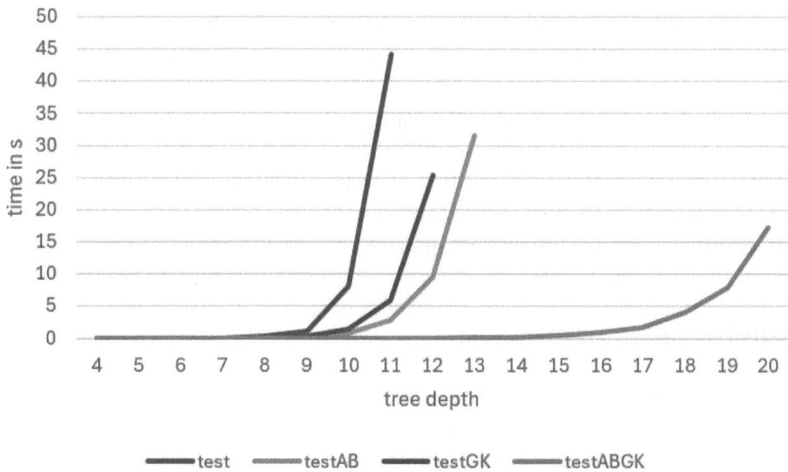

Fig. 3. Runtime in seconds for different tree depths and constant leaf label

As shown in Fig. 3, the runtime improvements are even more pronounced in this scenario, with the generalized selection monad combined with alpha-beta pruning (testC4) achieving the best performance.

These figures demonstrate a clear performance improvement when utilizing alpha-beta pruning within the selection monad. Furthermore, the tests suggest that the performance gains achieved are comparable to those obtained with the generalized selection monad. However, the true potential of alpha-beta pruning is realized when both the generalized selection monad and alpha-beta pruning are employed in combination, significantly outpacing the performance of the other implementations.

7 Related and Future Work

This work builds upon prior research concerning the selection monad in the context of sequential games. The selection monad has been extensively utilized to solve games with perfect information, as evidenced by previous studies exploring its applications in decision-making and game-theoretic reasoning. Research by Escardó and Oliva [2–4] has laid its theoretical foundations, while subsequent work by Hedges and others [1,8,9] has expanded its application in formalizing strategic interactions. However, despite these advancements, little attention has been given to optimizing the efficiency of the selection monad in practical game-solving scenarios. This work addresses that gap by integrating alpha-beta pruning with both the standard and generalized selection monads, thereby enhancing their computational performance in sequential decision processes.

Future research could explore additional optimizations by incorporating state or reader monads to carry extra contextual information, potentially reducing redundant computations and improving efficiency further. Another promising direction is to extend this approach to non-deterministic or probabilistic game trees, where outcomes are not solely determined by player actions but also involve elements of chance. Adapting the selection monad to such environments would provide a more general framework applicable to a wider range of games. Finally, implementing these methods in a full-scale game setting and benchmarking their performance against existing algorithms would offer valuable insights into their practical viability and real-world impact.

8 Conclusion

The selection monad serves as an elegant framework for describing algorithms that explore search trees. In its simplest form, it conducts a depth-first search and then selects an optimal path. Enhancements—such as incorporating game history and alpha-beta pruning—enable the monad to efficiently implement the minimax algorithm.

This paper presented a concrete method to extend the selection monad with alpha-beta pruning capabilities. We provided implementations for both the standard selection monad and its generalized variant, demonstrating significant reductions in unnecessary computations. Our performance analysis indicates that these techniques not only reduce the number of predicate evaluations but also scale effectively with the complexity of the game tree. Consequently, these methods hold promise for achieving more efficient evaluations in games with perfect information.

References

1. Bolt, J., Hedges, J., Zahn, P.: Sequential games and nondeterministic selection functions. arXiv preprint arXiv:1811.06810 (2018)
2. Escardó, M., Oliva, P.: Selection functions, bar recursion and backward induction. Math. Struct. Comput. Sci. **20**(2), 127–168 (2010)
3. Escardó, M., Oliva, P.: What sequential games, the Tychonoff Theorem and the double-negation shift have in common. In: Proceedings of the third ACM SIGPLAN Workshop on Mathematically Structured Functional Programming, pp. 21–32 (2010)
4. Escardó, M., Oliva, P.: Sequential games and optimal strategies. Proc. Royal Soc. A: Math. Phys. Eng. Sci. **467**(2130), 1519–1545 (2011)
5. Hartmann, J., Gibbons, J.: Algorithm design with the selection monad. In: International Symposium on Trends in Functional Programming, pp. 126–143. Springer (2022). https://doi.org/10.1007/978-3-031-21314-4_7
6. Hartmann, J., Schrijvers, T., Gibbons, J.: Towards a more efficient selection monad. Trends in Functional Programming, Proceedings (2024)
7. Hedges, J.: Monad transformers for backtracking search. In: Levy, P.B., Krishnaswami, N. (eds.) Mathematically Structured Functional Programming. EPTCS, vol. 153, pp. 31–50 (2014)
8. Hedges, J.: The selection monad as a CPS transformation. arXiv preprint arXiv:1503.06061 (2015)
9. Hedges, J.M.: Towards compositional game theory. Ph.D. thesis, Queen Mary University of London (2016)
10. Wikipedia contributors: Alpha-beta pruning (2025). https://en.wikipedia.org/wiki/Alpha-beta_pruning

On the Correctness of Barron and Strachey's Cartesian Product Function

Wouter Swierstra[1(✉)] and Jason Hemann[2]

[1] Utrecht University, Utrecht, The Netherlands
w.s.swierstra@uu.nl
[2] Seton Hall University, South Orange, USA
jason.hemann@shu.edu

Abstract. This paper shows how to verify Barron and Strachey's Cartesian product function. Doing so is not only a useful exercise in the specification and verification of a classic functional program—but gives insight into the importance of formulating soundness and completeness as symmetrical properties.

Keywords: Functional programming · verification · specification · Agda

1 Introduction

Christopher Strachey is one of the founding fathers of functional programming. His lecture notes from 1963 together with David Barron, as transcribed in *Advances in Programming and Non-Numerical Computation*, contain several examples of CPL programs [1]. Among these is a function for computing the Cartesian product of a list of lists. Consider the following example call:

```
Main> product [[1,2],[3,4,5],[6,7]]
  [[1 , 3 , 6 ], [1 , 3 , 7 ], [1 , 4 , 6 ],
   [1 , 4 , 7 ], [1 , 5 , 6 ], [1 , 5 , 7 ],
   [2 , 3 , 6 ], [2 , 3 , 7 ], [2 , 4 , 6 ],
   [2 , 4 , 7 ], [2 , 5,  6 ], [2 , 5 , 7 ]]
```

Barron and Strachey's definition of *product* is quite puzzling at first glance. We present it here, based on the modern implementation in Haskell by Danvy and Spivey [4]:

$$\begin{aligned}
&\mathit{product} :: [[a]] \rightarrow [[a]]\\
&\mathit{product}\ \mathit{xss} = \mathit{foldr}\ f\ [[\,]]\ \mathit{xss}\\
&\quad \textbf{where}\\
&\quad f :: [a] \rightarrow [[a]] \rightarrow [[a]]\\
&\quad f\ \mathit{xs}\ \mathit{yss} = \mathit{foldr}\ g\ [\,]\ \mathit{xs}
\end{aligned}$$

J. Gibbons (Ed.): TFP 2025, LNCS 15652, pp. 392–405, 2026.
https://doi.org/10.1007/978-3-031-99751-8_17

$$
\begin{aligned}
&\textbf{where} \\
&g :: a \rightarrow [[a]] \rightarrow [[a]] \\
&g\ x\ zss = \mathit{foldr}\ (\lambda\ ys\ qss \rightarrow (x : ys) : qss)\ zss\ yss
\end{aligned}
$$

This definition uses three calls to *foldr*, lexical scoping, and several higher order functions—all rather unusual for a program that is over sixty years old! Danvy and Spivey [4] have carefully dissected Barron and Strachey's Cartesian product function, and refer to it as 'possibly the first ever functional pearl.' What more could there possibly be to say about this mother of pearls?

One issue that remains unexplored is a mechanized formal correctness proof of Barron and Strachey's Cartesian product function. Mechanization would certainly have been out of reach for those authors back in 1963—four years before even the start of the Automath project [2,8]. We believe there is still mystery to be wrung out of this definition.

In writing our proofs, the inductive argument will elucidate the inductive structure of the functions themselves—giving a better insight into *how* this function computes a Cartesian product.

Throughout the remainder of this paper, we will use the programming language and proof assistant Agda [9] to specify and verify the Cartesian product function. The key technique, inspired by Danielsson's work on bag equivalence [3], is to verify that the desired soundness and completeness properties not only hold, but form an *isomorphism*, establishing a much stronger result. The underlying technique for specifications and proofs—establishing an isomorphism between two symmetric components of the specification—deserves to be more widely known. More generally, this technique illustrates the importance of proof relevance, where we are interested not only in whether or not a given statement is true, but also in accounting for the different possible proofs. The code associated with this paper has been published separately [10].

2 Warm-Up: Permutations

Rather than study the Cartesian product function immediately, we begin by a slightly simpler case study: computing all the permutations of a list. This is a typical exercise in functional programming; the verification of this function will introduce some of the scaffolding and specifications used in the remainder of the paper.

The permute function computes all the possible permutations of its input list:

```
permute : List A → List (List A)
permute []       = [ [] ]
permute (x : xs) = concatMap (sprinkle x) (permute xs)
```

The work is done by the sprinkle function that sprinkles its first argument in all the possible positions in its second argument:

```
sprinkle : A → List A → List (List A)
sprinkle y []        = [ [ y ] ]
sprinkle y (x :: xs) = (y :: x :: xs) :: map (x ::_) (sprinkle y xs)
```

So far so good—but we still need state what 'correctness' means for computing permutations and to prove that our function satisfies this specification. In the case of permutations, we are interested in two separate properties:

- *soundness* states that all the elements of the resulting list are permutations of the input;
- *completeness* states that every possible permutation of the input appears in the output.

The problem with writing such specifications in English is that we have cleverly side-stepped the problem of specifying when one list is a permutation of another—which is not necessarily any easier than the problem we set out to solve in the first place!

There are many different ways to specify that two lists are permutations of one another: by repeatedly swapping adjacent elements (as is done in the Rocq standard library); by quotienting the laws of commutative monoids [5]; by counting the number of occurrences of each element in the list; or, as we shall see shortly, by establishing an isomorphism between membership *proofs*.

To start our exploration of list processing functions, we begin with defining the binary relation, written x ∈ xs, that states that an element x occurs in a list xs:

```
data _∈_ (x : A) : List A → Set where
  here  : x ∈ (x :: xs)
  there : x ∈ xs → x ∈ (y :: xs)
```

This definition is reminiscent of the Haskell *elem* function: if the list is empty, the property is false and hence there is no corresponding constructor. If the list is non-empty, there are two alternatives: either the element we are looking is the first element, here, or it occurs in the tail of the list, there.

Besides this relation, our specification will use an additional *predicate transformer* on lists, given by the All data type below:

```
data All (P : A → Set) : List A → Set where
  []   : All P []
  _::_ : P x → All P xs → All P (x :: xs)
```

The proposition All P xs holds precisely when we have a proof of P x for each element x of of xs.

As a first approximation, we might define the following types to formalize our notions of soundness and completeness for our permute function:

```
soundness : (xs : List A) →
  ∀ ys → ys ∈ permute xs → All (_∈ xs) ys
completeness : (xs : List A) →
  ∀ ys → All (_∈ xs) ys → ys ∈ permute xs
```

This specification, however, is not very good. In words, the soundness property states that every list ys in permute xs draws its elements from xs. As it is stated, however, this property fails to prohibit illegal 'permutations' that might duplicate elements or discard elements. To illustrate this point, consider the following lists:

```
one-one  = 1 : []
two-ones = 1 : 1 : []
```

Now both All (_∈ one-one) two-ones and All (_∈ two-ones) one-one hold—yet clearly the lists are not permutations of one another. The completeness property is similarly problematic: just because the list ys contains all the elements in xs does not make ys a permutation of xs. Clearly we need to account for the *number* of occurrences of each element more carefully. In a way, the soundness and completeness properties as formulated above consider lists as *sets* rather than *bags*.

To address this problem, we take inspiration from Danielsson's work on defining bag equivalence using a proof relevant membership relation [3]. The key idea is to consider two lists to be bag equivalent if there is an *isomorphism* between their membership relations. To make this more precise, we begin by defining the notion of isomorphism:

```
record _≃_ (A B : Set) : Set where
  field
    to     : A → B
    fro    : B → A
    to-fro : ∀ x → fro (to x) ≡ x
    fro-to : ∀ y → to (fro y) ≡ y
```

Two lists are bag equivalent if there is an isomorphism between membership proofs. We formalise this relation as follows:

```
_≈_ : List A → List A → Set
xs ≈ ys = ∀ x → x ∈ xs ≃ x ∈ ys
```

In words, two lists xs and ys are bag equivalent, written xs ≈ ys, when there is a one-to-one correspondence between the proof of x ∈ xs and x ∈ ys, for every x. It is straightforward to prove that this definition of bag equivalence does form an equivalence relation.

A better specification for our permutation function now states:

$$\begin{array}{l}\mathsf{soundness} : (\mathsf{xs} : \mathsf{List\ A}) \rightarrow \\ \quad \forall\, \mathsf{ys} \rightarrow \mathsf{ys} \in \mathsf{permute\ xs} \rightarrow \mathsf{xs} \approx \mathsf{ys} \\ \mathsf{completeness} : (\mathsf{xs} : \mathsf{List\ A}) \rightarrow \\ \quad \forall\, \mathsf{ys} \rightarrow \mathsf{xs} \approx \mathsf{ys} \rightarrow \mathsf{ys} \in \mathsf{permute\ xs}\end{array}$$

We will now briefly sketch the key lemmas used to prove these two properties of the permute function.

Soundness. The proof of soundness relies on the property that sprinkle 'preserves' bag equivalence:

$$\mathsf{sprinkle\text{-}equiv} : \mathsf{ys} \in \mathsf{sprinkle\ x\ xs} \rightarrow \mathsf{ys} \approx (\mathsf{x} :: \mathsf{xs})$$

More precisely, we should say that each list ys in the list of lists produced by a call to sprinkle x xs is bag equivalent to x :: xs.

To establish soundness, however, needs a bit more work. In particular, it is not immediately obvious how to use an assumption of the form:

$$\mathsf{ys} \in \mathsf{concatMap\ (sprinkle\ x)\ xs}$$

To do so, we prove an equivalence between the elements of a list we generated by a call to concatMap:

$$\begin{array}{l}(\mathsf{y} : \mathsf{B})\ (\mathsf{f} : \mathsf{A} \rightarrow \mathsf{List\ B})\ (\mathsf{xs} : \mathsf{List\ A}) \rightarrow \\ \quad \mathsf{y} \in \mathsf{concatMap\ f\ xs} \simeq \exists\, [\, \mathsf{x} : \mathsf{A}\,]\ (\mathsf{x} \in \mathsf{xs} \wedge \mathsf{y} \in \mathsf{f\ x})\end{array}$$

Here we use the logical conjunction symbol, $\wedge$, to create a pair of proofs; the prevalent notation $\mathsf{A} \times \mathsf{B}$ is confusing when the types A and B also contain the variable x. In our implementation, we have packaged the fact of the concatMap membership equivalence into a custom *view* [7], letting us tease apart our assumption more easily. The proof of soundness follows from these ingredients using a straightforward inductive argument.

Completeness. To prove completeness is a bit trickier. In particular, our assumption that some list ys is a permutation of xs is itself not an inductively defined relation. Instead, we use the isomorphism between the elements of a concatMap in the other direction. Doing so, relies on a corresponding completeness result for sprinkle:

$$\mathsf{sprinkle\text{-}complete} : (\mathsf{p} : \mathsf{x} \in \mathsf{xs}) \rightarrow \mathsf{xs} \in \mathsf{sprinkle\ x\ (remove\ xs\ p)}$$

This proves that the sprinkle at least recovers the original list xs, after removing an arbitrary element from it. Here the remove function deletes the occurrence referenced by the proof p:

$$\begin{array}{lcl}\mathsf{remove} : (\mathsf{xs} : \mathsf{List\ A}) \rightarrow \mathsf{x} \in \mathsf{xs} \rightarrow \mathsf{List\ A} && \\ \mathsf{remove\ (x :: xs)\ here} & = & \mathsf{xs} \\ \mathsf{remove\ (x :: xs)\ (there\ i)} & = & \mathsf{x :: remove\ i}\end{array}$$

To prove completeness, we perform induction on the list ys. When this list is empty, our hypothesis tells us that xs must also be empty, and the proof is trivial. In the inductive case, however, we need to do a bit more work. We use the concatMap-isomorphism from the previous section in the opposite direction. The sprinkle-complete lemma and our induction hypothesis finish the proof. To use our inductive hypothesis, however, we need to establish that if x ∷ xs ≈ ys, then xs is bag equivalent to removing some particular element of ys, which we leave as a finicky proof for the reader.

Correctness. Even if we establish soundness and completeness, this is *still* not sufficient to guarantee the correctness of our permute function. There is nothing ruling out the following (incorrect) variation of the permute function:

```
wrong-permute : List A → List (List A)
wrong-permute xs = permute xs ++ permute xs
```

Indeed, we should prove that the soundness and completeness functions are mutual inverses, which involves equivalences of (bag) equivalences —the mind boggles.... Rather than go down this particular homotopical rabbit hole, however, we now return to our original problem: proving the correctness of the Cartesian product function.

3 Cartesian Products

We now turn our attention to the verification of the Cartesian product function from the introduction. We verify the function in two steps. First, we show how the version by Barron and Strachey is equivalent to a simpler definition using concatMap. Next, we establish the correctness of this second version. Arguably, this style of proof introduces an unnecessary indirection; we briefly sketch the direct proof in Sect. 4.

3.1 From ConcatMap to Nested Folds

Barron and Strachey's definition of Cartesian product seems perplexing at first and what's more, as Danvy and Spivey write, the authors seem almost to pull this startling definition out of thin air. To better explain how the triply nested fold arises, we have formalised a derivation of this function, suggested by a reviewer, starting from a simpler definition. The proof sketch of this derivation is in Fig. 1.

The following reference implementation of the Cartesian product function is a bit easier to understand and corresponds more closely to what one might write initially:

```
product-spec : List (List A) → List (List A)
product-spec []          = [ [] ]
product-spec (xs ∷ xss) =
  concatMap (λ x → concatMap (λ ys → [ x ∷ ys ]) (product-spec xss)) xs
```

The derivation in Fig. 1 illustrates the inductive case, establishing that this reference implementation is the same as the one from Barron and Strachey given in our introduction. After applying the induction hypothesis, the next two steps replace the calls to concatMap with the corresponding fold, using the following identity:

```
concatMap f xs ≡ foldr (λ x ys → f x ++ ys) [] xs
```

The penultimate step relies on the following property, essentially allowing us to fuse a call to map and append into a single fold:

```
foldr (λ x ys → f x : ys) [] xs ++ zs ≡ foldr (λ x ys → f x : ys) zs xs
```

This is used to replace the empty list in the base case with the previously computed elements of the Cartesian product, zss. To achieve the definition from the introduction, we would need to introduce the auxiliary functions, f and g, explicitly; Agda happily unfolds these definitions, however, completing the proof for us. The complete listing of the Agda reimplementation of Barron and Strachey's function is in Fig. 2.

```
product-spec (xs : xss)
  ≡⟨ definition of product-spec ⟩
concatMap (λ x → concatMap (λ ys → [ x : ys ]) (product-spec xss)) xs
  ≡⟨ induction hypothesis ⟩
concatMap (λ x → concatMap (λ ys → [ x : ys ]) (product xss)) xs
  ≡⟨ concatMap as foldr ⟩
foldr (λ x zss → concatMap (λ ys → [ x : ys ]) (product xss) ++ zss) [] xs
  ≡⟨ concatMap as foldr ⟩
foldr (λ x zss → foldr (λ ys qss → (x : ys) : qss) [] (product xss) ++ zss) [] xs
  ≡⟨ property of foldr ⟩
foldr (λ x zss → foldr (λ ys qss → (x : ys) : qss) zss (product xss)) [] xs
  ≡⟨ definition of product ⟩
product (xs : xss)
□
```

Fig. 1. Derivation of Barron and Strachey's Cartesian product function

3.2 Verification

With this simpler definition in place, we finally give the specification and correctness proof of the Cartesian product function. To specify the desired behaviour, we define another predicate transformer. The Pairwise data type lifts a relation between A and B to one over lists of A and lists of B:

```
data Pairwise (P : A → B → Set) : List A → List B → Set where
  []   : Pairwise P [] []
  _::_ : P x y → Pairwise P xs ys → Pairwise P (x :: xs) (y :: ys)
```

The Pairwise predicate transformer is similar to Haskell's zipWith function, requiring a proof of P x y for all elements x and y that occur at the same position in xs and ys respectively. Note that, unlike zipWith, the Pairwise predicate enforces that both lists have *exactly* the same length. There is no possible proof of a pairwise predicate if the argument lists have different lengths.

Just as we saw in the previous section, we formulate both *soundness* and *completeness* properties:

```
soundness : List (List A) → List (List A) → Set
soundness xss yss = ∀ ys → ys ∈ yss → Pairwise _∈_ ys xss

completeness : List (List A) → List (List A) → Set
completeness xss yss = ∀ ys → Pairwise _∈_ ys xss → ys ∈ yss
```

Both of these properties are slightly more general than necessary: rather than mention product xss, we refer to an arbitrary list yss. Instantiating yss to the list produced by product xss gives the soundness and correctness properties you might expect. The soundness property then states that all the elements listed by the product function must draw their elements from the input lists; the completeness property then states that any list that does so must be in the list computed by the product function. By generalizing over the list yss, however, we can re-use these properties to talk about the soundness and completeness of other functions—as we shall see in the next section.

Inspired by the bag equivalence relation from the previous section, we now formulate the overall correctness result we wish to establish:

```
correctness : List (List A) → Set
correctness xss = ∀ ys → ys ∈ product-spec xss ≃ Pairwise _∈_ ys xss
```

The soundness and completeness results each form one of the functions in this isomorphism. This overall correctness result ensures that the two functions are each other's inverse. This stronger property ensures that the Cartesian product function does not duplicate or discard elements: there is always a unique proof that each element in the Cartesian product draws its elements from the input lists.

Soundness. The soundness proof is somewhat involved. Given the assumption that ys ∈ product-spec xss, we need to establish that ys draws its elements pairwise from xss. In the inductive case, we deconstruct our assumption into several smaller parts:

```
ys ∈ concatMap f (product-spec xss) →
  ∃ [ xs : List A ] ((xs ∈ product-spec xss) ∧ (ys ∈ f xs))
```

Using this lemma twice, we produce the desired proof that the head of ys occurs in the head of xss; the inductive hypothesis then completes the proof.

Completeness. Somewhat surprisingly, the proof of completeness is almost trivial. We perform induction on our assumption that ys draws its elements pairwise from product-spec xss. In the inductive case, we have all the ingredients necessary to establish that ys ∈ product-spec (xs :: xss). We use the lemma from the previous section to establish that ys is an element of a list in the image of two calls to concatMap.

Correctness. The overall correctness proof establishes that the soundness and completeness proofs are mutual inverses. The proof itself is tedious, but technical, following the inductive structure of both lemmas.

The overall strategy for the proof in this section has been relate the Cartesian product from Sect. 1 to a simpler reference implementation, followed by the verification of this reference implementation. In the next section we show how to avoid this indirection and give a direct correctness proof Barron and Strachey's original implementation.

4 A Direct Proof

```
product : List (List A) → List (List A)
product xss = foldr f [ [] ] xss
  module F where
  f : List A → List (List A) → List (List A)
  f xs yss = foldr g [] xs
    module G where
    g : A → List (List A) → List (List A)
    g x zss = foldr (λ ys → (x :: ys) ::_) zss yss
```

Fig. 2. An Agda implementation of Barron and Strachey's Cartesian product function.

To prove the soundness and completeness of the original implementation, we begin by giving the complete definition in Agda in Fig. 2. A technical detail worth mentioning is that the additional local modules F and G enable us to refer to the locally defined functions f and g. These functions also generalize over all local variables in scope, in their order of occurrence. For example, the function g takes arguments xss, xs, yss, x and zss in that order; the function f takes arguments xss, xs and yss, even though it does not directly use xss.

4.1 Soundness

To establish the soundness of the original Cartesian product function, we need to prove:

soundness-direct : (xss : List (List A)) → soundness xss (product xss)

The base case follows readily enough; the inductive step requires an auxiliary lemma about the auxiliary function f:

f-soundness : ∀ xs → soundness xss yss → soundness (xs ∷ xss) (f xss xs yss)

The corresponding proof defers all the work to a final lemma about the function g:

```
g-soundness : soundness xss yss →
              soundness (xs ∷ xss) zss →
              soundness ((x ∷ xs) ∷ xss) (g xss xs yss x zss)
```

This lemma makes the inductive nature of the nested-fold explicit: the outermost fold traverses the outermost list of lists; the auxiliary function f adds a new list xs to this list of lists; and finally, the function g adds elements the inner list xs. The proof itself requires two lemmas:

```
sound-there : Pairwise _∈_ xs (ys ∷ yss) → Pairwise _∈_ xs ((y ∷ ys) ∷ yss)
elem-destruct : ys ∈ foldr (λ zs → _∷_ (x ∷ zs)) yss xss →
  Either (∃ [xs : List A] (ys ≡ x ∷ xs  ∧  xs ∈ xss))
         (ys ∈ yss)
```

The first lemma is used to extend the inner list with new elements. The second is used to decompose the hypothesis that ys occurs in the fused map-fold: either ys is in the image of map (x ∷_) or it occurs in the list yss, returned when xss is empty.

4.2 Completeness

The completeness proof is simpler, following exactly the same inductive structure. The types of the three key lemmas follow the same pattern as we saw for soundness:

```
product-complete : (xss : List (List A)) → completeness xss (product xss)
f-complete : completeness xss yss → completeness (xs ∷ xss) (f xss xs yss)
g-complete : completeness xss yss →
             completeness (xs ∷ xss) zss →
             completeness ((x ∷ xs) ∷ xss) (g xss xs yss x zss)
```

Once again, the only work is done by the last lemma about the auxiliary function g. This lemma traverses its argument Pairwise proof, using the following properties of g:

```
g-in-xss : ys ∈ xss → (y ∷ ys) ∈ g yss xs xss y zss
g-in-zss : ys ∈ zss → ys ∈ g xss xs yss x zss
```

Essentially, both these properties illustrate how the elements produced by g are either in the remainder of the Cartesian product (zss) or produced by adding the current head of the first list, y, to another list. The proofs of both these properties follow by a simple inductive argument.

5 Intrinsic Verification

Now that the inductive structure of the proof and program both coincide closely: why not do both at once? To achieve this, we need to abandon the simply typed folds used in Haskell, in favor of the dependently typed *induction principle* or *eliminator*:

```
elim : {P : List A → Set} →
  (∀ x {xs} → P xs → P (x ∷ xs)) →
  P [] →
  ∀ xs → P xs
elim step base []        = base
elim step base (x ∷ xs)  = step x (elim step base xs)
```

Operationally, the functions foldr and elim behave the same. The key difference is in the *return type*. A simply typed fold produces a value of the same type, irrespective of its input. On the other hand, the return type of the eliminator *depends* on its input value xs. As we have set out to define a function returning both a list and the proof that this resulting list is the Cartesian product of its input, we need this extra generality.

To make this even more clear, we introduce a type for 'correct Cartesian product', or CCP for short:

```
data CCP (xss : List (List A)) : Set where
  _,_ : (yss : List (List A)) → correctness xss yss → CCP xss
```

Such a correct Cartesian product of the list xss consists of an output list yss, together with the desired correctness proof relating xss and yss. The CCP type will form the first (implicit) argument P to the eliminator, sometimes referred to as the *motive* [6].

We now define a correct by construction Cartesian product function. The complete listing is given in Fig. 3, lightly edited for the sake of legibility. Replacing elim with foldr yields almost exactly the same function as the one in the introduction, only we now return both a list and a correctness proof. We have

```
product : (xss : List (List A)) → CCP xss
product xss = elim f ([ [] ] , base) xss
  where
  base : correctness [] [ [] ]
  f : (xs : List A) → {xss : List (List A)} → CCP xss → CCP (xs :: xss)
  f xs (yss , yss-c) = elim g ([] , f-base) xs
    where
    f-base : correctness ([] :: xss) []
    g : (x : A) → {xs : List A} → CCP (xs :: xss) → CCP ((x :: xs) :: xss)
    g x (zss , zss-c) =
      (foldr (λ ys → (x :: ys) ::_) zss yss , g-correct yss-c zss-c)
```

Fig. 3. A correct-by-construction Cartesian product

two base cases for our proofs, base and f-base, but we omit their definitions. The type signatures of the auxiliary functions, f and g, mention an additional (implicit) argument—but this is not used in the function's definition. The only real work—as always—is done by the innermost function, g, that uses a simple fold to construct the desired list and assembles the desired correctness proof—phrased in this way, we do not need the extra generality of the dependently typed elim function as we merely compute a list. The proof component is built by the function g-correct, that calls the soundness and completeness results from the previous section. Written in this way, the correct by construction Cartesian product function is only slightly more complicated than the original definition.

6 Discussion

It is unsurprising that a pure function defined using a fold is (relatively) easy to test and verify. Nonetheless, establishing the correctness of a triply nested fold that makes clever use of lexical scoping is still an amusing puzzle: finding a suitable specification, proving the required lemmata, and assembling the pieces all require a bit of thought. In particular, the symmetry in our specifications enables us to express the isomorphism of proofs succinctly.

This symmetry between the soundness and completeness is no accident. We have tried several other equivalent formulations. Although these alternative formulations are logically equivalent, they make it harder to express the required property that soundness and completeness are mutual inverses.

All Soundness. Rather than express soundness by mentioning individual elements of the output list, we can give an alternative, capturing the desired characteristic property of all the results returned by the Cartesian product function:

```
soundness : List (List A) → List (List A) → Set
soundness xss yss = All (λ ys → Pairwise _∈_ ys xss) yss
```

This definition is equivalent to the one introduced previously in Sect. 3. This follows readily from the following property, relating individual elements and the All predicate:

$$\text{all}{\in} : (x \in xs \rightarrow P\ x) \Leftrightarrow \text{All}\ P\ xs$$

Accumulating Completeness. The definition above shows how to specify soundness without mentioning individual elements. In the quest for symmetry, we have also considered alternative notions of completeness. Defining a suitable notion of completeness in this style is not entirely straightforward. One way to do so is using an *accumulating parameter*:

```
accumulate : (P : List A → Set) → List (List A) → Set
accumulate P []          = P []
accumulate P (xs :: xss) = All (λ x → accumulate (P ∘ (x ::_)) xss) xs

complete-acc : List (List A) → List (List A) → Set
complete-acc xss yss = accumulate (_∈ yss) xss
```

This avoids the additional quantification of the list ys. Like the notion of soundness above, this notion of completeness is described in terms of All. Once again, this definition is logically equivalent to the one we have seen previously. *A fortiori*, we show that for any predicate P the accumulating and pairwise specifications are equivalent:

```
acc-equiv : {P : List A → Set} (xss : List (List A)) →
  accumulate P xss ⇔ ((∀ xs → Pairwise _∈_ xs xss → P xs))
```

This directly implies that the accumulating and direct definitions of completeness are equivalent—but the formulation used in the paper makes it easier to express the isomorphism. The required proofs mirror the inductive structure of the underlying definitions. The proof from left to right is defined tail-recursively, extending the predicate P as we recurse over the input list and pairwise proofs. The other direction follows by induction on the input list, using the following lemma to accumulate the elements of the input list accordingly:

```
all-map : (∀ x → P x → Q x) → All P xs → All Q xs
```

Conclusion. Even setting aside the challenges of proving correspondence to an implementation, writing good specifications is hard. A specification that is too loose leaves room for incorrect implementations, as we saw with the wrong-permute function. Conversely, one that is too strict rules out valid programs, for example, by fixing the order in which the elements of a Cartesian product function must be generated. Expressing soundness and completeness symmetrically, however, has paid dividends: we establish a one-to-one correspondence between the elements of our Cartesian product and the proofs that these are valid.

Acknowledgments. We would like to thank the reviewers and attendees of TFP for their helpful feedback and suggestions. They have helped improve the paper enormously. Nicolas Wu suggested studying permutations before moving on to the Cartesian product function itself. The research of Jason Hemann has been partially supported by NSF grant CCF-2348408.

Disclosure of Interests. The authors have no competing interests to declare that are relevant to the content of this article.

References

1. Barron, D.W., Strachey, C.: Programming. In: Fox, L. (ed.) Advances in Programming and Non-Numerical Computation, pp. 49–82. Pergammon Press (1966)
2. de Bruijn, N.G.: Automath: a language for mathematics. EUT report 68-WSK-05, Technische Hogeschool Eindhoven (1968). https://pure.tue.nl/ws/portalfiles/portal/2039924/256169.pdf. wSK, Dept. of Mathematics and Computing Science
3. Danielsson, N.A.: Bag equivalence via a proof-relevant membership relation. In: Beringer, L., Felty, A. (eds.) ITP 2012. LNCS, vol. 7406, pp. 149–165. Springer, Heidelberg (2012). https://doi.org/10.1007/978-3-642-32347-8_11
4. Danvy, O., Spivey, M.: On Barron and Strachey's cartesian product function. In: Proceedings of the 12th ACM SIGPLAN International Conference on Functional Programming, ICFP 2007, pp. 41–46. Association for Computing Machinery (2007). https://doi.org/10.1145/1291151.1291161
5. Dinges, A., Hinze, R.: What's in a bag?: an "application proving interface" for finite bags and its implementation. In: Proceedings of the 35th Symposium on Implementation and Application of Functional Languages. IFL 2023. Association for Computing Machinery, New York (2024). https://doi.org/10.1145/3652561.3652563
6. McBride, C.: Elimination with a motive. In: International Workshop on Types for Proofs and Programs, pp. 197–216. Springer (2000)
7. McBride, C., McKinna, J.: The view from the left. J. Funct. Program. **14**(1), 69–111 (2004)
8. Nederpelt, R.P., Geuvers, J.H., de Vrijer, R.C.: Selected Papers on Automath. Studies in Logic and the Foundations of Mathematics. Elsevier, Netherlands (1994). https://doi.org/10.1016/s0049-237x(08)70226-x
9. Norell, U.: Towards a practical programming language based on dependent type theory. Ph.D. thesis, Department of Computer Science and Engineering, Chalmers University of Technology, SE-412 96 Göteborg, Sweden (2007)
10. Swierstra, W., Hemann, J.: Proofs associated with the paper *'On the Correctness of Barron and Strachey's Cartesian Product Function'* (2025). https://doi.org/10.5281/zenodo.15118185

Distribution

Formal Specification and Implementation of Distributed Lazy Group Membership Protocol

Jianhao Li(✉) and Viktória Zsók

Faculty of Informatics, Department of Programming Languages and Compilers, Eötvös Loránd University, 1117 Budapest, Pázmány Péter sétány 1/C, Hungary
{lijianhao,zsv}@inf.elte.hu

Abstract. In distributed systems, nodes typically collaborate to perform tasks. Many distributed systems adopt groups or clusters as architectural units to improve the management and coordination of nodes. The group membership protocol serves a crucial role in ensuring a consistent understanding of member status across all nodes in the group. Group membership protocols are essential in various distributed real-world systems, such as IoT sensor networks, smart agriculture, environmental monitoring, satellite communications, remote infrastructure monitoring, smart buildings, industrial automation, intelligent transportation systems, and medical monitoring systems. Group membership protocols are traditionally classified as heartbeat-based or gossip-based. Both protocol categories require frequent heartbeat or ping messages, facing challenges in energy efficiency, especially in systems with low failure rates and high energy consumption requirements. This paper introduces a novel group membership protocol with two main algorithms that eliminate the need for periodic ping or heartbeat messages. This protocol is designed for Symmetric P2P Systems using the actor model and ensures strong consistency. We provide formal specifications and verifications using TLA+ to ensure the correctness of our algorithms. The safety and liveness properties of the specifications are verified with the TLC model checker. In addition, the implementation of the protocol in the functional programming language is provided.

Keywords: Distributed systems · Group membership protocol · Formal specification · Actor model · Concurrent functional programming

1 Introduction

The group membership protocol in distributed systems involves ensuring that all members of the group maintain an up-to-date and consistent list of active group members [6].

J. Gibbons (Ed.): TFP 2025, LNCS 15652, pp. 409–434, 2026.
https://doi.org/10.1007/978-3-031-99751-8_18

Group membership protocols [20] are essential in distributed systems. Take smart agriculture as an example: as agricultural needs, farming practices, or seasonal changes, sensors must be added or removed accordingly. This environment needs a group membership protocol to manage the dynamic group coordination.

Group membership protocols can also play a critical role in other distributed systems, such as environmental monitoring systems, satellite communication systems, remote infrastructure monitoring systems, building management systems (BMS) [24], intelligent transportation systems (ITS) [4], and medical monitoring systems. Nodes in some of these systems typically experience very low failure rates, but have high energy consumption requirements. For example, sensors in smart agriculture are usually battery-powered and seldom fail due to rigorous environmental testing. Environmental monitoring system [21] sensors are often installed in fixed positions, requiring high energy efficiency and experiencing rare failures due to stable environments.

This combination of low failure rate and high energy efficiency requirements uncovers the unsustainability of the traditional group membership protocol that relies on periodic messages. In this context, the system needs to reduce unnecessary communication overhead and consider the consistency and real-time response in a dynamic network environment. Therefore, reducing energy costs while ensuring strong consistency of the group member list has become an urgent problem that needs to be solved.

The current group membership protocols can be categorized into two types: the heartbeat-based group membership protocol and the gossip-based group membership protocol. The heart-beating group membership protocol is the traditional type. However, implementations of the heart beating suffer from scalability limitations, which impose network loads that grow quadratically with group size, compromise response times, or false positive frequency [8]. Gossip-based group membership protocol is created to provide greater scalability than the heart-beat-based group membership protocol. Each node forwards messages to a small set of "gossip partners" chosen randomly from the entire group members in a gossip-based group membership protocol [2].

However, taking the well-known SWIM algorithm [8] as an example, the gossip-based protocol still needs each node to periodically send ping messages to a random number of other nodes in the local table and to initiate a failure confirmation based on the acknowledgment timeout, requesting assistance from several other nodes to verify the failure. SWIM uses an infection-style dissemination mechanism because hardware and IP multicasts are infrequently enabled on most networks and operating systems due to administrative reasons. These are also the reasons why the basic SWIM protocol can only utilize a costly broadcast or an inefficient point-to-point messaging scheme [8].

In systems where node failures are rare, and energy efficiency is critical, traditional group membership protocols with periodic messages are unsustainable. Reducing the frequency of heartbeat messages still results in unnecessary periodic communications, which consume significant network bandwidth. Moreover, many sensor networks use a duty cycling strategy to save energy by periodically switching sensors between active and sleep states. Protocols like SWIM, gossip-based protocols, and Chord [22] rely on periodic messages, which can conflict with duty cycling strategies since the system with periodic messages requires nodes to wake up regularly for communication, increasing energy consumption.

To address the above issues, we have designed a novel group membership protocol with two key components: a group list consistency algorithm and a lazy failure detection algorithm. We implemented our protocol in HASKELL, a pure functional programming language. The robust static type system, immutability, and purity improve code reliability and maintainability. These features simplify the analysis of state transitions and the debugging of concurrent processes.

The group list consistency algorithm ensures that all group members are aware of group list updates after a complete system operation.

Our lazy failure detection algorithm significantly reduces communication overhead by avoiding periodic ping or heartbeat messages. When no tasks are present, the communication overhead is nearly non-existent. In the lazy failure detection algorithm, the ping messages are not sent based on time intervals. Only when a task-related message transmission fails does the sending node become suspicious of the receiving node's potential failure. Ping messages are only used when a node suspects another node's failure and seeks other nodes' assistance for confirmation during the failure confirmation phase.

Our protocol design is for Symmetric P2P Systems. In Symmetric P2P Systems [13], all nodes have peer-to-peer status, no central control point or master-slave relationship, and all nodes have the same roles and rights. Symmetric P2P systems are more suitable for the above sensor systems because the decentralized architecture can avoid single points of failure and improve the scalability and fault tolerance of the system. The P2P system can easily add or remove nodes to adapt to dynamic changes in the system. Our protocol leverages the actor model [1], where each actor is an independent computational entity with its state and behavior. Actors communicate asynchronously through message passing instead of directly accessing shared resources, which is well-suited for handling concurrent communication tasks efficiently. The design of the protocol adheres to the non-Byzantine model [15], where the nodes fail by stopping operations without sending false or malicious messages.

We define the specification of the two algorithms of the group membership protocol using TLA+ [16,25], which enables us to express the algorithm designs precisely. Moreover, formal verification with TLA+ provides us with more information about the correctness of the algorithms since TLA+ is a formal specification language, functioning as a high-level language for modeling distributed programs and systems. The specification contains specific safety and liveness properties that ensure the group list consistency, and the failure is eventually confirmed.

In summary, this paper introduces a novel group membership protocol containing two algorithms. It also provides formal specifications, verifications and implementations for these two algorithms.

In the following sections, first, the design of two algorithms is introduced with the problem, methodology, algorithm description, formal specification, and message complexity in Sect. 2 and in Sect. 3, respectively; next, the specification verification is presented in Sect. 4; afterward, the functional programming implementation is described in Sect. 5; next, the algorithms' features, limitations and future work are discussed in Sect. 6; next, related work is analyzed in Sect. 7; finally, the conclusion is summarized in Sect. 8.

2 Group List Consistency Algorithm

In this section, the group list consistency algorithm is introduced. The description of the algorithm in natural language is easier to understand than in formal specifications. However, it is easier to produce ambiguity. Therefore, it is suggested that the implementation be constructed according to the specifications.

The challenge in designing this group list consistency algorithm is that we need to consider the possibility of node failure and messages being received unordered. In addition, under the architecture requirements of symmetry P2P and the actor model, as few messages as possible are used to achieve strong consistency in the group list.

2.1 Problems Addressed by Group List Consistency Algorithm

The problem addressed in this paper is how to achieve the group list consistency following the actor model and the symmetric P2P architecture. Sustainability and scalability should also be considered during the design phase.

The group list consistency algorithm specification assumes that:

(A1) *The receiver will eventually receive the message as long as it is active.* This assumption is fulfilled by the underlying communication method.

(A2) *Nodes may experience non-byzantine failures* [3]. The nodes that have not failed will send responses in a certain amount of time for the message they have to respond to. The failed node loses all the information. (The nodes do not have stable storage that can survive failure and restart). Considering the existence of the environment without stable storage and the high cost of stable storage, we do not assume all the nodes in the system has stable storage that can survive failure and restart. Therefore, the restarted node needs to rejoin the group.

The requirements of the algorithm specification:

(R1) *Group list consistency*: The algorithm must ensure that the group membership list is consistent across all nodes. This requirement is decomposed into three properties in the specification for this protocol:

Single introducer constraint: Only at most one node in the group is in the *introducer* state, which can send the group structure to the new group member and inform the existing group members about the new member.

This requirement prevents the group list inconsistency caused by synchronous group joining. Suppose two new group members join the group simultaneously; if two nodes are processing their joining requests separately and simultaneously, the group structure sent back to the new group members may not contain another new group member.

Idle group consistency: If all the group members are idle (which means no changing is happening; there can be changes before or after), then their group list is consistent (for every member u, the group list of u equals the set of all members excluding u).

Eventually group idle: Eventually, for all n in the set of members, the node state of n will become idle. Those properties imply the eventual consistency of the group lists among the group members.

(R2) *Reliability*: the design considers the non-byzantine failure of a node and message delays. The specification contains the action that lets the node fail. The nodes' failure does not block the system before they recover.

(R3) *Decentralization, symmetry, independence of nodes, and adherence to the actor model:* Symmetry is a property of P2P systems that declares that all nodes do not have unique capabilities that distinguish them from the rest of the nodes [13]. There is no static centralized manager role of the algorithm. The new member can send the join request to any existing group member. Each existing member in the group has the same role and can temporarily become the *introducer* after receiving the join request. There is no need for a particular node to be more powerful. Additionally, we do not use shared resources (shared variable, shared database) and do not use one node or several nodes to maintain the group structure specifically. All the group nodes keep their own local group structure list. It is also for the scalability consideration (no central bottleneck) and for reliability consideration (inherently free of a single point of failure).

It is essential to specify the system following the actor model to meet this requirement. Since each node performs computations and sends messages based solely on its local states without using shared variables, also, the actor model assumes distributed systems are composed of distributed components that can interact with each other asynchronously [1], it is necessary to specify the mailbox of nodes and the asynchronous communication among them.

(R4) *Sustainability*: the system decreases the number of messages and the hops of each message. The amount of messages should be as low as possible when the new members join the group.

Existing distributed algorithms do not fully align with the assumptions and requirements of our target scenario. Distributed mutual-exclusion algorithm [14] does not account for node failures and assumes ordered message reception. At the same time, the commit protocols (like two-phase commit protocol [5], three-phase commit protocol [5] and Paxos commit algorithm [9]) and the consensus algorithms (like Paxos [15] and Raft [18]) do not meet the assumptions of symmetric P2P systems. Therefore, we have developed a new group list consistency algorithm tailored to these needs. Detailed related work can be found in Sect. 7.

2.2 Design Methodology for Group List Consistency Algorithm

The algorithm is designed to coordinate the nodes through message passing, like most of the existing distributed algorithms. Under the requirements of the actor model and symmetric P2P architecture (nodes have equal roles, no shared resources, and unordered messages), the algorithm achieves group list consistency considering possible node failures. Unnecessary features, such as aborts and event ordering, are excluded. To enhance energy efficiency, we minimize the number of messages and communication rounds in different design versions. Additionally, scalability is addressed by implementing the forwarding and batch processing mechanism of join requests.

2.3 Group List Consistency Algorithm Description

Initially, a node outside the group begins as a *joiner* and sends a joining request to any existing group member B to start the joining process with a joining timeout. If the *joiner* receives a group structure message from any existing group member, it joins the group successfully, updates its local group list according to the group information it receives, and becomes an idle group member. If the *joiner* receives a join fail message, it knows it failed to join the group. Suppose the group structure message does not arrive within the joining timeout. In that case, the *joiner* will check if B has failed (information provided by the lazy failure detection algorithm). If B fails, the *joiner* knows it failed to join the group; if B does not fail, reset the joining timeout. Once the join request has been forwarded to other group members, the *joiner* will receive a handler update message and update the related local information.

When a failure is detected, the idle members update their deletion informing list. Nodes intending to leave voluntarily add themselves to the deletion informing list. The deletion informing list contains all the nodes that the member wants to inform other members to delete.

If an idle node finds out its group list except the deletion informing list is an empty set (which means it is the only member in the group), it updates its group list without sending any message.

After receiving a joining request or its delete inform list is not empty, the group node in *idle* state becomes *waitingInformAck* and sends informing messages to all the group members except the nodes in its deletion informing list. Then, it waits for the inform acknowledgments with an inform timeout. If It receives all the inform acknowledgments from all the not-failed nodes of the group list except the deletion informing list, it enters the *introducer* state.

For scalability, the node in *introducer* state can still receive joining requests from other new members or existing group members and detect failed nodes. The node in *introducer* state can also carry out the update operation by sending operation messages (ask the group members to deal with the group list update operation) to all the group members except the delete inform list. It also sends a group structure message to the *joiner* and updates its own local group list.

After the inform timeout of the node B in *waitingInformAck* state is exceeded, if B has not yet received lock acknowledgments from more than half of the not-failed nodes of its group list except the deletion informing list and it has received a lock request message from another node in the state *waitingInformAck* C with larger node ID, then will give up becoming *introducer* by sending:

- finish messages to all the nodes of its group list,
- fail joining message to the related *joiner*,
- inform acknowledgment message to the node C.

The node ID can be changed to other comparable unique values of nodes.

After receiving an inform message, the group members in state *idle* change to state *informed* with an informed timeout and send back the inform acknowledgment message.

For every group member D in the state *informed*: it changes to state *idle* after receiving a finish message; it forwards the join request to the node informed D after receiving a join request from a new group member; it includes the new group members to the local group list, sends back the operation acknowledgment message to the *introducer*, sends group information message to the *joiner* and change to state *idle* after receiving the operation message; if the node informed the node D failed and the informed timeout is elapsed, it changes to state *idle*.

The details of local information, such as the *informId*, are eliminated from this description.

2.4 Formal Specification of Group List Consistency Algorithm

As shown in Specification 2.1, *SingleIntroducerConstraint* formally specifies the safety property **R1** in Sect. 2. This property ensures that at most one node in the system is in the *introducer* state at any given time.

$$\begin{aligned}&\mathit{SingleIntroducerConstraint} \triangleq \mathit{Cardinality}(\{m \in \mathit{members} :\\ &\quad \mathit{localInfos}[m][\text{“}\mathsf{nodeState}\text{”}] = \text{“}\mathsf{introducer}\text{”}\}) \leq 1\end{aligned}$$

Specification 2.1: The *SingleIntroducerConstraint* invariant of the group list consistency algorithm

As shown in Specification 2.2, *IdleGroupConsistency* formally specifies the safety property **R2** in Sect. 2. This property guarantees that if every node is in the *idle* state, then each node's group list is consistent, which equals the set of all members except itself.

As shown in Specification 2.3, *EventuallyGroupIdle* specifies the liveness property **R3** in Sect. 2. This property states that the system will eventually reach a state where every node is in the *idle* state.

The Sect. A introduces all the actions of the group list consistency algorithm actions list and brief descriptions of the actions.

$$\mathit{IdleGroupConsistency} \triangleq$$
$$(\forall n \in \mathit{members} : \mathit{localInfos}[n][\text{"nodeState"}] = \text{"idle"})$$
$$\Rightarrow \forall u \in \mathit{members} : \mathit{localInfos}[u][\text{"groupList"}] = \mathit{members} \setminus \{u\}$$

Specification 2.2: The *IdleGroupConsistency* invariant of the group list consistency algorithm

$$\mathit{EventuallyGroupIdle} \triangleq \Diamond(\forall n \in \mathit{members} :$$
$$\mathit{localInfos}[n][\text{"nodeState"}] = \text{"idle"})$$

Specification 2.3: The *EventuallyGroupIdle* property of the group list consistency algorithm

Specification 2.4 shows the specification of one action, *RecvInform*. It defines that, after receiving the inform message, the group member nodes in the idle state are informed by the inform message sender, and they send an inform acknowledgment back.

$$
\begin{array}{l}
\mathit{RecvInform}(n) \triangleq \\
\quad \land\ \mathit{localInfos}[n][\text{"nodeState"}] = \text{"idle"} \\
\quad \land\ \exists\, i \in 1 \,..\, \mathit{Len}(\mathit{mailboxes}[n]) : \\
\qquad \text{LET} \\
\qquad\quad \mathit{Msg} \triangleq \mathit{mailboxes}[n][i] \\
\qquad\quad \mathit{InID} \triangleq \mathit{Msg}[\text{"informId"}] \\
\qquad\quad \mathit{IAck} \triangleq [\mathit{type} \mapsto \text{"informack"}, \\
\qquad\qquad \mathit{informId} \mapsto \mathit{InID},\ \mathit{sender} \mapsto n] \\
\qquad \text{IN} \\
\qquad\quad \land\ \mathit{Msg}[\text{"type"}] = \text{"inform"} \\
\qquad\quad \land\ \mathit{localInfos}' = [\mathit{localInfos}\ \text{EXCEPT} \\
\qquad\qquad !\,[n][\text{"nodeState"}] = \text{"informed"}, \\
\qquad\qquad !\,[n][\text{"informId"}] = \mathit{InID}] \\
\qquad\quad \land\ \mathit{mailboxes}' = [\mathit{mailboxes}\ \text{EXCEPT} \\
\qquad\qquad !\,[\mathit{InID}[\text{"intro"}]] = \mathit{Append}(@,\ \mathit{IAck}), \\
\qquad\qquad !\,[n] = \mathit{RemoveByIndex}(@,\ i)] \\
\qquad\quad \land\ \text{UNCHANGED}\ \langle \mathit{members} \rangle
\end{array}
$$

Specification 2.4: The *RecvInform* action of the group list consistency algorithm

2.5 Message Complexity Analysis of Group List Consistency Algorithm

The most significant energy consumption arises from CPU operations and network communication in many low-power devices [17]. In the group list consistency algorithm, we assume that the transmission distance of all communications is the same and only consider the impact of the number of messages on sustainability. In requirement (**R5**), we mentioned that this algorithm should have a low number of messages under the ideal situation (new members join the group in order with some intervals).

Within the context of the distributed transaction commit problem, transaction managers [9] are responsible for orchestrating the various steps involved in committing a transaction, managing resource locks, and handling any potential conflicts or failures that may arise during the process. Suppose N is the number of transaction managers (for the distributed transaction commit problem) and the number of existing group members (for the group joining problem). The number of messages in the ideal situation can be calculated: there is one joining request, $N-1$ of inform messages, $N-1$ of inform acknowledgments, N of operation and group structure messages, and $N-1$ of group structure information messages. There are $4*N-1$ messages in total. Accordingly, there are five message delays [9].

For comparison, we use two distributed asynchronous algorithms dealing with the distributed consistency problem: the two-phase commit protocol [5] and the Paxos commit algorithm [9]. The differences are discussed in detail in Sect. 7. The two-phase commit protocol requires four message delays and uses about $3*N$ messages for larger values of N [9]. The Paxos commit algorithm requires five message delays and uses about $4*N$ messages for larger values of N [9].

As shown in Table 1, the number of message delays and overall message counts are quite comparable despite the differences in system architecture and requirements among the protocols. Furthermore, if the underlying communication layer can reliably support message splitting and reassembly (allowing for larger message sizes), the algorithm could be further optimized by transmitting the complete group list to new members in a single message rather than requiring them to collect group information from multiple sources. This optimization has the potential to reduce both the delays and the total number of messages.

Table 1. Message complexity comparison

	Two-Phase Commit	Paxos Commit	Group list consistency
Message delays	4	5	5
Messages	3*N - 1	4*N	4*N-1

3 Lazy Failure Detection Algorithm

This algorithm can provide the fail information needed in the group list consistency algorithm.

Under sustainable consideration, in an actor model system, an actor does not need to be concerned by another node's failure status if there are no message interactions. Therefore, this algorithm achieves the *lazy* characteristic by not using a heartbeat and gossip mechanisms. The failure detection process is initiated only after the acknowledgment timeout of task-related messages rather than being performed periodically.

To provide the node failure-related information of the lazy failure detection algorithm to the group list consistency algorithm, we can set some messages in the group list consistency algorithm as task-related messages or send additional task-related messages when failure information is required.

3.1 Problems Addressed by Lazy Failure Detection Algorithm

The problem with designing the lazy failure detection algorithm is how to ensure specific safety and liveness properties without periodic messages.

The lazy failure detection algorithm shares the same assumptions as the group list consistency algorithm.

3.2 Design Methodology for Lazy Failure Detection Algorithm

This algorithm employs a timeout mechanism but replaces the conventional heartbeat mechanism with task-related message timeouts for failure detection. A consensus mechanism reduces false positives caused by transient network issues. The lazy failure detection algorithm is specialized. It utilizes a timeout-based failure detector within an asynchronous model, where no upper bounds on message delivery delays and processing times are assumed. Consequently, the timeout-based failure detector may incorrectly suspect failures due to message delays and processing times, thus not meeting the accuracy properties of conventional failure detectors.

Furthermore, eliminating periodic messages means it cannot satisfy the completeness properties typical of standard failure detection algorithms. Specifically, when there are no task-related messages, the algorithm cannot ensure that every failed node will eventually be permanently suspected by all (or some) running nodes. Therefore, unique properties need to be designed for this algorithm.

3.3 Lazy Failure Detection Algorithm Description

When a node fails to receive the acknowledgment of a task-related message, it starts the failure detection process by sending assist requests to a fixed number of nodes that are randomly chosen from the group nodes (except itself, the task-related message receiver, and the confirmed failed nodes). After receiving the assist requests, the group member nodes send detection messages to the task-related message receiver and send the detection results to the task-related message sender. The task-related message receiver sends detection responses once it receives detection messages.

3.4 Formal Specification of Lazy Failure Detection Algorithm

As shown in Specification 3.1, *NoFalseFailureDetection* specifies a liveness property: for every group node, if aways no messages are sent to the node, it will not be confirmed to failed.

$$
\begin{aligned}
&\mathit{NoFalseFailureDetection} \triangleq \\
&\quad \forall\, n \in \mathit{GroupNodes} : \\
&\qquad (\Box(\neg\exists\, i \in 1 \,..\, \mathit{Len}(\mathit{mailboxes}[n]) : \\
&\qquad\quad \mathit{mailboxes}[n][i][\text{"type"}] = \text{"CMsg"}) \\
&\qquad \Rightarrow n \notin \mathit{confirmedFailedNodes})
\end{aligned}
$$

Specification 3.1: The *NoFalseFailureDetection* property of the *lazy* failure detection algorithm

As shown in Specification 3.2, this algorithm has one more liveness property: for all the nodes, if a node A failed, and there is another node B that tried to send a message M to this failed node A and the detect process of this message M is completed, then eventually the node A will be confirmed failed.

$$
\begin{aligned}
&\mathit{EventualFailureConfirmation} \triangleq \\
&\quad \forall\, n \in \mathit{GroupNodes} : (((\exists\, i \in 1 \,..\, \mathit{Len}(\mathit{mailboxes}[n]) : \\
&\qquad \wedge\, \mathit{mailboxes}[n][i][\text{"type"}] = \text{"CMsg"} \\
&\qquad \wedge\, \mathit{mailboxes}[n][i][\text{"cMsgId"}] \in \mathit{detectRecords}) \\
&\qquad \wedge\, \mathit{localInfos}[n][\text{"nodeState"}] = \text{"Fail"}) \\
&\quad \leadsto (n \in \mathit{confirmedFailedNodes}))
\end{aligned}
$$

Specification 3.2: The *EventualFailureConfirmation* property of the *lazy* failure detection algorithm

The Sect. B introduces all the actions of the group list consistency algorithm actions list and brief descriptions of the actions.

3.5 Message Complexity Analysis of Lazy Failure Detection Algorithm

Assuming one actor (or node) will query other A nodes once it fails to receive the acknowledgment, the lazy failure detection algorithm needs $4 * A$ messages for the failure detection.

Assuming t is the time and N is a function of node number, $N(t)$ is the number of nodes present in the system at time t. Similarly, $M_j(t)$ is the number of the task-related message at time t, and $P_f(t)$ is the the probability that failed to receive acknowledgment in time for a task-related message at time t. Then, M_l equals the number of messages of the lazy failure detection algorithm in the time slot $[t_1, t_2]$.

$$M_l = (4A) \cdot \int_{t_1}^{t_2} N(t) \cdot M_j(t) \cdot P_f(t)\, dt$$

In comparison, assume the algorithms (or protocols) with heartbeat or ping messages have constants for the frequency of the heartbeat or ping message M_p and the number of nodes to which a node should send periodic messages, B. The constants M_p and B usually need to be configured according to the system, and the coverage rate and the number of messages need to be balanced. Then, the M_f stands for the number of messages of the algorithms (or protocols) with periodic messages in the time slot $[t_1, t_2]$.

$$M_f = M_p \cdot B \cdot \int_{t_1}^{t_2} N(t)\, dt$$

As we can see from the formulae, the lazy failure detection has a sustainability advantage when the $M_j(t) \cdot P_f(t)$ is smaller. In other words, this algorithm enhances system sustainability when the task-related messages are fewer or the probability that failed to receive an acknowledgment for a task-related message within the timeout is small. However, the task-related messages among all the group members with reasonable frequency can reduce the cases where failed nodes are not confirmed for a long time. Therefore, this algorithm suits systems with rare failures and reasonably configured timeouts.

4 Model Checking and Verification Results

This section presents the formal verification of the specifications of the algorithms. The TLC model checker is a type of formal verifier that can analyze the possible behaviors of the algorithms. TLC model checker enumerates all the possible behaviors of the systems or algorithm. It contains the combination within which there are many actions between the message-sending action and the message-receiving action, representing the message delay scenario. In that scenario, even if a message arrives early, it may be received (or processed) much later when multiple sub-actions are enabled simultaneously.

All the instances of model checking in this section passed the TLC model checking process, which indicates the specified safety properties are true in every reachable state and the liveness properties hold for every possible behavior of the algorithms. The machine used for model checking has the following specifications: AMD Ryzen 7 7840HS processor with Radeon 780M Graphics 3.80 GHz, 32 GB of RAM, and Windows 11 as operating system.

The duration the model checker requires to verify the specified properties is included in the following results. In this study, our primary concern is that the model-checking process is completed successfully and that all properties are verified. The process is notably time-consuming because it exhaustively explores all possible state transitions. Although the efficiency of the model checker is not within the scope of our work, these performance metrics may be valuable for developers of model-checking tools.

4.1 Group List Consistency Algorithm

Before the model checking, we include the formulae *TypeOK*, *SingleIntroducer-Constraint* and *IdleGroupConsistency* as invariants of the model and include the formula *EventuallyGroupIdle* as properties of the model. When we run the test, the TLC will check if those formulas are true in every reachable state (invariant) or for every possible behavior (properties). For the additional TLC options: we set the number of worker threads to 16; set the fraction of physical memory allocated to TCL to 90%; turned off the profiling feature; and checked the option of verifying temporal properties upon termination only.

To run the TLC model checker, we need to provide the value of the constants. When we provide the *{2,3,4}* and *{2,3}* for the constants *Nodes* and *InitMembers*, the TLC model checker console shows that no error was found when the model checking was completed. 44996269 states were generated, and 27320377 distinct states were found. The fingerprint collision probability is optimistically calculated as 2.6E-5. The depth of the complete state graph search is 75. The model-checking process finished in 153601 ms.

When we provide the *{2,3,4}* and *{2}* for the constants *Nodes* and *InitMembers*, the TLC model checker console shows that no error was found when the model checking was completed. 70485649 states were generated, and 43497354 distinct states were found. The fingerprint collision probability is optimistically calculated as 6.4E-5. The depth of the complete state graph search is 87. The model-checking process finished in 225163 ms.

All the results we show below have been confirmed by the TLC that the model checking was completed, and no error has been found. The states increase as the number of initial members decreases for the same number of nodes. It is reasonable because more nodes and fewer initial members result in more possible behaviors.

4.2 Lazy Failure Detection Algorithm

The algorithm has passed the TLC model checking, including checks for the conventional invariant *TypeOK*, liveness property *NoFalseFailureDetection* and *EventualFailureConfirmation*.

When we provide *{2,3,4}* (*GroupNodes*), *0* (*AssistNum*), and *1* (*MaxCMsgCount*) for the model, the TLC model checker console shows that no error was found when the model checking was completed. 246715 states were generated, and 59286 distinct states were found. The fingerprint collision probability is optimistically calculated as 6.0E-10. The depth of the complete state graph search is 18. The model-checking process finished in 12836 ms.

When we provide *{2,3,4}* (*GroupNodes*), *1* (*AssistNum*), and *1* (*MaxCMsgCount*) for the model, the TLC model checker console shows that no error was found when the model checking was completed. 132414253 states were generated, and 29259480 distinct states were found. The fingerprint collision probability is optimistically calculated as 1.6E-4. The depth of the complete state graph search is 30. The model-checking process finished in 2324489 ms.

5 Implementation in HASKELL

Using HASKELL to implement a TLA+ specification offers several advantages. HASKELL is a purely functional programming language. Reducing the impure code ensures that the software is solid [19]. Additionally, the functional nature of TLA+ closely matches functional programming paradigms, making HASKELL an ideal choice for translating specifications into code. This matching facilitates a more direct and intuitive mapping from mathematical models to executable code. It helps maintain the rigor and correctness of the original TLA+ definitions in the implementation process.

HASKELL has the advantage of providing a large number of reliable and robust packages. For instance, the `Data.Serialize` module from the `Cereal` package [11] enable us to facilitate straightforward encoding and decoding of various messages; the `Data.Set module from the containers` package [12] offers an efficient implementation of sets, making the transition from TLA+ specifications to HASKELL implementations smoother; and the `SecureUDP` package [10] ensures message delivery through mechanisms like resending and timeouts while preserving the asynchronous, out-of-order nature of communication, which also fulfills the assumption A1 in Subsect. 2.1.

The Listing 1.1 shows the implementation of the node state and the messages. The default generic implementations of the put and get functions can be included by making the `Message type deriving Generic` type class and declaring a `Serialize` instance for Message without any function definition when the `DeriveGeneric` and `DefaultSignatures` language extensions are enabled.

```
data NodeState = Idle | Informed
  | WaitingInformAck | Introducer
  | NotInGroup | Joining
  | FailedJoin | Leave | GsCollecting deriving (Show, Eq)

data NodeId = NodeId
  { host :: (Word8, Word8, Word8, Word8)
  , port :: Int
  } deriving (Eq, Ord, Show, Generic)
instance Ser.Serialize NodeId

type InformID = (NodeId, Word64)

zeroNodeID :: NodeId
zeroNodeID = NodeId { host = (0,0,0,0), port = 0 }

zeroInformID :: InformID
zeroInformID = (zeroNodeID, 0)

data Message
    = Inform { informId :: InformID }
    | Finish { informId :: InformID }
    | Gsack { sender :: NodeId }
    | Joinreq { sender :: NodeId }
    | Joinfail { sender :: NodeId }
    | Handlerupdate { new :: NodeId,
      sender :: NodeId }
    | Groupstruct { memberNum :: Word64,
        informId :: InformID, introLeave :: Bool }
    | Informack { informId :: InformID, sender :: NodeId }
    | Gsinfo { informId :: InformID, sender :: NodeId }
```

```
    | Operation { informId :: InformID,
        newMembers :: Set.Set NodeId,
        removeMembers :: Set.Set NodeId }
    deriving (Eq, Show, Generic)

instance Ser.Serialize Message
```

Listing 1.1. The NodeState and Message

As shown in Listing 1.2, we define the core data types that represent the state and configuration of a node. Each node is defined as a tuple comprising its configuration (`NodeConfig`), local state (`LocalInfo`) stored in a mutable concurrent variable (`MVar`), and a message list (`MsgList`) also maintained in an `MVar`.

```
data NodeConfig = NodeConfig
  { selfNodeID :: NodeId
  , secureUDP :: Sec.ChannelSt
  , msgFetchInterval :: Int
  }

data LocalInfo = LocalInfo
  { nodeState     :: !NodeState
  , localInformId:: !InformID
  , introCounter :: !Word64
  , inMemory      :: !NodeId
  , numInMemory   :: !Word64
  , toAdd         :: !(Set.Set NodeId)
  , toDelete      :: !(Set.Set NodeId)
  , deleteInform :: !(Set.Set NodeId)
  , ack           :: !(Set.Set NodeId)
  , groupList     :: !(Set.Set NodeId)
  } deriving (Show)

data MsgList = MsgList
  { clientMsgs :: ![ClientMsg]
  , groupCtrlMsgs :: ![Message]
  } deriving (Show)

type ClientMsg = (Soc.SockAddr, Bs.ByteString)

type Node = (NodeConfig, C.MVar LocalInfo, C.MVar MsgList)
```

Listing 1.2. The LocalInfo and function examples

Listing 1.3 illustrates the initialization of a node, where the `createNode` function sets up the node configuration and spawns three concurrent threads. These threads handle different aspects of the node's operation: receiving messages, detecting message loss (and consequently node failures), and processing group control messages to maintain a consistent group list.

```
createNode :: String -> Int -> Int -> IO Node
createNode hostStr portInt interval = do
...
  _ <- C.forkIO $ handleReceive channel msgListMVar nodeCfg
  _ <- C.forkIO $ handleLoss channel localInfoMVar nodeCfg
  _ <- C.forkIO $ handleGroup msgListMVar localInfoMVar nodeCfg
  putStrLn $ ‘‘Node created with NodeId: ‘‘ ++ show nodeId
  return (nodeCfg, localInfoMVar, msgListMVar)
```

Listing 1.3. The main threads of node

As shown in Listing 1.4, the **handleReceive** thread continuously retrieves incoming messages from a secure UDP channel, decodes them, and then categorizes them into client messages and group control messages. The received group control messages are appended to a local message list for further processing by the group management logic.

```
handleReceive :: Sec.ChannelSt -> C.MVar MsgList -> NodeConfig -> IO ()
handleReceive channel msgListMVar nodeCfg = forever $ do
  msgs <- Sec.getReceived channel
  forM_ msgs $ \(sAddr, bs) -> do
    case Ser.decode bs of
      Right message -> do
        C.modifyMVar_ msgListMVar $ \ml ->
          return ml { groupCtrlMsgs = groupCtrlMsgs ml ++ [message] }
      Left _ -> do
        putStrLn $ ''[handleReceive] client message from '' ++ show sAddr
        C.modifyMVar_ msgListMVar $ \ml ->
          return ml { clientMsgs = clientMsgs ml ++ [(sAddr, bs)] }
  C.threadDelay (msgFetchInterval nodeCfg)
```

Listing 1.4. handleReceive

Listing 1.5 shows the **handleLoss** thread, which is defined to handle the lost messages. When a loss is detected, the thread extracts the corresponding node identifiers and updates the node's local state accordingly. Depending on the current state of the node (e.g., Idle or Introducer), it triggers appropriate actions such as **idleDetectFail**.

```
handleLoss :: Sec.ChannelSt -> C.MVar LocalInfo -> NodeConfig -> IO ()
handleLoss channel localInfoMVar nodeCfg = forever $ do
  lostMsgs <- Sec.getLoss channel
  case lostMsgs of
    [] -> C.threadDelay (msgFetchInterval nodeCfg)
    _  -> do
      let lostIds = Set.fromList $ map (sockAddrToNodeId . fst) lostMsgs
      putStrLn $ ''lostIds:'' ++ show lostIds
      C.modifyMVar_ localInfoMVar $ \li -> do
        case nodeState li of
          Idle -> do
            idleDetectFail localInfoMVar lostIds
            selfUpdate nodeCfg localInfoMVar
            tryDeleteInform nodeCfg localInfoMVar
          Introducer -> introDetectFail nodeCfg localInfoMVar
          _ -> return ()
        return li
      C.threadDelay (msgFetchInterval nodeCfg)
```

Listing 1.5. handleLoss

As shown in Listing 1.6, the **handleGroup** thread processes group control messages. The function continuously retrieves and processes messages by invoking **processGroupMessage**, ensuring that the group membership information remains consistent across the system through the application of the Group List Consistency Algorithm.

```
handleGroup :: C.MVar MsgList -> C.MVar LocalInfo -> NodeConfig -> IO ()
handleGroup msgListMVar localInfoMVar nodeCfg = forever $ do
  maybeMsg <- C.modifyMVar msgListMVar $ \ml ->
    case groupCtrlMsgs ml of
      []     -> return (ml, Nothing)
```

```
      (m:ms) -> return (ml { groupCtrlMsgs = ms }, Just m)
  case maybeMsg of
    Nothing -> C.threadDelay (msgFetchInterval nodeCfg)
    Just msg -> processGroupMessage msg msgListMVar localInfoMVar nodeCfg
```

Listing 1.6. handleGroup

Listing 1.7 demonstrates the implementation for Specification 2.4. Once the message `Inform` is received, the enableRecvInform function checks if the node fulfills the enable condition of the action `RecvInform`. The receiveInform updates the node's state to Informed and sends back an inform acknowledgment.

```
processGroupMessage :: Message -> C.MVar MsgList
  -> C.MVar LocalInfo -> NodeConfig -> IO ()
processGroupMessage msg msgListMVar localInfoMVar nodeCfg =
  case msg of
    Inform { informId = inID } -> do
      en <- enableRecvInform inID localInfoMVar
      case en of
        True  -> do
          putStrLn $ ‘‘Processing Inform message’’ ++ show inID
          recvInform inID nodeCfg localInfoMVar
        False -> do
          putStrLn ‘‘enableRecvInform returned False. Re-enqueue message.’’
          reenqueue msg msgListMVar
...

enableRecvInform :: InformID -> C.MVar LocalInfo -> IO Bool
enableRecvInform _inID localInfoMVar = do
  li <- C.readMVar localInfoMVar
  putStrLn $ ‘‘[enableRecvInform] Current nodeState: ‘‘
    ++ show (nodeState li)
  return (nodeState li == Idle)

recvInform :: InformID -> NodeConfig -> C.MVar LocalInfo -> IO ()
recvInform inID nodeCfg localInfoMVar = do
  C.modifyMVar_ localInfoMVar $ \li -> do
    let newLi = li { nodeState = Informed, localInformId = inID }
    putStrLn $ ‘‘[recvInform] Updated localInfo: ‘‘ ++ show newLi
    return newLi
  let iackMsg = Informack { informId = inID,
    sender = selfNodeID nodeCfg }
      dest = nodeIdToSockAddr (fst inID)
      bsMsg = Ser.encode iackMsg
  putStrLn $ ‘‘[recvInform] Sending Informack message: ‘‘
    ++ show iackMsg ++ ‘‘ to ‘‘ ++ show dest
  _ <- Sec.sendMessages (secureUDP nodeCfg) [(dest, bsMsg)]
  return ()
```

Listing 1.7. The `RecvInform` implementation

Haskell also has well-designed testing frameworks, like Hspec [7]. As shown in Listing 1.8, a sample of tests with the Hspec framework is illustrated to validate the Haskell implementation we described. The test sample ensures the function `createNode`, `enableRecvInform`, and `recvInform` can run and the local state updates correctly. The output of the test sample execution can be found in Sect. C.

```
...
main :: IO ()
main = hspec $ do
  describe ‘‘createNode’’ $ do
```

```
    it ''successfully creates a node with correct return values'' $ do
      node <- P.createNode ''127.0.0.1'' 8080 1000
      case node of
        (nodeCfg, localInfoMVar, msgListMVar) -> do
          (P.selfNodeID nodeCfg) `shouldBe` P.NodeId { P.host = (127,0,0,1),
            P.port = 8080 }
          (P.msgFetchInterval nodeCfg) `shouldBe` 1000
          threadDelay 20000
          li <- MVar.readMVar localInfoMVar
          case li of
            P.LocalInfo { P.nodeState = st, P.localInformId = lid } -> do
              st `shouldBe` P.NotInGroup
              lid `shouldBe` P.zeroInformID
          ml <- MVar.readMVar msgListMVar
          case ml of
            P.MsgList { P.clientMsgs = cms, P.groupCtrlMsgs = gcms } -> do
              cms `shouldBe` []
              gcms `shouldBe` []
  describe ''enableRecvInform'' $ do
    it ''returns True when LocalInfo state is Idle'' $ do
      localInfoM <- initLocalInfo P.Idle
      res <- P.enableRecvInform P.zeroInformID localInfoM
      case res of
        True  -> return ()
        False -> error ''Expected True but got False''
    it ''returns False when LocalInfo state is not Idle'' $ do
      localInfoM <- initLocalInfo P.Informed
      res <- P.enableRecvInform P.zeroInformID localInfoM
      case res of
        False -> return ()
        True  -> error ''Expected False but got True''
  describe ''recvInform'' $ do
    it ''updates LocalInfo to Informed with new informID'' $ do
      localInfoM <- initLocalInfo P.Idle
      let testInformID = ( P.NodeId { P.host = (127,0,0,1),
        P.port = 9000 }, 42 )
          cfg = testNodeConfig
      _ <- (P.recvInform testInformID cfg localInfoM)
           `catch` (\(_ :: SomeException) -> return ())
      threadDelay 20000
      li <- MVar.readMVar localInfoM
      case li of
        P.LocalInfo { P.nodeState = st, P.localInformId = iid } -> do
          st `shouldBe` P.Informed
          iid `shouldBe` testInformID
```

Listing 1.8. The tests of the Haskell implementation

The HASKELL implementation in this section demonstrates a translation from TLA+ specifications into executable functional programming code. The strength of functional programming is leveraged to deliver a solution for dynamic group membership management.

6 Discussion

Using the protocol presented in this paper, after the network is partitioned, based on the failure detection results, a large group of nodes will gradually be divided into multiple small groups according to the network partition. We are designing protocol supplementary algorithms related to group merge, node self-checking, and security. After the network partition is restored, the small groups can be restored to a large group by merging.

Lazy failure detection can be converted to an algorithm similar to the heartbeat mechanism by disguising heartbeat information as job information and sending it periodically. Compared with heartbeat information, it should be called periodical detection information; however, the principle is similar: sacrificing sustainability in exchange for sensitivity to failure.

When the nodes exchange task-related messages frequently, the speed of detecting failures is not compromised in the lazy failure detection algorithm. However, this approach sacrifices the speed of failure detection when task-related messages between nodes are infrequent. In extreme cases where no nodes in the group are functioning, and there is no communication, failures will not be detected. Such scenarios are acceptable under this protocol. In other words, this algorithm permits the failure of permanently isolated nodes undetected.

From the protocol's perspective, the failure status of nodes in an inactive system (assuming the system activity of the actor model is mainly message communication) is non-essential. During idle periods, all machines should conserve energy and rest. When tasks emerge, it will then be determined which nodes have failed. Therefore, this protocol is unsuitable for systems with strict requirements on the detection speed of failed nodes or that rarely communicate between nodes.

Most distributed algorithms rely on a large number of message passing to ensure consistency. As the number of nodes increases, the message overhead will increase linearly. This increased communication demand can lead to network congestion and higher latency, which imposes natural limits on the system's scalability. The group list consistency algorithm includes a join requests forwarding mechanism under scalability consideration to ease the problem. The join requests are processed in a bunch to decrease the round of consistency coordination and the number of messages. However, scalability limitations still exist.

In the group list consistency algorithm, the node in *introducer* state only plays a temporary role as a guide when a new node joins and does not have permanent special privileges or control capabilities. Therefore, the existence of the *introducer* does not violate the principle of the symmetric P2P system.

Since network delay and system load vary, a fixed timeout will cause additional communication overhead in group list consistency algorithm and lead to misjudgment in lazy failure detection algorithm. Therefore, according to the network conditions and system load, a mechanism for dynamically adjusting the timeout can be added to this protocol in the actual implementation.

This protocol is designed for systems with rare failures and communication overhead-reduction requirements. According to the lazy feature, it may also suit data centers with reliable nodes and an upper limit of message delivery delay. However, evaluations of the implementations in different environments are needed to confirm this statement.

7 Related Work

The group list consistency algorithm's primary distinctions from other distributed algorithms or protocols are the requirements and the solved problems.

Lamport's distributed mutual-exclusion algorithm [14] is a prominent solution often considered for addressing mutual exclusion and synchronization in distributed systems. It can be used to create a distributed mutex to lock the distributed group list modification. However, upon reviewing the algorithm, we discovered that its assumptions and requirements do not match our specific scenario. Our system does not assume the message can be received in order, as we designed it based on the actor model and connectionless transportation protocol.

Moreover, the distributed mutual-exclusion algorithm requires the active participation of all processes, whereas we must account for potential node failures in our system. The primary variation is that our system does not require the total ordering of events. In our scenario, it is possible for the *introducer* who made the earlier lock requests to give up the lock requests. Although we still require mutual exclusion to ensure only one *introducer* enters the critical section, we do not require enforcing a specific order.

Distributed transaction commit algorithms or protocols, like the two-phase commit protocol [5], the three-phase commit protocol [5], and the Paxos commit algorithm [9], can also maintain the group list consistency in a group membership protocol: the group members decide about the group list modifications. However, comparing the group list consistency algorithm with the distributed transaction commit algorithm, the members in our system do not need to abort; our system has a decentralized symmetry architecture requirement. Furthermore, this algorithm solves the blocking problem using timeouts (JoinReqTimeout, InformTimeout, InformedTimeout) and failure detection, which differs from the approach of the three-phase commit protocol. Besides, this algorithm has a forward join requests mechanism to increase the scalability.

In our design, to ensure the independence of nodes, each node has a local group list that contains information about group member nodes' addresses or node IDs, excluding itself. Therefore, we also need to ensure the distributed consistency of the local group list. Since distributed consistency is involved, we also considered two classic distributed consensus algorithms: Paxos [15], and Raft [18]. We can also develop a group membership protocol using distributed consensus algorithms. However, these algorithms do not match our sustainability requirements because of the periodical messages. Additionally, this algorithm is designed specifically for group member updates. Furthermore, the group list consistency algorithm needs to be designed with the actor model for symmetric P2P systems.

8 Conclusion

The paper presented a novel sustainable group membership protocol containing two main algorithms. The design, formal specification, verification, and functional programming implementation of the two main algorithms of the protocol were introduced. Our approach eliminates the need for periodic messages, reducing communication overhead through a lazy failure detection algorithm. The group list consistency algorithm provides a consistency solution for a decentralized distributed system following the actor model and symmetric P2P systems architecture. Scalability and sustainability are both considered during the design phase.

This work represents a method to formally specify and verify distributed systems or algorithms under specific conditions. High-level abstract mathematical languages (such as TLA+) can significantly assist system architects in the design and verification phases, improving confidence in the system's correctness.

Although some research uses TLA+ for formal verification of distributed systems, TLA+ specifications specifically targeting algorithms of group membership protocol are relatively less. Existing TLA+ applications are more concentrated in distributed databases, consensus algorithms (such as Paxos and Raft), and other fields. We hope our work can be seen as one more step towards formalizing and proofing distributed algorithms and providing other software architects with practical experience in formal specification.

In future work, our protocol can be enhanced with more supplementary algorithms for advanced functional features and security considerations. It can be further proved with the help of the symbolic model checker APALACHE, property reduction methodology, and the SMT-based interactive theorem prover Ivy [23]. Further optimization of the protocol can be done for different types of distributed systems and exploration of additional applications in environments with varying failure rates and communication patterns.

A Group List Consistency Algorithm Actions List

As shown in Specification A.1, the *Next* defines the possible transitions of a system from one state to another in TLA+. The *Next* action of the group list consistency specification comprises 22 sub-actions, each representing a distinct possible subsequent behavior of the system:

SendJoinRequest allows a node in the *notInGroup* state to send a join request to an *idle* node, transitioning to the *joining* state.

This *RecvGroupStruct* allows a node in the *joining* state to receive a group structure message. Upon receipt, the node transitions to the *gsCollecting* state and updates its *informId*, *groupList*, and the expected number of group members.

The *RecvGsInfo* enables a node in the *gsCollecting* state to receive a *gsinfo* message. When a message with an *informId* matching the node's current informId is received, the sender is added to the node's groupList.

The action *RecvAllGsInfo* checks whether a node in the *gsCollecting* state has received all group information. Once confirmed, the node resets its *informId* and *inMemory* fields and transitions its state to *idle*.

RecvJoinFail facilitates a *joining* node in handling a join failure message, transitioning to *failedJoin* and updating local information.

RecvHandlerUpdate allows a *joining* node to update its handler based on the received message while retaining the *joining* state.

JoinReqTimeout causes a *joining* node to time out due to an introducer's failure, transitioning to *failedJoin*.

RecvJoinRequest enables an *idle* node to process a join request, update its state to *waitingInformAck*, and broadcast the request to its group.

IdleDetectFail allows an *idle* node to detect a failure in its group and mark the failed node for deletion locally.

IdleLeave enables an *idle* node to leave the group, marking itself for deletion.

TryDeleteInform allows an *idle* node to initiate a deletion broadcast for locally marked nodes, transitioning to

waitingInformAck. *SelfUpdate* facilitates an *idle* node with no remaining group members to reset its group list and become the sole member.

RecvInformAck enables a node in various states to acknowledge receipt of an inform message.

RecvAllInformAck enables a *waitingInformAck* node's transition to *introducer* after receiving acknowledgments from a majority of active nodes.

InformTimeout allows a *waitingInformAck* node to time out due to insufficient acknowledgments, updating its state and sending appropriate messages.

IntroRecvJoinRequest enables an *introducer* to process a join request and add the sender to its pending group member addition list.

IntroDetectFail allows an *introducer* to detect a failure in the group and mark the node for deletion.

UpdateOp facilitates an *introducer*'s execution of group membership updates, sending operation and group structure messages.

RecvInform allows an *idle* node to receive an inform message and update its state to *informed*.

RecvFinish enables an *informed* node to transition back to *idle* upon receiving a finish message.

InformedTimeout causes an *informed* node to time out due to the introducer's failure, reverting to *idle*.

ForwardJoinReq enables an *informed* node to forward a join request to the introducer and inform the joiner.

RecvOp allows an *informed* node to apply membership changes, send *gsinfo* messages to the new members and transition to *idle*.

Finally, *NodeFail* causes a node in an active state to transition to *fail*.

B Lazy Failure Detection Algorithm Actions List

As shown in Specification B.1, the *Next* action of the lazy failure detection specification consists of 12 sub-actions:

SendCMsg enables an *idle* node to select a group member as a target for a message, updating its state to *Sending* and incrementing its message count.

ReceiveCMsg allows a node to process a message by replying with an acknowledgment if it is the intended recipient or discarding the message otherwise.

$$
\begin{array}{l}
Next \triangleq \\
\quad \lor \exists i \in Nodes : \exists n \in Nodes : \\
\quad\quad SendJoinRequest(n, i) \\
\quad \lor \exists n \in Nodes : RecvGroupStruct(n) \\
\quad \lor \exists n \in Nodes : RecvGsInfo(n) \\
\quad \lor \exists n \in Nodes : RecvAllGsInfo(n) \\
\quad \lor \exists n \in Nodes : RecvJoinFail(n) \\
\quad \lor \exists n \in Nodes : RecvHandlerUpdate(n) \\
\quad \lor \exists n \in Nodes : JoinReqTimeout(n) \\
\quad \lor \exists n \in Nodes : RecvJoinRequest(n) \\
\quad \lor \exists n \in Nodes : IdleDetectFail(n) \\
\quad \lor \exists n \in Nodes : IdleLeave(n) \\
\quad \lor \exists n \in Nodes : TryDeleteInform(n) \\
\quad \lor \exists n \in Nodes : SelfUpdate(n) \\
\quad \lor \exists n \in Nodes : RecvInformAck(n) \\
\quad \lor \exists n \in Nodes : RecvAllInformAck(n) \\
\quad \lor \exists n \in Nodes : InformTimeout(n) \\
\quad \lor \exists n \in Nodes : IntroRecvJoinRequest(n) \\
\quad \lor \exists n \in Nodes : IntroDetectFail(n) \\
\quad \lor \exists n \in Nodes : UpdateOp(n) \\
\quad \lor \exists n \in Nodes : RecvInform(n) \\
\quad \lor \exists n \in Nodes : RecvFinish(n) \\
\quad \lor \exists n \in Nodes : InformedTimeout(n) \\
\quad \lor \exists n \in Nodes : ForwardJoinReq(n) \\
\quad \lor \exists n \in Nodes : RecvOp(n) \\
\quad \lor \exists n \in Nodes : NodeFail(n)
\end{array}
$$

Specification A.1: The *Next* of the group list consistency algorithm

ReceiveCAck facilitates a *sending* node's return to the *idle* state upon receiving an acknowledgment for its message.

CMsgSendTimeout transitions a node from *Sending* to *Skeptic* if no acknowledgment is received within the timeout period.

SendAssistRequests enables skeptical nodes to request assistance from other group members, transitioning their state to *Collecting*.

ReceiveAssistResult allows a *collecting* node to update its detection results based on responses from assist responders.

CollectedAssistResults reduces these results, confirming or dismissing the suspected failure and resetting the node to *idle*.

ReceiveAssistRequest facilitates nodes in handling assist requests by sending detection messages to the specified target.

ReceiveDetectResp allows nodes to process responses to detection messages and add the results to the requestor's detection set.

DetectTimeout ensures that when the detect process timeout, detected nodes are marked as failed, sending results back to the requestor.

ReceiveDetectMsg enables nodes to process detection messages and reply with detection responses.

Finally, *Fail* transitions any node to the *Fail* state, clearing its mailboxes.

$$
\begin{array}{l}
\mathit{Next} \triangleq \\
\quad \lor \exists\, n \in \mathit{GroupNodes} : \\
\quad\quad \exists\, r \in \mathit{GroupNodes} : \\
\quad\quad \mathit{SendCMsg}(n, r) \\
\quad \lor \exists\, n \in \mathit{GroupNodes} : \mathit{ReceiveCMsg}(n) \\
\quad \lor \exists\, n \in \mathit{GroupNodes} : \mathit{ReceiveCAck}(n) \\
\quad \lor \exists\, n \in \mathit{GroupNodes} : \mathit{CMsgSendTimeout}(n) \\
\quad \lor \exists\, n \in \mathit{GroupNodes} : \mathit{SendAssistRequests}(n) \\
\quad \lor \exists\, n \in \mathit{GroupNodes} : \mathit{ReceiveAssistResult}(n) \\
\quad \lor \exists\, n \in \mathit{GroupNodes} : \mathit{CollectedAssistResults}(n) \\
\quad \lor \exists\, n \in \mathit{GroupNodes} : \mathit{ReceiveAssistRequest}(n) \\
\quad \lor \exists\, n \in \mathit{GroupNodes} : \mathit{ReceiveDetectResp}(n) \\
\quad \lor \exists\, n \in \mathit{GroupNodes} : \mathit{DetectTimeout}(n) \\
\quad \lor \exists\, n \in \mathit{GroupNodes} : \mathit{ReceiveDetectMsg}(n) \\
\quad \lor \exists\, n \in \mathit{GroupNodes} : \mathit{Fail}(n)
\end{array}
$$

Specification B.1: The *Next* of the lazy failure detection algorithm

C Execution Output of the Test Sample

```
>stack test
lazy-0.1.0.0: unregistering (local file changes: test\Spec.hs)
lazy> build (lib + exe + test) with ghc-8.4.3
Preprocessing library for lazy-0.1.0.0..
Building library for lazy-0.1.0.0..
ignoring (possibly broken) abi-depends field for packages
Preprocessing executable 'lazy-exe' for lazy-0.1.0.0..
Building executable 'lazy-exe' for lazy-0.1.0.0..
Preprocessing test suite 'lazy-test' for lazy-0.1.0.0..
Building test suite 'lazy-test' for lazy-0.1.0.0..
[2 of 2] Compiling Main
Linking .stack-work\\dist\\61e22556\\build\\lazy-test
\\lazy-test.exe ...
lazy> copy/register
Installing library in
...
Registering library for lazy-0.1.0.0..
lazy> test (suite: lazy-test)
createNode
Node created with NodeId: NodeId {host = (127,0,0,1), port = 8080}
  successfully creates a node with correct return values
enableRecvInform
```

```
[enableRecvInform] Current nodeState: Idle
  returns True when LocalInfo state is Idle
[enableRecvInform] Current nodeState: Informed
  returns False when LocalInfo state is not Idle
recvInform
[recvInform] Updated localInfo: LocalInfo {nodeState = Informed,
localInformId = (NodeId {host = (127,0,0,1), port = 9000},42),
introCounter = 1, inMemory = NodeId {host = (0,0,0,0), port = 0},
numInMemory = 0, toAdd = fromList [], toDelete = fromList [],
deleteInform = fromList [], ack = fromList [],
groupList = fromList []}
[recvInform] Sending Informack message: Informack {informId =
(NodeId {host = (127,0,0,1),
port = 9000},42),
sender = NodeId {host = (127,0,0,1), port = 8080}} to 127.0.0.1:9000
  updates LocalInfo to Informed with new informID

Finished in 0.0683 seconds
4 examples, 0 failures
lazy> Test suite lazy-test passed
Completed 2 action(s).
```

References

1. Agha, G.A., Kim, W.: Actors: a unifying model for parallel and distributed computing. J. Syst. Architect. **45**(15), 1263–1277 (1999)
2. Allavena, A., Demers, A.J., Hopcroft, J.E.: Correctness of a gossip based membership protocol. In: Aguilera, M.K., Aspnes, J. (eds.) Proceedings of the Twenty-Fourth Annual ACM Symposium on Principles of Distributed Computing, PODC 2005, Las Vegas, NV, USA, 17-20 July 2005, pp. 292–301. ACM (2005)
3. Aspnes, J.: Notes on theory of distributed systems. CoRR arXiv, abs/arXiv: 2001.04235 (2020)
4. Bazzan, A.L., Klügl, F.: Introduction to intelligent systems in traffic and transportation. Springer Nature (2022)
5. Bernstein, P.A., Hadzilacos, V., Goodman, N., et al.: Concurrency control and recovery in database systems, vol. 370. Addison-wesley Reading (1987)
6. Birman, K.P.: Guide to reliable distributed systems: building high-assurance applications and cloud-hosted services. Springer Science & Business Media (2012)
7. Bragilevsky, V.: Haskell in Depth. Simon and Schuster (2021)
8. Das, A., Gupta, I., Motivala, A.: Swim: scalable weakly-consistent infection-style process group membership protocol. In: Proceedings International Conference on Dependable Systems and Networks, pp. 303–312 (2002)
9. Gray, J., Lamport, L.: Consensus on transaction commit. ACM Trans. Database Syst. **31**(1), 133–160 (2006)
10. Hackage Contributors: secureudp - haskell package. https://hackage.haskell.org/package/secureUDP (2017), Accessed 10 Dec 2024

11. Hackage Contributors: cereal - Haskell package. https://hackage.haskell.org/package/cereal (2022), Accessed 10 Dec 2024
12. Hackage Contributors: containers - Haskell package. https://hackage.haskell.org/package/containers (2023), Accessed 10 Dec 2024
13. Hasan, R., Anwar, Z., Yurcik, W., Brumbaugh, L., Campbell, R.: A survey of peer-to-peer storage techniques for distributed file systems. In: International Conference on Information Technology: Coding and Computing (ITCC 2005), vol. 2, pp. 205–213. IEEE (2005)
14. Lamport, L.: Time, clocks and the ordering of events in a distributed system. Commun. ACM **21**, 558-565 (1978)
15. Lamport, L.: Paxos made simple. ACM SIGACT News (Distributed Computing Column) 32, 4 (Whole Number 121, December 2001) pp. 51–58 (December 2001)
16. Lamport, L.: Specifying Systems: The TLA+ Language and Tools for Hardware and Software Engineers. Addison-Wesley Longman Publishing Co., Inc, USA (2002)
17. Mohapatra, S., Rahimi, M.R., Venkatasubramanian, N.: Power-aware middleware for mobile applications. In: Ahmad, I., Ranka, S. (eds.) Handbook of Energy-Aware and Green Computing - Two Volume Set, pp. 193–224. Chapman and Hall/CRC (2012)
18. Ongaro, D., Ousterhout, J.: In search of an understandable consensus algorithm. In: Proceedings of the 2014 USENIX Conference on USENIX Annual Technical Conference, USENIX ATC 2014, pp. 305–320. USENIX Association, USA (2014)
19. O'Sullivan, B., Goerzen, J., Stewart, D.B.: Real world haskell: Code you can believe in. O'Reilly Media, Inc. (2008)
20. Reiter, M.: A secure group membership protocol. IEEE Trans. Software Eng. **22**(1), 31–42 (1996). https://doi.org/10.1109/32.481515
21. Saputri, F.R., Dhaneswari, S.F.: Sensor design for building environment monitoring system based on blynk. Ultima Comput.: Jurnal Sistem Komputer **14**(1), 36–41 (2022)
22. Stoica, I., et al.: Chord: a scalable peer-to-peer lookup protocol for internet applications. IEEE/ACM Trans. Netw. **11**(1), 17–32 (2003). https://doi.org/10.1109/TNET.2002.808407
23. Tran, T.H.: Symbolic Verification of TLA+ Specifications with Applications to Distributed Algorithms. Ph. D. thesis, Technische Universität Wien (2023)
24. Uzair, M., Yacoub Al-Kafrawi, S., Manaf Al-Janadi, K., Abdulrahman Al-Bulushi, I.: A low-cost iot based buildings management system (bms) using arduino mega 2560 and raspberry pi 4 for smart monitoring and automation. Inter. J. Electr. Comput. Eng. Syst. **13**(3), 219–236 (2022)
25. Wayne, H.: Practical TLA+: Planning Driven Development. Apress (2018)

Energy-Aware Dynamic Adaptation of Runtime Systems

Jordy Aaldering(✉), Bernard van Gastel, and Sven-Bodo Scholz

Radboud University, Nijmegen, The Netherlands
{Jordy.Aaldering,Bernard.vanGastel,SvenBodo.Scholz}@ru.nl

Abstract. In recent years the energy-efficiency of software has become a key focus for both researchers and software developers, aiming to reduce greenhouse-gas emissions and operational costs. Despite this growing awareness, developers still lack effective strategies to improve the energy-efficiency of their programs beyond the well-established approaches that optimize for runtime performance. In this paper we present a dynamic adaptation algorithm that uses energy consumption feedback to optimize the energy-efficiency of data-parallel applications, by steering the level of parallelism during runtime through external control. This approach is especially suited to functional languages, whose side-effect-free nature and strong semantic guarantees allow for easier code generation and straightforward scalability of the parallelism of programs.

Through a series of experiments we evaluate the effectiveness of our approach. We measure how well the adaptation algorithm adapts to runtime changes, and we evaluate its effectiveness compared to a hypothesized oracle that knows the optimal level of parallelism, as well as a runtime-optimising-based approach. We show that in a fixed-workload scenario we approach the theoretical best energy-efficiency, and that in changing workload scenarios the adaptation algorithm converges towards an optimal level of parallelism that minimizes energy consumption.

Keywords: Dynamic Adaptation · Runtime Systems · Energy-Efficiency · Sustainability · High-Performance Computing · Parallel Programming

1 Introduction

The importance of software sustainability has grown rapidly in recent years, alongside an increasing awareness of environmental concerns. From mobile applications to data centres, minimizing the energy consumption of software has become essential for mitigating environmental impact, increasing battery life, and reducing operational costs. Traditional software systems often focus on maximizing runtime performance without adequately considering energy consumption. However, as sustainability becomes a priority, there is a growing need for approaches that balance runtime performance and energy-efficiency.

The current landscape of computing hardware is characterized by its heterogeneity, with a shift towards multicore and many-core systems. High-performance computing applications typically aim to fully utilize all available resources

J. Gibbons (Ed.): TFP 2025, LNCS 15652, pp. 435–458, 2026.
https://doi.org/10.1007/978-3-031-99751-8_19

on these systems, with the goal of maximizing runtime performance. Determining efficient resource allocation for optimizing performance – be it runtime or energy-efficiency – depends not only on an algorithm's implementation, but also on input data size, hardware characteristics, cache utilization, and system-specific configurations such as thread pinning. This makes static approaches for determining resource allocation increasingly difficult, as they fail to account for variations in hardware capabilities [4]. Furthermore, it has been shown that optimizing for runtime is not always equivalent to optimizing for energy-efficiency, and that optimizing runtime can have a negative effect on energy consumption [3,34].

A key candidate for improving the energy-efficiency through more efficient resource allocation is the thread management of an application. Traditionally, thread management in software systems has focused primarily on performance metrics such as execution time and operations per second. A notable approach in the context of the Single assignment C (SaC) language uses a dynamic adaptation algorithm that adjusts the thread-count of a program by observing changes in runtime metrics [18]. This technique enables SaC applications to adapt to varying workloads and resource availability, improving runtime performance by efficiently utilizing computational resources. This method optimizes for runtime performance, but does not directly address energy consumption.

We present a method that extends existing runtime adaptation techniques by incorporating energy consumption as the primary factor in decision-making. By dynamically adjusting the number of threads based on real-time energy consumption metrics, we show that it is possible to achieve a more sustainable balance between runtime performance and energy-efficiency. Functional languages are an especially suitable target for this dynamic adaptation algorithm, as their side-effect-free nature and strong semantic guarantees allow for easier code generation and straightforward scalability of the parallelism of programs.

Our contributions are:

- A static analysis of data-parallel programs that investigates the relation between the level of parallelism and overall energy consumption (Sect. 4).
- A dynamic adaptation algorithm that aims to minimize energy consumption of data-parallel programs at runtime through external control (Sect. 5).
- An implementation of a thread-steering mechanism in the data-parallel functional language SaC, based on this adaptation algorithm (Sect. 6.1).
- An evaluation of how close the adaptation algorithm comes to the energy-efficiency of a theoretical optimum (Sects. 6.3 and 6.4).
- An evaluation of the energy-efficiency of the adaptation algorithm compared a runtime-based approach and static approaches (Sect. 6.5 and 6.6).

2 Single Assignment C

Single assignment C (SaC) is a functional array language that resembles the imperative syntax of languages such as C, whilst remaining side-effect-free [20,21]. It aims to generate high-performance parallel code for a wide range of multicore and many-core architectures from a single source code.

One of the key design choices that makes this possible is the use of a single language construct for all array operations, named a tensor comprehension [39]. These tensor comprehensions are side-effect-free mappings from index spaces to element values, based on the set builder notation.

Take for example the following tensor comprehension:

```
res = { iv -> arr[iv] + 1 | [0,0] <= iv < [9,9] };
```

It constitutes an index vector `iv` that ranges over the index set with lower bound `[0,0]` and upper bound `[9,9]`. If the lower or upper bound can be inferred from the usage of `iv` in the inner expression, they may be left out. In the example, the upper bound would be inferred as the shape of `arr`. For each index vector in this range, the result is a selection into the array `arr` incremented by one.

All array types in SaC consist of an element type followed by a shape specification in square brackets. In simple cases, such shape specifications are lists of numbers describing the length of each dimension of the array. To express relations between shape components, these shape lengths can be replaced by variables, where identical variable names require identical lengths in the corresponding positions. For example, an integer vector of length 100 can be defined as `int[100]`, and a square integer matrix of size $n \times n$ can be referred to as `int[n,n]`. A multi-dimensional array of doubles with rank d and shape vector shp can be described by `double[d:shp]`. This notation is referred to as type patterns [2]. It allows not only to express constraints within shapes but also between different function arguments and return types. Take for example the shape constraints of a matrix multiplication. It requires that the multiplied matrices are of shapes $u \times v$ and $v \times w$, resulting in a $u \times w$ matrix.

This can be expressed as:

```
double[u,w] matmul(double[u,v] a, double[v,w] b)
```

Furthermore, shape variables such as `u`, `v`, and `w` can be used in function bodies as if they are user-defined variables. In combination with variable-rank type patterns, this allows for the embeddings of complicated shape expressions within type patterns, simplifying the function bodies.

2.1 Parallelism in Single Assignment C

The SaC compiler is able to generate parallel code for a range of parallel architectures, including multicore machines [19], GPUs [23,26], and clusters [31]. In this paper, we extend the work on code generation for multicore machines.

Before the actual generation of multithreaded code, the high-level optimization phase of the compiler extensively fuses tensor comprehensions to increase the granularity of parallelism and to improve the locality of code [21]. The multicore back-end then generates code to execute all top-level tensor comprehensions of sufficiently large size in parallel [19]. Each of these regions is executed in a fork-join style of bulk synchronous computing. To avoid the overhead of thread creation and termination for each such parallel region, threads are created only once upon program startup and kept active throughout the execution.

We refer to such a set of threads as *bees* in a *bee hive*. One designated thread, the *queen bee*, executes the entire program including the sequential sections, and coordinates all the other bees. The other bees wait until the start of a parallel section is signalled to them by the queen, and they return to the waiting state thereafter. More details on the multithreaded back-end can be found in [19].

3 Defining "Energy Consumption"

To quantify the energy-efficiency of a program, it is essential that we accurately define what we mean by its "energy consumption". Ideally we would isolate the total amount of energy consumed by the hardware to run one specific program, separating it from other sources of energy consumption such as operating system overhead, background tasks, and the baseline power required to keep the hardware operational. However, fully isolating the energy consumption of a single process remains a challenge.

Currently, separating a program's energy consumption from that of other programs is only possible in certain environments. On Apple Silicon, for example, this is possible through the use of the `task_info` API, which returns a per-process energy consumption value [37]. For Apple's Intel-based machines, the `diagCall64` function can be used instead. On Linux-based operating systems, separating the energy consumption is theoretically possible by extending the scheduler statistics, however to our knowledge there is no implementation available. Although these methods provide potential solutions, they lack necessary documentation and would require specific hardware and elevated permissions, which go against our goal of making a broadly applicable adaptation algorithm. Furthermore, these methods still fail to exclude the baseline power required to keep the hardware operational, for which currently no solution exists.

For the purposes of this study we define the energy consumption of a program as the total amount of energy consumed by the CPU throughout the entire runtime of that program, given that no other user-defined programs are running on that device. This implies that operating system overhead and baseline power required to keep the hardware operational are included in these measurements, as we cannot control or isolate these. We hypothesize that: if we succeed in improving the energy-efficiency of a program, this will result in a measurable decrease in total energy consumption across the runtime of that program.

3.1 Measuring Energy Consumption

Running Average Power Limit (RAPL) is a technology developed by Intel to measure and control the energy consumption of the CPU. It can be used to measure the total amount of energy consumed by the CPU throughout the runtime of a program. Although initially based on estimation models, thanks to improvements in hardware support, RAPL has evolved into a precise energy measurement tool. RAPL reports fine-grained and reliable energy consumption data across various CPU domains, such as the package, PSys, and DRAM [28].

RAPL operates using a running counter that tracks the cumulative energy consumed by each of these domains. The energy consumption in micro-Joules over a time interval is calculated as the difference in counter values at the start and end of that time period. RAPL is available on Intel CPUs since the Sandy Bridge architecture (2011), and AMD supports a similar feature starting with their Zen architecture (2017). In addition to its wide availability over the past decade, RAPL requires only slightly elevated privileges [42], making it accessible on most systems.

4 Energy Consumption Patterns

We perform a set of static experiments to determine which factors affect the energy consumption patterns of programs. Our aim is to determine whether there are cases where using all available resources is not optimal, and whether optimizing for energy-efficiency always correlates with optimizing for runtime. We do this to gain insight that informs the design process of the dynamic adaptation algorithm in Sect. 5.

Presumably, using all available resources of a system does not necessarily lead to the lowest energy consumption. Energy consumption patterns of programs are influenced by a wide range of factors, such as algorithm implementation, workload behaviour, and hardware characteristics. To illustrate this we investigate the effect these factors have on the energy consumption pattern of the N-body, nine-point stencil, and matrix multiplication algorithms. Within the context of data-parallel programming, these algorithms provide an interesting mix of CPU-bound and memory-bound applications.

Benchmarks are conducted on an Intel Xeon E-2378 server, maintained by the Radboud University. The system is accessible through Slurm, and contains a single 8 core 16 thread CPU, running at a base clock of 2.60GHz. The CPU has 16MB of level three cache, and the system itself provides 32GB of RAM.

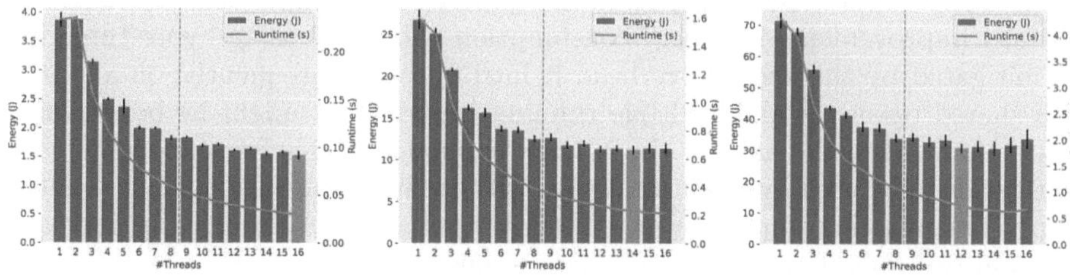

(a) 10000 elements. (b) 25000 elements. (c) 40000 elements.

Fig. 1. Average energy consumption and runtime of 250 N-body simulation in SaC. Bars denote energy consumption, with corresponding values in the left y-axis. The line denotes runtime, corresponding to the right y-axis.

4.1 N-Body Simulation

As our first benchmark we measure the energy consumption and runtime of a SaC implementation of the N-body algorithm, given three different problem input sizes. The N-body algorithm is typically applied in physics and astronomy to simulate the effect of physical sources, like gravity, on systems of bodies such as particles and celestial objects. Each body is defined by a record type, containing its current position, velocity, and mass. Although records in SaC use a similar notation as in C, they are fully flattened into arrays of the record's fields, improving data locality [25].

A single time step of the N-body simulation with delta-time `dt` on an array of bodies is defined as follows, where `acc` is a function that returns the acceleration vector between two bodies.

```
struct Body[n] nbody(struct Body[n] bodies, double dt)
{
    accel = { [i] -> sum({ [j] -> acc(bodies[i], bodies[j]) }) };
    bodies.pos += bodies.vel * dt;
    bodies.vel += accel * dt;
    return bodies;
}
```

For these case studies only the relevant parallel codes are measured, namely the tensor comprehensions. The runtime and energy measurements start right before those parallel regions, and stop immediately after their synchronization. The average runtime and energy consumption for the three input sizes are shown in Fig. 1. Along the x-axis is the number of threads, ranging from one to sixteen. Bars denote the average energy consumption of a single time step, and the line denotes its average runtime.

For an N-body simulation with 10000 elements in Fig. 1a we observe that although increasing the thread-count strictly decreases the runtime, for simulations with 25000 and 40000 elements in Figs. 1b and 1c respectively, the energy consumption plateaus when using more than eight threads. It seems that any improvements in energy consumption gained by using hyper-threading are mitigated by the energy overhead it introduces. Consequently, on a system with shared resources and multiple running processes, it might be beneficial to select a lower thread-count for the N-body simulation. This frees up the remaining threads to be used by other processes, without incurring a significant negative energy consumption impact on the N-body simulation. Although this increases the total runtime, it can conversely lead to energy savings.

An interesting observation, seen in the following benchmarks as well, is that increasing the thread-count has a greater effect on runtime performance than on energy-efficiency. This suggests that the overhead caused by having to manage multiple threads has a stronger negative effect on the energy consumption of a program than on its runtime performance, and that optimizing for runtime performance has diminishing returns for decreasing energy consumption.

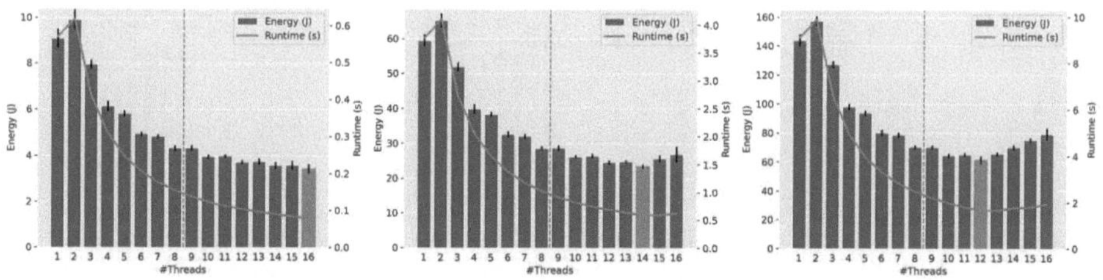

(a) 10000×10000 points. (b) 25000×25000 points. (c) 40000×40000 points.

Fig. 2. Average energy consumption and runtime of 250 nine-point stencil operations in SaC. Bars denote energy consumption, with corresponding values in the left y-axis. The line denotes runtime, corresponding to the right y-axis.

4.2 Nine-Point Stencil

The nine-point stencil operation is used for image processing, computer simulations, and for solving partial differential equations. Perhaps the most common application of the stencil operation nowadays is in the training process of Convolutional Neural Networks (CNN). In this context, the stencil operation is applied for edge-detection and other image processing tasks, as well as for providing a means for spatial awareness. Most relevant to us is the application of the stencil operation for resizing arrays in CNNs, which highlights a real-world scenario where the input data size changes during the runtime of a program.

The nine-point stencil is defined as a weighted sum of each point in an array and its eight immediate neighbours, where each weight depends on the corresponding value in a 3×3 array of weights. It is defined in SaC as:

```
double[2:shp] stencil(double[2:shp] arr, double[3,3] w)
{
    return { iv -> sum({ jv -> w[jv] * arr[mod(iv+jv-1, shp)] })
           | iv < shp };
}
```

For a 10000×10000 input matrix in Fig. 2a we observe that both the runtime and energy consumption decrease as the number of threads increases. However, for 25000×25000 and 40000×40000 inputs, using all available threads is no longer optimal for both the energy-efficiency and runtime performance. We see this in Figs. 2b and 2c respectively, whereas the input size increases, the optimum thread-count decreases.

4.3 Matrix Multiplication

The matrix multiplication algorithm is used across a variety of domains, from solving linear equations, to machine learning, to computer graphics. Whereas more sophisticated approaches aim to have consistent cache locality [41], the cache locality of the naive approach decreases as the input size increases, shifting

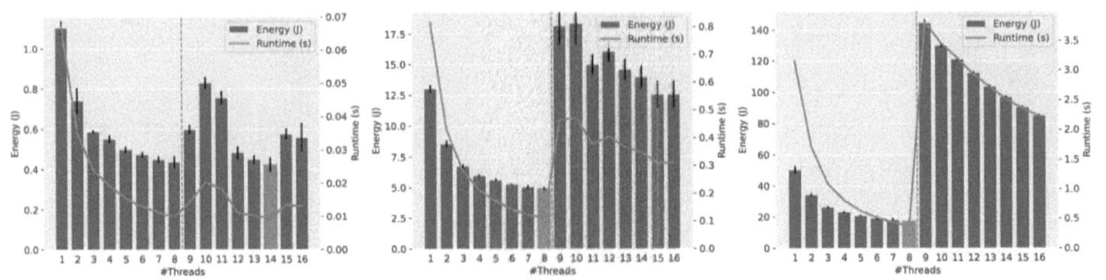

(a) 500 × 500 matrix. (b) 1000 × 1000 matrix. (c) 1500 × 1500 matrix.

Fig. 3. Average energy consumption and runtime of 250 naive matrix multiplications in SaC. Bars denote energy consumption, with corresponding values in the left y-axis. The line denotes runtime, corresponding to the right y-axis.

the bottleneck from CPU to memory. We implement the naive algorithm, since this behaviour provides us with an interesting case study.

The SaC implementation closely resembles the mathematical definition:

```
double[u,w] matmul(double[u,v] a, double[v,w] b)
{
    return { [i,j] -> sum({ [k] -> a[i,k] * b[k,j] }) };
}
```

Due to cache behaviour of the naive implementation, manual tuning is required to ensure an efficient thread layout. When using eight or fewer threads, an interleaved mode is optimal, ensuring each thread executes on a different physical core. However, since the system only has eight physical cores, using nine or more threads requires multi-threading. At this point an interleaved mode is no longer beneficial as it increases the amount of false sharing, drastically decreasing performance. It should be noted that choosing a different thread pinning strategy leads to significantly different observations, and that choosing an efficient thread layout is crucial to the performance of this benchmark.

The results of a 500 × 500 matrix multiplication in Fig. 3a align with our expectations; increasing the number of threads up to eight threads improves both the energy-efficiency and the runtime performance. Using more threads causes a decrease in performance, likely due to additional thread management overhead. This overhead is somewhat overcome by the increase in thread-count, making a thread-count of fourteen threads similar in performance to a thread-count of eight. However, as observed in Figs. 3b and 3c, increasing the matrix size to 1000 × 1000 and 1500 × 1500 changes this energy consumption pattern, resulting from the shift of being CPU-bound to being memory-bound. Even with an efficient thread pinning strategy, using more than eight threads causes a significant increase in both the energy consumption and runtime, making those approaches worse for energy-efficiency than even a single-threaded approach.

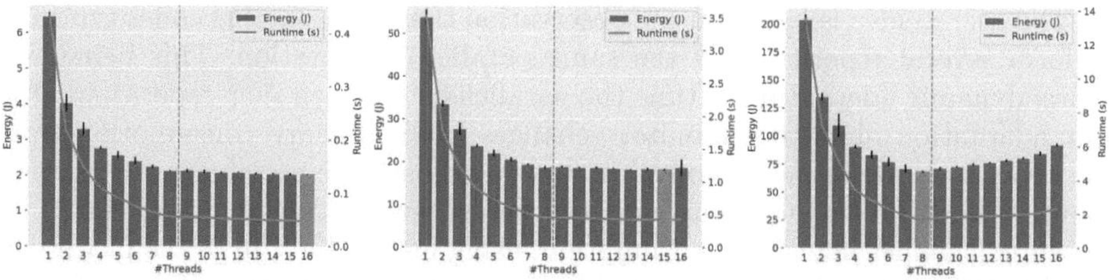

(a) 500 × 500 matrix. (b) 1000 × 1000 matrix. (c) 1500 × 1500 matrix.

Fig. 4. Average energy consumption and runtime of 250 naive matrix multiplications in Rust. Bars denote energy consumption, with corresponding values in the left y-axis. The line denotes runtime, corresponding to the right y-axis.

4.4 Implementation Language

To validate that these observations are not specific to SaC, we also evaluate a manually parallelized implementation of the matrix multiplication algorithm in Rust. We observe in Fig. 4 that switching the implementation language from SaC to Rust produces a significantly different energy consumption pattern. In Figs. 4a and 4b we observe that up until eight threads, increasing the thread-count improves both the energy-efficiency and runtime. When using more than eight threads, both the energy consumption and runtime plateau, suggesting that we gain no additional benefits by using hyper-threading. As the matrix size increases to 1500 × 1500, there is a shift in the energy consumption pattern. As the number of threads increases from 8 to 16, the energy consumption gradually increases again. This suggests that the overhead associated with hyper-threading outweighs the benefits of further parallelization.

Interestingly, although the SaC and Rust implementations provide a similar level of performance when using nine or more threads, comparing the best-case scenarios we find that the SaC implementation performs roughly four times better in terms of energy consumption and roughly five times better in terms of runtime. As discussed previously, thread pinning and cache behaviour have a significant impact on the performance characteristics of this benchmark. Although we suspect that these are the main reasons for this performance difference, it is unclear why exactly this behaviour occurs, complicating the task of determining an optimal thread-count and emphasizing the need for a dynamic approach.

5 Energy-Aware Dynamic Adaptation

In Sect. 4 we determine a multitude of running conditions that affect the selection of a thread-count for maximal energy-efficiency. Given the multitude of effects, a static cost-model-based approach seems infeasible. A profiling-based approach might provide better data but would incur a significant energy overhead. Consequently, we look for a solution that avoids the need for manual tuning by dynamically adapting to runtime changes.

The overall idea is based on the observation that data-parallel codes typically perform several repetitions of the same parallel computation. This behaviour allows dynamic adaptation to tune the parallelism between such repetitions [18]. Our adaptation algorithm monitors changes in the energy consumption from one repetition to the next, and periodically adjusts the recommended thread-count to find the thread-count with the lowest energy consumption. Based on measured changes in energy consumption, using meters built in to the processor, the algorithm determines whether to increase or decrease the thread count for the next iteration, and by what amount. The hypothesis is that with this approach, we can adapt the thread-count during runtime in correspondence to changes in energy consumption, converging to a (local) optimum for energy-efficiency.

The algorithm recomputes the recommended thread-count at a fixed interval; waiting for a fixed amount of energy measurements to arrive. Each of these energy measurements is the energy consumed during a single iteration of the parallel region, measured using RAPL (Sect. 3). The frequency is configurable, but we find for our benchmarks that a frequency of ten iterations per thread-count adjustment strikes a balance between a high adaptation speed whilst also being resilient against noise such as short-running background tasks and operating system overhead. The algorithm uses two variables for steering the thread-count of an application: a step direction, and a step size. The step direction describes whether the number of threads will be increased or decreased, corresponding to a value of 1 or -1. The step size gives the amount of threads that will be added or removed from the current thread-count, respectively.

When the median energy consumption of an iteration differs more than a factor α compared to the energy consumption of the previous iteration, we hypothesize that there is likely a change in workload behaviour or system configuration. To quickly converge to the new optimal thread-count, the step size is reset to half the number of maximum threads. For our benchmarks we observe that a value of 0.5 for α works well. Otherwise, if there was an increase in energy consumption that is less than factor α, this means that the previous iteration was more energy-efficient. We predict that the optimal thread-count is somewhere in between the current thread-count and the previous thread-count. Therefore, the step direction is inverted, and the current step size is halved.

As we observe in Sect. 4, changing the thread-count by even a single thread can have a significant negative impact on the energy consumption of a program. In an attempt to minimize this overhead, alongside the intrinsic scheduling overhead for making changes to the thread-count, we aim to settle into a fixed thread-count when we are close to the (local) optimum. To this end we use a real-valued step size that nears zero as we get close to this optimum, as opposed to a positive integer step size that always results in a change to the thread-count. Whereas typically the step size is halved in each iteration, as it reaches zero we gradually decrease it by a lower amount, ensuring that changes to the thread-count do still occur occasionally. This change to the step size is defined by a function $\Delta t \,/\, (\Delta t + \beta)$, where a lower value for β results in smaller changes to the step size. For our benchmarks we find that a value of 0.85 for β works well.

Eventually the step size reaches zero, and the thread-count will stagnate. In an attempt to escape potential local optima, the step size is reset to half the maximum number of threads when it becomes less than γ. The lower the value of γ, the more iterations are required until the step size is reset. Given our choice for β, a value of 0.155 for γ works well for our benchmarks.

A formal definition of this algorithm is described in Algorithm 1.

Algorithm 1. Algorithm for repeatedly updating the thread-count n_t based on energy measurements S, using step direction $\hat{d}$ and step size Δt.

$\hat{d} \leftarrow -1$
$\Delta t \leftarrow m_t \,/\, 2$
$E_{old} \leftarrow 0$
loop
$S \leftarrow$ Wait for samples
$E_{new} \leftarrow median(S)$
if $E_{new} \,/\, E_{old} < (1-\alpha) \vee E_{new} \,/\, E_{old} > (1+\alpha)$ **then**
$\hat{d} \leftarrow sign(m_t - 2n_t)$
$\Delta t \leftarrow m_t \,/\, 2$
else
if $E_{new} > E_{old}$ **then**
$\hat{d} \leftarrow -\hat{d}$
if $\Delta t > \gamma$ **then**
$\Delta t \leftarrow max(\Delta t \,/\, 2,\ \Delta t \,/\, (\Delta t + \beta))$
else
$\hat{d} \leftarrow sign(m_t - 2n_t)$
$\Delta t \leftarrow m_t \,/\, 2$
$E_{old} \leftarrow E_{new}$
$n_t \leftarrow n_t + \hat{d} \cdot \Delta t$
$n_t \leftarrow max(1,\ min(m_t,\ n_t))$

A limitation of this approach are its manually tuned variables, which may require reconfiguration in different contexts. The main challenge arises from variations in energy-efficiency across hardware, and run-to-run fluctuations due to input-dependent behaviour and changes in the software environment. While control theory [9] appears promising, it is not easily applicable to discrete values like thread-count, as it is designed for continuous systems. We believe genetic algorithms may be more suitable, which we plan to explore in future work.

6 Case-Studies

We conduct a series of experiments to evaluate the effectiveness of the dynamic adaptation algorithm. First we evaluate the ability of the algorithm to adapt to runtime changes and reach an optimal thread-count, by comparing the thread-count given by the adaptation algorithm to an optimal thread-count that can be derived from the observations in Sect. 4.

To evaluate how close the adaptation algorithm comes to the performance of a theoretical optimum, we compare its effectiveness against a hypothesized oracle that always determines the most energy-efficient number of threads. To investigate whether there are differences between our energy-optimising approach and a runtime-optimising approach, we similarly compare our solution to the runtime-based adaptation algorithm described by Gordon et al. [18]. We investigate whether the adaptation algorithm introduces significant energy overhead, and finally we measure how much energy the adaptation algorithm saves compared to multiple static approaches.

Both the energy-based and runtime-based dynamic adaptation algorithms, the benchmark scripts, and the benchmark results are publicly available on GitHub [1]. The implementation of the thread-switching beehive system and adaptation algorithm in SaC are available on the SaC GitLab project [22].

6.1 Thread-Management in Single Assignment C

We hook into SaC's beehive system, explained in Sect. 2.1, to control the number of threads of SaC programs dynamically. Before sending a signal to the worker bees to start processing, the queen requests the recommended thread-count and decreases or increases the size of the hive by putting worker bees to sleep or waking up sleeping bees, respectively. Since the actual thread-count is fixed, we selectively put bees to sleep through the use of a semaphore. The side-effect-free nature of the parallel code enables the required workload redistributions through the queen bee without any potential impact on the semantics of the program. Instead of SaC's standard busy wait, we use a semaphore to ensures that the threads of sleeping bees incur no additional energy consumption, and are free to be used by other processes on the system. The queen bee wakes sleeping bees sending a message to their semaphore, after which these bees enter the busy wait state again, waiting for the signal to start working.

6.2 Energy Overhead

With our goal of minimizing the energy consumption of programs, it is crucial that the adaptation algorithm itself does not introduce a significant amount of energy overhead. We measure the overhead introduced by the adaptation algorithm by applying it to a function with an empty body. The measured sources of overhead include the starting and stopping of each energy measurement, and the re-computation of the suggested thread-count when ten energy measurements have been supplied. The energy consumption and runtime overhead are measured by repeating this process one million times. We find that on average the algorithm has an energy overhead of $48\mu J$ and a runtime overhead of $5\mu s$. Considering that even a single 500×500 matrix multiplication consumes around half a Joule in the best case, we conclude that the adaptation algorithm does not introduce significant energy overhead.

While there might be additional effects of the adaptation that cause overhead, such as context switches or other operating system effects, we fail to identify

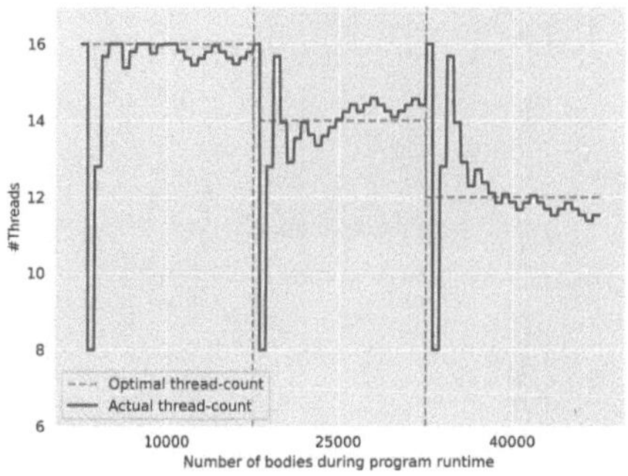

Fig. 5. Adaptation quality on the SaC implementation of the N-body simulation.

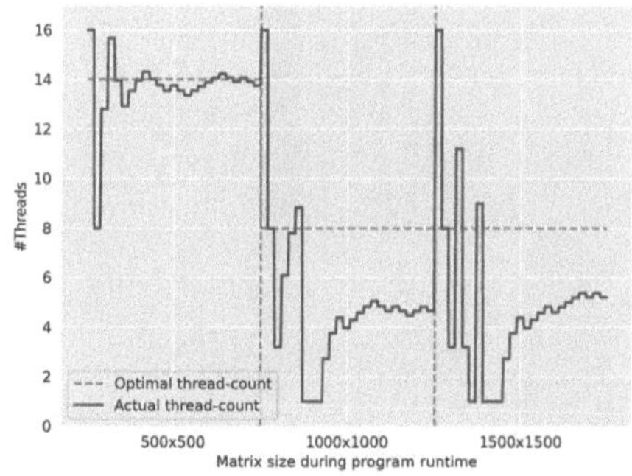

Fig. 6. Adaptation quality on the SaC implementation of the matrix multiplication algorithm.

experiments that would quantify these effects. We study the overhead that stems from the adjustment process itself in a series of experiments where we look at an execution where the problem-size is being changed over time.

6.3 Adaptation Quality

Factors such as input data size often change during the execution of a program. A prominent real-world example this is observed in the training process of Convolutional Neural Networks, where each layer of the network operates on differently sized arrays. We have observed in Sect. 4 that these changes can cause changes to the optimal thread-count. A key requirement for the adaptation algorithm is its ability to adjust to those changes during the runtime of programs. The objective is to dynamically converge towards the optimal thread-count under changing workload behaviours and system configurations. We evaluate the adaptation quality of the algorithm by gradually changing the input data size to the examples from Sect. 4, and assessing how effectively the adaptation algorithm converges to the thread-count with minimal energy consumption.

Figure 5 shows the actual thread-count suggested by the adaptation algorithm across the runtime of the N-body simulation, alongside the optimum thread-count determined in Sect. 4. The x-axis represents the iterations of the program, where the input data size, denoted by the x-axis labels, changes at fixed intervals. The orange dashed line shows the optimal thread-count derived from the observations in Sect. 4, and the blue line shows the thread-count suggested by the adaptation algorithm. The closer the suggested thread-count comes to the derived optimum, the better the adaptation quality of the algorithm.

In Fig. 5 we observe that the energy consumption plateaus when using eight or more threads. Thread-counts between eight and sixteen threads are close in terms of energy-efficiency. Even so, we see that the adaptation algorithm is able to find the optimum thread-count for the N-body simulation for each of the three input sizes. For brevity we exclude the N-body simulation from the remaining

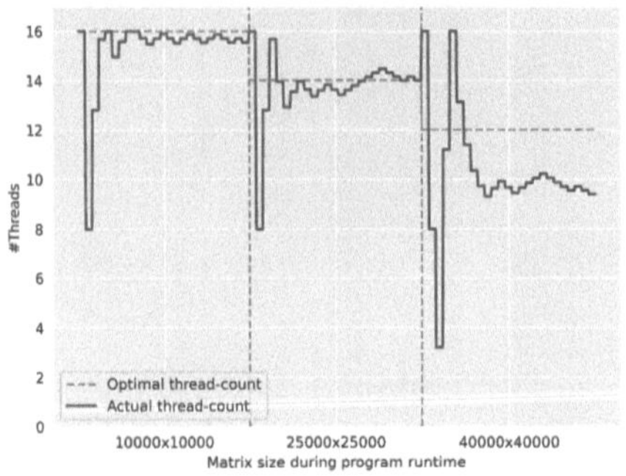

Fig. 7. Adaptation quality on the SaC implementation of the nine-point stencil operation.

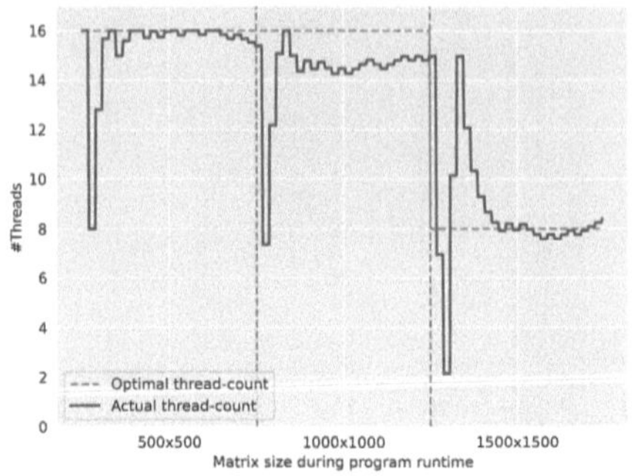

Fig. 8. Adaptation quality on the Rust implementation of the matrix multiplication algorithm.

benchmarks, as it provides a slightly better, but similar, level of performance compared to the nine-point stencil benchmark, and presents no further noteworthy results or insights.

The SaC implementation of the matrix multiplication algorithm presents an interesting challenge. As discussed in Sect. 4, choosing an effective thread pinning strategy is crucial to performance. Whereas an interleaved pinning strategy is optimal when using eight or fewer threads, a contiguous strategy is more effective when using more than eight threads. A drawback of our approach is that threads are disabled in a contiguous order, which results in a suboptimal pinning strategy for this benchmark. In Fig. 6 we see that for 500×500 inputs we converge to the optimal thread-count at fourteen threads, even though the local optimum at eight threads only consumes slightly more energy. However, for the other two input sizes the recommended thread-count around four threads, instead of eight. This happens because the dynamic algorithm disables threads in a contiguous order, resulting in a poor thread pinning strategy.

In Sect. 4 we observe for the nine-point stencil benchmark that as the input data size increases, the optimal thread-count gradually decreases. Applying the adaptation algorithm we see in Fig. 7 that it is able to converge to the optimal thread-count in these cases. Although for 40000×40000 inputs the algorithm suggests a thread-count of ten instead of twelve threads, Fig. 2c shows that the energy consumption at these two thread-counts are within margin of error.

Figure 8 shows the adaptation quality for the Rust implementation. The adaptation algorithm is able to quickly find the optimal thread-count after a change in the matrix size or system configuration.

These experiments show that the dynamic adaptation algorithm is capable of adequately adapting to runtime changes, except in outlier cases such as the 1500×1500 matrix multiplication in SaC where we do however find the local optimum given the suboptimal thread pinning strategy. When a change in the energy consumption pattern occurs, the adaptation algorithm is able to convert to the optimal thread-count within a few thread-count adjustments.

6.4 Comparison to Oracle-Based Approach

To further evaluate the effectiveness of the dynamic adaptation algorithm we compare its performance against a theoretical "oracle" approach. This theoretical oracle knows which thread-count will result in the lowest energy consumption for the current implementation, workload behaviour, and hardware characteristics. Although in general this level of foresight is unattainable without an analysis like the one in Sect. 4, it provides a theoretical upper bound for the performance of the chosen benchmarks. These optimums serve as the baseline to simulate the decision-making process of the oracle. This oracle represents the best possible energy consumption, so any solution that closely approaches its performance can be considered highly effective.

Table 1. Energy and runtime difference of the energy-based approach compared to the theoretical best performance of the oracle-based approach.

Input	Energy	Runtime
10000^2	5%	4%
25000^2	5%	5%
40000^2	15%	33%

(a) Nine-point stencil.

Input	Energy	Runtime
500^2	8%	8%
1000^2	46%	93%
1500^2	68%	100%

(b) Matrix multiplication.

Input	Energy	Runtime
500^2	1%	1%
1000^2	1%	0%
1500^2	10%	16%

(c) Rust implementation.

The comparison to the nine-point stencil operation is shown in Table 1a. It shows that, for 10000×10000 and 25000×25000 inputs, the dynamic approach provides a similar level of performance compared to the oracle, with only a 5% increase in energy consumption. However, for 40000×40000 inputs the energy consumption is increased by 15% compared to the oracle. In Fig. 7 we observed that for this input size the adaptation algorithm recommends ten threads, instead of the optimal thread-count of twelve threads. Although this thread-count has a similar energy consumption compared to running at twelve threads, it does have significantly worse runtime, leading to a 33% increase in runtime. The decrease in energy-efficiency can be attributed to the additional energy cost introduced by the operating system, as well as the power required to keep the hardware operational (Sect. 3), which increases as the runtime increases. Considering these additional energy requirements due to an increase in runtime, a 15% increase in energy consumption compared to a 33% increase in runtime seems reasonable.

Table 1b shows how close the adaptive algorithm comes to the theoretical best performance on the matrix multiplication algorithm, provided by the oracle. For 500×500 inputs we are within 8% of the energy consumption and runtime of the oracle-based approach. However, for the larger input sizes the performance deteriorates. As discussed in Sect. 6.3, this decrease in performance is due to the inability of our controller to switch its pinning strategy. A more sophisticated method might be able to provide a level of performance similar to the 500×500 input, and to the other three benchmarks.

For the Rust implementation of the matrix multiplication algorithm we see in Table 1c that the energy overhead of the dynamic approach is minimal. Even in the case where the dynamic approach has an 18% longer runtime, the increase in energy consumption is only 8%. In the other two cases, the energy-efficiency is within margin of error of the oracle.

These results demonstrate that while this theoretical oracle requires a level of manual tuning that is not feasible in practise, our dynamic approach provides a practical solution for reasonably approximating the theoretical optimal energy-efficiency in most cases.

6.5 Comparison to Runtime-Based Approach

We repeat the same benchmark as in Sect. 6.4, however we now compare the energy-based dynamic adaptation algorithm against an implementation of the dynamic runtime-optimising algorithm described by Gordon et al. [18].

Table 2. Energy and runtime difference of the energy-based approach compared to the runtime-based approach.

Input	Energy	Runtime
10000^2	-2%	-8%
25000^2	-4%	-3%
40000^2	7%	25%

(a) Nine-point stencil.

Input	Energy	Runtime
500^2	-7%	-13%
1000^2	10%	41%
1500^2	-3%	14%

(b) Matrix multiplication.

Input	Energy	Runtime
500^2	-2%	-3%
1000^2	-1%	-1%
1500^2	1%	-2%

(c) Rust implementation.

In Table 2a we see that for the two smaller input sizes the difference in energy consumption between the energy-optimising and runtime-optimising approach is within a few percent. However, the energy-optimising approach does have a 25% greater runtime than the runtime-optimising approach for a 40000×40000 input. As we discuss in the comparison to the oracle-based approach, this is likely due to the fact that the energy-aware algorithm recommends a threat-count of ten, which is similar to using twelve threads in terms of energy consumption, but is significantly worse in terms of runtime. Consequently, the increase in runtime introduces inherent additional energy consumption of the operating system and the hardware itself. Keeping this in mind, compared to the stark increase in runtime, a 7% increase in energy consumption seems reasonable.

In Table 2b we see that for the matrix multiplication benchmark our approach fares better against the runtime-based approach than compared to the oracle. This is due to the fact that the runtime-based implementation is unable to select an effective pinning strategy. Interestingly, for 1500×1500 we observe that the energy-optimising approach decreases energy consumption, but increases runtime, showing that optimizing for energy consumption is not necessarily equivalent to optimizing for runtime.

In Sect. 4 we observe that the energy consumption and runtime performance of the Rust implementation of the matrix multiplication algorithm are strongly correlation. As expected, in Table 2c we see that the energy-based approach and runtime-based approach provide a similar level of performance, both in terms of energy-efficiency and runtime performance.

These results demonstrate that, while a runtime-based method can provide a similar level of performance in cases where energy consumption scales linearly with the number of threads, in cases where the energy consumption or runtime is not strictly decreasing with respect to the thread-count, the runtime-based approach is not able to achieve the same level of energy-efficiency – or even runtime performance – as our energy-based approach.

6.6 Comparison to Static Approaches

Finally, we compare the performance of our dynamic approach to static approaches that run at typically effective thread-counts. Besides running single-threaded, typical choices for threat-count are based on the number of physical cores or the number of available threads. In Sect. 4 we observe that for our examples, choosing twelve threads often also leads to lower energy consumption.

Table 3. Energy and runtime difference of the energy-based approach compared to four fixed thread-count approaches.

Threads	Energy	Runtime
1	–79%	-137%
8	–10%	-39%
12	4%	0%
16	–5%	7%

(a) Nine-point stencil.

Threads	Energy	Runtime
1	–55%	–110%
8	41%	67%
12	–58%	–40%
16	–49%	–29%

(b) Matrix multiplication.

Threads	Energy	Runtime
1	–100%	-157%
8	1%	-3%
12	–2%	-4%
16	–7%	-7%

(c) Rust implementation.

Table 3a describes the difference in energy consumption and runtime between the dynamic adaptation algorithm and static thread-count methods. If a reasonable, but ineffective, choice in thread-count is made for the nine-point stencil operation we observe that 10% of energy can be saved with our dynamic approach. Compared to the single-threaded case, our dynamic approach consumes 79% less energy on average. Statically choosing twelve threads leads to a slightly lower energy consumption, however in practise this is not a thread-count that is typically chosen without an extensive analysis of the optimal thread-count for energy consumption, as we have performed in Sect. 4.

The results of the matrix multiplication example are shown in Table 3b. If a poor choice is made for the static thread-count, we save around 50% of energy, even without an optimal pinning strategy. However, when a static thread-count of eight threads is chosen, which we observed in Sect. 4 is always optimal or near-optimal, our approach consumes 41% more energy.

For the Rust implementation of the matrix multiplication algorithm, Table 3c shows that we save a significant amount of energy compared to a single-threaded approach or when running at sixteen threads, whereas the performance difference is within margin of error when using eight or twelve threads.

From this evaluation we conclude that improvements in energy consumption can be significant in cases where a reasonable but non-optimal choice was made for the static thread-count. When a program-specific and system-specific analysis is applied to determine an optimal static thread count, our dynamic approach still results in similar energy consumption, except for outlier cases such as the naive matrix multiplication where we observe an increase in energy consumption due to an inefficient thread pinning strategy. However, we argue that in general such an analysis is infeasible, and that our approach in most cases provides a reasonable solution for approximating these optimums.

7 Related Work

Dynamic Adaptation Algorithms. Besides the runtime-based dynamic adaptation algorithm[18], there are more approaches that steer the resource allocation of a system through dynamic control, in an attempt to improve runtime performance.

Grand Central Dispatch (GCD) is a technology developed by Apple that aids developers in writing parallel programs [17,33,38]. GCD is integrated into the host operating system and provides an integrated approach for thread management, shifting this load from the developer to the scheduler. However, GCD still requires some manual instrumentation from developers. They must define blocks of code that are dispatched to GCD synchronously or asynchronously, using one of several types of waiting queues. Parallel Dispatch Queues (PDQ) are a similar programming abstraction [8]. By synchronizing messages in a queue, it aims to reduce the overhead caused by acquiring and releasing synchronization primitives, as well as preventing busy waiting within handlers. These approaches do not consider energy-efficiency, and only optimize for runtime performance.

Related is Dynamic Voltage Frequency Scaling (DVFS). Instead of trying to increase energy-efficiency or runtime performance by instrumenting the software, this approach aims to instrument the hardware by scaling the voltage supplied to the CPU. Dynamic programming approaches have been applied to further improve the effectiveness of DVFS [24].

Profile-Based Optimization. Profile-based optimizations use the results of profiling runs to select an optimal implementation of an algorithm for the given input or hardware configuration. A prominent example of this is FFTW3, which selects one of many discrete Fourier transformation implementations through profiling [10]. They achieve this through the use of a special-purpose compiler, that generates optimized code for the given hardware in a planning phase. It would be interesting to investigate whether similar results can be obtained by optimizing for energy-efficiency instead.

Profile-based optimization of virtual machine scheduling is a popular avenue of research in the context of data-centres [5–7,32]. These approaches focus on the development of resource allocation policies and scheduling algorithms that aim to decrease the carbon footprint of data-centres without compromising on the required quality of service.

Static Methods for Optimizing Energy. Although there exists a myriad of compiler optimizations that aim to minimize the runtime of programs, not many optimizations exist that aim to specifically reduce energy consumption [34]. Pallister et al. have provided several optimizations that aim to reduce the energy consumption of programs, in the context of embedded devices [35,36]. As have we, they have found that for optimal energy-efficiency gains a vertical integration process that exploits hardware-specific energy characteristics is needed, to bridge the gap between hardware and software.

Bangash et al. have investigated byte-code transformations in the context of Android applications, determining whether certain (combinations of) transformations lead to in increase or decrease in energy consumption [3]. They found that certain combinations of byte-code transformations can actually increase energy consumption, whereas choosing the right combination of transformation can lead to a reduction of up to 11% in energy consumption.

Energy Visualization and Analysis. One of the key requirements in allowing developers to increase the energy-efficiency of their software is the ability to visualize and analyse the energy consumption of their code [40]. There exist semantics for programming languages that can calculate the energy consumption of their programs, and allow for calculation of break even points of algorithms [12, 13,15]. However, making these semantics work for a full language is hard [14].

Another approach uses model checking to detecting energy bugs and hotspots in control software [16]. The control software targetted with this model does have key interaction between software and hardware made explicit in the source code This is not the case for our target domain, in which all interactions are implicit. This makes using model checking harder. Using the same explicit interaction, energy consumption graphs can be generated next to control software source code inside an IDE [30]. Although it allows for near instant feedback to programmers, which is great for improving the code, it does not fit our target domain.

Energy-Optimizing Strategies. There is a handful of programming patterns that are known to improve the energy-efficiency of programs. These include application-level techniques such as caching, buffering, and batching, but also system-wide techniques such as retention policies and data compression. The effectiveness and adoption of such techniques have been previously investigated [11,27].

Another prominent example of a well-known pattern for reducing energy consumption is load balancing. Multiple approaches exist, however these make generalized assumptions about the energy-efficiency of the hardware. Kistowski et al. have compared a variety of load distribution strategies, and propose a new strategy that reduces a system's energy consumption even further [29].

8 Conclusion

We present a dynamic adaptation algorithm aimed at minimizing the energy consumption of data-parallel applications. It is based on the observation that data-parallel programs typically apply the same parallel operations in a repetitive fashion. This property allows for a dynamic feedback loop that reacts to changes in energy consumption from one repetition to the next. Our experiments show that such a non-intrusive method, in a functional context where scaling the level of parallelism is straightforward, can be very effective while requiring no in-depth program analysis, involving no programmer effort at all and causing negligible overhead. Looking at four different use cases with dynamically changing behaviour, we can see that our adaptation approach in most cases gets within 15% of a manually generated, ideally adapting runtime. The only remarkable outlier is the case of matrix multiplication where the ideal case depends on the thread pinning strategy, which our adaptation algorithm fails to find. However, we also find that optimizing these cases is highly context-dependent and that slight variations in configuration or implementation can introduce significant changes to the energy consumption characteristics of a program.

Furthermore, we observe that the dynamic approach yields energy improvements over static approaches. Depending on the number of threads chosen, the gains are up to 79% for any reasonable choice, and up to 100% if a poor decision is made. We also notice that in many cases our energy-optimising algorithm improves slightly over the runtime-optimising approach. This is reflected by our static analyses, which show that, while there is a correlation between overall runtime and energy use, the energy minima usually are reached before runtime minima when increasing the number of threads. Overall, we show that our method provides a feasible method for lowering the energy footprint of data-parallel applications solely based on automatic code instrumentation.

Whilst our adaptation algorithm proves effective across a range of data-parallel workloads, future work could explore the capability of the algorithm to adapt to changes in runtime conditions caused by other processes running in the background. Furthermore, it would be interesting to investigate whether the same approach can be applied to switch between devices in a heterogeneous system, such as CPU and GPU implementation of an algorithm, or to switch between thread pinning strategies. Beyond the array based domain, there is potential for applying this approach in other contexts that handle a large amount of similar computational complexity. For example, by adjusting resources dynamically in response to workload demands, web-servers could decrease their energy consumption, potentially without compromising on responsiveness.

Acknowledgements. We thank Thomas Koopman and the anonymous reviewers for proofreading the paper and providing helpful suggestions to improve it.

References

1. Aaldering, J.: Dynamic adaptation controller repository (2025). https://github.com/JordyAaldering/mtdynamic/tree/tfp25. branch tfp25, commit fea397d
2. Aaldering, J., Scholz, S.B., van Gastel, B.: Type patterns: pattern matching on shape-carrying array types. In: Proceedings of the 35th Symposium on Implementation and Application of Functional Languages. IFL '23. Association for Computing Machinery (2024). https://doi.org/10.1145/3652561.3652572
3. Bangash, A.A., Ali, K., Hindle, A.: A black box technique to reduce energy consumption of android apps. In: Proceedings of the ACM/IEEE 44th International Conference on Software Engineering: New Ideas and Emerging Results, ICSE-NIER '22, pp. 1—-5. Association for Computing Machinery, New York (2022). https://doi.org/10.1145/3510455.3512795
4. Buchty, R., Heuveline, V., Karl, W., Weiss, J.P.: A survey on hardware-aware and heterogeneous computing on multicore processors and accelerators. Concurr. Comput. Pract. Exp. **24**(7), 663–675 (2012). https://doi.org/10.1002/cpe.1904
5. Buyya, R., Beloglazov, A., Abawajy, J.: Energy-efficient management of data center resources for cloud computing: a vision, architectural elements, and open challenges (2010). https://arxiv.org/abs/1006.0308
6. Dai, X., Wang, J.M., Bensaou, B.: Energy-efficient virtual machines scheduling in multi-tenant data centers. IEEE Trans. Cloud Comput. **4**(2), 210–221 (2016). https://doi.org/10.1109/TCC.2015.2481401
7. Ding, Z.: Profile-based virtual machine placement for energy optimization of data centers. Ph.D. thesis, Queensland University of Technology (2017)
8. Falsafi, B., Wood, D.: Parallel dispatch queue: a queue-based programming abstraction to parallelize fine-grain communication protocols. In: Proceedings Fifth International Symposium on High-Performance Computer Architecture, pp. 182–192. IEEE, Piscataway (1999). https://doi.org/10.1109/HPCA.1999.744362
9. Filieri, A., et al.: Software engineering meets control theory. In: 2015 IEEE/ACM 10th International Symposium on Software Engineering for Adaptive and Self-Managing Systems, pp. 71–82. IEEE (2015). https://doi.org/10.1109/SEAMS.2015.12
10. Frigo, M., Johnson, S.G.: The design and implementation of fftw3. Proc. IEEE **93**(2), 216–231 (2005). https://doi.org/10.1109/JPROC.2004.840301
11. Funke, M., Lago, P., Adenekan, E., Malavolta, I., Heitlager, I.: Experimental evaluation of energy efficiency tactics in industry: results and lessons learned. In: 21st IEEE International Conference on Software Architecture (ICSA), pp. 1–12. IEEE, Piscataway (2024)
12. van Gastel, B.: Assessing sustainability of software: analysing correctness, memory and energy consumption. Ph.D. thesis, Open University, the Netherlands (2016)
13. van Gastel, B., van Eekelen, M.: Towards practical, precise and parametric energy analysis of it controlled systems. In: Proceedings 8th Workshop on Developments in Implicit Computational Complexity and 5th Workshop on Foundational and Practical Aspects of Resource Analysis. EPTCS '17, vol. 248, pp. 24–37. Open Publishing Association (2017). https://doi.org/10.4204/EPTCS.248.7

14. van Gastel, B., van Eekelen, M.: Towards practical, precise and parametric energy analysis of it controlled systems. Electron. Proc. Theor. Comput. Sci. **248**, 24–37 (2017). https://doi.org/10.4204/eptcs.248.7
15. van Gastel, B., Kersten, R., van Eekelen, M.: Using dependent types to define energy augmented semantics of programs. In: Foundational and Practical Aspects of Resource Analysis, FOPARA '15, pp. 20–39. Springer, New York (2016). https://doi.org/10.1007/978-3-319-46559-3_2
16. van Gastel, P., van Gastel, B., van Eekelen, M.: Detecting energy bugs and hotspots in control software using model checking. In: Companion Proceedings of the 2nd International Conference on the Art, Science, and Engineering of Programming, Programming '18, pp. 93–98. Association for Computing Machinery, New York (2018). https://doi.org/10.1145/3191697.3213805
17. Geeraerts, G., Heußner, A., Raskin, J.F.: Queue-dispatch asynchronous systems. In: 2013 13th International Conference on Application of Concurrency to System Design, pp. 150–159. IEEE, Piscataway (2013). https://doi.org/10.1109/ACSD.2013.18
18. Gordon, S., Scholz, S.B.: Dynamic adaptation of functional runtime systems through external control. In: Proceedings of the 27th Symposium on the Implementation and Application of Functional Programming Languages, IFL '15, pp. 10:1–10:13. Association for Computing Machinery, New York 2015). https://doi.org/10.1145/2897336.2897347
19. Grelck, C.: Shared memory multiprocessor support for functional array processing in SaC. J. Funct. Program. **15**(3), 353–401 (2005). https://doi.org/10.1017/S0956796805005538
20. Grelck, C.: Single Assignment C (SAC) high productivity meets high performance. In: Zsók, V., Horváth, Z., Plasmeijer, R. (eds.) CEFP 2011. LNCS, vol. 7241, pp. 207–278. Springer, Heidelberg (2012). https://doi.org/10.1007/978-3-642-32096-5_5
21. Grelck, C., Scholz, S.B.: SaC - a functional array language for efficient multi-threaded execution. Int. J. Parallel Prog. **34**(4), 383–427 (2006). https://doi.org/10.1007/s10766-006-0018-x
22. SaC group: SaC repository (2024). https://gitlab.sac-home.org/JordyAaldering/sac2c-mtdynamic, branch mtdynamic, commit 6cddce74
23. Guo, J., Thiyagalingam, J., Scholz, S.B.: Breaking the gpu programming barrier with the auto-parallelising SaC compiler. In: 6th Workshop on Declarative Aspects of Multicore Programming (DAMP'11), pp. 15–24. ACM Press, New York (2011). https://doi.org/10.1145/1926354.1926359
24. Hajiamini, S., Shirazi, B., Crandall, A., Ghasemzadeh, H.: A dynamic programming framework for dvfs-based energy-efficiency in multicore systems. IEEE Trans. Sustain. Comput. **5**(1), 1–12 (2020). https://doi.org/10.1109/TSUSC.2019.2911471
25. Huijben, R., Aaldering, J., Achten, P., Scholz, S.B.: Flattening combinations of arrays and records. In: International Symposium on Trends in Functional Programming, TFP '24, pp. 220–240. Springer, Cham (2025). https://doi.org/10.1007/978-3-031-74558-4_10
26. Janssen, N., Scholz, S.B.: On mapping n-dimensional data-parallelism efficiently into gpu-thread-spaces. In: Proceedings of the 33rd Symposium on Implementation and Application of Functional Languages, IFL '21, pp. 54—-66. Association for Computing Machinery, New York (2022). https://doi.org/10.1145/3544885.3544894

27. Jin, C., et al.: A survey on software methods to improve the energy efficiency of parallel computing. Int. J. High Perf. Comput. Appl. **31**(6), 517–549 (2017). https://doi.org/10.1177/1094342016665471
28. Khan, K.N., Hirki, M., Niemi, T., Nurminen, J.K., Ou, Z.: Rapl in action: experiences in using rapl for power measurements. ACM Trans. Model. Perf. Eval. Comput. Syst. (TOMPECS) **3**(2), 1–26 (2018). https://doi.org/10.1145/3177754
29. von Kistowski, J., Beckett, J., Lange, K.D., Block, H., Arnold, J.A., Kounev, S.: Energy efficiency of hierarchical server load distribution strategies. In: 2015 IEEE 23rd International Symposium on Modeling, Analysis, and Simulation of Computer and Telecommunication Systems, pp. 75–84. IEEE, Piscataway (2015). https://doi.org/10.1109/MASCOTS.2015.11
30. Klinik, M., Gastel, B., Kop, C., Eekelen, M.: Skylines for symbolic energy consumption analysis. In: ter Beek, M.H., Ničković, D. (eds.) FMICS 2020. LNCS, vol. 12327, pp. 93–112. Springer, Cham (2020). https://doi.org/10.1007/978-3-030-58298-2_3
31. Macht, T., Grelck, C.: SaC goes cluster: fully implicit distributed computing. In: 2019 IEEE International Parallel and Distributed Processing Symposium (IPDPS), pp. 996–1006. IEEE Computer Society, Los Alamitos (2019). https://doi.org/10.1109/IPDPS.2019.00107
32. Minarolli, D., Freisleben, B.: Utility-based resource allocation for virtual machines in cloud computing. In: 2011 IEEE Symposium on Computers and Communications (ISCC), pp. 410–417. IEEE, Piscataway (2011). https://doi.org/10.1109/ISCC.2011.5983872
33. Nutting, J., Olsson, F., Mark, D., LaMarche, J.: Grand Central Dispatch, Background Processing, and You, pp. 455–487. Apress, Berkeley (2014). https://doi.org/10.1007/978-1-4302-6023-3_15
34. Pallister, J.: Exploring the fundamental differences between compiler optimisations for energy and for performance. Ph.D. thesis, University of Bristol (2016). https://jpallister.com/documents/thesis_final.pdf
35. Pallister, J., Eder, K., Hollis, S.J.: Optimizing the flash-ram energy trade-off in deeply embedded systems. In: 2015 IEEE/ACM International Symposium on Code Generation and Optimization (CGO), pp. 115–124. IEEE, Piscataway (2015). https://doi.org/10.1109/CGO.2015.7054192
36. Pallister, J., Hollis, S.J., Bennett, J.: Identifying compiler options to minimize energy consumption for embedded platforms. Comput. J. **58**(1), 95–109 (2013). https://doi.org/10.1093/comjnl/bxt129
37. Quèze, F.: Power profiling with the firefox profiler (fosdem'23) (2023)., https://archive.fosdem.org/2023/schedule/event/energy_power_profiling_firefox/. Accessed 11 Nov 2024
38. Sakamoto, K., Furumoto, T.: Grand Central Dispatch, pp. 139–145. Apress, Berkeley (2012). https://doi.org/10.1007/978-1-4302-4117-1_6
39. Scholz, S.B., Šinkarovs, A.: Tensor comprehensions in SaC. In: Proceedings of the 31st Symposium on Implementation and Application of Functional Languages. IFL '19. Association for Computing Machinery, New York (2021). https://doi.org/10.1145/3412932.3412947
40. van der Steen, R., van Gastel, B.: The organizational hurdles of structurally reducing the energy consumption of software. In: BENEVOL, pp. 25–32 (2023)

41. Šinkarovs, A., Koopman, T., Scholz, S.B.: Rank-polymorphism for shape-guided blocking. In: Proceedings of the 11th ACM SIGPLAN International Workshop on Functional High-Performance and Numerical Computing, FHPNC 2023, pp. 1–14. Association for Computing Machinery, New York (2023). https://doi.org/10.1145/3609024.3609410
42. Zhang, Z., Liang, S., Yao, F., Gao, X.: Red alert for power leakage: exploiting intel rapl-induced side channels. In: Proceedings of the 2021 ACM Asia Conference on Computer and Communications Security, ASIA CCS '21, pp. 162–175. Association for Computing Machinery, New York (2021). https://doi.org/10.1145/3433210.3437517

Communication for Task-Oriented Systems with Edge Devices

Niek Janssen(✉), Mart Lubbers, and Pieter Koopman

Institute for Computing and Information Sciences, Radboud University, Nijmegen, The Netherlands
niek.janssen3@ru.nl, {mart,pieter}@cs.ru.nl

Abstract. Implementing communication between edge devices and their server in IoT systems is often a tedious and bug-prone task, since different programming languages with distinct underlying paradigms need to cooperate. The mTask system prevents this semantic friction by providing a single task-oriented framework for the whole system. Shared data sources provide flexible communication between tasks running on the server and tasks running on edge devices, however the current implementation has some drawbacks. We introduce an improved version of these shares with a clearer semantics. To improve the communication between edge devices and the server, we introduce the possibility to start parametrized server tasks from the edge device.

1 Introduction

Implementing communication between an edge device in an IoT system and the server is typically a tedious and bug-prone task. The server software is written in high-level languages or frameworks providing automated memory management, and other high-level features. Edge devices are still mostly programmed in low-level languages like C, due to their tight resource constraints. As these languages are vastly different and lack tooling that covers the entire system, it is difficult to get the server and edge device to cooperate smoothly. The problems caused by the discrepancy between levels of abstraction in the programming languages are called semantic friction [6].

For the communication code, the semantic friction is even more apparent than in the rest of the code base. Firstly, all communication code has to be written twice: once for the server-side and once for the client-side. These two implementations have to semantically complement each other exactly to provide correct communication. Furthermore, all this duplicated code has to be maintained, every change can break this exact match between the two implementations.

To prevent those problems, we use a tierless approach to program IoT systems; the server and edge code is generated from a single high level source [11]. The mTask system brings task-oriented programming (TOP) to edge devices [8]. It integrates directly with iTask, a TOP system for web servers [17]. Both are implemented as shallowly embedded DSL's in the host language Clean [15,18].

J. Gibbons (Ed.): TFP 2025, LNCS 15652, pp. 459–482, 2026.
https://doi.org/10.1007/978-3-031-99751-8_20

With iTask and mTask, a programmer writes a single program of which a part is executed on the server, and other parts are executed on the edge devices. The existing mTask system clones an iTask share to an edge device. These copies of the share are automatically synchronized when one of them is changed. This is convenient, but race conditions can cause incorrect updates. Moreover, the automatic synchronization can invoke superfluous communication. This paper introduces an improved design where shares are hosted either on the server, or on an edge device. The new system has simple and safe ways to update remote shares by executing a remote task. The ability to execute a task from the server on the edge device was part of the core of mTask. The possibility to start a task on the server from an edge device is new.

In Sect. 2, we discuss the current state of task-oriented programming and shared data sources, focussing on communication. In Sect. 3, we improve on the implementation of shared data sources, using friction points identified in Sect. 2. We discuss cross-platform access of shares, moving shares from task-level to device-level so that they are accessible from multiple tasks, and synchronization between edge device and server.

We then informally discuss some properties of the semantics of shared data sources in Sect. 4. We start with the existing properties of iTasks shared data source semantics, and see that these semantics hold for cross-platform access. We also see that one-way synchronization is semantically safe, whereas two-way synchronization is not.

In Sect. 5, we look at how we implement the features used in section Sect. 3. We conclude that with only one added combinator, it is possible to implement all features discussed in this paper. Finally, in Sect. 6 we discuss a bigger example and see how our new shared data sources perform in practice, in terms of possibilities and ease of use.

1.1 Research Contributions

- We introduce a new design for shared data sources on edge devices (Sect. 3) that prevents race conditions.
- The functionality of the new shares is a strict subset of shared data sources available on servers (Sect. 2.3). We sketch the semantic equality of these types of shares in (Sect. 4).
- We introduce a way to invoke parametrized server tasks from the edge devices (Sects. 5.1 and 5.2). We use this general mechanism to update shares on the server from the edge devices.

2 Task-Oriented Programming for the IoT

In this section, we discuss the current state of task-oriented programming for the IoT. We briefly explore TOP in iTask and mTask. We then implement a simple thermostat program as a vessel to discuss problems and limitations in the current version of mTask. We first focus on task parameters/results and later shared data sources to implement communication.

2.1 Tasks, iTask and mTask

At the core of TOP are tasks. Tasks are an abstract representation of work. This can be a wide variety of things. For example, in iTask, a task might be: fill in this form using the web interface. An example of an mTask task is: read the temperature using a certain sensor. Tasks are constructed from task primitives or by combining smaller tasks. For many tasks requiring user interaction, a user interface can be generated.

In its simplest form, tasks are combined either sequential or parallel. Sequential combinators are also called step combinators. An example use of a step combinator is: let a user fill in this form, *then* display the filled in form values on the screen for confirmation. An example use of a parallel combinator is: let the user fill in this form, and *at the same time* show a countdown of a time limit.

In this paper, we use two different implementations of task-oriented programming: iTask and mTask. Both are implemented as a shallow embedded DSL [15] in the host language Clean [18]. For programmers familiar to Haskell, a document comparing the two is available [10]. Whereas iTask is used to create multi-user distributed web applications [17,19], mTask is used to create applications for edge devices [8]. Due to the tighter resources on edge devices, the language of mTask is more restricted. As iTask sends mTask programs to embedded devices, and both languages are written as embedded DSL's in Clean, a full system containing iTask and mTask code can be written in a single source file.

As applications written with iTask and mTask are single-threaded applications, parallel tasks cannot run truly in parallel. Instead, the semantics of iTask and the parallel combinators run the two tasks interleaved, using small step rewrites.

The implementations of mTask and iTask are fully separated. As they each have their own combinator implementation, we cannot use the same combinator symbols to implement for example the sequential and parallel combinators. To distinguish them and avoid naming conflicts, mTask combinators usually contain a period character (.), whereas iTask combinators do not.

2.2 A Simple Thermostat

Using iTask and mTask, we create an example implementation of a simple thermostat. We assume an mTask device exists, which is equipped with a temperature sensor and a heater. In all our examples, a `TCPSettings` object is provided, containing all necessary information to create a connection with the embedded device. This device is controlled from a web server, which sets the target temperature. This example is used to introduce iTask and mTask gradually, so no shared data sources are used yet. Both the iTask and mTask code are implemented in the same source code file; iTask sends the mTask bytecode to the device over the network.

```
thermostat1 :: TCPSettings → Task Bool
thermostat1 deviceInfo =
    updateInformation [] 20.0 >>? λtargetTemp →
```

```
4     withDevice deviceInfo λdevice →
5     liftmTask (onDevice targetTemp) device
6 where
7     onDevice :: Real → Main (MTask v Bool) | mtask,dht v
8     onDevice targetTemp =
9         dhThermometer λthermometer →
10        declarePin D4 PMOutput λheater →
11        { main = rpeatEvery (BeforeSec $ lit 30) (
12            temperature thermometer >>~. λcurrentTemp →
13            writeD heater (currentTemp <. lit targetTemp)
14        )}
```

Listing 1. In the design of thermostat v1, the target temperature is set once via iTask, and then maintained using the thermometer and heater on the mTask device.

In Listing 1, we create a function `thermostat1`, hosting the iTask code. The function `updateInformation` on line 3 generates a user interface on the server, where the user can edit the target temperature that the thermostat should strive towards. We also create an `onDevice` function, hosting the mTask code. This code takes the temperature set within iTask, and uses a temperature sensor and heater to keep the temperature stable around the target temperature. The difference between iTask and mTask is visible in their types: whereas iTask tasks have type `Task a` (as visible in the type of `thermostat1`), mTask tasks have type `Main (MTask v a)` (as visible in the type of `onDevice`).

In Listing 1, some basic tasks are clearly visible. For example, on line 3 the `updateInformation` in iTask, displays a web form to the user. In mTask, the `temperature` task on line 12 uses the `thermometer` to read the current temperature.

On line 3, we also see a sequential combinator. As soon as the user clicks the submit button on the form, the sequential combinator executes the rest of the program. Listing 1 does not have parallel combinators, but we see some later in the paper.

The function `withDevice` on line 4 sets up a connection between the server running iTask and an edge device running the mTask runtime system. The `liftmTask` function on line 5 compiles an mTask program and starts it on a connected edge device. This way, iTask controls the placement of any mTask device [11].

An Interactive Thermostat. The example in Listing 1 is nice, but we can only set the temperature once. The thermostat then executes the loop to maintain this temperature indefinitely. If we want a thermostat where the user can change the target temperature at any time, and also see the current temperature, we end up with a relatively convoluted and cumbersome implementation. The idea is that we keep restarting the task running on the edge device using a new target temperature, and use the task value to communicate back the current temperature. The iTask main body necessary to accomplish this is shown in Listing 2

```
/* Part of thermostat v2 */
    mainLoop :: MTDevice (Real, Real) → Task ()
```

```
mainLoop device (targetTemp, currentTemp) =
    (   liftmTask (onDevice targetTemp) device >>- λcurrentTemp →
        waitForTimer False 30 >-| return (targetTemp, currentTemp))
    -||-
    ((updateInformation [] targetTemp -|| viewInformation [] currentTemp)
        >>- λtargetTemp → return (targetTemp, currentTemp))
    >>- λtemperatures → mainLoop device temperatures
```

Listing 2. Where thermostat v1 only allows the user to set the target temperature once, v2 continuously show the interface to set the target temperature and view the current temperature. Every 30 seconds everything refreshes.

Communication and Limitations. To understand why this implementation is so cumbersome, we first look at the communication present in the previous example thermostat 1 in Listing 1. In this example, we only communicate the target temperature to the device, by embedding it into the mTask program. We see on line 13 that `lit targetTemp` is used to lift the target temperature into the mTask domain. The mTask language is implemented as a shallow embedded DSL. When this DSL is executed at runtime, the mTask code is compiled into bytecode and sent to the mTask device. The target temperature is embedded into this bytecode as a constant. Once the task ends, the result of the mTask task becomes the result of the `liftmTask` combinator on line 5 in Listing 1. This mechanism could be leveraged to communicate a value back to the server.

One major limitation of this approach is the lack of modularity. As we can see in the main loop in Listing 2, program logic is interleaved with communication logic and the creation of user interfaces. Another limitation of this approach is the continuous recompilation and re-uploading of the mTask task.

First of all, this is a burden for the programmer. In this case, we needed a relatively complex loop structure with several parallel tasks to perform a relatively simple task. This code needs to be written and maintained by the programmers.

Secondly, it is a waste of resources. Every 30 s, the entire mTask program is recompiled and sent over the network. Especially on mTask devices that run on batteries, this accelerates battery depletion. Moreover, some devices are connected by relatively low-bandwidth connections, which has to be shared with other devices. Currently, we are only looking at a basic thermostat implementation which restarts every 30 s, but it is easy to imagine systems with more volatile variables, generating many more recompilation cycles.

2.3 Shared Data Sources

When communicating using task parameters and results, parallel running tasks only communicate by being restarted. Shared data sources allow for communication between parallel running tasks without the requirement of being restarted. In iTask, shared data sources are only a programmer interface containing a read and a write function. Since their first implementation, they have been extended with some extra functionality, like parametric lenses and a notification system [4]. Shared data sources in mTask are a strict subset of shared data sources in iTask. Everything that is not supported by mTask, is outside the scope of this paper.

In mTask, only simple shared data sources are supported that act as type-safe data storages. Neither parametric lenses nor the notification system are available. Furthermore, mTask shared data sources are limited to fixed-size data structures.

In iTask, such a simple shared data source acting like a variable is created using the function `withShared`. It takes an initial value for the shared data source, and a callback function with the shared data source as an argument. This shared data source can then be used in child-tasks.

```
shares :: Task Real
shares = withShared 20.0 λsds →
        updateSharedInformation [] sds -||
        viewSharedInformation [] sds
```

Listing 3. This small iTask program uses shared data sources.

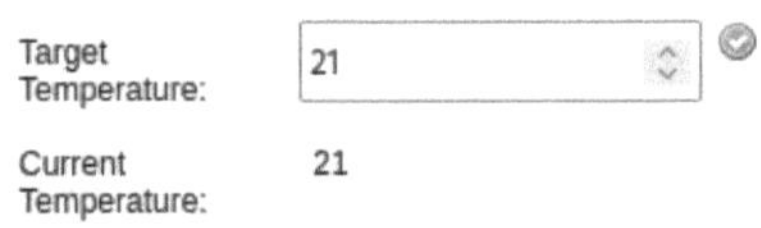

Fig. 1. This interface is being generated by the program on the left.

For example, in Listing 3, we have a shared data source used by two parallel tasks. The tasks generate an interface containing an input field and a numerical written value, as can be seen in Fig. 1. The form task updates the value of the shared data source when the form value changes, and the display task updates the displayed value when the value of the shared data source changes. Whenever the form value is changed, the value below changes with it. This process continues indefinitely, or until it is stopped by a parent task.

These shared data sources are used to improve the modularity and separation of concerns in source code. Take for example our thermostat implementation in Listing 2. There, we have a single main loop, handling the user interface and mTask device in a big ball of spaghetti. Using a shared data source, we separate these concerns in Listing 4.

```
thermostat3 :: TCPSettings → Task Real
thermostat3 deviceInfo =
    withShared 20.0 λiTargetTempShare →
    withShared 20.0 λiCurrentTempShare →
    updateSharedInformation [] iTargetTempShare -||
    viewSharedInformation [] iCurrentTempShare -||
    withDevice deviceInfo λdevice →
    mainLoop device iTargetTempShare iCurrentTempShare
where
    mainLoop device iTargetTempShare iCurrentTempShare =
        (forever $ get iTargetTempShare >>- λtargetTemp →
        liftmTask (onDevice targetTemp) device >>- λcurrentTemp →
        set currentTemp iCurrentTempShare >-|
        waitForTimer False 30)

```

```
16     onDevice :: Real → Main (MTask v Real) | mtask,dht v
17         // Identical to onDevice in Listing 2
```

Listing 4. Whereas thermostat v2 has to restart the interface every 30 seconds to update it, v3 uses shared data sources to automate this task. The mTask device code still has to be restarted every 30 seconds to synchronize the target and current temperatures.

On lines 5 and 6, we see the forms being created and linked to their respective shared data sources. All input/output of these form fields are handled directly via shared data sources. The form is now created outside the thermostat loop.

On lines 3 and 4, we create the shares to be used in the temperature form fields and the main loop. In the main loop itself, we only have to regularly run the thermostat using the values present in the shared data sources. We see on lines 11 and 13 that the values are retrieved from and updated to the shared data sources.

3 Improving Shared Data Sources

Up to here, we have implemented our thermostat solely using techniques already available in iTask and mTask. However, we still have a relatively monolithic implementation, with a big main loop (the `forever` on line 11) starting both the iTask and mTask parts of the code repeatedly. We would like our implementation to be more modular, similar to how `updateSharedInformation` detaches the form logic from the edge device logic. In this section, we introduce a new design for shared data sources and use it to implement communication between the server and the device.

3.1 Cross-Platform Shared Data Source Access

To accomplish this detachment of iTask and mTask logic, we introduce interfacing to access shared data sources cross-platform. We provide the functions `iGet` and `iSet` to access iTask shares from within mTask. To access mTask shares from within iTask, we provide `mGet` and `mSet`. Overloading the existing `get` and `set` methods is not possible, as `mGet` and `mSet` need the extra device argument. This further allows us to separate the communication from the control structure. Communication between the iTask server and the mTask device is no longer dependent on starting or restarting the mTask program.

In the next version of our thermostat, we no longer restart the thermostat task every 30 s. Instead, we provide the device with a task that uses the shared data source to update the target temperature. This way, we overcome the limitations posed in Sect. 2.2. We use our newly introduced cross platform access functions where necessary. As a small optimization, we compare the current value to the previous one, and only update it once the value changes.

```
thermostat4 :: TCPSettings → Task Bool
thermostat4 deviceInfo =
    withShared 20.0 λiTargetTempShare →
    withShared 20.0 λiCurrentTempShare →
```

```
5     updateSharedInformation [] iTargetTempShare ||-
6     viewSharedInformation [] iCurrentTempShare ||-
7     withDevice deviceInfo λdevice →
8     liftmTask (onDevice iTargetTempShare iCurrentTempShare) device
9  where
10    onDevice :: (Shared sds Real) (Shared sds Real)
11        → Main (MTask v Bool)
12        | RWShared sds & mtask,dht,lowerSds v
13    onDevice iTargetTempShare iCurrentTempShare =
14        dhThermometer λthermometer →
15        declarePin D4 PMOutput λheater →
16        withmTaskShared 20.0 λoldCurrentShare →
17        { main = rpeatEvery (BeforeSec $ lit 30) (
18            temperature thermometer ≫~. λcurrentTemp →
19            getSds oldCurrentShare ≫~. λoldCurrent→
20            If (currentTemp ==. oldCurrent) (rtrn currentTemp)
21                (iSet iCurrentTempShare currentTemp ≫|.
22                setSds oldCurrentShare currentTemp) ≫|.
23            iGet iTargetTempShare ≫~. λtargetTemp →
24            writeD heater (currentTemp <. targetTemp)
25        ) }
```

Listing 5. Where thermostat v3 only used shared data sources on the server, v4 uses shared data sources for all communication.

The function `thermostat4` in Listing 5 is very similar to `thermostat3` in Listing 4. The only difference is that on line 8 of Listing 5, the call to the main loop is replaced by `liftmTask`.

Then, in the mTask code, `withmTaskShared` is used to create a new shared data source on line 16. We start the device loop using `rpeatEvery` on line 17, and in the loop on line 18 to line 24 we implement our thermostat logic. When we get or set the current or target temperatures on lines 21 and 23, the data is directly retrieved from or written to the corresponding shared data source on the server.

Communication and Limitations. In this example, all communication is fully handled by reading to or writing from shared data sources. The shared data sources can be directly used from the server. However, as we do not expect the current temperature to change every 30 s, we have saved a lot of network traffic (and battery life) by checking whether the value is actually new. We can see on line 19 to line 22 that some scaffolding is necessary to implement this behaviour.

To implement the same behaviour on the server side for the target temperature, we have to take a different approach. On the client side, we have our own `iGet` every time the value changes. However, on the server side, the updating of the shared data source is fully handled using `updateSharedInformation`. We discuss this approach in more detail in Sect. 3.3.

Finally, one of the goals we described at the end of Sect. 2.2, was to have a less monolithic implementation. However, if we try to split our code into separate tasks for the thermometer and heater control, we encounter a problem. As we create a shared data source from within a task, the scope of that shared data source is limited to that task only. In another task, we can create a separate shared data source, but all communication between them has to go via the server, even though they exist on the same device. This approach causes a lot of network traffic, which is also something we want to avoid.

3.2 Task-Independent Shares

To get a grasp of why exactly it is not possible to fully separate communication logic, we consider Fig. 2. On the left hand side, we see the current situation, where shared data sources are created by and belong to a certain mTask task. This creates a scope, containing a task along with all the shares it needs. It also illustrates the inability for any other task to access these shares. As stated before, this situation is undesirable.

We now lift the creation of shared data sources out of the task creation, to the iTask domain. Once such a shared data source is created, any task can access these shares, as illustrated by the right hand side of Fig. 2.

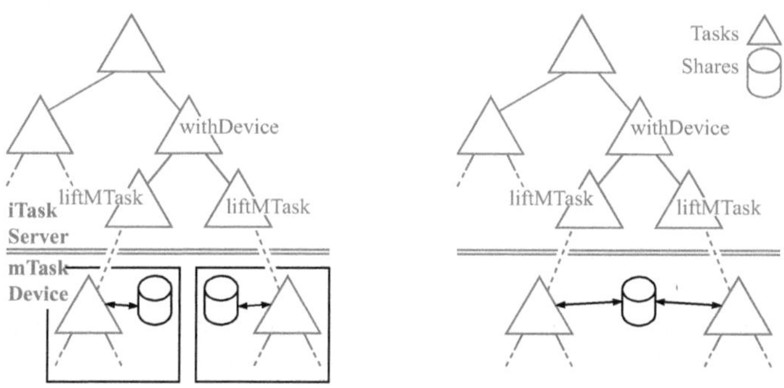

Fig. 2. This diagram visualizes the communication between the server and a device. The left hand side displays the old variant with a limited scope for shared data sources. The right hand side displays the new design, which is demonstrated in Listing 6.

To come back to our thermostat example, this change now allows us to create separate tasks for the heater and temperature controllers. This reduces the monolithicness of our implementation, and improves maintainability and the separation of concerns.

```
thermostat5 :: TCPSettings → Task Bool
thermostat5 deviceInfo =
    withShared 20.0 λiTargetTempShare →
    withShared 20.0 λiCurrentTempShare →
    updateSharedInformation [] iTargetTempShare ||-
    viewSharedInformation [] iCurrentTempShare ||-
    withDevice deviceInfo λdevice →
    withmTaskShared device 20.0 λmCurrentTempShare →
```

```
9      liftmTask (sensor mCurrentTempShare iCurrentTempShare) device ||-
10     liftmTask (heater mCurrentTempShare iTargetTempShare) device
11  where
12     sensor mCurrentTempShare iCurrentTempShare =
13        dhThermometer λthermometer →                /* No share creation here */
14        { main = rpeatEvery (BeforeSec $ lit 30) (
15           temperature thermometer ≫=. λtemp →
16           getSds mCurrentTempShare ≫~. λoldCurrent →
17           If (currentTemp ==. oldCurrent) (rtrn temp)
18              (iSet iCurrentTempShare temp ≫|.
19              setSds mCurrentTempShare temp)}
20
21     heater mCurrentTempShare iTargetTempShare =
22        declarePin A4 PMOutput λheater →             /* No share creation here */
23        { main = rpeatEvery (BeforeSec $ lit 30) (
24           getSds mCurrentTempShare ≫~. λcurrent →
25           iGet iTargetTempShare ≫~. λgoal →
26           writeD heater (current <. goal))}
```

Listing 6. Whereas thermostat v4 had to be implemented as a single mTask task, it is now possible to separate tasks for the heater and temperature controllers due to the possibility of accessing a shared data source from multiple tasks.

The thermostat version of Listing 6 contains a few updates from the previous version in Listing 5. Firstly, the `onDevice` task has been split into a `sensor` task on line 12, which is responsible for reading the thermometer and updating the current temperature, and a `heater` task on line 21, which is responsible for controlling the heater from the target and current temperatures. Secondly, the creation of the shared data source has been taken out of the individual mTask tasks, and has moved to the iTask code on line 8.

Communication and Limitations. The current version allows us to separate the concerns of the heater control and the temperature sensor. However, as we see on lines 19 and 18, we still need to update both the mTask and iTask version of the share. On line 25, we see that every iteration of the temperature check still requires a network call to the iTask shared data source, even though the temperature probably only changes sporadically. The communication logic is still interleaved with the two controllers.

3.3 Synchronizing Shares

We now would like to go one step further, and fully separate the thermostat logic from the communication logic. We provide the synchronization tasks `syncItoM` and `syncMtoI`. These functions take an iTask and an mTask shared data source, and synchronize the value from one side to the other whenever the value changes. Their implementation is further discussed in Sect. 5.3. These are simply functions we can insert alongside the temperature, heater and form tasks, in the same manner as we use `updateSharedInformation` in Sect. 2.3 to offload the handling of the user interface. In mTask, we can now focus solely on implementing our device code, knowing the communication is fully handled elsewhere.

In this final version of our thermostat in Listing 7, we outsource the synchronization of shares between server side and client side to the new tasks `syncItoM` and `syncMtoI`. We run the synchronization tasks parallel to the rest in lines 10 and 11. Note that on line 19, we do not update the iTask shared data source anymore. Data synchronization does come with a few caveats. We discuss the exact semantics and limitations of synchronization in Sect. 4.3.

4 Semantics of Shared Data Sources

In this section, we discuss the informal semantics of shared data sources and how they relate to cross platform access and synchronization, as described in Sect. 3. We define some properties on these semantics, and show that they hold for cross-platform access, but not for all cases of synchronized shared data sources. The full formal semantics are outside the scope of this paper.

```
1  thermostat6 :: TCPSettings → Task Bool
2  thermostat6 deviceInfo =
3      withShared 20.0 λiTargetTempShare →
4      withShared 20.0 λiCurrentTempShare →
5      updateSharedInformation [] iTargetTempShare ||-
6      viewSharedInformation [] iCurrentTempShare ||-
7      withDevice deviceInfo λdevice →
8      withmTaskShared device 20.0 λmTargetTempShare →
9      withmTaskShared device 20.0 λmCurrentTempShare →
10     syncIToM device iTargetTempShare mTargetTempShare ||-
11     syncMtoI device mCurrentTempShare iCurrentTempShare ||-
12     liftmTask (sensor mCurrentTempShare) device ||-
13     liftmTask (heater mCurrentTempShare mTargetTempShare) device
14 where
15     sensor mCurrentTempShare=
16         dhThermometer λthermometer →
17         { main=rpeatEvery (BeforeSec $ lit 30) (
18             temperature thermometer ¿¿=. λtemp →
19             setSds mCurrentTempShare temp)}
20
21     heater mCurrentTempShare mTargetTempShare=
22         declarePin A4 PMOutput λheater →
23         { main=rpeatEvery (BeforeSec $ lit 30) (
24             getSds mCurrentTempShare ¿¿~. λcurrent →
25             getSds mTargetTempShare ¿¿~. λgoal →
26             writeD heater (current <. goal))}
```

Listing 7. Whereas thermostat v5 had to do manual synchronization every time we write to a shared data source, v6 have background tasks on lines 10 and 11 to automate these tasks.

4.1 Semantic Properties on Shared Data Sources

We now look at the informal semantics of the operations `get`, `watch`, `set` and `upd`[1]. In the thermostat examples of Sect. 3, we only used `get` and `set`, together with their mTask (`getSds`, `setSds`) and cross-platform (`iGet`, `iSet`, `mGet`, `mSet`) variants. We introduce the full set of operations on shared data sources first.

- `get` takes the shared data source and returns its value.
- `watch` continuously reads the shared data source, and updates the task result with the value. Opposed to all other operations on shared data sources, this task does not terminate immediately, but only when it is discarded.
- `set` takes a value and a shared data source. It writes this value to the shared data source once, and returns it as well.
- `upd` takes a transformation function of type `a → a` and a shared data source of type `a`. It applies the transformation function to the value of the shared data source. The resulting value is both written back to the shared data source, and returned by the `upd` function.

The type signatures of operations on shared data sources in iTask, and the mTask counterpart, are found in Listing 8. Note that `get` is a special case of `watch`. In iTask, the choice has been made to specify both operations, where `get` is an optimized version that cannot be used to perform a `watch`. In mTask, the `get` is used for both.

```
// Given a shared data source of type (Shared a):
/* iTask signature */                          /* mTask variant */
   get :: (Shared a) → Task a                  // getSds
   watch :: (Shared a) → Task a                // getSds
   set :: a (Shared a) → Task a                // setSds
   upd :: (a → a) (Shared a) → Task a          // updSds
```

Listing 8. We define the type signatures of the operations on shared data sources.

We define five properties on the shared data sources as implemented in iTask:

- *Atomicity*: The operations are guaranteed to be *atomic*. While reading, writing, or updating, it is guaranteed that no other task can access the share. This is especially important for the `upd` operation.
- *Incompleteness*: It is *not* guaranteed that all tasks observing the shared data source see all changes. If two updates happen before a task gets a chance to observe the share, the first update is missed.
- *Ordering*: It is guaranteed that all tasks observing the shared data source see changes in the same order.
- *Convergence*: After a finite amount of time without any updates, all tasks observing the shared data source see the same value.

[1] The full iTask shared data source implementation supports several features that mTask shared data sources do not. For the sake of simplicity, we only discuss features of iTask shared data sources that mTask supports as well. More info about full iTask shared data sources can be found in [2,4].

To give a bit more intuition for the properties *Incompleteness*, *Ordering* and *Convergence*, let us look at the example of Listing 9. In this example, we run tasks `a` and `b` in parallel. Each of them sets the value of the shared data source, and then forever reads the shared data source to do something with it.

The *Incompleteness* non-guarantee tells us that it is undefined whether any of these tasks sees both values. It is possible that either, or both, only see the value that is written last. This simply has to do with the fact that there are defined moments on which the task looks at the value of the share. If the value of the shared data source changes twice between two observations, the task misses the first value. When it is important that no updates are missed, the programmer can employ a queue in the shared data source.

The *Ordering* property guarantees that the values that are seen by the tasks are always seen in the same order. It is not possible that task `a` first sees value 12 and then 42, while task `b` first sees 42 and then 12, or vice versa.

The *Convergence* property guarantees that, eventually, both tasks will observe the last written task value.

```
both = withShared 0 λshare →
    a share -&&- b share

a sds = set 12 sds >-|                 b sds = set 42 sds >-|
    watch sds >>* /* ... */                watch sds >>* /* ... */
```

Listing 9. We define two iTask tasks to illustrate that both tasks see values in the same order (*Ordering*), but not necessarily all values (*Incompleteness*).

The *Atomicity* property demonstrates the need for the `upd` operation nicely. As an example, we consider a program where multiple parallel running tasks increase a counter by one throughout the code. Were this `+1` implemented by a `get share >>- v→ set (v+1) share`, we would have a race condition in our code [13]. Implementing it with the atomic `upd` operator instead, we get `upd ((+ ) 1) share`. This version performs the whole operation in a single step, avoiding race conditions.

4.2 Semantics of Cross-Platform Access

In the previous section, we discussed the semantics of iTask's and mTask's shared data sources. The properties of *Atomicity*, *Ordering* and *Convergence* are guaranteed on these systems, as the host/server is the sole controller. The iTask and mTask runtime systems tightly control how operations on shared data sources are performed, and ensure these properties.

However, as iTask is run on a server and mTask is run on an embedded device, a system employing both is inherently a multiprocessor system. If we want to implement this combination in some kind of distributed manner, we run into all kinds of synchronization problems. The old implementation of shared data sources for mTask has exactly this problem. A more elegant approach is to handle updates of the shared data source on the runtime system where the shared data source exists. This is the approach we used in Sect. 3.1. It has also been used in distributed iTasks [14, Section 4.2]. However, as mTask shares differ from iTask shares, we cannot simply overload the shared data source access operations like they do.

Let us look at this approach more closely. As an example, we take the `upd` operation. In Fig. 3, on the left hand side, we see a visualization of the `upd` operation using a single runtime (either iTask or mTask) setting. Time is represented on the y-axis. On the x-axis, we have space for two tasks A and B, and a shared data source they can use. At some point, task A wants to perform an `upd` operation. As any kind of parallelism is implemented single-threadedly by the iTask combinators, the `upd` function can, in this case, control exactly what gets executed before other tasks get execution time again. The programmer gives it a transformation function, and the `upd` operation performs the get, function and set in one single rewrite step. The result of the function is also used as the task result.

Figure 3 on the right hand side shows the same process, but in a cross-platform setting. The platforms are separated by a network layer in the middle. In this case, we again take the transformation function provided by the programmer. This time we send it over the network to give it to our own task C running on the side containing the shared data source. This task C then runs the `upd` operation with the transformation function, which is executed like in the single-platform situation (Fig. 3, right). Finally, task C sends the task result back to task A, so it can resume execution as well.

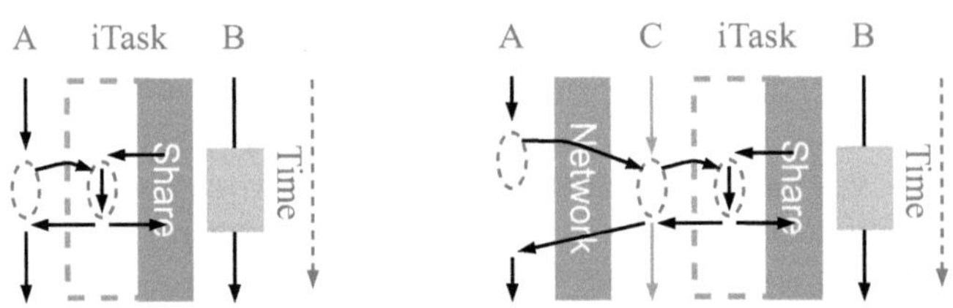

Fig. 3. These sequence diagrams show how an `upd` operation is performed. The left hand side has tasks A and B running on the same device, while the right hand side performs the `upd` over the network.

Using this approach, we guarantee that all semantics introduced in Sect. 4.1 hold. All operations on shares are performed on the single-threaded system where the shared data source lives, as if it were a single-core system. There is, of course, a networking delay in reading or writing a shared data source, but our semantics do not disallow such delay. The *Atomicity* property is guaranteed directly in this way. However, for *Ordering* we do require that messages do not get reordered in the network connection, and for *Convergence* we require that messages always eventually arrive. These requirements are easily fulfilled by using a communication protocol that gives us such guarantees, such as TCP or MQTT. The mTask implementation currently supports either of those.

4.3 Semantics of One-Way Synchronization

In Sect. 3.3, we introduced synchronization functions `syncItoM` and `syncMtoI` to synchronize two shares existing in iTask and mTask. This synchronization is useful only if reading from the synchronized shared data source is semantically equivalent to reading from the original share. In this section, we show that this equivalence holds for one-way synchronization. For two-way synchronization, it is much harder and much more costly to ensure these semantics. These synchronization issues are well documented and out of the scope of this paper [13]. As we use one-way synchronization only, writing has to be done to the *original* shared data source. For convenience, we define the original shared data source as side A, and the synchronized share as side B.

We now check our synchronization from side A to B against the semantic guarantees defined in Sect. 4.1. Writing to the shared data source is only possible on side A. As side A is a shared data source, all semantics for shared data sources hold on side A automatically. For side B, only the semantics for read operations have to hold. *Atomicity* holds, as reading from side B is still atomic. *Ordering* holds as well, as the semantics of cross platform shared data source access ensure this property. The same holds for *Convergence*.

Another way of looking at this setup is by considering B as a read-only cache for the shared data source. In this case, the updates are pushed proactively to side B by the synchronization function, instead of retrieved from side A on-demand by the cross-platform `get` function.

If a write from side B is still necessary, we can always use a cross-platform write to the shared data source on side A, so that the semantics are preserved.

5 Implementation

In this section, we discuss the implementation of the techniques above. We discuss that the implementation of cross-platform shared data source access only requires one extra combinator `loweriTask`. We look at `loweritask` and discuss what constructs we require for its implementation. Finally, we show that synchronization in its simplest form also only requires constructs previously defined in this paper.

5.1 Cross-Platform Access

To perform cross-platform communication safely, we need to execute the read and/or write on the other side of the network. As we discussed in Sect. 4.2, the safest and simplest way to do this while maintaining all guarantees and no code duplication is to insert a task actually performing the `get`, `watch`, `set` or `upd` on the side where the shared data source in question lives.

iTask Access to mTask Shares. For iTask to work with mTask shares we already have the `liftmTask` combinator to perform any mTask operation on the device. We can utilize this to transfer our operation to mTask.

```
mGet :: MTDevice (BCInterpret (Sds a)) → Task a | type a
mGet dev sds = liftmTask {main = getSds sds >>~. rtrn} dev

mSet :: MTDevice (BCInterpret (Sds a)) a → Task a | type a
mSet dev sds a = liftmTask {main = setSds sds (lit a)} dev

mUpd :: MTDevice ((BCInterpret a) → BCInterpret a) (BCInterpret (Sds a))
     → Task a | type a
mUpd dev fndef sds = liftmTask (
  fun λfn=fndef In
  {main=updSds sds fn}) dev
```

Listing 10. Using `liftmTask`, we implement iTask access to mTask shares.

Listing 10 shows the implementations for `get`, `set` and `upd`. The `BCInterpret` type is the mTask compilation monad. For simplicity, we omit the `watch`, as it is similar to `get`. For `get` and `set`, the implementation is trivial. We simply wrap the mTask version of the operation in a `liftmTask`. The `upd`, however, needs a function, which needs to be provided by the programmer. Due to how functions definitions are implemented in the shallow embedding of mTask, this function needs to be defined in the same mTask program as it is used, so the programmer only needs to give the function body. The exact semantics of mTask functions are described by [9, Section 5.3.2].

mTask Access to iTask Shares. To provide mTask access to iTask shares, we use an approach that is inverse of the approach of providing iTask access to mTask shares. For this, we need an operator inverse of `liftmTask`, which we define in Sect. 5.2. Listing 11 how we use this combinator to implement iTask shared data source access from mTask.

```
iGet :: (Shared a) → BCInterpret (TaskValue a)
  | Readable sds & TC a & type a
iGet sds = loweriTask (λ_ → get sds) (lit ())

iSet :: (Shared a) (BCInterpret a) → (BCInterpret (TaskValue a))
  | Writeable sds &  TC a & type a
iSet sds value = loweriTask (λa → set a sds) value

iUpd :: (Shared a) (b a → a) (BCInterpret b) → (BCInterpret (TaskValue a))
  | RWShared sds & TC a & type a & type b
iUpd sds fn value = loweriTask (λb → (upd (fn b) sds)) value
```

Listing 11. Using `loweriTask`, we implement mTask access to iTask shares.

5.2 LoweriTask

As mentioned in Sect. 5.1, we need a `loweriTask` combinator to implement mTask access to iTask shares. Such a combinator contacts the server, executes a task there, and synchronizes the task value generated by the iTask task with the mTask task. The signature of loweriTask is given in Listing 12.

```
loweriTask :: (a → Task b) (BCInterpret a) → MTask BCInterpret b
```

Listing 12. We define the type signature of `loweriTask`.

The function to be executed in iTask (the first argument) expects exactly one argument to be passed to the task. Zero or more than one arguments can be passed by using a unit type or a tuple. This value is sent to the server, along with the request to start the task. Every time the task value changes, it is sent back to the mTask device, and set to be the task result of the `loweriTask` combinator.

To allow for this execution to happen, we need two components: (1) we need to be able to create an iTask task from the mTask system, and (2) we need to communicate with the server to be able to start the task.

Creating an iTask Task from mTask. We want to be able to execute any arbitrary Clean/iTask code from our `loweriTask` combinator. However, mTask is an embedded DSL, which is restricted in its features compared to the host language. If we were to implement functions to execute on the server using the mTask DSL, these restrictions would apply. To circumvent this, we give `loweriTask` a task implemented in iTask instead, which is then labelled and stored on the server. The mTask program then uses this label to instruct the server on which stored task to execute.

Communicating with the Server. The `loweriTask` function sends a message to the server to start the iTask task. The iTask server already has an established communication channel with the mTask device to start mTask tasks and obtain task values when completed, which is visualized in the left hand side of Fig. 4. When a connection with a device running the mTask client is made, a communication task is started. This communication task handles the connection with the mTask client. The device handle then contains a shared data source which is used as a communication channel between the communication task and any other task who needs to communicate with the mTask client. For example, `liftmTask` uses these channels to upload a new mTask program to the mTask device.

We extend this communication infrastructure with the necessary messages for `loweriTask`, as visualized on the right hand side of Fig. 4. As the `liftmTask` function holds all labelled iTask tasks, it listens to task starting requests in the channel's shared data source. Once this task is started, it watches task value updates, and sends them back to the mTask client. Note that the iTask/mTask programmer does not see any of this; All communication is abstracted away.

5.3 Synchronization

In this section, we provide an implementation of the one-way synchronization as discussed in Sect. 3.3. We rely heavily on the cross-platform shared data source

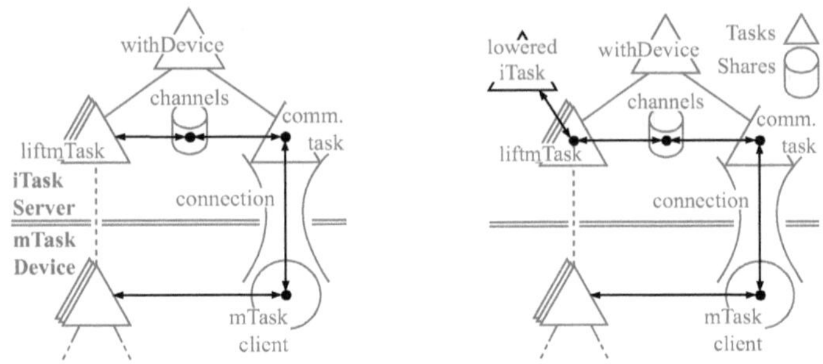

Fig. 4. We show that the existing communication channels can be reused. The left hand side displays the communication channels used for `liftmTask`. The right hand side reuses these channels to implement `loweriTask`.

access for the implementation. A one-way synchronization algorithm is relatively straightforward. We watch the shared data source for updates. As an optimization, we check if the updated value is actually different from the previous one. If it is, we update the share on the other side to this new value. The algorithm to synchronize an iTask share with an mTask shared data source is given in Listing 13.

```
1  syncIToM :: MTDevice (Shared a) (BCInterpret (Sds a)) → Task ()
2    | RWShared sds & iTask a & type a
3  syncIToM dev isds msds =
4    get isds ≫- λv →
5    detectLoop dev isds msds v
6  where
7    detectLoop :: MTDevice (Shared a) (BCInterpret (Sds a)) a → Task ()
8      | RWShared sds & iTask a & type a
9    detectLoop dev isds msds oldValue =
10     watch isds ≫* [OnValue $ ifValue ((=!=) oldValue) $ \newValue →
11     mSet dev msds newValue >-|
12     detectLoop dev isds msds newValue]
```

Listing 13. `syncIToM` synchronizes the value of an iTask shared data sourceto an mTask shared data source using the techniques shown in section 3.1.

We see a `watch` being used on line 10 to detect updates of the shared data source on the iTask side. This is followed by a ≫* step combinator. The ≫* is a generalized step combinator, which allows choosing for different task continuations based on certain conditions. We use it here to step only if the value of the shared data source is actually different from the old one. If it is, we continue execution and update the shared data source on the mTask side on line 11. Finally we recursively start the detection algorithm using a recursive call on line 12.

Finally, to start our algorithm, we have to retrieve the value of the shared data source, to provide an initial *old* value to the algorithm. This bootstrapping is done on line 4.

Again, to synchronize an mTask shared data source to an iTask shared data source, the implementation is inverse of the synchronization of an iTask shared data source to an mTask shared data source, where the iTask combinators are exchanged for mTask combinators.

6 Case Study

In this section, we implement a system monitoring air quality as a case study. The example makes use of a few different methods of working with shared data sources across iTask and mTask. The mTask device is equipped with a DHT sensor and an air quality sensor. The DHT sensor measures temperature and humidity. The air quality sensor measures CO2, but needs to be calibrated using the temperature and humidity.

We create two tasks `tempAndHum` (line 25) and `co2sensor` (line 38), that respectively read the temperature, humidity and co2 level from their respective sensors. The `co2sensor` task uses the temperature and humidity values to calibrate the co2 sensor.

Any time the temperature or co2 level strays too far from their optimal values, an alarm level is increased. An interface to set these optimal values, as well as view the alarm level and co2 level, is implemented in the function `interface` (line 17). The functions `updateInformation` (lines 19 and 20) and `viewInformation` (lines 22 and 23) provide this functionality.

The shared data sources necessary to communicate between tasks are defined in the main function `start` (line 1). They consist of:

- `iOptTempSds`, `mOptTempSds`, `iMaxCO2Sds` and `mMaxCO2Sds` (lines 4 and 5) form two pairs of synchronized shares, created by `withDoublyShared`. Because of the `ItoM`, the value of the iTask share is synchronized to the mTask share.
- `iAlarmSds` (line 7) counts the alarms, and only has a copy on the server. The device accesses this share directly to set the alarm (lines 36 and 46).
- `iAirQualitySds` (line 8) holds the co2 value, and only has a copy on the client. The server accesses this share directly to display the value (line 21).
- `mCurTempSds` and `mCurHumSds` (lines 9 and 10) are only accessed on the device to communicate the current temperature and humidity to the co2 sensor task.

The implementation is available in Listing 14.

```
1 start :: TCPSettings → Task ()
2 start deviceInfo =
3   withDevice deviceInfo λdevice →
4   withDoublyShared device ItoM 20.0 λiOptTempSds mOptTempSds →
5   withDoublyShared device ItoM 1200 λiMaxCO2Sds mMaxCO2Sds →
6
7   withShared 0 λiAlarmSds →
8   withMTaskShared device 0    λmAirqualitySds →
9   withMTaskShared device 0.0 λmCurTempSds →
```

```
  withMTaskShared device 0.0 λmCurHumSds →

  interface device iOptTempSds mAirqualitySds iMaxCO2Sds iAlarmSds -||
  liftmTask (tempAndHum mCurTempSds mCurHumSds mOptTempSds iAlarmSds) device -||
  liftmTask (co2monitor mCurTempSds mCurHumSds mAirqualitySds mMaxCO2Sds iAlarmSds)
      device

interface :: MTDevice (ISDS Real) (MSDS Int) (ISDS Int ) (ISDS Int) → Task ()
interface device iOptTempSds mAirqualitySds iMaxCO2Sds iAlarmSds =
  (updateSharedInformation [] iOptTempSds ¡¡@ Label "Optimal temperature (C)") ||-
  (updateSharedInformation [] iMaxCO2Sds ¡¡@ Label "Maximum co2 (ppm)") ||-
  mWatch device mAirqualitySds >&> λiAirQualitySds →
  (viewSharedInformation [] iAirQualitySds ¡¡@ Label "Current air quality") ||-
  (viewSharedInformation [] iAlarmSds ¡¡@ Label "Alarm level") @! ()

tempAndHum :: (MSDS Real) (MSDS Real) (MSDS Real) (ISDS Int) → MTaskMain ()
tempAndHum mCurTempSds mCurHumSds mOptTempSds iAlarmSds =
  dht (DHT_DHT (DigitalPin D2) DHT22) λdht → main (

  rpeatEvery (BeforeSec $ lit 30) (
    temperature dht ¿¿~. λtemp →
    humidity dht ¿¿~. λhum →
    setSds mCurTempSds temp ¿¿|.
    setSds mCurHumSds hum ¿¿|.
    getSds mOptTempSds ¿¿~. λoptTemp →
    Iff (mAbs (optTemp -. temp) >. lit 2.0)
        (iUpd iAlarmSds (λ_ i → i+1) (lit ())))))

co2monitor :: (MSDS Real) (MSDS Real) (MSDS Int) (MSDS Int) (ISDS Int)→MTaskMain()
co2monitor mCurTempSds mCurHumSds mAirqualitySds mMaxCO2Sds iAlarmSds =
  airqualitySensor AQS_SGP30 λsensor → main (

  rpeatEvery (BeforeSec $ lit 30) ( // Check CO2 level every 30 seconds
    co2 sensor ¿¿~. λco2level →
    setSds mAirqualitySds co2level ¿¿|.
    getSds mMaxCO2Sds ¿¿~. λmaxCO2 →
    Iff (co2level >. maxCO2) (iUpd iAlarmSds (λ_ i → i+1) (lit ()))
  ) .||.
  rpeatEvery (BeforeSec $ lit 600) ( // Recalibrate sensor every 10 minutes
    getSds mCurTempSds ¿¿~. λtemp →
    getSds mCurHumSds ¿¿~. λhum →
    setEnvironmentalData sensor temp hum
  ))
```

Listing 14. The source code for the air quality monitoring system.

In this example we see several utilisations of shared data sources that were not possible in the old implementation. There are four major usages of these new shared data sources that were not possible in the old situation:

In the new implementation...	**In the old implementation ...**
The shared data sources for the optimal temperature and max CO2 values (lines 4 and 5) are created, and synchronized only from the server to the client.	The old implementation only has bi-directionally linked shared data sources.
The shared data sources for current temperature and current humidity (lines 9 and 10) only exist on the device.	Each mTask task needs to have its own shared data source, both connected to the same shared data source on the server. Everything is synchronized automatically, and all communication has to go via the server.
The shared data source for air quality (line 8) is directly accessible from the server. If we only occasionally needed the value for something, we only occasionally have to retrieve the value.	The server has its own shared data source that is linked, always keeping it up to date. Communication would take place whenever the client has a new value.
The shared data source counting the alarms (line 7) is safely updated from both the `tempAndHum` task (line 25) and the `airQuality` task (line 38) by directly performing the +1 operation on the server.	Both the `tempAndHum` task (line 25) and the `airQuality` task (line 38) have their own copy. The +1 operation is performed on the copy, and afterwards synchronized to the rest of the linked shared data sources, leading to race conditions.

7 Related Work

On smaller IoT devices using microcontrollers, the industry standard for writing applications is the programming language C. The simplest, most bare-bones option for the implementation of communication, is to use TCP or UDP connections directly [20]. On top of this, high-level communication protocols like HTTP or web sockets can be used. Alternatively, a message broker like MQTT or AMQP can be used. These options are explored and compared in a paper by [12]. The mTask system supports both TCP and MQTT for communication. The programmer, however, never needs to send TCP/MQTT messages directly. This communication is all fully implied by starting/ending tasks, or writing to shared data sources cross platform.

On bigger IoT devices running a full operating system, any solution that also runs on normal computers and web servers can be employed. While this paper focusses on smaller IoT devices using microcontrollers, the same principles can be applied to bigger IoT devices. Distributed iTask implements proxy access to shared data sources similar to the interface of this paper [14, Section 4.2].

Another possibility is to run a full-fledged distributed memory system like Erlang [1].

mTask provides fine-grained control over what code gets executed on what device, using the `liftmTask` and `loweriTask` combinators. Other systems determine automatically what code runs on the server, and what runs on the client. In contrast to our solution, these systems assume that all nodes are powerful enough to execute any code fragment. A tierless JavaScript project created by [16] uses static code analysis, and inserts remote calls automatically into the code where necessary. JavaScript is an object-oriented language with extensive access to program state, so shared data sources and/or synchronization are not implemented. Potato is a reactive programming solution for IoT problems in the Elixir/Erlang world, using a similar approach [3]. Potato is a specific version of functional reactive programming [5]. A (remote) observable in Potato is somewhat similar to a SDS in task-oriented programming. The main difference is that an observable produces a stream of values, while a SDS only has a single current value that changes over time.

Our implementation of `loweriTask` uses tagged functions which are then remotely triggered to be executed. This is similar to remote function calls in other programming languages or frameworks. Because of our tierless setup [11], the mTask programmer does not need to define these tags and/or interfaces themselves. Instead, these tasks are generated from the single source file, and automatically inserted into the compiled mTask program.

8 Conclusion

In this paper, we improve our single source solution for communication between edge devices in IoT systems with their server. In the existing solution, the server could spawn tasks on the edge device. The tasks on the server and edge device can communicate via shared data sources during their execution.

We introduce separate shares on the server and the device. The interface to these shares on the server and the edge device is very similar. The semantics of the shares on the edge device is a proper subset of the server-based shares.

The server updates or reads a shared data source on the device by spawning an appropriate task. This requires the edge device-wide shared data sources introduced here. In the previous system, every task on the edge device had its own copy of the shared data source on the server.

To facilitate easy and efficient communication from edge device tasks to server tasks, the device tasks can invoke a parameterized task on the server. Our examples show that this yields a convenient abstraction level for safe communication.

Unidirectional synchronization from server to device, or vice versa, has still a well-defined semantics. This is easily expressed as a general task in our new abstraction level. The remote shared data source will reflect any value that lasts long enough with some delay.

All code shown here is implemented in the existing iTask system for the server and mTask system for task-oriented programming. All code shown in this paper is available online [7].

9 Future Work

In this paper, we have shown how shares can be used to greatly improve communication between an mTask device and a web server. However, there are still some open questions.

Currently, all types in mTask are required to be of fixed size, including values for shared data sources. This means that recursive abstract data types like lists/queues/trees are not supported. It is an open problem to see how we can add support for those data types on mTask devices, given the fact that the amount of memory is very limited, and no memory virtualization exists. This could be very useful when we want to implement for example a message queue. This message queue could use an actual queue data structure inside a shared data source.

Secondly, we only discussed one-on-one communication for shares, between a server and a device. Communication between two mTask devices is forced to take a detour via the server. When two devices are on the same end of a low-bandwidth connection, direct device to device communication is preferable. This could also be used for swarm behaviour, or mesh networks of mTask devices.

References

1. Armstrong, J.: Concurrent Programming in ERLANG. Prentice Hall, London. New York, 2nd edn. (1996)
2. Böhm, H.: Asynchronous Actions in a Synchronous World. Master's thesis, Radboud University, Nijmegen, Netherlands (2019)
3. De Troyer, C., Nicolay, J., De Meuter, W.: Building IoT systems using distributed first-class reactive programming. In: 2018 IEEE International Conference on Cloud Computing Technology and Science (CloudCom), pp. 185–192. IEEE, Nicosia (2018). https://doi.org/10.1109/CloudCom2018.2018.00045
4. Domoszlai, L., Lijnse, B., Plasmeijer, R.: Parametric lenses: change notification for bidirectional lenses. In: Proceedings of the 26nd 2014 International Symposium on Implementation and Application of Functional Languages, pp. 1–11. ACM, Boston MA USA (2014). https://doi.org/10.1145/2746325.2746333
5. Hudak, P.: Functional reactive programming. In: Swierstra, S.D. (ed.) Programming Languages and Systems, pp. 1–1. Springer, Heidelberg (1999)
6. Ireland, C., Bowers, D., Newton, M., Waugh, K.: A classification of object-relational impedance mismatch. In: First International Conference on Advances in Databases, Knowledge, and Data Applications, pp. 36–43. IEEE, Cancun, Mexico (2009). https://doi.org/10.1109/DBKDA.2009.11
7. Janssen, N., Lubbers, M., Koopman, P.: Source code for paper distributed data in task-oriented programming on edge devices (2024). https://doi.org/10.5281/zenodo.14236133
8. Koopman, P., Lubbers, M., Plasmeijer, R.: A task-based DSL for microcomputers. In: Proceedings of the Real World Domain Specific Languages Workshop 2018, pp. 1–11. ACM, Vienna Austria (2018). https://doi.org/10.1145/3183895.3183902
9. Lubbers, M.: Orchestrating the Internet of Things with Task-Oriented Programming. Radboud University Press, 1 edn. (2023). https://doi.org/10.54195/9789493296114

10. Lubbers, M., Achten, P.: Clean for haskell programmers (2024). https://arxiv.org/abs/2411.00037
11. Lubbers, M., Koopman, P., Ramsingh, A., Singer, J., Trinder, P.: Could tierless languages reduce IoT development grief? ACM Trans. Internet Things **4**(1), 1–35 (2023). https://doi.org/10.1145/3572901
12. Naik, N.: Choice of effective messaging protocols for IoT systems: MQTT, CoAP, AMQP and HTTP. In: 2017 IEEE International Systems Engineering Symposium (ISSE), pp. 1–7. IEEE, Vienna, Austria (2017). https://doi.org/10.1109/SysEng.2017.8088251
13. Netzer, R.H.B., Miller, B.P.: What are race conditions?: some issues and formalizations. ACM Lett. Program. Lang. Syst. **1**(1), 74–88 (1992). https://doi.org/10.1145/130616.130623
14. Oortgiese, A., Van Groningen, J., Achten, P., Plasmeijer, R.: A distributed dynamic architecture for task oriented programming. In: Proceedings of the 29th Symposium on the Implementation and Application of Functional Programming Languages, pp. 1–12. ACM, Bristol United Kingdom (2017). https://doi.org/10.1145/3205368.3205375
15. Pfenning, F., Elliott, C.: Higher-order abstract syntax. In: Proceedings of the ACM SIGPLAN 1988 Conference on Programming Language Design and Implementation, pp. 199–208. ACM, Atlanta Georgia USA (1988). https://doi.org/10.1145/53990.54010
16. Philips, L., De Roover, C., Van Cutsem, T., De Meuter, W.: Towards tierless web development without tierless languages. In: Proceedings of the 2014 ACM International Symposium on New Ideas, New Paradigms, and Reflections on Programming & Software, pp. 69–81. ACM, Portland Oregon USA (2014). https://doi.org/10.1145/2661136.2661146
17. Plasmeijer, R., Achten, P., Koopman, P.: iTasks: executable specifications of interactive work flow systems for the web. ACM SIGPLAN Not. **42**(9), 141–152 (2007). https://doi.org/10.1145/1291220.1291174
18. Plasmeijer, R., Eekelen, M.V.: Keep it clean: a unique approach to functional programming. ACM SIGPLAN Not. **34**(6), 23–31 (1999). https://doi.org/10.1145/606666.606670
19. Plasmeijer, R., Lijnse, B., Michels, S., Achten, P., Koopman, P.: Task-oriented programming in a pure functional language. In: Proceedings of the 14th Symposium on Principles and Practice of Declarative Programming. PPDP 2012, pp. 195–206. ACM, New York (2012). https://doi.org/10.1145/2370776.2370801
20. Stevens, W.R., Fall, K.W.: TCP/IP Illustrated. Volume 1, The Protocols. Addison-Wesley, Boston, MA, 2nd edn. (1994)

Teaching

Exploring Female and Male Student Perceptions in a Functional-Programming-Based Automata Theory Course

Marco T. Morazán(✉), Tijana Minić, and Andrés M. Garced

Seton Hall University, South Orange, USA
{morazanm,minictij,maldona2}@shu.edu

Abstract. Historically, it has been challenging for students to get interested in and for instructors to teach Formal Languages and Automata Theory courses. The challenges stem from a multitude of reasons including the theoretical nature of the material, the use of formal notation, student lack of experience with problem solving and proof development, and the student perception that the material is not relevant to majoring in Computer Science. In this article, we illustrate our novel design- and programming-based approach to building state machines and developing constructive proofs. Student perceptions, both overall and by gender, are explored to determine if this approach effectively addresses some of the negative historical trends. Our empirical results suggest that the approach has a positive impact overall and by gender. In addition, the results reveal nuanced differences between female and male students and areas for future improvements.

1 Introduction

Historically, among Computer Science students, it has been difficult to motivate interest in Formal Languages and Automata Theory (FLAT) courses. The lack of interest is due to a plethora of reasons that include: student perceptions of no association with other courses in the Computer Science curriculum [8,22,47,51], student difficulty to understand abstract mathematical topics [8,17,66], student difficulty to understand formal notation [6], lack of problem-solving skills [52,66], and lack of proof-development skills [8,51]. Most of these reasons are likely to resonate with FLAT instructors that need to deliver a Computer Science theory course to an audience trained to program and with an appetite for software development. These are all general problems in the FLAT student population that have led to high drop-out rates [28,47,64]. At a more human level, readers of this article are likely to recall multiple occasions when they have witnessed the enthusiasm in students when they get a program to run. The same readers are less likely to have witnessed the same enthusiasm when a student gets a proof right. We are trying to get students enthusiastic about FLAT without sacrificing content nor rigor.

In addition to the problems above, many female students have further compounding problems in Computer Science that include: the perception that "hacking" abilities are a required prerequisite skill in Computer Science [15,29], the

J. Gibbons (Ed.): TFP 2025, LNCS 15652, pp. 485–510, 2026.
https://doi.org/10.1007/978-3-031-99751-8_21

perception that male students know much more [15,29], the need to survive the "boys' club" [15,29], a stronger need to connect computing to other fields and to see the computer as a tool to use in a broader context [15,29], lower self-confidence [7,15,20,23,29,63], and the perception that Computer Science is narrowly focused on programming [15]. Many of these problems come from a male-dominated discipline that, indifferently or unconsciously, perpetuates stereotypes about persons in Computer Science. By listing the problems that tend to affect female students more, we are not suggesting that female students perform worse than male students in Computer Science. Studies have suggested, for example, that there are no differences between female and male students in programming performance [24,32].

In the literature, there is a clear emphasis on practices that discourage Computer Science students with many articles focusing on the practices that discourage women. In this article, we break away from this norm and try to shed light on practices that encourage students (both women and men), in a new programming-based `FLAT` curriculum tightly-coupled with `FSM`–a functional programming language for the `FLAT` classroom. We present data collected through anonymous surveys at two universities, Seton Hall University (`SHU`) and Worcester Polytechnic Institute (`WPI`), using the programming-based `FLAT` curriculum put forth in *Programming-Based Formal Languages and Automata Theory: Design, Implement, Validate, and Prove* [38]. We analyze the collected data in aggregate to capture overall perceptions across our sample population as well as by gender[1] to determine any differences. Our focus is on the following research questions:

- RQ1 Do students feel that programming state machines is straightforward?
- RQ2 Do students feel that Automata Theory, programming state machines, and programming constructive algorithms is intellectually stimulating?
- RQ3 Do students feel that Automata Theory is relevant to their Computer Science education?
- RQ4 Is programming in `FSM` useful to understand Automata Theory and to develop constructive proofs?

The article is organized as follows. Section 2 presents a brief introduction to `FSM`, the design-based programming methodology used to instruct students, and examples of machine and constructive algorithm implementations. Section 3 presents the collected empirical data. Section 4 compares and contrasts with related work. Section 5 presents a discussion of the results and threats to validity. Finally, Sect. 6 presents concluding remarks and directions for future work.

2 Programming in `FSM`

To illustrate the design methodology and the style used in class instruction, two examples are presented. The first is the design and implementation of a `dfa`. The

[1] In this article, the term gender refers to female and male, given that our sample population only contains two individuals that do not self-identify as such. In the empirical analysis, therefore, their responses were removed from the data set.

second is the implementation of an algorithm developed as part of a constructive proof. Specifically, we outline the design and implementation of a construction algorithm developed to prove the closure of regular languages under Kleene star (e.g., as discussed in [25,27,38,53,57]).

2.1 The Language

`FSM` [39] is a domain-specific language embedded in Racket [16]. It provides constructors for state machines: deterministic finite-state automata (`dfa`), non-deterministic finite-state automata (`ndfa`), pushdown automata (`pda`), Turing machines (`tms`), composed Turing machines (`ctms`) [33], and multitape Turing machines (`mttms`)[2]. For instance, the constructor for deterministic finite-state automata has the following signature:

make-dfa: S Σ s F δ ['no-dead] $\rightarrow$ dfa

`S` denotes the set of states. Σ denotes the input alphabet. The starting state is denoted by `s`. `F` denotes a set of final states. The transition function is denoted by δ. Finally, the optional argument, `'no-dead`, informs the constructor that the transition function is fully specified. When this argument is omitted, the constructor adds a dead/trap state and adds transitions to this state to fully specify the transition function. Constructors for other machines are similar in nature. Readers may consult the `FSM` documentation for all constructors [37].

The language also provides observers to extract the components of a machine, observers to apply a machine to a word, unit testing facilities using `RackUnit` [67], and random testing facilities. In addition, integrated into `FSM` is a powerful suite of static and dynamic visualization tools. On the static side, `FSM` offers the automatic generation of transition diagrams [45] and computation graphs [41]. On the dynamic side, `FSM` offers tools to trace machine application [45] and to trace the conversion between computation models (e.g., from an `ndfa` to a `dfa` [43] and from an `ndfa` to a regular expression and vice versa [42]).

Finally, `FSM` offers a tailor-made error-messaging system that associates a machine constructor misuse with an informative error message [10,40]. The error messaging system is tightly-coupled with the design-based methodology put forth by Morazán [38]. Each error message includes the step of the design recipe that has not been successfully completed along with a short, nonprescriptive, and jargon-free problem description. We name such errors *recipe-based errors*[3] [10] and they use the same vocabulary found in the textbook of instruction [38], which instructors are encouraged to employ in class.

2.2 Design-Based Programming Methodology

The design methodology put forth by Morazán uses design recipes [38]. A design recipe is a series of steps, each with a concrete outcome, that guides a student

[2] Constructors for grammars and regular expressions are also provided, but these are not addressed in this article.

[3] We thank Rose Bohrer for suggesting this term to us.

1. Name the machine, specify the alphabets, and formulate, if applicable, the pre and post conditions.
2. Write unit tests
3. Identify conditions that must be tracked as input is consumed, associate a state with each condition, and determine the start and final states.
4. Formulate the transition relation
5. Implement the machine
6. Run the tests and, if necessary, redesign
7. Design, implement, and test an invariant predicate for each state
8. Prove L = L(M)

Fig. 1. The design recipe for state machines.

from a problem statement to a solution. Design recipes were first introduced by Felleisen et al. to instruct beginners in programming [13] and later expanded by Morazán to a 2-semester introduction for beginners [34–36]. The design recipe for state machines is displayed in Fig. 1. Unlike most design recipes for beginners, this design recipe includes machine verification steps (i.e., steps 7 and 8). Such steps are appropriate and necessary for students starting to formally explore the realm of theoretical Computer Science. We note, however, that we are not suggesting that such steps are inappropriate for beginners. On the contrary, beginners have successfully been introduced to program correctness using Hoare logic [18,19] as part of designing `while`-loops [36,46].

Steps 1 and 2 ask for a descriptive machine name, the needed alphabets, and a thorough set of unit tests. Step 3 asks for the conditions that must be tracked as the machine processes the input and associating a state with each. In design recipes for beginners, this step is equivalent to developing a design idea. Step 4 asks for the development of the transition relation. Each transition is developed assuming that the condition describing the source state holds. The actions taken by a transition must guarantee that the condition of the destination state holds. Steps 5 and 6 ask for the machine's implementation and the running of tests. If errors are thrown or tests fail, students must revisit the steps of the design recipe to debug. Step 7 asks students to formalize the conditions that are tracked by the states (developed for step 3) as a computation advances. This is done by designing and implementing an invariant predicate for each state to affirm its design role. Step 8 asks for a proof of partial correctness. This is done in two steps. First, students prove by induction that state invariants hold during a computation. Second, once established that state invariants always hold, students prove that the machine's language is correct.

2.3 Programming Machines

To illustrate how students are instructed to design state machines, consider using the design recipe to implement a deterministic finite-state automaton for

```
1  #lang fsm
2  ;; State Documentation
3  ;; S aaba not in the consumed input and no proper prefix of aaba is at the end
4  ;;   of the consumed input, starting state
5  ;; A aaba not in the consumed input and a is detected at the end of the
6  ;;   consumed input
7  ;; B aaba not in the consumed input and aa is detected at the end of the
8  ;;   consumed input
9  ;; C aaba not in the consumed input and aab is detected at the end of the
10 ;;   consumed input
11 ;; F aaba is detected in the consumed input, final state
12 (define has-aaba (make-dfa '(S A B C F)
13                            '(a b)
14                            'S
15                            '(F)
16                            '((S a A) (S b S)
17                              (A a B) (A b S)
18                              (B a B) (B b C)
19                              (C a F) (C b S)
20                              (F a F) (F b F))
21                            'no-dead))
22
23 (check-equal? (sm-apply has-aaba '())                    'reject)
24 (check-equal? (sm-apply has-aaba '(a))                   'reject)
25 (check-equal? (sm-apply has-aaba '(a a))                 'reject)
26 (check-equal? (sm-apply has-aaba '(a a b))               'reject)
27 (check-equal? (sm-apply has-aaba '(a a a b))             'reject)
28 (check-equal? (sm-apply has-aaba '(b b a a b))           'reject)
29 (check-equal? (sm-apply has-aaba '(a a b a))             'accept)
30 (check-equal? (sm-apply has-aaba '(b b a a a b a b b))   'accept)
31 (check-equal? (sm-apply has-aaba '(b b b a a a b a a a)) 'accept)
```

Fig. 2. `dfa` for L=$\{$`w`$|$`w`$\in$(a b)* $\wedge$ `w contains aaba`$\}$.

L=$\{$`w`$|$`w`$\in\{$a b$\}^*$ $\wedge$ **`w contains aaba`**$\}$. The reader is sure to recognize this as an instance of the problem of finding a pattern (i.e., a subword) in a word. Such an example is a good pedagogic choice as it serves as en effective introduction to illustrate the development of the `KMP` algorithm [21].

The machine implementation after following the first 6 steps of the design recipe is displayed in Fig. 2. The first step of the design recipe is satisfied by lines 12 and 13 using the descriptive name `has-aaba` and identifying the alphabet as `(a b)`. The second step of the design recipe is satisfied with the unit tests in lines 23–31. It is emphasized to students that tests must be thorough and, when a machine decides a language, include words that are in and that are not in the machine's language. In this example, the tests are written using `FSM`'s observer, sm-apply, to apply a machine to a word. Step 3 is satisfied by (informally) documenting the meaning of each state as done in lines 2–11 and providing the states to the constructor as done in line 12. Based on the result of step 3, the transition function is formulated to satisfy step 4. Students are taught to assume that the role of a state, say `M`, is satisfied and that the action taken by a transition out of `M` to state `N` must guarantee that the role of `N` is satisfied. For instance, consider developing the transitions out of `A`. In this state, the consumed input ends with an `a` and does not contain `aaba`. Upon reading an `a`, the consumed input does not contain `aaba` and ends with `aa`, thus, satisfying the role of state `B`. Therefore, the transition needed is `(A a B)`. Upon reading a `b`, the consumed input does not contain `aaba` and does not end with a proper prefix of `aaba`, thus, satisfying the role of state `S`. Therefore, the transition needed is `(A a S)`. Lines 16–20 in Fig. 2 display the result of performing this analysis for each state to satisfy Step 4. Steps 5 and 6 are satisfied by the code in Fig. 2 and running the program to establish that all the tests pass. If syntax or constructor misuse errors are thrown or if any tests fail, students debug by revisiting the steps of the design recipe. In our experience, the scaffolding provided by the design recipe and by the `FSM` error messaging system reduce student frustration stemming from sitting in front of a monitor not knowing what to do.

To satisfy step 7, the predicates are designed starting with the state roles identified in step 3. Figure 3 displays the state invariant predicates developed for `has-aaba`[4]. For instance, the invariant predicate, `C-INV` (lines 23–27 in Fig. 3) for state `C` takes as input, `ci`, the consumed input. This predicate may be used by the `FSM` visualization tool when the machine transitions into `C`. It checks that `ci` does not contain `aaba` and that it ends with `aab`. If this predicate holds, then the role of `C` is affirmed and the visualization tool renders the state in green. Otherwise, the state is rendered in red. In this manner, students may validate their design before attempting to develop a proof of partial correctness.

To satisfy step 8, it must be established that `has-aaba`'s language is equal to `L`. This is done in two steps. The first establishes by induction, on the number of transitions performed, that the invariant predicates hold during machine execution. In the interest of brevity, we do not outline the entire proof. Instead, we provide proof snippets to communicate the spirit of what is done in the classroom. For the base case, we argue that `S-INV` holds as follows:

```
When the machine starts, the consumed input is empty. Given
that (eq? ci '()) holds, we have that S-INV holds.
```

For the inductive step, each transition rule is proven correct by assuming that the predicate invariant for the source state holds and establishing that, after the actions performed by the transition, the predicate invariant for the destination state holds. For instance, consider using `(A a B)`:

```
    By inductive hypothesis, A-INV holds. This means that the
```

[4] In the interest of brevity, neither the unit tests for each invariant predicate nor the implementation of the auxiliary functions (i.e., `contains?`, `ends-with?`, and `does-not-end-with?`) are displayed. We trust that enough context is provided to understand the invariant predicates.

```
;; word → Boolean
;; Purpose: Determine that aaba not in the consumed input and no subword
;;          of aaba is at the end of the consumed input
(define (S-INV ci)
  (or (eq? ci '())
      (and (does-not-end-with? ci '(a))
           (does-not-end-with? ci '(a a))
           (does-not-end-with? ci '(a a b))
           (not (contains? ci '(a a b a))))))

;; word → Boolean
;; Purpose: Determine if aaba not in the consumed input and a is detected
;;          at the end of the consumed input
(define (A-INV ci)
  (and (not (contains? ci '(a a b a))) (ends-with? ci '(a))))

;; word → Boolean
;; Purpose: Determine that aaba not in the consumed input and aa is detected
;;          at the end of the consumed input
(define (B-INV ci)
  (and (not (contains? ci quot(a a b a))) (ends-with? ci '(a a))))

;; word → Boolean
;; Purpose: Determine that aaba not in the consumed input and aab is detected
;;          at the end of the consumed input
(define (C-INV ci)
  (and (not (contains? ci '(a a b a))) (ends-with? ci '(a a b))))

;; word → Boolean
;; Purpose: Determine that aaba is detected in the consumed input
(define (F-INV ci) (contains? ci '(a a b a)))
```

Fig. 3. State invariant predicates for has-aaba.

consumed input does not contain aaba and that it ends with an a. This transition reads an a. Therefore, after performing this transition, the consumed input ends with aa and does not contain aaba. Thus, B-INV holds.

Finally, to argue for the correctness of the machine, students assume predicate invariants hold and prove the following equivalences:

$$w \in L \Leftrightarrow w \in L(\texttt{has-aaba}) \qquad w \notin L \Leftrightarrow w \notin L(\texttt{has-aaba})$$

Briefly, for example, students argue that $w \in L(\texttt{has-abaa}) \Rightarrow w \in L$ holds as follows:

Assume w∈L(has-aaba). Given that predicate invariants always hold, this means that w contains abaa. Thus, w∈L.

The remaining implications are established in a similar manner. In the interest of brevity, their proofs are omitted.

This completes our presentation of how students are taught to design, implement, validate, and verify machines. The reader can appreciate that none of the steps of the design recipe are beyond an advanced undergraduate that has taken an introduction to Discrete Mathematics course and has taken an introduction to programming course. We note that for students that are introduced to programming using HtDP [13] or APS [35] and APD [36], as is the case at WPI and at SHU, the use of FSM quickly becomes natural given that its syntax is familiar to students. For students that are not familiar with Lisp-like syntax, feeling comfortable with FSM may take a little longer and students are helped by the syntax explanations found in the textbook used for instruction [38].

2.4 Programming Constructive Proofs

To illustrate our approach to teaching students about constructive proofs, we outline an algorithm to establish the closure of regular languages under Kleene star. Let M = (make-ndfa S Σ s F R). We denote M's language as L(M).

After a brief class discussion, most students understand that a machine, say M*, that accepts words obtained by concatenating zero or more words in L(M) needs to be designed. With a bit more effort, class discussion defines:

$$L(M^*) = \{w | w=\epsilon \vee w=w_0...w_n, \text{ where } w_i \in L(M)\}$$

The definition above is not an algorithm for constructing M*, but students are encouraged to use it to start designing such an algorithm. Based on it, students assert the following about M*:

- needs M's states and δ
- starting state ought to be an accepting state, given that $\epsilon \in$L(M*)
- M* needs to loop
- M's starting state cannot be made M*'s starting state
- M* may nondeterministically move from a final state to its starting state

The first two assertions stem from class discussion observing that words in L(M*) are constructed from words in L(M) and that $\epsilon\in$L(M*). The third assertion stems from observing that multiple words in L(M) may need to be read by M*. The fourth assertion stems from class discussion and/or a homework exercise illustrating what goes wrong if M's starting state is arbitrarily made a final state in M*. This observation naturally leads to concluding that a new starting state, say Z, is needed for L(M*). The fifth assertion stems from realizing that M* needs to loop after reading a word in L(M).

Based on this discussion, both the graphical description of the construction algorithm displayed in Fig. 4 and the following formal description are developed:

$$M^* = (\text{make-ndfa } S\cup\{Z\}\ \Sigma\ Z\ F\cup\{Z\}\ R\cup\{(f\ \epsilon\ Z) | f\in F\}), \text{ where } Z\notin S$$

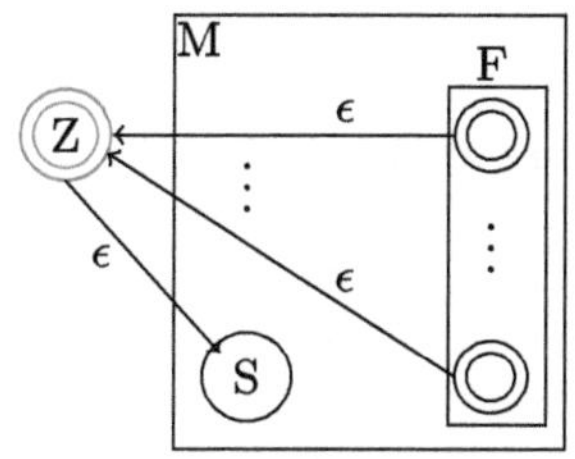

Fig. 4. Graphical description of the construction algorithm for L = L(M)*.

Invariably, a significant number of students find both descriptions difficult to understand. A sample of questions/comments raised by students include[5]:

1. *What is Z?*
2. *What is little f?*
3. *Where did all those arrows labeled with the empty word come from?*
4. *This is unreadable.*
5. *Why is Z a final state?*
6. *Why is there an or-statement?*[6]

We observe that such questions are consistent with the historical observations that students struggle with formal notation.

In our experience, an instructor may repeatedly answer such questions for students, but the answers are not fully assimilated until they are tied to design and programming. To this end, we use the ideas outlined above as a draft design idea, use elements from the design recipe for state machines, and follow the design recipe for function development taught to beginners [13,35,36] to complete the implementation. The developed constructor is displayed in Fig. 5. For step 1, the constructor's signature, purpose, and header are displayed in lines 1–3[7]. To satisfy step 2, the unit tests displayed on lines 23–28 are developed using a sample constructor application displayed on line 21. To design and implement the body of the constructor, the input machine and the design of the new machine are considered. Locally, variables are defined for the components of the input machine. In addition, a local variable, `Z`, is defined for the needed new state, using `FSM`'s `gen-state`[8]. The roles of `M`'s states remain unchanged in the constructed machine. Students must, however, define `Z`'s role. An immediate answer provided by some students is that `Z` is the starting state of the constructed machine, which is not enough. It is during this design step that students begin to understand that if the constructed machine is in `Z` then the consumed input is the concatenation of zero or more words in the language of the input machine. This is reflected in lines 10–12 in Fig. 5 and provides answers to the first and

[5] These are presented verbatim without any editing.
[6] The student is referring to "|" on the formal description of M*.
[7] The type `fsa` (i.e., finite-state automaton) denotes either a `dfa` or an `ndfa`.
[8] Generates a state guaranteeing that it does not match any state in its given input.

```
;; fsa → ndfa
;; Purpose: Build the ndfa for L(M)*
(define (build-Kleene*-machine M)
  (let* [(Mstates (sm-states M))
         (Msigma  (sm-sigma M))
         (Mstart  (sm-start M))
         (Mfinals (sm-finals M))
         (Mrules  (sm-rules M))
         (Z       (gen-state Mstates))]
         ;; New state documentation
         ;;  Z the consumed input is the concatenation of 0 or more words
         ;;  in L(M), starting state
    (make-ndfa (cons Z Mstates)
               Msigma
               Z
               (cons Z Mfinals)
               (append
                (cons (list Z 'ϵ Mstart) Mrules)
                (map (λ (f) (list f 'ϵ Z)) Mfinals)))))

(define has-aaba-Kstar (build-Kleene*-machine has-aaba))

(check-equal? (sm-apply has-aaba-Kstar '(a b b))         'reject)
(check-equal? (sm-apply has-aaba-Kstar '(a a b b a a b)) 'reject)
(check-equal? (sm-apply has-aaba-Kstar '())              'accept)
(check-equal? (sm-apply has-aaba-Kstar '(a a b a))       'accept)
(check-equal? (sm-apply has-aaba-Kstar '( b a a b b a a b a b))
              'accept)
```

Fig. 5. Constructor for regular language closure under Kleene star.

fifth student questions above. With this new found understanding, most students now understand that the constructed machine may nondeterministically transition from Z to S to start reading (another) word in the input machine's language and that ϵ-transitions are needed from the input machine's final states to Z to loop. Thus, providing concrete answers to the second, third, and sixth student questions above that resonate with most students. Finally, after designing and implementing the constructor most students state that Fig. 4 and its formal description are understandable.

Finally, the proof of correctness follows in two steps as done in Sect. 2.3. First, students assume that state roles hold for the input machine and argue by induction that for the constructed machine the state roles hold. Second, assuming state roles hold, students argue that L(M*)=L(M)*, where M* is the constructed machine and M is the given machine.

3 Empirical Data

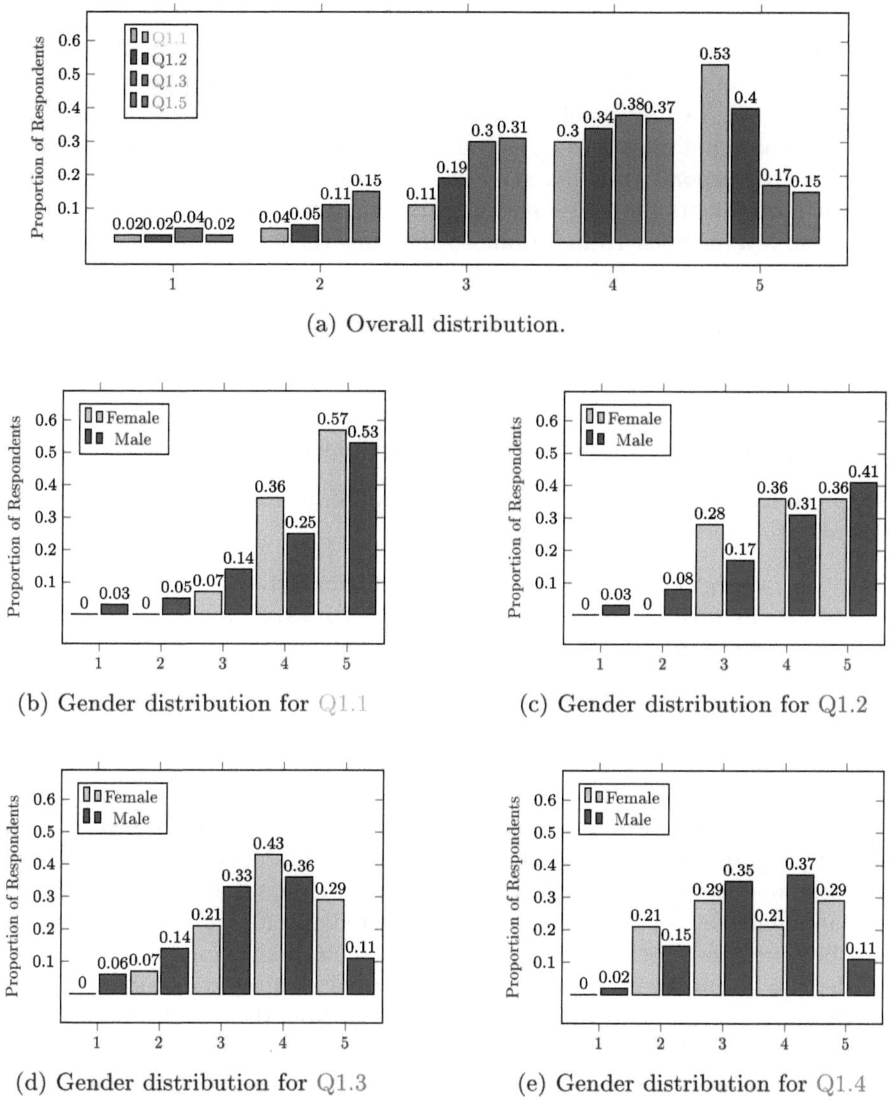

(a) Overall distribution.

(b) Gender distribution for Q1.1

(c) Gender distribution for Q1.2

(d) Gender distribution for Q1.3

(e) Gender distribution for Q1.4

Fig. 6. Programming `dfa`/`ndfa`/`pda`/`tm` machines is straightforward.

To answer RQ1–RQ4, students enrolled in their first `FLAT` course at `SHU` and at `WPI` were anonymously surveyed. The two courses enrolled a total of 106 students, 11 at `SHU` and 95 at `WPI`. A total of 53 students volunteered to participate in the survey, 10 from `SHU` and 43 from `WPI`, making the overall response rate among registered students 43% (the response rate among registered students is 91% at `SHU` and 45% at `WPI`). The day the survey was administered, a total of 43 students attended class at `WPI` (31 in-person and 12 remotely) and 10 students attended class at SHU (all in-person). This attendance rate is typical for both institutions. The responses, therefore, reflect the perceptions of students that regularly attend class and not the perceptions of all students registered for these courses. Among the respondents, 14 (26%) self identified as female, 36 (68%) self identified as male, and the remaining 3 (6%) self identified as: 1 nonbinary, 1 agender, and 1 declined to respond. Finally, students at both institutions received neither payment nor benefits for participating in the survey.

The survey includes 10 questions to measure their perceptions. Each question presents a statement and the respondent is asked to identify their level of agreement using using a Likert scale [26]: `[1] Strongly disagree`...Strongly agree [5] (including [3], a neutral category). The overall response distributions as well as the distributions by gender are presented.

3.1 Programming Machines Is Straightforward

To explore RQ1, *Do students feel that programming state machines is straightforward?*, the following statements are used:

Q1.1. **Programming dfas is straightforward.**
Q1.2. **Programming ndfas is straightforward.**
Q1.3. **Programming pdas is straightforward.**
Q1.4. **Programming tms is straightforward**[9]**.**

The overall distribution of responses is displayed in Fig. 6a. We observe that for all machine types a majority of respondents tend to agree (responses 4 and 5) with the statements: 83%, 74%, 55%, and 52%, respectively for `dfas`, `ndfas`, `pdas`, and `tms`. Thus, for our sample at large, the answer to RQ1 is that students feel that programming state machines is straightforward. As machine complexity increases, we observe that the proportion of respondents that tend to agree with the statements decreases. This is to be expected given that the programming tasks become more difficult for most students. Students, for instance, do not consider programming an `ndfa` as straightforward as programming a `dfa`, given that they are not accustomed to nondeterminism. Nonetheless, the data suggests that students found the experience of programming state machines straightforward. It is also noteworthy that only a small proportion of respondents tend to disagree (responses 1 and 2) with the statements: 6%, 7%, 15%, and 17%, respectively, for `dfas`, `ndfas`, `pdas`, and `tms`. We interpret this as further evidence is support of our answer to RQ1. These results are very encouraging considering that Computer Science popular culture states: *Beware of the Turing tar-pit in which everything is possible but nothing of interest is easy* [50]. *Easy* may or may not be interchangeable with *straightforward* in this context, but it is certainly the case that anything easy is likely to also be straightforward.

Figures 6b to 6e presents the distributions for females and males. For all machine types, female students tend to agree (i.e., responses 4 and 5) more or the same with the statements than male students: 93% versus 78%, 72% versus 72%,

[9] One respondent failed to provide a valid response.

72% versus 47%, and 50% versus 47%, respectively, for `dfa`s, `ndfa`s, `pda`s, and `tm`s. Among male students, the proportion agreeing with the statements tends to decrease more sharply as machine complexity increases and drops just under 50% for the two most complex machine types (i.e., `pda` and `tm`). Among females, no such tendency is observed. The female proportion agreeing with the statements drops from `dfa` to `ndfa`, remains steady from `ndfa` to `pda`, and drops from `pda` to `tm`. The first drop coincides with student's first exposure to nondeterminism and, therefore, is expected regardless of gender. The female proportion agreeing remains steady for `pda`s and presents the widest gap with male students. It is difficult to explain why this occurs, but a plausible explanation is that female students tend to do less unguided exploration and adhere more closely to the steps of the design recipe. Thus, they assimilate nondeterminism better than male students. The next drop in the female agreeing proportion, from `pda` to `tm`, coincides with the introduction of mutation (i.e., `tm`s mutating their tape), which is also expected regardless of gender given that reasoning about mutations is challenging. The challenge appears significant enough to virtually make the levels of agreement among female and male students the same. Our answer for RQ1, when examined by gender, is that both genders agree that programming state machines is straightforward. However, female students tend to feel stronger on this dimension.

3.2 Intellectual Stimulation and CS Education Relevance

To explore RQ2, *Do students feel that Automata Theory, programming state machines, and programming constructive algorithms is intellectually stimulating?*, and RQ3, *Do students feel that Automata Theory is relevant to their Computer Science education?*, the following statements are used:

```
Q2.1. Automata Theory is intellectually stimulating.
Q2.2. Programming state machines [grammars and regular
      expressions][10] is intellectually stimulating.
Q2.3. Programming constructive algorithms is intellectually
      stimulating.
Q2.4. The course is relevant to my Computer Science education.
```

The overall distribution is displayed in Fig. 7a. We observe that for all statements a majority of respondents tend to agree (responses 4 and 5). An unexpected result is that 61% of the respondents tend to agree that Automata Theory is intellectually stimulating. A further unexpected result is that only a small minority, 14%, tend to disagree. This bucks the historical trend that suggests that students do not feel stimulated by Automata Theory. Given that our curriculum covers all the classical topics taught in a first Automata Theory course, we interpret this as evidence that a programming-based approach makes Automata Theory more stimulating for students. Another encouraging result is

[10] The survey studied topics beyond the scope of this article. Square brackets are used to indicate full question text where not the entire text is relevant to this article.

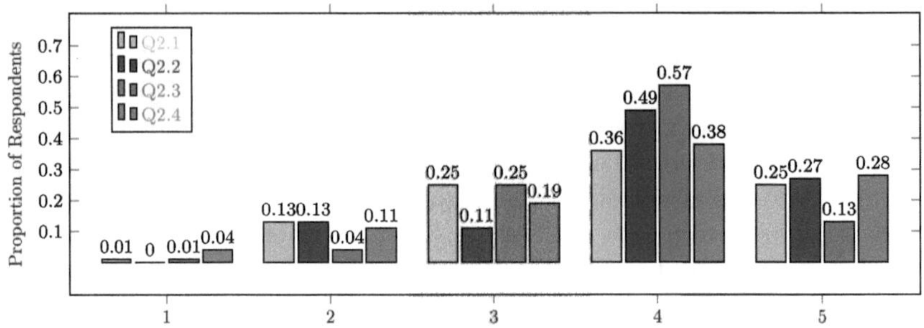

(a) Overall intellectual stimulation and relevance to CS education.

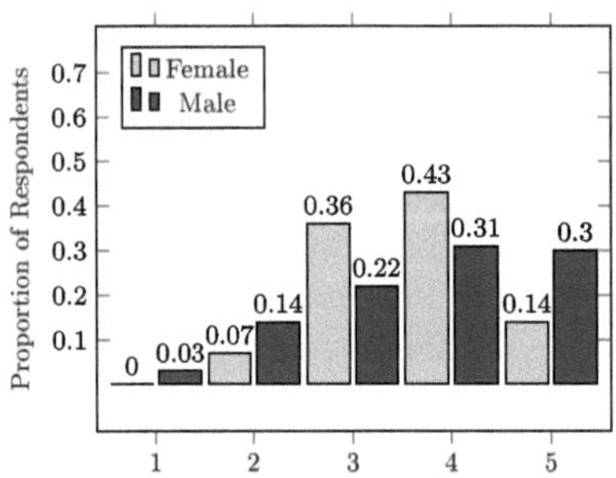

(b) Gender distribution for Q2.1.

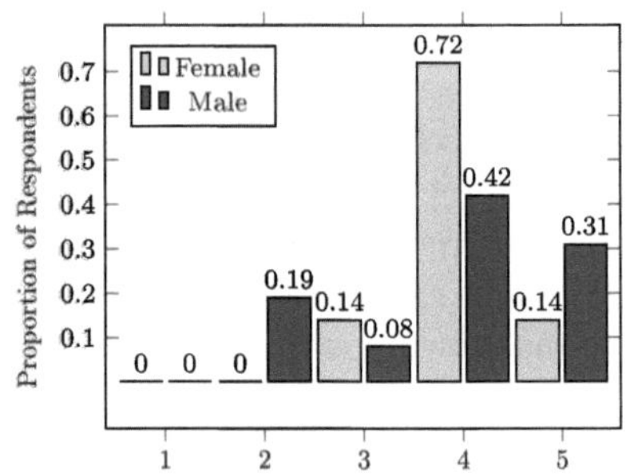

(c) Gender distribution for Q2.2.

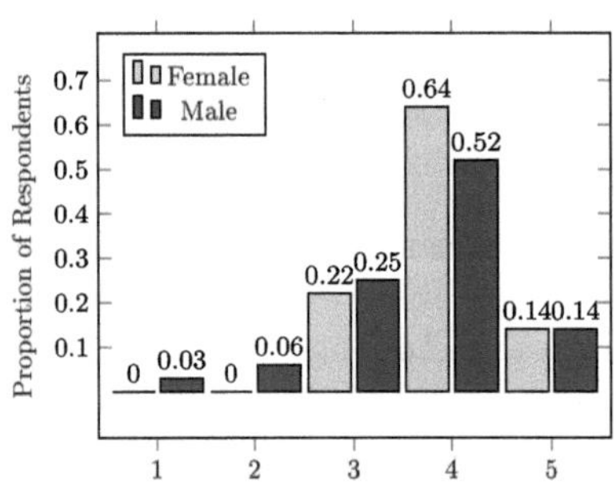

(d) Gender distribution for Q2.3.

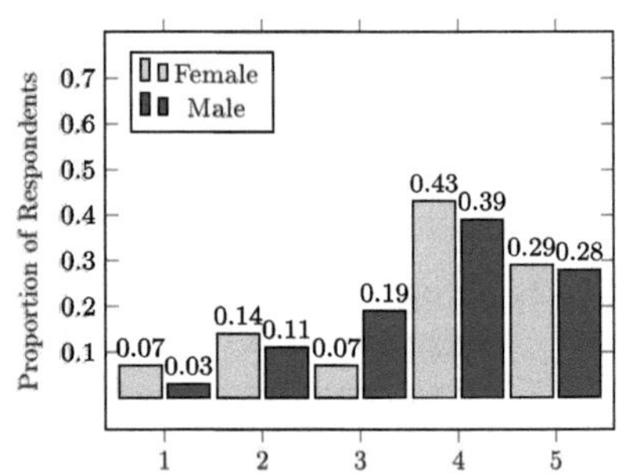

(e) Gender distribution for Q2.4.

Fig. 7. Intellectual stimulation and relevance to CS education.

that an overwhelming majority (i.e., > 67%), respectively 75% and 70%, tend to agree that programming state machines and programming constructive algorithms is intellectually stimulating. Therefore, the respondents feel more strongly about programming in Automata Theory than about Automata Theory itself. We interpret this as evidence that programming is an effective means to engage Computer Science students in Automata Theory. Thus, our answer to RQ2, for our sample at large, is that students feel that Automata Theory, programming state machines, and programming constructive algorithms is intellectually stimulating.

A majority of respondents, 66%, tend to agree that the course in relevant to their Computer Science education. Besides unexpected, this result, once again, goes against what is reported in the literature. To us, it suggests that a programming approach is a key that makes Automata Theory appealing and relevant to Computer Science majors. Therefore, for our sample at large, our answer to RQ3 is that students feel that course is relevant to their Computer Science education.

The distributions by gender are displayed in Figs. 7b to 7e. We observe that a larger proportion of female students, 57%, than males students, 34%, tend to agree (responses 4 and 5) that Automata Theory is intellectually stimulating. This suggests that our design- and programming-based approach makes Automata Theory significantly more stimulating for female students. We also observe that a larger proportion of female students, 86%, than males students, 73%, tend to agree that programming state machines is intellectually stimulating. In addition, we see a larger proportion among females, 78% versus 66%, agreeing that programming constructive algorithms is intellectually stimulating. These results suggest that connecting Automata Theory with programming is more intellectually stimulating for females students. Our answer for RQ2, under the lens of gender, is that female students find Automata Theory, when connected with programming, more intellectually stimulating than male students and that both genders find programming in `FLAT` intellectually stimulating.

Finally, we observe that both genders exhibit overwhelming majorities, 72% for females and 67% for males, that tend to agree (responses 4 and 5) that the course is relevant to their Computer Science education. This is a rather astonishing result considering decades of research suggesting that students feel that Automata Theory has little relevance to their major. It suggests that a design- and programming-based methodology in `FLAT` is an effective means to make it relevant for male and female Computer Science students. Our answer for RQ3, under the lens of gender, is that both genders in our sample feel very strongly that `FLAT` is relevant to their Computer Science education.

3.3 `FSM` Programming Helpfulness

To explore RQ4, *Is programming in FSM useful to understand Automata Theory and to develop constructive proofs?*, the survey presents the following statements:

- Q3.1 `Programming in FSM helped me understand Automata Theory.`
- Q3.2 `Writing programs in FSM helped me develop constructive proofs.`

The overall distribution of responses is displayed in Fig. 8. We observe that the majority of respondents, 64%, tend to agree (responses 4 and 5) that programming in `FSM` is useful to understand Automata Theory. We interpret this as evidence that programming helps elucidate topics in Automata Theory. This

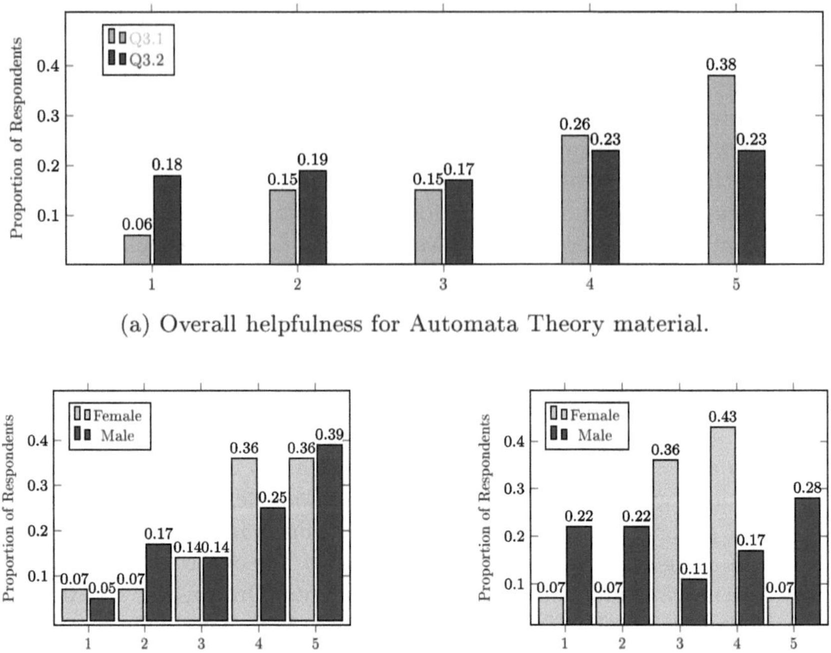

(a) Overall helpfulness for Automata Theory material.

(b) Gender distribution for Q3.1.

(c) Gender distribution for Q3.2.

Fig. 8. FSM Programming helpfulness.

suggests that future studies ought to tease out what topics are elucidated. We hypothesize, for example, that programming helps students understand nondeterminism.

In contrast, the distribution for Q3.2 is polarized. Just less than half of the respondents, 46%, tend to agree that writing programs in FSM helps them develop constructive proofs while 37% tend to disagree. This polarization is unexpected. It can be argued that the act of only writing, not designing, a machine definition in FSM provides little help in developing a proof. Our curriculum, however, requires students to carefully elaborate the meaning of each state and develop invariant predicates that can be validated with FSM visualization tools. Both of these activities have a direct bearing on the development of correctness proofs. This suggest that there is room for improvement in tying together design and proof development or that the survey statement is not detailed enough causing students to equate "writing programs" with only writing machine definitions. Therefore, our answer to RQ4, for the sample population at large, is that the results are inconclusive.

The distributions by gender are displayed in Figs. 8b to 8c. It paints a much more nuanced picture. A larger proportion of female students, 72%, tend to agree (responses 4 and 5) with Q3.1 versus 64% for male students. A similar disparity is observed with the proportions, 14% and 22%, that disagree (responses 1 and 2).

This suggests that female students find programming in FSM is more elucidating regarding Automata Theory topics. For Q3.2, we observe that half of the female respondents tend to agree (responses 4 and 5) and about a third, 36%, are neutral. The distribution for male students is polarized with 45% that tend to agree and 44% that tend to disagree. This suggests that female students are more likely than male students to see the connection between designing and implementing construction algorithms and the development of correctness proofs. A plausible explanation for this, once again, is that female students adhere more closely to following the steps of the design recipe. Thus, our answer for RQ4, under the lens of gender, is that female students find programming in FSM useful to understand Automata Theory and to develop constructive proofs. On the other hand, the results are mixed for male students. Male students find programming in FSM useful to understand Automata Theory. However, the results are inconclusive for male students regarding whether programming in FSM is useful to develop constructive proofs. These results, indeed, suggest that future research is required to explain this gender difference in more detail.

4 Related Work

4.1 FLAT Instruction

A significant hurdle that many FLAT students need to overcome is the intrinsic mathematical/theoretical nature of the material [6,8,12,28,48,51,65,66]. For Computer Science students, this problem can be compounded by a lack of experience with formal notation [6,28], a lack of a natural programming component that permeates most other courses in the curriculum [55,64], a lack of maturity in developing proofs [8], and a lack of problem-solving abilities [52,66]. Collectively, these problems lead students to feel that FLAT courses present a high risk of failure [66] and can lead to high drop-out rates [51,64]. Furthermore, students fail to develop motivation to master the material given that they perceive it as having little or no relevance to the Computer Science major [8,48,51]. If a FLAT course is taught using a traditional "chalkboard approach," it is common for students to also have difficulty piecing together the details of machine execution [31] and of construction algorithms [51,52] resulting in students only achieving a superficial understanding of the material [5,64].

To address these problems, many FLAT instructors have turned to constructivism [5,51,64]. Constructivism is a theory of learning that postulates that knowledge is constructed by students engaged in building activities [3,49]. In FLAT education, this has taken two primary approaches. The first (and most common) approach uses visualizations to engage students in building instances of the models of computations they study (e.g., [2,4,11,17,30,54–56,58,64]). These tools can help students develop conceptual models, but must be used with care. Visualization tools by themselves do not help students develop knowledge nor their problem-solving skills [3,52,64]. The second approach uses (textual) programming to engage students in building instances of the models of computations they study (e.g., [8,59,68]). Such approaches promote deep learning and encourage exploration by having students, carefully think about a programming implementation. For example, a library implemented using Standard ML of New Jersey [1], `Forlan` [59–61], students may define deterministic and nondeterministic finite automata and program their own constructors based on the algorithms typically studied in `FLAT` courses. In addition, `Forlan` is supported by `JFORLAN` [62], a graphical tool in which machine editing is done in a manner similar to `JFLAP` [54,56].

In contrast, `FSM` and its design-based methodology is the first effort to fully unite both approaches: textual programming and visualization. Programmers may define machines, implement their construction algorithms, and visualize results both statically (e.g., transition diagrams [44,45] and computation graphs [41]) and dynamically (e.g., machine execution [45] and machine transformations [42,43]). `FSM`'s visualization tools are designed to engage students in thinking by providing informative messages that explain the (currently) displayed graphic. In this manner, `FSM` helps students by presenting two views of `FLAT` algorithms and helps instructors by providing the means to move away from static images to explain dynamic processes.

4.2 Female Students in Computer Science

It is widely recognized that the female Computer Science student population faces unique obstacles. Perhaps, the most accentuated problem is self-confidence [9,14,15,20,29]. In this population, low self-confidence is attributed to many factors including stereotypes about hacking skills being a prerequisite to study Computer Science [15], about needing to be narrowly focused on programming [15,23,63], about women's abilities in science [29], and about Computer Science being mundane and tedious [23]. These stereotypes create a hostile environment, for example, by suggesting that others know so much more [15,29], by suggesting that the study of Computer Science is unrelated to its usefulness in the real world [63], by intimidating those that do not finish assignments quickly [69], and by suggesting that long hours of unguided exploration (i.e., hacking) or luck is rewarded when completing assignments [69].

To combat these stereotypes, the literature suggests taking actions outside and inside of the classroom. Outside classroom, universities can increase the number of female role models by increasing the number of female faculty members [69] and create a departmental environment that highlights the creative, the interesting, and the challenging opportunities found in Computer Science. Inside the classroom, instructors can use examples that highlight the benefits of Computer Science in real life [63], can create an environment that encourages questions [69], can highlight that successes are not due to luck and failures are not due to lack of ability [69], and can actively discourage the belief that "you are only here because you are a girl" [29].

5 Discussion

In this section, we summarize how we believe the FSM methodology addresses the challenges in teaching FLAT courses. We address some of the challenges faced by all students and some of the compounding challenges faced by female students. In addition, we discuss threats to validity and limitations of the study.

5.1 Addressing Challenges in Teaching FLAT Courses

Providing a programming language is not enough to make FLAT courses attractive to students. The programming language must not require skills beyond those expected from students taking their first FLAT course and must provide the proper abstractions to build instances of computation models and to implement construction algorithms. For instance, we would not expect programming state machines using assembly to satisfy this criteria neither would we expect this result if students had to implement the searches necessary to determine if a nondeterministic machine accepts or rejects a given word. The results obtained for RQ1, suggest that FSM meets this criteria for programming state machines and associated construction algorithms. If the use of FSM abstractions were beyond the skills of our students, then it is unlikely that students would find programming them straightforward.

When the language provides an environment in which programming is straightforward, it provides a natural programming component that permeates most other courses in the Computer Science curriculum. Students have the opportunity to focus on problem solving and cast theory problems, expressed in formal notation, as programming problems. Thus, helping students understand the material's intrinsic theoretical nature and the formal notation used by creating an environment for exploration and knowledge-building that provides immediate feedback upon running programs. In turn, this sparks intellectual interest and provides the sense that FLAT is relevant to a student's Computer Science education as reflected in the responses obtained for RQ2 and RQ3. Furthermore, it helps understand the responses obtained for RQ4: implementing a machine or an algorithm that works confirms understanding and is a step towards developing a constructive proof.

The lack of problem solving and proof development skills commonly reported by FLAT instructors is, in part, addressed by providing students with a design recipe for state machines. The design recipe provides scaffolding to guide students in the problem solving process. This scaffolding does not exist in most FLAT textbooks and, therefore, probably in most FLAT courses. Thus, feeding student fears that they are at high risk for failure, which is likely to prompt higher drop-out rates. For students that are introduced to programming using a design-based methodology [13,35,36], this approach creates a stronger connection with other Computer Science courses, which reinforces the feeling of relevance to their major. In addition, it also provides scaffolding for proof development, which elucidates the results seen for RQ4.

The use of a design recipe also addresses some of the concerns we face with female students. It emphasizes design over hacking, expands problem solving beyond coding, and moves FLAT beyond (the perception of) its mundane and tedious mathematical nature. Female students see themselves, as well as their male counterparts, work hard to fulfill the steps of the design recipe, thus, eliminating to some degree the perceptions that unguided exploration and luck is rewarded and that others know more because they finish assignments quickly. In addition, using examples, like finding a pattern from Sect. 2.3, reinforces (to students of all genders) that FLAT is relevant in the real world.

Finally, using a design recipe encourages questions. It provides a *lingua franca* in which students and instructors can discuss FLAT programs. Instead of not knowing what to ask when they are confused, students can ask questions about a design recipe step they are stuck on. Furthermore, instructors can ask questions about a student's design in the language used in class and found in the textbook.

5.2 Threats to Validity and Limitations

The empirical data collected comes from students at two universities in northeast USA. Thus, the diversity of the sample population is limited (at both universities most Computer Science students are male and Caucasian). As a result, it is unclear if the observed results are generalizable to a more diverse student population or to populations in different regions of the world. Future work includes collecting data from students, over several iterations of the course, from a larger number of universities in different geographical locations.

The study presented only includes data collected through anonymous surveys. Although this facilitates numerical analysis, it fails to capture the personal experiences of students. Capturing these experiences can help pinpoint elements in our methodology that work well or that present difficulties for students. Future work includes the collection of data through open-ended questions and observational studies to better capture personal student experiences.

Finally, the results reported are from classrooms led by professors that have fully adopted the design-based approach presented. It is unclear if the same results would be observed in classrooms led by professors that only partially adopt design methodology described. For instance, we doubt that the same results would be observed in a classroom that only adopts the use of FSM without adopting the design-based methodology. Similarly, we doubt that the same results would be observed in a classroom that simply adopts the use of the FSM visualization tools without requiring students to program their own machines and constructors. To this end, our expectation is that the data presented helps convince potential instructors to fully embrace the design- and programming-based approach presented.

6 Concluding Remarks and Future Work

This paper illustrates a design- and programming-based methodology to teach students about state machines in a Formal Languages and Automata Theory course using the domain-specific language FSM. In addition, it explores student perceptions, overall and by gender, about programming state machines, about how intellectually stimulating Automata Theory, programming state machines, and programming constructive proofs are, about the relevance of Automata Theory to majoring in Computer Science, and about the usefulness of programming to understand Automata Theory and to develop constructive proofs. The empirical results suggest the following conclusions:

- students of both genders feel that programming state machines in FSM is straightforward
- students feel that Automata Theory, programming state machines, and programming constructive algorithms is intellectually stimulating, but female students feel stronger than male students that programming state machines and construction algorithms is intellectually stimulating
- female students feel more strongly that Automata Theory is intellectually stimulating
- students of both genders feel that Automata Theory is relevant to majoring in Computer Science
- students feel that programming in FSM helps them understand Automata Theory, but female students feel more strongly about it
- female students tend not to disagree with and male students are polarized over the statement that FSM programming helps them develop constructive proofs

Future work includes more nuanced studies to better understand what topics students feel are most elucidated by our design- and programming-based approach using state machines. Future work also includes studies to measure student perceptions about our design- and programming-based approach using grammars (i.e., regular, context-free, and context-sensitive). Finally, future work will explore the effectiveness of FSM visualizations to help students understand and to motivate interest in FLAT.

References

1. Appel, A.W., MacQueen, D.B.: Standard ML of New Jersey. In: Maluszyński, J., Wirsing, M. (eds.) PLILP 1991. LNCS, vol. 528, pp. 1–13. Springer, Heidelberg (1991). https://doi.org/10.1007/3-540-54444-5_83
2. Barwise, J., Etchemendy, J.: Turing's World. J. Symb. Log. **55**(1), 370–371 (1990). https://doi.org/10.2307/2275002
3. Ben-Ari, M.: Constructivism in computer science education. In: Proceedings of the Twenty-Ninth SIGCSE Technical Symposium on Computer Science Education, SIGCSE 1998, pp. 257–261. Association for Computing Machinery, New York (1998). https://doi.org/10.1145/273133.274308
4. Castro-Schez, J.J., del Castillo, E., Hortolano, J., Rodriguez, A.: Designing and using software tools for educational purposes: FLAT, a case study. IEEE Trans. Educ. **52**(1), 66–74 (2009). https://doi.org/10.1109/TE.2008.917197

5. Chesñevar, C.I., González, M.P., Maguitman, A.G.: Didactic strategies for promoting significant learning in formal languages and automata theory. In: Proceedings of the 9th Annual SIGCSE Conference on Innovation and Technology in Computer Science Education, ITiCSE 2004, pp. 7–11. Association for Computing Machinery, New York (2004). https://doi.org/10.1145/1007996.1008002
6. Chesñevar, C.I., Cobo, M.L., Yurcik, W.: Using theoretical computer simulators for formal languages and automata theory. ACM SIGCSE Bull. **35**(2), 33–37 (2003). https://doi.org/10.1145/782941.782975
7. Christensen, M.A.: Tracing the gender confidence gap in computing: a cross-national meta-analysis of gender differences in self-assessed technological ability. Soc. Sci. Res. **111**, 102853 (2023). https://doi.org/10.1016/j.ssresearch.2023.102853
8. Chua, Y.S., Winton, C.N.: Teaching theory of computation at the junior level. In: Proceedings of the International Conference on APL: APL in Transition, APL 1987, pp. 69–78. Association for Computing Machinery, New York (1987). https://doi.org/10.1145/28315.28324
9. Du, J., Wimmer, H.: Hour of code: a study of gender differences in computing. Inf. Syst. Educ. J. **17** (2019)
10. Dzhatdoyev, S., Rosiers, J.A.D., Morazán, M.T.: Error messages for students taught using a systematic program design curriculum. In: Hemann, J., Chang, S. (eds.) Trends in Functional Programming - 25th International Symposium, TFP 2024, South Orange, NJ, USA, January 10–12, 2024, Revised Selected Papers. Lecture Notes in Computer Science, vol. 14843, pp. 195–219. Springer (2024). https://doi.org/10.1007/978-3-031-74558-4_9
11. D'Antoni, L., Helfrich, M., Kretinsky, J., Ramneantu, E., Weininger, M.: Automata tutor v3. In: Lahiri, S.K., Wang, C. (eds.) CAV 2020. LNCS, vol. 12225, pp. 3–14. Springer, Cham (2020). https://doi.org/10.1007/978-3-030-53291-8_1
12. Estrebou, F.C., Lanza, M., Mauco, V., Barbuzza, R., Favre, L.: Minerva: Una Herramienta para un Curso de Lenguajes Formales y Autómatas. https://www.researchgate.net/publication/266384889_Minerva_Una_Herramienta_para_un_Curso_de_Lenguajes_Formales_y_Automatas (2002), last accessed: March 2025
13. Felleisen, M., Findler, R.B., Flatt, M., Krishnamurthi, S.: How to Design Programs: An Introduction to Programming and Computing, 2nd edn. MIT Press, Cambridge (2018)
14. Fisher, A., Margolis, J.: Unlocking the clubhouse: the Carnegie Mellon experience. SIGCSE Bull. **34**(2), 79–83 (2002). https://doi.org/10.1145/543812.543836
15. Fisher, A., Margolis, J., Miller, F.: Undergraduate women in computer science: experience, motivation and culture. SIGCSE Bull. **29**(1), 106–110 (1997). https://doi.org/10.1145/268085.268127
16. Flatt, M., Findler, R.B., PLT: The Racket Guide. PLT (2024). https://docs.racket-lang.org/guide/. Accessed Mar 2025
17. García-Osorio, C., Mediavilla-Sáiz, I.n., Jimeno-Visitación, J., García-Pedrajas, N.: Teaching push-down automata and Turing machines. In: Proceedings of the 13th Annual Conference on Innovation and Technology in Computer Science Education, ITiCSE 2008, pp. 316. Association for Computing Machinery, New York (2008). https://doi.org/10.1145/1384271.1384359
18. Hoare, C.A.R.: An axiomatic basis for computer programming. Commun. ACM **12**(10), 576–580 (1969). https://doi.org/10.1145/363235.363259
19. Hoare, C., Jifeng, H.: Unifying Theories of Programming. Prentice Hall Series in Computer Science, Prentice Hall, Hoboken (1998)

20. Kemp, P.E.J., Wong, B., Berry, M.G.: Female performance and participation in computer science: a national picture. ACM Trans. Comput. Educ. **20**(1) (2019). https://doi.org/10.1145/3366016
21. Knuth, D.E., Morris, J.H., Jr., Pratt, V.R.: Fast pattern matching in strings. SIAM J. Comput. **6**(2), 323–350 (1977). https://doi.org/10.1137/0206024
22. Korte, L., Anderson, S., Pain, H., Good, J.: Learning by game-building: a novel approach to theoretical computer science education. SIGCSE Bull. **39**(3), 53–57 (2007). https://doi.org/10.1145/1269900.1268802
23. Lasen, M.: Education and career pathways in information communication technology: what are schoolgirls saying? Comput. Educ. **54**(4), 1117–1126 (2010). https://doi.org/10.1016/j.compedu.2009.10.018
24. Lau, W.W.F., Yuen, A.H.K.: Exploring the effects of gender and learning styles on computer programming performance: implications for programming pedagogy. Br. J. Edu. Technol. **40**(4), 696–712 (2009). https://doi.org/10.1111/j.1467-8535.2008.00847.x
25. Lewis, H.R., Papadimitriou, C.H.: Elements of the Theory of Computation. 2nd edn. Prentice Hall PTR, Upper Saddle River (1997). https://doi.org/10.1145/300307.1040360
26. Likert, R.: A technique for the measurement of attitudes. Arch. Psychol. **140**, 1–55 (1932)
27. Linz, P.: An Introduction to Formal Languages and Automata, 5th edn. Jones and Bartlett Publishers Inc, USA (2011)
28. Mane, D.T., Howal, S.S., Lokare, V.T.: Problem-based learning using simulation tools for automata theory. J. Eng. Educ. Transformations **30** (2016). https://doi.org/10.16920/jeet/2016/v0i0/85708
29. Margolis, J., Fisher, A.: Unlocking the Clubhouse: Women in Computing. MIT Press, Cambridge (2001)
30. Martínez, M., Barbuzza, R., Mauco, M.V., Favre, L.: MTSolution: A visual and interactive tool for a formal languages and automata course. Inf. Syst. Educ. J. **7**(10) (2009). http://isedj.org/7/10/
31. McDonald, J.: Interactive pushdown automata animation. SIGCSE Bull. **34**(1), 376–380 (2002). https://doi.org/10.1145/563517.563489
32. McDowell, C., Werner, L.L., Bullock, H.E., Fernald, J.: The impact of pair programming on student performance, perception and persistence. In: Clarke, L.A., Dillon, L., Tichy, W.F. (eds.) Proceedings of the 25th International Conference on Software Engineering, May 3–10, 2003, Portland, Oregon, USA, pp. 602–607. IEEE Computer Society (2003). https://doi.org/10.1109/ICSE.2003.1201243
33. Morazán, M.: Composing turing machines in FSM. In: Proceedings of the 2023 ACM SIGPLAN International Symposium on SPLASH-E, SPLASH-E 2023, pp. 38–49. Association for Computing Machinery, New York (2023). https://doi.org/10.1145/3622780.3623647
34. Morazán, M.T.: Infusing an HtDP-based CS1 with distributed programming using functional video games. J. Funct. Program. **28**, e5 (2018). https://doi.org/10.1017/S0956796818000059
35. Morazán, M.T.: Animated Problem Solving - An Introduction to Program Design Using Video Game Development. Texts in Computer Science, Springer, Cham (2022). https://doi.org/10.1007/978-3-030-85091-3
36. Morazán, M.T.: Animated Program Design - Intermediate Program Design Using Video Game Development. Texts in Computer Science, Springer, Cham (2022). https://doi.org/10.1007/978-3-031-04317-8

37. Morazán, M.T.: FSM. Seton Hall University, South Orange, NJ, USA (2024). https://morazanm.github.io/fsm/fsm/index.html. Accessed Mar 2025
38. Morazán, M.T.: Programming-Based Formal Languages and Automata Theory - Design, Implement, Validate, and Prove. Texts in Computer Science, Springer, Cham (2024). https://doi.org/10.1007/978-3-031-43973-5
39. Morazán, M.T., Antunez, R.: Functional Automata–Formal Languages for Computer Science Students. In: Caldwell, J.L., Hölzenspies, P.K.F., Achten, P. (eds.) Proceedings 3rd International Workshop on Trends in Functional Programming in Education, TFPIE 2014, Soesterberg, The Netherlands, 25th May 2014. EPTCS, vol. 170, pp. 19–32 (2014). https://doi.org/10.4204/EPTCS.170.2
40. Morazán, M.T., Des Rosiers, J.A.: FSM error messages. In: Achten, P., Miller, H. (eds.) Proceedings Seventh International Workshop on Trends in Functional Programming in Education, TFPIE@TFP 2018, Chalmers University, Gothenburg, Sweden, 14th June 2018. EPTCS, vol. 295, pp. 1–16 (2018). https://doi.org/10.4204/EPTCS.295.1
41. Morazán, M.T., Kempinski, O.: Using computation graphs to explain nondeterminism to students. In: Proceedings of the 2024 ACM SIGPLAN International Symposium on SPLASH-E, SPLASH-E 2024, pp. 23–33. Association for Computing Machinery, New York (2024). https://doi.org/10.1145/3689493.3689978
42. Morazán, M.T., Minić, T.: Finite-state automaton to/from regular expression visualization. Electron. Proc. Theor. Comput. Sci. **405**, 36–55 (2024). https://doi.org/10.4204/eptcs.405.3. In: Proceedings TFPIE 2024
43. Morazán, M.T., Minić, T.: Nondeterministic to deterministic finite-state machine visualization: implementation and evaluation. In: ITiCSE 2024: Proceedings of the 2024 Conference on Innovation and Technology in Computer Science Education V. 1, ITiCSE 2024, pp. 262–268. Association for Computing Machinery, New York (2024). https://doi.org/10.1145/3649217.3653641
44. Morazán, M.T., Minić, T., Kempinski, O.: Visualizing composed turing machines. In: Proceedings of the 2024 ACM SIGPLAN International Symposium on SPLASH-E. SPLASH-E 2024, pp. 34–44. Association for Computing Machinery, New York (2024). https://doi.org/10.1145/3689493.3689979
45. Morazán, M.T., Schappel, J.M., Mahashabde, S.: Visual designing and debugging of deterministic finite-state machines in FSM. Electron. Proc. Theor. Comput. Sci. **321**, 55–77 (2020). https://doi.org/10.4204/eptcs.321.4
46. Morazán, M.T.: How to design while loops. Electron. Proc. Theor. Comput. Sci. **321**, 1–18 (2020). https://doi.org/10.4204/eptcs.321.1
47. Naveed, M.S., Sarim, M.: Didactic strategy for learning theory of automata and formal languages. Proc. Pak. Acad. Sci. A. Phys. Comput. Sci. **55**(2), 55–67 (2018), https://www.ppaspk.org/index.php/PPAS-A/article/view/171
48. Neeman, A.: Buy one get one free: automata theory concepts through software test. J. Comput. Sci. Coll. **31**(6), 90–96 (2016)
49. Papert, S., Harel, I.: Situating constructionism. In: Papert, S., Harel, I. (eds.) Constructionism, chap. 1. Ablex Publishing Corporation, Norwood, NJ (1991). http://www.papert.org/articles/SituatingConstructionism.html
50. Perlis, A.J.: Special feature: epigrams on programming. Sigplan Not. **17**(9), 7–13 (1982). https://doi.org/10.1145/947955.1083808
51. Pillay, N.: Teaching the theory of formal languages and automata in the computer science undergraduate curriculum. South Afr. Comput. J. **42**, 87–94 (2008). http://reference.sabinet.co.za/document/EJC28069

52. Pillay, N.: Learning difficulties experienced by students in a course on formal languages and automata theory. SIGCSE Bull. **41**(4), 48–52 (2010). https://doi.org/10.1145/1709424.1709444
53. Rich, E.: Automata, Computability and Complexity: Theory and Applications. Pearson Prentice Hall, Hoboken (2019)
54. Rodger, S.H.: JFLAP: An Interactive Formal Languages and Automata Package. Jones and Bartlett Publishers Inc, USA (2006)
55. Rodger, S.H., et al.: A collection of tools for making automata theory and formal languages come alive. SIGCSE Bull. **29**(1), 15–19 (1997). https://doi.org/10.1145/268085.268089
56. Rodger, S.H., Bressler, B., Finley, T., Reading, S.: Turning automata theory into a hands-on course. In: Baldwin, D., Tymann, P.T., Haller, S.M., Russell, I. (eds.) Proceedings of the 37th SIGCSE Technical Symposium on Computer Science Education, SIGCSE 2006, Houston, Texas, USA, March 3–5, 2006, pp. 379–383. ACM (2006). https://doi.org/10.1145/1121341.1121459
57. Sipser, M.: Introduction to the Theory of Computation, 3rd edn. Cengage Learning, USA (2013)
58. Stallmann, M.F., Balik, S.P., Rodman, R.D., Bahram, S., Grace, M.C., High, S.D.: ProofChecker: an accessible environment for automata theory correctness proofs. In: Proceedings of the 12th Annual SIGCSE Conference on Innovation and Technology in Computer Science Education, ITiCSE 2007, pp. 48–52. Association for Computing Machinery, New York (2007). https://doi.org/10.1145/1268784.1268801
59. Stoughton, A.: Formal Language Theory: Integrating Experimentation and Proof. https://alleystoughton.us/forlan/book.pdf (2003–2022). Accessed Mar 2025
60. Stoughton, A.: The Forlan Project. https://alleystoughton.us/forlan (2003–2022). Accessed Mar 2025
61. Stoughton, A.: Experimenting with formal languages using forlan. In: Proceedings of the 2008 International Workshop on Functional and Declarative Programming in Education, FDPE 2008, pp. 41–50. Association for Computing Machinery, New York (2008). https://doi.org/10.1145/1411260.1411267
62. Uppi, S.A.: JFORLAN Tool. Kansas State University, Manhattan, Kansas, USA (2009)
63. Vekiri, I.: Information science instruction and changes in girls' and boy's expectancy and value beliefs: in search of gender-equitable pedagogical practices. Comput. Educ. **64**, 104–115 (2013). https://doi.org/10.1016/j.compedu.2013.01.011
64. Verma, R.M.: A visual and interactive automata theory course emphasizing breadth of automata. In: Proceedings of the 10th Annual SIGCSE Conference on Innovation and Technology in Computer Science Education, ITiCSE 2005, pp. 325–329. Association for Computing Machinery, New York (2005). https://doi.org/10.1145/1067445.1067535
65. Vieira, L.F.M., Vieira, M.A.M., Vieira, N.J.: Language emulator, a helpful toolkit in the learning process of computer theory. SIGCSE Bull. **36**(1), 135–139 (2004). https://doi.org/10.1145/1028174.971348
66. Vijayalaskhmi, M., Karibasappa, K.: Activity based teaching learning in formal languages and automata theory - an experience. In: 2012 IEEE International Conference on Engineering Education: Innovative Practices and Future Trends (AICERA), pp. 1–5. IEEE (2012). https://doi.org/10.1109/AICERA.2012.6306722
67. Welsh, N., Culpepper, R.: RackUnit: Unit Testing. PLT Racket, v8.12 edn. (2024). https://docs.racket-lang.org/rackunit/index.html. Accessed Mar 2025

68. Wermelinger, M., Dias, A.M.: A prolog toolkit for formal languages and automata. In: Proceedings of the 10th Annual SIGCSE Conference on Innovation and Technology in Computer Science Education, ITiCSE 2005, pp. 330–334. Association for Computing Machinery, New York (2005). https://doi.org/10.1145/1067445.1067536
69. Wilson, B.C.: A study of factors promoting success in computer science including gender differences. Comput. Sci. Educ. **12**(1–2), 141–164 (2002). https://doi.org/10.1076/csed.12.1.141.8211

Using GHC CORE to Normalise Student Programs

Matilda Blomqvist[1] and Alex Gerdes[2,3](✉)

[1] Uppsala University, Uppsala, Sweden
matilda.blomqvist@it.uu.se
[2] University of Gothenburg, Gothenburg, Sweden
[3] Chalmers University of Technology, Gothenburg, Sweden
alexg@chalmers.se

Abstract. ASK-ELLE is an online tutor for solving small programming exercises in Haskell. It provides feedback by first determining whether a student's submission matches one of the teacher-provided model solutions. However, Haskell's rich syntax allows for semantically equivalent but syntactically different programs, making direct comparison challenging. To address this, ASK-ELLE applies normalizing program transformations to reduce such syntactic differences. Despite this, some correct programs remain unrecognised. We have developed a new approach to feedback generation that leverages GHC's internal transformations and warning messages. This method improves the recognition of correct programs while also being much faster. Additionally, we share our experiences using GHC as a library.

Keywords: Programming tutor · Functional programming · Haskell · GHC · Program normalisation

1 Introduction

Learning to program is challenging, even with access to suitable course materials and good teachers [17]. It requires practice, and the teacher may not always be around to guide students. Usually, students write source code, compile it, and then run the program to test if it works as expected. Modern compilers point out errors at different levels in the source code, but these are often difficult to decipher for beginners [18]. Intelligent tutor systems aim to do a better job and support students by giving *semantically rich feedback* [2,13,25].

A review study by VanLehn concluded that intelligent tutor systems are almost as efficient as human tutors [24]. Including intelligent tutors in education can have many benefits. For example, they are always available, can give instant feedback, can handle large student numbers, and may save course instructors' time. In addition, a study by Kumar [14] showed that using intelligent programming tutors can help improve female computer science (CS) students' confidence. Several studies [9,21] have shown that the confidence of female CS students is

J. Gibbons (Ed.): TFP 2025, LNCS 15652, pp. 511–532, 2026.
https://doi.org/10.1007/978-3-031-99751-8_22

lower than their male counterparts and if digital tutors can enhance their confidence, we have a strong motivation to keep developing them.

Ask-Elle is an online tutor aiming to improve students' programming skills in the functional language Haskell by providing comprehensive feedback [7]. Figure 1 displays a screenshot of the learning environment. The tutor focuses on small programming tasks and allows a student to *stepwise* solve an exercise. A teacher can specify an exercise by defining a number of model solutions and properties that a solution should have. Ask-Elle uses *model tracing* based on strategies [10] to match a student program with one of the model solutions, and if it succeeds, it can generate feedback on different levels. If a student program cannot be matched, Ask-Elle reverts to property-based testing with QuickCheck [4] to validate that the program has the expected behaviour.

We show a fictional interaction with Ask-Elle, where we ask a student to define a function that duplicates all elements in a list. Suppose a student has implemented the base case, but gets stuck defining the recursive case:

```
dupli []     = []
dupli (x:xs) = ?
```

In Ask-Elle, a student can ask for help even if parts of the program are yet to be defined. The undefined parts are indicated by a question mark and correspond to a (typed) *hole*. Using these holes, a student can check if she is on the right track and ask how to continue. Ask-Elle will respond that the student can use explicit recursion and refine the program by introducing the cons-operator (:). It can also show the result of the proposed refinement to the student:

```
dupli []     = []
dupli (x:xs) = ? : ?
```

or show a complete derivation of how to construct a solution.

Although Ask-Elle can recognise many incomplete programs and guide students towards a solution, it does have its limitations. Consider the following incomplete program:

```
dupli = \xs -> case xs of
  []        -> []
  (:) x xs -> ?
```

Ask-Elle unfortunately fails to recognise this program, even though it is essentially the same partial solution we saw before. The problem is that the strategies, on which our model tracing is based, are too strict and do not recognise such variations.

To be more flexible, Ask-Elle uses *program transformations* to ignore non-essential differences. Ask-Elle normalises a student program while doing model

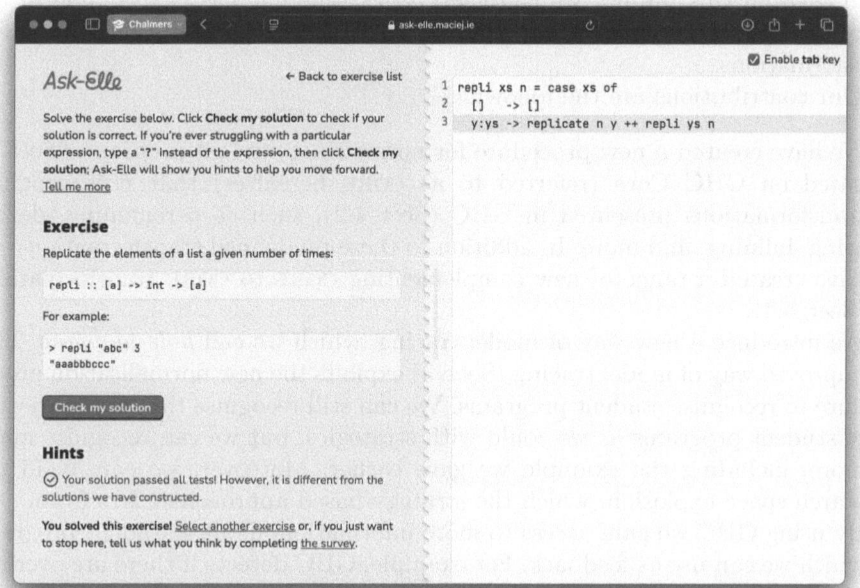

Fig. 1. Screenshot of the ASK-ELLE web interface. The student writes code in the editor to the right, and the exercise description and generated feedback are displayed in the panel to the left.

tracing. It uses, for example, a program transformation for rewriting `where`-clauses to `let`-expressions and another transformation that does α-renaming, such that a student can use different variable names.

To also recognise the above (and other) variations of a simple Haskell program, we could improve the existing normalisation procedure by adding more program transformations. The problem is that we would need to implement numerous program transformations and, in doing so, duplicate most, if not all, of the program transformations found in a Haskell compiler. In addition, ASK-ELLE has its own abstract syntax for expressions. We would likely need to restrict it to a subset of possible Haskell expressions to enable the implementation of necessary program transformations. Such a subset would resemble an intermediate (core) language in a Haskell compiler, where syntactic variations have been desugared.

Another issue with our current model tracing approach is that it can only handle small programs. The use of strategies causes a search space explosion. We explain this in more detail in Sect. 2.

Instead of reinventing the wheel, we propose to use the program transformations and core language (GHC Core) of the 'de facto' standard Haskell compiler GHC [19]. GHC is written in Haskell and offers much of its functionality via a library. Using this library, we can cherry-pick different passes available in the compiler, such as the parser, type checker, and, most importantly, the program transformations.

Our contributions are the following:

- We have created a new procedure for normalising student programs (Sect. 4) based on GHC Core (referred to as CORE hereafter) that uses program transformations presented in GHC (Sect. 4.2), such as α-renaming, desugaring, inlining, and more. In addition to these predefined transformations, we have created a range of new complementing CORE to CORE transformations (Sect. 4.3).
- We introduce a new way of model tracing, which we call *hole-mapping*. This improved way of model tracing (Sect. 3) exploits the new normalisation procedure to recognise student programs. We can still recognise the same variation of student programs as we could with strategies, but we can recognise many more, including the example we gave earlier. Moreover, we can avoid the search space explosion, which the strategy-based approach suffers from.
- By using GHC we gain access to more information about a student program, which we can use as feedback. For example, GHC detects if there are overlapping patterns in a definition. We show how we can generate feedback (Sect. 5) when we tap into this source of information.
- We evaluate and share our experiences we gained with using GHC as a library (Sect. 6.3). In addition, we evaluate the improved feedback generation and compare it with the existing version (Sect. 6.1).

Before we delve into the intricacies of our improvements, we first detail the problems with the existing way of model tracing.

2 The Problem

The `dupli` example in the previous section shows that ASK-ELLE has its limitations and that we cannot recognise particular variations of a model solution. On top of this, ASK-ELLE can only handle relatively small programs. The next paragraphs describe the causes for these limitations.

Strategies. The current version of ASK-ELLE is based on strategies [10], which is a description of valid sequences of rewrite rules to solve a class of exercises in a particular domain. A strategy can be regarded a context-free grammar, and recognising a valid sequence of steps boils down to parsing a sentence. Strategies are implemented as an embedded domain-specific language in Haskell, and the library offers many combinators for creating strategies, such as sequence, choice, interleave, etc. It has been used for generating feedback in many domains, for example, in propositional logic [16].

Using strategies, we view solving a programming exercise as a sequence of *refinement steps* where the student refines a program step by step. For example, she first introduces a function binding, then a pattern match, then a function application, and so on. A model solution is translated automatically to such a strategy, the teacher does not need to do this by hand. Using the strategy, we generate intermediate solutions and check if a student program matches one of these, if so, we can conclude that the student is making progress towards one of the model solutions. Furthermore, we then know at what stage a student is in the development of a solution, and we can provide hints on how to continue.

The domain of functional programming is a bit special in the context of strategies, since there are many ways in which a student can stepwise develop a solution to a programming exercise. This variation is captured in the strategy for a given exercise. We use the choice combinator to let a student solve an exercise with different model solutions. The interleave combinator is used to allow a student to work on different parts of a solution. Consider a variant of the `dupli` example:

```
dupli []     = ?1
dupli (x:xs) = ?2 : ?3
```

A student is not forced to refine the `dupli` in a particular order, she can choose to refine the hole `?1` to the empty list, or the second hole to the variable `x` or to continue with the third hole and introduce another cons operator.

This degree of freedom is, however, quite problematic since the number of intermediate solutions has a factorial order of growth ($O(n!)$), where n is the number of holes. The above `dupli` example can be solved in six different ways. To counter this ASK-ELLE implements a number of improvements:

- We assume that a student usually finishes a particular construct (e.g., a function binding), before continuing to the next. So, we do a depth first search when we try to match a student program to an intermediate solution.
- We try to rule out other model solutions as quickly as possible, which limits the search space drastically.
- Many permutations of the possible refinements will lead to the same intermediate solution. For example, refining the first hole and then the second, or vice versa, will lead to the same intermediate solution where just the third hole is left. In which order we have arrived at a particular intermediate solution does not affect whether it can be recognised. Therefore, ASK-ELLE has a different semantic interpretation of the interleave combinator that prevents generating duplicate intermediate programs.

These improvements make ASK-ELLE much faster, but the order of growth of the number of intermediate solutions remains factorial.

Helium. Until now ASK-ELLE has used the Helium [11] compiler, known for its good (type) error messages. We reuse a large part of the front-end of the Helium compiler. After the type checking stage, we convert the program from Helium's abstract syntax tree (AST) into ASK-ELLE's AST. This AST is smaller than the one in Helium, easing the definition of refinement rules because there are fewer language constructs to cover. The Helium compiler has been a great aid in developing ASK-ELLE, but it has a few disadvantages. One issue is that the Helium codebase is no longer actively maintained; its last update on the Haskell package repository Hackage was ten years ago[1]. Exchanging Helium with GHC will make ASK-ELLE more future-proof since GHC is more actively developed.

3 Model Tracing Based on Normalisation

Model tracing based on strategies has served ASK-ELLE well for many years. However, the enumeration of intermediate solutions leads to a factorial search space explosion, limiting the size of possible exercises. To accommodate larger programs in exercises, we introduce a technique we have coined 'hole-mapping'. The idea is as follows, suppose a teacher has defined the following model solution for the `dupli` exercise:

```
dupli :: [a] -> [a]
dupli []     = []
dupli (x:xs) = x : x : dupli xs
```

and that a student submits the following incomplete program:

```
dupli []     = []
dupli (x:xs) = x : ?1 : ?2
```

Instead of using strategies to enumerate all intermediate solutions, we compare the student program syntactically with the teacher-defined model solution and *map* holes in the student solution with the corresponding expression in the model solution. In this example, we can match the hole `?1` with the variable `x` in the model solution and the second hole with the expression `dupli xs`. We can thus create a mapping from holes to expressions.

If we succeed in creating such a mapping and the two programs are syntactically equivalent (modulo holes), we can conclude that the student is on their way to creating a program that we consider to be a solution to the exercise. That is good to know in itself, because we can signal to the student that she is making progress. In addition, we can use the mapping to provide the student with a hint on how to continue. We can, for example, show that the first hole needs to be replaced with the variable `x`, just like we were able to do with strategies. However, there is a catch. Because we match a hole with an entire expression, we will give the it as the next refinement step if a student asks for help, whereas with strategies, we can present the student with more fine-grained steps. In the above example, our new approach would suggest refining the second hole to `dupli xs` while using strategies we can give `dupli ?` or `dupli xs` as the next steps for the recursive call.

Now suppose a student submits the following program we showed earlier:

[1] Checked at 2025-02-17.

```
dupli = \xs -> case xs of
  []        -> []
  (:) x xs -> ?1 : ?2
```

Syntactically matching this program with the model solution we have considered will fail. However, as we argued before, this is essentially the same program as the model solution, and we want to be able to match it. Now we need to introduce the second part of our new model tracing approach: we are going to *normalise* both the student program and model solution *before* matching them. Assume that the following program is the normalised form of the model solution:

```
dupli = \x0 -> case x0 of
  []        -> []
  (:) x1 x2 -> (:) x1 ((:) x1 (dupli x2))
```

The infix operators are written prefix, new unique names have been introduced, the function bindings have been rewritten as a `case` expression, etc. This is a simplification and in the next section we will explain the actual normalisation procedure, but it comes quite close. If we also normalise the student program it would now match this normalised model solution. However, now the resulting mapping contains normalised expressions, that is, the hole `?1` is matched with the variable `x1` (which is not even bound in the student program) and the second hole is paired with `(:) x1 (dupli xs)`. We cannot give this as feedback to the student.

To solve this problem we need to remember during normalisation to which part of the original model solution a rewritten (normalised) subexpression belongs. For example, we need to remember that the subexpression `x1` is the variable `x`. We are in a good spot here using GHC because every (sub)expression is annotated with its origin in the concrete syntax. We get this information (nearly) for free when using GHC. With this information we can make a mapping again from holes in a student program to parts of a model solution, and present these as next steps.

The above procedure does not take care of different variable names. In such a case the student would get a hint with the names from a model solution, instead of her own. These names may be unbound or capture something else. Again, GHC comes to the rescue, because it gives all variable a new unique name, and it remembers the original name (for error reporting purposes). We can use this information to create a mapping from student variable names to model variable names. For example, if we know that the student variable `y` is renamed to `x1`, and the model variable name from `x` to `x1`, then we know that need to substitute `x` with `y` in our next step hints.

We are well aware that it is in general undecidable to validate if two programs are equal, and there will always be cases where we fail to match equal programs, but that does not mean that you can come quite far in practice. Say that a student submits an intrinsically different program, for example:

```
dupli xs = concatMap (\x -> [x, x]) xs
```

We will not be able to match it with the given model solution. In such a case, we need to revert to property-based testing, to validate whether the student program at least has the expected behaviour. If you also want to recognise this student program, you can add it to the collection of model solutions.

We have, with some simplifications, explained the new 'hole-mapping' procedure to convey the general idea. In the next section, we demonstrate how GHC's intermediate CORE language is used to normalise programs.

4 Normalisation Using GHC Core

GHC contains several compilation passes that transform Haskell source code into executable code[2]. The program transformations of interest for normalisation are mainly part of the *desugarer* that translates a program to CORE, and the *simplifier* that performs additional transformations.

CORE is an implementation of System FC [8], an extension of System F, and shares some of the most fundamental constructs found in regular Haskell, but is much smaller. CORE consists of a collection of data types and type synonyms. The most central data type is `Expr`:

```
data Expr b
  = Var      Id
  | Lit      Literal
  | App      (Expr b) (Expr b)
  | Lam      b (Expr b)
  | Let      (Bind b) (Expr b)
  | Case     (Expr b) b Type [Alt b]
  | Cast     (Expr b) Type
  | Tick     (GenTickish Id) (Expr b)
  | Type     Type
  | Coercion Type
```

which only has a handful of constructors and abstracts over the type of a binding. The `Expr` data type uses other data types, but we omit them for brevity. A direct implication of the small number of expression constructors is the loss of specificity. CORE expressions are purposely general to capture a lot of different Haskell concepts with the same constructor. The `Bind` data type used in a `Let` supports two types of binders: recursive and non-recursive. The `Case` constructor corresponds to a `case` expression in Haskell, enabling pattern matching on the evaluation of a given expression, known as the scrutinee. The scrutinee's value is bound to a variable, allowing it to be reused in alternative cases. CORE `Case` expressions are also used to represent the different pattern-matching options in,

[2] https://gitlab.haskell.org/ghc/ghc/-/wikis/commentary/compiler/hsc-main.

for example, a function with multiple function bindings, guarded expressions or if-then-else expressions. In other words, `Case`-expressions appear frequently. In addition, `Case` expressions are exhaustive in the sense that they always cover all reachable alternatives but not necessarily all available constructors. If GHC detects that a function or other structure has non-exhaustive patterns, a "pattern error" alternative is generated. Furthermore, expressions can be annotated with extra information using the `Tick` constructor, such as breakpoints or source locations. As we will see, this is important for our feedback generation.

4.1 Representing Holes

Since holes are an essential concept in how ASK-ELLE provides incremental feedback, changing from the customised AST of ASK-ELLE that allows holes as a replacement for any term requires a suitable counterpart that is also parsable by GHC. GHC's *typed holes*, denoted _, is a good candidate for representing holes in ASK-ELLE for two main reasons. First, they are a built-in feature of GHC, and their types can be inferred automatically. Second, GHC has support for reporting possible valid hole fits for typed holes, which allows extending ASK-ELLE with simple program synthesis in the future. We can enable the "defer typed holes" option in GHC to avoid the compilation terminating with a type error and let the compilation continue past the type checker. However, no explicit constructs exist for holes on the CORE syntax level that is convenient for our purposes. Holes are treated as type errors and are compiled into CORE `Case` expressions.

4.2 Using GHC's CORE TRANSFORMATIONS

Many program transformations needed for normalising programs in ASK-ELLE, like β-conversion, η-conversion and other program rewrite transformations, are already implemented in GHC. Using GHC as a library, we can leverage these internal transformations. GHC's main purpose, though, is to optimise the compiled code, which is different from ASK-ELLE's goal to determine if two programs are syntactically equal. Hence, GHC's transformations are not always helpful in normalisation. It is important to find an appropriate configuration of GHC through compilation options, such that GHC's transformations can be maximally utilised while at the same time not losing information from the original program.

The transformations GHC applies while translating Haskell source code into CORE solve the following normalisation steps directly:

Local and top-level functions: GHC's inlining of non-recursive local definitions from `where`-clauses and `let`-expressions, in many cases, allows arbitrary use of local helper functions. An exception to this is where type differences may arise if local functions are given explicit type signatures, or if the inferred type of a local function is more general than the top-level function it is defined in.

Overlapping patterns: Overlapping patterns are removed by GHC and a warning is generated. We pass this information on to the student as feedback.

Capture avoiding renaming: GHC's renamer allows keeping the name as declared in the source code while still avoiding name capture by attaching unique identifiers to variables.

β-abstraction: this is always performed.

Pattern matching and cases: Functions that use several pattern bindings and functions that use a `case`-expression on a single variable pattern are α-equivalent in CORE.

Including GHC's simplifier pass in compilation also removes redundant equality checks, e.g., an expression like `if x == y then True else False` is simplified to `x == y`. However, the simplifier pass is quite aggressive and might remove code that we want to retain.

It is not possible to rely solely on GHC's internal transformations to normalise Haskell programs in ASK-ELLE. Before GHC applies a particular transformation or rewrite rule to an expression, it analyses if it will lead to a performance gain. For example, the inlining of expressions is based on heuristics, which makes it non-deterministic. For normalisation, it is desirable to deterministically apply transformations to know that a particular expression is always normalised in a certain way. The GHC API does not offer any ways to control these heuristics, and changing this behaviour would require changes to the GHC source code. Instead, we have implemented several new CORE-to-CORE transformations to control the application of some transformations.

4.3 New Program Transformations

When a CORE program is obtained, many of the transformations we want to include in normalisation are already applied as described in the previous section. The remaining issues (syntactical variations) are due to a lack of control over which transformations GHC performs, especially in the simplifier, and the non-determinism in GHC's application of its transformations mentioned above. We improve normalisation by adding the following program transformations:

- Replacing error expressions with variables
- Inlining and non-heuristical η-reduction
- Rewriting recursive functions to non-recursive functions with local recursive `let`-expressions
- Renaming variables
- Removing type variables

First, the transformations replacing error expressions are injected between the desugarer and the simplifier to remove redundant information from the AST and avoid losing information in the simplifier. For instance, typed holes are treated as type errors and are, like other errors (e.g., *pattern errors*, which are inserted into the AST when GHC detects an incomplete pattern), compiled into CORE `Case` expressions. Since `Case` expressions are strict, code occurring after a hole, for example, might be removed by the simplifier. We traverse the AST and replace all typed hole `Case` expressions with variables (`Var`) named `hole1`, `hole2`, and so on. Similarly, we remove all *pattern error* `Case` expressions having an empty list of `Case` alternatives and replace them with a variable `patError`.

The remaining transformations are applied after simplification. We explicitly revert a non-configurable transformation from the simplifier that replaces default `Case` alternatives with concrete `Case` alternatives. For particular programs, all occurrences of the scrutinee in the alternatives of a `Case` expression are replaced by the `Case` binder. Of course, this is better for performance since the scrutinee does not have to be re-evaluated, but it creates a problem when trying to match an incomplete student program with a single function binding and thus no `Case` expressions.

Moreover, both inlining and η-conversion are reimplemented to obtain a deterministic version of these transformations that operates on the CORE data types. In addition, We rewrite recursive top-level functions with recursive `let`-expressions. There are separate constructors for recursive and non-recursive binders: `Rec` and `NonRec`. If we find a `Rec` constructor, we substitute the function name with a fresh one and wrap it into a `Let`-expression inside a new `NonRec` constructor with the original function name. We exemplify this transformation by applying it to the `length` function:

```
length []     = 0
length (x:xs) = 1 + length xs
```

which is rewritten into:

```
length = let fresh []     = 0
             fresh (x:xs) = 1 + fresh xs
         in fresh
```

CORE programs must also be renamed for student programs to match a model solution. It is relatively straightforward to implement since GHC already assigned unique names to all variables. Any variable matching the exercise name is *not* renamed, while all other non-special variables are renamed with fresh names in a predefined order. The renaming procedure is applied after the previously discussed transformations since these transformations might reorder, remove or introduce new variables. ASK-ELLE must handle matching of *incomplete* programs, so the renaming procedure must be slightly more clever than simply renaming all variables in the order they appear. For instance, when a student only defines a single function binding with no or general pattern for the input argument, the compiled CORE program will not contain a `Case` expression. Renaming the `Case` binder in the model solution would offset all succeeding variable names, and there would be a name mismatch when trying to match the single function binding from the student program with any of the `Case` alternatives in the model solution. How partial and complete programs are matched is described in Sect. 5.1.

Finally, type variables and type evidence variables are passed around in CORE expressions and are needed to type check CORE programs [22] but clutter the AST with lots of irrelevant information for checking if any two programs are syntactically equal. They can also, depending on how the original source program was written have slightly different placements in the AST. We simply remove any type variables from the AST since any ill-typed program would already have been rejected by GHC's type checker.

5 Generating Feedback

Feedback on whether an exercise is complete or if a student's program is on track toward a solution is determined by *matching* the normalized student submission with (one of) the normalized model solution. Additional suggestions are extracted from GHC warning messages, the hole-mapping procedure, and HLint, as discussed in the following subsections.

5.1 Matching Programs

Recognising that student input matches a model solution requires a definition of what matching programs means. Matching CORE programs is implemented as two different relations defined in a type class `Similar`[3]:

```
class Similar a where
  (~>) :: a -> a -> Bool
  (~=) :: a -> a -> Bool
```

Relating two CORE programs `s ~> m` can be read as "`s` is a predecessor of `m`", meaning that a student program `s` can be *refined* into a model solution `m`. For example, (using concrete syntax) `dupli [] = _ ~> dupli [] = []`. The `~=` relation can sloppily be read as "is syntactically equal to". These two relations compare two CORE programs construct by construct, so we define a `Similar` instance for all CORE data types. The predecessor relation is more liberal and can consider two *different* terms `t` and `s` to be similar (`t ~> s`) if `t` can be refined into `t'` in one or more steps such that, in principle, `t' ~= s`. For example, consider the following definitions for lambda expressions in the `Similar` instance for expressions:

```
instance Similar (Expr Var) where
  (Lam b e) ~> (Lam b' e') = b ~> b' && e ~> e'
  (Lam b e) ~= (Lam b' e') = b ~= b' && e ~= e'
```

---
[3] We have chosen the terminology similarity over equality to account for syntactical dissimilarities we want to disregard.

where `b ~> b'` if `b` is either a hole variable or `b ~= b'`. Here, `b` is a variable of type `Var` and `b ~= b'` if the strings contained in the variables `b` and `b'` are equal. If both the lambda parameters and bodies are similar, we consider the lambda expressions similar.

In general, `t` is considered a predecessor of `s` (`t ~> s`) despite differences like differently ordered or different number of function bindings (`Case` alternatives) or occurrences of holes, for example. This requires special checks for some data types, making the implementation somewhat intricate. We will not go into every detail here – instead, we will start by showing two examples to give some intuition for the special cases of the predecessor relation and briefly mention the remaining ones. A more thorough explanation can be found in [3].

First, consider the following model solution:

```
dupli []     = []
dupli (x:xs) = x:x:dupli xs
```

and that a student submits the following partial solution:

```
dupli _ = []
```

The student program is not equal to the model solution but could be considered a predecessor of the model solution. The model solution has two function bindings, one for the empty list and one for non-empty list, which are translated into a `Case` expression with two alternatives in CORE. On the other hand, the wildcard pattern in the function binding of the student program matches *all* input, and thus, the corresponding CORE program will not contain a `Case` expression since the given pattern covers all cases. When comparing these two programs, we will not compare two `Case` expressions against each other - checking syntactic equality (~=) would immediately fail. In the predecessor relation, we *also* check if the student expression matches *any* `Case` alternative in the model solution, which is true in this case. This also entails a special check for nested `Case` expressions to avoid false positives. Second, assume that the student refines the program from before:

```
dupli []     = []
dupli (x:xs) = _
```

Compiled into CORE, the top-level binder for `dupli` is non-recursive since there's no recursive call. The model solution above uses explicit recursion and will, on the other hand, be bound with a recursive binder. Despite having different types of binders, the student program should be considered a predecessor to the model solution since the other parts of the programs match (a hole is a predecessor to any term).

Additionally, if a student has at least one missing case in their function definition, it will compile to a `Case` expression containing at least one "pattern error" alternative. As long as the other alternatives match a model solution, we will regard this as a predecessor. Another exception is function application, for which we check for commutativity to prevent student solutions like `x == y` from being disregarded if the model solution is defined as `y == x`. Since functions and operators simply are variables in CORE, there is no elegant way to test commutativity. Currently, we only check for some common binary operators, but a more general solution would be a nice improvement for future work.

5.2 Hole-Mapping

The new normalisation procedure allows matching student programs with holes directly against model solutions to relate holes with terms from the model solution. We call such a term a *hole-match*, which we can use to generate feedback. The first step is to find all the CORE expressions that match the holes in the student solution (hole-matches). If the outermost expression of a hole-match is a `Tick`, we can use the source location to extract the corresponding parsed expression. Consider once again one of the solutions to the `dupli` exercise:

```
dupli = concatMap (replicate 2)
```

and that the student attempts

```
dupli xs = concatMap _ xs
```

The hole-mapping function will return the following CORE expression:

```
Tick src<studentfiles/Tmp.hs:4:19-31> (App (Var replicate)
(Tick src<studentfiles/Tmp.hs:4:30> (App (Var I#) (Lit 2))))
```

The outermost expression is a `Tick`, which contains the source location. The source location can be used to extract the corresponding parsed expression from the parsed source (the AST returned by the parser), which is stored separately. GHC's API also provides functionality to print a parsed expression as defined originally, e.g., `(replicate 2)` in the above example. In this case, the printed parsed expression could be used directly as feedback. If, instead, the hole-match expression includes a user- (or teacher-) defined variable it must be translated to the corresponding variable in the student solution before it is used in feedback to the student. For example, consider the model solution and the following student solution to an exercise on a function that, given a list and an integer index, returns the element at the given index (starting from 1):

```
elementat :: [a] -> Int -> a
elementat list n = list !! (n-1)
```

```
elementat :: [a] -> Int -> a
elementat xs i = _ !! _
```

The hole-mapping procedure will return this list of two matching expressions, one for each hole: `["list","(n-1)"]`. To give feedback with the same names the student used, we have stored maps containing the renamed and original variables of the student and model solution, respectively. The student variables corresponding to the variables in the list of hole-fit expressions can then be looked up in the substitution map. In the above example, we can retrieve the translated expressions `xs` and `(i-1)` and use it in the feedback to the student.

Retrieving hole-matches might require additional work, for example, if the hole matches a local helper function in a model solution or the whole right-hand side of a function definition. How to retrieve hole-fits in these cases is described in [3]. Matters are also complicated by the sparse control over `Tick` placements, which is limited to the GHC API.

5.3 HLint

Using GHC allows us to conveniently integrate HLint[4], a tool that suggests possible improvements to Haskell code, for generating additional feedback. To ensure HLint's feedback is formatted consistently with other GHC warnings, we use Splint[5], an existing HLint compiler plugin for GHC. Splint converts HLint suggestions into standard GHC warnings, seamlessly integrating them into the feedback process.

HLint suggestions are valuable for teaching coding style and best practices. For example: when to avoid lambdas, if the program contains redundant brackets, or when η-reduction is possible. HLint can also suggest possible rewrites, for example, if defining `dupli` as:

```
dupli  = concat . map (replicate 2)
```

HLint would give the following suggestion:

```
Use concatMap, perhaps: concatMap (replicate 2)
```

6 Evaluation

Our overall goal is to improve the feedback that we can give to a student during a programming exercise. Recognising a student program is important in generating this feedback, and we evaluate if the new approach improves the recognition of student programs. Our new approach also makes it possible to use GHC warnings, and we evaluate if this improves our generated feedback. Furthermore, we compare the execution time of the new normalisation procedure against the current procedure in ASK-ELLE.

[4] https://github.com/ndmitchell/hlint.
[5] https://github.com/tfausak/splint.

Evaluation Data. We use a data set containing programs from both real-world student interactions with ASK-ELLE and artificial ones. The latter are designed to capture particular Haskell constructs that are expected to be normalised in a certain way. The student programs are gathered from two experiments conducted in 2015 and 2023, where students were asked to solve exercises in ASK-ELLE while logging their interactions with the system. The experiment from 2015 consisted of 889 logged student programs, and the one from 2023 of 448 programs. Both data sets include duplicate programs and programs that do not compile or have other errors. We discard duplicate programs[6] and programs having syntax or type errors or don't pass the tests. Of course, when a student submits a program with any of these types of errors, ASK-ELLE gives a proper feedback message, but they are not relevant for evaluating the recognition rate. After excluding such programs, 197 and 113 student programs in the respective data sets remain.

6.1 Evaluating Feedback

The student programs are categorised as follows:

Complete Programs without holes that match at least one of the model solutions.
OnTrack Incomplete programs that contain at least one hole, and match at least one of the model solutions.
HLint Programs that cannot be matched, but where we can give a HLint feedback message that leads to a model solution.
Missing Cases Programs with missing cases, such as functions that are not defined on all possible inputs.
TestPassed Programs for which all tests pass. We don't run the tests in this evaluation since these use the unmodified student programs. Hence, these programs are assumed to remain in this category if not recognised.
Unknown Programs that cannot be matched and are not complete enough to test. In other words, programs for which we cannot generate meaningful feedback.

The results of our comparison are summarised in Table 1. The aim is to have as many programs in the Complete, OnTrack, and HLint categories as possible because that means we can give better feedback (and that the student has not submitted complete nonsensical programs). With the new approach, the number of student programs in those categories went up from 150 to 175 (around 56% of the total number of programs), an increase of about 17%. This might seem like a low figure, but if we count all diagnosed student programs (including programs that contain either syntax or type errors) ASK-ELLE can give proper feedback in 1027 of the 1337 cases, which is about 77%.

These results raised the question of whether the new normalisation procedure is still too weak to recognise more of the *probably* correct (TestPassed) or

[6] Duplicates were only checked by comparing the input strings. Hence, some duplicates may remain depending on variable names and if parentheses were used.

Table 1. Comparison of the old and new approach. The HLint category is specific to the new approach.

	Existing procedure			New procedure		
Category	2015	2023	Tot	2015	2023	Tot
Complete	37	21	58	40	25	65
OnTrack	68	25	92	81	27	107
HLint	-	-	-	2	1	3
Missing	43	8	51	32	8	40
TestPassed	33	52	85	30	47	77
Unknown	16	7	23	12	5	17
All	197	113	310	197	113	310

Unknown programs. We analysed the 94 programs that fell into the TestPassed and Unknown categories and noticed the following patterns:

Using disallowed functions: Six programs used a function from the Prelude (Haskell's standard library) corresponding to the exercise they were supposed to implement (e.g., `myreverse = reverse`).

Using other Prelude functions: Eleven programs failed due to using other Prelude functions not used in any of the model solutions.

Point-free: Three attempts failed where the model solution used point-free style and the student used normal application and parenthesis or the application operator.

Redundant patterns: 20 attempts could not be matched due to redundant patterns in the function bindings. Another four programs could not be matched due to redundant 'patterns' on the expression level.

Complicated or other solutions: Most of the remaining programs could not be recognised due to overly complicated solutions or different approaches to the model solutions.

We will not be able to recognise all of these (and, in some cases, we don't want to), but there is room for improvement. For example, detecting redundant patterns and signalling this to the student.

6.2 Execution Time

Enumerating all possible intermediate model solutions and searching for a matching one, as is the modus operandi currently in ASK-ELLE, takes time. The hypothesis is that the 'hole-mapping' approach described in Sect. 3 will be faster. To assert this, we have created simple benchmark tests using the Criterion[7] library to measure the execution times for generating feedback for both the

[7] https://hackage.haskell.org/package/criterion.

strategy-based and our new approach. The exact measured execution times are irrelevant, but rather the comparison between the two approaches. The results displayed in Table 2 confirm our hypothesis and show that the new approach is faster than the current approach in ASK-ELLE.

Table 2. Benchmark results

		Strategy-based		New approach	
	Number	Avg. time	σ	Avg. time	σ
Complete 2015	37	41.80 s	76.21ms	17.07 s	299.3ms
Complete 2023	21	24.19 s	40.29ms	10.79 s	76.21ms
OnTrack 2015	68	73.29 s	517.7ms	55.57 s	790ms
OnTrack 2023	25	27.88 s	74.77ms	20.03 s	342.2ms

For complete student programs the new approach is more than twice as fast and in case of incomplete (OnTrack) there is a performance gain of about 27%. Note, that we have not optimised the new approach yet, whereas the strategy-based approach is. Supporting larger exercises is likely to increase this difference.

6.3 Using GHC as a Library

The small number of constructors in the CORE expression data type makes some transformations on the CORE syntax harder to implement and require string comparisons and other "hacks" to check certain conditions that are not directly available in a constructor. For example, any kind of conditional, like pattern matching, guards, `if`-expressions, as well as pattern errors and typed holes, are compiled into a `Case`-expression in CORE. To know if a particular CORE `Case`-expression corresponds to, for example, a typed hole requires checking that the expression contains a variable called `typeError`. For our purposes, having a few more (specialised) data constructors to distinguish between expression would probably have been beneficial.

We found the main difficulties of using the GHC API to be finding the correct functions in the vast code base and understanding the, sometimes sparse, documentation. A piece of advice to anyone wanting to work with the GHC API, but does not know where to start: search GHC's code repository for things you would expect to find! The names of functions, modules, data types, etc., are most often reasonable and what you would expect. We found the easiest way of getting acquainted with the code base was to browse the GHC source code from the package documentation and follow links in the source code to inspect data types and functions. It is especially useful due to the extensive use of type synonyms and type families - you might require further investigation to find the actual type of a function or composite data type you are looking for. Finally, the notes and comments added directly in the source code can often provide a better understanding of certain concepts than the documentation pages.

A helpful entry point for understanding CORE is the informal overview provided in the GHC Compilation System User's Guide [23], along with a series of blog posts [5], though some of the material is slightly outdated. Another resource that gives some insight into how the simplifier operates in general and how GHC's inliner works in particular is [20] by Peyton Jones. A more general description of the CORE to CORE transformations in GHC can be found in [12]. Although this paper is a bit outdated, the main ideas are still valid.

An additional problem with using the GHC API is that not all functions and data types are exported, which can sometimes be inconvenient. A simple thing like inspecting the CORE AST requires writing `Show` instances for all CORE data types (and their underlying data types).

7 Related Work

Using GHC for normalisation in a programming tutor is a quite specific, and there is not (expectedly so) a lot of related work on this subject. Related work has been done by the Hermit tool [6] with GHC's CORE language, implementing optimising transformations as a CORE plugin. The tool is used for interactive exploration of optimisations of Haskell programs in a command line tool. The presented program transformations could have also been implemented as a CORE plugin, allowing reuse for normalisation purposes.

There also exists work on refactoring Haskell programs like HaRe [15], which can be seen as applying program transformations directly to the source code. HaRe operates on the parsed AST to easily retain source locations and keep as much information as possible after refactoring. It implements transformations such as rewriting `if`-expressions to `case`-expressions and lifting definitions to the top level, but the number of available refactorisations is limited. It is available as a Haskell library and allows implementation of new transformations, although it is only compatible with earlier versions of GHC. It would be interesting to explore if refactoring tools like HaRe could be used to rewrite student programs as a first step to match student programs with model solutions. An advantage of performing transformations over the parsed AST is that it is possible to retrieve the source code representation directly when generating feedback. However, matching programs and performing hole-mapping on a richer AST likely requires more normalisation efforts.

In this paper, we have only discussed normalisation achieved by applying a number of rewrite rules on a program. Another approach to normalisation is normalisation by evaluation (NBE). The idea of NBE is to translate a source language into some underlying host language, evaluate it in the host language and *reify*, or translate it back to the source language. Aehlig et al. [1] presents an NBE approach for functional languages, which translate a source language into some underlying functional language, evaluating and translating back to the source language.

7.1 Future Work

There is ample room for improvement and future work on the new approach for recognising and giving feedback in Ask-Elle. Here we highlight several possibilities.

η-Conversion and Holes Representing holes in Ask-Elle with GHC's typed holes has many benefits but, unfortunately, η-conversion works poorly in both directions if a program contains holes. Since we perform η-reduction instead of η-expansion, Ask-Elle can run into trouble when trying to match an incomplete student solution. Consider the following student program:

```
dupli :: [a] -> [a]
dupli xs = concatMap (replicate 2) _
```

Since `xs` is not used on the right-hand side in the definition, this cannot be reduced to `dupli = concatMap (replicate 2)`, which is the model solution. However, `xs` is detected as a valid hole-fit by the typed holes mechanism. Hence, if the hole-fit suggestions for typed holes are used in the future, the hint that `xs` could replace the hole could come from program synthesis instead.

Allowing Teacher-Defined Feedback. Ask-Elle's current implementation allows teachers to annotate model solutions with descriptive feedback using pragmas. The annotation pragmas used in Ask-Elle are not standard GHC pragmas; they cannot be parsed by GHC and will therefore not end up in the core AST. When we integrate the new normalisation approach in Ask-Elle, the annotation parser should be refined to include source locations, such that it can be used when creating feedback for hole-mappings.

Parameter Permutation. Despite our normalization procedure applying numerous program transformations, many equivalent programs remain unrecognised. Our evaluation in Sect. 6.1 confirms this and highlights several categories. In particular, our approach does not currently recognize functions where the order of arguments is permuted. However, for commutative operators, we attempt to account for both application orders. An interesting direction for future work would be developing a unification procedure for argument permutations.

8 Conclusion

We have shown that we can successfully use GHC's core language and program transformations to normalise student programs such that we can generate semantically rich feedback. We have introduced a new way of model tracing to generate this feedback. This new method circumvents the search space explosion inherent to the strategy-based approach. The new approach can recognise even more student programs and can thus deliver good feedback. Furthermore, the new 'hole-mapping' is much faster than its predecessor.

Using GHC to normalise Haskell programs improved the recognition of student programs in ASK-ELLE without too much programming effort spent at reimplementing common program transformations. With this said, using GHC's API has been a struggle at times. We have shared our experiences with using GHC as a library, such that others can get a head start and know what to look out for.

Acknowledgments. We would like to thank Maciej Goszczycki for generously allowing us to use valuable experiment data he collected for his master's thesis using ASK-ELLE.

References

1. Aehlig, K., Haftmann, F., Nipkow, T.: A compiled implementation of normalization by evaluation. In: Mohamed, O.A., Muñoz, C., Tahar, S. (eds.) TPHOLs 2008. LNCS, vol. 5170, pp. 39–54. Springer, Heidelberg (2008). https://doi.org/10.1007/978-3-540-71067-7_8
2. Algaraibeh, S.M., Dousay, T.A., Jeffery, C.L.: Integrated learning development environment for learning and teaching C/C++ language to novice programmers. In: IEEE Frontiers in Education Conference (FIE), pp. 1–5 (2020)
3. Blomqvist, M.: Improving Recognition of Student Programs in Ask-Elle. Master's thesis, Chalmers University of Technology (2023)
4. Claessen, K., Hughes, J.: QuickCheck: A lightweight tool for random testing of Haskell programs. SIGPLAN Not. **35**(9), 268–279 (2000)
5. Diehl, S.: https://www.stephendiehl.com/posts/ghc_01.html
6. Farmer, A., Gill, A., Komp, E., Sculthorpe, N.: The HERMIT in the machine: a plugin for the interactive transformation of GHC core language programs. SIGPLAN Not. **47**(12), 1–12 (2012)
7. Gerdes, A., Heeren, B., Jeuring, J., van Binsbergen, L.T.: Ask-Elle: an adaptable programming tutor for Haskell giving automated feedback. Int. J. Artif. Intell. Educ. **27** (2016)
8. Girard, J.Y.: The system F of variable types, fifteen years later. Theoret. Comput. Sci. **45**, 159–192 (1986)
9. Harrington, B., Peng, S., Jin, X., Khan, M.: Gender, confidence, and mark prediction in CS examinations. In: Proceedings of the 23rd Annual ACM Conference on Innovation and Technology in Computer Science Education, pp. 230–235. ITiCSE 2018, ACM (2018)
10. Heeren, B., Jeuring, J., Gerdes, A.: Specifying rewrite strategies for interactive exercises. Math. Comput. Sci. **3**, 349–370 (2010)
11. Heeren, B., Leijen, D., van IJzendoorn, A.: Helium, for learning Haskell. In: Proceedings of the 2003 ACM SIGPLAN Workshop on Haskell, pp. 62–71. Haskell '03, ACM (2003)
12. Jones, S.L.P.: Compiling Haskell by program transformation: a report from the trenches. In: Nielson, H.R. (ed.) Programming Languages and Systems — ESOP '96, pp. 18–44. Springer (1996)

13. Kölling, M., Quig, B., Patterson, A., Rosenberg, J.: The BlueJ System and its Pedagogy. Comput. Sci. Educ. **13** (2003)
14. Kumar, A.N.: The effect of using problem-solving software tutors on the self-confidence of female students. In: Proceedings of the 39th SIGCSE Technical Symposium on Computer Science Education, pp. 523–527. ACM (2008)
15. Li, H., Thompson, S., Reinke, C.: The Haskell Refactorer, HaRe, and its API. Electr. Notes Theor. Comput. Sci. **141**(4), 29–34 (2005)
16. Lodder, J., Heeren, B., Jeuring, J., Neijenhuis, W.: Generation and use of hints and feedback in a hilbert-style axiomatic proof tutor. Int. J. Artif. Intell. Educ. **31**(1), 99–133 (2021)
17. McCracken, M., et al.: A multi-national, multi-institutional study of assessment of programming skills of first-year CS students. In: Working Group Reports from ITiCSE on Innovation and Technology in Computer Science Education, pp. 125–180. ACM (2001)
18. Nienaltowski, M.H., Pedroni, M., Meyer, B.: Compiler error messages: what can help novices? In: Proceedings of the 39th SIGCSE Technical Symposium on Computer Science Education, pp. 168–172. SIGCSE '08, ACM (2008)
19. Peyton Jones, S.: Haskell 98 language and libraries: the revised report. Cambridge University Press (2003)
20. Peyton Jones, S., Marlow, S.: Secrets of the glasgow Haskell compiler inliner. J. Funct. Program. **12**, 393–433 (2002)
21. Spieler, B., Oates-Indruchova, L., Slany, W.: Female students in computer science education: understanding stereotypes, negative impacts, and positive motivation. J. Women Minorities Sci. Eng. **26**, 473–510 (2020)
22. Sulzmann, M., Chakravarty, M.M.T., Jones, S.P., Donnelly, K.: System f with type equality coercions. In: Proceedings of the 2007 ACM SIGPLAN International Workshop on Types in Languages Design and Implementation, pp. 53–66. TLDI '07, Association for Computing Machinery, New York, NY, USA (2007). https://doi.org/10.1145/1190315.1190324
23. Tolmach, A., Chevalier, T., GHC Team: An External Representation for the GHC Core Language (For GHC 6.10). GHC online documentation
24. VanLehn, K.: The relative effectiveness of human tutoring, intelligent tutoring systems, and other tutoring systems. Educ. Psychol. **46**(4), 197–221 (2011)
25. Whittall, S.J., Prashandi, W.A.C., Himasha, G.L.S., De Silva, D.I., Suriyawansa, T.K.: CodeMage: Educational programming environment for beginners. In: 9th International Conference on Knowledge and Smart Technology (KST), pp. 311–316 (2017)

Correction to: Functional Reactive GUI Programming with Modal Types

Jean-Claude Disch, Asger Heegaard, and Patrick Bahr

Correction to:
Chapter 5 in: J. Gibbons (Ed.): *Trends in Functional Programming*, LNCS 15652, https://doi.org/10.1007/978-3-031-99751-8_5

An error occurred during the production process of Chapter 5, Functional Reactive GUI Programming with Modal Types. The sentence originally published as: "to indicate that a tick a clock" instead of "to indicate that a tick on a clock".

The updated version of this chapter can be found at
https://doi.org/10.1007/978-3-031-99751-8_5

J. Gibbons (Ed.): TFP 2025, LNCS 15652, p. C1, 2026.
https://doi.org/10.1007/978-3-031-99751-8_23

Author Index

J. Gibbons (Ed.): TFP 2025, LNCS 15652, pp. 533–534, 2026.
https://doi.org/10.1007/978-3-031-99751-8

MIX
Papier aus verantwortungsvollen Quellen
Paper from responsible sources
FSC® C105338

If you have any concerns about our products,
you can contact us on
ProductSafety@springernature.com

In case Publisher is established outside the EU,
the EU authorized representative is:
Springer Nature Customer Service Center GmbH
Europaplatz 3, 69115 Heidelberg, Germany

Printed by Libri Plureos GmbH
in Hamburg, Germany